THE ROUGH GUIDE TO

Dominican Republic

This sixth edition updated by

Matt Norman and Charles Young

ROUGH
GUIDES

roughguides.com

Contents

Introduction to

The Dominican Republic

A world-famous magnet for sun worshippers and a celebrated baseball powerhouse, the Dominican Republic is the Caribbean's most visited tourist destination – yet it still holds plenty of surprises. There's the geographic diversity, for starters – how many outsiders know that the country boasts five distinct mountain ranges, seemingly endless swathes of rainforest, regions of cactus-strewn semi-desert, plus the Caribbean's largest metropolis, highest peak and biggest lake? Or that the capital, Santo Domingo, is the oldest colonial city in the Americas, home to the continent's first cathedral, university and hospital? For a country significantly smaller than Scotland, the DR, as it's commonly known, certainly packs a lot in.

As for that celebrated **coastline** – all 1000km and more of it – you can count on hundreds of beautiful, white-sand beaches, 166km of coral reefs and 325 square kilometres of mangroves. Besides **rainforest** there are vast tracts of **pine forest**, much of which can be found in the country's many **national parks** and **nature reserves**. Occupying gentler plots of land are the manicured greens of over 25 designer **golf courses**, complementing the countless spots for other **outdoor pursuits**, including mountain **rapids** for whitewater rafting, extensive limestone **cave** systems for spelunking, dirt tracks on the slopes of **sierras** for mountain biking, one of the world's best kitesurfing spots in Cabarete, and the largest breeding ground for the North Atlantic **humpback whale** population in the Samaná Bay, providing the scene for some of the most unforgettable nautical excursions anywhere.

Next, throw rich and theatrical Dominican **culture** into the mix. Locals let themselves go to the sophisticated and intoxicating rhythms of **merengue** and **bachata** – musical styles native to the DR – while **religion** remains an overt and integral part of life, with

ABOVE CAYO LEVANTADO, SAMANÁ **OPPOSITE** FRUIT STALL, NEAR PUNTA CANA crucifixes hanging around millions of necks, Jesus praised on countless bus and car stickers and – adding an enthralling Caribbean twist – Catholic symbolism mixed with African religious custom. The exhibitionist streak accompanying all this can be experienced first-hand at a vibrant **fiesta patronal**. Held in every town across the country, these celebrations in the name of a patron saint usually involve music-driven, round-the-clock processions and street parties that can last several days.

Even outside of festival times most towns in the DR, whether large or small, are boisterous places with a lively **street life**, an apparently lawless **traffic** system, especially in Santo Domingo, and always a buzzing sense of **commerce**. While vast supermarkets and swish shopping malls point to the strong **North American** influence on society, a huge number of independent, family-run businesses provide every town centre with a distinctly Dominican flavour, packed with colourful shop fronts, grocery stores crammed ceiling-high with cans, tins and jars, uninhibited salesmen and a strong sense of **community**. Around a third of the population live in **rural areas**, which, though unsurprisingly more subdued than the towns and cities, often throw up a quirky mix of modern and traditional, with block-rocking sound systems mounted in SUVs engulfing entire villages in reggaeton, and mobile-phone shops selling iPhones to tobacco farmers.

Another surprising discovery for many visitors is how well set up the DR is for **independent travellers** as well as **package holiday** tourists. Public **transport** is very cheap but relatively efficient and reaches the remotest corners of the country, while finding budget

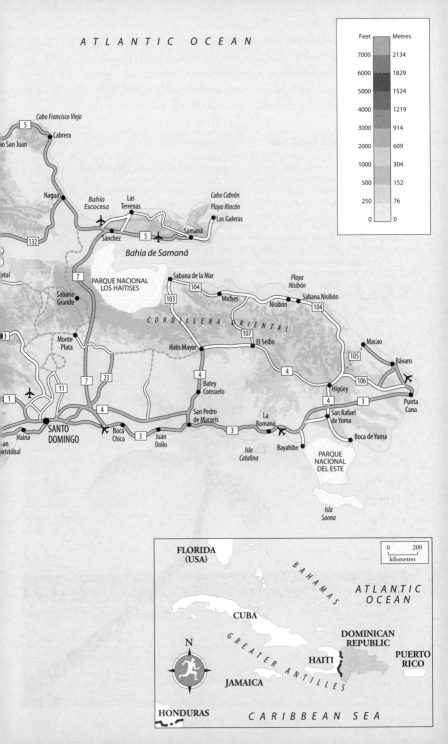

accommodation is becoming increasingly easy as hostels spring up around the resort areas, guesthouses abound and average prices, even for boutique hotels, are invitingly low. Many are also struck by the **friendliness** and **helpfulness** of Dominicans – they won't stop at giving you a few directions, they'll walk you there; and just when you think they're about to ask for something in return, they shake your hand and wish you luck.

CROWD-FREE BEACHES

With hundreds of kilometres of **beach** spread around every part of the meandering coastline, you needn't go far to find a sandy shore. The likes of **Punta Cana** and **Playa Dorada** are world-famous, but there are innumerable lesser-known gems worth seeking out. In the north, along the Silver Coast west of Puerto Plata, the poor state of the roads ensures that relatively few visitors make it as far as **Laguna Estero Hondo**, a great spot for snorkelling and one where you might – just might – spot a manatee in the protected waters. At the other end of the north coast, at the extreme east of the Samaná Peninsula, make for secluded **Playa Frontón**, hiding behind sheltering cliffs, **Playa Madama**, a tiny, serene beach, only reachable by boat, horseback or hiking, and increasingly popular **Playa Rincón**, a spectacular curve of sand that is still quite empty some days. Also on the peninsula is **Playa Bonita** near Las Terrenas, which is easy to get to but surprisingly calm and peaceful, particularly if you walk around its western point. In the southeast, just up the coast from the busiest beach in the country, are **Playa Nisibón** and **Playa Limón**, whose mountain backdrop provide both the gorgeous setting and the barrier to getting there easily. Remotest and least accessible of the lot is the beach at **Bahía de las Águilas** in the distant southwest, where stunningly beautiful white powdery sand is lapped by azure water.

ABOVE PLAYA BONITA **OPPOSITE** A GUITAR LESSON OUTSIDE CONVENTO DE LOS DOMINICOS, SANTO DOMINGO

Where to go

Many visitors head directly for beachfront resorts, and there's much at these holiday retreats to admire. The southeastern part of the country has the largest all-inclusive resort zone, **Punta Cana** and **Bávaro**, which has pristine coastline stretching for kilometres on end and is increasingly accessible to backpackers, with several hostels in among the giant sprawling hotels. Up on the north coast, and also dedicated to mass tourism, is the mega-complex **Playa Dorada**, whose appeal is enhanced by its proximity to the historic city of **Puerto Plata** – with its wealth of Victorian architecture – and to wind- and kitesurfing capital **Cabarete**.

Of course, you needn't base yourself in a resort in order to visit the DR's most popular sights, and there are plenty of opportunities for independent travellers to range further afield. A quest for immaculate beaches may take you to the most remote corners of the southwest, where your efforts will be rewarded with the breathtaking sands of the **Jaragua peninsula**. This little-visited corner of the country is also home to impressive **Lago Enriquillo**, a huge salt-water lake full of crocodiles and a truly fabulous array of tropical birds. There are some beautiful, and far more accessible, beaches scattered about the **Samaná Peninsula**, poking out at the country's extreme northeast. Its provincial capital, the small city of Samaná, serves as a base for checking out the humpback whales that migrate to the Bahía de Samaná each winter, while **Las Terrenas** is the peninsula's liveliest town. Its long, sandy seafront is lined with expat-owned hotels, tour operators and popular restaurants and bars; secluded paradise isn't far away, either, at the beaches of playas **Bonita** and **Rincón**.

On the central southern coast the capital, **Santo Domingo**, is among the most cosmopolitan cities in the Caribbean, with a collection of excellent museums and galleries, three huge city parks, an expanding metro system and a vibrant social scene. The historic forts, churches and the elegant homes of the **Zona Colonial** form its compact centre, with the modern, high-rise-heavy financial and shopping

BASEBALL STADIUM CULTURE

Baseball is an integral part of Dominican culture and it's inside the stadiums of the six Winter League teams that the **national passion** for the sport and the idiosyncrasies of the game here are at their most addictive. With capacities ranging between 8000 and 18,000, Dominican ball parks are relatively small, certainly compared to MLB stadiums, lending them an appealing intimacy and, when they are full, an **intensity** that can be electrifying. Games are at their most animated and crowded when the **Aguilas Cibaeñas** of Santiago match up against Santo Domingo's **Tigres del Licey**, and more still if it's a Sunday game, especially during the playoffs. The atmosphere in general is animated and festive: merengue blasts over the public address system and music is played live by bands in the stands. Adding to the **noise** are whistles, horns, vuvuzelas and drums making some games cacophonous but always imbued with a sense of fun, and fans are never less than expressive when their team delivers so much as a base hit, jumping up on their seats, dancing and waving flags. **Cheerleaders**, dancers and mascots perform on the pitch during breaks in play and, throughout games, old men in the back of the bleachers are making and taking **bets** on every movement going on in the field.

ABOVE DOMINCAN FANS AT A GAME **OPPOSITE** MERCADO MODELO, SANTO DOMINGO

districts stretching out beyond it, home to impressive upscale restaurants and trendy nightclubs.

If you're seeking a bit more adventure and outdoor life, head for the **Cordillera Central**, the island's largest and the Caribbean's highest mountain range, providing the stunning setting for multiday treks through the wilderness to the summit of the tallest peak, **Pico Duarte**. The most popular starting point for these treks is **Jarabacoa**, a resort town just two hours by bus from Santo Domingo, which is blessed with a cluster of four waterfalls in its immediate vicinity and features all manner of mountain sports. Another great base for hiking here is breathtakingly beautiful **Constanza**, a farmed valley with a small town at its heart, all perfectly packaged by the surrounding mountains.

When to go

There are two distinct tourist **high seasons** in the Dominican Republic: the summer months of **July** and **August**, when travellers from the northern hemisphere fill the resorts and all but the most out-of-the-way beaches; and the **winter season** between **December** and the **start of April**, when the Dominican climate is at its optimum, having cooled down a little from the summer. You'll therefore save a bit of money – and have an easier time booking a hotel room on the spot – if you arrive during the **spring** or the **autumn**, which is just fine, as the temperature doesn't really vary all that much from season to season, with the annual average temperature around 25°C (see p.42). Bear in mind that **May** to **mid-November** constitutes the DR's **rainy season**, though not all heavy rains are concentrated into these months (see p.42) – you can often get two weeks of unbroken sunshine in the summer and torrential downpours in January.

The **humidity** is relatively low during the winter months and it tends to cool down in the evenings much more than in the summer months. Furthermore, in the mountainous interior of the country, particularly in the Cordillera Central, it is always significantly cooler, and on the highest mountain peaks the **temperatures** have been known to drop below zero. Be aware also that the Dominican Republic is in the centre of the Caribbean hurricane belt, and gets hit with a major storm every decade or so. The **hurricane season** runs roughly from June to November with the stormiest months usually **August** and **September**.

THE DR'S FIVE MOUNTAIN RANGES

There are **five** major mountain ranges in the Dominican Republic, four of which bisect the entire island. By far the grandest – and the biggest in the Caribbean – is the **Cordillera Central**, which takes up a third of the island's mass, including a broad section of the DR's centre, before continuing through Haiti as the Massif Central and then ploughing underwater to Cuba and Honduras. These are extremely steep, craggy mountains that climb to a height of more than three thousand metres and are often covered with pine forests, some of them still virgin. After a brief trough, the mountains continue into the nation's southeast as the **Cordillera Oriental**, though here they're somewhat smaller, more humid and dominated by palm forest. South of the Cordillera Central the **Sierra de Neiba** holds the most extensive virgin rainforest left on the island, though along its southwestern slopes the range is parched limestone terrain.

The **Sierra Bahoruco**, south of the Sierra de Neiba and separated from it by the Neiba valley, is the second largest of the island's ranges, stretching west through Haiti – where it's known as the Massif du Sud – and encompassing the most diverse mix of mountain environments of all the ranges. Along the eastern half, where the semiprecious stone larimar is mined, rainforest predominates, while out west an enormous pine forest thrives; the range's northern segment is dominated by a mixture of deciduous forest and rainforest, before semi-arid, deforested farmland takes over along the southern section.

The **Cordillera Septentrional** along the country's north is dominated by a mix of tropical rainforest and evergreen forest, and separates off a valley ribbon along the coastline from the larger Cibao valley. The range stretches from Monte Cristi to Nagua where, after a brief trough, it continues on to the Samaná Peninsula as the Cordillera Samaná.

ABOVE THE CORDILLERA CENTRAL **OPPOSITE FROM TOP** LOCAL MINIBUS; *CASA SÁNCHEZ; SOLES* BEACH BAR

Author picks

Seafront bars at sunset The *Cafe del Mar* formula of music, drink and the setting sun has been perfectly captured at several cool beach and seafront bars – there's the Ibiza legend's own offshoot in Samaná (see p.131), *Soles* and *Huracán Café* in Bávaro (see pp.115–116), and *El Lobo y La Sal* in Juan Dolio (see p.93). Lounge about with a beer in your hand, as the sounds of the waves and the ambient soundtrack wash over you.

Live music and dance at Ruinas de San Francisco Join the concert-goers and swirling dancers on Sunday evenings in the atmospheric ruins of the first monastery in the Americas (see p.78) – the rum and community spirit flow, and locals mix with visitors, dancing and enjoying the merengue, bolero, son and other Latin American sounds of Grupo Bonyé.

Guaguas and conchos Whether sitting in the back of a pick-up truck rolling through the Cordillera Central or squeezed into a minibus on a highway, guaguas and *conchos* (see p.25) are central to the DR experience – they're cheap, sociable and will get you almost anywhere.

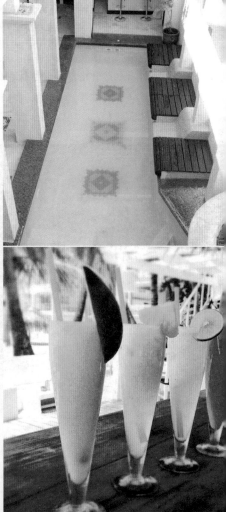

Colonial interiors in Santo Domingo Enjoy the beautiful architecture of some of the most captivating buildings in the country in Santo Domingo's Colonial Zone – by sleeping, eating or drinking in them. Dine in style at *La Taberna Vasca* and *La Bríciola* (see p.75); sleep between the arches at *Casa Sánchez*, *Villa Colonial* or *El Beaterio* (see pp.73–74) and sink a beer in the *Casa de Teatro* (see p.77) before catching a performance.

Parque Duarte One of the capital's most sociable and feel-good spots, well-kept Parque Duarte (see p.77) simply buzzes at weekends – with its easy co-existence of gay and straight revellers, it goes some way to destroying the idea that the Caribbean is rabidly homophobic, too. Dominican street life at its best.

Salcedo in the Cibao This Dominican Bedford Falls is the best of small-town DR in its simplicity and friendliness – there are colourful murals on many of the buildings, merengue echoes through the streets and it's one of the safest urban centres in the country (see p.231).

Our author recommendations don't end here. We've flagged up our favourite places – a perfectly sited hotel, an atmospheric café, a special restaurant – throughout the guide, highlighted with the ★ symbol.

things not to miss

It's not possible to see everything the Dominican Republic has to offer in one trip – and we don't suggest you try. What follows is a selective and subjective taste of the country's highlights: gorgeous beaches, colonial relics, outdoor activities and plenty of dancing. All highlights have a page reference to take you straight into the guide, where you can find out more; coloured numbers refer to chapters in the guide section.

1

1 PLAYA FRONTÓN
Page 139
Shielded from the rest of the world by encapsulating cliffs, this fabulous beach is hard to get to and hard to forget.

2 SANTO DOMINGO'S ZONA COLONIAL
Page 49
Santo Domingo's compact treasure-trove of colonial architecture.

3 CABARETE
Page 177
This lively beach town boasts the best windsurfing and kiteboarding in the Caribbean.

4 CONSTANZA
Page 228
A circular Shangri-La valley set deep in the heart of the Caribbean's tallest mountains.

12 MERENGUE DANCING
Page 280

The stuttering, fast-paced national music has been around in various forms for the past three hundred years.

13 EL LIMÓN WATERFALL
Page 148

Hidden deep within the Samaná mountains, but accessible on horseback, this pristine 150m waterfall is one of the loveliest spots on the island.

14 MOUNTAIN BIKING IN THE CORDILLERA SEPTENTRIONAL
Page 164

Choose from all-day downhill rides to multiday treks for experts, with stunning mountain scenery as your backdrop.

15 PICO DUARTE
Page 226

Climb to the rooftop of the Caribbean along five strenuous hikes of varying lengths – sublime views guaranteed.

16 AMBER
Page 41

Unbeatable as an authentic, locally produced souvenir, this semiprecious stone is stunning when set in jewellery.

17 MUSEO DEL HOMBRE DOMINICANO, SANTO DOMINGO
Page 64

This impressive museum, one of four in Santo Domingo's Plaza de la Cultura, houses an outstanding collection of Taino artefacts, plus exhibits on the island's African heritage.

Itineraries

Size-wise, the DR isn't daunting – but it does an awful lot with the available space. Our Grand Tour is a jam-packed, two-week route around the headline acts, while the other two itineraries can be done in a shorter space of time – or at a more leisurely pace – with no need to stay the night at every stop.

GRAND TOUR

Allow two weeks for this whistle-stop tour, taking in distinctly wild, remote-feeling landscapes and the largest city in the Caribbean.

❶ **Punta Cana and Bávaro** Start at the country's largest resort zone, which offers a good selection of inexpensive, independent hotels nestled amid the all-inclusives. **See p.110**

❷ **Santo Domingo** Give yourself at least three days to see the capital, prioritizing the Zona Colonial, but taking in at least one of the museums, restaurants or parks beyond the old city. **See p.46**

❸ **Samaná Peninsula** The Samaná Peninsula is mesmerizingly picturesque and perfect for independent tourists, with loads of great, affordable places to stay and unforgettable whale-watching. **See p.122**

❹ **Cabarete** One of the premier spots in the country for watersports, Cabarete can lay claim to near-perfect kiteboarding conditions. **See p.177**

❺ **Santiago** The DR's second city has plenty going on and combines a lively going-out scene with a laidback charm. **See p.207**

❻ **Cordillera Central** Pick your base for hiking in the "Dominican Alps" – Jarabacoa, the town best set up for tourism; San José de las Matas, a sleepy mountain village with breathtaking views

of the mountains; or Constanza, a lush, scenic valley. **See p.219**

❼ **Lago Enriquillo** Enormous Lago Enriquillo is the headline attraction in the remote southwest, home to a large population of American crocodiles and tropical birds. **See p.258**

CITIES, BEACHES AND MOUNTAINS

Travel from the south to the north coast via the Cordillera Central, the largest mountain range in the Caribbean, taking in the DR's two main cities.

❶ **Santo Domingo** If short on time in the capital, restrict yourself to the Zona Colonial, with its historic sights, excellent restaurants and nightlife. **See p.46**

❷ **Jarabacoa** Right in the thick of the Cordillera Central, Jarabacoa gives easy access to whitewater rafting, hiking trails and four memorable waterfalls. **See p.221**

❸ **Constanza** At 1300m above sea level, breathtakingly beautiful Constanza is the highest populated mountain valley in the country and another great base for hiking. **See p.228**

❹ **Santiago** The country's second city offers an entirely different experience to the capital – set against a mountainous backdrop and with its roots in agriculture, it's less cosmopolitan and less urban but rich in cultural heritage. **See p.207**

ABOVE FROM LEFT CORDILLERA ORIENTAL, THE SOUTHEAST; PLAYA RINCÓN, SAMANÁ

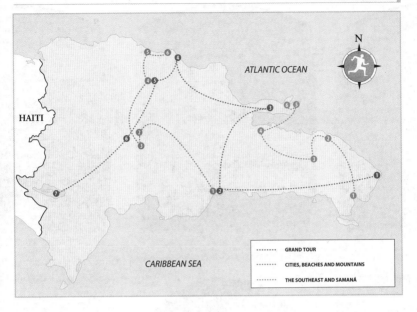

⑤ Puerto Plata and Playa Dorada Playa Dorada has passed the mantle of premier DR beach resort to Punta Cana, but with marvellous beaches and a cultural, history-rich neighbour in Puerto Plata, it still has the edge over its southern rival. **See p.157**

⑥ Sosúa A pleasant little place with a set of inviting beaches, more tranquil than Puerto Plata to the west and Cabarete to the east, this charming resort town is a fine place to unwind. From here there are regular buses back to Santo Domingo, four hours away. See p.171

THE SOUTHEAST AND SAMANÁ

It's at the heart of the package tourism industry, but the southeast has gorgeous, little-visited beaches, virtually tourist-free towns and a ferry link to the Samaná Peninsula.

① Boca de Yuma Just 40km down the coast from Punta Cana but not connected directly by public transport, Boca de Yuma may only have a pin-prick of a beach in comparison – but its end-of-the-road appeal makes up for it. See p.107

② Playas Limón and Nisibón These long stretches of pristine beach at the rugged edges of the Cordillera Oriental are two of the southeast's hidden highlights. **See p.119**

③ El Seibo This pleasant little town is as much about the journey as the destination, the twisting road from Miches passing through the most scenic part of the unspoilt Cordillera Oriental. See p.116

④ Parque Nacional Los Haitises Few travellers actually spend the night at this unmissable national park, but they're missing out on one of the most memorable hotels in the country: *Paraíso de Caño Hondo*. See p.132

⑤ Las Galeras Catch the small ferry boat from Sabana de la Mar and head straight from Samaná to Las Galeras, a sleepy place full of fantastic independent hotels. **See p.135**

⑥ Playa Rincón and Playa Frontón While in Las Galeras make at least one boat trip out to one of these outlying beaches – Playa Rincón with its 2km-curve of sand or isolated Playa Frontón, protected by black cliffs. **See p.139**

HOTEL FRANCÉS, SANTO DOMINGO

Basics

Getting there

The Dominican Republic is well connected to the outside world and you'll find a plethora of flight options from North America and Europe. The primary points of entry into the country by air are Santo Domingo, Puerto Plata and Punta Cana, with additional international airports at Santiago and Samaná.

When travelling to the Dominican Republic, it's often cheaper to come via a **charter flight**. Most of these are a result of the huge all-inclusive tourism industry built up along Dominican shores; package deals for airfare, hotel and food abound, with astounding rates available to those willing to shop around. But even if you don't want to go all-inclusive, the air charters that transfer package tourists to their all-inclusive destinations regularly offer extra seats to independent travellers for a surprisingly low price. Those headed here from South Africa will find fewer bargains, but with a bit of stamina you can make your way to the DR via the major airlines, though you won't be able to avoid a transfer at some point along the way.

Flights from the UK and Ireland

British Airways (Ⓦ britishairways.com) runs **direct flights** from London to Punta Cana; they currently fly on Wednesdays, Fridays and Sundays in both directions and cost around £650 year-round. American Airlines (Ⓦ aa.com) flights to Punta Cana travel via Miami or New York and so are slightly cheaper at £540. To Santo Domingo, both airlines code-share, along with Iberia (Ⓦ iberia.com), with **multi-stop** flights via Miami or Madrid for £530–550 also year-round.

Alternatively, there are a number of **charter flights** that fly direct to Punta Cana or Puerto Plata from London Gatwick and Birmingham; these are typically offered in conjunction with all-inclusive hotel stays, but you can also book empty seats on these at one of several charter flight wholesaler websites (such as Ⓦ cheapflights.co.uk or Ⓦ skyscanner.net)for as little as £450–500. All scheduled services to the Dominican Republic run daily from both **Heathrow** and **Gatwick**; Punta Cana trips typically fly via Paris, with Puerto Plata flights stopping off in New York.

Flights from the US and Canada

There are **flights** to the Dominican Republic from most major Canadian and US cities (some west-coast connections require an overnight stay in Miami or New York), but the cheapest and most frequent depart from the "gateway" cities of Miami, New York, Montréal and Toronto. The **budget airline** JetBlue (Ⓦ jetblue.com) offers cheap flights from North America to Santo Domingo, Samana, Punto Cana, La Romana, Puerto Plata and Santiago. All flights go through New York City, requiring a transfer here if coming from elsewhere on the continent.

A number of companies offer good-value **package tours** to Dominican resorts, usually for one or two weeks. Packages are generally only available to the more commercialized destinations, such as Puerto Plata, Sosúa and Cabarete in the north and Boca Chica, Juan Dolio and Punta Cana/Bávaro in the south. In the **US**, package tour operators usually operate out of a particular city and can't book connecting flights from elsewhere; one online operator, cheapcaribbean.com, books flights with American Airlines and can get you to the DR from any major city in the US, though their prices are a bit higher. In **Canada**, Dominican packages are serviced by a number of giant travel "wholesalers" and charter airlines which don't deal directly with the public; if you want to book one of their packages, you'll have to go through a local travel agent.

Flights from Australia, New Zealand and South Africa

The Caribbean is not a bargain destination from **Australia** or **New Zealand**. Because there are **no direct flights** to the Dominican Republic, you'll need

---

A BETTER KIND OF TRAVEL

At Rough Guides we are passionately committed to travel. We believe it helps us understand the world we live in and the people we share it with – and of course tourism is vital to many developing economies. But the scale of modern tourism has also damaged some places irreparably, and climate change is accelerated by most forms of transport, especially flying. All Rough Guides' flights are carbon-offset, and every year we donate money to a variety of environmental charities.

to travel first to the US or Europe. It's a day-long slog whichever way you go, but most convenient **from Australia** is a non-stop from Sydney to New York City via Qantas (W qantas.com), American or United (W united.com), followed by an onward connection to the DR via one of the North American airlines listed below. From **New Zealand** you can take a direct flight from Auckland to New York with a stop in Los Angeles and get an onward connection from there.

Travellers from **South Africa** can get to Santo Domingo via Iberia airlines, though stops at Madrid and/or London are involved, and to Puerto Plata and Punta Cana via British Airways with stops in London and/or Miami.

Agents and operators

Apple Vacations W applevacations.com. Online package-holiday company with all-inclusive trips from most of the US to Puerto Plata, Punta Cana, Samana, Santiago, and La Romana.

Aquatic Adventures T 954 382 0024, W aquaticadventures.com. Florida-based outfit that offers US$3695 week-long whale-watching cruises in the Silver Banks Sanctuary, departing from Puerto Plata, which is all-inclusive but doesn't include airfare.

ebookers UK T 0800 082 3000, W ebookers.com; Republic of Ireland T 01 488 3507, W ebookers.ie. Low fares on an extensive selection of scheduled flights and package deals.

W cheapcaribbean.com. All-inclusive North America package holidays using American Airlines instead of the charter-flight operators. Trips are slightly more expensive as a result, averaging around US$1500–2000.

STA Travel US T 800 781 4040; UK T 0333 321 0099; Australia T 134782; New Zealand T 0800 474 400; SA T 0861 781 781; W statravel.com. Worldwide specialists in independent travel; also student IDs, travel insurance, car rental, rail passes and more. Good discounts for students and under-26s.

Sunquest T 1 877 485 6060, W sunquestvacations.ca. All-inclusive holidays to Punta Cana, Puerto Plata, Sosúa, Cabarete Samana and La Romana from Toronto and Ottawa, with connections from all major Canadian cities.

Tours, Trips, Treks & Travel T 809 867 8884, W 4tdomrep.com. First-class tour operator focusing on combination culture tours and adventure trips across the island.

Trailfinders UK T 0845 058 5858; Republic of Ireland T 01 677 7888; Australia T 1300 780 212; W trailfinders.com. One of the best-informed and most efficient agents for independent travellers. They also run medical travel clinics offering a twenty percent discount on vaccinations for customers.

Getting around

Although you can get just about everywhere in the Dominican Republic by public transport, the downside is that recent statistics show the country to the worst in the Americas – and possibly the world – for road fatalities. It's vital to exercise every precaution outlined below with the pre-eminent advice being to avoid travelling by road at night.

The DR's **bus companies** provide an excellent, inexpensive service over much of the country. Queues at the stations move quickly, there's plenty of room for luggage on the vehicles and – aside from the quality of the movies screened on cross-country rides – trips are relatively pleasant and hassle-free. Even more extensive and cheap is the informal network of **guaguas**, ranging from fairly decent minibuses with on-board wi-fi to battered vans, that cover every inch of the DR; in most cases, you should be prepared for some discomfort – and you'll have a hard time fitting in much luggage, as every square inch of space is packed with passengers. Within towns there's usually a reliable formal 24-hour **taxi service** that you can call for pick-up as well, though they typically cost a bit more. **Car rental** affords a freedom you'll greatly appreciate after a few days going from town to town on the guaguas, but the cost is .generally high, due to petrol prices, import duties and high accident rates. Also, a number of **tour operators** in Santo Domingo, Puerto Plata and the all-inclusive resorts organize individual itineraries and packages with transport included.

By bus

Santo Domingo and Santiago are the major hubs for **bus travel** and some companies do little more than shuttle between the two. You generally have to buy your ticket the day you travel, though **Caribe Tours** (T 802 221 4422, W caribetours.com.do) allows you to reserve online, provided you confirm two hours before departure. Caribe Tours boasts by far the most extensive network of bus lines – with connections to the Cibao, the Samaná Peninsula, the Barahona region, the entire Silver Coast and even Port-au-Prince, Haiti – while **Metro** (T 809 227 0101, W metroservicios-turisticos.com) can get you from the capital to the Cibao, Puerto Plata and the Samaná Peninsula. Both of these companies have comprehensive brochures available in their stations, listing destinations and departure times and you can also book online.

In addition to these two, you'll find several regional bus companies that cover one particular part of the country, though vehicles and drivers tend to vary more in quality; negotiating the regional connections is detailed throughout the guide. Unless it's a public holiday, you won't need **advance reservations**, but you should arrive at least an hour before the bus leaves to be sure of getting a seat. A good source of information on buses, and many guagua routes is ⓦ horariodebuses.com/EN/do.

The bus companies strive to stay in competition with guaguas and so **fares** are extremely cheap. Even a cross-country trip from Santo Domingo to Sosúa will set you back no more than RD$320, while shorter trips fall in the RD$150 range. Make sure that the date and time are correct on your ticket; even if the mistake isn't yours, you cannot normally change your ticket or get a refund. All Dominican buses have toilets at the back and on trips of more than two hours a rest stop will be taken at a roadside restaurant or service station.

By guagua, público, taxi and motoconcho

The Dominican Republic's informal system of **guaguas**, an unregulated nationwide network of private operators, is a distinctive experience that you should try at least once. **Vans** are the most prevalent types of guagua, though there are other manifestations as well, such as **pick-up trucks** or comfortable, air-conditioned **minibuses** (sometimes even with wi-fi) on busy inter-city routes. You'll find a higher volume of guagua traffic in the **morning**, but there are occasionally very limited overnight services as well. In the southeast and other parts of the country not serviced by Caribe Tours and Metro, they're your best option for public transport.

An instant bond of familiarity is formed as passengers – mostly locals – are crammed four and five to a seat in these half-wrecked vans that often seem held together with little more than packing tape and a strategically placed bit of rope. Journeys are typically colourful: Amway salespeople pester fellow passengers, Pentecostals proselytize to heathens, a bottle of rum is passed around and – on night runs when the guaguas are less crowded – somebody pulls out a guitar and everyone breaks into song. Aside from the fun, they're worth using for the cheap fares and comprehensive coverage to all parts of the country. Guaguas are operated by teams of two, the **driver** and the **cobrador**, who sticks his head out of the sliding side door and drums up business. If you want to catch one, just stand by the side of the road and wave your arms at one as it passes. Often the **destination** will be emblazoned on the side, but always ask before you hop aboard.

For longer trips, you'll often have to change guaguas at major towns, but even the longest leg of the trip will cost no more than RD$100; more often, you'll be paying RD$50–60. Be aware, though, that attempted **rip-offs** of tourists are not unheard of. You should ask around and find out how much a given guagua ride costs before flagging one down – don't ask the driver or you may be quoted a rate ten times higher than the norm; instead, clamber into the vehicle and hand over your money immediately without saying a word. If the *cobrador* won't take the money, get out and wait for the next. Keep a careful eye on the road as you go; you'll have to shout for the driver to pull over when you want to get out: even if you ask them to alert you at your stop, they sometimes forget.

Along the Silver Coast, guaguas are augmented by private cars called **públicos**, which charge around RD$40–50 and only go to the next nearest town and wait to fill up before heading off. *Carros públicos* (often beat-up taxis or even more beat-up door-less vans) also make up part of the city transport system in Santo Domingo and other cities, and dominate it in Santiago. City routes rarely cost more than RD$20–30, though you'll have to put up with blaring music and some daredevil driving manoeuvres.

Taxis are relatively expensive, especially in tourist areas and at airports and hotels, where prices are up to double the normal. Rates are often set, with meters rarely used, so you should **negotiate** the price beforehand – your best bet is to ring one of the firms listed in the chapters, or use a taxi stand where the usually exorbitant prices are posted. In whichever case, they should have an **official ID** in the windscreen and their union's logo somewhere on the car's exterior – unlicensed taxi drivers known as *pirates* often cruise the streets at night looking for business, but using these is not recommended at all. It is possible to hire a taxi by the day or half-day which can work out cheaper (and certainly less hassle) than a hire car, depending on your negotiation skills.

A cheaper form of city transport, most prevalent in smaller places, are **motoconchos**, inexpensive, small-engine motorbikes that ferry you from place to place, often at high speed. They're faster than the *públicos* and should cost around RD$30/km, but be warned that they can often be dangerous.

By car

With an infamous record on **road safety** you should only consider driving in the DR if you have

CROSSING THE HAITIAN BORDER

Technically, there are **three legal border crossings**: Ouanaminthe–Dajabón; Malpasse–Jimaní; and the remote Pedernales Anse-à-Pitre, all open daily from 8am to 4pm (Dominican time), but it's easier to cross with one of the major bus companies, which both use the Jimaní crossing. Terrabus (☎809 531 0383) is a very efficient company with comfortable buses that runs a daily service at 11.30am (US$40) from Santo Domingo to Port-au-Prince, while Caribe Tours (☎809 221 4422, ⓦcaribetours.com.do) offers trips to Port-au-Prince that depart Santo Domingo daily at 9am and 11am (RD$1680).

No one is allowed to bring a **rental car** across the Haitian–Dominican border, so unless you own a car in the DR, you won't be able to drive into Haiti or vice versa. In Haiti there's a **guagua network** – they're called *taptaps* – as well as *motoconchos*, which are much better ridden, and safer than those in the DR. Otherwise you'll be stuck with the often bizarre Haitian modes of public transport; among the most popular are school buses with their front end chopped off, soldered onto a Mack truck cab – and with the eardrum-pulverizing horn pointed directly at passengers.

Crossing the border involves some **extra costs**, as you'll have to pay the US$20 leaving tax (usually included in flight tickets), often along with an unregistered payment of US$5 to the Haitian officials. Returning from Haiti, there's another (official) US$20 departure tax, plus a further US$10 for a new Dominican tourist card.

experience of taking to the wheel in developing countries. Moreover, **never drive at night** – drink-driving is relatively common, headlights are never dipped, and many road users don't have working lights. Be wary, too, of stopping for people who look to have broken down, particularly on quiet roads – it may be a trap.

If you do take the plunge, you'll find that **car rental** is expensive in the DR, though you can cut your costs a bit – and avoid a lot of hassle – by booking in advance with reputable Dominican agency Nelly or an **international operator** – Dollar and National are generally the best value and both offer decent **4WDs** (essential for the beautiful coastal and mountain back roads that give access to the DR's finest scenery) for from US$50/day. The international firms have branches at the airport and are far less likely to rip you off; if you don't have a credit card, though, you'll be stuck with the local companies, who accept passports in lieu of a security deposit, which is technically illegal. Take extra care in documenting any **pre-existing damage** to the car at the outset.

Rates start at around US$35–40 per day, with unlimited mileage but no discount for longer rental periods. Note that if renting a 4WD, some rental firms may try to entice you into choosing the cheaper Suzukis, which are the same price as standard cars, but they aren't really intended for rough mountain travel and, after the first bone-wrenching hour along a Dominican dirt road, you'll curse yourself for not spending more. You should also get **full collision insurance**; even with

collision, though, you're usually contractually responsible for any damage up to RD$120,000. You should therefore take special care to note *all* dents, scratches and missing parts before signing off; nor should you sign the contract if a total price, including all hidden charges, taxes and fees, is not filled out. You can also check to see if you're insured by a **credit card company** (they sometimes provide it if you use it to pay for car hire) or your home/travel insurance cover, but check the details with a fine-tooth comb.

Americans can anticipate high **petrol** costs, while everyone else will find the prices about average at around RD$200 per gallon. Premium costs a little extra, but seems to be worth it, especially if you need that tad more power in the mountains. Most petrol stations close around 8pm – and there are none whatsoever in the most remote regions – so keep a careful eye on your tank. If all else fails, look for one of the many roadside tables that offer individual bottles of petrol (usually in small/big beer bottles) for around RD$60/100.

Rental firms here charge exorbitant rates for **repairs**; if your car is dented you're far better off going to one of the local mechanics, who will charge at most RD$300 (as opposed to as much as RD$25,000). Because of the poor quality of many roads, **flat tyres** are a common occurrence; fortunately, every town has at least one *gomero*, independent tyre shops that work miracles for as little as RD$50.

Motorcycles can also be rented at many local firms, from around US$15–20 per day for a moped, though bigger machines (including dirt bikes) are also available, and necessary if you want to explore the rough back roads. When riding, stay as much to the edge of the road as possible (on bigger roads the emergency lane is for use by bikes) and sound your horn frequently. A motorcycle **helmet law** was enacted several years ago, but it's only really adhered to in the cities – if you're stopped by the cops it's a RD$1400 fine – and laughable local attempts to comply generally utilize baseball batting helmets or plastic American football gear intended for children. That doesn't mean that you should follow suit – insist that a proper helmet comes with your bike. Be warned that **motorbike thefts** are extremely common, especially in resort areas, so you'll have to keep it locked up when you're not riding it.

Road rules and dangers

Dominicans drive on the **right-hand side of the road**, usually at a breakneck pace. You'll have to keep a careful eye out along the highways, as large commercial buses and cargo trucks constantly veer into the opposite lane to pass slower vehicles, and other drivers often stay near the centre of the road to avoid the many motorbikes.

An array of **signals** using car horns and lights are employed by local motorists. Frequent honking is highly advised to stay safe; you should at least sound the horn while overtaking or – especially – passing parked cars. A driver about to pass you will often blink the headlights, while one coming towards you doing this is signalling that they're in your lane and you should slow down or get out of the way. One other important rule is that if you hesitate it means you've given way, even if you have the right of way.

You'll also find a bewildering variety of **obstacles** in your path, including turtle-paced ice-cream trucks, *motoconchos* with comical cargoes of piled chicken coops or construction equipment (which the driver holds down with one arm) and children running back and forth along the freeway. Potholes are common and you must be wary of vehicles suddenly swerving to avoid them, and of course be wary of hitting them yourself. Note that some towns have convoluted **one-way systems**, often not signposted as such – keep a close eye on which way the cars are parked.

As you approach towns, also watch out for the nasty **speed bumps** which are often unmarked and obscured under the shade of trees. Originally intended to prevent accidents, they are now sometimes used by local police to slow passing cars enough that **bribes** can be exacted from them, though this has been become much less

common in recent years due to government campaigns. In the fairly unlikely event you get waved down, either pretend not to see them and carry on, or to speak no Spanish and keep repeating the word "tourist" and they'll usually let you go – otherwise you should only give them RD$100.

CAR RENTAL AGENCIES

Alamo US ☎ 1 800 462 5266, ⓦ alamo.com.
Avis US & Canada ☎ 1 800 633 3469; UK ☎ 0845 44 55 66; Republic of Ireland ☎ 021 428 1111; Australia ☎ 13 63 33 (toll-free) or ☎ 02 9353 9000; New Zealand ☎ 09 526 2847 or, ☎ 0800 655 111 (toll-free); ⓦ avis.com.
Budget US ☎ 800 472 3325; Canada ☎ 1 800 268 8900; UK ☎ 084 4544 3455; Australia ☎ 13 0036 2848; New Zealand ☎ 0800 283 438; ⓦ budget.com.
Dollar US and Worldwide ☎ 1 800 800 4000, ⓦ dollar.com.
Enterprise Rent-a-Car UK ☎ 0800 800 227; **Canada and US** ☎ 1 800 261 7331; ⓦ enterprise.com.
Hertz US & Canada ☎ 1 800 654 3131; UK ☎ 0843 309 3099; Republic of Ireland ☎ 01 676 7476; New Zealand ☎ 0800 654 321; ⓦ hertz.com.
National US ☎ 1 877 222 9058; Australia ☎ 0870 600 6666; New Zealand ☎ 03 366 5574; ⓦ nationalcar.com, ⓦ nellyrac.com.
Nelly ☎ 809 687 7997 or ☎ 1 809 687 7263 from outside the DR, ⓦ nellyrac.com.
Thrifty US & Canada ☎ 1 800 541 7044; UK ☎ 0203 468 7686; Republic of Ireland ☎ 01 844 1950; Australia ☎ 1300 367 227; New Zealand ☎ 03 359 2721; ⓦ thrifty.com.

Accommodation

The Dominican Republic has become the most visited destination in the Caribbean thanks to its preponderance of all-inclusive hotels, which make package vacations here far cheaper than elsewhere. The all-inclusives do have their downsides: the food is usually mediocre and you'll be stuck in a walled-off complex for your entire trip, which can get claustrophobic. Plenty of other options exist for travellers who want to get out and see the country: luxury high-rise resorts along the capital's Malecón, independently operated beach hotels, rooms for rent in Dominican family homes and an assortment of bearable budget hotels – many with private bath, hot water and air conditioning – and a gradually growing range of independent hostels.

Away from the main tourist spots you can expect to pay around US$20–40/UK£10–20 for the night; in resort towns prices rise to US$40–100/UK£20–50. Throughout the guide, unless otherwise stated, the price listed is for the **cheapest double room in high season**. Reservations are essential for the all-inclusives, where you'll get up to 75 percent off the price by booking with a travel agent as part of a package before you arrive. If you want to stay in an independent hotel during the high season, you will need to book in advance in the major resort towns, but should be able to wing it elsewhere.

Independent hotels, hostels and pensiones

When travelling, most Dominicans stay at the spartan **budget hotels** that you'll find dotted throughout the country. If you do likewise you'll save a lot of money, but beware – you often get what you pay for. That means fairly nondescript, box-like rooms, best avoided except for sleep. Some of them have a shared bath and the majority have cold showers. Keep in mind also that when a budget hotel boasts "hot water" showers, this often means a large plastic nozzle on the showerhead that heats the water on the spot, making for a somewhat tepid temperature. Whatever you do, don't touch the nozzles when wet, or you'll risk a painful **electric shock**. Look to spend about RD$500–1000 (US$12–25) for these establishments, though some, especially in the cities, also offer rooms with a/c and television for around RD$200 (US$5) extra. It's easy to mistake the many roadside **cabañas turísticas** for budget traveller hotels; identifiable by their garish decor and the words "Cabañas Turísticas" emblazoned on the outside, these are in fact the type of hotel that charges by the hour and are mainly used by local couples.

There are no official **HI (Hostelling International)** venues in the DR, but the expanding range of **independent hostels** is making budget travel a little easier. Another good way to cut expenses is to use the traditional **pensiones** that you'll still find in many towns, though over the past two decades they've begun to die out. These are rooms within a private Dominican home and so offer an excellent opportunity for contact with local people. Pensiones vary widely in quality, so you should have a good look at your room before deciding. If you want to shop around, don't feel guilty about seeing the room and then moving on; expect to pay RD$500–700.

Nicer, **mid-range hotels** are available in areas regularly frequented by foreigners. Ranging between US$35 and US$60, they feature air conditioning, hot water and more pleasant rooms. Hotels at the lower end of this price range are often especially good value; at the higher end you'll get a few luxuries thrown in, like cable TV or breakfast.

If there's one around and you can afford it, you might want to consider the independent **luxury hotels** as well, which will accept US dollars (US$80–150). The majority are clustered in Santo Domingo, but you'll also find one or two in most other major cities and a couple along the rural coast. They range from well-appointed beach hotels and seaside high-rises to full-service, two-storey apartments and renovated colonial stone mansions furnished with sixteenth-century pieces. You can often get better rates (up to thirty percent off) at these hotels on weekends, as they cater mostly to business travellers.

All-inclusive hotels

The Dominican Republic is the archetypal, high-volume **all-inclusive** destination, where a single price covers your room, all meals and drinks and a variety of activities. If you go all-inclusive, you should do so through a **package** arranged by a travel agent in your home country, which will cost you substantially less than arriving at the reception desk and asking for a room.

For couples and families on a tight budget, the all-inclusives can be a wonderful opportunity for a peaceful beach vacation in relative luxury – these places are usually stationed right on the country's prime beachfront. The product offered is usually good and despite a blanket no-tips policy, the staff are generally pleasant and accommodating. It's remarkable that the hotels – most owned by large foreign chains – can maintain their high level of quality given the dirt-cheap price of their packages.

A long-standing issue, though, is the omnipresent **buffet food**, which is often below par; at many resorts you'll have the option of going one or two nights a week to a better restaurant with individual main courses and a few hotels also reserve a few spaces for room-only deals, which will allow you to spend your money at restaurants in town. Nevertheless, the idea of having unlimited access to a resort's facilities at no additional cost is undeniably attractive and it's possible to counteract the claustrophobia that often comes with several days spent in the grounds by taking an organized tour or a guagua ride into the beautiful countryside beyond.

Camping

There are several **campgrounds** in the southwest Dominican Republic and along the Pico Duarte trails, though camping is a fairly new concept here. Outside of the Barahona region though, your best bet is to ask permission first – from village residents if you're on the beach, or from a farmer with a large property if you're in the mountains.

Food and drink

If you take all your meals at an all-inclusive hotel, you'll get little sense of how Dominicans eat and drink; the bland "international" buffet fare and watered-down daiquiris on offer at these resorts just can't compete with the delicious, no-nonsense cooking at the many family-run restaurants, or the rum drinks on offer at locals' bars just outside the compound walls.

Meals and cooking styles

Dominicans call their cuisine **comida criolla** and it's a delicious – if often rather greasy – blend of Spanish, African and Taino elements, with interesting regional variants across the island. Dishes usually include rice and beans – referred to locally as *la bandera dominicana* (the Dominican flag) – using either *habichuelas* (red beans) or the tiny black peas known as *morros*. Most often the rice is supplemented with chicken either fried, grilled or served *asopao* (in a rich, soupy sauce). Invariably, main courses come with *plátanos* (deep-fried green plantains), which locals often inundate with ketchup, and a small coleslaw salad.

Local **breakfasts** – traditionally starchy and huge, designed for people who are about to go and work the calories off – typically include *huevos revueltos* (scrambled eggs), sometimes *con jamón* (with bits of ham mixed in); *mangú*, mashed plantains mixed with oil and bits of fried onion; *queso frito*, a deep-fried cheese; *jugo de naranja* (orange juice; also called *jugo de china* in the southwest); and a strong cup of coffee, either *sólo* or *con leche*, but always with a healthy dose of sugar.

Dominican **lunches** are quite hearty and are generally consumed between noon and 2pm, but **dinner** is still the day's main meal and is almost always a family affair. Aside from the omnipresent chicken, popular main courses include *mondongo*, a tripe stew strictly for the strong of stomach; *mofongo*, a tasty blend of plantains, pork rinds and garlic; and *bistec encebollado*, grilled steak topped with onions and peppers. Special occasions, particularly in rural areas, call for either *chivo* (roast goat) with *cassava*, a crispy, flat bread inherited from the Tainos, made with ground yucca roots; or *sancocho*, considered the national delicacy, a hearty stew with five different kinds of meat, four types of tuber and a bewildering array of vegetables and spices.

For the best Dominican offerings, go for the **seafood**, which is traditionally prepared one of five ways: *criolla*, in a tasty, slightly spicy tomato sauce; *al ajillo*, doused in a rich garlic sauce; *al horno*, roasted with lemon; *al orégano*, in a tangy sauce with fresh oregano and heavy cream; and *con coco*, in a tomato, garlic and coconut milk blend especially prevalent on the Samaná Peninsula. You'll find that the tastiest local fish are the *mero* (sea bass), *chillo* (red snapper) and *carite* (kingfish). Other popular seafoods include *langosta* (clawless lobster), *lambí* (conch), *camarones* (shrimp), *pulpo* (octopus) and *cangrejo* (crab).

Dominican **desserts** are good but extremely sweet; the best of the many types are the *dulces con coco*, made with molasses and coconut shavings. Also popular are *dulces de leche*, usually a bit bland, and *dulces de naranja*, composed of a molasses-orange marmalade that can send you into instant sugar shock. You'll also find a wide variety of cakes, custards and flans on offer, including a distinctive corn custard, *flan de maíz*. A healthier and usually tastier option is to explore the tremendous variety of **tropical fruits**. *Guineos* (bananas), *lechoza* (papaya) and *piña* (pineapple) are the most popular, but you won't regret trying the local *limoncillos*, tiny, delicious lime-like fruits sold in bunches, and *chinola*, Dominican passion fruit. The DR is especially known, though, for its out-of-this-world **mangos**; less famous, but simply delicious, are the *fresas* (strawberries) that are widely cultivated in the Constanza region and grow wild in the Sierra Bahoruco.

Where to eat

Eating out can be extremely cheap in the Dominican Republic, provided you stick to the modest-looking local establishments, many of which serve outstanding food. In the more formal dining rooms, prices are higher but are usually still a bargain by European and North American standards. Either way, with the exception of the *cafeterías*, you'll be charged an eighteen percent **sales tax** on your meal and a ten percent "service" charge, though these often find their way into the hands of neither the government nor the waiting staff and instead are kept by the proprietors. if you've had particularly good service then an additional tip of five to ten percent is a nice gesture. Outside of the major cities **vegetarians** will often have to make do with rice and beans.

The cheapest places to dine are the **cafeterías**, humble establishments with a few tables and a glass case displaying a variety of typical foods such as fried fish, chicken stew, rice and beans, *mangú* and *plátanos*. You can generally get a meal here for under RD$100, but you're best off frequenting them only at lunch, when the food is fresh; by dinnertime the dishes may have been standing for hours under the heat lamps. Also under glass cases are the fried chicken dishes served at the many Dominican **pica pollos**, popular chain outlets with neon, fast-food decor; but far tastier and less aggressively lit are the **pollo al carbón** shacks that serve heaped portions of grilled chicken, rice and beans, and salad; always a good bet for a cheap meal.

Only slightly more expensive, the many Dominican **comedores** are a great resource: unpretentious, family-run restaurants, generally little more than a hole in the wall but often dishing up incredible *comida criolla*, which will set you back around RD$125–150 for a full meal. For a quick snack, check out the greasy goods of the various **street vendors** hawking empanadas, flat fried pastries with a ground-beef filling; *chicharrones*, crunchy bits of deep-fried chicken or pork; shredded barbecue pork sandwiches; boiled corn; and split coconuts all for around RD$10; and peeled oranges for RD$3. From time to time you'll also see small children selling trays of home-made *dulces* for RD$2.

You'll find plenty of **high-end** dining in the major cities and the resort towns, generally featuring an array of authentic international cuisine including French, Italian, Chinese, Korean, Japanese, Indian and Basque. Count on spending around RD$300–600 at these and don't expect to be seated if you're wearing shorts, a bikini top or a short skirt. Dress codes are far less formal in the **all-inclusive buffet halls**, but the food is a lot more bland. Even at the best of them, don't expect anything special.

Shopping for food

Most Dominicans do their shopping at the many small **colmados** that dot the country, little more than shacks packed with various basic food supplies, an ample selection of liquors and some fresh produce. The *colmados* generally extend a line of credit to their local customers, allowing them to purchase a single spoon of tomato paste, for example, for RD$5, which is added to the running tab. These small portions are necessary because most *campesinos* don't have refrigerators and so only purchase what they need for the day. In the cities and resort centres, you'll find more traditional **grocery stores**, laid out much as they are at home.

Drinking

Dominican **coffee** is among the best in the world. Grown in the heights of the Cordillera Central mountain range, it's a major export earner for the country, sold in the coffee bars and grocery stores of North America and Europe, often misleadingly labelled Costa Rican or Colombian because these nations are more closely associated in the public mind with high-quality coffee production. Most Dominicans take it *sólo*, with a great deal of sugar added, which is the way it's sold for RD$5 by omnipresent morning street vendors and handed out for free in the petrol stations. Dominican *café con leche* is made with steamed milk and is extremely good; the best place to get it is a *comedor*, where you'll pay RD$20–40.

Jugo de naranja, fresh orange juice squeezed as and when you order it, is another ubiquitous Dominican morning drink and makes for a good reason to get up; keep in mind that they tend to add piles of sugar to it unless you ask them not to. Later in the day you should sample the fresh **coconut milk** sold by street vendors. Dominican **batidas** are popular fruit shakes made with ice, milk and either papaya, mango, pineapple or banana – freshly made in a *comedor*, they bear no relation to the cartoned stuff bearing the same name. A similar drink that's traditionally served in Dominican homes is the **morir soñando**, a heavenly concoction of orange juice, condensed milk, sugar and crushed ice. Meanwhile, Coca-Cola and Pepsi have long been popular throughout the country. Once they were drunk as a matter of national pride, because the beverage companies used Dominican sugar to sweeten them. Today, the drinks are laced with American-made corn syrup, but you'll still find them almost everywhere.

There are several Dominican **beer** brands, but by far the most popular is **Presidente**, which is served in both normal-sized (RD$70) and surreally large (RD$100) bottles and compares favourably with beers from across the world. Similarly priced, but not as widespread, is **Bohemia**, which is more flavoursome and probably better suited to European tastes. Dominicans are obsessed with getting their beer as ice-cold as possible – if you don't want it to be a block of ice when you open it, do as they do and rub your hand under the bottom of the bottle before popping the cap. Also popular are the very good, inexpensive local **rums**, Brugal, Barceló and Bermúdez. Of these Bermúdez is the very best, but the dark, aged versions made by all three are quite good. A popular way to drink it is with Coke as a **Cuba libre**. In the discos and bars, ask for a *Cuba libre servicio*: a bottle of rum, two Cokes and a bucket of ice.

Watch out also for a potent local drink called **Mama Juana**, a sometimes hard-to-stomach concoction of local wines, rum, honey, and leaves and bark from various trees, which locals claim prolongs both sexual potency and life span. After hearing them go on (and on) about its miraculous properties, you may want to try it at least once. Traditionally, it's supposed to be buried underground for at least three months, then laid out in the sun for another three before consumption. You'll find Mama Juana bottles in the souvenir shops that circumvent this extended process, with the appropriate leaves and bark already added and a recipe for finishing the brew on the label.

Festivals

The Dominican Republic has a bewildering barrage of festivals. On every day of the year, there seems to be some kind of celebration somewhere. The majority are the regional fiestas patronales, held in honour of the city's or town's patron saint, who is often an amalgamation with an African god.

These traditional fiestas are one of the great pleasures of a trip to the DR; there's at least one in every city, pueblo and *campo*. The date is dictated by the saint's day as stated in the **Bristol Almanac** (published by pharmaceutical giant Bristol-Myers-Squibb), considered the authoritative source for such matters throughout Latin America. In addition to the actual saint's day, there will often be a nine-night celebration, called a **novena**, leading up to it.

The format of the fiesta follows one of the two models. In more remote parts of the country, the *fiestas patronales* have retained their original character and are syncretic religious ceremonies that feature large **processions** carrying an icon of the saint, religious folk songs accompanied by enormous **palos drums** fashioned from tree trunks, Haitian **gagá** music employing long wooden tubes and keyless metal trumpets that are both blown through and rattled with a stick, and **spirit possession**. Many others in the major towns and tourist areas have shed this religious affiliation and are today merely vibrant outdoor parties with a lot of drinking and a few traditional **contests** like a race to climb up a greased pole. An intermediate version are the many **cattle festivals** of the southeast, where processions of cattle and cowboys descend on the city from all sides. Regardless, they're invariably lively and will certainly be one of the highlights of your trip. In the big city festivals, though, **women travellers** should be prepared to deal with unwanted sexual advances and everyone should take precautions against pickpockets.

Major holidays and festivals

January

Jan 1 Santo Cristo de Bayaguana. A major procession of local bulls to the church in Bayaguana, where some are given to a local priest as a sign of devotion and thanksgiving.

Jan 1 Guloya Festival. The famous mummers of San Pedro de Macorís run a morning procession through the streets of San Pedro's Miramar barrio. A great opportunity to see this unique subculture's music, costumes and mini dance dramas.

Jan 5–6 Three Kings' Day. The major gift-giving day of the Dominican year.

Jan 21 Virgen de Altagracia. By far the most important religious day on the Dominican calendar, a prayer-of-intercession day to the country's patron and a massive gathering of celebrants in Higüey.

Jan 26 Duarte Day. Holiday in honour of the Father of the Country, with public fiestas in all major towns, biggest in Santiago and La Vega.

February

Feb Carnival. The pre-eminent celebration of the year, held on every Sunday in February and culminating on February 27. La Vega, Monte Cristi and Santo Domingo are your best bets.

Feb 2 Virgen de Candelaria. A religious procession in the capital's barrio San Carlos, in honour of this aspect of the Virgin.

Feb 27 Independence Day. Celebration of independence from Haiti and the culmination of the Dominican Carnival. Battle re-enactments in Santo Domingo and major parties in other big Carnival towns.

March–April

March 19 de Marzo. The major fiesta in Azua, in honour of the battle in which the Haitians were defeated here, ensuring Dominican independence.

Variable, usually early to mid-April Semana Santa. The Christian Holy Week is also the most important week of Haitian and Dominican *Vodú*. Traditional *gagá* festivals take place in the Haitian *bateyes*. Meanwhile, the town of Cabral holds its famous Carnival Cimarrón, in which townspeople adorned with demon masks descend on the city from the lagoon and castigate passers-by with whips.

May

May 2–3 Santa Cruz. A popular nine-night celebration in El Seibo, with a cattle procession to the sixteenth-century church on the final day and a very different spring festival in Azua and Baní, where all of the crosses in the area are covered with bright-coloured paper.

May 3 San Felipe. A huge cultural celebration on Puerto Plata's Malecón, with lots of live music. Seven weeks after Semana Santa.

May 3 Espíritu Santo. In honour of the Holy Spirit, syncretized to the Congo region's supreme deity Kalunda. Best in Santo Domingo's Villa Mella barrio.

June–July

June 3 San Antonio. Great, authentic celebration in the town of Yamasá, two hours north of Santo Domingo.

June 17–24 San Juan Bautista. A religious festival in San Juan de la Maguana in honour of John the Baptist and his African counterpart Chango, plus a smaller fiesta in Baní that features a distinctive style of music called *sarandunga*, a rapid-fire African drum-and-chorus rhythm that's beaten out in drum circles.

June 29 San Pedro Apóstol. A magnificent Cocolo festival in San Pedro de Macorís, with roving bands of *guloyas* performing dance dramas on the street.

July 24–26 Santiago Apóstol. Celebrating Santiago, the warrior patron saint of the Christian armies that conquered Moorish Spain. A large civic festival in Santiago with a lot of requisite partying around the Monument.

August–September

Aug 14 Festival of the Bulls. Higüey's *fiesta patronal*, featuring cowboys on horseback, large herds of cattle, and women carrying an icon of the Virgin on their shoulders and singing traditional *rosarios*.

Aug 16 Restoration Day. Nationwide celebration of independence from Spain, with large parties in Santiago around the Monument and around Plaza España in Santo Domingo.

Sept 24 Virgen de la Merced. A traditional *fiesta patronal* in the small Santo Domingo barrio Mata Los Indios, beginning mid-month, plus nationwide festivities.

Sept 29 San Miguel. This saint's also known as Belíe Belcán and is honoured with major festivals taking place in the capital's Villa Mella and barrio San Miguel, Haina and across the country. Look for the green-and-white-frosted cakes consumed on this day.

October

Oct 14–15 Santa Teresa de Ávila. The patron saint of Elías Piña, where you'll see a wonderful syncretic celebration using *palos* drums, *rosario* processions and *gagá*, plus a less traditional merengue party around the Parque Central.

Third week of October Merengue Festival. A major music festival in Puerto Plata, with major acts playing all over town; lots of partying on the Malecón. Date varies slightly from year to year.

October 24 San Rafael. In Samaná you'll see a procession through the town, partying on the Malecón and a traditional Dominican dance called the *bambulá*, which has died out in the rest of the country.

Last week of October DR Jazz Festival. Four-day jazz festival (ⓦ drjazzfestival.com) with venues in Puerto Plata, Sosuá, and Cabarete.

November–December

Nov 1 Todos los Santos. A major *Vodú* festival in the San Juan de la Maguana and southern border region, especially in nearby pueblo Maguana Arriba, where locals proceed to the cemetery to ask for the release of their relatives for the day.

Dec 4 Santa Bárbara. *Fiesta patronal* for the city of Samaná, including a procession that features the music of Doña Bertilia, queen of the *bambulá*, which is a major popular music on the peninsula.

Dec 28 Festival of the Bulls. Traditional cattle festival in Bayaguana, featuring unique traditional "cattle songs" that are sung to the bulls in order to bless them and prepare them for the January 1 procession to the local church.

Sports and outdoor activities

Not surprisingly, the majority of the country's tourism industry centres on its endless supply of idyllic, palm-fringed beaches and crystalline-clear turquoise waters. Watersports range from swimming, snorkelling, scuba diving, windsurfing and surfing to deep-sea fishing and whale watching.

Though many beaches are protected from powerful ocean currents by natural barriers, others have dangerous rip-tides and should be avoided by all but the strongest swimmers; also worth noting is that the waters off Santo Domingo are shark infested and should be eschewed by all. Inland, the island's many rivers and lakes are perfect for white-water rafting, canoeing and lake fishing. The country's five separate mountain ranges are popular for mountain biking, horseriding and trekking. In the resorts you'll also find golf courses, tennis courts and, in La Romana's *Casa de Campo*, polo grounds.

Snorkelling and scuba diving

The vast majority of **Dominican reefs** have been damaged beyond repair by careless local fishing practices, notably the daily dropping of anchors by thousands of small vessels. However, in recent years there has been a concerted effort at **conservation**, and coral is returning slowly to many areas. The only region where you'll still find a large system of intact coral reefs lies west of **Puerto Plata**, between La Isabela and Monte Cristi. By no coincidence, this is the most remote coastal region in the country and devilishly difficult to access for scuba diving and snorkelling. A number of tour operators, however, can take you out to parts of the reef from Sosúa or Cabarete.

Along the southern coast, the best snorkelling is at **Isla Catalina**, a small, heavily visited island near La Romana where the fish have been known to eat out of snorkellers' hands; at **Isla Saona**, an enormous mangrove island with decent reefs, just east of Bayahibe; and at **Parque Nacional La Caleta**, just east of Santo Domingo, where the National Parks Department sank a retired treasure-hunting ship called the *Hickory* in 1984, which has since been calcified with new reef that is a feeding ground for an array of sea creatures. Numerous private operators and most all-inclusive hotels offer trips to the reefs, wrecks and caves that dot the southeast coast, along with diving instruction. These are listed throughout the guide.

Surfing, windsurfing and kitesurfing

The north coast resort of Cabarete is known internationally as the **windsurfing** capital of the Americas and is the venue for the Cabarete Race Week and the Encuentra Classic, both major world competitions. There are a dozen different windsurfing clubs that offer equipment rental and high-quality tutoring, but the strength of the waves and wind makes it a daunting region for beginners.

Perhaps more appealing for beginners, though, is the burgeoning sport of **kitesurfing**, which takes much less time to learn and is truly exhilarating – even beginners are often shot up in the air by their kites as they skate along the waves. Once surfers have mastered Playa Cabarete's waters, many experts often try their hand at Playa Encuentro several kilometres west, where the waves are titanic and conditions extreme.

Surfing is less organized and done mostly by locals, though there are surf camps at Playa Encuentro, one of the less exploited beaches in the region, on a much smaller scale at Playas Grande and Preciosa, just east of Río San Juan, and Playa Boba north of Nagua. Be aware, though, that these are challenging spots for the sport and most have

no posted lifeguard, though they do have schools; they should only be used without supervision by those with a good deal of experience.

Sailing, fishing and whale watching

The DR is a major port of call for Caribbean **sailors**, with especially good marinas in Luperón, Manzanillo and Samaná, where you'll come across a network of dozens of fellow independent sea-travellers. Be warned, though, that the Puerto Turístico in Puerto Plata should be avoided at all costs, due to a high frequency of robberies and acts of sabotage. Nautical maps of the surrounding waters are hard to come by; your best bet is to pick one up at the marina in Luperón, though some of them will be a bit out of date. **Day-sailors** will find tour operators and independent boats in Puerto Plata, Cabarete, Luperón and Bayahibe that regularly take small groups of passengers on sailing day-trips; prices can run anywhere between RD$700 and RD$2000 for the day, depending on location and length of the excursion.

Many of the all-inclusive resorts feature daily **deep-sea fishing** tours that run around RD$1500 for the day per person, though you typically have to stay at the hotel in order to book them. Standard catches include sea bass, red snapper and kingfish, though you can get good game fish from tours along the southeast coast, including wahoo, porpoise and marlin. Along the northwest coast between Monte Cristi and Luperón the remarkable reef makes for some tremendous fishing; expect to catch wahoo, king mackerel and dorado year-round, with lots of tuna between June and August, blue marlin from May to September, white marlin between August and October and sailfish from November to April. Away from the hotels, you'll find good big-game fishing, especially for marlin, in southern coastal towns Boca de Yuma and Palmar de Ocóa. There's little in the way of tourist infrastructure in these towns, so ask around at the hotels for a good boat captain and make sure he or she has a working radio and safety equipment. On the south coast, the best months for fishing are from June until early September and you should expect to catch blue and white marlin, dorado and barracuda. From October to January you can still catch abundant sailfish and wahoo. The best **lake fishing** is near remote inland town Cotuí, where the Lago Hatillo, a pretty reservoir surrounded by rolling hills, holds large quantities of lake bass.

DOMINICAN NATIONAL PARKS

In the 1970s, ten percent of Dominican land was set aside for inclusion in a new state-run national park system. This foresight has resulted in the preservation of a diverse range of **ecosystems**, many of which seem out of place in the Caribbean, for example the karst moonscape desert of **Jaragua National Park** in the southwest, or the craggy, pine-forested alpine peaks of the **Bermúdez** and **Ramírez** national parks in the Cordillera Central, which are taller than any North American mountains east of the Mississippi River.

Other popular parks are the mangrove-laden cave system of **Los Haitises** in the northeast, and archetypal **desert island** Isla Saona in the southeast near Punta Cana. There are also lesser-known mountainous parks in the Sierra Bahoruco, arid desert in Jaragua National Park and a dozen different protected cave systems and **lagoons**.

The most popular parks, such as Bermúdez and Ramírez, have a reasonable amount of **infrastructure** with park offices and marked trails with cabins for spending the night mid-trek. More secluded and better-preserved areas along the Haitian border or in the **Sierra Bahoruco** are less geared towards tourism, although every year a new crop of independent tourist operations springs up catering to those looking for no-frills wilderness. We've covered these at the appropriate points in the guide.

Every winter, over four thousand **humpback whales** from across the Atlantic come to the DR's Bahía de Samaná and Silver Banks Sanctuary to mate, give birth and nurse infants. High season is January and February, with some early arrivals in December and a number of hangers-on in March. Whale-watching boats set out from the town of Samaná every day in high season and you'll also find tour operators that feature week-long boat excursions to Silver Banks, during which you'll have the opportunity to swim with the whales.

NATIONAL PARKS

Laguna Cabral	15	Parque Nacional Jaragua	17
Laguna Estero Hondo	2	Parque Nacional Monte Cristi	1
Lagunas Redondo y Limón	10	Parque Nacional Nalga de Maco	5
Parque Nacional Bahoruco	16	Parque Nacional Ramírez	8
Parque Nacional Bermúdez	7	Reserva El Pomier	12
Parque Nacional Cabo Francisco Viejo	4	Reserva Isabela de Torres	3
Parque Nacional del Este	14	Reserva Valle Nuevo	11
Parque Nacional Los Haitises	9	La Vega Vieja	6
Parque Nacional Isla Cabritos	13		

River sports

Mountain resort town Jarabacoa, deep in the heart of the Cordillera Central, is the centre for **white-water rafting** and **kayaking**. Several tour operators with experienced guides run daily trips down the turbulent Río Yaque del Norte. Expect a moderately challenging trip with several tricky twists and turns and a couple of steep drops. You can also spend as long as a week kayaking through the Cordillera Central rivers on excursions from operators Rancho Baiguate and Iguana Mama (see box, p.222). Jarabacoa, Cabarete and Las Terrenas also have terrific opportunities for cascading (descending a rock face on elastic cords) down various waterfalls as high as 75m, which when accompanied by experienced guides is far less dangerous than it sounds.

Mountain biking

The DR has five separate mountain ranges (see box, p.12) that afford almost infinite opportunities for **mountain biking**. Cabarete's Iguana Mama (see p.181) is the one major mountain-bike tour outfit in the country, offering challenging day-trips into the Cordillera Septentrional and week-long mountain-bike and camping excursions from one side of the country to the other. They're also the best place in the DR to go for **bicycle rental**, as they rent out several well-serviced Cannondales for US$30 per day. You'll find **bike clubs** in Santo Domingo and Santiago that go on major mountain-bike excursions across the island on weekends. Be forewarned, though, that if you can't keep up with their pace, they'll have no qualms about leaving you behind; if you're interested, ask first at Iguana Mama for a personal reference.

Hiking

The best **hiking** can be found along the five separate trails (see p.226) that lead from disparate parts of the Cordillera Central to Pico Duarte, the

---

SPECTATOR SPORTS

Baseball is the national spectator sport, and many of the top American major leaguers have come from the DR, including Alex Rodríguez, Sammy Sosa and Pedro Martínez (see p.287). A professional **winter season** is held from mid-November to mid-February, after which the winners go on to compete in the Caribbean Series (Serie del Caribe), along with the champion teams of Mexico, Puerto Rico, Venezuela and Cuba. The series is held in the DR every five years; they're next hosting in 2016. The **standard** of play in these games is quite high, with teams featuring the hottest up-and-coming Dominican kids along with veteran Dominican major leaguers and promising North American prospects sent here by their organization. Cities that boast **professional teams** are Santo Domingo (which has two), Santiago, San Pedro de Macorís, La Romana and Puerto Plata. These teams are often coached by former stars such as Tony Peña or Juan Marichal.

Tickets are available at all venues on the night of the game (from both the box office and touts) for RD$50–150, depending on where you want to sit – given that there's plenty of other entertainment going on (see p.10), it's a good-value night out. In addition to this professional season, **amateur winter seasons** take place in San Francisco de Macorís, San Juan de la Maguana, San Cristóbal and a few other towns. In **summer** you can check out the workouts and intramural play in the many **baseball camps**, run by teams such as the Los Angeles Dodgers, the San Francisco Giants, the Boston Red Sox and even Japan's Hiroshima Toyo Carp.

Surpassing baseball in terms of its history, if not popularity is **cockfighting**, which was brought over from Spain during the colonial era and is still largely considered the national "sport". Fights are typically held in a two-tiered, circular venue called a **club gallístico**, and more informal events take place in backyards. Throughout the countryside you'll see fighting roosters being carried, groomed and cooed at by starry-eyed owners who see them as a potential meal ticket, with **gambling** central to the sport. Watching the two birds peck at each other for ten minutes (sometimes killing one another but more often inflicting little damage) is less exciting than observing the rabid **crowd**. Fight preparations are also fascinating: the owners glue translucent brown claws (once made of turtle shell but now more often plastic) onto the feet, and then spew mouthfuls of water and oil over the feathers, making them more slippery and harder to claw through. The cocks are displayed to the crowd, bets are barked out in a flurry, the birds are let loose in the ring and the mayhem begins.

highest peak in the Caribbean. Hikes range from three to six days in length. The even more adventurous might want to take the rugged two-day trail from Río Limpio near the Haitian border to Nalga de Maco, an enormous system of caverns that's little visited by outsiders. If you're not up for a multiday excursion, try one of the several great day-trip hiking trails near Puerto Plata, Monte Cristi, Jarabacoa and Constanza, each outlined in the appropriate section of the guide.

Horseriding

Horseriding excursions are also quite popular. In addition to the plethora of outfits that offer day-rides along the country's many beaches, you'll find good-quality operators in Cabarete, Punta Cana, Las Terrenas, Jarabacoa, San José de las Matas and Río San Juan.

Caving

Another tempting outdoor option available is **caving** in one of the numerous extensive systems throughout the island, many bearing vast collections of Taino rock art. Among the easiest to see are the coastal caves in Parque Nacional Los Haitises, accessible by boat tour, but the most rewarding of all are the series of Taino caves in Parque Nacional del Este near Bayahibe, where Taino art references to Christopher Columbus and the early Spaniards have been discovered. Other prime places for exploration include caves near San Cristóbal, Monción, Cabarete, Las Galeras, Boca de Yuma, Loma de Cabrera, Bánica and Hato Mayor. There aren't a lot of organized caving tours, though; typically you'll have to hook up with a local guide and do them on your own, so be sure to bring your own boots and a torch.

Golf

Though there are several small, nondescript **golf courses** spread across the island, three of them stand head and shoulders above the pack: the Pete Dye-designed Teeth of the Dog course at *Casa de Campo* in La Romana and the excellent Robert Trent Jones courses at Playa Dorada and Playa Grande on the Silver Coast. All three have the majority of their holes set on spectacular open oceanfront and are occasionally used as tournament venues.

Travel essentials

Costs

Costs are **creeping up** in the Dominican Republic, for tourists as well as for locals. It is still cheap compared to other Caribbean destinations, with reasonable prices on the ground for independent travellers and budget package deals from the UK, Ireland and the US that include hotel, food and flight for those who want beach on a budget. In many parts of the country shoestring travellers can survive on as little as **US$25 per day** by getting by as the locals do; having a beer or eating in a local cafeteria can cost less than US$2/UK£1.20 for example, and in some places you can get the cheapest rooms for as little as RD$250–500. The savings are spread unevenly, though: riding from town to town via public transport can cost as little as US$0.50/£0.30, but car rental (including fuel and insurance) will set you back at least US$50/£30 a day. You may also want to set aside US$200/UK£120 or so for **unexpected splurges** such as an outdoor activity tour, which are priced to tourist, not local, budgets.

Crime and personal safety

The Dominican Republic is a **relatively safe** place, though in the cities you should take the same precautions that you would anywhere else – don't flaunt fat rolls of pesos, leave your expensive jewellery at home and definitely avoid walking alone late at night, or wandering around unknown barrios. You can tell you're in (or heading into) a **bad neighbourhood** as you will get a lot of discomforting stares and locals may warn you – the key words are *caliente* (literally "hot", meaning dangerous), or *tigre* (literally "tiger", meaning robber or hooligan). If you find yourself alone in a bad area, walk in the middle of the road and get to a main street or anywhere there are people. You need to be **especially careful** anywhere outside the Colonial Zone in Santo Domingo, including when leaving the airport (usually early morning hours or late at night), as the city (along with other big cities such as Santiago, Bonao, Moca, Barahona and La Vega) is experiencing a **crime wave** at time of writing due to high youth unemployment. Tourists are particularly targeted for both pickpocketing and armed muggings in broad daylight – though a crackdown by authorities is under way.

Rural areas are much, much safer, although travelling along little-used or remote roads alone is ill-advised – and it's best not to stop for anyone along them – as is travel after dark. **Tourist areas** are also pretty safe, though if you are staying on a resort, take off your wristband before going exploring as it is like drawing a target on yourself, increasing the likelihood of being robbed, overcharged or scammed.

The most likely danger you'll face is small-scale **rip-offs**, but even these can usually be avoided by not changing money on the street and by following the hints regarding guaguas (see p.25). **Sex tourism** is visible in tourist towns like Boca Chica, Sosúa and Las Terrenas but it's mostly kept to particular bars and so you are unlikely to be hassled on the street.

However, all that being said, if you use your common sense, you should get through your trip unscathed as the majority of Dominicans are honest, friendly and helpful. It's best to keep a copy of your passport, airplane ticket and all travellers' cheques at home and another at your hotel. You will need your tourist card (see right) and a photo ID on you at all times; a photocopy of your passport is acceptable. A few additional precautions will help keep your belongings safe: use the lock box in your room if there is one; take a room on an upper storey if you can; always keep an eye on your things while you're on the beach and on your luggage at the airport.

Dress

The Dominican Republic is a relatively conservative culture and while T-shirts and shorts are expected and entirely acceptable in resort areas, elsewhere both men and women should avoid wearing shorts and overly revealing clothing; topless men and women with bikini tops, for example, are frowned upon and will offend.

Electricity

Electricity service in the DR has become a lot more reliable in recent years, and blackouts are experienced less frequently and only in the more remote corners of the country. Plugs are standard American two-pins, so European visitors should bring suitable adaptors. The voltage is 110v AC. Intermittent, chronic power outages throughout the country mean that you may want to ask if your hotel has a generator that they're willing to use 24 hours a day.

Entry requirements

All visitors are obliged to pay a US$10 cash-only **entry tax** on arrival. Citizens and permanent residents of the US, Canada, the UK, Ireland, New Zealand, Australia, South Africa and all EU countries don't need a **visa** when visiting the Dominican Republic, but must obtain a thirty-day Dominican Republic **tourist card** for US$10 (US dollars only) at the airport on arrival; check first with your airline to see if the price of the tourist card is included in your flight. If you stay for a longer period of time, on departure you will have to pay an additional RD$1000 for up to a 90-day stay. Whatever your nationality, you'll have to show a return ticket home before boarding your flight, and your passport on arrival. Leaving the DR incurs a US$20 departure tax, although this is routinely included in most airfares, but not bus tickets.

Gay and lesbian travellers

Many resort towns like Boca Chica, Sosúa, Cabarete and Las Terrenas have a small yet fairly open **gay and lesbian** component but, although homosexuality is legal here, the only parts of the country that have a gay club scene are Santo Domingo (see p.79) and, to a lesser extent, Santiago. In other places, gay cruising usually takes place along the Malécon in town. The best **website** for gay and lesbian life in the DR is Ⓦmonaga.net, which includes a list of gay-friendly hotels. Bear in mind that the DR is a conservative, Catholic society at heart so overt public displays of affection may well be met with negative responses and you need to be especially careful as you enter and leave gay nightclubs.

Health

The standards of Dominican **health care** vary widely from institution to institution, even in the capital. Some hospitals don't properly sterilize operating rooms and there are a good number of frauds among the ranks of private doctors. But there are also a number of excellent institutions where you can get high-quality medical care; we've noted outstanding facilities in the appropriate sections of the guide. In emergencies you can dial ☎911 for ambulance and emergency medical care. No specific inoculations are required but it's strongly recommended that you be up to date with your hepatitis A vaccination in particular;

the virus is not unheard of in the DR and can be contracted more casually than other forms of hepatitis (eg contaminated drinking water). In general, you should do as the locals do and don't drink the **water**. Stick with bottled water for both drinking and brushing your teeth. For longer stays you might want to buy purified water in four-gallon jugs; if you return the bottle for deposit when you're done, it will cost you only RD$40.

There have been occasional reports of **malaria** and **dengue fever** in the Dominican Republic, though the risk of becoming infected is still quite low. Check with your doctor about the necessity of malaria pills; most people don't bother because of the extremely low rate of incidence. If you do opt to take medication, pay the extra cash and use malarone, as it has few side effects and will not interfere with your enjoyment of the trip.

HIV is a particular concern, as it is around the world. Roughly 1.1 percent of the adult population is HIV positive, and the rate among sex workers is twenty times higher than that. Unprotected sex with a stranger is a bad idea, full stop, and condoms are readily available.

Swimming in or drinking from **rivers** and streams also has risks, particularly the dreaded *Giardia*, a bacterium that causes stomach upset, fever and diarrhoea, and *Schistosomiasis*, a freshwater flatworm that can penetrate unbroken skin; both are treatable with antibiotics.

MEDICAL RESOURCES FOR TRAVELLERS

US and Canada

Canadian Society for International Health W csih.org. Extensive list of travel health centres.
CDC T 1 800 232 4636, W cdc.gov/travel. Official US government travel health site.
International Society for Travel Medicine T 1 770 736 7060, W istm.org. Has a full list of travel health clinics.

Australia, New Zealand and South Africa

Travellers' Medical and Vaccination Centre W tmvc.com.au. Lists travel clinics in Australia, New Zealand and South Africa as well as a few in East and Southeast Asia.

UK and Ireland

Hospital for Tropical Diseases Travel Clinic, London
T 020 3447 5999, W thehtd.org. Only for travellers with complex pre-existing medical problems or going abroad for more than 6 months. Open Wed & Fri, by appointment only.
MASTA (Medical Advisory Service for Travellers Abroad)
T 0870 606 2782, W masta.org. See website for the nearest vaccination clinic.
Tropical Medical Bureau Republic of Ireland
T 1 850 487 674, W tmb.ie.

Insurance

It is a sound idea to take out **travel insurance** coverage to cover against theft, loss and illness or injury. Before paying for a new policy, however, it's worth checking whether you are already covered: some all-risks home insurance policies may cover your possessions when overseas and many private medical schemes include cover when abroad. In Canada, provincial health plans usually provide partial cover for medical mishaps overseas, while holders of official student/teacher/youth cards in Canada and the US are entitled to meagre accident coverage and hospital in-patient benefits.

Students in the US will often find that their student health coverage extends during the vacations and for one term beyond the date of last enrolment.

After checking out the possibilities above, you might want to contact a specialist travel insurance company. A typical travel insurance policy usually provides cover for the loss of baggage, tickets and – up to a certain limit – cash or cheques, as well as cancellation or curtailment of your journey. Most of them exclude so-called dangerous sports unless an **extra premium** is paid: in the Dominican Republic this can mean scuba diving, whitewater rafting, windsurfing and trekking, though probably not kayaking or jeep safaris.

ROUGH GUIDES TRAVEL INSURANCE

Rough Guides has teamed up with WorldNomads.com to offer great travel insurance deals. Policies are available to residents of over 150 countries, with cover for a wide range of adventure sports, 24hr emergency assistance, high levels of medical and evacuation cover and a stream of travel safety information. Roughguides.com users can take advantage of their policies online 24/7, from anywhere in the world – even if you're already travelling. And since plans often change when you're on the road, you can extend your policy and even claim online. Roughguides.com users who buy travel insurance with WorldNomads.com can also leave a positive footprint and donate to a community development project. For more information, go to W roughguides.com/travel-insurance.

Internet

Virtually every town in the Dominican Republic has public **internet** access by way of phone centres, internet cafés and wi-fi access in restaurants, and from almost all mid-range and luxury hotels; the latter also tend to have at least one computer available for guests. Connection speed is not a problem in the DR, and you'll find using high-bandwidth services like Skype relatively easy. The going rate is typically RD$30 per 30min.

Laundry

Hotels typically offer **laundry service** and there are laundrettes in the major cities of the DR where you can get it done by weight, which costs much less than hotel prices, at around RD$100/kg. In a hotel, it's normal to have to pay per item, with the following prices a rough guide to what you should expect: trousers RD$40, men's shirt RD$20, blouses RD$25, underwear RD$5 and socks RD$5.

Living in the Dominican Republic

Many foreigners work in the tourism industry as adventure sport instructors or reps for all-inclusive resorts; most of these people work illegally on a tourist card, as it's phenomenally expensive and time-consuming to obtain an official **work permit**. If you're at a North American college, it's worth checking whether your school is one of the many to operate an exchange programme with the Catholic University in Santiago. Study, work and volunteer opportunities are listed below.

STUDY AND WORK PROGRAMMES

BTCV (British Trust for Conservation Volunteers) 📞 01302 388 883, 🌐 btcv.org.uk. One of the largest environmental charities in Britain, with a programme of national and international working holidays (as a paying volunteer).

BUNAC US 📞 1-800 GO-BUNAC; UK 📞 020 7870 9570; Republic of Ireland 📞 1477 3027; 🌐 bunac.org. Organizes working holidays in a range of destinations for students.

Camp America UK 📞 020 7581 7373; Canada 📞 902 422 1455; Australia 📞 1300 889 067; NZ 📞 9416 5337; SA 📧 lisajnel@gmail .com; 🌐 campamerica.co.uk. Organizes cultural exchange programmes all over the world.

Council on International Educational Exchange (CIEE) US 📞 1 207 553 4000; UK 📞 020 8939 9057; 🌐 ciee.org. Leading NGO offering study programmes and volunteer projects around the world.

Peace Corps 1111 20th Street, NW Washington, DC 20526 📞 855 855 1961, 🌐 peacecorps.gov. Maintains a large presence in the Dominican Republic, placing people with specialist qualifications or skills in two-year postings. Their operation in the Dominican Republic is considered one of their best.

Transformational Journeys 📞 816 808 3668, 🌐 tjourneys.com. Organizes mission trips to the Barahona region, particularly around the sugar-growing regions, in which you'll help build a piece of community infrastructure and stay in the home of a local family.

Mail

Dominican *correos*, or **post offices** (🌐 inposdom .gob.do), are notoriously slow if you use the normal mail so EMS **special delivery** is highly recommended as you'll only have to allow 3–5 days for North America and 6–8 days for mail to reach Europe or Australasia. EMS postage costs start at RD$878 to North America and RD$1175 to Europe, and elsewhere further afield. **Normal mail**, by comparison, costs from between RD$20–46, though it will take weeks rather than days. You can cut these delivery times by as much as a week if you use the central *correos* in Santo Domingo, Puerto Plata or Santiago, which have specific special-delivery windows; look for the "*entrega especial*" sign. Sending **packages** is unreliable (damage and theft are frequent) and not recommended unless absolutely necessary; if you must send parcels, bring them unsealed to the post office for inspection. Whatever you do, don't use the **postal boxes** that you'll see on the streets of many towns – you'll be lucky if the mail is picked up once a month – and don't ever send money or other valuables. A **private postal service** operates in Cabarete and Las Terrenas (see p.147). The most convenient way to **receive mail** is to have it sent to your hotel.

The media

It ranges from difficult to impossible to get magazines or newspapers from home, but virtually all hotels will have some form of US news on the TV and many of the high-end hotels get BBC as well. There are virtually no English-language newspapers and magazines available in the country, but there is a vibrant Spanish-language local media that can keep you up to date on the world's events.

Century-old **Listin Diario** is the most reputable of the Dominican daily newspapers, a broadsheet that has weathered a dozen different repressions of the free press over its history and still produces the best investigative journalism in the country, along with excellent sports coverage and a decent international roundup. **El Siglo** is a more recent arrival and a bit more plebeian in its outlook, mixing equal-opportunity haranguing of the three major political parties with good coverage of local music events as well as news stories on violent crime. **Hoy** is less enlightening than the other two, with rather perfunctory political coverage and a major emphasis on sports. You should be able to find the **Miami Herald** at the airports and **The New York Times** in high-end hotel gift shops; the odd copy of **Time** and **Newsweek** is available in bookstores.

On **Dominican radio**, you'll find only one American and European pop station in most areas, surrounded by a dozen Latin stations and at least one with 24-hour Pentecostal programming. Flip around a bit and you're likely to come up with a station playing old-style *merengue périco ripao*. In the most rural mountain areas, however, you'll be lucky to tune in to even one station. If you're in the south of the country, tune in to *Radio Millon* at 107.9, which features the golden age of Latin music, a real treat and a nice break from the omnipresent thud of merengue everywhere else.

Dominicans have access to cable **television**, which sends out over eighty channels, half in Spanish and half English-language American fare with subtitles, including CNN, various sports channels, the American networks and a number of others that will be familiar to North Americans. Without cable you'll be stuck with, at most, six local stations; one or two will feature the dregs of American cinema past – some with subtitles, some dubbed – while the rest focus on merengue videos, Venezuelan and Mexican soap operas, local talk shows and baseball games.

Most larger towns and cities will have at least one **cinema**, with foreign-language films usually dubbed, although occasionally they'll be subtitled. Check out ⓦcinema.com.do for an up-to-date list of cinemas and showings.

Money

There are two distinct economies within the Dominican Republic, the **US dollar** economy of the all-inclusive hotels and tour operators and that of the official Dominican currency, the **peso** (RD$). Throughout most of the country, you will have to change any foreign currency into pesos in order to conduct transactions. At the all-inclusive resorts and other foreign-owned tourism companies, though, all prices will be quoted in US dollars and Dominican pesos are accepted reluctantly – and at a poor rate.

Today the peso floats freely against the dollar, which means that there's some variation in exchange rate from day to day; it hovered at 43 pesos to the US dollar and 71 pesos to the British pound at the time this book went to press.

ATM machines are available across the country, even in fairly small towns. The most reliable ATMs are those run by Banco Popular – they can give you up to RD$10,000 at a time, while the more common **Banreservas** will only give you RD$2000. **Visa** and **MasterCard** are accepted in major cities and tourist destinations, and Amex is accepted in most large hotels and resorts, but when travelling in the countryside expect to pay in pesos.

You will at some point be approached by **moneychangers** in the street who will quote you unbelievably good exchange rates, but this is in no way advisable as you're most likely to end up ripped-off or even robbed.

Opening hours and public holidays

Banks and most businesses are typically open Mon–Fri 9am–12.30pm & 2–5pm, Sat 9am–12.30pm, though retail and other shops often stay open all afternoon and on weekends. There is no standard set of opening hours applicable to museums and colonial landmarks, but the opening hours of each are outlined in the guide.

Phones

Phone rates are typically expensive from your hotel room, but there are phone centres in every town that will allow you to call home. The going rate is RD$6 per minute to North America, RD$16 to Europe and RD$3.50 for calls within the country. It's much cheaper, of course, to call with an **online service** such as Skype, and you can either use your own device and the wi-fi in your hotel (most places have it these days), or use an internet/phone centre which are common all over the DR. You can also purchase local **sim cards** for your mobile device for under RD$500. Orange is by far the best-value vendor with the most national coverage and offices across the country. Their **phone cards** are sold in stores as well as by street vendors at major intersections of the cities and major highways. If you do bring your own mobile phone, keep in mind that radical **roaming charges** can be applied to calls made in the Dominican Republic; it's best to check roaming rates with your carrier ahead of time.

Making calls

The Dominican Republic shares the same dialling prefix as the US (1), and the vast majority of phone numbers share three **countrywide area codes** ❶809, ❶829 and ❶849. To call the Dominican Republic **from the US or Canada**, or to call from one region of the DR to another, you simply dial 1 plus the area code and the seven-digit local number. From all other countries, dial ❶001 plus the area code and seven-digit number.

Shopping

You'll probably be disappointed with the thin selection of local crafts on offer in the DR. Typical are the tacky "faceless dolls of Higüerito" sold in souvenir shops across the country, glazed clay statuettes of featureless, pale-skinned women in Victorian garb. Your best bet for an ostentatious piece of local folk craft is to buy one of the elaborate **papier-mâché Carnival masks**, though finding them can take some effort if you're not in Santo Domingo (where you can pick them up in Zona Colonial gift shops). Try in one of the major Carnival towns, preferably La Vega, Santiago or Cabral and ask around. They're easier to track down just before or after February; if you come during the festivities and see someone wearing a particularly interesting one, ask and they may well sell it to you at the month's end for around RD$500–1000.

Other good options are the stores that specialize in jewellery made with **larimar**, a turquoise, semiprecious stone found only in the DR, and **amber**, which is mined in the Cordillera Septentrional. You'll find outlets across the island, but if you go to the locations where these substances are mined, it's possible to get large chunks of the stuff for a few pesos; local miners sometimes even sell bits of amber with insects embedded inside them. Beware, though, as many souvenir stores try to rip off tourists with fake amber or larimar. The museums of larimar and amber in Santo Domingo (as well as the amber museum in Puerto Plata) will show you how to identify fakes. A good place to go for quality jewellery is **Harrisons**, a high-end Dominican jewellery store with outlets all over the country; you'll find an array of beautiful craftsmanship at these stores for half the price the same piece would cost at home. They're also working hard to preserve the nation's dwindling coral reefs by removing all of their black coral in favour of **black jade**, another indigenous, semiprecious stone.

The most popular souvenirs of all are the local **cigars**, considered by aficionados to be the equal of Cuban cigars. They're easy enough to purchase at souvenir shops across the country, but for a freshly rolled packet that's boxed while you watch, you'll have to go to one of the major cigar towns such as Santiago or nearby Tamboril. **Rum** is another major takeaway for visitors, as the local dark, aged rums are among the world's finest. You can find gift packages of Barceló and Brugal's very best *ron añejo* at stores across the country, and in Puerto Plata you can get a decent discount on Brugal's aged rums at their bottling factory tour.

Time

The Dominican Republic is in North America's Eastern Standard Time Zone (same time as New York and Atlanta) and five hours behind GMT. There is no daylight savings time.

Tourist information

The Dominican government also maintains **tourist offices** and toll-free tourist **hotlines** throughout the country and in the UK and North America (see p.42), which can be helpful in hooking you up with tour operators and package travel agents. The glossy promotional materials handed out by Dominican consuls and tourist agencies are pretty to look at but seriously lacking in hard facts.

The tourist office **maps** aren't especially good, but you can find several excellent ones of the country in travel bookstores and online; National Geographic's Dominican *Republic Adventure Map* is

TEMPERATURES AND RAINFALL

PUERTO PLATA

	Jan	Feb	Mar	Apr	May	Jun	Jul	Aug	Sep	Oct	Nov	Dec
Avg temp °F	73	73	75	75	79	81	81	81	81	81	79	75
Avg temp °C	23	23	24	24	26	27	27	27	27	27	26	24
Rainfall (mm)	193	154	121	157	128	62	71	82	91	137	293	280

CONSTANZA

	Jan	Feb	Mar	Apr	May	Jun	Jul	Aug	Sep	Oct	Nov	Dec
Avg temp °F	61	63	63	64	66	68	68	68	68	66	64	63
Avg temp °C	16	17	17	18	19	20	20	20	20	19	18	17
Rainfall (mm)	200	83	129	167	130	74	70	69	88	131	194	179

PUNTA CANA

	Jan	Feb	Mar	Apr	May	Jun	Jul	Aug	Sep	Oct	Nov	Dec
Avg temp °F	79	79	79	79	81	81	82	82	82	81	79	79
Avg temp °C	26	26	26	26	27	27	28	28	28	27	26	26
Rainfall (mm)	58	44	46	58	113	113	84	93	78	120	130	87

especially accurate and detailed. Mapas Gaar, El Conde 502, 3rd Floor, Santo Domingo, RD (☎809 888004; closed Sun), has navigational charts of the surrounding waters and wall-sized, detailed blueprints of most Dominican towns.

The Dominican Republic maintains a large presence on the internet although ferreting out a specific piece of information can take some time. Below are a few **tried-and-tested sites**.

TOURISM OFFICES

Canada 2055 Peel Street, suite 550, Montreal, H3A 1V4 2B8 ☎ 514 499 1918; 26 Wellington Street East Suite 201, Toronto, M5E-1S2 ☎ 416 361 2126.
UK Dominican Republic Tourist Board, 18–22 Hand Court, High Holborn, London WC1 ☎ 020 7242 7778,
✉ uk@godominicanrepublic.com.
US 136 E. 57 St. Suite 805, New York, NY 10022 ☎ 1 888 374 6361; 180 North LaSalle St. Suite 3757, 37th Floor. Chicago, IL 60601 ☎ 312 981 0325; 848 Brickell Ave. Suite 747 Miami, FL 3313 ☎ 1 888 358 9594.

USEFUL WEBSITES

Ⓦ **activecabarete.com** Terrific website devoted to Cabarete, with a detailed interactive map and a complete listing of hotels, restaurants, bars, current wind conditions, a calendar of events and other local services.
Ⓦ **debbiesdominicantravel.com** A dizzying array of links to hundreds of Dominican-related sites and a deep archive of travellers' personal accounts of all-inclusive vacations.
Ⓦ **dr1.com** The most heavily trafficked Dominican message board and the best place to get information on the web. Also has a good daily news bulletin that you can sign up for.
Ⓦ **ecoturismo.com**.do Great portal for finding out about

ecotourism trips and accommodation throughout the country.
Ⓦ **godominicanrepublic.com** Official website of the Dominican Republic Ministry of Tourism site, which is most useful for its info on visas and tourism offices.
Ⓦ **hispaniola.com** A site dedicated to Dominican tourism, with a talking Dominican Spanish phrasebook, daily weather, and a message board.
Ⓦ **listindiario.com.do** Online version of the DR's most venerable newspaper, with the best Dominican news coverage on the internet.
Ⓦ **paginasamarillas.com.do** Home page of the Dominican Republic's premier phone company, with a comprehensive Yellow Pages covering the entire country.
Ⓦ **popreport.com** An exhaustive news bulletin and comprehensive roundup of tourist attractions and businesses in the Puerto Plata area.

Travellers with children

The all-inclusive resorts are especially helpful when you're travelling with children, as they're in self-contained spaces, provide three meals a day and are generally designed to take care of the daily tasks of life for you. All resorts make at least some token effort towards **children's activities** and some are quite good at it. Independent travellers will find that the DR is a family-oriented place, and that locals are welcoming to small children.

You should watch out particularly for the **sun** – which is dangerously strong; SPF 25 and above is recommended – and the **water**: children are particularly susceptible to gastrointestinal problems caused by tap water and you should make sure that the whole family brush their teeth with bottled water.

You'll find that Dominicans love children and will focus a lot of positive attention on them. They're also more accepting of them in **restaurants** and hotels, and are unlikely to be bothered by any ancillary small-children chaos or noise; public **breastfeeding**, though, is pretty much unheard of. It's easy enough to buy **nappies** and the like in grocery stores, pharmacies and even rural *colmados*.

Travellers with disabilities

There are, unfortunately, few facilities that make independent travelling easier for the disabled in the DR, and no rental cars come with hand controls, though certain major monuments have access ramps. Most of the **all-inclusives**, though, have wheelchair access to certain rooms and all of their restaurants, casinos, bars and beaches. Call the hotel directly before booking a package for specific details regarding the hotel's infrastructure.

Women travellers

Though violent attacks against female tourists are relatively uncommon, many **women** find that the constant barrage of hisses, hoots and comments comes close to spoiling their holiday. Dominican men are quite aggressive and women travellers should come armed with the knowledge that they will draw incessant attention whether they like it or not – especially if you're blonde. Also, at major festivals, in guaguas, and on crowded streets, you may be subjected to a lot of groping hands. Whatever you do, don't be afraid to seem rude.

Santo Domingo

THE MALÉCON

1

Santo Domingo

It may not be the tropical paradise for which most travellers come to the Caribbean, but Santo Domingo has a past and a present as lively and fascinating as anywhere in the region. As the oldest colonial city in the Americas, an extraordinary number of New World firsts took place here – not least the building of the first cathedral, university, monastery, nunnery and hospital. But the capital throngs with far more than just history: as the modern face of the Dominican Republic, with a population of over two million, the city's heartbeat is loud and fast, propelled by everything from Latin music and baseball to ballet and opera.

Most visitors make a beeline for the **Zona Colonial**, the first European city of the New World, which remains magically intact along the western bank of the Río Ozama. Drawn in by the wonderful old buildings, memorable boutique hotels, delightful little parks and squares, and an eating and drinking scene equal to any in the city, many never bother to venture outside this neighbourhood – perhaps put off by their first impressions of the sprawling outer districts on their way into the centre.

Yet there's plenty more to see and do outside the boundaries of the Zona Colonial's sixteenth-century walls. Neighbouring **Gazcue** is home to the city's largest museums: the wonderful **Museo del Hombre Dominicano,** dedicated to the Taino civilization that thrived here before Columbus; and the **Museo de Arte Moderno** with its display of contemporary Dominican visual art. There are plenty of restaurants in Gazcue and along the city's seafront, the Malecón, where you'll also find some of the more spectacular nightlife venues. Few tourists stay in **Arroyo Hondo**, north of Avenida Kennedy, but with several fine museums in the vicinity and as the site of the **Jardín Botánico Nacional** it does entice some visitors away from the seafront neighbourhoods. Of course, the city isn't perfect: traffic screeches and stampedes through its streets, the air pollution is epic and the only relief from the monotonous vista of concrete-box construction in its outer neighbourhoods are the neon signs of strip malls and motor repair shops. Equally jarring is the visibly uneven distribution of wealth in a city that's dominated by ramshackle slums but has the highest per capita of Mercedes-Benz owners in the hemisphere. If you stick to the Zona Colonial you'll be blissfully unaware of all this – but Santo Domingo's frantic, less comfortable side is part of what lends the capital its arresting energy.

Brief history

The Río Haina, which borders Santo Domingo to the west, was once the site of a Taino village discovered by Spaniard Miguel Díaz, who fled Columbus's first settlement, La Isabela, after stabbing a fellow colonist in a drunken brawl. Locals gave him a gold nugget found near the river, which he brought back to the Spanish outpost where Christopher's brother **Bartolomé Columbus** was in charge while his brother was in

PARQUE COLÓN, ZONA COLONIAL

Highlights

❶ The Zona Colonial Pick through the sixteenth-century ruins of the first European city in the Americas, founded and ruled by the Columbus family. **See p.49**

❷ Plaza de la Cultura Four large museums and the sumptuous National Theatre. Especially memorable are the Museo de Arte Moderno and the Museo del Hombre Dominicano. **See p.64**

❸ Weekend nights at Parque Duarte The Dominican spirit is at its best at this pretty park on weekend nights – gay and straight revellers party in harmony at one of the most sociable feel-good spots in the city. **See p.77**

❹ Old-style Cuban son Several clubs across town feature some of the best Buena Vista-style old-school son in the world. **See box, p.78**

❺ La Guácara Taina Unique disco set in a massive five-storey cave, with live music and a thriving rave scene. **See p.78**

❻ Baseball at Estadio Quisqueya The enthusiasm of the crowd makes watching a baseball game in the heart of the DR a thrill regardless of whether or not you're a baseball fan. **See p.79**

HIGHLIGHTS ARE MARKED ON THE MAP ON PP.50–51

1

Spain. The La Isabela outpost had been a complete disaster and most colonists who hadn't already died of yellow fever had mutinied and abandoned the town. Spurred on, however, by dreams of gold, Bartolomé set sail with his remaining men in 1496 to establish a colony on the eastern bank of the Ozama. When Columbus returned in 1498, he took command of the new town, but he had trouble controlling the colonists and was recalled by Spain two years later. His replacement, **Nicolás de Ovando**, moved the city to the western bank and began the monumental stone construction that remains to this day, work that was continued by Columbus's son Diego when he took over in 1509. During their rule the city was a satellite capital of Spanish possessions, from which conquistadors set out to colonize and rule the rest of the Caribbean and the American mainland.

Invasions, occupations and ruin

Once Spain found greater wealth in the silver mines of Mexico and Peru, Santo Domingo's power and influence quickly eroded. An earthquake in 1562 destroyed much of the town and in 1586 **Sir Francis Drake** captured Santo Domingo, looted it and burned it down. Once rebuilt, the city failed to regain its strategic relevance and instead became subject to more attacks by the British and French over the next century until finally, in 1801, Haitian **Touissant L'Ouverture** took it without a fight. A succession of short-lived occupations followed, including the French in 1802, the British in 1803, the French again in 1804, the British again in 1809 and the Spaniards in the same year. By the time this spate of invasions was over, the city was economically devastated.

From Haitian city to Ciudad Trujillo

A much longer occupation was to follow – the Haitian domination from 1822 to 1843. They quickly alienated the Dominicans by implementing a land reform programme that robbed the Church and many wealthy white colonists of most of their land. As a result, Spanish merchants in the capital joined with the Catholic hierarchy to form the **Trinitarian movement** – named for its three leaders, the "Trinity" of Duarte, Mella and

SANTO DOMINGO

1

Sánchez – that led to independence after a long partisan war. But self-determination immediately devolved into internal strife as the city was besieged and captured again and again by competing Dominican *caudillos*, a cycle that ended only with the brutal regime of **Rafael Leonidas Trujillo**, who renamed the capital Ciudad Trujillo in 1936 (though it was changed back immediately on his death in 1961) and transformed it from a mere administrative capital to the national centre of shipping and industry.

American influence

A military coup and American invasion in 1965 were the last major battles to take place here, during which the Americans cordoned off the city along avenidas Mella and Independencia; the pro-democracy demonstrators were kept in check within it, while the Dominican military controlled the territory outside it and butchered hundreds of their enemies. Since then, industrialization and urban migration have forced the city outwards and, though the last forty years have been the longest stretch of peace Santo Domingo has seen in two centuries, the tough living conditions of many inhabitants make it less than idyllic.

Zona Colonial

"Its buildings are as tall and beautiful as those in Italy and its streets, wide and straight, are far superior to those of Florence."

Spanish Bishop Geraldini, on his arrival in 1525

The **Zona Colonial** – a square-shaped district nestling at the mouth of the Río Ozama and encircled by the ruins of the original city walls – is crammed with monumental architecture, and yet it's very much a living neighbourhood, thanks to the trendy cafés, locals' bars and rows of clapboard houses where thousands of people live and work. This was the domain of **Christopher Columbus**: founded by his brother Bartolomé, ruled by him for a time and claimed a decade later by his son Diego. After five centuries, the Columbus palace can still be found alongside the cobbled streets and grand old buildings of the walled, limestone city the family built. It was here that decisions with major repercussions for the rest of the hemisphere were made, for better or worse. A multimillion-dollar renovation, begun in the 1970s in preparation for the Columbus Centenary, has brought a number of the historic buildings back to their original state, giving you a real sense of how the city looked when first developed, and the piecemeal renovation continues as new businesses occupy the stone mansions and set up shop. Many of the important monuments can be seen in a single day if you keep to a brisk pace, although thorough exploration requires at least two or three. Wandering about, you'll no doubt be accosted by freelance guides, who are generally very friendly and sometimes quite knowledgeable; if you tell them you don't want assistance they'll leave you in peace.

Parque Colón

Museo de Ámbar Mon–Fri 9.30am–7pm, Sat 9.30am–6.30pm • Free

Everything emanates from **Parque Colón**: on the whole, the further you get from it, the less touristy the area becomes. A pleasant open space surrounded by beautiful colonial and Victorian buildings, the park centres on a statue of Columbus, standing heroically with an adoring, topless Taino maiden at his feet. Though the park is largely given over to tourism – as signalled by the *Hard Rock Café* at its northern end – it's still a remarkably pleasant place to hang out.

At the west end of the park lies the Victorian-style nineteenth-century town hall, no longer a seat of government but still used for municipal office space, while to the north

1

sit cafés and restaurants, a cigar dealer and, in the oldest colonial home on the park, a high-end jewellery store with a small museum upstairs, the **Museo de Ámbar**, featuring ants, termites, wasps and other insects trapped in amber. On the park's east side are more municipal and administrative buildings including **Casa de Abogados**, the old town jail, and **Palacio Borghella** – both early nineteenth-century edifices constructed by the Haitians. Borghella was once especially beautiful, but Hurricane Georges destroyed its stunning facade in 1998.

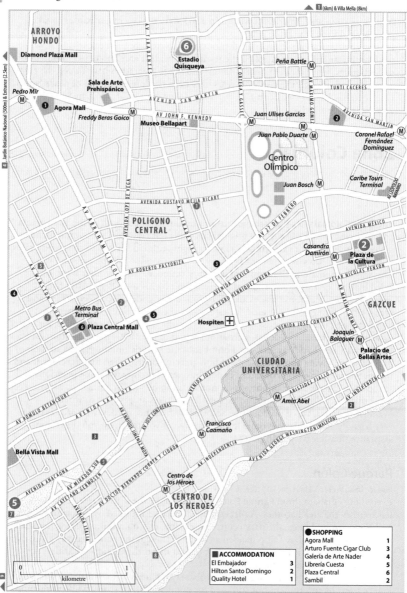

■ ACCOMMODATION	
El Embajador	3
Hilton Santo Domingo	2
Quality Hotel	1

● SHOPPING	
Agora Mall	1
Arturo Fuente Cigar Club	3
Galería de Arte Nader	4
Librería Cuesta	5
Plaza Central	6
Sambil	2

Basílica Catedral Santa María de la Encarnación

Parque Colón, entry on La Plazoleta de los Curas, accessed either via the gate on Isabel La Católica or the Alley of the Priests off Padre Billini • Mon–Sat 9am–4.30pm • RD\$40 or RD\$60 with audio guide, under-13s free • ☎ 809 685 2302 • No thigh-revealing shorts or skirts; trousers forbidden for women

Most imposing of the buildings on Parque Colón is the **Basílica Catedral Santa María de la Encarnación**, intended, when constructed by the Vatican, to be the religious centre of the West Indies and the base for proselytizing all the indigenous peoples of the Americas. It

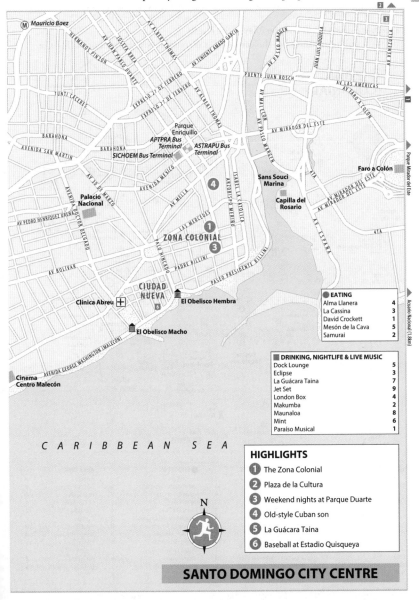

EATING

Alma Llanera	4
La Cassina	3
David Crockett	1
Mesón de la Cava	5
Samurai	2

DRINKING, NIGHTLIFE & LIVE MUSIC

Dock Lounge	5
Eclipse	3
La Guácara Taina	7
Jet Set	9
London Box	4
Makumba	2
Maunaloa	8
Mint	6
Paraíso Musical	1

HIGHLIGHTS

1 The Zona Colonial

2 Plaza de la Cultura

3 Weekend nights at Parque Duarte

4 Old-style Cuban son

5 La Guácara Taina

6 Baseball at Estadio Quisqueya

N

SANTO DOMINGO CITY CENTRE

also played a formative role in the birth of New World Voodoo, when imported slaves appropriated the practices of the sixteenth-century Spanish religious brotherhoods called *cofradías*, an Iberian institution since the Middle Ages. The *cofradías* used the cathedral for their patron-saint parades, and the slaves followed suit, except that West African god Chango was worshipped under the guise of Christian St John, in religious processions involving traditional drum music, dancing and possession. As the century wore on, the clergy realized that the African *cofradías* were incorporating some distinctly unorthodox practices and banished them to the churches along the city's northern wall.

La Plazoleta de los Curas and the Alley of the Priests
The entry point for visitors to the cathedral is through its southern door, facing the

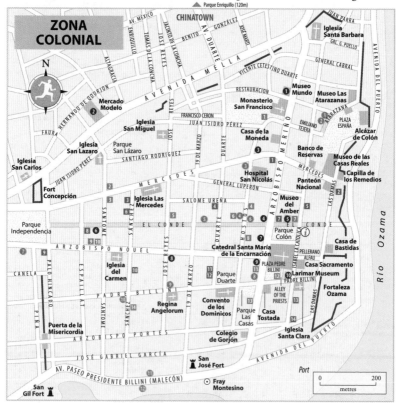

■ DRINKING, NIGHTLIFE & LIVE MUSIC		■ ACCOMMODATION		● SHOPPING		● EATING	
Bio	14	Aida	8	Caoba Cigars		Angelo	1
Casa de Teatro	13	El Beaterio	11	Boutique del Fumador	5	Antica Pizzeria	9
Doubles	11	Hostel Casa Grande	6	Columbus Plaza	7	La Bríciola	8
Esedeku	2	Casa Naemie	13	De Mi País	9	La Cafetera	5
La Espiral	5	Casa Sánchez	3	Joyería DiCarlo	4	D'Luis Parrillada	12
Fogoo	9	Casa Del Sol	14	La Leyenda del Cigarro	3	Dumbo	7
G Lounge	10	Conde de Peñalba	7	Librería La Trinitaria	8	Falafel	10
Hard Rock Café	7	Discovery	9	Mercado Modelo	2	Mesón d' Bari	4
Lucia 203	4	Dominico Mundial	12	Museo del Ámbar	5	Mesón de la Rioja	11
Lulú	12	Francés	1	Museo Larimar		Mesón de Luís	6
Mesón d'Bari	6	Hodelpa Caribe Colonial	5	Museo Mundo de Ámbar	1	Pat'e Palo	2
NYC	3	Hotel Nicolás de Ovando	2	Dominicano	10	La Taberna Vasca	3
Ruinas de San Francisco	1	Palacio	4	Musicalia	6		
El Sarten	8	Villa Colonial	10				

enclosed **Plazoleta de los Curas**, the Plaza of the Priests. This little square was once the city cemetery, but Drake burned the cathedral's records and now no one knows who was buried here. Across the plaza, the **Alley of the Priests**, an attractive walkway lined with bougainvillea, leads past the old priests' quarters; note the decorative Islamic brick arches over the doorways.

The northern and western facades

Built between 1521 and 1540, only the fortifed **northern facade** bears the traces of the cathedral's Gothic roots in the minimalist stud ornaments around the windows. The **western facade** is instead Plateresque, a style that predominated in Santo Domingo during the reign of Diego Columbus, with an overabundance of friezes and fanciful ornamentation: look for the allegorical frieze above the portals – meant to symbolize the ocean journey of the colonists – that depicts a flight of cherubs making their way past horse-headed sea creatures and impious women. The original mahogany doors here remain intact, and priests still use the same 500-year-old key to lock them at night. The gold Habsburg seal and statuary that once surrounded the portals, however, were pilfered by Sir Francis Drake – the current ones are modest reproductions. Look around to the right and you'll see the cathedral's exposed bell tower; the original covering was demolished by Drake (who turned the church into a barracks during his stay) and never replaced.

The interior

Inside the cathedral, under a Gothic ribbed vault, a few items are worth seeking out, including a seventeenth-century marble altar and a sixteenth-century altar, pulpit and pews of mahogany. Beneath the marble floor a tunnel, now sealed off, led to the archbishop's palace across the street. Just to the right of the pulpit is one of the thirteen church chapels, **Santa Ana**, which bears the tomb of colonial administrator Rodrigo de Bastidas and the only surviving original stained-glass window, an angel hovering over Virgin and Child. Beside it the **Chapel of Life and Death**, where baptism and extreme unction are performed, has a Rincón Mora window – reminiscent of Chagall – showing a deranged-looking John the Baptist baptizing a clean-shaven Christ. Continue down the southern wall and you'll come to the **Chapel of the Apostles**, which holds an original mural on its 1556 vault, a beautiful mahogany altar with a silver retable (framed altarpiece) and the grave of Royal Secretary Diego Caballero. On the northern wall you'll find the **Chapel of the Virgin of Antigua**, with its gorgeous groined vault and a beautiful 1520 painting of Mary, shipped to Spain by Santana upon annexation and returned in terrible shape in 1892 (it's since been restored); the **Chapel of the Virgin of the Light**, where Columbus was interred for a time; and the **Chapel of Christ in Agony**, where two stone lions stand guard over the grave of Santo Domingo's first bishop, Alejandro Geraldini.

El Conde

El Conde, stretching west from Parque Colón and linking directly to Parque Independencia, was once Santo Domingo's main thoroughfare but was closed off to motorized traffic in the 1970s. It is now a busy pedestrian boulevard cutting right through the heart of the Zona Colonial, and is lined with touristy gift shops, cafés, fast-food restaurants, cheap clothing stores, tattoo parlours and bookstalls. It's an ideal place to people-watch, with hundreds of city-dwellers passing through at all hours, locals playing chess and pavement vendors selling everything from pirated CDs to split coconuts.

Puerta del Conde

Opposite the western end of El Conde

The **Puerta del Conde** (Gate of the Count), part of what was a military fort in the seventeenth century, was named for Count Bernardo Bracamonte, whose military tactics

1

saved the city from British invasion in 1655. It's an imposing stone structure adorned with a decorative, red-brick belfry, where Mella raised the new national flag for the first time.

Parque Independencia

Altar de la Patria daily 8.30am–6pm • Free • No shorts or short skirts

The Puerta del Conde leads into the interior of beautiful **Parque Independencia**, a popular meeting place encircled by a traffic-choked ring road, with shaded benches and a stone slab that serves as a marker from which all distances in the capital are calculated. Near the park's centre is the honour-guarded **Altar de la Patria**, a marble mausoleum in which Mella is buried beside his compatriots Duarte and Sánchez. At the north end of the park, look for the fenced-off, fortified ramp that leads to the **Fort Concepción** (1678), just beyond the park boundaries, a pentagonal cannon platform with tremendous limestone walls.

Plaza Padre Billini and Casa de Tostado

Plaza Padre Billini, corner of Arzobispo Meriño and Padre Billini • **Museum** Mon–Sat 9am–5pm, Sun 9am–4pm • RD$100 • ☎ 809 689 5000

Behind the cathedral is **Plaza Padre Billini**, a neat little public plaza enclosed by several very appealing places to eat and drink (see p.75 & p.77). Over the road from its southeast corner you'll find **Casa de Tostado**, built in 1503 by scrivener Francisco Tostado, whose son was later killed by a Drake cannonball. The exterior's most notable feature is the Gothic double window above the front door, the only one of its kind in this hemisphere. Inside you'll find the **Museum of the Nineteenth-Century Dominican Family**, featuring a number of attractive (if unspectacular) antique furnishings, some of which are Art Nouveau. Check out the geometric Mudéjar tiling on the courtyard well and ask to climb the circular mahogany staircase that leads to the roof.

Iglesia Santa Clara

Padre Billini and Isabel La Católica

Built in 1552, the largely unadorned **Iglesia Santa Clara** was the New World's first nunnery. The Catholic primary school that's here now is not technically open to the public, but the nuns will let you wander into the grounds to see the chapel on, with its single nave supported by five Gothic arches.

Casa del Sacramento

Isabel La Católica and Pellerano Alfau • Free entry but no formal visiting times

Just north of the Iglesia Santa Clara nunnery lies another important relic owned by the Church, the peach-coloured **Casa del Sacramento** (House of the Sacrament), built in 1520 by Diego Caballero and now the residence of the archbishop. Legend ascribes the building's name to an apocryphal sixteenth-century event in which the owner purchased a large orangutan from a passing merchant. The animal somehow got loose in the courtyard and threatened to hurl an infant off the roof until the baby's mother began repeating the rosary, upon which the primate put the child down and went to sleep. Renovations in the 1930s disguised the building's colonial bulk in a decorative Victorian wrap. You can sometimes walk through the two connecting courtyard gardens, or up to the viewing platforms of the towers, which offer scenic rooftop views of the neighbourhood.

Museo Larimar Dominicano

Isabel La Católica 54 • Mon–Sat 9am–6pm • Free • ☎ 809 682 3309, ⓦ larimarmuseum.com

A remodelled house from the late 1700s, the **Museo Larimar Dominicano** holds a variety of English-captioned exhibits on larimar, a turquoise-coloured stone that exists only in the Dominican Republic. In addition to a number of particularly beautiful examples of raw larimar as it is mined from the Bahoruco Mountains (see p.257), the museum shows how the semiprecious gem was created by local volcanic activity, how it is mined, a number of larimar-embedded leaf and wood fossils and some pieces of larimar art. You'll also find out how to tell real from fake larimar and there's a very nice jewellery shop on the ground floor.

Colegio de Gorjón

Corner of Meriño and García

The sixteenth-century **Colegio de Gorjón** served as the New World's second university, after San Tomé de Aquino (see p.59). As with all early colonial structures, the stonework was originally exposed but, acting under a misconception that the plague was transmitted through bare masonry, Philip V decreed in 1712 that all buildings in the empire be plastered; this building is a beautifully whitewashed example. Check out as well the stunning courtyard on Calle García, which has a delightful ocean view.

Calle Las Damas

A block east of the cathedral

Calle Las Damas (Ladies' Street) was the first road laid out by Ovando when he moved the town to this side of the river, which might just make it the oldest surviving street on the American continent. It got its name in 1509, thanks to the retinue of women who would accompany Diego Columbus's wife María de Toledo down it to church every Sunday morning; their proximity to María reflected their standing in the city's social hierarchy. Today it's mostly tourists treading its cobblestones, and many of the early sixteenth-century mansions now house museums or prestigious institutions, including the French Embassy on the corner of El Conde, originally the home of conquistador Hernán Cortes, and, opposite, the high-end *Hotel Nicolás de Ovando* (see p.73).

Fortaleza Ozama

Southern end of Las Damas • Tues–Sun 9am–5pm • RD$70, students RD$10, under-10s free • ☎ 809 688 1553

Fortaleza Ozama, where Diego and María lived while their palace was under construction, was long Santo Domingo's most strategic site. Built in 1502 and enlarged over the centuries, it's set on a steep bank over the mouth of the Ozama and was the departure point for the Spanish conquests of Cuba, Colombia, Jamaica, Peru and Mexico – it was finally decommissioned after the American invasion of 1965. Today it's also known as the **Museo Fortaleza de Santo Domingo**. Beyond the Neoclassical main gate, the courtyard features a statue (with definite shades of Rodin) of González Oviedo, author of the first *History of the Indies* and commander of the fort from 1533 to 1557. The largest structure is the bulky medieval **Torre de Homenaje** (Tower of Homage), the most impenetrable part of the fortress and used for centuries as a prison. Climb to the top for panoramic views, or head inside where you'll find the hole through which prisoners were dropped to their cell. Also on the grounds are the old **arsenal** (with a niche bearing an icon of Santa Bárbara, patron of the military), the excavated remains of the provisional fort from 1502, and the intact wall of Fort Santiago, the first line of defence against potential invaders.

Casa de Bastidas and Museo Infantil Trampolín

Southern end of Calle Las Damas, next to Fortaleza Ozama • Museum Tues–Sat 9am–5pm • RD$60 children, RD$100 adults • ☎ 809 685 5551, ⓦ trampolin.org.do

Sharing Fortaleza Ozama's northern wall is **Casa de Bastidas**, built around 1510 by Bishop Rodrigo Bastidas, who was the king's tax collector and went on to colonize Colombia. Since then the house has been associated with the fort, often serving as an

1

officers' residence; the seventeenth-century statue of Santa Bárbara above the main entrance signifies its link with the military. These days it serves as a children's science museum, the **Museo Infantil Trampolín**, with a planetarium and exhibits on geography, paleontology, energy, ecology and social sciences. All in all, it's a great place for kids, but exhibits are in Spanish only.

Panteón Nacional

Las Damas between El Conde and Las Mercedes • Tues–Sun 8am–6pm, Mon 12–6pm • Free

The **Panteón Nacional** was built from 1714 to 1745 as a Jesuit convent, not long before the order was expelled from the colonies. Today it's a nationalist monument where most of the major military and political figures from Dominican history are interred. The building's Neoclassical, martial facade seems particularly suited to its sober task, topped with a prominent cupola flanked by statues of Loyola and Jesus. The interior has been completely redone, with Italian marble floors, an enormous central chandelier donated by Spanish dictator Franco and a massive central mausoleum. The serenity and patriotic uniformity of the elevated marble caskets around a large eternal flame is at odds with the competing *caudillos'* legacies – nineteenth-century dictator Pedro Santana, for example, is surrounded by his enemies (and successors) Pepillo Salcedo, Gaspar Polanco, Pedro Antonio Pimentel, José María Cabral and Gregorio Luperón, each of whom briefly served as president before being deposed by the next.

Casa de los Jesuítas

Las Damas, corner of Las Mercedes

Beside the Panteón Nacional is **Casa de los Jesuitas**, built in 1508 by Diego Caballero's brother Hernán and taken over in 1701 by the Jesuits, who turned it into a renowned school of rhetoric; now it holds the administrative offices of the Museo de las Casas Reales (see p.57). Check out the beautiful Islamic portal in the courtyard.

Casa de las Gárgolas

Las Mercedes 6 between Las Damas and Isabel La Católica

Another sixteenth-century Jesuit property, **Casa de las Gárgolas** is named for the prominent row of five grimacing gargoyles above the front door. Their state of decay is due in part to the vagaries of time and in part to a seventeenth-century incident in which they were pelted with stones by a mob, who believed them supernaturally responsible for a series of local murders.

Casa de Juan Viloria

Las Mercedes 4 between Las Damas and Isabel La Católica • Dominican Development Foundation ⓦ fdd.org.do

Next door to the Casa de las Gárgolas, **Casa Viloria**, built by the king's chamberlain Juan de Viloria in 1520, continues the supernatural theme: supposedly haunted by Viloria's ghost, some locals claim that he appears one night a year and offers to reveal the location of his buried treasure to anyone willing to follow; apparently enough folks took up this offer to dig several holes in the courtyard's tile floor, found when work was begun on the house's restoration. Today it houses the headquarters of the Dominican Development Foundation.

Plaza de España

Calle Las Damas ends at **Plaza de España**, the colonial zone's widest open space, an attractive tiled expanse with terrific views across the river, which you can enjoy from one of its many breezy outdoor cafés. This was the centre of colonial power and commerce, with sailors disembarking from the adjoining port, foreign merchants auctioning slaves and Spain's high officials administering their empire from the Casas Reales. An intact section of the old town wall still skirts the eastern plaza, extending to

1

Puerta San Diego, the colonial-era entrance from the port. More decorative than functionally defensive, at night the plaza's arcades are a favourite local hangout but during the day it can feel a little deserted; on its eastern face you'll find the excavated foundations of the colony's arrow-shaped, riverfront fort. At the centre a statue of Ovando stands on the previous site of an enormous pillar that was to support an aqueduct from the Río Haina (the Ozama's water being too brackish to drink).

Museo de las Casas Reales

Entrance just off the southern end of Plaza de España on Las Damas • Mon–Sat 9am–5pm, Sun 9am–4pm • RD$100 including audio guide • ☎ 809 686 0414

Built between 1503 and 1520, **Museo de las Casas Reales** was the administrative centre of the West Indies, housing the Royal Court, Treasury and Office of the Governor. Opposite the entrance, an eighteenth-century sundial sits on a pedestal, positioned so bureaucrats could tell the time by simply looking out the window. The museum's ground-floor collection is a bit of a hotchpotch, with a few Taino artefacts and Spanish navigational instruments. Near the back you'll find a rickshaw, in which Spanish judges were carried to court by Tainos, and a sixteenth-century apothecary crammed with colourful glass vials. The floor above is more coherent, holding an armoury donated by Trujillo, with examples of weaponry used here since the time of Columbus.

Alcázar de Colón

Plaza de España • Tues–Sat 9am–5pm, Sun 9am–4pm • RD$100 including audio guide; tickets sold in building adjacent to palace • ☎ 809 221 1737

In the northeastern corner of Plaza de España is the **Alcázar de Colón**, the fortified palace of the Columbus family, built by Diego from 1511 to 1515 without the use of a single nail. He chose the site because of its easy proximity to the Casas Reales (see above), where he conducted official business, and so that it would be the first building seen by disembarking sailors and merchants. Also, from its terrace he could look across the Ozama and see the remains of the wooden colony his father Christopher had built. The palace grounds would also decay, hastened by the family's departure for Spain in 1577; a nineteenth-century illustration by American traveller Samuel Hazard depicts them scarred, overgrown with weeds and fronted by two thatch huts. You'd never know it today – the portal's flattened arches, framed by rectangular panels, are pristine. They're also the finest local example of the late Gothic style called **Isabelline**, characterized by plain, linear surfaces adorned only with Islamic portals and delicate vine ornaments.

Inside, a **museum** assembles an array of sixteenth-century pieces, evocative of the life of early Spanish nobility. Reproductions of the stone gargoyles that held up the first-floor ceiling leer down at the collection of mahogany furniture, religious tapestries and period silverware. A narrow, circular stone staircase leads to the second floor, where the private study showcases illuminated manuscripts from Spain and the music salon holds a sixteenth-century harp and clavichord. From the second floor, you can walk to the terrace fortifications, the construction of which led Spanish officials to fear Diego intended to barricade his followers inside and declare himself "Emperor of the Americas".

La Atarazana

Tucked behind the Plaza de España to the north is a short street known as **La Atarazana**. In the old days the buildings that now house shops, restaurants and bars held taverns frequented by passing mariners and the city's large public market, where ships stocked up on tropical fruit to combat scurvy. Follow it round the corner to the Reales Atarazanas, once the port authority, and more recently the **Museo de las Atarazanas**, which displayed the recovered booty from the wreck of the

1

sixteenth-century Spanish galleon *Concepción*, sunk during a hurricane in the Bahía de Samaná. It has undergone a lengthy period of renovation and was still closed in 2014.

Museo Mundo de Ámbar

Arzobispo Meriño 452 and Restauración • Mon–Sat 9am–6pm, Sun 9am–2pm • Free • ☎ 809 682 3309, ⊗ amberworldmuseum.com

Not to be confused with the Museo de Ámbar on Parque Colón (see p.50), the **Museo Mundo de Ámbar**, at the less visited end of Arzobispo Meriño, is based on the popular amber museum in Puerto Plata (see p.162). Inside is a nice little exhibit on the origins of amber, a set of Triassic-era insects trapped in the translucent goo, and a gift shop with a generous sampling of amber jewellery.

Banco de Reservas

Isabel La Católica 201 and Mercedes • Mon–Fri 8am–5pm, Sat 9am–1pm • Free

This Art Deco branch of the **Banco de Reservas** is worth a visit for the social-realist mural *Moneda* displayed in its lobby. It's the work of **José Vela Zanetti**, an anarchist exile of the Spanish Civil War who lived and worked in the Zona Colonial during the 1940s and 1950s, gleefully tattooing subversive, anti-capitalist statements on the many public commissions he received. Here labourers slaving in factories and fields surround a heroic figure stolidly grasping a gold coin.

Monasterio San Francisco

End of Emiliano Tejera, corner of Hostos

Perched atop a hill at one of the highest points in the Colonial Zone lie the atmospheric ruins of the **Monasterio San Francisco.** Begun in 1544 when the Catholic Church was transforming Santo Domingo into the religious capital of the hemisphere, the Franciscan monastery weathered an artillery assault from Sir Francis Drake and the brunt of several earthquakes, which levelled the main building and the original chapel adjacent to it. Still visible above the entrance are the curling stone belt of the Franciscan order and a Renaissance bust of Bishop Geraldini, who oversaw its initial construction. The Gothic portal below leads to the **Chapel of the Third Order**, built in 1704 after the original was flattened; the Third Order was an organization of spiritual laymen who followed the Franciscan lifestyle. The coral-pink arcade opens onto the cloisters and the monastery church – also in ruins but with enough of the structure remaining to make it a popular, atmospheric spot for local weddings. All that's left of the main building, however, are the foundations, a few mounds of rubble and, poignantly, some metal studs in the walls: these once held the leg chains of inmates when the site served as a mental asylum during the nineteenth century.

Hospital San Nicolás de Bari

Hostos between Las Mercedes and General Luperón • No formal timetable for visits • Free entry

Not much remains of the **Hospital San Nicolás de Bari**, built in 1503 and mostly torn down in 1911 after being devastated by a hurricane. The most impressive feature left in the pigeon-haunted ruins is the two-storey portal with Renaissance pillars on the ground floor and a tremendous Gothic arch on the top. The Victorian **Iglesia Altagracia** beside it – associated locally with miraculous healing – incorporates the hospital's eighteenth-century chapel. Within it you'll find a life-size statue of **Dr José Gregorio Hernández**, a Venezuelan medical doctor from the 1930s, worshipped throughout Latin America as a saint who performs operations on believers while they sleep.

Convento de los Dominicos

1

Convento de los Dominicos: Hostos 64 and Padre Billini • Mon–Sat 8.30am–12.30pm & 3–6pm • Free • ☎ 809 682 3780,
ⓦ conventodominico.org

Just south of El Conde are three ancient churches worth a detour: **Regina Angelorum**, **Iglesia del Carmen** and, oldest of the trio, the 1510 **Convento de los Dominicos**, which held the New World's first university, San Tomé de Aquino. Its striking stone facade is framed by decorative two-dimensional pillars, blue Mudéjar tiling runs along the top of the portal, and a profusion of red Isabelline vine ornamentation surrounds the circular window in the centre. Inside, on the vault of the sanctuary's Chapel of the Rosary (the first chapel to the right of the entrance) you'll find an impressive reminder that European Christianity was a syncretic religion (see box, p.60) long before it came to the New World: an enormous pagan **zodiac wheel** is guarded by Jupiter (spring), Mars (summer), Mercury (autumn) and Saturn (winter), each identified not only with a season but as one of the gospel authors as well. Though there were once many such syncretic church illustrations in Europe, most were destroyed during the Counter-Reformation. The simple but attractive **Chapel of the Third Dominican Order** across the plaza once held the studies of famed Taino defenders Las Casas and Montesino. In colonial times the cobblestone path between the chapel and the church was known as the Street of the Cobblers, as it was home to the city's shoemakers.

Regina Angelorum

Padre Billini and José Reyes

A monumental piece of architecture that took nearly a century to build, the **Regina Angelorum** (Queen of the Angels) nunnery features huge external buttressing, decaying gargoyles and a sombre stone facade. Knock on the caretaker's door in the back to have a peek inside, where you'll find a Baroque eighteenth-century altar with a stunning silver retable and the marble grave of Padre Francisco Billini.

Iglesia del Carmen

Arzobispo Nouel and Santomé • Opening hours vary but services usually held Mon–Sat 5pm and Sun 9.30am

Smaller than Regina Angelorum, but far prettier, is nearby **Iglesia del Carmen**, once the secret meeting place of the Trinitarian rebels. Its facade boasts a decorative Isabelline red-brick portal topped by a fanciful Islamic peak and a niche holding a statuette of the Virgin. Erected as a neighbourhood church in the 1590s (after Drake burned down the original), the building manages to retain a cohesive look despite numerous renovations made over the centuries, such as the addition of the **Capilla San Andrés** chapel and the philanthropic **Hospital Padre Billini** in the seventeenth. The life-size wooden statue of Christ above the chapel's intricately patterned mahogany altar is brought out every Ash Wednesday and paraded through the streets, a tradition that began in 1630.

The northern wall and around

The area around the old **northern wall** that marks the edge of the Zona Colonial holds a number of lovely **churches** worth a peek, though the run-down barrio alongside, running roughly parallel with Avenida Mella, is equally interesting. In the sixteenth century this was the city slum, populated by subsistence farmers and stonecutters who laboured alongside natives in the nearby Santa Bárbara limestone quarry.

Iglesia Santa Bárbara and the fort

Isabel La Católica and General Gabino Puello • Daily 8.30am–7pm

Iglesia Santa Bárbara is a handsome whitewashed church that honours the military's patron saint. Behind it are the remains of the **Santa Bárbara Fort**, to which the church

1

DOMINICAN SYNCRETISM

Syncretic religion – the mixing of European and African religions in South America and the Caribbean – is very much a part of Dominican culture, though Eurocentrism and official disfavour make it an object of shame. Cousin to Haitian Voodoo, it came about during the colonial era, when European Christianity was imposed on African slaves from the Congo and West Africa; the slaves mixed Catholicism, along with elements from European paganism, freemasonry and Taino religion, with their own belief system. Over time, various Christian saints came to be linked to deities imported from Africa, allowing the slaves to practise their religion in peace. St Patrick, for example, was the equivalent of Damballa, a powerful Dominican *Vodú* deity, because both were associated with snakes; St Elias was identified with Samedi, guardian of the cemetery; while St John the Baptist's association with water has connected him to Chango, Dahomeyan god of the ocean, lightning and tempests.

SANTERA AND VODÚ

Practising Dominicans make a distinction between *Santera* and *Vodú*, categories that correspond roughly to the Haitian *Rada* and *Petwo* classes of spirit – the *Rada* are benevolent but less powerful, while the *Petwo* are stronger but amoral and mercenary and require specific sacrifices for their interventions. Known in the DR as the **misterios**, the *Petwo* adherents are a select few who have some sort of transcendent religious experience in which they're forcibly "called" into service by their patron spirit. Rural groups also worship Taino spirits thought to inhabit caves, pools and streams, leaving offerings of food and flowers at their holy sites. Though largely attributed to Haitian influence, Dominican *Vodú* was practised in the early sixteenth century and thus actually predates Voodoo.

Vodú practice involves private ceremonies using large altars covered with depictions of saints, offertory candles, plastic cups of rum and numerous crosses honouring the **gedes**, bawdy cemetery spirits known to spout lascivious songs when they possess humans. **Possession** is an integral part of *Vodú* ceremonies, both by saints and the spirits of dead Taino warriors. You'll see *Vodú* paraphernalia, including love potions, spray cans that impart good luck in the lottery and Catholic icons, at the many *botánicas* throughout the country. For more intractable problems, followers will consult a **brujo**, or spiritual medium, who offers herbal healing remedies and acts as a go-between in barter deals made with the saints; in exchange for good health, for example, you might trade daily prayers for a year, a week-long pilgrimage to Higüey on foot, or a direct cash payment to the *brujo*.

COFRADÍAS

Syncretic **cofradías** – religious brotherhoods – began among black slaves in Spain and Portugal in the fourteenth century, before the discovery of the New World. The societies, an amalgamation of Spanish Catholic fraternities and West African secret societies, were officially sanctioned by the Church and allowed to use the cathedral for their annual processions. Most were then dedicated, in Santo Domingo's early days to San Juan Bautista – who represented the Dahomeyan Chango – but in time the societies were taken over by their incorporeal supreme deity Kalunda, who is identified with the Holy Spirit; these *cofradías* are usually named **Hermandad del Congo**. *Cofradía* activities include funeral rites for dead members. After the funeral, a nine-day second wake is held to assist in the passing on of the dead to the spirit world; on the anniversary of the person's death, the brotherhood then holds a ceremony with the family which often involves possession of a family member by the deceased, who doles out practical advice.

FESTIVALS

All the aspects of Dominican syncretism can be witnessed at the **fiestas patronales**. These festivals vary quite a bit in the amount of folk religion they exhibit (some have had most of the religion leeched out of them). In Nigua, 12km west of Santo Domingo, you may also stumble onto a **rosario**, a penitent procession entreating the Virgin of Altagracia in times of drought or distress, with townsfolk marching behind the banner of their patron saint, singing folk songs structured in the manner of the Catholic "Hail Mary" (sung fifty times each in three sessions) and playing tambourines and drums; some devotees carry boulders on their head as an act of penance. Devout individuals and *cofradías* also sponsor private festivals called **velaciones** in their home barrios.

was once attached, and a large chunk of the old city wall, mostly in ruins – what's left has been converted into a neighbourhood park. Ostensibly part of the city's riverfront defences, the garrison was used mostly to keep the Taino (and later African) slaves in line as they laboured in the quarry – this has long since been paved over and is now part of the city's shabby shopping district, running along Avenida Mella and the surrounding streets.

Iglesia San Miguel

José Reyes and Juan Isidro Pérez • Daily 8.30am–6pm

From Santa Bárbara, walk ten minutes west through a pretty residential area, to **Iglesia San Miguel**, a small seventeenth-century chapel facing a park with an enormous pigeon coop. The old priests' quarters beside the church are used as private apartments; the fort that once stood across the street is in rubble. In the 1650s Spain ordered that San Miguel was to become a hospital for slaves, but local administrators ignored the decree.

Iglesia San Lazaro

Juan Isidro Pérez and Santomé • Daily 8.30am–2.30pm

Opposite a small neighbourhood park in the northwestern corner of the Zona Colonial lies **Iglesia San Lazaro**, which once adjoined a hospital for lepers built in 1573. The hospital, deliberately built on the outskirts of the old city to avoid disease spreading to the wider population, was destroyed in an earthquake in 1751 and in the rebuilding that followed the church was added and finally completed in 1759. A bad nineteenth-century plaster job has defaced the red-brick facade, but the Tuscan columns and triple-arched belfry are still intact.

Iglesia Las Mercedes

Mercedes • Daily 8.30am–7pm

One of the more imposing churches in the northern section of the Zona Colonial is the Gothic **Iglesia Las Mercedes**, its mahogany altar carved in the shape of a serpent. Built in the 1530s, the church was used during Haitian rule to house six thousand African-American immigrants who were eventually shipped off to Puerto Plata and Samaná.

Puerta de la Misericordia

Corner of Palo Hincado and Arzobispo Portes, just north of the Malecón

Working your way down through the Zona Colonial towards the Malecón it's worth passing by the massive **Puerta de la Misericordia** (Gate of Mercy), an early sixteenth-century fortified city entrance in the southwestern corner of the district. Connected to it from the south are the rubble remains of its watchtower, the San Gil Fort. The gate earned its name during the devastating earthquake of 1842, when local priests erected a tent city beneath it to treat the sick and shelter the homeless. Two years later, on February 27, 1844, freedom fighter Ramón Mella made a dramatic speech here inciting the city to insurrection and fired off the first shot of the revolution against Haiti. A re-enactment of the event is staged every Independence Day.

The Malecón

The capital's famous oceanfront promenade, the **Malecón** is best enjoyed on Sundays, when all motorized vehicles are banned and it becomes a broad pedestrian-only thoroughfare. Despite the tempting and stereotypically Caribbean waters that the Malecón skirts, **swimming** here is a very bad idea. Not only is it polluted, but the food waste being dumped into it from the mouth of the Río Ozama attracts **sharks**. Though

1

known popularly as the Malecón, officially the seafront road is divided into several separately named sections, the most central of which is Avenida George Washington.

Around the San José Fort

The Malecón starts within the Zona Colonial, at the large industrial port by the mouth of the Río Ozama, where an intact section of the old city wall follows it for 100m to the seventeenth-century **San José Fort**. Built on a strategic oceanfront promontory after an attempted invasion by the British in 1655, the cannon that remain here appear to point across the street at a 50m-high statue of **Fray Anton de Montesinos**, a sixteenth-century priest who preached against the Taino genocide, his legendary rage manifested in the flame-like spikes of his hair. This section of the boardwalk is extremely popular at night, with massive crowds and weekend live music at the commercial port below Puerta San Diego; there's also usually a lively crowd at *D'Luis Parrillada* (see p.75), an outdoor restaurant with dancing at night that's right next to the Montesino statue.

The obelisks

A few metres west of the Zona Colonial section of the Malecón, more or less at the foot of Palo Hincado, you'll find what is popularly referred to as **El Obelisco Hembra** (The Female Obelisk), a large, two-pronged monument that locals equate with parted legs. Officially known as the **Monumento a la Independencia Financiera**, it was placed there by Trujillo in 1941 to honour repayment of a long-outstanding debt to the United States, incurred over the decades by less budget-conscious Dominican administrations. Another kilometre west is a second obelisk, **El Obelisco Macho** (The Male Obelisk), built in 1936 to commemorate Santo Domingo's temporary re-christening as Ciudad Trujillo, though now bearing distinctly anti-Trujillo murals depicting the Mirabal sisters – whom he assassinated – as nature goddesses capturing rainbows in a gourd. Beyond here, a line of high-rise hotels, restaurants, discos and festive outdoor parks stretches for 4km. Dotted all along are a series of **outdoor party zones** (notably at avenidas Sánchez and Máximo Gómez) where you'll see plenty of dancing and activity every evening, though between these bright spots you're likely to be accosted from time to time by local hustlers acting as freelance "tour guides".

West to the Teatro de Agua y Luz

At the southern end of two of the capital's major streets, the Avenida Winston Churchill and Avenida Abraham Lincoln, is the **Centro de los Héroes**, the nation's administrative centre and home of parliament, marked along the promenade by a large pink arch and accompanying globe. In the southwestern corner the **Teatro de Agua y Luz**, an outdoor amphitheatre built in 1955, once renowned for its spectacular fountain and light displays, now stands derelict. From here the waterfront becomes mostly residential, though closer to the **Río Haina**, a 2km stretch of gaudy Vegas-style cabañas turísticas marks the longest zone of "hourly" motels in the country (see p.299). This is also where you'll find the Centro de los Heroes station, marking the southern end of the Metro and making it a convenient place to come if you want to visit places further north from here, such as the Plaza de la Cultura, the Sala de Arte Prehispánico and the Jardín Botánico, all close to Metro stations.

Gazcue

Immediately west of the Zona Colonial is rambling, tree-shaded **Gazcue**, the city's prettiest residential district, a mostly middle-class neighbourhood whose highlight is the **Plaza de la Cultura**, a complex of four museums sitting alongside the National

1

Theatre and Library (see below & p.64). Eastern Gazcue is within easy walking distance of Parque Independencia and the Colonial Zone. It'll be easier on your feet, however, to take a taxi or guagua to reach the Plaza.

Further north on Máximo Gómez from the Plaza de la Cultura is the leafy expanse of the **Centro Olímpico** – it is not set up for visitors but is helpful if only as an unmistakable landmark. Beyond Gazcue, two kilometres to the west of Máximo Gómez, begins the **Parque Mirador del Sur**, a 7km-long walking and cycling area scattered with baseball diamonds.

Museo de Arte Moderno

Plaza de la Cultura • Tues–Sun 9am–5pm • RD$50 • ☎ 809 682 4750 • Metro station Casandra Damirón (Linea 1)

Of the museums in the Plaza de la Cultura, the first stop should be the **Museo de Arte Moderno**, four storeys dedicated to modernist and postmodern Dominican art, with a magnificent permanent collection and a lively programme of temporary exhibits. At times the assemblage can seem a bit random, exacerbated by the frequent rotation of pieces within the museum space, but certain themes are discernible, not least a reliance on Taino influences.

Among the abstract works on permanent display is the arresting *El sacrificio del chivo* by **Elegio Pichardo**, which won the Santo Domingo Biennial in 1958. It's a

● EATING		● SHOPPING		■ ACCOMMODATION		■ DRINKING, NIGHTLIFE	
Adrian Tropical	7	Galería Bidó	1	La Casona Dorada	3	**& LIVE MUSIC**	
Ananda	2			La Grand Mansión	2	Cinema Café	1
Cantabrico	1			La Morada	1	La Parada Cervecera	3
El Conuco	5			Maison Gautreaux	4	Salón de los Espejos	2
Manolo	6			Hotel Shaky	5		
Sabor y Especias	3			Sheraton Santo Domingo	6		
Trattoria Vesuvio	8						
Vesuvio	9						
Villar Hermanos	4						

1

dark depiction of a family meal that interprets the everyday ritual of dinner as a pagan rite – note the shrunken head in the hand of the child as he waits for the mother to carve the goat.

The most highly regarded proponent of a more pastoral strain in modern Dominican art is **Cándido Bidó**, whose stylized idealizations of *campesino* life have won international acclaim. Bidó's father was a Carnival mask maker in Bonao – the influence is apparent in the faces with hollowed-out eyes, straight noses and exaggerated lips. The museum owns six Bidós, including his most famous, *El Paseo a las 10am*, a painting of a Dominican woman in a sunhat with a handful of flowers. The pigeon fluttering by her side is a typical Bidó gesture, as is the use of colour: his serene, distinctive world contains a generous application of indigo blue and almost no green, with yellow fields, black mountains and the sun surrounded by a subduing, dark cyst.

Among the works of **Alberto Bass**, one-time director of the museum, is *La Vida del Dominicano en Nueva York*, an enormous triptych depicting a family divided by American immigration. The first panel is of a sleepy Dominican fishing village, the second of the emigrant's cramped Manhattan apartment (with a letter home in the typewriter), and the third of the alien, neon rumble of Times Square. Don't miss, either, **Silvano Lora**'s *Flor Endemica*, a mixed-media commentary on the bombed-out urban environment that many of the country's children live in. Lora was renowned as an outspoken defender of the oppressed – in 1992, when replicas of Columbus's three ships tried to dock in Santo Domingo in honour of the 500th anniversary of his voyage, Lora dressed up like a Taino, paddled out to the boats in a canoe and fired arrows at them until his vessel was capsized by the Coast Guard.

Museo del Hombre Dominicano

Plaza de la Cultura • Tues–Sun 9am–5pm • RD$100; English-language guide RD$50 • ☎ 809 687 3622 • Metro station Casandra Damirón (Linea 1)

One of the Plaza de la Cultura's main attractions is the **Museo del Hombre Dominicano**, which holds an extraordinary collection of Taino artefacts and an anthropological exhibit on Dominican *fiestas patronales*. The **ground floor** is mostly concerned with the gift shop, but does display a dozen stone obelisks and Taino burial mounds found near Boca Chica in the 1970s. The first floor is office space; the **second floor** consists of one large room bearing display cases of Taino sculpture, beginning with seated human figures and *cemis* – small stone idols that stood in for the gods during rituals, possessing large, inward-spiralling eyes and flared nostrils. Further down the room is an extensive collection of flints, hatchets and stone spearheads, which can be scanned over before passing to the two cases bearing beautiful animal sculptures and ceremonial daggers. At the far end of the space you'll find jewellery with incredibly intricate carvings made from coral, tooth, stone and conch shell, a case filled with spectacularly nasty-looking death heads and a few examples of the artwork created by the Tainos' ancestors in the Amazon basin.

The **third floor** moves on to Dominican culture after Columbus, with emphasis on the African influence. The first room focuses on the slave trade; the next room is taken up by a comparison of the rural dwellings of African peasants and Dominican *campesinos*. These are followed by a terrific exhibition on **syncretist religious practices** in the DR, including photographs of various rural *fiestas patronales* and a Dominican *Vodú* altar, with Catholic iconography standing in for African gods, votive candles and a sacrifice of cigarettes, a chicken and a bottle of rum. From here walk past the display of local musical instruments that originated in Africa to three large glass cases depicting costumed Carnival celebrations in Monte Cristi, La Vega and Santo Domingo.

Palacio Nacional

Av. Mexico and 30 de Marzo; visitors' entrance at back of palace on Calle Dr Báez • Mon–Fri 8am–6.30pm • Visits only via organized tour and submission of passport; call ☎ 809 695 8347 or ☎ 809 695 8359 two days in advance

East of the Plaza de la Cultura stands the heavily guarded office of the president, the **Palacio Nacional**, an attractive, coral-pink marble edifice that's even better on the inside. Contemplating the decadent glory of the interior is worth the effort it takes to get a tour: mahogany furnishings, marble floors, gold and silver inlay, monumental murals depicting major historical events and an enormous hall of mirrors with fifty caryatids (pillars sculpted into the shape of women) and six chandeliers.

Palacio de Bellas Artes

Corner of Independencia and Máximo Gómez • Art galleries usually Tues–Sat 9am–noon & 3–6pm • ☎ 809 687 0504, a useful website for performance schedules is ⓦ santo-domingo-live.com

South of the Plaza de la Cultura is the sumptuous **Palacio de Bellas Artes**, a rectangular Neoclassical temple to high art housing the National Dominican Ballet, the School of Dramatic Art, the National School of Visual Arts and a host of other prestigious arts institutions. It holds regular classical music performances by touring ensembles, theatrical productions and "merenjazz" concerts from top local musicians. On the whole you'll need to attend a performance here to appreciate its interior but there are often fine art displays in the exhibition rooms, usually free to view.

Galería Bidó

Dr Báez 5, half a block north of Independencia • Mon–Fri 9am–5pm • Free • ☎ 809 682 5310, ⓦ galeriacandidobido.com

If you were taken with the works of Cándido Bidó in the Museo de Arte Moderno, it's worth making a detour to **Galería Bidó**, set in a rambling home whose first floor holds one of the city's best private galleries. Bidó died in 2011 at the age of 74 and his work went through some interesting transformations towards the end of his life. The doll-like, hollow-eyed faces – which once conveyed pastoral innocence – were latterly exploited for their ability to convey existential angst. One piece consists of a series of still lifes in which discarded piles of these open-mouthed dolls stare eyeless from a pastel tablecloth. The gallery also features rotating exhibits of other top Dominican artists.

Polígono Central and Arroyo Hondo

West of Gazcue is the downtown area of Santo Domingo, sometimes referred to as the **Polígono Central**, framed by Avenida John F Kennedy to the north, Avenida Winston Chruchill to the west, Avenida 27 de Febrero to the south and Avenida Máximo Gómez to the east. This group of neighbourhoods, among them Paraíso and Piantini, form the business and commercial centre of the city, characterized by huge shopping malls, swanky apartment buildings and high-rise office blocks as well as some upmarket clubs, bars and restaurants.

Neither as wealthy as the downtown area below it nor as desperate as the barrios beyond it, **Arroyo Hondo** is a fairly bland expanse of residential neighbourhoods that shifts from upper-crust mansions in the south to makeshift shacks in the north but it does feature some expansive green spaces, including the impressive **Jardín Botánico Nacional**, which make it well worth a visit.

On the border between these two areas, marked by the Avenida John F Kennedy, are two of the city's best museums – the **Sala de Arte Prehispánico** and the **Museo Bellapart**.

Dotted along Avenida John F Kennedy are half a dozen Metro stations on the east-west Metro line, Linea 2.

Jardín Botánico Nacional

Av. República de Colombia • Daily 9am–6pm • Dominicans RD$50, non-Dominicans RD$175; train RD$20 • ☎ 809 385 2611 • ⓦ jbn.gob. do • Metro station Francisco G Billini (Linea 2)

The **Jardín Botánico Nacional** has samples of flora from every part of the island, a pavilion with three hundred types of orchid (most endemic), and greenhouses for bromeliads and aquatic plants. Less indigenous but quite striking is the manicured Japanese garden with a maze of shrubs and a pagoda with shaded benches beside a babbling brook. A train ride will take you through the length of the park with a stop-off at some of the highlights, but it's far more pleasant to wander about the grounds at your leisure.

Sala de Arte Prehispánico

San Martín between Av. John F Kennedy and Lopé de Vega • Mon–Fri 9am–5pm • Free • ☎ 809 540 7777 ext. 235 • Metro station Freddy Beras Goico (Linea 2)

The **Sala de Arte Prehispánico** is a private collection of Taino artefacts housed in a large room within the Pepsi-Cola corporate building. At the entrance are a few pieces from Venezuela (the Tainos' ancestral home), while nearby you'll find fossilized mastodon and armadillo remains, animals that the natives hunted to extinction on the island. There are display cases laying out the history of indigenous ceramics, plus intricate tooth and bone sculptures used in necklaces – one is so small you need a magnifying glass to see the carving. At the far end of the room you'll see jewellery made from conch shells, coral, teeth or clay; at its opposite end you can inspect an intact wooden *duho* – a chair carved with the face of a Taino god, used by *caciques* as a throne during religious ceremonies. Along the wall beside it is a collection of clay animals that represented various deities, including a dozen frogs, a few turtles, a crocodile and two owls, which were believed to ferry souls to the afterlife. The exhibit turns to more practical items as you double back towards the entrance, but the intricate ornamentation on the pots, cassava grinders and ceremonial axe heads keeps your attention from flagging. Especially arresting is the jet-black monolith of a Taino deity with an ostentatious phallus – used to guard the entrance to a cave.

Museo Bellapart

Av. John F Kennedy and Dr Lembert Peguero • Mon–Fri 9am–6pm, Sat 9am–noon • Free • ☎ 809 541 7721 ext. 296, ⓦ museobellapart. com • Metro station Freddy Beras Goico (Linea 2)

The **Museo Bellapart**, located in a single large room on the first floor of a massive Honda dealership, is well worth a visit. This small private art museum holds one of the country's best collections of Dominican art from the first half of the twentieth century – over 2000 pieces in all. The paintings follow a timeline from the 1890s to the late 1950s. Highlights include social-realist Jaime Colsón's *Merengue* at the entrance, a lively, expressive rendition of a traditional Dominican fiesta, which is strongly influenced by Mexican muralist art; the subdued aesthetic of Celeste Woss y Gill's *Retrato sin fecha*, a sombre portrait of a Latin flapper from the Roaring Twenties, gracefully scanning a book; and folk artist Yoryi Morel's ragged depiction of a Dominican *campo* entitled *Dedicado a Mi Madre*. The crowning glory of the collection, though, is the *La Vida de los Campesinos* series by Spanish exile **José Vela Zanetti**, whose work also graces the walls of the UN Security Council in New York. The painting here marks a stylistic break from the monumental social – realism of his public building commissions: sketchier, with rough-hewn peasants in front of a whorling, almost formless background of barren rolling hills, it is more attuned to the modernism of Van Gogh. Especially arresting are *Familia Campesina* and *Retrato Paño Azul*, which offer a poignant human intimacy absent in his more ambitious, sweeping social statements.

East of the Ozama

Though most of Santo Domingo's attractions lie west of the **Río Ozama**, there are a few scattered points of interest along the eastern bank and beyond. It's best to visit this part of the city by car or taxi as distances between attractions are quite substantial. Two main highways plough through this area: the Avenida Las Americas, which becomes the Autopista Las Americas, the main route out of the city heading east; and Avenida España which follows the river down from the Puente Juan Bosch, past the developing Bartolomé Colón Marina, and then curves round and becomes a seaside road, skirting the rocky shore.

Parque Mirador del Este and Los Tres Ojos

Av. Las Américas • Caves daily 8.30am–5.30pm • RD$50 • ☎ 809 788 7056

Occupying a large swathe of land in this part of the city, **Parque Mirador del Este** is a pleasant 3km stretch of manicured woodlands spanning the length of the barrios east of the Ozama. At the park's far eastern tip is a series of large caves dotted with freshwater lagoons. Known as **Los Tres Ojos** ("The Three Eyes"), the caves were used by the Tainos for religious ceremonies; more recently they've been the setting for no fewer than six Tarzan movies. Walkways lead you to three of the lagoons and a manually powered pulley conducts a ferry to a fourth.

Faro a Colón

Just under 1km east along Av. Las Américas from the Puente Juan Bosch, turn right onto the Av. Faro a Colón and follow it to the end • Tues–Sun 9am–5.30pm • RD$100 • ☎ 809 591 1492

At the western end of the Parque Mirador del Este is the controversial Faro a Colón, or Columbus Lighthouse. Known locally as **El Faro** – simply, "the lighthouse" – it is actually nothing of the sort, its imposing, hulking structure resembling an immaculately scrubbed prison. After decades in the making, the project was finally completed in 1992, the 500th anniversary of Columbus's "discovery" of the Americas. The idea for such a tribute dates to the 1850s, when several prominent intellectuals signed an editorial in *Listin Diario* calling for its creation, and an international competition was held in 1929 for its design. Given that there were over 450 contestants from fifty countries, it's hard to understand how British architect J.C. Gleave's monstrous, cross-shaped entry managed to beat off all competition. The building's most impressive feature is the 250-laser cross of light that it projects onto the city's night sky (hence the lighthouse moniker), though even that is resented by many here – it's said that whenever it turns on, power goes out in villages across the country. Columbus's role in the Taino genocide led to protests in the capital when the lighthouse was opened and the government's razing of one of the city's poorest neighbourhoods to build it didn't help. Another sticking point was the price tag, estimated to be US$100–150 million.

Within the bombastic eyesore that is El Faro stands the Baroque **mausoleum of Christopher Columbus**, with dozens of flowery angels hovering above the marble casket alongside a more corporeal 24-hour honour guard. Whether Columbus's remains are actually here is disputed most strongly by Seville in Spain, who also claim to have them in their possession – his posthumous globetrotting took in the Cuban capital, Havana, too. Also on the ground floor, look for a series of galleries with paintings of the Virgin

Mary from every country in the Americas, while on the third floor you'll find a modest Naval Museum.

Capilla del Rosario

70m south of the Sans Souci Marina • Daily 10.30am–4.30pm • Free

The eastern bank of the Ozama was the first part of the city that was settled, but Christopher Columbus's outpost was constructed from timber and the lone colonial relic left here is the early sixteenth-century **Capilla del Rosario**, a pretty, single-nave church with three brick portals supposedly built on the site of Columbus's home.

Acuario Nacional

Av. España 75, San Souci, around 3km from the river • Tues–Sun 9am–5.30pm • RD$50 • ☎ 809 766 1709, Ⓦ acuarionacional.gob.do

By international standards, the **Acuario Nacional** is a rather modest 'national' aquarium but, sited atop cliffs looking out over the Caribbean, it's undoubtedly enhanced by the setting. The highlight is the large Plexiglas tunnel passing through a tank full of sharks, manta rays, moray eels and other sea creatures. There are frustratingly few plaques with information on what's on display and where they do appear they are in Spanish only.

The outer barrios

The city's **outer barrios** are, for the most part, extremely poor industrial zones with a mix of concrete-box homes and thatch huts. There are no tourist sights in the traditional sense and if you want to explore them for a sense of how people here live, you should do so only during the day, as they become dangerous at night. Buses leave Parque Enriquillo (see p.70) every twenty minutes or so to northwestern barrio **Los Alcarrizos**, a concrete suburb buzzing with swarms of motorcycles and studded with dozens of storefront Pentecostal churches; **La Ciénaga**, a riverside barrio that was hit hard by Hurricane Georges; **Sabana Perdida**, a moderately prosperous, sprawling residential zone northeast of the city; and **Yamasá**, a moderately rural area well north of the city where you can visit a local factory to find out how Taino ceramics were made.

Parque Mirador del Norte

6km north of the Malecón on Máximo Gómez, between Av. Hermanas Mirabal, Av. Mirador del Norte, Av. Jacobo Majluta Azar and the Río Isabela • Daily 8am–5pm • Adults RD$30, children RD$20; rowing boats RD$40/30min, pedal boats RD$60/30min, bike hire RD$35/30min • ☎ 809 328 0112, Ⓦ parquemiradornorte.gob.do • Metro station Hermanas Mirabal (Linea 1)

Parque Mirador del Norte is Santo Domingo's largest public park, though it actually sees far less use than the two smaller city parks closer to the seafront. Its nine square kilometres are dominated by chinaberry trees, bisected by an enormous artificial lake and walking trails. The rolling terrain provides a number of spots for lovely slope-top views across the park and beyond, with viewing platforms dotted around from which you can sit down and drink it all in. Access to the park is through any of its six gates, spaced around its eastern, western and northern borders. Gate 4, on Avenida Mirador del Norte, is the closest to the lake and the most popular entrance point. You can rent rowing boats and pedal boats and this is also the gate to come through for bicycle hire. There are basic cafés at points around all six gates but only one proper restaurant, inside Gate 3, also on the Avenida Mirador del Norte.

Villa Mella

1

12km north of the Malecón on Máximo Gómez and then Av. Hermanas Mirabal; for Mata los Indios turn left at the second dirt road after the Nativa petrol station • Metro station Mamá Tingó (Línea 1)

A poor, semi-rural district right on the northern outskirts of the city and dissected by several main roads, **Villa Mella** plays host to the most interesting syncretic religious festivals in Santo Domingo. The local population is largely descended from Congolese slaves, and elements of Congo culture are still evident in the local language, religion and music, particularly in the tiny community of **Mata Los Indios**, whose inhabitants maintain an ancient brotherhood known as the Cofradía de los Congos del Espíritu Santo (see below). Indeed, during the festivities of **Espíritu Santo** (seven weeks after Semana Santa), congo drums are played round the clock for nine straight days at both the Parque Central and Iglesia Espíritu Santo.

Museo de la Cofradía del Espíritu Santo

Calle 30 no. 39, Mata los Indios • Daily 9am–5pm • RD$20 donation suggested • ☎ 809 239 9506

To get a taste of syncretic culture in Villa Mella at any time of year head for the **Museo de la Cofradía del Espíritu Santo** which displays photographs of the brotherhood's rituals and festivities, plus some strikingly beautiful paper floats that are created for the anniversaries of dead loved ones. The museum's manager is friendly and a great source of local lore: she'll take you to see Joselito, a local drum-maker, in remarkable shape given his 100-odd years, who still makes his own congos and *palos* drums by hollowing out tree trunks by hand with a blunt steel tool. The drums are colourful and truly remarkable, quite possibly the finest opportunity for a local souvenir on the island (they cost RD$3000–7000 depending on the size).

Taina Cerámica factory

In Yamasá village, 15km north of Villa Mella; take the Metro to the northern end of Línea 1 at Villa Mella, then switch to a guagua (around RD$100); by car, head straight up Máximo Gómez, turn left at the fork in the road a few kilometres north of Villa Mella and then left again at the fork with a statue of Taino Queen Anacaona; once in town turn right at the first street after Parque Central, or just call Yamasá Taxi (☎ 809 535 0709) • No official visiting hours; ring in advance to arrange visit and any costs • ☎ 809 525 0756, ⓦ artesaniaguillen.com

The **Taina Cerámica factory** was founded by the locally famous Hermanos Guillen, artist brothers who carefully studied the ceramic artwork of the Tainos and now

---

DAY-TRIPS FROM SANTO DOMINGO

Beyond the belt of industrial barrios that encases Santo Domingo are a variety of **day-trips** within easy striking distance, including two very reachable beaches. Those looking for a slice of Caribbean fun in the sun, with nighttime action to match, could try **Boca Chica** (see p.90), an overcrowded resort town 10km east of the airport, about halfway between the capital and San Pedro de Macorís. Less seedy but a little further away is **Juan Dolio** (see p.92), where there is more beachfront, albeit one that is dominated by all-inclusive hotels. You could also try its sister town **Guayacanes**, which has great beaches and lacks tourist development. You can easily make it to these places independently, whether by catching a guagua from Parque Enriquillo or by driving yourself, but for day-trips further afield, consider paying for an organized excursion. The travel agents below will whisk you as far away as the **Samaná Peninsula**, where you can spend a day whale-watching (see p.130), or to Isla Saona in the **Parque Nacional del Este** (see p.105). Expect to pay upwards of US$70 for most full day tours and as much as US$300 for a private two-person tour to Samaná.

Colonial Tour and Travel Arzobispo Meriño 209, Zona Colonial ☎ 809 688 5285, ⓦ colonialtours.com.do.
Explora Ecotour Gustavo Mejia Ricart 43, Suite 209, Naco ☎ 809 567 1852, ⓦ exploraecotour.com.

Metro Tours Francisco Prats Ramirez, corner of Av. Winston Churchill ☎ 809 544 4580, ⓦ metrotours.com.do.
Viajes Bohío Benito Moncion 161, Gazcue ☎ 809 686 2992, ⓦ viajesbohio.com.

1

produce replicas so authentic that most archeologists can't tell the difference – if it wasn't for the brothers' signature on each piece, that is. Their handiwork is sold in shops throughout the country, but you can save more than 75 percent by buying at the factory. They're happy to take visitors on a **tour** of the multi-step process, too, which involves digging for clay, mashing the material with their feet, shaping the sculpture by hand, drawing the symbols and finally cooking it in an old-fashioned kiln. They also run a cocoa factory at the same location where you can watch the process of making chocolate and taste the local variety; the factory itself is very no-frills, but the hot chocolate they serve at the end is delicious.

ARRIVAL AND DEPARTURE   SANTO DOMINGO

BY AIR

AEROPUERTO INTERNACIONAL LAS AMÉRICAS

Most visitors arrive at Aeropuerto Internacional Las Américas (☎ 809 947 2225 & 809 947 2297, ⓦ aerodom .com), 13km east of the city proper, and the country's largest. There are currently no domestic scheduled flights from the airport but plenty of charter flights to destinations around the country.

Getting into town The easiest way into the city centre is by taxi; look for the official brown sticker on the windshield and expect to pay around US$40/RD$1600, though you can usually negotiate drivers down during daylight hours. Much cheaper but considerably more hassle, especially if you have bulky bags, is to catch a guagua. The pick-up point is outside the departures section of the airport, upstairs from the arrival hall: turn left once outside the building; expect to pay RD$100–150 to get to Parque Enriquillo in town. If renting a car, avoid the touts who'll accost you once through customs and go directly to the agency booths: though the price is a bit higher, it's safer to stick with established international agencies; better still, arrange rental beforehand (see p.72). Keep in mind that there's an RD$30 toll as you leave the airport by car.

Facilities There's a Banco de Reservas currency exchange at the exit to the luggage pick-up area, an ATM at the airport exit, a bank of car rental agency booths just south of the luggage-area exit and a few fast-food restaurants scattered within the terminal.

AEROPUERTO INTERNACIONAL LA ISABELA

The smaller Aeropuerto Internacional La Isabela-Dr Joaquín Balaguer (☎ 809 826 4019) operates mostly charter domestic routes, the majority to Punta Cana, but there are also services to Haiti and elsewhere in the Caribbean. It lies on Av. Presidente Antonio Guzman Fernández, to the northwest of the city's outskirts, 20km from the Zona Colonial. Taxis from here to the Zona Colonial cost around $US20/RD$700.

AIRLINES

Air France, Máximo Gómez 15 ☎ 809 686 8432, ⓦ airfrance .com.do; American Airlines, Av. Winston Churchill 2, corner of Max Henriquez Ureña ☎ 809 542 5151, ⓦ aa.com;

Cubana, 27 de Febrero 227 and Av. Tiradentes ☎ 809 227 2040, ⓦ cubana.cu; JetBlue Airways, Plaza Las Américas II, Av. Winston Churchill ☎ 809 200 9898, ⓦ jetblue.com; United Airlines, Av. Winston Churchill 1 ☎ 809 262 1060, ⓦ united.com.

BY BUS AND GUAGUA

As the transport centre of the country, even the smallest villages at the far end of the north coast are connected to Santo Domingo by either bus or guagua. If arriving in Santo Domingo by **bus**, you'll have no trouble finding a taxi or public transport from your terminal (see below). The majority of **guaguas** and many buses arrive at and depart from Parque Enriquillo, with stops along the Malecón for destinations to the east and west. From Parque Enriquillo you can catch a *público* to Parque Independencia and the Zona Colonial, four blocks away. The park is safe enough during the day, but take a taxi at night. Guaguas from the north typically drop you off at a chaotic traffic circle that intersects 27 de Febrero and Charles de Gaulle at the northwestern city limits, from where you can catch a guagua or *público* to the centre of town.

BUS AND GUAGUA COMPANIES AND DESTINATIONS

There is no central bus station and buses depart from the depot of the relevant operator while guaguas depart either from their own depots or the relevant public transport hub, in many cases **Parque Enriquillo**, where a number of bus company depots are also located, or **Kilómetro 9**, to the west of the city at the busy junction where the Autopista Duarte meets Avenida John F Kennedy. There are many more bus and guagua companies than are listed here but these are among the most reliable services and should suffice for almost all destinations. There are guaguas to **Boca Chica** every 15 minutes from Parque Enriquillo.

ASTRAPU José Martí and Ravelo, just off Parque Enriquillo (☎ 809 221 4006).

Destinations Juan Dolio (every 25min from 6am–9.30pm; 1hr 10min); San Pedro de Macorís (every 25min from 6am–9.30pm; 1hr 30min).

APTPRA Ravelo 92 on Parque Enriquillo (☎ 809 686 0637).

Destinations Higuey (every 20min 5.30am–8pm; 2hr

30min); Bavaro (every 20min 5.30am–8pm; 4hr 30min); Punta Cana (every 20min 5.30am–8pm; 4hr).

Caribe Tours Av. 27 de Febrero and Av. Leopoldo Navarro (📞 809 221 4422, 🌐 caribetours.com.do). Has by far the most connections, stopping at towns along the Autopista Duarte on its way to Santiago, then Puerto Plata and Sosúa, as well as nearly every region in the country, save the southeast and the southwest past Barahona.

Destinations Azua (for Lago Enriquillo; 8 daily; 2hr 30min); Barahona (4 daily; 3hr); Cabrera (8 daily; 6hr 30min); Castillo (bus: 8 daily; 4hr); Dajabón (6 daily; 5hr 15min); Guayacanes (10 daily; 4hr 40min); Haiti (2 daily; 8hr); Jarabacoa (4 daily; 2hr); La Vega (41 daily; 1hr 45min); Loma de Cabrera (3 daily; 6hr 15min); Monte Cristi (6 daily; 4hr 30min); Puerto Plata (14 daily; 3hr 30min); Río San Juan (8 daily; 3hr 45min); Samaná (8 daily; 4 via San Francisco de Macorís 4hr 30min; 4 Express buses 2hr 30min); San Francisco de Macorís (13 daily; 2hr); San Juan de la Maguana (for Las Matas de Farfán; 4 daily; 3hr 50min); Sánchez (8 daily; 4 via San Francisco de Macorís 4hr; 4 Express buses 2hr); Santiago (25 daily; 2hr 15min); Sosúa (14 daily; 4hr 10min).

Expreso Bávaro Juan Sánchez Ramirez, just a few metres from Av. Máximo Gómez; also picks up passengers at Parque Enriquillo (📞 809 682 9670). Shuttles between the capital and Bávaro.

Destinations Friusa and Bávaro (4 daily; 3hr 30min); Punta Cana Airport (4 daily; 2hr 45min).

Expreso Vegano Av. 27 de Febrero and San Martín (📞 809 573 4446).

Destination La Vega (every 30min; 2hr).

Metro Av. Winston Churchill and Francisco Prats Ramirez Piantini (📞 809 227 0101, 🌐 metroserviciosturisticos.com).

Destinations Puerto Plata (6 daily; 3hr 30min); Santiago (14 daily; 2hr 15min); Sosúa (3 daily; 4hr).

SICHOEM Ravelo and Av. Duarte, just off Parque Enriquillo (📞 809 687 2190 & 829 537 5480).

Destinations Juan Dolio (every 20min 5am–9pm; 1hr 10min); La Romana (every 20min 5am–9pm; 2hr).

Transporte del Valle Av. Independencia, behind Parque Independencia (📞 809 557 6200).

Destination San Juan de la Maguana (every 30min 7am–6pm; 3hr).

Transporte Espinal Av. París 69, between Juana Saltitopa and Dr Betances, about five blocks west of the Río Ozamae; stops at Kilómetro 9 too (📞 809 689 9301 🌐 transporteespinal.com).

Destinations Santiago (every 20min 5am–8.40pm; 2hr 30min).

BY CAR

Those with their own wheels should note that city traffic can be tremendously heavy and that the highways are insufficiently signposted. If you're simply passing through the city from one region to another, it's best to take the bypass, which is called Av. Azar from the west (where it connects from the Autopista Duarte) or Av. Charles de Gaulle from the east (from Av. Las Américas).

Arrival Coming from the Cibao or the Silver Coast you'll hit the northern end of town on the Autopista Duarte, which becomes Av. Kennedy once you reach the city limits. Arriving from the east, follow the signs marked "Centro Ciudad" until you cross the Río Ozama on the Duarte bridge: this takes you onto Av. Mexico, where a left onto Calle 30 de Marzo will lead you directly to Parque Independencia in the Zona Colonial. From the west via the Carretera San Cristóbal, follow the signs that lead to the Malecón.

Departure To head north and west, take the 27 de Febrero elevated highway west through town. Those heading east from the city should get on the eastbound 27 de Febrero, which crosses the Río Ozama as the Duarte Bridge and then turns into the Carretera las Américas, skirting the ocean all the way to San Pedro de Macorís and beyond.

GETTING AROUND

BY METRO

The Metro runs Mon–Fri 6.45am–10.30pm and at weekends 6.35am–10pm. It is clean and safe, with its own security guards, and if you're in the right part of town it's by far the quickest and easiest way to get around.

Network There are two Metro train lines in Santo Domingo, with a third on the way and three more planned, though the completion of all six lines is likely to be more than a decade away. The existing lines run north–south, following the route of Avenida Máximo Gómez, and east–west following Av. John F Kennedy, terminating (at the eastern end) 3km north of the Zona Colonial and bypassing that part of the city altogether. The most convenient downtown stop is currently at the Plaza de la Cultura. Unhelpfully, most stations have geographically meaningless names, and are named instead after people. However, on the trains themselves there are street maps with stations marked and announcements at every stop with useful information on what significant streets or buildings the station is close to.

Fares To use the Metro you'll need to purchase either a one-charge card (*tarjeta carga única*) for RD$15 or a rechargeable card (*tarjeta recargable*) for RD$60. Fares are very reasonable at RD$20 flat rate per journey, with discounts available if you buy a day pass (RD$80) or charge your card with ten trips (RD$185) or twenty trips (RD$360).

BY PÚBLICO AND GUAGUA

They may not be as safe or as straightforward as the Metro, but the **informal network** of *públicos* and guaguas (see p.25) cover every inch of the city and its outer districts and

1

CHU CHU COLONIAL

If you want the Zona Colonial experience without wearing out too much shoe leather then consider the Chu Chu Colonial (☎809 686 2303 ⊛chuchucolonial.com) tourist 'train'. The whistle-stop tour lasts 45 minutes, taking in the area between Las Mercedes and Padre Billini. Departures are hourly between 9am and 5pm from Parque Colón. Adults US$12, children under 12 US$7.

can get you pretty much anywhere for around RD$30; most *público* rides cost RD$10–20. Just stand on the corner of a major street and wave your arms at the first car with a taxi sign on the roof, provided you don't mind being crammed in with as many other people as can fit. Parque Independencia and Parque Enriquillo are among the more convenient **hubs** for anyone staying in the Zona Colonial.

BY TAXI

Taxis can be found at the Parque Independencia, at the road junctions along El Conde and in front of the large Malecón hotels. Alternatively you can call a taxi from other locations – Apolo (☎809 537 0000) is the best taxi service in town; you can trust them to charge a fair price, typically RD$150–300. Other reliable operators include Taxi Rondon (☎809 599 4444), Maxi (☎809 544 0077), Millennium (☎809 532 0303) and Tropical (☎809 262 3333).

BY CAR

Driving is daunting given the chaotic nature of traffic in the capital and current mass construction along several major roads to accommodate the new subway, but if you're planning on taking a few day-trips it could be worthwhile renting one. The best roads to take from one end of the city to the other are Av. 27 de Febrero and Av. JFK; both roads have elevated freeways above them for large stretches, with turn-offs every few kilometres.

Car rental There are rental outlets at the Las Américas airport, while city-based offices include Avis on the Malecón (☎809 535 7191, ⊛avis.com); Budget at Av. Kennedy Km 6 (☎809 566 6666, ⊛budget.com.do); Europcar at Av. Independencia 354 in Gazcue (☎809 688 2121, ⊛europcar.com.do); and Honda at Kennedy and Pepillo Salcedo (☎809 567 1015).

INFORMATION AND TOURS

Tourist information There's an inconspicuous Tourist Information Office at Isabel La Católica 103 on Parque Colón (Mon–Fri 9am–3pm; ☎809 686 3858) with very little in the way of printed or published resources but the staff can answer questions. You're generally just as well asking at your hotel.

Guides There are always freelance guides, some of them with official state tourism licences, hanging around Parque Colón who will provide tours of the Zona Colonial for a negotiated fee. Expect to pay upwards of US$20 for a two-hour tour.

ACCOMMODATION

There's a wide variety of accommodation in the city, but budget rooms in decent neighbourhoods are hard to come by. Most expensive are the high-rises along the **Malecón**, frequented predominantly by business travellers. If you've got this kind of budget, though, you're probably better off in the smaller luxury boutique hotels tucked away in the **Zona Colonial**, some of them in sixteenth-century mansions, all with bags more character than the high-rises. The Zona Colonial also has a good spread of mid-range options, where rooms are typically between US$50 and US$100, but keep in mind that things can get a bit noisy at night. If you want peace and quiet, head to one of the small hotels in residential **Gazcue**, most of which come with hot water, TV and optional a/c. Be sure to check out your room before paying for it: quality can vary widely within a single establishment. There are also plenty of less expensive, basic rooms available in the shopping district around **Av. Duarte**, but that neighbourhood gets very dicey at night. Wherever you go, you may want to check that your hotel has a **generator** that provides power during the frequent city blackouts and that the management is willing to run it on a 24-hour basis.

LONG-TERM STAYS

For stays of a month or more it's worth renting an apartment in a residential complex. Starting from around US$1000 a month and dropping below that for stays of over two months, you can stay in top-notch apartments at the same daily rate as a budget hotel. There is a particular concentration of these on Calle 19 de Marzo in the Zona Colonial, including Residencial Paseo (⊛residencialpaseocolonial.com) which offers reasonable rates for between a week and a year; and the upmarket La Castilla complex (⊛lacastillacolonial.com).

1

ZONA COLONIAL

Aida El Conde 474 and Espaillat ☎809 685 7692; map p.52. One of the cheapest hotels on El Conde, with clean, simple accommodation, but be wary – the place has a reputation for turning a blind eye to prostitution. You'll have to decide whether paying a bargain price to relax on your private balcony and watch the street life down below is worth having some of that street life inside your hotel. RD$1200

★ El Beaterio Duarte 8 ☎809 687 8657, ⓦelbeaterio .com; map p.52. Magnificently renovated sixteenth-century convent declared a World Heritage Site by UNESCO. The beautiful rooms are simple but distinguished, with cast-iron furniture and wooden ceiling beams, all overlooking the verdant patio. There's a knockout lounge area too. US$100

Hostel Casa Grande Sánchez 254 ☎809 686 1199, ⓔreservacion@hotelcasagrande.com; map p.52. The cheapest rooms in the Zona Colonial are the snug backpacker-friendly dorms at this capacious, well-equipped and sociable hostel. There are six private rooms too, plus a host of very spacious communal areas including a large yard, a kitchen and dining area on a balcony terrace, a leisure room with pool table and TV, and a roof terrace where they hold barbecues. There's also internet access, a washing machine and even a little swimming pool. Dorm RD$640, double RD$1100

Casa Naemie Isabel La Católica 11 ☎809 689 2215, ⓦcasanaemie.com; map p.52. A charming little bed and breakfast dotted with memorable colonial and neo-colonial hallmarks – such as mahogany furniture and brick arches – and enchanting communal spaces, from the rooftop lounge to the breakfast bar. Rooms are clean and comfortable and some have views of the local neighbourhood. US$65

★ Casa Sánchez Sánchez 260 between Las Mercedes and El Conde ☎829 947 9002, ⓦcasasanchezhotel .com; map p.52. Style and comfort married with high levels of cleanliness, service and security make this place hard to beat – for the price, it's the best in the city. Highlights include thoughtfully furnished rooms, a dinky patio pool and an upstairs terrace area, where you can sunbathe on the loungers or relax on the shaded sofas. US$75

Casa del Sol Isabel La Católica 1 on the corner of Arz. Portes ☎849 936 4033, ⓦhotel-casadelsol.com; map p.52. Tucked into the southeastern corner of the Colonial Zone, a block from the Malecón, this simple guesthouse makes good use of its location with its roof terrace, where meals are served, providing views of the Caribbean Sea. Rooms are nothing special but perfectly adequate. One of the better deals at this price. US$55

Conde de Peñalba El Conde 111 and Meriño ☎809 688 7121, ⓦcondepenalba.com; map p.52. A fair compromise between comfort and colonial character, this 20-room hotel in a century-old building on Parque Duarte is right in the thick of the most touristy part of the city. The hotel boasts good service, comfortable rooms (a/c, cable TV, phone) and strong, hot showers. The ground-floor restaurant, although lively, is nothing special, and you undoubtedly pay for the location. US$85

Discovery Arz. Nouel, corner of Palo Hincado on Parque Independencia ☎809 687 4048, ⓦdiscoverygranhotel .com; map p.52. A nice enough place with standard amenities and nondescript but well-maintained rooms. The central location is hard to beat, while the rooftop bar and hot tub aren't bad either. US$45

Dominico Mundial Duarte 6 on Parque Duarte ☎809 682 6197, ⓦapartahoteldominicomundial.com; map p.52. The rooms are clean and cheap but a little basic and uninspiring at this no-frills hotel. The pleasant central patio lifts the mood inside while the location, overlooking pretty Parque Duarte, is a definite bonus – it gets either annoyingly noisy or irresistibly inviting at weekends, depending on your perspective. Rooms are priced according to six different grades, with breakfast optional for an extra US$10. US$28

Francés Las Mercedes 106 and Arz. Meriño ☎809 685 9331, ⓦmgallery.com; map p.52. Beautiful sixteenth-century building decorated with period furnishings, this cosy boutique hotel's best feature is the quiet, starlit, leafy courtyard. The 19 deluxe rooms are large and very comfortable; amenities include cable TV, a/c and minibar, with bathtubs and hairdryers in the en suite. The attached Le Patio restaurant is pretty good but overpriced. US$145

Hodelpa Caribe Colonial Isabel La Católica 159 ☎809 688 7799, ⓦhodelpa.com; map p.52. A bit of an anomaly within the Zona Colonial: a modern, almost flash hotel with nice but somewhat cramped rooms and eleven suites with balcony and hot tubs. The place is lacking in charm, but the staff are multilingual, there's 24hr room service and a taxi is on hand in the form of a snazzy, remodelled 1950s Cadillac. US$97

Hotel Nicolás de Ovando Las Damas and El Conde ☎809 685 9955, ⓦaccorhotels.com; map p.52. High-priced luxury hotel in the former home of conquistador Nicolás de Ovando (see p.263). The gorgeous rooms have authentic sixteenth-century decor, while offering every modern amenity (including high-speed internet). Half the rooms have great river views; the others overlook the colonial city – either way, you can't really lose. US$250

★ Palacio Duarte 106 and Ureña ☎809 682 4730, ⓦhotel-palacio.com; map p.52. Formerly the residence of infamous *caudillo* Buenaventura Báez (see p.266), this 1628 mansion has been very well maintained and boasts a dozen large, well-appointed rooms, quality service and all the mod cons. It's a pleasure just to walk the brick-arched corridors here, the walls lined with portraits of the island's first Spanish nobles. Free parking. US$125

1

★**Villa Colonial** Sánchez 157 ☎809 221 1049, ⓦvillacolonial.net; map p.52. Eleven tastefully understated, high-quality rooms, some opening up onto a narrow, plant-lined lawn, the others along an upstairs balcony. Away from the main building, a lovely dining area is sunk into the back of the garden, overlooking a small swimming pool, while the lobby and patio are filled with beautifully crafted Indonesian furniture, including a striking, ornately carved canopy couch. Overall the feeling is of calming harmony, making this a wonderful place to stay. US$85

THE MALECÓN

Hilton Santo Domingo Malecón 500 ☎809 685 0202, ⓦhiltonsantodomingo.com; map pp.50–51. Among the swishest of the city's waterfront hotel options, featuring very comfy but generically decorated rooms with work desks, great service and views of endless ocean. Geared toward high-end business travellers, so the place is run extremely well. US$129

Sheraton Santo Domingo Malecón 365 ☎809 221 6666, ⓦstarwoodhotels.com; map p.63. Launched as a Sheraton hotel in 2014, what was the *Hotel Magna 365* has been completely renovated but maintains an excellent level of service. It has spacious, modern rooms and boasts a shopping arcade, casino, three restaurants, swimming pool, hot tub and excellent rooms with cable TV, a/c, coffee-maker and phone. US$220

GAZCUE

La Casona Dorada Independencia 255 and Osvaldo Báez ☎809 221 3535, ✉casonadorada00@hotmail.com; map p.63. Set in quiet grounds away from the road, this refurbished nineteenth-century mansion has drab rooms, but features a restaurant-bar, swimming pool, hot tub, laundry service and free parking by way of recompense. Gay-friendly and a good price given the 24-hour security. RD$2300

La Grand Mansión Danae 26 ☎809 689 8758, ✉johanny_v@hotmail.com; map p.63. An unpretentious, clean and functional guesthouse on a quiet residential street, with private hot-water bathrooms, fan or a/c (a/c US$2.50 extra). Request a second-floor room for a pleasant tree-filled view. RD$1200

Maison Gautreaux Felix Mariano Llúberes 8 ☎809 412 7838, ⓦmaisongautreaux.net; map p.63. Large, clean rooms come with a/c, comfortable beds and especially strong hot showers – far better than what you'll find at most mid-budget hotels, though the front desk is not especially friendly. US$2 extra for cable TV. US$50

La Morada Santiago 104 ☎809 689 1088, ⓦhotellamorada.com; map p.63. This small, relatively new hotel has a quirky, colourful, almost Cubist exterior and some striking, slightly offbeat communal spaces too, including an upstairs terrace nightclub-style bar and dining area, a rooftop hot tub and loungers with nice views of the local area, and a small lounge resembling a set from *Miami Vice* with its tropical-island mural and leather couches. By contrast, the rooms are simple. US$55

Hotel Shakey Av. Pasteur ☎809 689 1237, ⓦhotelshakey.com; map p.63. Sparkling white aparthotel whose very clean apartments are somewhat plain and charmless but come suitably equipped with kitchen and living room. TV, a/c, free wi-fi and two bathrooms are all standard features. Offers very good service. US$92

POLÍGONO CENTRAL AND ARROYO HONDO

El Embajador Sarasota 65 ☎809 221 2131, ⓦoccidentalhotels.com; map pp.50–51. A grand hotel with a great deal of history (it was where American troops bunkered down during the invasion of 1965), this is the best of the supersized upmarket hotels in the capital, but is unfortunately quite far from the action – come here only if you have your own rental car. Set around ten blocks back from the Malecón but tall enough that many rooms offer ocean views from their terraces. The gorgeous grounds include gardens, tennis courts and a great swimming pool. US$119

EAST OF THE OZAMA

Quality Hotel Carretera Las Américas, 2km west of the Las Américas airport ☎809 549 2525, ⓦqualityinn .com; map pp.50–51. This is the best place to spend the night if you have an early flight, with good chain-style rooms offering comfort and modern amenities. It's used primarily by foreign executives heading in and out of town, but don't let that stop you. US$134

EATING

Dining options in the capital range from the small family **comedores** and ubiquitous *pica pollos* fried-chicken joints to **gourmet** restaurants with ethnic cuisines as diverse as Basque, North African and Japanese. At the more expensive places, expect to spend about US$25–40 including tax and tip (but not drinks). For **groceries**, there are numerous small *colmados* spread throughout the city; the nearest large supermarket to the Zona Colonial is La Sirena on Av. Mella and Duarte while there's a branch of Jumbo Express on El Conde. Most of the shopping malls also have large supermarkets. **Gazcue** is the city's swankiest restaurant district but options are widely spread – there are plenty of great places within the **Zona Colonial** and all within a much smaller, walkable area. Food shacks and stands dot **the Malecón**, where you'll be able to get pulled-pork sandwiches, grilled chicken with rice and beans, or a burger for as little as RD$60.

1

ZONA COLONIAL

Angelo Atarazana 21 ☎ 809 686 3586; map p.52. This pizzeria on the Plaza de España makes for a great mellow evening hangout, with outdoor tables on an attractive terrace and a good range of thin-crust options. Expect to spend around US$20 per person. Mon–Fri noon–midnight, Sat & Sun noon–1am.

Antica Pizzeria Padre Billini, corner of José Reyes ☎ 809 689 4040; map p.52. Good-value pizza and pasta in a smart yet rustic dining room. The straightforward menu features the usual classics, most of which are priced between RD$250 and RD$380, along with a small selection of filled pastries such as *panzerotti* and *calzoni*. Wed–Mon 5–11pm.

★**La Briciola** Arz. Meriño 152, corner of Padre Billini ☎ 809 688 5055, ⓦ labriciola.com.do; map p.52. Impeccable service and elegant, candlelit ambience in a restored colonial palace. Prices are high but justifiably so – the home-made pastas are top quality, such as the seafood spaghetti (RD$690) overflowing with shrimp, squid, mussels, clams and octopus. The seafood itself starts around the RD$800 mark. Daily 11am–midnight.

La Cafetera El Conde 253 ☎ 809 682 7114; map p.52. Best of the cafés along El Conde and a popular haunt for local painters and musicians. Come for the delicious but greasy traditional Dominican breakfasts with fresh orange juice and *café con leche*. Also sells bottles of the best local rums at great prices, and cutting-edge Spanish literature too – the perfect combo. Mon–Sat 7.30am–10.30pm, Sun 7.30am–6pm.

Dumbo Arz. Nouel 454 and Piña at Parque Independencia ☎ 809 687 1204; map p.52. Great workaday Dominican grub in a diner setting for around US$5 a plate. Peppered beefsteaks, several tasty chicken dishes, sandwiches and surprisingly good fish. Mon–Sat 7am–9pm, Sun 7am–6pm.

Falafel Billini and Sánchez ☎ 809 688 9714; map p.52. Israeli immigrants run this truly awesome little Mediterranean bistro, where tables are located in a delightful multilevel courtyard. Locals like the excellent falafel with mayo, so be sure to let them know if you want it without, while the shish kebabs are succulent and there's a nice selection of salads. You'll get a full meal here for less than RD$1000. Mon–Fri 5pm–midnight, Sat & Sun 5pm–2am.

Mesón d'Bari Hostos 302 and Ureña ☎ 809 687 4091; map p.52. This tavern serves some of the best food in the Zona Colonial, with their take on *filete encebollado* (RD$600) – a Dominican Republic national dish – arguably the finest you'll find anywhere. The exceptionally fresh seafood includes *cangrejo guisado*, a house speciality that features local soft-shell crabs in a garlic sauce. Note that it gets rather noisy at weekends when the music is cranked up several notches and the place doubles as a popular bar. Daily noon–midnight.

Mesón de Luís Hostos 201 between El Conde and General Luperón ☎ 809 689 4640; map p.52. Run by a friendly Dominican family, this rustic, cosy tavern-diner with tables huddled closely together and plenty of local flavour, serves up breakfasts (the best time to come) and typical Dominican dishes for between RD$90 and RD$400. Daily 8am–midnight.

★**Pat'e Palo** Atarazana 25, Plaza de España ☎ 809 687 8089, ⓦ patepalo.com; map p.52. Take a seat looking out over Plaza de España or in the atmospheric brick-walled interior – either way, this renowned restaurant offers top-notch dining. Dishes are mouthwatering, from killer burgers and steaks to seafood delights such as lobster in creamy white-wine sauce with gnocchi and truffles. The hearty salads are jam-packed with the likes of Roquefort cheese and roasted piquillo peppers. Mains RD$500–1000. Daily noon–midnight, Fri & Sat until 1am.

★**La Taberna Vasca** Hostos 356, corner of Las Mercedes ☎ 809 221 0079, ⓦ latabernavasca.com; map p.52. Exquisite French and Spanish food, including the Zona Colonial's finest paella, in an atmospheric 500-year-old building with some captivating, antique-laden private dining rooms that are well worth booking if you're in a large group. The menu is big on flavour – think shrimps in honey and ginger sauce or beef tenderloin in porcini mushroom sauce. Mains RD$450–1000. Mon–Sat 7pm–midnight.

THE MALECÓN

Adrian Tropical Av. George Washington near the foot of José Maria Heredia ☎ 809 221 1764; map p.63. A great place to eat authentically traditional Dominican cooking, with unbeatable sea views from several levels of decked terraces. Among the most spectacular outdoor dining spots in the city. There are several other branches elsewhere in the city. Mains RD$300–700. 24hr.

D'Luis Parrillada Malecón between Sánchez and 19 de Marzo ☎ 809 686 2940; map p.52. One of the capital's most popular late-night dining spots, with outdoor seating along the ocean, cheap food and a revved-up merengue atmosphere. The speciality here is Argentine-style grilled meat dishes and they're worth what can often be a long wait. Mon–Thurs 8am–1am, Fri–Sun 8am–3am; sometimes 24hr.

Mesón de la Rioja Malecón 25 between Sánchez and 19 de Marzo ☎ 809 685 0064; map p.52. As one of the only Malecón restaurants in the Zona Colonial, with a captivating interior akin to an aristocratic wine cellar and perfectly reasonable, mid-priced creole cuisine, this place should be more popular than it is. But its reputation for slow service is not undeserved. Daily 11.30am–midnight, Fri & Sat until 1am.

Trattoria Vesuvio Malecón 523 ☎ 809 221 1954; map p.63. Come for the best pizza in town (around US$20 for a large that can feed 3–4) or the decent pasta, sandwiches and crepes. Run by the same management as next door's *Vesuvio* but more casual and family-oriented. Daily midday–1am.

Vesuvio Malecón 521 ☎809 221 1954, ⓦvesuvio .com.do; map p.63. One of the most renowned restaurants in the city, deservedly so for its excellent, expensive seafood and fabulous location. Don't miss the knockout desserts either. Daily midday–1am.

GAZCUE

Ananda Av. Casimiro de Moya 7 ☎809 682 7153; map p.63. Popular vegetarian cafeteria and arty crowd hangout, with live merengue sometimes featuring on Monday nights. Food is good but fairly bland, though the tempuras are nicely done. Mains RD$50–200. Mon–Fri 11am–9pm, Sat & Sun 11am–4pm.

Cantabrico Independencia 54 between Las Carreras and the Shell garage ☎809 687 5101, ⓦrestaurantcantabrico.com; map p.63. A romantic, old-school spot that's known for its great service. Food is served in a simple but classy dining room, with high-priced specialities like Valencian-style paellas and Segovian suckling pig. Daily noon–midnight.

El Conuco Casimiro de Moya 152 ☎809 686 0129, ⓦelconuco.com.do; map p.63. This popular place on a pretty suburban street is set in an oversized *bohío* (a traditional thatched-roof *campesino* common area inherited from the Tainos). The daily RD$75 buffet is a bargain and the menu features traditional treats such as *sancocho* and *chivo orégano*. You'll be attended to by singing, dancing waiters, too. Daily 11.30am–11.30pm.

Manolo Av. Independencia, corner of Hermanos Deligne ☎809 687 7670; map p.63. They turn out a decent *mofongo* or *mondongo* at this reliable establishment, and you can enjoy their Dominican cuisine at any time of the day or night. Choose from the enclosed dining room or the covered, roadside terrace, which is a great people-watching spot. Open 24hr.

Sabor y Especias Santiago 302 ☎809 682 1204; map p.63. Great little neighbourhood diner serving good-quality creole cuisine like stewed beef or fried chicken in a very simple but clean and pleasant environment. There's a different good-value *menú del día* for each day of the week. Perfect for a laidback lunch. Mon–Sat 11.30am–midnight.

Villar Hermanos Av. Independencia 312, corner of

Pasteur ☎809 682 1433; map p.63. This local institution draws in a great mix of people with its affordable, homely Dominican food. The variety's another bonus – grab a pastry from the excellent bakery, take an easy-going lunch at the buffet cafeteria or enjoy a formal dinner at the Garden Café set at the back of the complex. Daily 7am–midnight; Garden Café 11am–11pm.

POLÍGONO CENTRAL AND ARROYO HONDO

Alma Llanera Av. Churchill 51 just south of 27 de Febrero ☎809 508 6327; map p.50–51. A small, easily missed little kitchen which serves tremendous Venezuelan dishes like shredded beef in creole sauce and a variety of *cachapas* – cornbread pancakes stuffed with beef, chicken, shredded pork or cheese. Good for those on a tight budget. Daily 11am–midnight.

La Cassina Av. Roberto Pastoriza 504 ☎809 363 4444; map pp.50–51. Fine Italian dining in a large, upscale restaurant with an elegant main salon and a more laidback terrace. Mouthwateringly rich ravioli and risotto options (RD$460–740), flavoursome steaks (RD$990–1495), seafood and pizzas. Live traditional Latin music features on Thursdays. Fri & Sat noon–2am, Sun–Thurs noon–midnight.

David Crockett Ricart 34 ☎809 565 8898; map pp.50–51. Excellent steak house with corny "Wild West" decor, which makes it quite popular with kids. The massive porterhouse steaks go under the name "Cowboy Filet"; rack of lamb and prime rib are also favourites. Expect to spend US$50 here for two. Daily noon–midnight.

Mesón de la Cava J. Contreras 237, Mirador del Sur at eastern end of park ☎809 533 2818, ⓦelmesondelacava .com; map pp.50–51. Funky restaurant in a large cave once used by the Taimos – though not as a restaurant. The food is decent enough, with lobster, garlicky shrimp *ajillo* and ribeye steaks all featuring, but it's more notable for the unique setting. Only a small percentage of main dishes are less than RD$800. Daily noon–midnight.

Samurai Seminario 57, a block from Av. 27 de Febrero and Av. Abraham Lincoln ☎809 565 1621, ⓦsamurairestaurante.com; map pp.50–51. Japanese sushi bars are thin on the ground in Santo Domingo, so enjoy this place's *shabu-shabu*, mixed sushi and sashimi platters, hibachi platters and sake while you have the chance. It's surprisingly inexpensive, too, considering the high quality. Daily noon–11pm.

DRINKING, NIGHTLIFE AND LIVE MUSIC

The **Malecón** and the **Zona Colonial** are the focal points for nightlife. The Malecón venues tend to be a little more raucous (lapsing occasionally into seediness) and include some of the city's finest dancehalls. Some of the biggest **parties** happen outdoors, fuelled by food and drink shacks that slowly start getting crowded around 10pm and stay open until the early hours. The Zona Colonial is the place for **bar-hopping**: dotted around the atmospheric ruins are a variety of working-class joints, jazz bars and slick clubs. Less known to outsiders are the nightclubs along **Av. Venezuela**, 1km east of the Río

PARQUE DUARTE

The liveliest outdoor spot in the Zona Colonial at weekends is **Parque Duarte**, where the crowd slowly builds from around 10pm. Come the wee hours it's heaving with locals, who buy their drinks from the little bar on the park or at the *colmado* over the road. The Duarte side is **gay** and the Hostos side straight but there's a fantastically **harmonious** and feel-good atmosphere – you'll find no better place in the city to socialize with locals and soak up the best of the tolerant, friendly Dominican spirit.

Ozama, and on the section of **Av. Abraham Lincoln** that lies north of 27 de Febrero: these are easily the most popular clubs with locals and they are less safe than the venues in the Zona Colonial. In addition to the clubs listed below, Av. Venezuela is home to a host of smaller beer halls and pool halls that attract huge crowds nightly, as do some of the *colmados* here, often a focus for Dominican night-time street life. For some informal Dominican entertainment, check out the **merengue périco ripao** bands that wander the crowded *colmados* along Avenida Duarte, just north of the Zona Colonial, in the early evening. There are also several clubs across the city that specialize in **son** (see box, p.78).

ESSENTIALS

When to go out It's counter-intuitive, but along with the weekend the busiest night for heading out to the city's bars and clubs is Monday, perhaps because locals need to fortify themselves in the face of a new week at work. Big-name acts, whose reputation will raise the cover charge by RD$200, often perform on this unlikeliest of nights; street-side banners across the city advertise any notable concert.

Listings There are several Spanish-language websites devoted exclusively to covering the latest events in the city's nightlife. Covering cinema, comedy, live music and restaurants is ⓦ uepa.com. *Hoy's* "Agenda" section (ⓦ hoy .com.do) has event listings, as does *Listin Diario's* "Entretenimiento" (ⓦ listin.com.do).

ZONA COLONIAL

Bio Sánchez 125 and Padre Billini ☎ 809 686 0147; map p.52. This two-storey lounge is one of the hippest bars in the zone, a with a great mix of western and Latin music. Undoubtedly one for the poseurs but it's still a must on anyone's Zona Colonial bar-hopping itinerary. Thurs–Sat 9pm–3am, Sun 9pm–midnight.

Casa de Teatro Arz. Meriño 110 ☎ 809 689 3430, ⓦ casateatro.com; map p.52. Classy courtyard café in the nineteenth-century Casa de Teatro, a drama venue that also features live jazz and jazz-influenced Latin combos. Mon–Fri 9am–1am, Sat & Sun 9am–3am.

Doubles Arz. Meriño 54A ☎ 809 688 3833; map p.52. This is a great-looking place – a smart yet comfortable joint just off the Plaza Padre Billini, invitingly decked out with easy chairs and couches, coolly complemented by the dark wood panelling, candelabra wall lights and well-stocked backlit bar. Daily 6pm–1am, Fri & Sat until 3am.

La Espiral José Reyes 107 ☎ 809 686 1765; map p.52. The granddaddy of the local rave clubs, formerly known as *Ocho Puertas*, has tamed down over time and is now more of a bar with music than a club. It's housed in a gorgeously restored colonial mansion, and there's a couch-filled

lounge, outdoor plaza and a straight-up stool-lined bar. The music, both live and recorded, is a mix of everything from trance to reggae and rock to funk. Tues–Sun 8pm–late.

Hard Rock Café El Conde at Parque Duarte ☎ 809 686 7771; map p.52. Believe it or not this worldwide chain is one of the big live-music venues in the Zona Colonial, with some good "unplugged" Latin acts and the occasional techno night. Daily 9am–1am, Fri & Sat until 3am.

Lulú Arz. Meriño, corner of Padre Billini ☎ 809 687 8360 ⓦ lulu.do; map p.52. Very trendy tapas bar, or "tasting bar" – as the proprietors insist on calling it – with aspirations of sophistication. Thankfully, the atmosphere is convivial, with well-dressed punters sitting at tables on the lovely patio or along the smart bar chin-wagging over *croquetas*, teriyaki, wine and cocktails. A good spot for a laidback evening. Daily 6pm–2am.

Mesón d' Bari Hostos and Ureña; map p.52. An atmospheric after-work gathering place, notable for its soundtrack of traditional bachata, Sinatra, jazz and old-style Cuban son. The seafood dishes are quite good here as well (see p.75). Daily noon–midnight.

THE MALECÓN

Maunaloa Calle Héroes de Luperón at Malecón, Centro de los Héroes ☎ 809 533 2151; map pp.50–51. This nightclub and casino is super-suave and gorgeous to boot, with two floors of tables looking out onto a big-band stage reminiscent of the Roaring Twenties. The music is not as good as in the outer barrio son clubs, but it's a lot more convenient to get to. RD$100 cover most nights and a one-drink minimum; the music doesn't start until 11pm. Daily 6pm until late.

Mint Av. George Washington 51, *Hotel El Napolitano* ☎ 809 687 1131 ext. 704; map pp.50–51. Surprisingly, this mid-range hotel has the most popular disco on the boardwalk these days, in large part because working-class twentysomethings can come without paying a steep cover charge. Cover RD$150. Tues–Sun 10pm–6am.

1

SON RISE

There are several venues across the city where you can listen to live **son** – a melodious and traditional style of Cuban music featuring acoustic guitars and percussion, reintroduced to much of the world in the 1990s by the **Buena Vista Social Club**. Some Dominicans claim the style was born here, where it has always been popular, and the form is enjoying something of a **revival**, as evidenced by a citywide festival each March (see box, p.80). Below are some of the venues where you can enjoy dancing and listening to son throughout the year.

★ **Lucia 203** Hostos 203 ☎ 809 689 5546; map p.52. Open throughout the week but only Thurs and Sat are Cuban son nights at this inviting venue, featuring a lounge bar full of designer seating and exposed sections of the original brick walls, plus a nice bamboo-lined courtyard and a restaurant upstairs. There are jazz nights here too. Son nights 8pm–1am.

★ **Ruinas de San Francisco** End of Emiliano Tejera, corner of Hostos; map p.52. For years now sixteen-piece band Grupo Bonyé have been playing their mix of traditional Dominican and Cuban music to enthusiastic crowds here in the old open-air ruins of the Monasterio de San Francisco. Free entry. Usually kicks off around 6pm.

Salón de los Espejos Palacio de Bellas Artes, corner of Independencia and Máximo Gómez ☎ 809 689 8720; map p.63. Live son acts perform here every Sunday in the refined surroundings of a bar at one of the country's premier cultural institutions. RD$100. From 6pm.

★ **El Sarten** Hostos 153 ☎ 809 686 9621; map p.52. Traditional Dominican and Cuban music set the tone at this dinky, lovable bar where old couples drift around the small space in front of the bar dancing, and everyone else squeezes in around them. Notable for its down-to-earth, friendly vibe. Daily from around 7pm.

La Parada Cervecera Plaza D'Frank, just west of the *Crowne Plaza Santo Domingo* hotel, Malecón ☎ 809 683 2258; map p.63. The most popular of the outdoor beer joints dotting the boardwalk and a favourite hangout of baseball legend Sammy Sosa. They claim to have the coldest beer in town, for what it's worth. Food served too. Daily 8am–midnight.

GAZCUE

★ **Cinema Café** Plaza de la Cultura, Av. Pedro Henríquez Ureña ☎ 809 221 7555, ⓦ cinemacafe.com .do; map p.63. Creatively designed and run venue with an interesting schedule of events and an imaginative set of largely open-air spaces. Live and recorded music from heavy metal gigs to eighties nights. Daily happy hour 5–8pm. Cover charge at weekends RD$200–300. Daily 5pm–midnight, Fri & Sat until 2am.

POLÍGONO CENTRAL AND ARROYO HONDO

Dock Lounge Acropolis Center, second level, Av. Winston Churchill between Andre Julio Aybar and Rafael Augusto Sánchez ☎ 829 719 0368; map pp.50–51. This popular lounge bar is a good place for an early drink if you're going out in this part of town. DJs some nights, when the small dancefloor comes into its own. Daily 4pm–midnight, Fri & Sat until 2am.

★ **La Guácara Taina** Av. Mirador del Sur ☎ 809 530 2151; map pp.50–51. Set in a huge, multilevel natural cave and known locally as "La Cueva", this remains probably the most famous club in the city and is a popular spot for tourists. The music focuses almost exclusively on electronica. RD$300 cover. Thurs–Sun 9pm–3am.

Jet Set Independencia 2253, corner of Proyecto ☎ 809 535 4145; map pp.50–51. Inconveniently located at the far western end of Independencia is this venerable old merengue club. It's always packed with a local crowd and lots of top-name acts appear here on weekends; the dancehall sometimes doesn't close down until around 6am. Cover is RD$300–1200 depending on who's playing. Mon–Thurs 8pm–1am, Fri–Sun 8pm–5am.

London Box Plaza Andalucia II, 2nd floor, Av. Abraham Lincoln and Gustavo Mejía Ricart ☎ 829 864 0610; map pp.50–51. A pretty mixed crowd and nothing too posey, nights here can get very lively and this relatively intimate club packed out. Music policy is equally mixed and nights range from reggaeton, hip-hop and house to eighties and nineties nostalgia. Free or cover charges up to RD$500. Mon–Thurs 9pm–1am, Fri–Sun 9pm–4am.

EAST OF THE OZAMA

Eclipse Av. Venezuela 64 and Bonaire ☎ 809 597 2089; map pp.50–51. The hottest spot on Av. Venezuela, this club seems to net major live acts every weekend, though the cover can be as steep as RD$400. Closed Mon.

Makumba Av. Venezuela and Cabrera ☎ 809 803 3366; map pp.50–51. After you enter through the mammoth Sphinx that serves as the building's entrance, you'll find an extremely dark, ridiculously crowded dance club that's one of the most popular on the Venezuela strip. Local acts play frequently as well. RD$120 cover. Wed–Sun 8pm–3am.

THE OUTER BARRIOS
Paraíso Musical Av. Hermanas Mirabal, Villa Mella ☎ 809 569 5959; map pp.50–51. About 250m south of the Gregorio Gilbert Metro stop, music events here vary greatly, from afternoons and evenings of bachata and Cuban son to heavy nights of hip-hop and reggaeton. Opening hours vary.

GAY CLUBS AND BARS

The Zona Colonial is becoming increasingly popular with gay visitors and stands out as one of the most **gay-friendly** places in the Caribbean. Gay clubs come and go in Santo Domingo so it's often best to take a look at ⓦ monaga.net for the latest news on the scene. Free entry unless stated.

Esedeku Mercedes and San Tomé, Zona Colonial ☎ 809 869 6322; map p.52. At the time of writing this was the newest and hippest bar in town, frequented mostly by a local, welcoming crowd, though they can be a little snooty on the door. Wed–Sun from 9pm.

Fogoo Arz. Nouel 307 ☎ 809 514 7777 & 829 433 4472, ⓦ fogoord.com; map p.52. Among the hottest nightclubs on the city's gay scene in recent times, featuring drag shows, live music, karaoke nights and strippers. Cover RD$100–300. Thurs–Sat 11pm–3am, Sun 11pm–4am.

G Lounge Arz. Nouel 305, Zona Colonial ☎ 829 745 2724; map p.52. One of the newer gay nightlife venues in the Zona Colonial (next door to *Fogoo*) and one of the liveliest at weekends, when the party spills out onto the street. Cover is free before 11pm and RD$200 after. Tues–Thurs 9pm–2am, Fri–Sun 10pm–4am.

NYC Mercedes 263, corner of Santomé ☎ 809 653 2879, ⓦ nycbardr.com; map p.52. With its 1980s-style shiny black and white interior, this bar is best known for its weekend strip shows. Daily 8pm–1am, Fri–Sun until 3am.

CINEMAS

Most Santo Domingo cinemas are large **multiplexes** with a focus on first-run American action flicks, which hit the screens at the same time as they do in the US. Unfortunately, almost every theatre in the city shows the same two or three Hollywood blockbusters and there are no cinemas at all in the **Zona Colonial**. You'll be able to check at the ticket booth whether the film is in English with Spanish subtitles or dubbed. Either way, expect the audience to be as much a part of the show as the movie – locals often derive most of their pleasure from making fun of the action on screen. **Tickets** are generally between RD$100 and RD$200; check ⓦ supercartelera.com or the cinema chain websites given below for **listings**.

Broadway Cinema Plaza Central, 27 de Febrero and Churchill ☎ 809 872 0000, ⓦ caribbeancinemasrd.com. Offers alternative films unavailable elsewhere, along with the usual hits.

Cinema Centro Malecón Av. George Washington 457, just east of Máximo Gómez, Gazcue ☎ 809 685 2898, ⓦ caribbeancinemasrd.com. The usual set of blockbuster American films in a rowdy atmosphere. Conveniently located close to the Malecón hotels.

Hollywood Diamond Diamond Plaza at Av. Proceres just north of Kennedy ☎ 809 565 8877, ⓦ caribbean cinemasrd.com. This multilevel theatre with two 3D

SPORTS AND OTHER ACTIVITIES IN SANTO DOMINGO

The most exciting spectator sport in Santo Domingo is **baseball**. Two separate professional teams, Licey and Escogido, play in the winter professional league between October and early February. There are games most days of the week in the regular season at **Estadio Quisqueya**, located on Avenida Tiradentes, a few blocks north of Avenida John F Kennedy (tickets RD$300–1000; ☎ 809 616 1224, ⓦ estadioquisqueya.com.do). Tickets are generally available on the night of the game, or you can purchase in advance online, from the stadium ticket office and elsewhere – see local newspapers for up-to-date ticket purchasing locations. Though more and more Dominican major-leaguers are opting out of the winter season, you'll still find a few famous Dominican players along with some of America's top minor-league prospects.

Most foreign visitors find **cockfighting**, the other local obsession, less easy to stomach, but it's a central part of Dominican culture. The city's grand Coliséo Gallístico Alberto Bonetti Burgos on Av. Luperón just south of the Autopista Duarte (RD$250 for ground floor, RD$100 for first-floor stands; ☎ 809 548 7045), effectively transforms this traditionally rural pastime into something of an upper-class diversion – indeed, smart dress is required. There are plenty of other, smaller venues spread across the city's outer barrios, but this is by far the best place for visitors to come. Finally, the entire city is dotted with **pool halls**. The best places to shoot a few games are the second-floor halls that you'll find along El Conde – though as with most male-dominated Dominican hangouts, the atmosphere is hyper-macho.

1

SANTO DOMINGO FESTIVALS

CARNIVAL

Partying, live music and elaborate costumes along El Conde and the Malecón **every Sunday in February**, especially the last of the month. Expect to be pelted with inflated sheep bladders and balloons.

INDEPENDENCE DAY

A citywide celebration on the final day of Carnival (**February 27**), with a raucous re-enactment of the Trinitarians' 1844 torchlit march to El Conde, to the tune of the *1812 Overture*, accompanied by live cannon. Afterwards, head to Puerta San Diego where you'll almost certainly be able to hear big-name merengue acts..

SON FESTIVAL

Dozens of events take place in the **last two weeks of March** celebrating this popular Cuban musical form that many Dominicans claim as their own. *Mesón d' Bari* (see p.77) posts a list of all events on its wall in early February.

SEMANA SANTA

On the morning of **Ash Wednesday**, go to the Zona Colonial's Iglesia del Carmen, where a statue of Christ is paraded through the streets, serenaded and draped in money. In Haina, on the city's western outskirts, you'll find a Hispanicized version of the Haitian Semana Santa festivities also found in the *bateyes*.

ESPÍRITU SANTO

Taking place **seven weeks after Semana Santa**, this full week of fervent religious processions and conga drums in the Villa Mella district is undoubtedly the most spirited and visually interesting of the local festivals.

SAN ANTONIO

Large festival on the **first Sunday before June 13** in the rural northern suburb of Yamasá. The Hermanos Guillen (see p.69) pump a lot of money into the proceedings (including free food and drink for everyone) with the purpose of preserving traditional rural Dominican musical forms *gagá*, *gajumbe* and *bambulá*.

MERENGUE FESTIVAL

Loud outdoor concerts in the **last two weeks of July** on the Malecón by big-name *merengueros*, plus traditional accordion merengue groups performing at the Palacio de Bellas Artes and merengue-based "folklore" shows at the National Theatre that feature the *Vodú*-based *palos* musicians of Villa Mella with the National Folklore Ballet.

VIRGEN DE LAS MERCEDES

Syncretic religious ceremony and neighbourhood street party in Mata Los Indios near Villa Mella on **September 15–24**. Famous for its African-style drumming and music.

SAN MIGUEL

Fiesta patronal in honour of one of the country's most important saints, celebrated in Villa Mella and the Zona Colonial's barrio San Miguel on **September 29**. A large procession carries an effigy of the saint accompanied by drums and *gagá* band.

FIESTA ORIENTAL

The eastern side of the city had the first recorded Dominican Carnival (1520) and in recent years the Zona Oriental now finally has its share of festivities again. This massive Carnival on **October 7** in honour of the barrios east of the Ozama is heavier on the African syncretic elements of Dominican culture than the February event, including traditional local dances like the *mandinga* and *bailan pri-pri*, as well as *guloya* performances from the Cocolos of San Pedro. Runs the length of Av. Venezuela and ends up in Parque Mirador del Este.

screens attracts plenty of families, so it helps to be good-natured about the crowd noise.

Palacio del Cine Sambil, Av. John F Kennedy, corner of Av. Máximo Gómez ☎809 633 0505, Ⓦpalaciodelcine.com.do. One of five Palacios del Cine around the city, this one is the biggest of the lot with nine screens. Like the others, it's a pretty slick affair with large screens, comfy seating and good levels of cleanliness.

SHOPPING

High-end boutiques and shopping malls, known in Dominican Spanish as *plazas*, spread outward from the **Plaza Central** at 27 de Febrero and Troncoso, marking the city's main shopping district. More tourist-oriented shops can be found along **El Conde** in the Zona Colonial. Most Dominicans shop for clothing and electronics at the budget stores that line **Av. Duarte**, especially La Sirena, Mella 258 and Duarte, which has inexpensive counterfeit designer clothes purchased en masse at the markets along the Haitian border.

ARTS, CRAFTS AND JEWELLERY

There are arts and crafts shops and indoor markets the length of El Conde and a few more on Isabel La Católica within a block of El Conde.

Columbus Plaza Arz. Meriño 206 at Parque Colón ☎809 689 0565; map p.52. An arts, crafts and gifts department store with three floors of merchandise and above them a cafeteria. As well as all the paintings, ceramics, jewellery and T-shirts, there is an excellent selection of Dominican coffee, rum and cigars. One of the best places for a prolonged browse. Mon–Sat 8.30am–5.30pm.

De Mi País Arz. Meriño 164, corner of Arz. Nouel ☎809 689 3972; map p.52. There's nothing for sale here that you can't buy elsewhere but it's a slightly more relaxed atmosphere and a less crowded store than most of the gift shops on El Conde. The speciality is jewellery, including mother of pearl, jade and turquoise as well as the ubiquitous amber and larimar, and there are paintings and other crafts too. Mon–Sat 9am–6pm.

Joyería DiCarlo El Conde and Meriño ☎809 682 2026; map p.52. High-end jewellery shop on Parque Colón that's a cut above the usual tourist-shop fare. Features quality amber and larimar offerings, but also a range of stylish gold and silver earrings and necklaces. Mon–Sat 9am–6pm.

Mercado Modelo Av. Mella between Santomé and Montey Tejada ☎809 686 6772; map p.52. The largest arts and crafts market in the city – aimed squarely at tourists – is an indoor set-up, tightly packed with dozens and dozens of separate units, almost all of them run by pushy salespeople. You'll find every type of handmade sculpture, souvenir and trinket but be prepared for some lively haggling. Mon–Fri 9am–6pm, Sat 9am–2pm.

Museo del Ámbar El Conde 107 at Parque Colón ☎809 221 1333; map p.52. Excellent but pricey jewellery shop with the highest-quality amber and larimar, including some amber pieces with insects suspended inside them and knock-off colonial coins made into necklaces and bracelets. There's also a museum on the first floor (see p.50). Mon–Fri 9.30am–7pm, Sat 9.30am–6.30pm.

Museo Larimar Dominicano Isabela la Católica 54 ☎809 689 6605, Ⓦlarimarmuseum.com; map p.52. A generous selection of all manner of quality larimar jewellery is for sale here once you've taken in the exhibits at the museum itself (see p.54). Mon–Sat 9am–6pm.

Museo Mundo de Ámbar Arz. Meriño 452 and Restauración ☎809 682 3309, Ⓦamberworldmuseum .com; map p.52. This amber museum (see p.58) actually has a better exhibit than the one on Parque Duarte and a comparable gift shop stocked with all sorts of amber jewellery. Mon–Sat 9am–6pm, Sun 9am–2pm.

BOOKS AND MUSIC

El Conde has several **CD** shops. The best places for secondhand **books** are on Arz. Nouel and Parque Enriquillo, where the entire northern border of the park is chock-a-block with stalls.

Librería Cuesta Av. 27 de Febrero, corner of Av. Abraham Lincoln ☎809 473 4020, Ⓦcuestalibros.com; map pp.50–51. The biggest and best bookshop in the city spans just two floors but is a very pleasant place to browse; it has a good selection of foreign and Dominican literature, sizeable history and social science sections and a considerable selection of English-language titles. Mon–Sat 9am–9pm, Sun 10am–8pm.

Librería La Trinitaria Arz. Nouel 160 and José Reyes ☎809 082 1032; map p.52. Best of the many small bookshops that surround El Conde, with a host of great Spanish-language tomes on every aspect of Dominican life and culture imaginable. Mon–Sat 8.30am–6pm.

Musicalia El Conde 464 ☎809 687 5051; map p.52. This renowned bachata record outlet has the best of the Dominican golden oldies, including operatic favourites Eduardo Brito and María Montéz, old *bachateros* like Luis Segura and *típico merengueros* from Francisco Ulloa to Tavito Vasquez. Mon–Sat 10am–7pm.

CIGARS

Arturo Fuente Cigar Club Av. 27 de Febrero 211, near corner of Av. Tiradentes ☎809 683 2771;

1

map pp.50–51. This is a cigar shop, lounge and bar for the connoisseur or the very brave beginner. Dress formally (no trainers, shorts, sports gear or T-shirts) and act like you know what you're talking about – otherwise you'll feel very uncomfortable no matter which of the sumptuous sofas and chairs you sit in. Shop Mon–Sat 9am–midnight; bar Mon–Thurs 3pm–midnight, Fri & Sat 3pm–2am.

Caoba Cigars Boutique del Fumador El Conde 109 at Parque Colón ☎ 809 685 6425; map p.52. A variety of top Cuban and Dominican cigars at reasonable prices. There's also a cigar roller on hand to teach you how to roll your own. Mon–Sat 9am–7pm, Sun 10am–3pm.

La Leyenda del Cigarro Mercedes 107, corner of Hostos ☎ 809 682 6490; map p.52. One of three city branches of this excellent cigar dealer and manufacturer. The staff are very knowledgeable about their product and the selection is first class. Daily 9am–9pm.

GALLERIES

Galería de Arte Nader Rafael Augusto Sánchez 22 and Geraldino, Polígono Central ☎ 809 544 0878; map pp.50–51. A prestigious gallery, displaying big-name contemporary Dominican painters. Mon–Fri 9.30am–7pm, Sat 9.30am–1pm.

Galería Bidó Dr Báez 5 ☎ 809 682 5310; map p.63. Art gallery set on a residential block, run by the famous Dominican painter Bidó (see p.64); there's a selection of his own work and exhibits from other Dominican modernists like Picasso-influenced Cristian Tiburcio, whose massive

sculptures of musicians flank the gallery's front door. Mon–Fri 9am–5pm.

MALLS

Agora Mall Av. John F Kennedy, corner of Av. Abraham Lincoln ☎ 809 363 2323; map pp.50–51. A sleek mall with four levels and an above-average food court. One of the highlights here is the branch of Cosas del País, a store selling all kinds of Dominican food stuffs (particularly sweets) and craftwork. On Saturdays independent traders set up stalls on the first floor and create a market of strictly Dominican wares. Shops Mon–Sat 9am–9pm, Sun 10am–8pm; food court daily 11am–midnight, Fri & Sat until 1am.

Plaza Central Av. 27 de Febrero, corner of Av. Winston Churchill ☎ 809 541 5929; map pp.50–51. Large mall with all the standard shops – largely clothing and beauty stores and salons, as well as shoe shops and a large cinema. There's live concert-band music on Sundays at 6pm in front of the mall. Mon–Sat 9am–8pm, Sun 10am–4pm.

Sambil Av. John F Kennedy, corner of Av. Máximo Gómez ☎ 809 234 5678; map pp.50–51. Wandering around the relatively empty hallways of this four-floor shopping centre does make you wonder whether Santo Domingo really needed yet another huge mall when this Venezuelan-owned complex was erected in 2012 – but the quietness does make for a stress-free visit to more than a hundred shops. There's a huge cinema too. Mon–Sat 10am–9pm, Sun noon–8pm.

DIRECTORY

Ambulance Dial ☎ 911 in case of emergency; for private, fee-charging ambulance call Movimed (☎ 809 532 0000).

Banks In the Zona Colonial go to Isabel La Católica where, on the two blocks between Emiliano Tejera and General Luperón, there are four large banks including branches of Banco Popular, Scotiabank and Banco de Reservas; in Gazcue, try Banco Popular at Av. Bolívar 357 between Av. Doctor Delgado and Tony Mota Ricart. There are also banks in all the malls (see above). There are three ATMs on El Conde between Hostos and Duarte in the Zona Colonial and in the malls.

Currency exchange There are plenty of small exchanges in the Zona Colonial, though withdrawing out of an ATM bank machine will get you a better exchange rate. If you don't have a bank card, go to the exchange desk at Caribe Tours (27 de Febrero and Navarro) which offers the city's best rates. Avoid any dealings with exchangers who approach you on the street, as rip-offs and counterfeit pesos are standard practice.

Dental For 24hr service go to Dr Melchor Fernandez at Plaza Central on Churchill and 27 de Febrero, suite 365 (☎ 809 547 3902).

Embassies Canada, Churchill 1099 ☎ 809 262 3100; United States, Edificio Corominas Pepin, 27 de Febrero

233 ☎ 809 472 7111; United States, Nicolás Penson 81 and Leopoldo Navarro ☎ 809 221 2171. There is no consular representation for Australia or New Zealand.

Gym The only gym in the Colonial Zone is the well-equipped Gimnasio Colonial at Sánchez 255. Membership-free access for tourists at US$10 per day.

Hospitals A good hospital with some English-speaking staff close to the Zona Colonial is Clínica Abreu, located 600m from Parque Independencia at Arzobispo Portes 853 (☎ 809 688 4411, ⓦ clinicaabreu.com.do); on the other side of Gazcue, in the university district, is another recommended hospital run by the Spanish Hospiten Group, the Hospiten Santo Domingo at Alma Máter on the corner of Av. Bolívar (☎ 809 541 3000, ⓦ hospiten.com).

Internet In the Zona Colonial there are several internet cafés along El Conde and a business centre (ⓦ businesscentercolonialzone.com) at Sánchez 255 with excellent facilities and good internet access. Rates in most places run about RD$1 per minute. Free wi-fi in the lobbies of all Malecón hotels and throughout many of the Zona Colonial hotels.

Laundry In the Zona Colonial, Lavandería Nacional at Santomé 399 and Lavandería Colonial at Padre Billini 205;

in Gazcue, Royal Lavandería at Av. Bolívar 354. Count on around US$3 per large load. Otherwise hotels often offer a laundry service, though they generally charge by the piece and are much more expensive.

Mobile phones There are Orange and Claro outlets on El Conde in the Zona Colonial and at the Sambil and Agora shopping malls (see opposite).

Pharmacies The Carol chain of pharmacies (w farmaciacarol) has branches all over the city, many of them open 24hr; there are Gazcue branches at Av. Bolívar 251 (daily 8am–midnight; ☎ 809 689 6000) and Independencia 57 (24hr; ☎ 809 685 8165), just a few blocks from the Zona Colonial.

Police The central police station is on Independencia (☎ 809 682 3151). More convenient if you're in the Zona Colonial is the small Politur tourist police station on El Conde and José Reyes (☎ 809 689 6464). Dial ☎ 911 in case of emergency.

Post office The main office is on Héroes de Luperón just off the Malecón (Mon–Fri 8am–5pm, Sat 8am–noon; ☎ 809 534 5838). In the Zona Colonial there's a branch at Isabel La Católica 103 on Parque Colón (Mon–Fri 8am–5pm, Sat 9am–1pm; ☎ 809 687 7991).

Telephone Public telephones are increasingly few and far between – try the hotels or shopping malls.

The southeast

BASÍLICA DE NUESTRA SEÑORA DE LA MERCED, HIGÜEY

The southeast

The Santo Domingo valley stretches east from the capital along the Caribbean coast all the way to the Mona Passage, the body of water separating the Dominican Republic from Puerto Rico, encompassing vast tracts of sugar cane along the way, once practically the nation's sole source of hard currency. North of these fields roll the verdant high hills of the Cordillera Oriental – really a final spur of the Cordillera Central. This sizeable region is the Dominican Republic's southeast, known primarily for its popular Punta Cana resort zone, a 45km strip of idyllic, uninterrupted sand lined with all-inclusive hotels that are far less expensive than what you'll find around most of the Caribbean. While these beaches may be a bit remote for extensive day-tripping and countryside exploration, they do make perfect spots for utterly relaxing holidays. And the upgrading of the region's roads – which has seen much of the coastal highway widened, and a new highway through to Punta Cana – means that the whole area is becoming ever more accessible.

Often visited on day-trips from Santo Domingo are the rather more accessible **Boca Chica**, **Juan Dolio** and **Guayacanes**, which are all a little rough around the edges but do feature some fine beaches. Aside from the resort areas, the southeast is fairly poor, rural and somewhat bereft of must-see sights – with the notable exception of the two national parks that help frame the region. One of these, **Parque Nacional del Este**, protruding into the Caribbean at the southeastern tip of the Dominican Republic, more or less continues the theme of great beachfront, especially in the case of **Isla Saona**'s remarkable nature reserve. The park features a number of **cave systems** – Peñon Gordo, Del Puente, José and Padre Nuestro – though the extensive Taino rock art that these caves hold is mostly off-limits to tourists. Not far to the west, the pretty seaside village **Bayahibe**, the latest centre of all-inclusive construction, is the best base from which to visit the park's various points of interest.

La Romana and **San Pedro de Macorís**, which lie on Highway 3 between Santo Domingo and Parque Nacional del Este, serve as urban exceptions to the backwater feel of much of the region. These two mid-sized towns, which both flourished during the glory era of the sugar industry, have enjoyed contrasting fortunes in recent years. La Romana has grown into a relaxing and prosperous place, having benefited quite a bit from Gulf & Western's investment in local industry and its been able to capitalize on some resort build-up – notably in the vast **Casa de Campo** complex just east of town.

ISLA SAONA

Highlights

❶ Bayahibe Unwind in this picturesque fishing village, enjoying a candelit dinner on the beach or a cool drink from one of the casual bars overlooking the bay. **See p.101**

❷ Boat trips to Isla Saona Embark on a memorable day-trip to island wildlife reserve, part of Parque Nacional del Este, which boasts untrammelled wilderness, beautiful beaches and manatees. **See p.103**

❸ Boca de Yuma Passed over by package tours, this laidback seafront village has bluffs with crashing surf, good fishing and caving, and the fortified lair of conquistador Ponce de León. **See p.107**

❹ Los Corales beach bars Sip and lounge your way through the afternoon and into the evening at one of the chill-out bars on the beach in Punta Cana. **See pp.115–116**

❺ Cueva Funfún One of the largest caves on the island features an otherworldly subterranean landscape with roaring underground rivers, towering stalactites and countless bats. **See p.118**

❻ Laguna Limón Take a fishing boat out on this tranquil lake fringed with wetlands and brimming with birdlife. **See p.119**

HIGHLIGHTS ARE MARKED ON THE MAP ON PP.88–89

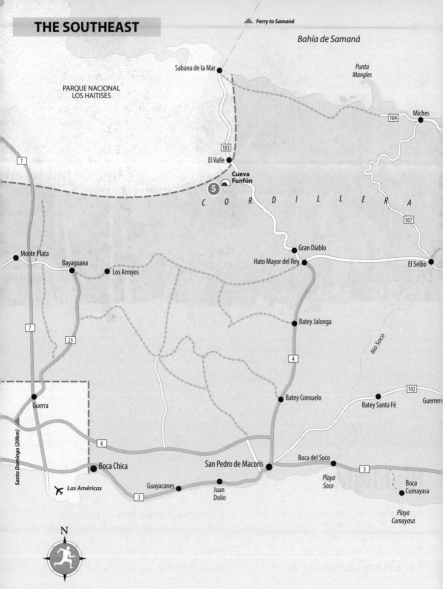

THE SOUTHEAST

Ferry to Samaná

Bahía de Samaná

Punta Mangles

PARQUE NACIONAL
LOS HAITISES

Sabana de la Mar

104

Miches

7

103

El Valle

Cueva
Funfún

⑤

C O R D I L L E R A

107

Monte Plata

Bayaguana

Los Arroyos

Gran Diablo

Hato Mayor del Rey

El Seibo

Batey Jalonga

Río Soco

7

23

4

Batey Consuelo

102

Batey Santa Fé

Guerrer

Guerra

Santo Domingo (20km)

4

Boca Chica

Las Américas

Guayacanes

Juan
Dolio

San Pedro de Macorís

Boca del Soco

Playa Soco

3

Boca
Cumayasa

Playa Cumayasa

N

CARIBBEAN SEA

HIGHLIGHTS

① Bayahibe
② Boat trips to Isla Saona
③ Boca de Yuma
④ Los Corales beach bars
⑤ Cueva Funfún
⑥ Laguna Limón

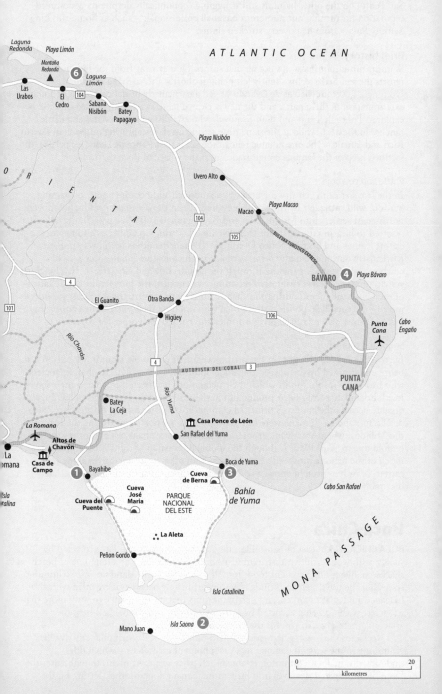

San Pedro, on the other hand, is still struggling economically despite its widespread reputation for turning out numerous **baseball** professionals – such as home-run king Sammy Sosa – from its poverty-stricken slums.

Brief history

With its tumultuous past, it's not all that surprising that away from the big tourist resorts the southeast seems slightly left behind. Shortly after arriving in Santo Domingo, governor **Nicolás de Ovando** waged a particularly brutal campaign of Taino extermination in these parts, and the newly cleared land was quickly settled in 1502 by explorers Ponce de León and Juan Esquivel, who established sugar estates and cattle ranches in the area, while at the same time setting up slave-capturing outposts in Puerto Rico and Jamaica. The one notable relic of the era is **Casa Ponce de León** (see p.108), the fortified keep of the famous conquistador near the village of Boca de Yuma.

Cattle and cowboys

In the late sixteenth century the area was abandoned and became home to roaming herds of **wild cattle** left by the Spanish estates. When the *devastaciones* forcibly moved north-coast settlers into Monte Plata and Bayaguana in 1605 (see p.265), the colonists resorted to hunting the cattle for their livelihood, setting up tanneries and ranches to export leather and beef via Santo Domingo. The **rancher ethos** is still very present, particularly during the many *fiestas patronales*, which feature long processions of cowboys and livestock parading through the countryside and city streets. This ranching system promoted a less egalitarian economic system than the prosperous family farms of the Cibao valley, and during the chaotic nineteenth century the southeast produced most of the **caudillos**, political strongmen who imposed their will on the country by force of arms, who recruited private armies and battled each other for supremacy.

Sugar and tourism

Even as the *caudillos* fought for national power, their economic clout in the region was being undermined by the burgeoning **sugar industry**. In the 1860s, Cuban financiers, who had fled a revolution in which their plantations had been burned and their slaves freed, began large-scale sugar production in the eastern Santo Domingo valley; sugar quickly became the country's principal commodity. Former fishing villages San Pedro de Macorís and La Romana were built up into bustling **port cities** during the Dance of the Millions, when American corporations pushed the Cubans out and prices increased tenfold due to World War I, though the **global depression** of the 1930s wiped out much of the region's prosperity. The construction of lavish all-inclusives along the eastern coast has brought about a revival of sort, though the pristine coastline has inevitably suffered.

Boca Chica

BOCA CHICA, 25km east of Santo Domingo, curves along a small bay protected by shoals, with wonderfully transparent Caribbean water lapping at a long line of beach shacks, many serving excellent food. It used to be one of the island's prime swimming spots, but the town that surrounds it has unfortunately become so crowded with freelance guides, sex workers and persistent touts that it's impossible to walk more than a few feet without being accosted by some enterprising individual hell-bent on attaching themselves to you for the duration of your stay.

At weekends the beach is jam-packed with thousands of day-tripping city dwellers swimming in the sea and dancing to a cacophony of car stereos – which does, undoubtedly, make for an unforgettable beach party scene. At night, though, after the Dominicans leave, it devolves into little more than a gringo brothel. Sitting on the

DIVING AND WATERSPORTS AROUND BOCA CHICA

Regular **dive trips** from Boca Chica are led by Caribbean Divers at Duarte 28 (☎809 854 3483, ⓦcaribbeandivers.de; single dive US$50, two dives US$90), a PADI- and PDIC-certified outfit. Dives head out to **La Caleta Submarine National Park**, a protected nearby coral reef at the bottom of which lie two sunken ships: the *Hickory*, once a treasure-hunting ship that salvaged two Spanish **shipwrecks** and now home to thousands of tropical sea creatures; and a bizarre-looking vehicle nicknamed "The UFO", which is touted on the tour as being potentially extraterrestrial, but is in fact an old oil rig. The outfit's other diving excursions go to the waters off Bayahibe, Isla Catalina and a **cave dive** near Santo Domingo.

2

beach is the main attraction, and the waters are calm and shallow enough to walk out to the bird-inhabited mangrove island **La Matica** just off shore. If you tire of swimming and sunbathing, you could opt for something a little more rigorous (see box above)

ARRIVAL, GETTING AROUND AND INFORMATION   BOCA CHICA

By guagua Guaguas drop off and pick up from the petrol station *Burger King* at the entrance to town on the coastal highway; from there you can get a guagua or *motoconcho* ride either to your hotel or to the beach. It takes about 20min to get here from Aeropuerto Internacional Las Américas by public transport, or a little less than an hour from central Santo Domingo.

By taxi There's a taxi stand on Duarte and Hungria on the west side of the town strip.
Tourist office San Rafael and Juanico García (Mon–Fri 9am–5pm; ☎809 523 5106). More an administrative office than a place for tourist information but the staff here can provide some useful advice.

ACCOMMODATION

There are plentiful **hotels**, most of which are rarely full; the only time you might have trouble finding a room is in Jan or Feb. Of the three **all-inclusive** hotels, two are set directly on the beach, though the third, the *Dominican Bay*, is the best of the bunch. There are lots of cheaper, smaller, independently run hotels set up by both European expats and locals all across town.

BOCA CHICA

● EATING, DRINKING & NIGHTLIFE

Boca Marina	1
Hamaca Hotel Disco	3
Neptuno's Club Restaurant	2
Pequeña Suiza	4

■ ACCOMMODATION

Dominican Bay	2
Hamaca	3
Neptuno's Refugio	1
Zapata	4

2 DE JUNIO
AUTOPISTA LAS AMERICAS
PROYECTO 3
PROYECTO 2
Baseball Field
AVENIDA DEL SUR
PROYECTO
20 DE DICIEMBRE
JUAN BAUTISTA VICINI
CARACOLES
PROLONGACIÓN DUARTE
SAN RAFAEL
PEDRO MELLA
DOMINGUEZ
SÁNCHEZ
Parque Central
Bank Machine
DUARTE
ABRAHAM NUÑEZ
Playa Boca Chica

0   200
metres

CARIBBEAN SEA

Zona Colonial Santo Domingo (35km)
San Pedro de Macorís (40km)

Dominican Bay Juan Bautista Vicini and 20 de Diciembre ☏809 412 2004, ⓦbellevuedominicanbay .com. Best of the local resorts, with beautiful grounds, clean, modern rooms, helpful service and good buffet food. Set back two blocks from the beach, but much quieter as a result. US$60/person

Hamaca Duarte 26 ☏809 563 4848, ⓦbelivehamaca .com. All-inclusive, split between a main building, where many rooms have balconies, and *Hamaca Gardens*, a complex of beachfront villas. Other amenities include a casino, five bars, decent food (for an all-inclusive) and free snorkelling equipment. They can also lay claim to the best disco in Boca Chica (see below). US$170

Neptuno's Refugio Duarte 17 ☏809 523 9934, ⓦrefugioneptunos.com. Comfortable if slightly dated rooms plus nice staff and good privacy make this a pleasant place to stay, though it's a bit of a walk off the main strip. They also offer several full-service apartments. US$55

★**Zapata** Abraham Núnez 27 ☏809 523 4777, ⓦhotelzapata.com. This hotel has some serious upsides for independent travellers, including a huge, secluded beachfront bar, a doorman, good showers and free breakfast for guests staying two nights or more. Some rooms were freshly renovated in 2014 and the hosts are friendly and helpful. US$70

EATING, DRINKING AND NIGHTLIFE

There are several quality **restaurants**, but the best place to eat during the day is at one of the **food shacks** serving fresh seafood dishes on the beach – try the tasty local dish *lambí criolla* (creole conch). All the **bars** are along the main strip (Calle Duarte), but go out of business with alarming rapidity. The **nightlife** scene here is quite rowdy and focused primarily on sex tourism but one or two venues buck that trend.

★**Boca Marina** Prolongación Duarte 12A ☏809 523 6702, ⓦbocamarina.com.do. The fantastic seafood here is relatively expensive but well worth it, not least because the service is second to none. Try the red snapper, dorado filet or overflowing portions of grilled shrimp, ceviche and fried calamari. The waterfront setting is also ideal; if you bring your bathing suit, you can take a dip between courses. Mains RD$350–1010 but most are over RD$600. Daily 10am–midnight, Fri & Sat until 1am.

Hamaca Hotel Disco Duarte 26 ☏809 523 4611. This hotel disco pulls in huge crowds from Santo Domingo and the surrounding barrios, largely because it offers a free bar once you pay the RD$700 for a night pass. One of the town's

slicker venues, though be warned that you may still see sleazy goings-on. Hours vary.

Neptuno's Club Restaurant Prolongación Duarte 12 ☏809 523 4703, ⓦneptunos.com.do. Popular gourmet seafood restaurant with great views of the ocean. Terrific mixed seafood platters, lobster ravioli and prawns. Booking recommended at weekends. Mains RD$470–1090. Daily 11am–midnight.

Pequeña Suiza Duarte 56 ☏809 523 4619. Pleasant spot for a snack, with an eclectic mix ranging from antipasti to fondue. Also good for a croissant or brioche with fresh orange juice or cappuccino at breakfast. Mains RD$250– 700. Daily 7am–12.30am.

Juan Dolio and Guayacanes

Ten kilometres east along the coast from Boca Chica begins a 9km-long stretch of more-or-less uninterrupted beach that holds a strip of holiday homes and all-inclusives collectively referred to as **JUAN DOLIO**, though the western section is actually in neighbouring **GUAYACANES**. The two bleed into one another with no obvious join, forming a package resort area created in response to the wild success of Playa Dorada (see p.164) in the early 1980s. Even though the slightly scrappy-looking resort has never quite matched its northern rival, with half-finished or run-down hotels and a beach that can be patchy in places, there are some wonderfully wide sections of fine, golden sand.

NOBODY'S POOL

If you're up for some out-of-the-way natural beauty, head 3km west of the beach at Guayacanes and you'll find a **long-abandoned beach home** with a natural swimming pool that was carved into the rock by its former owners – the spot is marked by the only highway overpass between Guayacanes and Boca Chica. It's perfectly safe to swim in the **pool**, which has rough-hewn steps leading into it from the ground and from here you can look out onto the Caribbean crashing against high, jagged cliffs.

ARRIVAL AND DEPARTURE

JUAN DOLIO AND GUAYACANES

By guagua and bus Guaguas arrive from Parque Enriquillo in Santo Domingo (every 20min, though less frequent after 5pm; 1hr 30min). Drivers drop passengers off along the highway (sometimes called the Boulevard de Juan Dolio) that runs in parallel with the coastal road – just 50m away in places – where all the hotels are. Leaving, you can flag down guaguas anywhere on this same road but if you have bulky baggage you're probably better off taking a taxi to San Pedro de Macorís (see p.94) and catching a bus or guagua from the ASTRAPU terminal there – the taxi fare shouldn't be more than RD$500 and the journey takes about fifteen minutes.

GETTING AROUND

There is very little consensus on what the coastal road that runs the length of Guayacanes and Juan Dolio is called. You will hear and see it referred to variously as Calle Principal, Calle Central, Calle Boulevard and Camino de la Playa (among others). Pretty much everything of any use is on this road – in this guide the newer, wider section at the eastern end of Juan Dolio where there are two lanes on both sides is referred to as **Av. Boulevard** and the rest, from the Barceló Capella Beach hotel westwards, is referred to as **Calle Principal**.

By taxi rental car or on foot Though many visitors get about solely on foot, as the main road runs for over 6km through Juan Dolio and for over 3km in Guayacanes, if you want to explore the whole of this section of coastline you'll need to take a taxi (try SICHATRATUR on ☎ 809 526 3110 or Dionisio, a local driver used by some of the hotels, on ☎ 809 913 1969) or rent your own transport which you can only do through the larger hotels, including the *Barceló Capella Beach*.

ACCOMMODATION

Juan Dolio has seen a decline in the quality and quantity of its accommodation over recent years, with **large chains** pulling out, ambitious projects going unfinished and some hotels looking increasingly in need of a revamp. Nevertheless, there are still options for **all budgets** and a sufficient number of small, affordable places to appeal to **independent travellers**. Addresses on the Carretera Las Américas reflect distance from San Pedro de Macorís to the east.

Barceló Capella Beach Villas del Mar, Carretera Las Américas Km 14 ☎ 809 526 1080, ⓦ barcelocapella .com. Expansive grounds, 500 quality rooms with private balcony, friendly service and a casino. The "beach" is a small strip of cement covered in sand but it's probably the best of the all-inclusives. US$104

Habitaciones Don Pedro Calle Principal 50 ☎ 809 526 2147, ⓦ habitaciones-donpedro.com. A very basic, independent cheapie in a three-floor villa over the road from a lively section of beach. Geared toward backpackers who don't mind the spartan rooms which come with ceiling fans, cable TV, fridge and safe. RD$200 extra for hot water and a/c. RD$1000

Fior di Loto Calle Principal 517 ☎ 809 526 1146, ⓦ fiordilotohotels.com. This is the best budget hotel around and a hangout for independent travellers, not least for its hot tub and sun deck. The India-themed rooms are simple but comfortable, with visitors encouraged to augment the Far East-inspired patterns painted on the walls. All rooms have hot water, cable TV and fan; some come with kitchenettes. Dorm US$5, double US$25, apartment US$40

Meridiana Residence Av. Boulevard ☎ 809 526 1689, ⓦ meridianaresidence.com. Time is beginning to take its toll on these decent-sized holiday apartments but they are still good value, with a small pool out the back and an on-site pizzeria. Housed in a seven-floor building, some also offer good views, and all have kitchenettes. US$45

EATING, DRINKING AND NIGHTLIFE

Outside of the all-inclusives, the **food** in Juan Dolio is actually not bad, with a number of Italian restaurants of some merit and some fantastic beachfront venues. They are, however, spread relatively thinly along the strip and distances between places mean it's tricky making on-spec comparisons without transport. There's not much **nightlife** in Juan Dolio, but you will find half a dozen local hangouts that can be fun when they get busy.

★ **Deli Swiss** Boulevard de Juan Dolio, Guayacanes, at the west end of town ☎ 809 526 1226, ⓦ deli-swiss-restaurant.com. Not much to look at from the outside, but venture in and you'll find tables nestled romantically on a rocky outcrop on the beach – perfect for gourmet seafood dishes that rank among the island's finest. Options typically include outrageously good grilled langoustines and fresh local fish. Note that you should expect to pay around US$50 per person. Daily 11am–9pm.

★ **El Lobo y La Sal** Calle Principal 570 ☎ 829 958 0701 or ☎ 809 526 1819. This chic yet laidback little place offers a reassuringly simple (yet relatively

2

expensive) menu of wide-ranging starters – including chorizo and cheese-filled croquettes (RD$200) and very tasty Italian sausages (RD$290) – and primarily seafood mains such as barbecued langoustines (RD$675 per pound) or garlic shrimps in white wine (RD$550). Choose from tables on the stylish wooden deck or out on the sand. A band sometimes plays here at weekends. Daily except Tues 11am–11pm.

El Mesón At the western end of Av. Boulevard, opposite the *Club Hemingway* Hotel ☎ 809 526 2666 or ☎ 809 526 2182. The most popular place to eat out in the eastern half of town is this accomplished Spanish restaurant that offers excellent paella and high-quality seafood such as red snapper stuffed with crabmeat. Mains start at around RD$300. Daily 11am–10.45pm, Fri & Sat until 11.45pm.

Soya Azul Calle Principal, 600m west of the *Fior di Loto* Hotel ☎ 809 526 2101. Stylish but down-to-earth, this reasonably priced restaurant at the quiet, western end of the beach offers authentic Japanese and Thai cuisine. With

tables and chairs spread out on the sand it's perfect for a drawn-out afternoon sipping drinks and snacking on sashimi. Tues–Sun 11am–9pm.

El Sueño Calle Principal 330 ☎ 809 526 3903. A local favourite, this delightful Italian restaurant is set on an outdoor patio with white linen tablecloths and has impeccable service. Try the chicken *scaloppini* in white-wine sauce, sea bass in mushroom sauce, or grilled dorado. Pasta RD$300–470; pizzas RD$300–450; meat and seafood mains RD$400–800. Tues–Sun noon–3pm & 7pm–midnight.

Wood Madera Café Carretera Nueva, Camino de la Playa 45 ☎ 809 526 1772, ◍ woodmaderacafe.com. Without doubt the hippest bar in the Juan Dolio area, with avant garde live music and video most nights, great bartenders and a fun, cool vibe. Also operates as a restaurant serving everything from steaks (RD$645–1095) and ribs (RD$525–825) to crepes (RD$365–465) and salads (RD$345–375). Mon–Fri 5–11pm, Sat & Sun noon–1am.

San Pedro de Macorís and around

The crowded city of **SAN PEDRO DE MACORÍS**, some 70km east of Santo Domingo, owes its uneven development to the boom-and-bust fortunes of the sugar industry. During the crop's glory years in the early twentieth century, grand homes and civic monuments were erected along the eastern bank of the Río Higuamo. Today these buildings are grimy and faded, and just one sugar mill remains: built by Cuban refugees and lying a few blocks east of Estadio Tetelo Vargas (see opposite), the 1879 **Ingenio Porvenir** (ironically, the "Engine of the Future") grinds slowly on.

The best time to visit is in the evening, especially at weekends, when **the Malecón** has a much greater buzz than anything in nearby Juan Dolio and when, during winter months, you can often catch a national league baseball game. The bulk of San Pedro, however, is a pretty uninspiring place, and the only good reason to linger any length of time is during **Semana Santa** (see p.97) and the **Cocolo festivals**. The latter are held at Christmas and during the Feast of San Pedro (June 24–30), and see two competing troupes of masked dancers known as **mummers** wander along the major thoroughfares in elaborate costumes adorned with feathers and baubles, and perform dance dramas that depict folk tales, biblical stories and events from Cocolo history (see box opposite), accompanied by fife-and-drum bands.

The Malecón

What redeems San Pedro for most residents and visitors alike is its **Malecón**, a wide seaside promenade, known officially as the Avenida Gastón Fernando Deligne, which hugs the coastline at the southwestern end of the city, with modest public beaches at either end. It is celebrated by bachata star Juan Luis Guerra (see p.280) in his song *Guavaberry*: "I like to sing my song in the middle of the Malecón watching the sun go down in San Pedro de Macorís". Though, easily the city's most attractive public space, the Malecón only comes to life at night and, particularly, at weekends. Then, the little green huts lining the seafront become busy bars and food stalls, the discos crank up their sound systems, the beer and rum flow, and vendors weave through the crowds hawking fast food, boiled corn, sweets and chewing gum. On weekdays, it's a mellow, sometimes almost deserted place to stroll in the cooling sea breeze; come Sunday, it's taken over by perambulating families.

THE COCOLOS

When the Dominican sugar industry was nearing its zenith in the late 1800s, plantation owners began to employ migrant labourers from a number of islands in the British Antilles to meet the increased work demand. These black English-speakers – many of whom prefer to be called "the English" – were termed **Cocolos**, a bastardization of Tortola, one of the islands from which the workers arrived. While many of them returned home to their respective islands each year with their harvest season earnings, growing numbers began to settle permanently in camps around San Pedro de Macorís.

The Cocolos lived in squalid **bateyes**, shantytowns that were infested with vermin and tended to lack running water. Disease – malaria, cholera and leprosy mainly – was widespread, and residents often starved during the off season. They were also the victims of widespread **racism**, which led many to embrace the pan-Africanism of **Marcus Garvey**, a Jamaica-born activist who moved to New York's Harlem to spread his message of black empowerment. Thousands joined his Universal Negro Improvement Association (UNIA), which encouraged community self-reliance and provided disability benefits for those injured in the mills, and donated a portion of their salaries to the Black Star Line, a black-owned and -operated fleet that was intended eventually to repatriate New World blacks to West Africa. In August 1921 the Garveyites organized a **strike** to protest against the inhuman conditions of the *bateyes*, but the unrest was broken up by US Marines who occupied the Dominican Republic, and the local leaders of the UNIA were deported.

The community infrastructure begun by UNIA soon evolved into **self-improvement organizations** that pooled resources to better the conditions in the *bateyes*, establish and enforce codes of conduct and provide medical care. During nonworking seasons, members formed cricket teams that evolved into the sugar-mill baseball squads, which eventually produced some of the world's finest players. Labour unrest continued as well – in 1946 the Cocolos staged the only successful strike of the Trujillo era – which resulted in sugar companies turning westward to Haiti for cheap migrant labour.

Parque Duarte and the city centre

Head north of the Malecón along Sánchez for around a dozen blocks to arrive at Avenida Independencia, one of San Pedro's main shopping streets. This southwestern end of Independencia is home to **Parque Duarte**, sometimes referred to as Parque Central, whose shady trees provide some welcome greenery amid all the surrounding concrete and traffic chaos. On Mondays traditional Cocolo bands gather there in the morning and play until noon – the only way to hear the great local *momise* music if you're not in town for a festival.

Three blocks along Independencia towards the river from Parque Duarte stands the improbably virginal-looking 1911 **Catedral San Pedro Apóstol**, whose bright whitewashed facade stands in gleaming contrast to the dilapidated dwellings opposite. The cathedral marks the town end of the grimy port road, Avenida F. D. Charro, which leads back down to the Malecón.

Also worth a look while in the city centre is the palatial **mansion** of local baseball hero George Bell (called Jorge Bell locally), which lies at the eastern end of Avenida 27 de Febrero, another of the city's main shopping drags, running east from Parque Duarte. It's certainly one of the city's most ostentatious buildings, a coral-coloured behemoth adorned with castle turrets, a drawbridge and a moat.

Estadio Tetelo Vargas

Av. Circunvalación and Carretera Mella • ☎ 809 529 3618, ⓦ estrellasorientales.com.do • Tickets are available on the night of the game for RD$50–400 (get there early)

Above all, San Pedro is famous for its baseball players, with **Sammy Sosa** just one of the modern greats who grew up locally, spending his free time playing stickball with a modified milk carton for a glove. The **Estadio Tetelo Vargas** is a tattered concrete temple to the sport. Named after one of the first great Dominican baseballers, it's a good place to catch a game – check Santo Domingo newspapers and the stadium website for schedules.

2

The main highway running east from Santo Domingo enters San Pedro as Av. Francisco A Caamaño.

By guagua Most buses to and from Santo Domingo, Juan Dolio and Boca Chica pull in and out at the ASTRAPU terminal (☎ 809 529 4840 and ☎ 809 339 8258) on Av. Francisco A Caamaño to the north of the centre. Along the same road you can flag down or jump off guaguas to and from La Romana, and sometimes on to Higüey; they pass at regular intervals from early morning until around 9pm. From the terminal it's a 1km-walk to Parque Duarte and a

further 1.5km to the Malecón but there are always *motoconchos* waiiting at the terminal (around RD$50 to ride to the centre). Local *públicos* (RD$20) run along Av. Independencia and the Malecón.

By car If driving from Santo Domingo, take the first right when you reach the roundabout after the bridge (it's the one with the iron baseball sculpture at its centre). This will lead you straight down Av. Charro to the Malecón. Any other option will take you into the city centre and a honking maelstrom of traffic.

ACCOMMODATION

Hotel Macoríx Av. Gastón Fernando Deligne, western end of the Malecón ☎ 809 339 2100. The largest hotel in town might be rather faded and overpriced but it's close to the night-time action and its swimming-pool area (open daily to all) thrums with live merengue at weekends. The 170 rooms are of variable quality – check before committing and ask for a sea view. **RD$1664**

Hotel Royal Calle Ramón Castillo 32, four blocks northeast of Parque Duarte ☎ 809 529 7105, ✉ hotelroyal32@hotmail.com. It says something about the standard of hotels in this town that the tagline for this one is "El más limpio" ("The cleanest"). Nevertheless, it is better value than the *Macoríx*, and its en-suite rooms, while smaller, are in better condition. **RD$1400**

EATING, DRINKING AND NIGHTLIFE

The best spot for a choice of decent restaurants is right on the **river** – head 200m north of the cathedral, past the basketball arena, then take a left down to the brightly coloured stalls where fishermen sell the day's catch. Here you'll find the best **seafood restaurants** in the city, including *Robby Mar* (see below). San Pedro's buzzing **nightlife**, the primary reason to visit the town, is centred on the western section of **the Malecón** (the river end) where over twenty bar-cum-food stalls line the front. It's less about specific venues and more the general buzz. Note that most only open for business in the evening and at weekends when the city's discos, which also line this stretch, are in full effect.

Café Caribe Av. G F Deligne 1 ☎ 809 529 4764. A stage venue on the Malecón with DJs and live bands packing out the dancefloor at weekends, this lively spot is one of the best places for a dance and a big night out. RD$350–500 for live shows. Wed–Sun from around 8pm.

Portofino Av. G F Deligne 21 ☎ 809 526 6107. A cheap and popular Italian patio restaurant churning out pizzas to punters on plastic tables and chairs. The best of a fairly

mediocre bunch on the Malecón, it's just past the roundabout to the east. Tues–Sun noon–10pm.

Robby Mar Av. F D Charro 35 ☎ 809 529 4926. You'll find the best food in town at this dependable seafood restaurant. The prices are reasonable and the menu includes a huge variety of local shrimp, lobster and grilled fish dishes, served in a romantic ambience, with candlelit outdoor tables that offer river views. Daily 8am–midnight.

Batey Consuelo

18km north of the Estadio Tetelo Vargas on Av. Laureano Cano and then Carretera Mella (Highway 4)

On the fringe of San Pedro begins *batey* country, where most of the baseball players grew up, in the midst of seemingly endless fields of sugar cane. **Batey Consuelo** is home to hundreds of Haitian cane cutters and a smattering of remaining Cocolos (see p.95), and has produced star baseball players such as Rico Carty, George Bell and Julio Franco. The neighbourhood is liveliest during Semana Santa (see box opposite), when a Haitian carnival with parades and traditional *gagá* music played on keyless wooden tubes heralds a bawdy religious ceremony.

Cueva de las Maravillas

17km east of San Pedro • Guided tours (40min) Tues–Sun 10am–5pm • RD$300; horseriding RD$400/hr • ☎ 809 696 1797 • Any of the frequent guaguas that shuttle between San Pedro and La Romana can drop you here, while a taxi there and back will cost around RD$2000, including wait time; aim to arrive at opening time, or after 2pm, if you want to avoid the tour groups

Following the highway to La Romana from San Pedro, just past the very prominent entrance to *Playa Nueva Romana* (a new residential complex and marina on the right-hand side of the highway), you'll spot prominent national park signs to the left that mark the entrance to the **Cueva de las Maravillas**. Translated into English as the Cave of Wonders, the caves won't quite make your jaw drop but nonetheless feature some beautifully odd geological formations, including plenty of stalactites and stalagmites. Though only thirty percent of the system is accessible, you get to see scores of **Taino pictographs** and witness plenty of bats flying about. The easy **walkways**, augmented by motion-sensor lighting, an elevator and wheelchair-accessible ramps, make the caverns easy to explore, though the obligatory guided tours arguably take away some of the mystery. There are English-speaking **guides**, well versed in the cave's history and the significance of the various pictographs. You can't take photographs once inside, although postcards are available at the gift shop. There's also a small, rather sparse café on site. The non-profit foundation that runs the cave also offers **horseriding** in the surrounding countryside.

2

La Romana and around

Visitors to **LA ROMANA**, 37km east of San Pedro, tend to be day-trippers – the blossoming Bayahibe beach resort is just down the road and the glamorous *Casa de Campo* complex also lies nearby. However, with some appealing riverside restaurants and its proximity to sights such as **Isla Catalina** (see p.101) and the **Cueva de las Maravillas** (see above), it's well worth stopping here for at least a night; the city is also well placed as a stop-off between Santo Domingo and the beaches on the east coast.

SEMANA SANTA

The Haitian *bateyes* that surround La Romana and San Pedro hold exuberant **Semana Santa** festivities during the Christian Holy Week, which is also the most important Voodoo celebration of the year. The various satellite *bateyes* surrounding a sugar mill each have their own religious brotherhoods, headed by a medium known as a *houngan* (male) or a *mambo* (female). Each worships a patron deity and has its own **gagá** band – called *rara* in Haiti – which plays a repertoire of religious and Carnival songs in a processional orchestra of one-note trumpets and bamboo tubes that are blown and beaten in a cacophonous procession that can play all night long. On **Ash Wednesday**, the groups carry their senior officers on their shoulders in chairs, accompanied by *gagá*. This is merely a warm-up to **Good Friday** when, just before dawn, four shrouded dancers parade into the *perestil* (the roofed court of a Voodoo temple), where religious services are performed. The *houngan* "breathes life" into them one at a time, and they throw off their shrouds and lead the *gagá* bands in a parade around their *batey*, playing, singing and dancing to songs with lascivious lyrics, in keeping with the festival's theme of regeneration and fertility. On Saturday and **Easter Sunday** they head out onto the road towards the sugar mill. Upon encountering another group along the way, a competitive jam session begins, which can, in cases, lead to fisticuffs. Though anyone is welcome to attend Semana Santa, if you look like you have money the *gagá* bands will repeatedly play for you, seeking money and rum in return: you're best off bringing plenty of small bills for tips to the band, and arriving in a small group.

To familiarize yourself with the music of Semana Santa, you should purchase two things: the Smithsonian Folkways CD *Caribbean Revels: Haitian Rara and Dominican Gagá*, which features live recordings from Semana Santa festivals across the island, and *Rara! Vodou, Power and Performance in Haiti and its Diaspora* by Elizabeth McAlister, a terrific book with companion CD on the music and the culture that surrounds it.

A good place to catch the celebrations is **Batey La Ceja**, 18km east of La Romana along the road to Higüey – largely because the local residents have been thoroughly recorded by anthropologists and are used to outside visitors so you are likely to feel a little more welcome. To get there turn right onto the unmarked dirt road exactly 1km after the town of Benerito on the road to Higüey.

2

The **downtown** itself is not especially interesting but its tidy streets lined with potted palms – combined with a sprinkling of cosy cafés, good bars and one or two excellent places to eat – make it a pleasant place to hang out. From most parts of the centre, however, the river is disappointingly hidden from view and its banks are not easily accessible. The delightfully shaded **Parque Central** is, instead, the major meeting place, dotted with an eclectic mix of metal sculptures and fibreglass statues of former local baseball heroes. You can check out the current crop of players during the winter fixtures at the **Estadio Francisco Micheli** (☎ 809 556 6188, ⌨ lostorosdeleste.com; tickets RD$50–400), home field of Los Toros del Este, which is located at Abreu and Luperón towards the western end of town – check the website or newspapers for details of matches. Just west of the arena the **municipal market** sells bountiful produce and meat; look also for the small *botánicas* selling various items related to *Vodú Dominicana*.

Brief history

Ever since the South Porto Rico Sugar Company built the mammoth **Central Romana** mill in 1917, La Romana has been a one-company town (the mill was the only sugar operation not taken over by Trujillo during his thirty-year reign). If you're here in the harvesting season (Dec–March), you'll hear the train hooting as it arrives from the surrounding plantations, laden with sugar cane. The mill was eventually sold to multinational Gulf & Western in 1967, which used the substantial profits to expand their holdings in the area, constructing the *Casa de Campo* resort just to the east and convincing the government to open the first of the country's industrial free-zones here.

LA ROMANA

The mill and the resort, sold in the 1980s to the wealthy Cuban-American Fanjul family, help make this one of the most highly employed parts of the country.

ARRIVAL AND GETTING AROUND   LA ROMANA

BY GUAGUA OR MINIBUS

Most guaguas drop you off in Parque Central, although those to and from **Bayahibe** and **Bávaro** also drop off and pick up on Av. de la Libertad at the city's east entrance. Guagua stations are scattered around the city, with the main one serving **Santo Domingo** and points **west** located right out on the western outskirts. For **Boca de Yuma** (every 35min 7am–7pm; 1hr 30min; RD$90) head for the small bus station with no branding on Calle Fray Juan de Utrera between Teofilo Ferry and Santa Rosa.

SICHOEM Station on Padre Abreu, the main highway heading west out of town, a 5km drive from Parque Central ☎ 809 550 4585. Frequent *públicos* ferry passengers for free from Parque Central to the station, the largest in La Romana.

Destinations Juan Dolio (every 30min 4am–8pm; 1hr); San Pedro de Macorís (every 30min 4am–8pm; 45min); Santo Domingo (every 30min 4am–8pm; 2hr).

SITRAIHR Station on Trinitaria 65, half a block north of Parque Central ☎ 809 554 1177 or ☎ 809 550 0880. Offers full-size coaches as well as guaguas.

Destinations Bavaro (6 daily between 5.40am and 6.20pm; 1hr 30min); Higüey (every 30min between 5.40am and 10pm; 2hr 30min); Punta Cana (6 daily between 5.40am and 6.20pm; 1hr 15min).

BY PLANE

If you're staying at *Casa de Campo* or one of the resorts in Bayahibe and arrive at the small La Romana airport, your hotel will almost certainly arrange the 40min transfer into town.

BY CAR

It's best to avoid driving within city limits, as there are a number of unmarked, and even mismarked, one-way streets, and traffic accidents are frequent. However, if you do want to hire a car, note that Avis (☎ 809 550 0600) has an office on Castillo Márquez and Duarte, one block east from the park, and Honda has one at Santa Rosa between Utrera and Miranda (☎ 809 556 3835).

BY TAXI

Sichotaxi (☎ 809 550 2222) has its "Estación de Taxis José Martí" at Av. Libertad 1 in a kind of bus shelter a few metres from where the minibuses set off for Bayahibe. Taxis can also be picked up at the southern end of the Parque Central. Most taxi rides in town should not cost more than RD$150. A taxi to Bayahibe costs US$35.

ACCOMMODATION

Casa de Campo Main entrance 1.5km east along Highway 3 from the river bridge at La Romana ☎ 809 523 3333 & ☎ 809 523 2161, ⓦ casadecampo.com.do. The country's top resort is a massive fantasy world of carefree luxury, encompassing almost thirty square kilometres of meticulously manicured rolling hills set along the Caribbean sea. Guests can choose between all-inclusive or room-only rates, high-spec hotel rooms or spacious three-to-seven-bedroom villas, with golf carts to get around and numerous extras. Non-guests can also make use of the extensive facilities (see box, p.100). Double US$325, villa US$1310

Hotel Condado Altagracia 55 ☎ 809 550 6757. Though rooms are small and dark with tiny bathrooms, and not all of them have windows, a recent renovation means that many are in good nick, with firm beds, cold water only, a/c

and cable TV. The quieter rooms are located at the back section of the hotel. RD$800

Hotel Olimpo Corner of Calle Padre Abreu and Pedro A Llúberes ☎ 809 550 7646, ⓦ olimpohotel.com. This functional but gloomy business hotel is inconveniently situated away from the city centre but has well-maintained modern facilities. Continental breakfast included. RD$1600

Hotel River View Restauración 17 ☎ 809 556 1181 or ☎ 809 813 0984, ⓔ hotelriverview@gmail.com. Enjoying the best location in town (though not the eponymous view), this place has great potential but is in need of some TLC. Rooms have slightly tired furnishings but are fairly comfortable, with a/c, hot water & cable TV. As it's not far from a major highway, some rooms can be noisy, so check before committing. RD$2250

EATING AND DRINKING

Increasing numbers of tourists from *Casa de Campo*, visiting **cruise ships** and the occasional tour bus help support a surprisingly **diverse** culinary scene, from candlelit riverside dining and delightful café-bars to excellent Dominican fast food and plentiful Italian restaurants.

China Town Altagracia ☎ 809 550 3838. It may be a clinical, neon-lit environment but you can't argue with the quality or the prices. Most dishes come in at around RD$180 – expect

excellent soups, chow mein and chop suey, plus some fancier, slightly more expensive options such as chilli filet mignon and breaded chicken in sesame seed sauce. Daily 8am–1am.

2

Pica Pollo Rodríguez Duarte 2B ☎ 809 813 3493. This popular spot is packed to the gills at lunchtimes with Dominicans tucking into tasty, inexpensive *comida criolla*, each portion ranging between RD$30–60. Excellent fresh juices are served at the kiosk outside. Daily 8am–midnight.

Portofino Monción 11 ☎ 809 349 9856 or ☎ 809 418 3333. Perched above the river, this open-sided restaurant offers fabulous views across the floodlit river. The cuisine is good too: a mix of Italian and Dominican favourites, with pizzas cooked in a wood-fired oven. There are several levels of terraces here, the lower levels occupied by a bar. Mains around RD$500. Daily 11am–11pm.

★ **Trigo de Oro** Eugenio A. Miranda 9 ☎ 809 550 5650. An excellent, moderately priced cake shop and café serving to-die-for French pastries (authentic specimens at that), cheesecakes and all manner of fantastic crepes, plus burgers, baguette sandwiches and salads. Set in a converted mansion and covered patio forecourt decked out with plants, it's an ideal place to enjoy a hot chocolate and brioche for breakfast, or a leisurely cocktail in the evening. There's free wi-fi too. Mon–Sat 7am–10pm, Sun 7am–2.30pm.

DRINKING AND NIGHTLIFE

More a place to enjoy **laidback dining** than to party, La Romana nevertheless has a couple of spots where you can swing your hips. Party time for the **fiestas patronales** occurs in the last week of August.

ACTIVITIES AROUND LA ROMANA

JEEP AND RIVER TOURS

Along the nearby Soca and Chavón rivers, you can take a variety of extremely popular **jeep and river tours**. These are available at each of the all-inclusive hotels from Juan Dolio to Punta Cana and various tour operators in Bayahibe (see box, p.103). They generally involve a drive into the countryside, stopping off at a farm or *batey* – perhaps with an hour or two on a horse or ATV – before gliding downriver on a raft-like boat, dancing to merengue, and downing copious rum punches.

DIVING AND SNORKELLING

You can access the tiny snorkelling haven of **Isla Catalina** (see p.101) by booking a day-trip there through Passion Paradise Adventures (☎ 809 446 9602, ⓦ passionparadise.co) or El Fiestón (☎ 809 455 1643, ⓦ elfiestonpuntacana.com) whose boats set off from the Marina Turística (☎ 809 550 8156), located on the city side of the river beside the bridge, accessed via Benito Monción. Both offer snorkelling trips out to the island by catamaran or yacht, with lunch, drinks and snorkel gear included for around US$50. They also lead scuba-diving excursions for certified PADI divers (US$120 for two tanks).

ACTIVITIES AT CASA DE CAMPO

By far the greatest variety of activities near La Romana can be found at the *Casa de Campo* resort (see p.99), which offers day passes to non-guests (US$25; food purchased separately) granting you access to the extensive luxury playground, including over a dozen restaurants, a variety of bars, and **Playa Minitas**, a delightful stretch of sand protected by a shallow reef. You can also sign up for the resort's plethora of excursions and activities (prices and details on website). The resort has its own **marina** so it should come as no surprise that an abundance of **watersports** are on offer, including practically everything from kayaking and windsurfing to scuba diving and serious deep-sea **sportfishing** (expect to catch wahoo, dorado, kingfish, sailfish, marlin and barracuda). Back on dry land, the resort also boasts one of the world's top **golf courses** – the Pete Dye-designed "Teeth of the Dog" (US$295 for non-guests), a second Pete Dye course called Dye Fore (US$230–295 for non-guests, depending on season) and a stunning links course (US$183–205 for non-guests, depending on season). Other options include a range of **horseriding** activities on horseback, a **tennis** centre and a world-class shooting range.

Finally, the day pass also gives you access to **Altos de Chavón**, a mock Tuscan medieval hilltop town that incorporates a **shopping village** overlooking the Río Chavón, an impressive 5000-seat open-air **amphitheatre** (previous concerts here have included Sting and Alicia Keys) and the excellent **archeology museum** (daily 8am–10pm; free; ☎ 809 682 3111), boasting some three thousand Taíno artefacts, including two intact canoes and a wooden idol found in Parque Nacional del Este.

Babylon Francisco del Castillo Márquez 00010, just down from the park ☎ 809 782 8733, ⊛ es-la.facebook .com/babylonvip. This chic glass-fronted club is the slickest, most glamorous operation in town, attracting crowds with a weekly roster of big-name live bands and DJs, though there are also occasional karaoke nights. On most nights drinks are free for women for the first few hours. Cover free–RD$300, depending on who's playing. Thurs & Fri from 7pm, Sat &

Sun matinees from 3pm and club nights from 9pm.
Bar Marinelly Av. Santa Rosa 25 and Dr Hernández ☎ 809 556 1111. A long-established bar-club that draws a varied, smartly dressed clientele. It has a pleasant, open-sided thatched-roof area plus a more flashy bar and dance space inside, where a DJ or band takes centre stage on Fri and Sat nights. The place also serves food and is open until 3am at weekends. Cover RD$50 females, RD$100 males. Open daily.

Isla Catalina

Two kilometres off shore from La Romana lies the small picture-postcard, palm-fringed **Isla Catalina**. The island has the southern coast's best **coral reef**, and the fish have grown tame enough that schools of them will swim up and eat food out of your hands. This makes it one of the island's prime spots for **scuba diving**: various dive shops and tour operators (see opposite & p.103) lead trips to a steep underwater drop-off called "The Wall", which holds an enviably intact coral reef that provides habitat for a virtual aquarium. There are also excellent beaches here, though several local tours and cruise ships drop anchor just off the island, ferrying thousands of passengers back and forth via speedboats, so expect large crowds.

Bayahibe

Not long ago **BAYAHIBE** was a pleasant, low-key place but this fishing village is now a significant tourist destination, providing the best base from which to explore the islands, beaches, caves and dive sites of the **Parque Nacional del Este** (see p.105). Despite the steady growth of sprawling all-inclusive hotels along the surrounding coast (in particular the resort zone of **Dominicus Americanus** to the east), Bayahibe village, where most independent travellers stay, retains much of its charm and laidback vibe, its idyllic setting round a sheltered bay still integral to its appeal.

There is a good selection of budget accommodation, as well as a row of atmospheric restaurants dotting the **waterfront** and miles of beach stretching out on either side of the village, although Bayahibe's own strip of sand is rather scrubby and uninviting. Where once a handful of fishing boats bobbed in the water, serried ranks of motorized launches and catamarans waiting to transfer tourists to **Isla Saona** pack the harbour while a plethora of agencies and operators provide access to the country's best **diving** and **snorkelling** nearby. The village is also characterized by a burgeoning expat community, most notably Italians.

The village

Bayahibe **village** consists of little more than a dozen or so blocks, with a main street now quite densely packed with inexpensive *comedores*, *pica pollos*, locally owned fast-food joints and various other businesses catering to the tourist trade. Other than this there's little more than dwellings, a row of arts and craft stalls down near the beach, a gaggle of dive outfits and tour operators, and a line of waterfront restaurants. A small rocky **peninsula**, the tip of which is known as La Punta, hosts the village's tiny painted wooden church, primary school and a rather neglected and somewhat brief interpretive walk outlining the village's history (in Spanish only).

Dominicus Americanus

A 2km coastal walk southeast from the village along the shady path that begins at the baseball pitch, or 3km by road from the Bayahibe turning (at the border of Parque

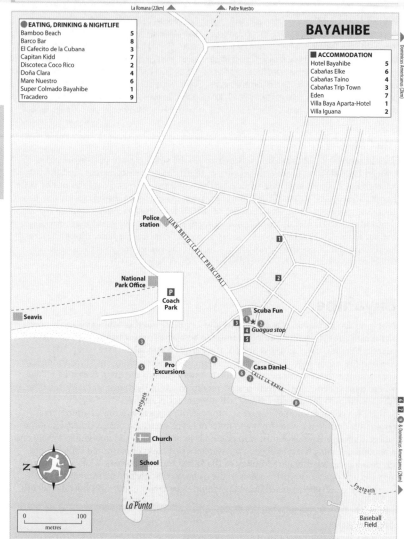

EATING, DRINKING & NIGHTLIFE

Bamboo Beach	5
Barco Bar	8
El Cafecito de la Cubana	3
Capitan Kidd	7
Discoteca Coco Rico	2
Doña Clara	4
Mare Nuestro	6
Super Colmado Bayahibe	1
Tracadero	9

BAYAHIBE

ACCOMMODATION

Hotel Bayahibe	5
Cabañas Elke	6
Cabañas Taíno	4
Cabañas Trip Town	3
Eden	7
Villa Baya Aparta-Hotel	1
Villa Iguana	2

Nacional del Este), lies the **Dominicus Americanus** strip, with its all-inclusive hotels and glut of beachfront, cafeteria-style restaurants. The custom-built shopping street and slightly incongruous casino produce a slightly contrived feel, but there are some nice places to eat and it does offer better shopping (mostly of the souvenir variety) than in Bayahibe.

ARRIVAL AND GETTING AROUND

BAYAHIBE

By guagua The easiest way to reach Bayahibe by public transport is from La Romana by guagua (25min); they stop frequently throughout the day in the centre of the village and go on from there to Dominicus Americanus (5–10min; RD$25). From Higüey or points east, you'll have to disembark either at the turn-off to Bayahibe or on the Av. Libertad in La Romana and catch one of the guaguas from there. On departure, if you're heading anywhere other than Dominicus, take the guagua to La Romana and find the relevant bus station there (see p.99).

BAYAHIBE TOURS, OPERATORS AND BOAT HIRE

Every morning coachloads of tourists from Dominicus Americanus and resorts elsewhere set off by boat from Bayahibe to the islands, reefs and beaches of the **Parque Nacional del Este** (see p.105) and to **Isla Catalina** (see p.101). Some also come for tours along mainland **hiking** trails and to local **caves**, even though you can more easily experience these independently (see p.107). Note that most of the resort hotels in the area and further afield offer excursions to the park but they usually contract out to the operators in Bayahibe – to **reduce costs**, book directly with one of them yourself (try their website as first port of call). To the west of La Punta, the mini-peninsula, is the small beach and harbour, where boats can be hired for trips to the national park (see p.103).

2

Casa Daniel Calle Principal 1, on the waterfront in Bayahibe ☎ 809 833 0050, ⊛ casa-daniel.com. A recommended diving operator running family-oriented snorkelling excursions from US$48, diving excursions to Isla Saona (US$162), Isla Catalina (US$156) and the less-visited Isla Catalinita (US$162), where you've a better chance of getting the remote sands mostly to yourself, plus all kinds of dive courses and packages.

ProExcursions On the waterfront in Bayahibe ☎ 829 659 4688, ⊛ proexcursionsbayahibe.com. This Canadian outfit offers a wide selection of sea and land excursions, a few of which they subcontract for other operators, though they do have an impressive roster of their own tours (look for the "Authentic House Tour" logo on their website), ranging from trips to Saona and Catalina islands (from US$99; children half-price) to half- and full-day safaris in all-terrain buggies in the countryside around Bayahibe and La Romana (US$69–109). Setting off from Punta Cana, Bávaro or

Juan Dolio, you pay an extra US$15 to include a bus transfer from your hotel.

Scubafun Calle Principal 28 in Bayahibe ☎ 809 833 0003, ⊛ scubafun.info. A good choice for divers, with scuba programmes including PADI-certified open-water courses (US$365) and dives to local coral reefs (US$135 for a half-day), plus advanced adventure dives into the Padre Nuestro caves (US$79 for two tanks) and night dives (US$69). Equipment rental costs another US$10 per day.

Seavis At the village end of Playa Bayahibe, in front of the *Viva Wyndham Dominicus Palace* ☎ 829 714 4947, ⊛ seavisbayahibe.com. Offers boat excursions to Isla Saona (US$85, including lunch), as well as two-island tour, which also visits Isla Catalinita (US$95). A good-value day-trip (US$85) takes in mainland hiking trails, caves, a trip up the River Chavón, a riverside ranch, canoeing on the river and a visit to Benerito, the village where the inhabitants of the park were relocated when it was cleared for preservation and tourism.

By car Driving is easy as the turn-off from the H3 highway is well signposted and paved. As you near Bayahibe, the road forks: left takes you to Dominicus Americanus, while right leads you to the village.

By taxi Call ☎ 809 833 0059 for the local taxi service (SICHOTUHBARED). Taxis between the village and Dominicus Americanus cost US$10 per trip. The fare between La Romana and Bayahibe is US$35; to Boca de Yuma from Bayahibe is US$40.

ACCOMMODATION

Most of the **budget accommodation** in the Bayahibe area is in the village, including a few sets of motel-like cabañas aimed primarily at Dominicans on a modest budget. There are currently seven large international-standard **all-inclusives** dotted along this stretch of coastline, most of them in **Dominicus Americanus** – you can try turning up on spec but you'll save a lot of money by booking a package holiday in advance. The hotel chains administering these resorts are *Dreams* (⊛ dreamresorts.com), *Iberostar* (⊛ iberostar.com), *Catalonia* (⊛ hoteles-catalonia.com), *Be Live Hotels* (⊛ belivehotels .com), *Viva Wyndham Resorts* (⊛ vivaresorts.com), who run two hotels here which share one another's facilities, and *Cadaques Caribe* (⊛ cadaquescariberesort.com), who are responsible for one of the most recently built complexes.

THE VILLAGE

Hotel Bayahibe Calle Principal ☎ 809 833 0159, ⊛ hotelbayahibe.net. This bright, modern hotel is one of the town's more salubrious offerings – all rooms are cheerily furnished with comfortable beds, fridges, a/c, cable TV and various trimmings. Ask for one of the lighter rooms on the upper floor. Prices include breakfast. US$60

Cabañas Taíno Calle Principal ☎ 829 924 9409. A short hop from the waterfront, these simple cabins are clean, neat, and equipped with the basics. The seven rooms are smallish, but come with TVs, fans (a/c extra), hot water and fridges, with a tiny outside patio. US$31/ RD$1000

Cabañas Trip Town Calle Prinicipal ☎ 809 833 0082.

2

On the other side of the road to *Cabañas Taíno* and a very similar set up – clean and tidy, simple pine-furnished rooms, with private solar-powered warm-water bathrooms and fans (a/c RD$200 extra) plus a small space to sit outside. RD$1000

Villa Baya Aparta-Hotel Tamarindo ☎809 833 0048, ⓦhotelvillabaya.com. In the heart of the village and offering good-value apartments and rooms (a/c or fan) in an attractive three-storey building. Italian restaurant on site. US$39, apartments US$50

★**Villa Iguana** Ocho ☎809 833 0203, ⓦvillaiguana.de. A German-owned guesthouse in the centre of the village, offering five spotless, well-maintained rooms (some with a/c) and three comfortable self-catering apartments with kitchenettes (two with balconies), plus a stunning penthouse that covers an entire floor and boasts its own sundeck and mini-pool. Breakfast is included for guests in the rooms and penthouse (US$120). US$39, apartments US$69

DOMINICUS AMERICANUS

Cabañas Elke Vía Eladia 7 ☎809 833 0024, ⓦcabanaelke.it. It looks a bit lost amid the massive hotels but this set of Italian-owned, fan-ventilated rooms and duplex apartments is the nearest you'll get to a budget option in Dominicus. A small pool and bar-restaurant are on site, but there's no beach access (the public beach is a short walk away). Some guests use the facilities at the nearby *Viva Wyndham Dominicus* but to do so you need to buy a day pass (US$77). Accommodation only or all-inclusive packages are available. US$70, apartments US$90

Eden Av. La Laguna 10 ☎809 833 0856, ⓦsantodomingovacanze.com. On the approach road into Dominicus (so not on the beach), this comfortable, family-oriented hotel is a good choice for those looking to avoid the all-inclusives. A selection of well-appointed rooms, apartments and bungalows are available, all set in pleasant grounds which also feature a decent restaurant, swimming pool, bar and games area. Rates include breakfast. US$60

EATING, DRINKING AND NIGHTLIFE

Bayahibe offers a good variety of **dining** as restaurateurs have been forced to up their game in the hope of luring some of the resort trade away from the all-you-can-eat buffets. **Seafood**, unsurprisingly, dominates the menus, although the blossoming **Italian expat** community ensures that pasta and pizzas abound. Calle Principal/Juan Brito is lined with good-value *comedores* and *pica pollos*. Most restaurants don't accept **credit cards**. The town's nightlife is hardly wild but it does at least make a change from the stale Vegas-lite atmosphere at the resorts, the vast **casino** with disco attached on Dominicus Avenue providing the starkest contrast with the **easy-going** streetlife that characterizes Bayahibe. As lively as anywhere is the area outside the collection of bars and restaurants between the coach park and La Punta, where locals and tourists mix in and see the night through together.

Bamboo Beach At the village end of the small peninsula, overlooking Playa Bayahibe ☎829 410 1326. This French-owned place does decent *camarones al ajillo* (shrimps in garlic) and offers crepes for dessert alongside some Breton specialities that may not be on the menu, so ask. No credit cards. Daily except Tues 11.45am–2pm & 6.30–10pm.

★**Barco Bar** Calle La Bahía ☎829 580 1436. A top choice right by the water and one of the few places you can actually get breakfast – there are fresh juices, crepes, sandwiches and cappuccinos for RD$100–200 with more substantial Dominican and Italian staples for lunch and dinner. The comfy wicker chairs on a raised, thatched deck are the perfect spot to enjoy a sundowner too. Expect occasional outbreaks of dancing. Daily 8am–2am.

★**El Cafecito de la Cubana** At the village edge of Playa Bayahibe ☎809 833 0159, ⓦcubanabayahibe.com. A fabulously friendly and intimate restaurant under a shady tree just off the beach, serving tasty, excellent-value dishes ranging from sandwiches and choice burgers through salads and seafood to more authentically Cuban *ropa vieja*. Also boasts mojitos made with Havana rum. Daily except Tues 11am–11pm.

Capitan Kidd Calle La Bahía ☎849 350 1977 or ☎829 513 3183 ⓦrestaurantecapitankidd.com. One of the most

expensive restaurants in town, but the seafront setting – with tables right up to the water's edge and some seats spread along a narrow, rocky jetty – goes a long way to justifying the prices. At night it becomes fantastically atmospheric, and the food isn't bad either, with wood-fired oven pizzas for around RD$400 and good-quality seafood mains starting at RD$400, averaging at around RD$600. Daily 11am–midnight.

Discoteca Coco Rico Half a block from Juan Brito, near the Super Colmado. Local box-like nightclub venue in the village centre, which doesn't get going until late. No cover charge. Daily except Tues 9pm–2am.

Doña Clara Calle La Bahía ☎809 833 0159. Belonging to *Hotel Bayahibe*, this bar and restaurant offers surprisingly inexpensive beer right on the waterfront and decent seafood lunches and dinners for RD$300–850. Daily 8am–10pm.

Mare Nuestro Calle La Bahía ☎809 833 0055, ⓦmarenuestro.com. A great location with a first-floor balcony offering incomparable views across the bay and elegant fine dining by candlelight. Unfortunately, the pricey, seafood-dominated menu (mains from around RD$350), which includes curried shrimps and vodka linguini with salmon, doesn't always live up to its reputation. Tues–Sun: restaurant 11am–11pm, bar 11am–2am.

Super Colmado Bayahibe Calle Principal. From sunset,

the music blares and the drink flows as the general store transforms into a bar for locals and expats alike, spilling out onto the street. It's certainly the cheapest place to get an ice-cold Presidente. Daily until 9 or 10pm.

Tracadero Los Corales, Dominicus ☏ 809 906 3664, ⊛ tracaderorestaurante.com. The most exclusive restaurant in the area is perfect for a special occasion, offering refined dining by torchlight and excellent service right by the ocean. The Italian cuisine and service are excellent though the menu is not particularly imaginative. Reserve one of the special tables that sit almost out on the rocks. Tues–Sun 11am–midnight.

Parque Nacional del Este

Bayahibe sits on the northwest edge of expansive **PARQUE NACIONAL DEL ESTE**, a broad peninsula jutting south into the Caribbean and also encompassing **Isla Saona**, just across a small bay and easily accessible by boat. The national park features a maze of forests, mangroves, trails, caves and cliffs, an impressive array of **birdlife** and, on the cultural side, some signs of early Taino activity. Not much of the park, however, is conveniently accessible; in fact, no roads lead directly into its interior, and the best method of approach is to **hire boats** from Bayahibe (see box, p.103) to hit specific points along the rim, from where you can hike inland. Wherever you go in the park, wear plenty of insect repellent against the ubiquitous mosquitoes and sizeable population of wasps. Watch out, too, for **tarantulas**, though they won't bother you unless they're antagonized. Note that there is no **accommodation** in the park.

Isla Saona

Around 20km by boat from Bayahibe village, or 30km to Mano Juan; 45min by speedboat or 1hr 30min by catamaran to Mano Juan from Bayahibe

The most popular part of Parque Nacional del Este, and rightly so, is **Isla Saona**, an island off the southern coast lined with alternating stretches of idyllic, coconut-tree-backed beach and mangrove swamp, and unpopulated except for one fishing hamlet

---

LA ALETA

On a 1988 expedition deep in the heart of Parque Nacional del Este, a team of archeologists from Indiana University discovered the most significant and extensive Taino excavation yet on record, four ceremonial plazas surrounding a *cenote* (natural well) – a site referred to as **La Aleta**. Evidence shows that natives came to this well to worship during pre-Columbian times from across the countryside, even as far away as the Tetero valley near Pico Duarte.

In his *History of the Indies*, Spanish priest Bartolomé de Las Casas recorded a journey to La Aleta in the late fifteenth century, noting that the natives lowered bowls into the well via a piece of rattan rope to pull up water, which was sweet at the surface and salty at the bottom – a stratification that still exists. He also described the slaughter of seven hundred people at La Aleta in 1503, the culmination of Nicolás de Ovando's campaign of **Taino extermination**, which he started after the Tainos killed three Spaniards on Isla Saona, itself a retaliation for an attack by a Spanish soldier. Bones from the mass killing have been found scattered throughout the site and within the well.

For the Tainos, caves served as the gateways to an underground **spirit world**. The well was apparently a site for subterranean ceremonies; fragments believed to have been parts of rafts lowered into the well have also been discovered. Other artefacts recovered from the site include clay pots and one straw basket, thought to contain offerings of food; a cassava cooking pan; axes and clubs; and an intact wooden *duho* (the seat from which the *caciques* prophesied to their people). On the four ceremonial plazas around the *cenote* – bounded by monumental limestone pillars – a **ball game** similar to modern-day soccer was played by those who attended the rituals.

The government hopes one day to create a trail between here and Peñon Gordo and open La Aleta to the public, but for now archeologists have to use a **helicopter** to get in, and no one else is supposedly allowed admittance. Still, the place has been ransacked twice by treasure hunters, and Dominican soldiers have been posted to prevent further looting.

called **Mano Juan** that has around three hundred families. That said, the tourist traffic on Saona has increased exponentially in recent years, prompting the more discerning operators to look for alternative spots, such as Isla Catalinita.

Most boats pull in to Isla Saona at Mano Juan, a picturesque strip of wooden huts painted in pastel shades on the southern side of the island with a 4km hiking trail that leads inland, an expensive restaurant, and a long line of beach chairs and umbrellas. An equally popular target is **Canto de la Playa**, another wonderful stretch of beach and coral reef, making it a good **snorkelling spot**. If you visit with an independent boat, avoid the hordes and head to one of the more isolated stretches of beach that dot the island, though in high season you may struggle to find anywhere that you have completely to yourself.

Isla Catalinita

Around 35km by boat from Bayahibe village; 20min by speedboat or 1hr by catamaran from Bayahibe

If you're keen to avoid the crowds on Isla Saona, one option is to have your boat captain skip Saona altogether, head into the Catuano Canal that separates Saona from the mainland, and stop off at the much smaller island of **Isla Catalinita**, which gets less tourist traffic and has some excellent reefs for diving (less so for snorkelling). Its beaches are littered with large conch shells and during the winter months you may be able to spot humpback whales and dolphins and even, if you're really lucky, an elusive manatee. In recent years the government has closed access to the island for months at a time to preserve it from the ravages of tourism.

Padre Nuestro trail and Cueva Chico

Entrance is marked 20m from the turning for Bayahibe village • Daily 9am–4.30pm • RD$200 includes entry and guide

The **Padre Nuestro** hiking trail cuts through densely vegetated landscape (excellent for birdwatching) then down into a remote cave system with four perfectly clear, deep, fresh springs that have been a source of potable water since pre-Columbian times. Archeologists regularly scour the depths on the hunt for Taino relics – they have previously unearthed a *poliza*, a ceremonial Taino vessel. Local tour operators lead cave-diving tours to **Cueva Chico** (US$79 with Scubafun; see p.103), the cave with the easiest access. You can make your way to this part of the park independently, though you will have to pick up a guide at the entrance.

Cueva del Puente

3km (30min hike) south of the national park entrance at El Guaraguao, which lies at the southern end of Dominicus Americanus • Guided tours daily 9am–4.30pm • RD$100; payable at national park office in Bayahibe

The park's limestone landscape is riddled with caves, many of which are adorned with Taino rock art. At the present time, the only cave system that is relatively straightforward to visit independently is the **Cueva del Puente**. You can sometimes hire a **guide** at the national park entrance to accompany you down to the caves but it's a fairly easy hike to do on your own. The system consists of three separate levels of caverns (the first gets some sunlight) with thousands of stalagmites and stalactites along with hundreds of bats and sparkling seams of bright, crystallized minerals. There are also Taino pictographs on the third level, though they're not accessible to tourists; one reason to hire a park ranger is that they might show you a Taino picture of a small-eared owl on the first level of caves – a bird that was thought by the Tainos to ferry dead souls to the afterlife.

Cueva de Berna

Eastern entrance to national park, a short walk west of Boca de Yuma (see opposite) • Locals offer boat trips up the River Yuma to the cave for a negotiated fee

From the park's eastern entrance, walk for an hour along the water to a natural land bridge from which turbulent jets of sea water rocket into the air against and through the porous rock. Just a short walk north of the park station lies the mouth of the cavernous **Cueva de Berna**, a large cave once inhabited by Tainos. It makes for an alternative (albeit less spectacular) goal than the caves near Bayahibe. Along with hundreds of bats and small birds, you'll see Taino *caritas* (little faces) carved on the walls, though some have been defaced by graffiti.

ARRIVAL, TOURS AND INFORMATION — PARQUE NACIONAL DEL ESTE

2

Entry points There are specific entry points into the mainland section of the park, at Padre Nuestro (see opposite), El Guaraguao (see opposite) and Boca de Yuma (see below).

Park offices and entry fee The Bayahibe national park station (daily 8am–4pm; ☎ 809 467 6412) is located on the opposite side of the coach park to the village. It's a simple green and white bungalow with very little printed information on the park and no maps, other than the large billboard map posted outside, but is a necessary stop if you're heading into the national park solo as you'll need to pay a RD$100 entry fee here (tour operators should take care of your permits if on a tour).

Organized boat tours The majority of boat tours into the park take off from Bayahibe and are best booked in advance. Dozens of tour companies (see p.103) set off from here for Isla Saona.

Private boat tours The advantage of a private charter is that you can organize to be taken to a more remote, and therefore quieter, beach. You can hire one either by hanging around the seafront in Bayahibe where there are always boat owners touting for business or by calling in at the cabin belonging to ASPLABA (Bayahibe Boat Owners' Association; ☎ 829 254 8235 or ☎ 809 833 0474) on the seafront near the coach park. You will probably have to haggle for a good price; the going rate for Saona is around RD$5000 for a boat carrying six to eight passengers, or RD$1500 per person with a minimum of two.

Hiking If you're on your own and hiking into the park, you'll first have to get the RD$100 entrance ticket at the park station and then drive to the far southern end of the resort strip. From there, walk another kilometre along the beach until you arrive at the entrance to the park at El Guaraguao.

Boca de Yuma and around

On the northeastern tip of Parque Nacional del Este sits **Boca de Yuma**, a pueblo that has been passed over by mass tourism because of its lack of accessible beachfront, though there is one fairly nice stretch of sand across the river. Boca de Yuma's setting along squat, ocean-pounded bluffs is undeniably impressive and it makes for a pleasant stop, particularly if you fancy experiencing everyday life in one of the country's quieter corners. There's also great fishing in the area, and the town is a good alternate entry point to Parque Nacional del Este. From here you can also take in the former stronghold of conquistador **Ponce de León**.

The village and Playa Borinquen

Boat to Playa Borinquen RD$1200; boat and captain (for fishing) around RD$5000/day, though more if heading to Isla Saona

The appeal of the **village** lies simply in wandering along the shore, its rocks sculpted over time by the crashing surf, or paying a local fisherman to ferry you across the Río Yuma (and collect you later) to a pretty little beach called **Playa Borinquen** which you'll share only with a couple of grazing cows. Most of the little boats lining the beaches are still used primarily for fishing – this is one of the best hunting grounds for marlin in the entire Caribbean.

ARRIVAL AND DEPARTURE — BOCA DE YUMA AND AROUND

By bus Buses headed for Boca de Yuma leave La Romana (every 35min 7am–7pm; 50min) from the guagua station northwest of the park, and from Av. Trejol in Higüey (every 30min, 7am–6pm; 1hr). If there are no passengers headed as far as Boca de Yuma (most get off in San Rafael) then you'll need to catch one of the tatty minibuses that shuttle between the two places to complete the trip. They pass every 15–20min from roughly 7am–5pm. From San Rafael you can catch a guagua on to Higüey or La Romana (last bus leaves San Rafael at 6pm).

ACCOMMODATION AND EATING

El Arponero Malecón ☎809 493 5502. Fabulous Italian restaurant dishing up great pizzas and fresh seafood and offering a fantastic view. The owners intend to move the restaurant in the near future but wherever it ends up in the village, it'll likely still be the best place to eat. Main dishes RD$170–350. Daily 11am–10pm.

El Viejo Pirata Proyecto 33 ☎809 804 3151 or 809 780 3236, ⟨w⟩modna.com/vp/pirata_do.html. Boca de Yuma's main hotel is fronted by a plastic pirate effigy and the obligatory skull and crossbones, and the theme continues across a handful of comfortably furnished rooms. The place also has a small pool, a large tiled terrace overlooking the sea and a decent seafood restaurant. **RD$1300**

Casa Ponce de León

9km northwest of Boca de Yuma in pueblo San Rafael de Yuma • Tues–Sun 10am–1pm • RD$50; guided visits offered in Spanish (RD$100 tip expected; often unavailable noon–2pm) • ☎829 330 0803 or ☎809 551 0118

The fortified, early sixteenth-century **Casa Ponce de León**, a remote medieval keep built by Taino slaves for the noted explorer, was established as a working farm and sugar plantation during his rule of nearby Higüey. In 1508 he increased his holdings by setting up a slave-catching outpost in Puerto Rico, which quickly grew into a colony in its own right, proving more profitable than his Dominican estate. Following this venture he set off to Florida, where he died at the hands of natives while searching for the Fountain of Youth.

The parks department has renovated, and maintains, the two-storey residence, which is now a museum to the life and times of de León. Inside you'll find original mahogany furnishings and the restored mahogany floor, along with his suit of armour and bulky treasure chest. The **caretaker** takes visitors on a guided tour in Spanish, dispensing a lot of information about both the construction of the house and de León's exploits.

Higüey

Cramped, dusty and 100 percent concrete, **HIGÜEY** is a busy agro-commercial town of 150,000 that's generally passed through quickly en route to the eastern coast. Despite the uninviting setting, it's famous throughout the country as a Dominican **holy city**, and tens of thousands gather here each January 21 for a mammoth procession and prayer of intercession to the nation's patron saint, the Virgin of Altagracia, who supposedly provides miraculous healing to pilgrims. Even if you don't believe in the Virgin, you should not pass up the chance to take a peek at the **cathedral**, whose unprepossessing exterior belies a far more impressive interior. A couple of other sights will help you while away a pleasant hour or so: the more diminutive sixteenth-century **Iglesia San Dionisio** – goal of the annual pilgrimage before construction of the basilica began in the 1950s – lies on Parque Central; and a few blocks northeast from the church, along Las Carreras, you'll find the bustling **mercado**, which sells mounds of fresh fruit, vegetables and meat as well as the odd trussed chicken, still clucking. Check out the informal food stalls here too.

Basílica de Nuestra Señora de la Merced

Arzobispo Nouel between La Altagracia and Av. de la Libertad • Daily 6am–7pm • Free or voluntary donation • ☎809 554 4541

Rendered in concrete (of course), the 80m arch of the modernist **Basílica de Nuestra Señora de la Merced**, centre of Higüey's religious activity, is visible from   every point in the city, which makes it easy to get your bearings. Its design, which adorns the fifty-peso note, is supposed to represent two hands folded in prayer.

Two vast bronze doors covered in gold leaf mark the entrance, one depicting scenes from the history of the city, the other narrating the story behind the basilica. Love it or loathe it, you cannot fail to be impressed by the vast, vault-like interior comprising a further series of arches that frame the altar, which features a sacred painting of the Virgin. Assuming there's no queue, head up the steps in front of the altar to get a good

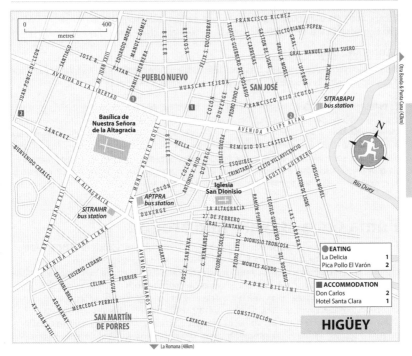

HIGÜEY

close-up of the exquisitely carved wooden leaves surrounding the icon. Most stunning when the sun is shining is the vast stained-glass window behind the altar, whose colours range from amber through to blood red.

ARRIVAL AND DEPARTURE
HIGÜEY

Higüey serves as a major public **transport hub** for the southeast, which means you'll probably be passing through (and may well have to change buses or guaguas if you're travelling within the region. Almost all buses and guaguas drop off passengers on Av. Mons. Adolfo Nouel outside the grounds of the Basilica, as well as at their respective terminals, listed below. Minivans to Boca de Yuma (every 30min; 1hr) leave a few blocks from the basilica, down Av. Trejo. The fare to Punta Cana and Bávaro is RD$130 and to Santo Domingo RD$200.

APTPRA Av. Hermanos Trejo 1, corner of Colón ☏ 809 554 2574.
Destinations San Pedro de Macorís (10 daily; 2hr); Santo Domingo (every 30min 4am–8pm; 3hr).
SITRABAPU Av. Felipe Alfau, on the main road heading out of town to Bávaro and the east ☏ 829 259 9900.

Guaguas to Miches (every 45min; 3hr) leave from the streets around here too.
Destinations Friusa in Bávaro (every 30min 5am–8pm; 1hr 15min); Punta Cana (every 30min 5am–8pm; 1hr).
SITRAIHR La Altagracia ☏ 809 550 0880.
Destination El Seibo (every 30min until 7pm; 1hr).

ACCOMMODATION

There is a particular concentration of hotels on or within a block or two of Av. Mons. Adolfo Nouel. If you're here for the **Altagracia** procession, you'll find these hotels fully booked, which means either checking into a less salubrious joint or, better, staying in La Romana or Punta Cana.

Don Carlos Ponce de León and Sánchez ☏ 809 554 2713. This is the best of a mediocre bunch, serving a business clientele and offering clean, bright rooms with

a/c, cable TV and hot water, plus a decent patio restaurant. **RD$1720/US$35**
Hotel Santa Clara F S Docudray 9, a block north of Av.

Libertad ☎809 554 2040, ✉ramonlao@hotmail.com. More basic and smaller than the *Don Carlos*, this boxy, white

and orange three-storey building has rooms with fan and cold water (extra for a/c) – it will do for a night or two. RD$900

EATING AND DRINKING

There are plenty of inexpensive restaurants and fast-food outlets round the centre of town. You'll also find a fair few dancefloors and beer halls, though nightlife is mostly of the male-dominated, hard-drinking variety.

La Delicia Av. Libertad 182 ☎809 554 9507 or ☎809 696 0596. One of the classier outfits in town, this seafood specialist is the best spot for a relaxing, drawn-out meal. Mussels (RD$550–700), octopus (RD$500–600), shrimp (RD$500) and lobster (RD$800) are all on the menu alongside a host of meat dishes. Bow-tied waiters serve it all up on a large terrace under a thatched palm roof. Daily

10am–midnight.

Pica Pollo El Varón Av. Felipe Alfau, corner of Gastón F Deligne ☎809 746 1525. One of three branches in the city of this locally founded fried-chicken chain, offering inexpensive and tasty cafeteria-style *comida criolla* as well as the artery-bunging chicken on which it has built its name. Daily 7am–midnight.

Punta Cana, Bávaro and around

From Higüey, a paved road winds 40km east to the tropical playlands of **PUNTA CANA** and **BÁVARO**. At one time, Punta Cana and Bávaro were two distinct areas lying at either end of a long curve of coconut-tree-lined beach. However, an extraordinary spate of construction over the past few decades has blurred the boundaries between them. Nowadays, "Punta Cana" is as much a marketing brand as a specific location, incorporated liberally into the title of most of the hotels in the region, even those 40km north of Punta Cana beach itself. There are actually very few services in what might be termed Punta Cana proper; most of the nightlife and daytime action occurs in Bávaro, which is also where all the budget accommodation is. The nearest town to Punta Cana proper is **Verón**, which most buses in and out of the area pass through but it is little frequented by visitors.

Despite its growth, Punta Cana has not yet reached the tipping point where the pace and size of construction begin to impinge on the holiday experience. With such an abundance of coast to play on, it has been possible to make sure that no hotel intrudes too greatly on any other. And you can still find, with a little exploration, glorious stretches of relatively uninterrupted sand, particularly in the north at **El Macao** and **Uvero Alto**. At points where resorts have cropped up, you'll find the requisite concentration of umbrellas, watersports outfitters and beach bars, with occasional souvenir shacks set up in between. Aside from the glass-bottom-boat operators trying to drum up business here and there, though, there's relatively little hassle – and the all-inclusives here are the nicest on the island.

Punta Cana

The vaguely defined area that is **PUNTA CANA** proper, occupying the southern section of this heavily developed curve of coastline, can be broken down very loosely into four sections: the **resort strip** where a number of the most exclusive hotels in the area have cordoned off their sections of the top-notch beach; the vast **Cap Cana** project south of the main strip (see box, p.112); the commercial complex known as **Punta Cana Village** right next to the airport, currently home to the densest concentration of non-hotel restaurants in this southern section; and the ambitiously named **Downtown Punta Cana**. The latter is not yet worthy of the name, but the already-completed San Juan shopping mall (🌐sanjuanshoppingcenter.com), situated at a junction known as the "cruce de Coco Loco", marks the beginning of the development of a visitor hub for the whole area, featuring housing, restaurants, nightlife, further shops and a luxury hotel on a man-made lake.

Bávaro

BÁVARO is at the heart of things round these parts, especially for the independent traveller. It's here that you'll find the bus station and most banks, shops, restaurants and bars, as well as the medical centre and police station. Its two main beaches – **El Cortecito** and **Los Corales** – and **Friusa**, the dusty urban area a couple of kilometres inland, are the hubs of activity, but there's also a splurge of life at the halfway point between these two poles, where Avenida España, Avenida Francia and Avenida Italia

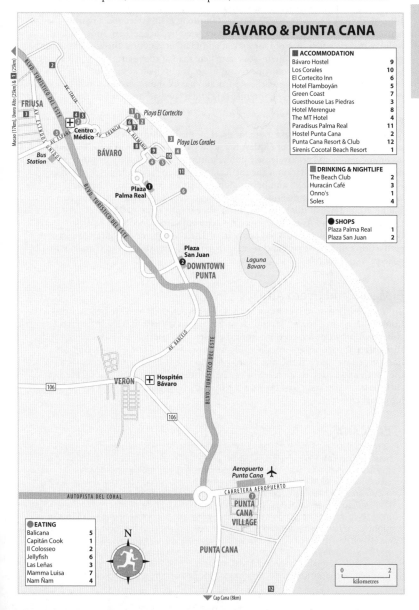

BÁVARO & PUNTA CANA

ACCOMMODATION

Bávaro Hostel	9
Los Corales	10
El Cortecito Inn	6
Hotel Flamboyán	5
Green Coast	7
Guesthouse Las Piedras	3
Hotel Merengue	8
The MT Hotel	4
Paradisus Palma Real	11
Hostel Punta Cana	2
Punta Cana Resort & Club	12
Sirenis Cocotal Beach Resort	1

DRINKING & NIGHTLIFE

The Beach Club	2
Huracán Café	3
Onno's	1
Soles	4

SHOPS

Plaza Palma Real	1
Plaza San Juan	2

EATING

Balicana	5
Capitán Cook	1
Il Colosseo	2
Jellyfish	6
Las Leñas	3
Mamma Luisa	7
Nam Ñam	4

meet. The largest shopping and commercial complex in the area is the Palma Real mall (ⓦpalmarealshoppingvillage.com), 2km south of Los Corales on Avenida Barceló.

El Cortecito and Los Corales

If you're not staying at one of the hotel resorts, head to **El Cortecito** or **Los Corales**, the only beachside options for budget travellers and the closest thing along this stretch of coastline to a town area. El Cortecito is the more built-up of the two neighbouring areas – which share their names with the beaches they sit alongside – and consists of little more than a touristy beachfront, a 200m-long main street and a narrow alley of souvenir stalls. It's an agreeable hangout populated by backpackers, independent holiday-makers and a slew of Dominican and Haitian vendors. The attitude towards commerce is necessarily more in-your-face here than at the resorts and you'll struggle to walk a few paces without someone trying to get you to look at their stall. Still, it's the liveliest stretch of coast around these parts and has all the services that independent travellers need: a supermarket, internet café and a few bars and restaurants.

Friusa

With more local flavour, and more locals, than the beachfront settlements, the small, scrappy, commercial town of **FRIUSA** is a good place to stay if you want inexpensive accommodation and relatively easy public transport access to the surrounding area and beyond. Its small bus station is the main transport hub for connections to Higüey, La Romana, Santo Domingo and points along the south coast between here and the capital. From the **Cruce de Friusa**, the bustling crossroads marked by a Texaco gas station around which this workaday little place revolves, the two main streets, Avenida Estados Unidos and Avenida España, emanate outwards, lined with hardware stores, banks, fast-food joints and a few seedy bars. There are one or two pleasant places to grab a drink or a bite to eat and it's easy to get El Cortecito and Los Corales either by guagua or *motoconcho*.

El Macao and Uvero Alto

To uncover the last remaining stretches of undeveloped, pristine **beach**, head to **EL MACAO**, a small town 9km north of Bávaro, or **UVERO ALTO**, a little further north still. Both provide some respite from the relentless resort sprawl and their windy, surf-battered beaches are usually quite empty, save for a few quad-biking or horse-trekking tours. But come soon – development has begun to encroach from the south and is due to increase in the near future. El Macao is among the best **surf spots** on the east coast (at its peak in the winter months), with an excellent local surf club.

CAP CANA

At the southern extreme of the resort zone, 10km south of the airport, past the Punta Cana hotels, is **Cap Cana** (ⓣ809 688 5587, ⓦcapcana.com), the would-be resort to end all resorts. This largely residential, rich man's playground, glistening with multimillion-dollar condominiums, high-end boutique hotels, a stretch of stunning beach, plus a state-of-the-art marina and Jack Nicklaus-designed golf courses, is Punta Cana's answer to *Casa de Campo* (see p.99). Although there are further developments to come, it is already the complete resort, with more than a dozen restaurants and a theatre thrown into the mix. At upwards of **$1000 a night** you might need a winning lottery ticket to stay here but, in theory, all you need to access the pristine beach is your own set of wheels (there's no public transport in these parts, and if you turn up on foot you'll almost certainly be turned away) and a self-assured demeanour – combined, they might well be enough to convince the guards at the gate to let you in. Note that you'll be asked to swap your passport or driver's license for a **day pass**.

ARRIVAL AND DEPARTURE

By plane All flights to the area arrive at Aeropuerto Punta Cana (☎809 959 2376 or ☎809 688 4749, ⓦpuntacanainternationalairport.com; for live arrivals and departures information see ⓦpunta-cana-airport.com), just 2km north of the beach hotels at Punta Cana proper, and 20km from El Cortecito and Friusa. Visitors flying to the resorts via a charter as part of a package-tour deal are ferried to hotels in air-conditioned buses but independent travellers will have to get a taxi.

By bus or guagua Guaguas head to Punta Cana hourly from the bus station in Higüey and cost RD$130 for an express. The daily Expreso Bávaro bus service which runs nonstop between here and Santo Domingo (7am, 9am,

PUNTA CANA, BÁVARO AND AROUND

11am, 1pm, 3pm and 4pm; RD$400; Santo Domingo office ☎809 682 9670; Bávaro office ☎809 552 1678; ⓦexpresobavaro.com) departs from just off Santo Domingo's Av. Máximo Gómez at Juan Sánchez Ramírez 31, picking up passengers at Parque Enriquillo en route (see p.71). The drop-off points for the bus service are just outside Aeropuerto Punta Cana and at the Friusa terminal in Bávaro, well away from most of the resorts, but if you speak to the bus conductor he may agree to drop you off somewhere more convenient. There is also a daily Expreso Bávaro–La Romana service (6am, 8.20am, 10.50am, 1.20pm, 3.50pm and 6.20pm; 1hr 30min).

GETTING AROUND

BY CAR

Roads Driving around the Punta Cana area has never been easier since the completion of the Bulevar Turístico Expreso (Tourist Express Boulevard) highway in late 2013, linking the airport to El Macao. The Santa Domingo–Punta Cana highway was completed in 2012 when the final stretch of the Autopista del Coral was laid down – journey times between the two are now down to around two hours.

Car rental National (☎809 959 0434) and Avis (☎809 688 1354) at the airport, with another Avis rental point near the San Juan shopping mall (☎809 688 1354); Budget (☎809 466 2028) on Av. Barcelo; Europcar on Av. España between Friusa and El Cortecito (☎809 686 2861).

BY GUAGUA

From opposite the Texaco station at the main junction in Friusa, you can catch a local guagua, which stops off at most of the major resorts along the coast (10min to El Cortecito and Los Corales; RD$30), following Avenidas España, Francia, Alemania and Barceló in a clockwise direction south to El Cruce (see p.110) and then back up the Bulevar Turístico. It may take a while to get where you're going, but at between RD$30 and RD$50 it will be a fraction of the taxi fare. They run until around 10pm.

BY MOTOCONCHO

There are legions of *motoconchos* in the area – if you have to wait for more than two minutes before one passes,

PUNTA CANA ACTIVITIES AND TOURS

Each resort will have plenty of **tours** on offer and many operate their own dive shops, but it's also possible, and sometimes cheaper, to book directly through an independent operator. For **deep-sea fishing** excursions, try First Class Fishing Charters (☎809 852 8737, ⓦfirstclassfishing.com; US$99 /person) or Fishing Punta Cana (☎809 552 1124, ⓦfishingpuntacana.com; from US$475 for five people).

The most established **diving** outfit is Sea Pro Divers (☎809 841 4800, ⓦseaprodivers.com) who operate out of around a dozen hotels on this stretch of coastline, but the easiest and best place to find them, unless you're staying in one of those hotels, is on the beach between Los Corales and El Cortecito. As well as diving excursions to locations around the Parque Nacional del Este (from US$89), they offer all kinds of other activities, from **parasailing** (US$55) to **kitesurfing** courses (US$299). A respected dive and watersports shop is Pelicano Sport, based at the *Ocean Blue and Sands Hotel* (☎809 729 4242, ⓦpelicanosport.com), which has low-priced dives to local reefs (US$49 per dive) as well as excursions to reefs and wrecks around Parque Nacional del Este (US$99 plus dive costs). They also organize other watersports and various beach-related activities such as **dune-buggy hire** (US$99) or horseriding (US$92).

Exclusively on dry land, Rancho Capote (☎809 553 2656, ⓦcuevafunfun.net), with an office at Av. Barcelo near the San Juan Shopping Centre, leads **caving** excursions to Parque Nacional Los Haitises (see p.132). Set in over 1000 acres of woods and parkland halfway between the airport and Bávaro, off the Blvd. Turístico del Este, the Bávaro Adventure Park (daily 8.30am–6.30pm; ☎809 933 3040, ⓦbavaroadventurepark.com; from US$89 for three activities) lets you try your hand at any of their nine energetic main activities, including **zipline** tours, **mountain biking** and a **flight simulator** operated by a crane.

something's wrong. Between Friusa and Los Corlaes or El Cortecito the fare should be RD$100.

BY TAXI

Taxis are usually waiting at the airport and the entrance to the resorts; if not, call the local taxi syndicate on ☎ 809 552 0617, ☎ 809 466 1133 or ☎ 809 221 2741 for pick-up. Standardized fares should mean you'll pay around US$20 from the airport to the nearby Punta Cana beach resorts; US$35 for any hotel in the Bávaro area including El Cortecito; US$50 for El Macao; and US$70 for Uvero Alto; from El Cortecito to Friusa is about US$10. Make sure you have the right change.

ACCOMMODATION

There are well over forty hotels along the coast between Punta Cana and El Macao and more inland. Most people staying in the **all-inclusives** are on package tours, so it's rare to actually call up a resort and request a room for the night. You'll get much better deals in any case by booking at home through a travel agent, though you can get some great last-minute deals online wherever you are. The *Melia* hotel group has three of its Paradisus-branded hotels here (ⓦ paradisus.com) while *Barceló* (ⓦ barcelo.com) also has a significant presence; dozens of other international hotel chains have at least one Punta Cana resort. The privilege of quieter beaches comes with a high price tag at a few **luxurious hotels** to the north (around Uvero Alto) and south of the main resort zone (Punta Cana and Cap Cana) – most have both standard room rates and an all-inclusive option. The **budget lodging** is around the beaches in El Cortecito and Los Corales – almost all of it set back from the beach itself – or in Friusa.

PUNTA CANA

Punta Cana Resort & Club ☎ 809 959 2262, ⓦ puntacana.com. This vast, tranquil resort, on 26 square miles of immaculately picturesque beachfront land, with enough space for two world-class golf courses, is a good choice for anyone with deep pockets. There are several completely separate accommodation options: luxury villas and elegant houses, plus two hotels. Double US$342, villa US$750

BÁVARO

★**Bávaro Hostel** Los Corales ☎ 809 931 6767, ⓦ bavarohostel.com. Friendly, well-run hostel, ideal for backpackers and only a minute's walk from the beach, with two dorms, private rooms with communal bathrooms and two-bedroom apartments. Gill, the amiable and helpful owner, of Dominican and English heritage, has created an appealingly relaxed vibe here, with the sociable communal spaces perfect for meeting fellow travellers. Dorm US$22, private room US$40, apartment US$80

Los Corales Bavaro Plaza Piazzetta ☎ 809 552 1262, ⓦ los-corales-villas.com. One- to four-bedroom kitchen apartments and villas, each with small garden or terrace, comparable to all-inclusive standard accommodation, a bit more spacious. Rates include maid service and access to a beach club. Prices drop by as much as fifty percent in low season. US$200

El Cortecito Inn Calle Pedro Mir, El Cortecito ☎ 809 552 0639, ⓔ cortecitoinn@codetel.net.do. In the heart of Cortecito, around 30m back from the beach, and undergoing a very slow refurbishment. Some rooms, updated relatively recently, are significantly better than others, but most are large and some have private balconies; there's also a swimming pool and restaurant. Breakfast included. US$60

Hotel Flamboyán Av. Italia across from the Bávaro Princess ☎ 809 552 0372, ⓦ bavaropuntacanahotel .com. Bars, shops, a casino and a club are conveniently close – obtrusively so for some – and both the location and plain building make this feel a bit like a business hotel. Rooms are bright and clean with the usual amenities, plus a small balcony. A five-minute bus ride from beach. Breakfast included. US$46

Green Coast Calle Pedro Mir, El Cortecito ☎ 809 552 0789, ⓦ puntacanagreencoast.com. Separated and obscured from the beach by a bar and restaurant strip, these apartments are not suitable for a tranquil holiday, despite the misleading images on the website, but are an excellent-value choice if you want to be at the centre of the action in El Cortecito. Only the bedrooms have a/c, not the whole apartments, and no hot water. US$60

★**Guesthouse Las Piedras** Guarionex 3, 100m off Av. Estados Unidos, Friusa ☎ 809 889 2873, ⓦ guesthousepuntacana.com. A 10min bus ride from the beach but you'd have to go a lot further to find as charming a place as this for the same price. Just four clean, understated rooms, spread around a lovely, spacious, leafy courtyard. The hosts are charming and operate a strict anti-sex tourism policy. No sign outside. US$50

Hotel Merengue Av. Alemania ☎ 809 552 9992 and ☎ 809 552 9993, ⓦ hotelmerenguepuntacana.com. Somewhere between the budget hotels and the all-inclusives, with a modest pool on a well-groomed, leafy little campus and very comfortable bedrooms. It's sited on the wrong side of the Av. Alemania for the beach but is still only a few hundred metres from the sand. Suitable for families, and breakfast included. US$96

★**The MT Hotel** Plaza Brisas, Av. España ☎ 809 552 0941, ⓦ themthotel.amawebs.com. A surprisingly pretty hotel given its location between Friusa and the beaches, in one of the roadside commercial plazas. Skirted by well-tended, shade-giving gardens and low hedges, the pleasant rooms are in attractive tiled-roof blocks, along balconied fresh-air corridors. There's a lovely pool area out back and several modest restaurant options on Plaza Brisas. All in all – a bargain. US$50

★**Paradisus Palma Real** Playa Bávaro ☎ 809 688 5000, ⓦ paradisuspalmareal.com. The top Bávaro resort, with opulent contemporary architecture, sculpted tropical gardens, luxury suites with whirlpool baths, plasma TVs and free minibars, Chinese, Japanese and Mediterranean restaurants, a spa and access to the Cocotal golf course. The resort's adjoining sibling, the *Meliá Caribe Tropical*, offers much the same setting (but a lot less pampering) for around half the price. US$560

Hostel Punta Cana Residencial Nautilus, Av. Italia, next to the White Sands Golf Course ☎ 809 488 8090, ⓦ puntacanahostel.net. This hostel is a mixed bag: it raises expectations with its hotel-standard pool and grounds but room maintenance can be hit and miss and not everything is in good working order. A perfectly acceptable choice as long as you don't forget that it's not a hotel. Dorm US$20, double US$50, suite/studio US$60

UVERO ALTO

Sirenis Cocotal Beach Resort Playa Uvero Alto ☎ 809 688 6490, ⓦ sirenishotels.com. Spacious rooms, a small casino and one of the finest pools around – it's shaped like a river winding through the resort grounds, with island bars at each end. The gym and spa facilities are also excellent, and activities for adults and children abound. Eight à la carte restaurants plus the usual buffet option. US$250

EATING, DRINKING AND NIGHTLIFE

You'll find a number of popular beachside **restaurants** in El Cortecito and Los Corales where many of the night-time venues double up as places to eat. In addition, most of the roadside commercial centres, or *plazas*, contain various fast-food options such as pizza and *pica pollo* though you'll find more sophisticated options, including sushi and tapas, in the classy, coral-stone Palma Real (see above) and San Juan (see p.110) shopping malls, both of which also have a cinema offering both subtitled and dubbed Hollywood fare.

PUNTA CANA

Mamma Luisa Galerías Comerciales ☎ 809 959 2013. Dependable Italian bar-restaurant in a handsome bungalow with wraparound verandah and an extensive menu of pasta, meat and fish dishes offering good value for money and prompt service. Daily 11am–4pm & 7–11pm.

BÁVARO

Balicana Los Corales ☎ 809 707 3433, ⓦ balicana.net. It bills itself as an Asian restaurant, and the tasty offerings here are mostly Thai, with some Japanese, Malaysian and Indonesian thrown into the mix. It's a really agreeable, verdant spot tucked away at the end of a drive, a stone's throw from the beach – you'll dine in the open air by a swimming pool, surrounded by palms. Mains RD$380–490. Mon–Sat noon–3pm & 7–11pm.

The Beach Club Calle Pedro Mir, Playa El Cortecito ☎ 809 552 6904, ⓦ thebeachbavaro.com. This spacious venue between the beach and the nightlife strip in El Cortecito has all bases covered: seafood grill, steakhouse and cocktail bar, as well as being a good place to catch televised sporting events; also occasional live music nights and hog roasts. Main dishes US$10–20. Daily 11am–11pm.

Capitán Cook Playa El Cortecito ☎ 809 552 0645 or ☎ 809 688 4577. A wonderful location with patio tables right on the sand and great fresh seafood (from lobster to sea snails) cooked on a mammoth barbecue grill then served in tomato-based creole sauces (mains RD$400–1200). Daily noon–midnight.

★**Huracán Café** Playa Los Corales, opposite the jetty where boat trips depart from ☎ 809 552 1046. A great place to enjoy a beer or cocktail at sunset, slumped on one of the comfy loungers, couches or easy chairs spread across this broad slice of beach. At night the two-floor, wooden, thatched-roof building springs into life – especially on Saturday nights when it hosts one of the most popular club nights in the area (entry RD$1000/$US25). You can eat here too. Daily 11am–11pm, until 3am Sat.

Il Colosseo Plaza Brisas, Av. España ☎ 849 210 4333. A choice of around twenty satisfyingly filling pizzas cooked in a wood-fired oven (RD$200–500) and a similar selection of pasta dishes. It's set on a covered terrace with a bar and backs onto the attractive gardens of a hotel and the hanging plants and wrought-iron lamps add to the leisurely feel of the place. Daily noon–midnight.

Jellyfish Playa Jellyfish ☎ 809 840 7684, ⓦ jellyfishrestaurant.com. Lovely, airy restaurant on the beach tastefully furnished in bamboo and rattan – book a table on the elevated top deck overlooking the ocean. The seafood mains are predictably pricey (from around RD$600), especially given that they make you pay extra for accompaniments. The place also has mounds of cushions and loungers laid out on the sand, making it a great place to unwind with a cocktail. Cash only. Daily 11am–11pm.

★**Las Leñas** Av. España, Gran Plaza Friusa ☎ 809 552 6776, ⓦ laslenascafe.com. This great little inexpensive bakery-café, with both comfy indoor and patio seating, provides a welcome oasis of calm amid the roaring traffic. Tasty rolls, pastries, cakes and empanadas are on offer, to be washed down with a selection of teas, coffees and *batidas* (fruit shakes). Free wi-fi. Mon–Sat 6am–8pm, Sun 6am–3pm.

★**Nam Ñam** Plaza Sol Caribe, Los Corales ☎ 809 988 3176, ⓦ nam-nams.com. The menu at this simple side-street café-restaurant has a distinctly European/North American flavour and is one of the most reliable places for an easy lunch in the whole of Bávaro. Succulent burgers, fresh salads and a good spread of vegetarian options are lovingly made and reasonably priced. Tues–Sat 11am–2.30pm & 6–11pm, Sun noon–3pm & 7–10pm.

Onno's Playa El Cortecito ☎ 809 552 0376, ⓦ onnosbar .com. This national chain of nightclubs is the slickest operation in El Cortecito. Though it suffers a little from a lack of individual character – replicating the look and feel characteristic of a *Hard Rock Café* or *TGI Fridays* – it is nevertheless quite atmospheric at night, with its red lighting, and its walled-in bar leading direct to the beach and balcony terrace. Happy hour 5–8pm. Daily 5pm–2am.

★**Soles** Playa Los Corales ☎ 809 552 0912 or ☎ 809 910 4371. They make it hard to leave this fantastic "chill-out bar" – it's invitingly comfortable, the cocktails are a knockout and the music suitably cool and calm. It's an informal restaurant too, serving crepes and sandwiches as well as more substantial seafood meals, with prices running US$7–20. Sunday afternoon DJ sessions and late evening live music during the week are the icing on the cake. Daily 10am–1/2am.

DIRECTORY

Banks Banco Popular has branches with ATMs on Av. España between Friusa and the turning for El Cortecito, and at the Palma Real shopping mall.

Hospital Centro Médico Punta Cana (☎ 809 552 1030, ⓦ centromedicopuntacana.com) on Av. España and Blvd. Turístico del Este, near Friusa; Hospiten Bávaro Hospital (☎ 809 686 1414, ⓦ hospiten.com) just outside Verón.

Laundry Punta Cana Laundromat, Plaza Arenal del Caribe, Av. Alemania, Los Corales (daily 7am–8.30pm; ☎ 809 552 9970)

Pharmacies Farmacia Dorado, Plaza El Dorado, Los Corales (daily 8am–7pm; ☎ 809 552 0476).

Police Politur, the tourist police, at Cruce de Friusa (☎ 809 688 8727 & ☎ 809 754 3082).

El Seibo

Well off the beaten path, the pleasant cattle town of **EL SEIBO**, smack in the middle of the Cordillera Oriental and a bumpy 40km drive south of Miches, was once the stomping ground of nineteenth-century *caudillo* Pedro Santana, who ruled the Dominican Republic off and on during the period of internecine strife that followed independence from Haiti and continued until annexation by Spain. Whenever Santana was booted out of office by his rival Buenaventura Báez, he would retreat here until the next Haitian invasion.

The only sight worthy of the name is the squat **Iglesia Santa Cruz**, a preserved piece of colonial architecture standing beside the Parque Central that's still used as the parish church. Occasional renovations have kept its red-brick dome and partially whitewashed limestone facade in good shape, though one of these "improvements" also resulted in the unfortunate plaster Victorian top to the bell tower.

North of the city a predominantly paved but potholed road winds its way to **Miches** (see opposite), passing through the most scenic part of the unspoilt Cordillera Oriental mountain range; the peaks here are shaped into spires and cones draped with a thick canopy of greenery.

ARRIVAL AND DEPARTURE   EL SEIBO

By guagua Guaguas heading for Higüey (every 30min until 7pm; 1hr; RD$100) leave from the main road south of Parque Central. If you're going west to San Pedro de Macorís (every 45min until 7.20pm; 1hr 30min; RD$175), Hato Mayor (every 30min until around 7pm; 25min; RD$50) or Santo Domingo (every 45min until 7.20pm; 2hr 30min; RD$175), look for the buses that gather west of the roundabout at the town's northern entrance. North of the roundabout, opposite the Shell station, battered minibuses set off for Miches (every 30min until 6pm; 1hr 15min; RD$110).

ACCOMMODATION, EATING AND NIGHTLIFE

Spreading out along the main road from either side of the church are numerous bars, dancehalls and restaurants – surprising for such a seemingly out-of-the-way town.

2

> ### EL SEIBO FESTIVALS
>
> The *fiestas patronales* in honour of **Santa Cruz**, which take place during the first week in **May**, see a spirited celebration converge on the otherwise slow-moving town. **Bullfighting** features on the calendar and cattle are paraded along the main road, serenaded with song and eventually blessed at Iglesia Santa Cruz. The **nine nights** leading up to the fiesta are known as *novenas*, similarly festive evening celebrations that are worth a look if you're in the area.

Genesis Av. Asomante 46 ☎ 809 552 3024. As comfortable a hotel as there is in El Seibo, yet this is still a pretty modest affair – but at least it's safe, (there's an overnight security guard), and also enjoys a quiet location tucked away on a back street. Rooms have a/c or fan and there's cable TV. RD$700

El Gran Taíno Av. Manuela Díaz. A leafy spot under a thatched roof serving classic Dominican seafood and meat dishes for very reasonable prices – this is about as close as the town gets to somewhere you'd honour with the name "restaurant". Daily noon–11pm.

Hato Mayor del Rey

Despite the lush surroundings of the Cordillera Oriental's rolling hills and orange groves, overcrowded **HATO MAYOR DEL REY** – to give it its full name – remains one of the poorest towns in the region. It has little of interest for visitors, even though Colinas del Rey (see below), the so-called "water park" just outside of town, whose aquatic attractions consist of little more than a couple of swimming pools, is very popular with locals. Most travellers get just a passing glance of Hato Mayor while taking Highway 103, but there is one worthwhile stop – lying just 8km north of town is the pueblo Gran Diablo, from where an extremely rocky dirt road leads 5km northeast to a Cordillera Oriental **cave system** (see box, p.118).

ARRIVAL AND DEPARTURE   HATO MAYOR DEL REY

By guagua On Carretera Mella near the Texaco gas station on the western side of town there are guaguas from and to El Seibo (every 30min 6am–7pm; 30min) and Higüey (every 30min 6am–9pm; 1hr 15min); for Santo Domingo

(every 30min 5am–7pm; 3hr) and San Pedro de Macorís (every 30min 5am–7pm; 2hr), guaguas operate from the corner of San Antonio and the highway, a little closer to the centre of town.

ACCOMMODATION AND EATING

Colinas del Rey Carretera Mella (the road to San Pedro de Macorís), just under 2km south of the town ☎ 809 553 1039, ✉ info@colinasdelrey.com. This "water park" just outside town counts among its facilities a hotel and restaurant. Dominican and Italian food are on offer as are seven double rooms – as long as you don't mind your meals and your evenings set to a blasting merengue and bachata soundtrack this is a good option. RD$1000

★ **Miguelina's Guesthouse** José Francisco Papaterra 21B, near corner of Francisco Ramírez Curro, a couple of blocks behind the city hall ☎ 809 553 4135, ✉ miguelinafranco51@hotmail.com. A memorable B&B in a large, elegant house on a quiet side street backed by fields, with the three clean and comfortable bedrooms all upstairs. Endearing, knowledgeable host Miguelina, a first-rate cook with excellent English, offers daytime and evening meals for an extra cost. US$35

Miches and around

MICHES is a little town on the Bahía de Samaná notorious for being the setting-off point for illegal immigration to Puerto Rico. Dominicans have been known to pay their life savings to local boat captains to be smuggled in small fishing vessels across the shark-infested Mona Passage. For visitors, the lone attraction is the **Costa Esmeralda**, a series of near-deserted sandy **beaches** extending for several kilometres east of town. The best access point is **Playa Miches**, directly across the Río Miches from town. To get there, cross the bridge over the river from the town centre side, turn immediately left and walk a few hundred metres down the road. Then you can

2

CUEVA FUNFÚN

Cueva Funfún (also called Boca de Diablo), a huge, stalactite-ridden, bat-infested cave system south of Parque Nacional Los Haitises, holds several separate chambers and an **underground river**. The only way to visit is on one of the popular organized day-trips run by **Rancho Capote** (☎809 553 2812, ⓦcuevafunfun.net; US$120/person) which involve riding on **horseback** from the ranch, 30km west of Hato Mayor, to the caves. You can book in Hato Mayo at Duarte 12 on the southern end of town (☎809 481 7773) or through the Rancho Capote website; pick-up can be arranged from Punta Cana, Bávaro or Bayahibe.

either walk along the beach or travel on horseback (organized by hotels; US$30); from here the sand continues 8km further, though there are a couple of small rivers to ford. You can also get local fishermen to take you out to **Media Luna**, a half-moon of sand that peeks out of the ocean at low tide, several kilometres off shore. Trips generally cost several hundred pesos; make sure that the boat is sturdy.

Around 40km west of Miches is Sabana de la Mar, a small town just outside the eastern border of the **Parque Nacional Los Haitises**. Though joined to Miches by a winding road, the park is more often and more easily visited from the Samaná Peninsula (see p.132).

ARRIVAL AND DEPARTURE   MICHES

By bus or guagua Guaguas approach Miches from all directions, though the quality of the roads leaves much to be desired, especially heading west. Public transport drops off passengers at the petrol station on the east side of town near the river, where decent-sized buses leave for Higüey (every hour until 5.20pm; 2hr) and pass within hiking distance of Laguna Redonda, Laguna Limón and Montaña Redonda on the way. Frequent guaguas to Sabana de la Mar leave from the western end of Mella, the main street through town, and around the corner from there for El Seibo, where the asphalt ends,

southwest of the plaza. The last transport leaves around 6pm.
By car From Punta Cana head along the road to Higüey, passing through Verón on the way to Carretera 104 which is paved – albeit in various states of repair from good to challenging – and head north along it from outside Higüey for 60km, passing through a series of small villages along the way. From El Seibo (and an alternative route from Punta Cana, via Higüey and the 41km road between there and El Seibo), follow the winding Highway 107 through the mountains for 37km.

ACCOMMODATION AND EATING

There are several decent options in town, though they all suffer from periodic cuts in **water supply**. The nearest hotels to the lagoons stand just before **Playa Limón**.

Coco Loco Playa Miches ☎809 886 8278, ⓦabatrex .com/cocoloco. The best option is located just across the river from town on pretty Playa Miches. Set back among the palms behind the beach, ten simple but comfortable bungalows have hot-water showers and an excellent restaurant with an ocean-view terrace. <u>US$40</u>
Hotel Comedor Orfelina Duarte 71 off San Antonio ☎809 553 5233. This friendly, family-run budget hotel has half a dozen tiny, no-frills en-suite rooms, though the new bar-disco next door will ensure you don't get to sleep early. It can also rustle up some tasty home-cooking for lunch or dinner. <u>RD$1000</u>
Hotel La Cueva Playa Limón ☎809 519 5271, ⓦrancholacueva.com. Part of Rancho La Cueva (see box

opposite), this rather laidback place is the more established of Playa Limón's hotels, though rooms are still pretty basic. It has an attached seafood restaurant, and organizes jeep tours and horse rides to Laguna Limón, and trips up Montaña Redondo. In high season, your tranquillity is likely to be interrupted on a regular basis by visiting tour groups from Punta Cana. <u>US$40</u>
Hotel La Loma ☎809 553 5562. Perched atop a high hill overlooking the town on the western edge of Miches, the poor state of the road means that this place is a little tricky to reach, even though its only 500m from the town square. Once there you're rewarded with spectacular ocean views, a small pool and cosy rooms with modern amenities. There's also an unremarkable on-site restaurant. <u>US$45</u>

EXCURSIONS IN THE LAGUNA LIMÓN AREA

One of the best ways to make the most of this corner of the southeast and explore its natural beauty is to hook yourself up with **Rancho La Cueva** (☎809 519 5271, ⊕rancholacueva.com), located 1km to the west of Laguna Limón and 100m from Playa Limón, on the road between Playa Limón and Carretera 104. As well as running a hotel (see opposite) they offer boat tours of Laguna Limón (US$15/40/person with at least four/two people), trips up Montaña Redonda by truck (US$20/person with a minimum of four people) and horseriding on Playa Limón (US$10/hr), among other activities.

2

Laguna Redonda

East of Miches via Highway 104 are twin mangrove lagoons protected as a single nature reserve that will captivate serious birdwatchers and casual nature-lovers alike. The westernmost lagoon, **Laguna Redonda**, is particularly difficult to reach – a rusted sign points to the turnoff but you can only get to its banks with a 4WD and there are no boats dedicated to taking travellers out, though occasionally a fishing boat nearby can be enticed to do the job for a few hundred pesos. Even if you're stuck on shore, you'll see many birds, including the predatory ospreys, egrets and herons.

Laguna Limón

Park station daily 9.30am–noon & 2–5pm • RD$100 park entrance fee

East of and more accessible than Laguna Redondo is the spectacularly beautiful and serene **Laguna Limón**, which feels extremely pristine and remote but has a couple of small outfits around it dedicated to tourism. Two separate entrances lead to it from the main road, the first of which is marked by a small **national park station**, where a local guide with a boat can be hired (expect to pay around RD$800). The second entrance is 2km further west; there's no park station here, so you won't be asked to pay the fee.

Montaña Redonda

Around 17km east of Miches is **Montaña Redonda**, which can be climbed for spectacular views of the lakes, Samaná bay and the Cordillera Oriental. The fairly arduous hike takes about an hour and a half but the going is scenic all the way and the grassy peak, complete with benches, makes a great place to sit down and rest. You can also drive to the top by taking the turnoff just after the village of Los Urabos.

Playa Limón and Playa Nisibón

About 20km east of Miches and 2km west of Laguna Limón, a dirt road at the village of El Cedro winds 3km down through pastureland to **Playa Limón**, one of the area's spectacular **beaches**, though the undertow is often strong enough to preclude swimming and it's plagued by sand fleas at dusk. It does, though, make for a scenic walk, and sea turtles lay their eggs here in the spring; take a left to reach the mouth of a local river, where the surf churns sea water into the brackish lagoon and the beach is adorned with patches of mangrove.

On the other side of Laguna Limón, a marked turnoff within the tiny town of Sabana de Nisibón leads northeast to **Playa Nisibón**, the entry point to a glorious, uninterrupted stretch of sand – picture Punta Cana and Bávaro without a single hotel.

The Samaná Peninsula and Parque Nacional Los Haitises

SAMANÁ HARBOUR

The Samaná Peninsula and Parque Nacional Los Haitises

It's easy to appreciate the beauty of the Samaná Peninsula, a thin strip of land poking out from the Dominican Republic's northeast corner into the Atlantic Ocean. Arguably the most appealing part of the whole country, the region boasts a coast lined with spectacular beaches that epitomize the glorious Caribbean archetype of powdery white sand, vast banks of swaying coconut trees and transparent green-blue sea. Away from the water, the Sierra de Samaná – a lush, forested mountain range with sixty different types of palm tree and a few impressive waterfalls – supports the peninsula, most of it penetrable only by horse.

As well as being drawn here by the beaches and spectacular geography, visitors come for the opportunity to see up close the thousands of **humpback whales** that migrate to the Bahía de Samaná during the winter. **Whale watching** has become a thriving local industry – with regulations in place to preserve the safety of the animals – that peaks between mid-January and mid-March, when there is a very high chance of a sighting. Most whale boats depart from the town of **Santa Bárbara de Samaná** (generally shortened to "Samaná"), the largest on the peninsula, with many of these boats also ferrying passengers to **Cayo Levantado** – the original Bacardi Island – and to the other side of the bay where the enchanting mangrove swamps of the **Parque Nacional Los Haitises** hide several Taino caves.

If the hustle and bustle of the towns becomes too much, head east to **Las Galeras**, a pristine horseshoe of sand that, despite some development in recent years, still maintains an air of tranquillity. Take a boat ride from here to two of the country's top beaches, picturesque **Playa Rincón** or isolated **Playa Frontón**.

Along the peninsula's north coast you'll find the expat colony of **Las Terrenas**, a burgeoning beachside hangout for independent travellers that is *the* popular holiday spot on the peninsula and lays claim to a decent nightlife scene. Easy day-trips from here include untamed **Playa Bonita**, the largest Samaná beach of all, and horseback excursions to the remote and thundering waterfall **Salto El Limón**.

Until the late nineteenth century, a narrow channel separated the Samaná Peninsula from the Dominican mainland, making it a hotbed for pirates, whose smaller ships used the channel to evade the bulkier galleons that couldn't make it through. Since then, sediment has slowly glued the peninsula onto the mainland; where once the water flowed, a fertile flood plain lies, packed with rice paddies. The peninsula's gateway town **Sánchez** is situated here – once a famous port, it now derives most of its income from shrimp farming and is of little intrinsic interest to visitors except as an important transportation hub, providing guagua connections with Samaná and Las Terrenas.

PARQUE NACIONAL LOS HAITISES

Highlights

❶ Whale watching, Samaná More than four thousand humpback whales visit Dominican waters from mid-January to mid-March, providing one of the world's finest – and most dependable – wildlife spectacles. **See p.130**

❷ Parque Nacional Los Haitises Take an atmospheric boat ride through a surreal snarl of mangrove swamps and prehistoric caves. See p.132

❸ Paraíso de Caño Hondo This is the most convenient base for exploring Parque Nacional Los Haitises – but it's worth staying at this unforgettable hilltop hotel in the trees even if you never leave its confines. **See p.134**

❹ Las Galeras With rugged cliff-top walks,

secluded coves and a number of great hotels and restaurants, you can truly get away from it all at this idyllic outpost near the peninsula's easternmost tip. **See p.135**

❺ Playa Frontón Relax beneath swaying palms and swim in clear waters at this beautiful beach hidden beneath a bank of black cliffs. **See p.139**

❻ Dining out in Las Terrenas Las Terrenas has a more diverse and higher-quality set of gourmet restaurants than anywhere in the country outside of the capital – and most of them are set right on the beach. **See p.144**

❼ El Salto de Limón An impressive 40m waterfall reached by a gentle horseback trek through pleasant countryside. **See p.148**

HIGHLIGHTS ARE MARKED ON THE MAP ON P.124

Samaná and around

Protected on its southern side by a protruding spur of land and two small islands, **SANTA BÁRBARA DE SAMANÁ** possesses a remarkably safe harbour. Naturally shaped to blunt the impact of hurricanes and tropical storms, and with shoals and breakers allowing entry via only one small bottleneck, it's the perfect spot to ward off unwelcome intruders. Strangely, this tremendous strategic potential has never been fully realized, despite five centuries of international political wrangling.

Looking out over Samaná harbour today, you can still get an idea of the great city **Napoleon** envisaged here when the French took over Hispaniola from Spain. A flotilla of sailboats stands behind the palm-ridged island chain; the **port** and the wide-open **promenade** that borders the water bustle with activity; and in place of the impenetrable French fortress that was to jut atop the rocky promontory across from the town is the whitewashed *Gran Bahía Principe Cayacoa* resort. A number of other **all-inclusive hotels** have been built just outside the town but they haven't yet fundamentally altered the appealing character of the place, which still acts as a focus for travellers wishing to get away from the larger resorts. Though Samaná lacks the **beaches** of Punta Cana and the other larger Dominican resorts, it more than makes up this lost ground on its rivals with its beauty and charm. Part neatly maintained holiday town, part forgotten haven of **tranquillity**, it is endowed with pretty, spacious neighbourhoods, winding streets that amble up the hills and a warm sense of community.

Samaná is also a convenient and inexpensive base from which to explore some of the peninsula's more compelling sights. Many visitors use it as a setting-off point for **whale watching** (see box, p.130) and to explore the attractive beaches on the north coast of the peninsula, especially untainted **Las Galeras** (see p.135). Several companies also offer

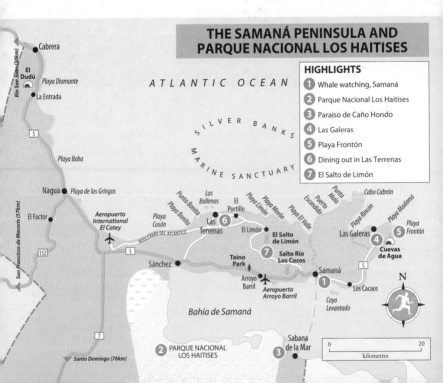

THE SAMANÁ PENINSULA AND PARQUE NACIONAL LOS HAITISES

HIGHLIGHTS

1. Whale watching, Samaná
2. Parque Nacional Los Haitises
3. Paraíso de Caño Hondo
4. Las Galeras
5. Playa Frontón
6. Dining out in Las Terrenas
7. El Salto de Limón

PIRACY IN THE SAMANÁ BAY

The Spaniards made little use of Samaná harbour for the first two centuries of their rule, paving the way for **pirates** to take advantage of the narrow Samaná Channel and the snarl of limestone caves within the dense swamps of Los Haitises. The most notorious of these ne'er-do-wells was England's **Joseph Bannister**, an official government privateer condemned to outlaw status by the 1670 Treaty of Madrid between England and Spain. In 1690 Bannister was anchored at Samaná with a frigate and another smaller vessel when two English warships tried to enter the harbour to arrest him. Bannister took his boats to the nearby island of **Cayo Levantado** and moved his men ashore along with some light artillery. The incoming warships were thus put directly in the line of fire and 125 English soldiers were killed as they cruised into the teeth of Bannister's defences. Bannister's large vessel was also destroyed in the melee; when his two-hundred-man crew found out that the ship was gone – and that the smaller one could accommodate only a quarter of them – they **stampeded** aboard the light craft, with forty of them killed in the process. Bannister, though, got away and the islands surrounding the Samaná harbour have been known ever since as the **Bannister Cays**.

---

boat tours of **Parque Nacional Los Haitises**, an enormous mangrove reserve across the bay (see p.132).

Also worth going out of your way to discover is Samaná's English-speaking community descended from African-American freemen and women (see p.128), who hold a series of interesting **harvest festivals** from August through October.

Brief history

Before European colonization the harbour was one of the settlements of the **Ciguayos** – an initially distinct ethnic group that was ultimately assimilated into Taino culture – that dotted the peninsula's south coast. The Ciguayos lived near the Caribes and borrowed some aspects of Caribe culture, including the bow and arrow, elements of their language, and black and red body paint. When **Columbus** landed at Playa Las Flechas just east of town in January 1493, the Ciguayos greeted his men with a flurry of arrows that forced the Spaniards back to their ships. A week later, the admiral met Chief Cayacoa aboard the *Niña*, repaired their differences and formed an alliance; the Ciguayos later assisted in subjugating the remaining four Taino *caciques*, only to be pacified themselves in the early sixteenth century.

Napoleon

Spain officially founded Santa Bárbara de Samaná in 1756 with transplants from the Canary Islands. In 1795, though, Spain handed the entire island over to **Napoleon Bonaparte** in exchange for territory he controlled in Spain. Bonaparte quickly had blueprints drawn up of his dream New World capital, to be located in Samaná, but widespread chaos on the island – including a revolution in Haiti, two British invasions and civil war among the French commanders – prevented Bonaparte from taking control of the Dominican Republic for almost a decade. When the French finally received their colony in 1802, they were besieged by both a well-organized Haitian force and another British invasion and they soon capitulated.

US interest

The **United States**, too, went to some effort to acquire Samaná, inadvertently toppling two regimes in the process. In 1855, **General Pedro Santana** entered into formal negotiations with the Americans to allow for the annexation of the peninsula and its harbour, a move that proved fatal to his government as **Haiti** – eager to prevent the US from gaining a foothold here – invaded and **Spain** sent aid to local rebels. Santana's successor, **Buenaventura Báez**, reopened negotiations in 1870 with President Ulysses S. Grant, who wanted Samaná to become the US's main Caribbean port, finally

3

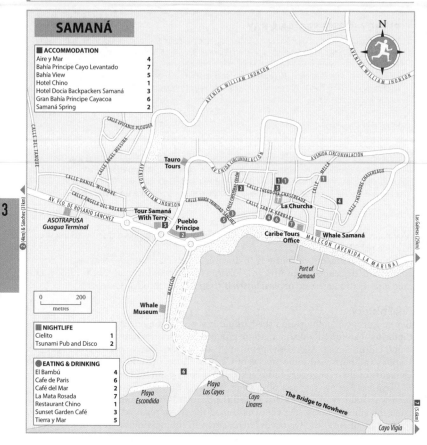

SAMANÁ

ACCOMMODATION
Aire y Mar	4
Bahía Principe Cayo Levantado	7
Bahía View	5
Hotel Chino	1
Hotel Docia Backpackers Samaná	3
Gran Bahía Principe Cayacoa	6
Samaná Spring	2

NIGHTLIFE
Cielito	1
Tsunami Pub and Disco	2

EATING & DRINKING
El Bambú	4
Cafe de Paris	6
Café del Mar	2
La Mata Rosada	7
Restaurant Chino	1
Sunset Garden Café	3
Tierra y Mar	5

agreeing to annex the island for US$150,000. The treaty was rejected by the isolationist US Senate, so the desperate Báez turned instead to private American investors, who signed a 99-year lease with him that gave them total political control over Samaná. Before the Americans were able to take it over, though, Báez was deposed and the contract rescinded.

The Malecón

The focus of activity for most visitors is the city's **Malecón**, also known as Avenida La Marina, a broad promenade dotted with outdoor cafés, storefront shops and patches of park. At its centre is tiny **Samaná port**, little more than two jetties, the departure point for ferries across to Cayo Levantado or Sabana de la Mar and whale-watching boats that cruise the bay in winter. Lying where the road from town meets the strip, **Pueblo Principe** is an incongruous-looking commercial centre in bright pastel colours built by the Bahía Principe group to service the clients of its three hotels on this side of the peninsula. Most of the **shops** time their openings around the comings and goings of the various hotel groups. Come night-time, during the busier seasons, the Malecón's **restaurants** and **bars** buzz with activity and music, a fairly mixed scene of Dominicans, expats and foreign visitors that's both lively and unthreatening.

Whale Museum

Western end of the Malecón • Mon–Fri 9am–2pm • RD$100 • ☎ 809 538 2042

The neglected western end of the Malecón, an otherwise fairly deserted cul-de-sac, is home to a small but fairly uninspiring **Whale Museum**, which has some limited but interesting insights into the lives of the town's annual visitors (see box below), including displays on the extraordinary migration they make every year across the Atlantic, recordings of whale song and a 12m-long skeleton.

HUMPBACK WHALES

Humpback whales have used the Dominican Republic's Samaná Bay and Silver Bank coral-reef sanctuary as a nursery and breeding ground for thousands of years. Taino drawings on the limestone caves of Los Haitises depict breaching whales in the Bahía de Samaná, and Columbus made note of their presence here in 1493. The whales return each **December** after nine months of relentless feeding in the North Atlantic; by **late January** more than four thousand of them, the entire northern Atlantic population, move around the waters of the country's northeastern coast. They're at their liveliest in Samaná's tepid depths, as males track females, compete for attention and engage in courting displays, while mothers teach their calves basic survival skills. Don't allow yourself to come here during the winter without taking an excursion to see them; the **season** generally runs from mid-January to mid-March.

Adult humpbacks grow to nearly 15m in length, weighing up to forty metric tonnes and are black with distinctive white patches. Their name comes from the singular arching of their backs when they dive. Their mouths are filled with **baleen**, hundreds of fibrous sheets that hang from the upper jaw and act as a sieve that traps tiny crustaceans. On their bellies are **ventral folds** – retractable pleats extending the length of their bodies – which expand, allowing the animals to hold massive amounts of food. Their enormous **tails** possess unique patterns of white blotches, which marine biologists use to identify individual whales in a similar way to human fingerprints.

Among the behaviours you may see while whale watching are: **breaching** – hurling the entire body above the surface before landing back down in a spectacular crash; **chin breaching** – bringing the head above water and slapping the chin against the surface; **lobtailing** – raising the tail and smacking it against the water; **flippering** – rolling the body and slapping the flipper against the water; **diving** – arching the back and then sticking the tail straight up in the air in preparation for a deep descent; and the **trumpet blow** – a tremendous, low blast that can be heard from several kilometres away.

Humpbacks also engage in the **whale songs** for which the species is well known – an eerie combination of moans and chirps formed into short phrases that are shuffled and put together in a basic form of communication. Only males sing and they do so far more frequently here than in the North Atlantic – which leads to speculation that songs are used to find a mate. Humpback groups in each region of the North Atlantic develop their own distinctive music, but a **single song** prevails while around the Dominican Republic. This is constantly evolving, probably due to the breeding success of the males who deviate from the original. Therefore, each winter starts with last year's song but this is slowly revised over the course of the ensuing three months.

All of this is done to advance the serious business of **mating and birthing** that takes place in Samaná. The female gestation period is a full year, so calves that are conceived in the bay one year are born here the next; there's a good chance you'll see at least one of the **babies**, which can weigh over a tonne and are light grey. Mothers give birth at two-year intervals and shed up to two-thirds of their body weight while nursing; if **twins** are born – as they sometimes are – the mother is forced to choose between them, as her body cannot feed them both. The thick milk enables infants to grow at the astonishing rate of over 40kg per day.

Whale watching as a local tourist industry was begun in the early 1980s by **Kim Beddall**, then an itinerant scuba instructor with no formal training as a marine biologist. She's spent the subsequent thirty-plus years lobbying for government protection of the whales and creating an economic incentive that will protect them should the **international whaling ban** ever cease. As a result, more than forty boats in Samaná offer whale-watching tours (see box, p.130) every winter and regulations are in place, again instigated by Beddall, to try to ensure that the vessels don't harass the animals.

3

The Bridge to Nowhere and the harbour cays

At the end of a 400m-long dirt track branching off the western end of the Malecón

Across from the harbour, accessed via a set of steps at the foot of the *Gran Bahía Principe Cayacoa* resort, you can walk along the narrow, pedestrian-only **Bridge to Nowhere** to the two cays bordering the harbour: **Cayo Linares** and **Cayo Vigía**. The bridge stands as a symbol of French-descended Dominican President Joaquin Balaguer's failed act of hubris – the transformation of this sleepy town into the largest **resort** complex on the planet, its design mirroring Napoleon's to the letter. In the early 1970s he tore down the city's remaining Victorian architecture, widened the streets, built three large resorts and secured a World Bank loan to construct several more hotels and an **international airport**. A restaurant was built on Cayo Vigía, the larger of the two islands, but when Balaguer lost the election in 1978 the whole project was scrapped and the tourism complex was moved to Playa Dorada near Puerto Plata (see p.164). The restaurant never opened and the bridge leads merely to its graffiti-ridden **ruins**. It's an intriguing spot to wander around and take in lovely views of the harbour and town, though be ready for some precarious steps as you arrive at the cay.

Playa Escondida and Playa Los Cayos

At the foot of the *Cayacoa* hotel are the two small city beaches, both mainly used by hotel guests but open to everyone: **Playa Escondida**, accessible via the road up to the hotel; and **Playa Los Cayos**, reachable via the dirt track connecting the Malecón to the Bridge to Nowhere. They are out of sight of the city itself and though they have nothing on their more spectacular competitors outside town, their setting, nestling inside their own cosy little bays and up against the green slopes of the hill holding the hotel, makes them as relaxing and pleasant a spot as anywhere in Samaná.

La Churcha

Calle Duarte • Sun 9am–noon

A few blocks back from the waterfront is the Iglesia San Peter, popularly known as **La Churcha**, or La Chorcha, whose Spanglish names, as well as the building itself, tangibly maintain what African-American culture is left in Samaná (see box below). The prefabricated, tin-roofed structure was originally shipped over in 1901 from

---

AFRICAN-AMERICANS IN SAMANÁ

A large portion of Samaná's residents are descendants of **African-American freemen and women** who emigrated here during Haitian rule in 1824–25. At the time, a movement in the United States worked to repatriate thousands of freed slaves – seeking to escape the pervasive racism in the States – to West Africa, but stories of malaria epidemics made Haiti, the world's only **black republic**, a more attractive option for many. Six thousand emigrants were temporarily housed in Santo Domingo's Iglesia Las Mercedes (see p.61) before travelling on to various points across the country. About half ended up in Samaná, which the Haitians wanted to develop into a naval base. Despite sustained persecution by the Trujillo dictatorship in the 1940s and a general lack of interest by today's younger generation, the settlers have managed to maintain their **culture** to some degree.

Some of Samaná's older African-American population – many of them clustered within the sprawling **Barrio Wilmore** that borders the C-5 from the town's west entrance – preserve an antiquated form of English, an oral history of the community's struggles and an array of folk tales and legends. One ongoing custom is the series of yearly **harvest festivals**, community feasts with African-American church music held every Friday from late August to the end of October, a tradition that harks back to the yam celebrations and rice festivals of West Africa – check the bulletin board at the back of **La Churcha** (see above) for dates and locations, if you're interested in attending.

England, following the arrival in 1823 of African-American emigrants, most of whom were freed slaves from Philadelphia and members of the African Methodist Episcopal Church, one of whose earliest ministers in the DR was an Englishman. This same religious community remains here today, though these days it's better known as the Dominican Evangelical Church. North of the church, a series of winding streets move up the hills through **residential neighbourhoods** filled with clapboard shacks, mule-riding *caballeros*, children playing stickball and the occasional grazing cow.

Cayo Levantado

The hotel runs a ferry service (10 daily; 10min; RD$200–400) in small boats between Samaná's tiny port on the Malecón and Cayo Levantado; there are also freelance boat owners offering the same trip

Six kilometres out in the bay lies **CAYO LEVANTADO**, the original Bacardi Island, photographed in the 1970s rum campaign. Although the famous swaying palm from the ad has since been uprooted in a tropical storm, hundreds of others still line the soft white sands. The island is now owned by the Bahía Principe group, who run the sole hotel, the *Gran Bahía Principe Levantado* (see p.130) – which takes up two-thirds of it – while welcoming a steady stream of cruise-ship passengers throughout the year to a **public beach** at the other end of the island. Yet more visitors take the ferry over from Samaná, and many whale-watching tours and excursions to the Parque de Los Haitises stop off here for an hour or so, which can make it very **crowded** in high season. Moreover, with the extortionate food and drink prices and the sometimes persistent hassling from vendors, this is no Robinson Crusoe-esque paradise. That said, the water here is warm and beautifully crystalline, the sand supremely soft, and the island small enough to afford the novel sense of being on a beach out at sea. There are many better and less crowded beaches on the peninsula but this is better than either **Playa Escondida** or **Playa Los Cayos** back in Samaná – if you are lucky enough to catch it when the crowds have dispersed (a rare event, admittedly), it's really very special.

ARRIVAL AND INFORMATION

SAMANÁ

By plane Aeropuerto Internacional El Catey (📞809 338 0147 or 📞809 338 5888), also known as Juan Bosch, is just west of the peninsula. The airport is served by about a dozen North American and European airlines, including Air Canada and JetBlue Airways, though some of them on a seasonal basis only. A taxi to or from the airport costs around US$70. Another much smaller airport, Aeropuerto Arroyo Barril (📞809 248 2566), is closer to Samaná, 12km from town on the road between Samaná and Sánchez, but serves domestic flights only. A taxi between the town and the airport costs around US$25.

By car A relatively new road (RD$600 toll charges), Highway 7, connects Santo Domingo's airport to the C-5 just west of Sánchez, reducing the travel time between Samaná and the capital to around two hours. The C-5, which stretches along the country's north coast, leads down to Samaná's Malecón as Av. Francisco de Rosario Sánchez, the two roads comprising the only major thoroughfare in the town.

By bus Caribe Tours runs buses to and from Santo Domingo on both an express service (4 daily 8am–4pm; 2hr 30min) and a normal service that goes via Nagua (4 daily 7am–3pm; 4hr). They arrive at and depart from outside the small office opposite the port (📞809 538 2229).

By guagua Guaguas congregate at and around the tiny ASOTRAPUSA terminal (📞809 664 7830) by the town market, on the main street a few hundred metres from the Malecón. There is a Puerto Plata service (1 daily; 3hr 30min) run separately (📞829 376 8346), sometimes offering pick up from your hotel. Numerous *motoconchos* are always available from this part of town.

Destinations El Limón (5am–5pm; 30min); Las Galeras (6am–6pm; 1hr); Las Terrenas (5am–5pm; 45min); Sánchez (5am–5.20pm; 45min); Santiago (8 daily 4.45am–2.30pm; 3hr); Santo Domingo (18 daily 4.30am–4.45pm; 2hr 30min).

By boat It's also possible to arrive at Samaná via the ferry from Sabana de la Mar (see p.134), which docks at the port. Return crossings leave daily at 7am, 9am, 11am and 3pm (1hr; RD$200). If you're sailing, the port of Samaná makes a good safe place to dock, but you'll have to get a permit from the port authority as soon as you arrive.

Tourist office The Ministry of Tourism has an administrative office in the Pueblo Principe commercial complex (Mon–Fri 8am–3pm; 📞809 538 2332) but you'll probably get more information from your hotel or from one of the tour operators.

WHALE WATCHING AND OTHER ACTIVITIES AROUND SAMANÁ

Whale watching is only possible in the winter months, with **peak season** between mid-January and mid-March. Tracking down a whale-watching **tour** will not be difficult – simply standing around by the port area is enough to guarantee attention from the men employed to rustle up trade for the various trips, but make sure that you travel with a **reputable operator** who adheres to the "no more than three boats to a group of whales" rule. Most tours whale-watch in the **Bahía de Samaná**, sometimes with an hour stop-off at **Cayo Levantado** (see p.129), which may cost extra, though **week-long expeditions** to the country's **Silver Banks Sanctuary** just north of the peninsula are also possible. None of the Samaná operators should offer swimming and snorkelling in the waters around the whales, though some out-of-town operators do, as it's against regulations to swim with the whales in the bay. Other activities in the area include **ziplining**, **quad-biking** and trips to **Parque Nacional Los Haitises**.

Runners Adventures ☎829 599 0622, ⓦrunnersadventures.com. A very professional and well-established operator with offices around the country whose offers include their specialist zipline adventure through the forest canopy, trips to El Salto de Limón (see p.148) and a choice of full-day, whistle-stop Samaná Peninsula tours (US$75–79; children US$38–50), pausing at places of interest amid spectacular scenery and including a dip in a river or in the sea.

Tauro Tours Av. Circunvalación, Building 16, Local no.4 ☎849 658 8997, ⓦtaurotours-excursionsamana.com. Successful and experienced tour operator with a whole host of different excursions on offer, from whale watching to trips to Parque Nacional Los Haitises and their flagship tour – the four-hour, cross-country quad-bike trip to Las Galeras (US$55–86).

Tour Samaná With Terry Opposite the second roundabout ☎809 538 3179, ⓦtoursamanawithterry.com. This highly recommended and conscientiously run operator has a programme designed specifically for visiting cruise-ship passengers, but also arranges tours for anyone staying in town, including whale watching (US$70; US$50 for children 11 and under). Though more expensive than Whale Samaná, this includes lunch and beach time at Cayo Levantado. The website has a schedule for the numerous other tours and activities on offer, from horseriding and trips to El Salto de Limón to ziplining, and a forum to help people hook up with other interested parties to make up numbers.

Whale Samaná Just off the Malecón ☎809 538 2494, ⓦwhalesamana.com. Run by Canadian conservationist Kim Beddall and her team, this is the best whale-watching outfit in Samaná. The commentary, which not all operators offer, is knowledgeable, well rehearsed and delivered in English, Spanish and other languages if there are enough passengers to warrant it. Departures are once or twice a day from the Samaná port throughout the whale-watching season and if you don't see any whales your next trip is free. Tours cost US$59 plus US$3 for Marine Mammal Sanctuary. During the whale off season, you can join one of the "caves and kayaks" excursions to the Los Haitises swamps (see p.132; US$58).

ACCOMMODATION

There are plenty of **cheap** options in Samaná but **mid-range** hotels are in short supply and there is just one **luxury** resort in the town itself – you'll find greater variety in nearby Las Terrenas or Las Galeras. On arrival at the Malecón, you may be beset by local *buscones* (literally "finders"), freelance assistants – some of whom speak fluent English – who will help you find whatever you need, be it a whale-watching tour, a hotel or a restaurant. If you're looking for good, cheap accommodation, they can make the task a bit easier – bear in mind, though, that they do have a vested interest in the places they recommend.

★**Aire y Mar** 27 de Febrero 4, on eastern side of town ☎809 820 7200, ✉aparthotel-aireymar@hotmail.com. This lovely house in a great hillside location has just six simple and unadorned but pleasantly spick-and-span rooms. It's well worth paying the extra US$10 for the sea-view rooms with a fantastic shared balcony verandah and a perfectly framed bay vista. US$25

Bahía Príncipe Cayo Levantado Cayo Levantado ⓦbahia-principe.com. If you're looking for luxury and relaxation in an idyllic location it doesn't get much better than this hotel, sited on its own palm-fringed island. Though the public beach gets crowded (see p.129), there are private beaches for guests plus four restaurants, six bars and two pools as well as a pool-side lounge, beautiful views from all over the property and free ferries to and from Samaná every day. Low-season prices can be more than 50 percent cheaper. US$350

Bahía View Circunvalación ☎809 538 2237 or ☎829 880 9653, ✉dgoreyes202@hotmail.com. The Pueblo Príncipe shopping complex now rather obscures the eponymous views, but this is still a good option for budget travellers, with a friendly proprietor, better-than-average rooms and private showers. The nice, small restaurant below has a great people-watching patio. RD$1000

Hotel Chino San Juan 1, on top of hill behind La Churcha ☏ 809 538 2215, ✉ hotelchino.samana @hotmail.com. You're paying more here for the great hilltop views of the bay, which you can appreciate from the exceedingly comfortable communal living-room terrace. The rooms themselves, while nicely tiled with firm beds, a/c and hot water, are rather small and humble. US$55

Hotel Docia Backpackers Samaná Duarte and Teodoro Chaseraux ☏ 809 538 2041, ⟨w⟩ backpackers-samana .com. Well situated a few blocks from the seafront, this youth hostel is one of the best budget options in town. Clean, though rather cramped private rooms with a/c, TV and proper shower heads in the bathroom, plus dorms and a communal kitchen. Dorm US$12 double $US30

Gran Bahía Principe Cayacoa Loma Puerto Escondido ☏ 809 538 3131, ⟨w⟩ bahia-principe.com. Imperiously overlooking the town, the *Cayacoa* is the most glamorous location in Samaná and good value for an all-inclusive. It makes full use of its vertical dimensions with a top-floor restaurant offering great views and an elevator lowering guests down to the dinky beach at the foot of the cliffs. In between, the rooms are large and attractively appointed. Entertainment is provided outside the hotel grounds in the town itself at the purpose-built Pueblo Principe complex (see p.126). Adults only. US$156

Samaná Spring San Cristobal 94 ☏ 809 538 2946 or ☏ 829 763 2048. Neat, unfussy, well-maintained rooms with decent amenities for a budget hotel (a/c, hot water, TV, wi-fi) in a large, good-looking, three-storey house with balconies and terracotta-tiled roofs. The location is conveniently central and side-street quiet. US$35

EATING, DRINKING AND NIGHTLIFE

Samaná's best **restaurants**, charging tourist prices, are concentrated on the four blocks of the Malecón around the port, but there are plenty of **cheaper** local establishments – mostly *comedores* and *pica pollos* – along Av. Francisco de Rosario Sánchez, sloping down towards the Malecón. The **drinking** and **nightlife** scene revolves largely around the restaurants and there are hardly any proper bars, with only a couple of clubs-cum-discos and a few open-air pool halls along the Malecón. **Cafe del Mar**, however, is well worth the short trip out of town.

El Bambú Malecón ☏ 809 538 2661. Serves a fairly basic, but perfectly acceptable menu of Dominican and international staples – steaks, pizza, pasta – plus some good, fresh seafood. They lay on daily lunch specials for as little as RD$150; at all other times mains start at around RD$300. Daily 10am–11pm.

★**Cafe del Mar** Carretera Sánchez-Samaná, 5km west of Samaná ☏ 809 732 2010, ⟨w⟩ cafedelmar.com.do. The famous sunset bar from Ibiza has opened its first branch in the Americas here at the tip of the classy marina in the posh Puerto Bahía complex. With lawns, a restaurant and a curving infinity pool, it feels more exclusive than its Spanish counterpart but the basic formula is the same and still unbeatable – ambient and other chill-out music played to drinkers and diners with a fantastic view of the setting sun against a spellbinding horizon. Daily 11am–9pm.

Cafe de Paris Malecón ☏ 809 538 2488. This cool and casual venue with a central bar surrounded by stools is the best spot for knocking back some beers. Softly lit at night and purposefully rough around the edges with mismatched furniture and decor, it's an inviting and sociable place to meet fellow travellers, and also works well for a no-frills, reasonably priced meal of Dominican staples and sandwiches. Daily 8am–midnight.

Cielito Rosa Duarte 2 ☏ 809 849 3024. One long-time favourite for dancing is the dark blue, bunker-like *Cielito*, where you can throw some shapes under the flashing lights

to merengue, bachata and salsa, plus European and North American dance. Entry for men is RD$50; free for women. Tues–Sun 9pm–2am.

★**La Mata Rosada** Malecón ☏ 809 833 0514. A graceful and stylish dining area plus an eclectic menu and excellent quality food make this the pick of the seafront restaurants. There are several curried dishes and some creations that are a refreshing break from the norm, such as chicken breast in orange and onion sauce (RD$400) and beef cooked with ginger (RD$430). Daily except Wed 10am–3pm & 6.30–11pm.

Restaurant Chino San Juan 1, on top of the hill behind La Churcha ☏ 809 538 2215. Perched on a high hill overlooking the bay with indoor and outdoor dining spaces, *Chino* serves generous, moderately priced portions of good but rather greasy Chinese food alongside popular Dominican, Italian and international standards. Mon–Thurs & Sun 11am–midnight, Fri & Sat 11am–2am.

Sunset Garden Café Av. Maria Trinidad Sánchez, just off the Malecón ☏ 809 906 4703. With its low-slung chairs and open-air setting, this is the perfect spot for a drawn-out afternoon sipping cocktails (RS$150–200) and nibbling tacos and burritos (RD$200–500) or Dominican seafood and meat dishes (RD$200–800). Also good for an easy-going Dominican breakfast of *mangú* or mashed potatoes with fried cheese, salami or eggs (RD$225). The neat little hedge hemming things in and obscuring the road enhances the relaxing vibe. Daily 9am–11.30pm.

3

Tierra y Mar Av. María Trinidad Sánchez, just off the Malecón ☎ 809 538 2436 or ☎ 809 209 6857. Run by Evelyn and David, a half-Dominican, half-American couple, this relaxing, gravel-floored joint under a thatched roof is a good place for simple breakfasts such as pancakes or cereal, and simple Dominican lunches and dinners – *lambí*

(RD$350) and the crabmeat *masa de cangrejo* (RD$500) are recommended. Free wi-fi. Daily 8am–11pm.

Tsunami Pub and Disco Pueblo Príncipe, Malecón ☎ 829 392 4344. Opened in 2014, this very touristy nightclub is the most polished and professional spot in town, with a neon-lit dancefloor and "international" music. Tues–Sun 9pm–3am.

Taino Park

Los Róbalos, Samaná–Sánchez road, 15km west of Samaná • Daily 9am–6pm • Entrance US$15; children under 12 free • ☎ 809 729 1514 or ☎ 809 2679531, ⓦ tainopark.com

With its tour of life-size recreations of pre-Columbian culture on the island, **Taino Park** may look at first like an attempt to Disneyfy history but, in fact, this is a relatively serious, sombre and honest attempt to depict the Taino people and their clash with the European colonizers (see box opposite). The undercover **walking tour**, through five acres of alluring tropical grounds, with a very worthwhile audio guide, takes in over twenty-five relatively well-crafted open-air scenes. Depicting both typical Taino life, such as hunting and ceremonial scenes, as well as encounters with the Spanish, including recreations of battle and slave labour, there's plenty to stimulate here. There's also a **museum** on site with one of the country's most complete collections of Taino artefacts.

Playa El Valle

North coast of peninsula, 11km north of Samaná

Just east of Samaná, a signposted turnoff leads north up a tortuously bad road to **Playa El Valle**, an entirely isolated beach cut off by steep mountains. A 4WD is recommended, as you'll have to ford a small river, but you're pretty much guaranteed to share the beach with only the inhabitants of the small fishing village on its western bank, though the place now features on the occasional jeep safari's itinerary. A couple of shacks in the village serve good fish with rice and plantains.

Parque Nacional Los Haitises

On the south of the Samaná Bay is **PARQUE NACIONAL LOS HAITISES**, a massive expanse of mangrove swamp that protects several Taino caves, 92 plant species, 112 bird species and a wide variety of marine life. It is not possible to visit independently – all visits must take place as part of the highly recommended **organized tours**, the majority of which leave from the Samaná Peninsula and are organized by operators in Samaná (see, p.130), Las Galeras (see p.136) and Las Terrenas (see, p.142), though excursions from resorts on the south coast are popular too, and you can also book a trip from the sole hotel on the park's edge (see p.134). Tour groups from Punta Cana and other southeastern resorts pass through **Sabana de la Mar**, a dusty little port town to the east of the park, which is where you will dock if you have taken the ferry over from Samaná – you can also book an excursion with locals from here on spec. Along the coast the park holds the country's largest unblemished expanse of red and white **mangroves**; in the near-impenetrable interior, dense, trail-less **rainforest** predominates, punctuated by the ruins of long-abandoned sugar plantations and numerous **cave systems**. What you'll see on the **boat tours**, some of which include a short forest walk, is a series of virtually untouched mangrove rivers along with small islands and coastal caves that provide habitat for untold numbers of tropical birds; some of the caves bear Taino petroglyphs.

Most tours stop at **Cueva Arena**, a large grotto that has numerous Taino drawings of families, men hunting, supernatural beings, whales and sharks. Some tours pause briefly at the beach cove here, offering the opportunity to get a good look at **Cayo Willy**

THE TAINO LEGACY

Over the past century a lot of impassioned debate has gone into the question of whether or not the **Tainos** who once inhabited Hispaniola – along with Puerto Rico and Cuba – were exterminated during the initial period of Spanish colonization. Certainly the majority were wiped out – by war, slave labour and epidemic smallpox – but a growing body of evidence points to the fact that some Tainos (perhaps quite a number of them) survived throughout the colonial era and intermarried with the Africans and Europeans who lived on the island from the time of Columbus onward.

The primary evidence for complete **genocide** comes from Spanish authors such as Las Casas and Montesino, who wrote of the absolute devastation wreaked upon the Tainos in the early years of European colonization. According to Las Casas, only a few thousand remained as long ago as 1518, and early sixteenth-century sugar-mill owners such as Juan de Viloria claimed that their entire Taino slave workforce had been destroyed by smallpox. Counter-evidence, though, can sometimes be seen at the margins; when Viloria died, his wife claimed that he had three hundred Taino slaves as part of his property, and it seems a reasonable assumption that he hid them in his report to the Crown in order to get a free allotment of several hundred African slaves as an additional labour force. In addition, early colonial records show that most of the first male colonists **intermarried** with locals; some records suggest that as the sixteenth century wore on, Tainos who married Europeans and converted to Catholicism began to be considered Spaniards. At the very least, the **historical record** is confused. Various wills and court documents continued to refer to "Indians" in a variety of contexts, and a 1545 census claimed that over half of the sugar-mill slaves were Indian – twenty years after the Tainos' supposed extermination. In addition, the vast majority of the island was not under European control and thus would have served as a safe harbour for Taino communities as well as *cimarones*; in 1555 four large Taino villages were discovered along the island's north coast, and there were likely many more in the isolated mountain regions.

Various tests of Dominican and Puerto Rican **genetics** have been performed in order to establish to what extent the current inhabitants of the Greater Antilles are descended from Tainos, and some have purported to find definitive traces of Taino in the current population. A recent study of DNA in hair samples of **Puerto Rican** citizens found that about half of them had some Taino heritage, while a study of blood types in the Dominican Republic indicated that today's Dominican people get around 15 percent of their genes from the Tainos.

The question of the Dominican Republic's continuing Taino heritage is a lot knottier than it looks at first sight, though – in large part because the Tainos have been used by Dominican intellectuals in the past to cover up the nation's more extensive **African** background. **Dominican mulattos**, for example, are still officially classified as "Indios", and many mainstream anthropologists become understandably suspicious whenever they hear someone pressing the case for the Taino heritage of the Dominican people. Even though it now appears that the Dominican people do possess significant Taino heritage, the African debt is much greater, and much harder for many to admit due to **racism** and widespread miseducation in schools.

Regardless, **Dominican culture** owes a profound debt to the Tainos. Dominican Spanish is interspersed with hundreds of Taino words and inflections, the pantheon of spirits in **Vodú dominicana** (see box, p.60) – a largely African religion – includes several divisions of Taino spirits, and the Taino methods of farming, cooking, weaving and boat-building are still widely performed throughout the country even today. In the most rural *campos*, villagers still call to each other from hill to hill with signals blown through conch shells whenever fresh meat or ice has arrived for sale.

3

Simons (once a hideout for the infamous pirate), recognizable by the dozens of birds circling around it: pelicans, herons, terns, frigates, even an occasional falcon.

Beyond Cueva Arena, you pass the ruins of a hundred-year-old banana wharf, with pelicans and terns perched on the remaining wooden pilings, before pulling up at **Cueva de la Linea**, once intended to hold a railroad station for the sugar cane that was grown in the area. In pre-Columbian times, the cave was a Taino temple; look for the guardian face carved at the entrance, and residues of ancient campfire smoke

PARQUE NACIONAL LOS HAITISES PRACTICALITIES

All visits to **Parque Nacional Los Haitises** must take place as part of an organized tour, many of which leave from the Samaná Peninsula and are arranged by tour operators in Samaná (see box p.130), Las Galeras (see box p.136) and Las Terrenas (see box p.142). The closest you can realistically get to Los Haitises **independently** is the *Paraíso de Caño Hondo* hotel (see below) at the **park entrance**, 12km west of Sabana de la Mar, an unexceptional little town that is missed out altogether by boat tours from the Samaná Peninsula (which head straight into the mangroves) but the only ferry port on this southern side of the bay. Boat tours organized from *Paraíso de Caño Hondo*, Punta Cana and the other resorts on the south coast depart from a jetty by the **park entrance** next to the hotel, and the standard trip around the park takes 2hr 30min. There is a park entrance **fee** of RD$100, usually included in the cost of a tour.

OPERATORS AND ACCOMMODATION

Paraíso de Caño Hondo Carretera Los Haitises, 12km west of Sabana de la Mar ☎ 829 259 8549 or ☎ 809 248 5995, ⌨ paraisocanohondo.com. This hotel (see below) and tour operator, located at the entrance to the park itself, offers a range of tours, including a trek through the forest, their "Two Caves" tour to Cueva Arena and Cueva de la Linea, or the five-hour "Aventura Ecológica" exploring caves, cays, rivers and beaches by boat. Prices range between US$50 and US$90 for boats tours.

Sabana Tours By the pier in Sabana de la Mar

☎ 809 868 4301 A slightly cheaper option – generally a negotiable RD$2000 per person – is to go with a local boatman operating from the Sabana Tours office. Some of them have been certified as guides by the park's office (ask to see their certification), and tours will be predominantly in Spanish. Their boats leave from the same jetty at the park entrance but transport to the entrance from Sabana de la Mar is not included in the tour price, though the guides can often arrange transportation by *motoconcho* to the jetty.

GETTING TO SABANA DE LA MAR AND THE PARK

By bus Buses run from Santo Domingo (3hr 30min), Miches (2hr) and Hato Mayor (1hr 15min).

By boat There's a ferry service (see p.129) between Samaná town and Sabana de la Mar. The ferry returns to Samaná at 9am, 11am, 3pm and 5pm (daily; 1hr;

RD$200). **The park entrance** is 12km west of Sabana de la Mar, in the same spot as the *Paraíso de Caño Hondo* hotel. You can take a *motoconcho* here for RD$250–300.

---

and innumerable pictographs along the inside walls. Another cave with Taino faces carved into its walls that features on many tours is **Cueva San Gabriel**, also once the temporary home of various pirates, including Cofresí, Jack Banister and John Rackham.

ACCOMMODATION AND EATING   PARQUE NACIONAL LOS HAITISES

There are no **accommodation** or **eating** facilities within the park itself, the nearest being at *Paraíso de Caño Hondo* at the park entrance and the rest in Sabana de la Mar, 12km east of the park entrance.

El Tres 3km south of Sabana de la Mar on the road to Hato Mayor ☎ 809 556 7575 or ☎ 829 797 6260. Around a dozen simple rooms on a farm ranch where the animals roam freely and the friendly hosts organize horseriding for guests (US$10 /person/hr). A relaxing spot if you don't mind animals. **RD$1100**

★**Paraíso de Caño Hondo** Carretera Los Haitises, 12km west of Sabana de la Mar ☎ 829 259 8549 or ☎ 809 248 5995, ⌨ paraisocanohondo.com. An amazing eco-lodge designed by its architect-owner that's like something straight out of Hans Christian Andersen, with rustic room furnishings fashioned from driftwood.

The stream that runs through the property has been diverted into a series of cascades and a large natural pool to bathe in, which is overlooked by one of the two restaurants. Twenty-eight spacious en-suite rooms (fan and hot-water showers), some with private balcony, are primarily divided between a hilltop lodge, affording magnificent views across the bay, and two smaller villas, one of which is situated next to the pools and waterfalls, where the noise of running water happily blocks out some of the rowdier day-trippers (the main downside of this otherwise idyllic place) even if you don't stay here, it's worth paying the place a visit and perhaps taking one of their excursions (see box opposite). All room rates include breakfast. <u>RD$1606</u>/person

Restaurant Jhonson Elupina Cordero 5, near Parque Central ☎ 809 556 7715. They may not be able to spell but they can certainly cook at this open-air, bay-view restaurant. The speciality is seafood, including lobster for around RD$600, with most other main dishes costing RD$250–450. Daily 9am–midnight.

Las Galeras and around

Set in a narrow horseshoe-shaped cove at the eastern end of the peninsula, the sleepy outpost of **LAS GALERAS** is gradually being brought into the mainstream. The road from Samaná has been improved in recent years and the number of lodgings and restaurants continues to rise steadily, though – mercifully – they have so far been small-scale, low-impact developments. Despite this growth, the small village has managed to maintain its peaceful and timeless ambience. Though there is a sweep of white sand **beach** here, upon which an almost unbelievably turquoise sea laps gently, Las Galeras is used as a launch pad to the more secluded beaches in the vicinity – **Playa Frontón**, **Playa Rincón** and others – as much as it is visited for its own sandy haven. If you're going to spend a few days in the area though, Las Galeras makes the perfect base, as the local amenities are spaced out along its main street, **Calle Principal**. Turn any corner along this road and you run out of town almost immediately, with all the other

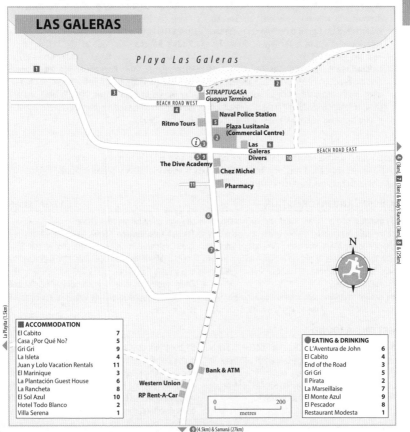

LAS GALERAS

Playa Las Galeras

SITRAPTUGASA Guagua Terminal

BEACH ROAD WEST

Naval Police Station

Ritmo Tours

Plaza Lusitania (Commercial Centre)

Las Galeras Divers

BEACH ROAD EAST

The Dive Academy

Chez Michel

Pharmacy

N

■ ACCOMMODATION

El Cabito	7
Casa ¿Por Qué No?	5
Gri Gri	9
La Isleta	4
Juan y Lolo Vacation Rentals	11
El Marinique	3
La Plantación Guest House	6
La Rancheta	8
El Sol Azul	10
Hotel Todo Blanco	2
Villa Serena	1

Bank & ATM

Western Union

RP Rent-A-Car

● EATING & DRINKING

C L'Aventura de John	6
El Cabito	4
End of the Road	3
Gri Gri	5
Il Pirata	2
La Marseillaise	7
El Monte Azul	9
El Pescador	8
Restaurant Modesta	1

0   200
metres

La Playita (1.5km)

● (3km), **7** (3km) & Rudy's Rancho (3km), **8** (25km)

● (4.5km) & Samaná (27km)

3

ACTIVITIES IN LAS GALERAS

There are plentiful ways to appreciate the area's outstanding **natural beauty**, both by **land** or **water**. Several **trails** have been marked extending out from the village into the surrounding countryside, though it is easy to get lost if you want to go all the way to Playa Frontón, Playa Madama or any of the other popular beach destinations – enquire about reliable guides at La Rancheta (see below), the End of the Road information centre (see below) or your accommodation. For **horseriding**, other than those mentioned below, you might also try La Loma-Cita (☎829 905 3272, ⊛lalomacita-lodge.com).

The Dive Academy At the crossroads in the village ☎829 577 5548, ⊛diveacademy.co. If you're keen to do a bit more than swim, check out this NAUI-certified outfit who charge US$55 for a single dive or US$85–90 for two successive dives (once the cost of equipment is included). They also offer various dive courses including the four- to five-day "Passport Course" (US$320) and organize diving trips around the tip of the peninsula to reefs, wrecks and underwater caves.

Las Galeras Divers At the crossroads in the village ☎809 538 0220, ⊛las-galeras-divers.com. Also at the crossroads and worth considering are Swiss-run, PADI-certified Las Galeras Divers, who offer the same prices and dive options as The Dive Academy, plus a beginners' course (US$75).

La Rancheta 3km east of the Las Galeras crossroads near the beach ☎829 939 8285, ⊛larancheta.com. Offers highly acclaimed riding excursions (half-day US$45–60; full day US$75–90) of the local area, taking in such highlights as Playa Madama, a thin curve of

sand in a sheltered bay surrounded by lush green hills, and Playa Frontón (see p.139) for US$90. You can even spend the night sleeping out under the stars at Playa Frontón, heading on to Boca del Diablo the next day (US$200).

Ritmo Tours In village, a few metres from the beach on the main street ☎829 916 8112, ⊛samanaritmotours.com. This local outfit runs a range of informative tours with multilingual guides. One of the most popular day-trips is an all-inclusive quad-bike excursion to Playa Rincón (see p.139) for US$80. They can also organize outings further afield to Parque Nacional Los Haitises (US$75) and El Limón (see p.148) for US$59.

Rudy's Rancho 2km east of the Las Galeras crossroads near the beach ☎829 305 3368, ⊛rudysrancho.com. Runs horseriding trips along the shore at US$20 for 2hr as well as whole- and half-day outings to Playa Rincón, Playa Frontón and a number of other beaches and places of natural beauty in the area.

---

restaurants and accommodation options in the area widely dispersed: a car, a willingness to walk a lot, or a budget for taxis is essential if you want to make the most of Las Galeras and its surroundings.

ARRIVAL AND INFORMATION   LAS GALERAS

By guagua The tiny SITRAPTUGASA terminal is at the end of the main road, almost on the beach. It is served by guaguas (every 20min 6am–6pm; 45min) from Samaná, with the last minibus or pick-up returning to Samaná at 6pm. To get to Las Terrenas, El Limón or Sánchez you have to travel via Samaná.

By car The lone 28km road connecting Las Galeras with Samaná and the rest of the peninsula is in good condition

and more or less follows the coastline.

Tourist information There's an independently run tourist information service in the End of the Road internet café on the main crossroads, 50m back from the beach (daily 8am–9pm; ☎829 797 9469). Diane, the British expat who runs it, is unendingly helpful and friendly and happy to provide unbiased advice on all local matters.

GETTING AROUND

By car and scooter You can rent a car (US$60–70/day) or an ATV (US$50/day) at RP Rent-Car (☎809 538 0249) on the main street, 1km from the beach. To rent scooters (RD$2000/day) go to Chez Michel (☎829 883 2644) next to The Dive Academy near the main crossroads.

By boat Turn up at Las Galeras beach almost any time during daylight hours and there will more than likely be a few local fishing-boat skippers touting boat trips. The going rate is around RD$1000 per person to most of the surrounding beaches but everything is by negotiation, with better deals for parties of two or more.

ACCOMMODATION

Accommodation options are **scattered** around a wide area, though quite a few are along the beach end of the main road and also on either side of the dirt roads that run parallel to the beach to the east and west. There are some fabulous, genuine **ecotourism** options just out of town in the wonderful surrounding countryside and something for every budget and preference, including the possibility of **camping**.

El Cabito 3km east of Las Galeras ☎829 697 9506, ⓦelcabito.net. Fabulous cliff-top location (4WD recommended to get there) close to Playa Madama offering a couple of wonderfully thatched cabañas with ocean-view terrace and breezy open-sided bedroom (mosquito net provided) plus camping facilities with shared showers, kitchen and BBQ. You can pitch your own tent, sleep in a hammock or even sleep in a treehouse. Two night minimum stay. Cabaña US$50, treehouse US$30, camping US$10, hammock US$7.50

Casa ¿Por Qué No? Calle Principal, between the main crossroads and the beach ☎809 712 5631, ⓔcasaporqueno@live.com. within stumbling distance of the beach, there are just two simple, tasteful rooms here, in a bungalow separated from the road and the noise by an idyllic garden with a sweeping lawn. It's a lovely, laid-back place to stay with the sense of calm augmented by the easy-going, likeable and unconventional nature of the French–Canadian couple who run it. Only open Nov–April. US$55

Gri Gri Calle Principal ☎809 705 2894. Extremely basic accommodation aimed squarely at backpackers on a budget. The rooms are spartan but clean with hot water, fan (and fridge in some cases), plus some wonderful reproduction furniture – even a four-poster bed in one room. Solid on-site restaurant. RD$1500

La Isleta Beach Rd West ☎809 538 0116, ⓦlaisletasamana.com. A stone's throw from the beach, set amid charming tropical gardens, these cheerfully decorated apartments come equipped with kitchens and sleep up to four, making them good value. Hot tub, barbecue and wi-fi available. US$89

Juan y Lolo Vacation Rentals Calle A no. 313 ☎809 538 0208, ⓦjuanylolo.com. A selection of rustic but rather attractive thatched and self-contained accommodation spread around Las Galeras, be it a bungalow for two or a three-bedroom villa to sleep six. Well equipped, with lounges, full-size bathrooms and fully functional kitchens, offering good long-term rental rates. Bungalow US$40, villa US$60

El Marinique Beach Rd West ☎809 538 0262, ⓦelmarinique.com. One of the first hotels in Las Galeras, *El Marinique* has three simple cottages (sleeping two) as well as two well-equipped two-storey apartments (sleeping four) set in a garden just back from the sea. The overpriced accommodation is offset by the warm, personalized service of the owners and the wonderful views and food from the restaurant. Cottage US$64, apartment US$89

La Plantación Guest House Beach Rd East ☎809 538 0079, ⓦvillalaplantacion.com. Sizeable and contemporary en-suite rooms attached to a modern house belonging to a friendly French couple. Rooms are set around a lovely garden with a circular pool and hot tub, very close to the beach. US$55

La Rancheta 2.5–3km east of Las Galeras from the crossroads near the beach ☎829 939 8285, ⓦlarancheta.com. Karin and Ron, the multilingual owners, offer a range of fairly rudimentary budget accommodation suitable for backpackers. The *La Rancheta Guesthouse*, set amid tropical gardens, has rooms with their own bathrooms, a basic kitchen and patio. *La Hacienda* is a kind of hostel set on a hill and has a mix of dorms and private rooms (fan-ventilated and each with private bath) – you can also camp on site in your own or rented tents. Alternatively there is a house and a cabin, both more upmarket and sleeping up to six, around 1km away, nearer the beach. Camping US$12, dorm US$14, private room US$35, house/cabin US$65

El Sol Azul Beach Rd East, one block inland from the beach ☎809 538 0001, ⓦelsolazul.com. Lovely B&B with four large, thatched-roof cabins arranged around a swimming pool and decorated with local flotsam – driftwood, shells, pieces of coral, etc. Generous breakfasts are served on your patio. US$65

Hotel Todo Blanco Facing the beach, 100m east of the main beach entrance ☎809 538 0201, ⓦhoteltodoblanco.com. Tasteful in the extreme and a genuine haven of tranquillity with huge airy rooms set in a pretty but enjoyably wild garden right on the beach. The hotel also boasts a superb and authentic Italian restaurant (open to non-guests) and gets discounted scuba-diving rates. US$90

★**Villa Serena** Beach Rd West ☎809 538 0000, ⓦvillaserena.com. Housed in an elegant faux-Victorian mansion with a large, manicured tropical garden, this place screams "honeymoon". Indeed, set right on the beach and facing a small deserted island, it's difficult to imagine a more idyllic location. All the rooms are exquisite, with great attention to detail, but try to reserve the one with the wraparound verandah facing the ocean. The restaurant, serving Caribbean cuisine based around locally caught seafood, is also one of the best in town (open to non-guests, but call first). US$120

3

3

EATING AND DRINKING

Options for **dining** in Las Galeras have increased as much as have places to stay. Most of the **hotels** can provide food, but if you want a change of scenery or menu, you'll find a mixed bag of eating options dotted along the main road, including lots of very affordable **comedores**. As far as **nightlife** goes, the village remains pretty quiet, although there are a couple of bars, pool halls and a disco (*Manuel's*, next to *La Marseillaise*).

C L'Aventura de John Calle Principal. A lively yet relaxed ambience pervades this casually sophisticated bar-restaurant that serves up excellent food. Tasty pizzas (RD$250–490), seafood mains (RD$390–590) or the house speciality – a huge seafood platter (RD$950). The bar area is a lively gathering spot for expats. Free wi-fi. Mon–Fri 4pm–1am, Sat & Sun 10am–3pm & 5pm–1am.

★ **El Cabito** 3km from Las Galeras ☎ 829 697 9506, ⓦ elcabito.net. You can't beat this cliff-top restaurant for magical sunsets, armchair whale-watching (in season) and superb food (RD$250 for pasta dishes; around RD$600 for fancier seafood mains), including weekly specials and vegetarian options. Pick-up from Las Galeras can be arranged. Fish or lobster dishes require advance reservation. Daily except Tues 11am–11pm.

End of the Road Calle Principal at the crossroads nearest the beach ☎ 829 797 9469. A good, easy place for a simple, inexpensive breakfast or lunch. The headliners are their generously filled burritos (RD$140–180) but you can't go wrong with the eggs and pancakes either. Daily 8am–9pm.

Gri Gri Calle Principal ☎ 809 705 2894. Right in the heart of the action in the hotel of the same name, *Gri Gri* dishes out some great Dominican fish and meat dishes with rice or pasta from around RD$350, with *sancocho* a weekend speciality. Located at the crossroads, it's a great people-watching spot. Daily except Sun 8am–10pm.

★ **Il Pirata** Plaza Lusitania. A lively outdoor patio pizzeria located in the Plaza Lusitania commercial complex, serving quite possibly the best thin-crust pizza outside Naples. It's one of the most sociable spots in the

evening, too, helped by the friendly proprietors. Daily except Tues 4–11pm.

La Marseillaise Calle Principal ☎ 829 461 1980. This low-key French bakery and patisserie is the ideal spot to grab a coffee and croissant for breakfast or stock up on baguettes for a picnic. Also sells burgers, salads, pasta and snacks. Daily 7am–2pm & 5–10pm.

★ **El Monte Azul** La Guázuma, 4km south of the village ☎ 849 249 3640 or ☎ 849 249 3641. The road up to this out-of-the-way hilltop restaurant is bumpy and steep but the rewards are tremendous. The 360-degree views are spectacular and the simplicity of the dining area – an open-air concrete platform under a thatched roof – is well judged given the ready-made, natural 'decor' all around. The eclectic, top-quality dishes feature French and Asian influences and include excellent steaks and a catch-of-the-day option. Daily 11am–10pm.

El Pescador Calle Principal, opposite the bank ☎ 829 502 7149, ⓦ restaurantpescador.com. Seafood paella is the house special at this patio restaurant but there are plenty of worthwhile fish and shellfish alternatives (from RD$420) and the wood-fired oven pizzas (RD$280–620) are very satisfying too. Daily except Tues 10am–8pm.

Restaurant Modesta Beach entrance. Not so much a restaurant but one of a number of shacks under a large thatched-roof hut run by a community association serving excellent, locally caught seafood dishes and cold beer. Prices can vary for tourists so check before eating, but expect to pay around RD$350 per head for fish with rice and plantains, and more for shrimp or lobster. Daily: usually 9am–9pm.

Cuevas de Agua and Boca del Diablo

Along the only road from Las Galeras to Samaná, an unmarked turning leads northeast to a series of prominent limestone caves, collectively known as **Cuevas de Agua**, which once served as homes for the local Ciguayo population. The tiny farms adjacent contain some of the most extensive archeological sites on the island – for a small fee, some of the residents will happily guide you round a selection of the petroglyphs and show you small Taino *cemi* sculptures that have been unearthed at the site.

The road continues for another 500m, ending at a high limestone cliff with more ocean views. Over millions of years, a blowhole – known locally as **Boca del Diablo** – has been gouged out of the cliff here, and the surf thunders up 50m, spraying anyone standing nearby. From here, a 2km footpath leads down to unforgettable **Playa Frontón** but most people arrive at this beach by boat (see p.136).

Playa Rincón

Tucked away from the rest of the peninsula on the upper prong of its easternmost end, **Playa Rincón** is one of the top Samaná beaches. More accessible than ever now that there is a good quality road all the way to the sand from the main road, this is not the hidden gem it once was but retains much of its appeal. Although rumours that a major **hotel chain** is set to start building on the beach have been doing the rounds for years, development has been kept mostly at bay save for a few low-key food shacks and restaurants.

Tucked away at the base of the **Bahía de Rincón** – which is buttressed on both sides by enormous capes – the beach has long been a favourite of wealthy Dominican city-dwellers who camp out here with their families for the night. Of all the warm, clear waters on the island, Rincón has the very finest – moderately deep with manageable waves and a bright turquoise transparency that can't be matched – combined with a 4km stretch of whiter-than-white sand and a sprawling coconut forest (see box below) behind it.

Both water-taxis and land vehicles approach the beach near its western end, which is bordered by high cliffs. From the road it's another 500m west to **Río Frío**, a freezing-cold river popular for washing off the salt at the end of the day. To the east, the beach stretches uninterrupted for another 3km.

ARRIVAL AND DEPARTURE

PLAYA RINCÓN

By car From the crossroads near the beach at Las Galeras it's a 5km drive along the main road towards Samaná, to a signposted turnoff heading west; the beach is about 12km from this turnoff. A local taxi from Las Galeras will set you back around RD$2000. There are no guaguas.

By boat There are always boats waiting to make the 4km trip along the coast from Las Galeras – ask around for the best price; around RD$1000 per person is the going rate.

ACCOMMODATION AND EATING

Rincón Ruby Eastern end of beach ☎ 829 380 7295. Generally considered the best of the bunch of local beach restaurants, serving fresh fish lunches, usually accompanied by rice and plantains – expect to pay around RD$350 per head. The owners also run a delightful hotel, a few minutes from the beach, with spacious, rustically decorated and furnished rooms. __US$75__

Playa Frontón

The beautiful, remote and unspoilt beach of **Playa Frontón**, whose long, thin strip of sand is buttressed along its length by imposing black cliffs and overhung with swaying palms, is the archetypal hidden paradise, surrounded by superb **coral reefs** and transparent turquoise waters. Arguably even more beautiful – and certainly more secluded – than Playa Rincón, it's definitely worth seeking out either on foot via the spectacular five-hour round trip through the bush and along the cliff-tops from east of Las Galeras, or by boat from the beach at Las Galeras itself for around RD$1000 per person (see p.136). There are no route maps for hiking and it's easy to get lost so you're better off hiring a guide or organizing a horseriding trip here (see box p.136); be sure to bring your own food and drink.

DEATH BY COCONUT

If you're in the vicinity of **coconut trees**, be careful where you park your car. All Dominican car rental agreements have a provision explicitly stating that insurance will not cover damage – usually shattered windshields or dented hoods – inflicted by a falling coconut. More seriously, an average of six people per year in the Dominican Republic **die** from being hit by one of the plummeting fruits. **Tropical storms** are the most frequent culprits; the high winds sometimes launch dozens of them through the air like cannon shot. Many of the larger resorts and hotels employ people with long poles to knock the fruits from their trees before they have a chance to fall.

Las Terrenas and around

Set on the peninsula's northern coast, **Las Terrenas** has grown over the past few decades from remote backwater to an expat-dominated resort town renowned for its buoyant nightlife and a strong French-speaking presence. A livelier, more crowded and more hectic place than the town of **Samaná**, it is now one of the country's tourist hotspots, especially since the arrival of the **international airport** at El Catey in 2006, and the new **highway** from Santo Domingo that has made Las Terrenas an easy weekend retreat for wealthy Dominicans from the capital. Getting there, whichever side you approach from, is an unbelievably scenic, twisting drive, whether along the cliff-edge road from the west or passing over the **Sierra de Samaná** from Samaná or Sánchez.

There are two distinct areas to the town: the **beachside** glitz and glamour of the hotels, bars and restaurants; and the inland **Dominican barrio**, which has been built up into a warren of rough dirt roads with dirt-cheap housing to accommodate the masses of workers needed to sustain the tourism. There is some resentment between the Dominican and foreign communities, centred on the well-founded perception that the expats are making all the money from the booming tourist business, which is busiest in summer (particularly July and August), when the town is swamped with Europeans. The larger hotels and resorts catch most of the traffic but there are enough **independent travellers** and backpackers to keep the smaller businesses busy, and everybody tends to come together later in the evening to crowd out the livelier bars and discos to the early hours.

The town makes a pleasant base camp (see box, p.142) from which to explore the northern part of the Samaná Peninsula, including the less developed beaches to the west, **Playa Bonita** and **Playa Cosón**, which hold at least as much appeal as the one in town, and **El Portillo** to the east – home to the principal package holiday hotel on the north coast. Aside from exploring these, a day-trip to the **El Limón waterfall** is highly recommended both for the journey there on horseback and the view of the fall itself.

Brief history

No village existed here at all until the 1940s, when Trujillo began, in a misguided effort to alleviate **urban poverty**, to forcibly move the lower classes from Santo Domingo to the countryside, in order that they fish and farm the land; thirty such families ended up in present-day Las Terrenas. Their quiet settlement was interrupted in the 1970s by an influx of **French expats** searching for a secluded patch of paradise; they were soon followed by waves of Swiss, Canadians, Germans and British. You are as likely to see men playing boules as dominoes while baguettes and croissants are as easy to come by as plates of rice and beans. In the bars and restaurants French satellite TV is as ubiquitous as Latin American *telenovelas*.

The town centre

In the bustling centre of the town, the three shopping complexes, **Plaza El Paseo**, **Plaza Taina** and **Casa Linda**, dominate the main intersection, with a number of souvenir

---

OLD AND NEW STREET NAMES

A few years ago the main streets in Las Terrenas were given **official names** for the first time, though you may see or hear them still referred to by their old, adopted names.

Old name	New name
Calle del Carmen	Avenida Nuestra Señora del Carmen (or just Carmen)
Calle de la Playa	Avenida Francisco Caamaño Deno
Calle Portillo	Avenida 27 de Febrero
Calle Principal	Avenida Juan Pablo Duarte (or just Duarte)

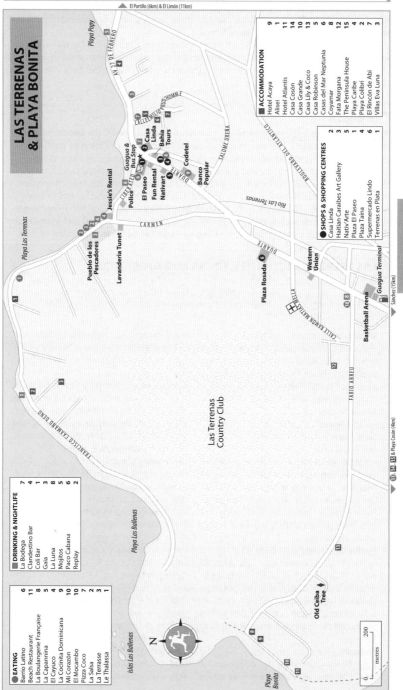

LAS TERRENAS & PLAYA BONITA

■ **ACCOMMODATION**
Hotel Acaya	9
Alisei	1
Hotel Atlantis	11
Casa Cosón	14
Casa Grande	10
Casa Lily & Coco	13
Casa Robinson	5
Casas del Mar Neptunia	6
Coyamar	8
Fata Morgana	12
The Peninsula House	15
Playa Caribe	4
Playa Colibrí	2
El Rincón de Abi	7
Villas Eva Luna	3

● **SHOPS & SHOPPING CENTRES**
Casa Linda	2
Haitian Caraïbes Art Gallery	3
Nativ'Arte	5
Plaza El Paseo	4
Supermercado Lindo	6
Terrenas en Plata	1

■ **DRINKING & NIGHTLIFE**
La Bodega	7
Clandestino Bar	4
Coli Bar	1
Gaia	3
La Luna	8
Mojitos	5
Paco Cabana	6
Replay	2

● **EATING**
Barrio Latino	6
Beach Restaurant	11
La Boulangerie Française	8
La Capannina	5
El Cayuco	4
La Cocinita Dominicana	9
Mi Corazón	10
El Mocambo	10
Pizza Coco	7
La Salsa	2
La Terrasse	3
Le Thalassa	1

3

shops tucked away in their corners; Plaza El Paseo holds a French-dominated **food and craft fair** on Saturday mornings until noon.

Further south along Duarte, you'll enter the original Dominican **barrio**. There's much more local flavour to the streets here and the souvenir shops tend to be cheaper, but the heady cloud of exhaust fumes that fills the air can be a little stifling at times.

The beach

Aside from spectacular day-trips to the surrounding countryside, the **beach**, which extends uninterrupted 2km in either direction from town, is the focus of daytime entertainment. The stretch to the **east** of the main intersection is the older, more established core of the resort, and is lined with hotels, low-end cabañas and bars until the construction suddenly peters out entirely. Of late, the waters here have become increasingly populated by kitesurfers, windsurfers and surfers at the far end of town near **Playa Portillo**. The ocean at the **western beach** is calm and good for **swimming** – albeit rather thick with seaweed in places – and protected by a coral reef 100m out that provides decent **snorkelling**. It stretches to **Playa Las Ballenas** – a section of the

---

LAS TERRENAS ACTIVITIES, TOURS AND OPERATORS

If you get tired of lounging on the beach, there's no end to the number of ways in which you can fill your days more actively, from **hiking** and **quad-bike tours** to **fishing**, **horseriding** and **kitesurfing**. Some of the specialist operators listed below sub-contract out to other specialists, usually at no greater cost – but check around.

Arena Tours Plaza Linda, Duarte ☏ 809 968 5474, ⊛ arenatours-lasterrenas.com. Covering everything from trips to El Salto de Limón (US$29–45), a once-weekly trip to Parque Nacional Los Haitises (US$65), whale watching (US$70–80) and day-trips to Santiago (US$120) and Santo Domingo (US$120), this excellent operator has one of the most comprehensive and well-run set of excursions in Las Terrenas.

Flora Tours Duarte 278, opposite Plaza Taina ☏ 809 240 5482, ⊛ flora-tours.net. The very personable Nicolas offers a chance to get out into the countryside with a selection of half-day and full-day hikes from the moderate to the strenuous (15km). Comfortable in Spanish and French, he employs English-speaking guides too. Trips across the peninsula to go whale watching and visit Los Haitises can also be organized.

Indrina Quad Tours Duarte 237 ☏ 829 717 2621 & ☏ 829 348 7245, ⊛ indrinaquad.com. All-terrain half-day (US$60) and full-day (US$80–120) quad-bike excursions into the countryside to visit local coffee plantations, waterfalls and beaches further afield (such as Playa Rincón). The staff are mainly French-speaking and they also offer longer excursions and hire out quads for the day.

Profundo Blue Punta Popy, next to the Hotel Playa Caribe ☏ 829 349 1913, ⊛ profundoblue .com. With some two decades of experience running

local diving excursions and courses, this outfit comes with a well-established reputation. They offer the PADI Discover Scuba Diving course for US$70 and more in-depth courses.

Rancho Cedric between Playa Las Ballenas and Playa Las Terrenas ☏ 809 847 4849. A simple local operation offering all kinds of horseriding excursions as well as simple rides along the beach. Ride to Playa Bonita (RD$800), Playa Cosón (RD$2800) or on an overnight trip all the way to El Limón (RD$4000).

Las Terrenas Kitesurf Club Punta Popy, Calle 27 de Febrero ☏ 809 801 5671, ⊛ lasterrenas-kitesurf.com. This friendly and enthusiastic team can help you learn to kitesurf or simply rent you equipment. Their courses start at US$110 for a two-hour session while rental rates range from US$70 for a day to US$300 for a week. Kitesurfing is usually possible at Las Terrenas in all months except October and November.

Turtle Dive Center Plaza El Paseo, corner of Duarte and Libertad ☏ 829 903 0659, ⊛ turtledivecenter .com. Philippe, the boss here, and his crew are very experienced and professional divers, catering to beginners and veterans alike. All kinds of SSI-certified training courses are offered (US$65–520), while a single dive costs US$60 or for an additional US$15 certified divers can explore a shipwreck. Cave diving and snorkelling trips also offered.

beach named for three oblong islands in the waters that resemble breaching humpback whales. The western beach is the more up-and-coming area, with a livelier, funkier feel. Here, a cluster of what were once old fishing shacks have been transformed into the **Pueblo de los Pescadores** (see p.144), a parade of hip, colourful restaurants and bars lined up along the sand, the previous constructions now undetectable after a fire destroyed the place in 2012.

ARRIVAL AND DEPARTURE   LAS TERRENAS

BY BUS AND GUAGUA
For Santo Domingo, Santiago and Puerto Plata Transporte Las Terrenas (☎809 240 5302; Santo Domingo office ☎809 687 1470) runs reasonably comfortable, air-conditioned buses between Las Terrenas and Santo Domingo (5 daily; 3hr), Santiago (3 daily; 3hr) and Puerto Plata (1 daily; 3hr 30min). Buses leave from outside Plaza El Paseo.

For Sánchez and Nagua Guaguas for Sánchez (7am–6pm; 40min) arrive and depart frequently from the tiny terminal next to the basketball arena at the far end of Duarte, from where you can also catch a guagua to Nagua (7.15am & 2pm).

For Samaná Guaguas run to Samaná on a fixed timetable (hourly to every 1hr 30min), offering departures from the main road outside Plaza El Paseo (this is sometimes referred to as the cemetery stop but the cemetery in question is out of sight behind a high wall); it's sometimes quicker to jump in a guagua (often a pick-up) to the village of El Limón, which leave at

regular 15min intervals throughout the day, and change there. All guaguas will drop off at the main junction in town if requested.

BY CAR
If arriving from outside the peninsula, the most direct route is the breathtaking coastal toll road, the Boulevard del Atlántico which turns into the town's Calle Principal (also known as Av. Duarte), and runs all the way to the sea, where it connects with the beachfront strip. If you're driving from Samaná or Las Galeras it's an equally scenic drive over the Cordillera Samaná, entering the town on the coast road from the east.

BY PLANE
Las Terrenas is served by Aeropuerto Internacional El Catey (☎809 338 0147 or ☎809 338 5888) at the western extreme of the peninsula. It's a US$70-, 30km-cab ride to Las Terrenas. The smaller Aeropuerto El Portillo just to the east of Las Terrenas hasn't received flights since 2012.

GETTING AROUND AND INFORMATION

There are no guaguas to **Playa Bonita** or **Playa Cosón** (see p.147), so you'll either have to catch a *motoconcho*, a taxi, or look into hiring a quad bike.

By motoconcho *Motoconchos* are in plentiful supply. Rides within town are between RD$50 and RD$100 and to Playa Bonita between RD$100 and RD$150.

By private taxi Taking acronyms to new heights, the local taxi syndicate ASOCHOTRATUTENA (☎809 240 6391) has an office on the beach and fixed rates to Playa Bonita (US$15), Playa Cosón (US$30), El Limón (US$30) and everywhere else on the peninsula and beyond.

By quad bike or car Quad bikes (ATVs), a common sight in Las Terrenas, are available from at least half a dozen agencies in town, many of which also rent cars. There's plenty of choice, so it's worth shopping around: two good bets are Indianapolis (☎829 539 5401 or ☎829 539 5402, ✉indianapolisrentacar@hotmail.com) and Fun Rental on

Carmen near the corner of Libertad (☎809 713 6666 or ☎849 350 9839, ✉funrental@hotmail.com). Quads cost from around US$50 and cars US$60 per day.

Tourist information Tourist information is available from the well-established Bahía Tours (☎809 979 1564, ⓦbahia-tours.com), though it's first and foremost a travel agent; it's located at the end of Duarte among the shops gathered around the Casa Linda commercial complex. They stock the very useful, free and annually updated *Info*, a guide to the Samaná Peninsula (also distributed to hotels), and arrange excursions to El Limón waterfall, whale watching in Samaná and trips to Los Haitises (see p.132). A good website for local info is ⓦlas-terrenas-live.com.

ACCOMMODATION

Las Terrenas is heaving with places to stay. With so much competition, **prices** have remained relatively low, although real rock-bottom bargains are scarce. Still, while there has inevitably been some inflation, with several hotels now pitching squarely for the luxury market, Las Terrenas remains a good deal cheaper than most other Caribbean destinations. It's best to make **reservations** before you arrive – the cheaper places in particular get booked up quickly. If it's peace and quiet you're after, **Playa Bonita** (see p.147) is your best bet.

Alisei Francisco Caamaño Deno ☎ 809 240 5555, ⓦ aliseihotel.com. One of the town's top-end modern hotels, boasting 54 luxury apartments (both one- and two-bedroom), nicely styled grounds, a large pool and fairly pricey restaurant/bar, plus a whole host of activities. The fact that it's on the same stretch of public beach as the rest of the hotels does, however, make it feel a bit overpriced. Breakfast included. US$134

Casa Lily & Coco On the road to Playa Bonita ☎ 809 240 5423, ⓦ casalilyecoco.com. Three nicely furnished and fully equipped studios (for one–two people) and two one-bedroom apartments (for two–four people). The larger upstairs units have delightful private patios looking out over lush countryside. Owned by a charming Dominican-Italian couple. No breakfasts. Free transfers to town or Playa Bonita. Studio US$45, apartment US$65

Casa Robinson Av. 27 Febrero ☎ 809 240 6496, ⓦ casarobinson.it. This Italian-owned affair has a collection of clean, cheerfully decorated rooms, studios and apartments (with kitchens, sleeping up to four) dotted about a shady and quiet garden. Room US$42, studio US$46, apartment US$53

★**Casas del Mar Neptunia** Emilio Prud'Homme ☎ 809 240 6884, ⓦ casadelmarneptunia.com. The nicest of this quiet side road's inexpensive accommodation, comprising ten spacious bungalows with private patios (though offering little privacy) decked out with brightly painted furniture and set amid a lovely lush garden. Bungalows have ceiling fans, fridges and hot water. Free wi-fi, with breakfast included. RD$2000/US$50

Fata Morgana Off the dirt road to Playa Bonita near the Escuela Francesa ☎ 809 836 5541, ⓦ fatamorganalasterrenas.com. Six simple but nice budget cabins (fan, mosquito screens and cold water) with a shared, fully functional kitchen, barbecue and book exchange, set in the garden of a house in a quiet

residential area, some way from the beach and centre. Internet access available. One of the cheapest deals in town and ideal for backpackers or long-term stays. US$24

Playa Caribe Av. 27 de Febrero, near Punta Popy ☎ 809 240 6661, ⓦ hotelplayacaribe.com. Just over the road from the beach this is great value given the location – rooms are comfortable and clean and the atmosphere is very laidback. There's a small on-site restaurant and a bar right on the beach. US$50

Playa Colibrí Francisco Caamaño Deno 31 ☎ 809 240 6434, ⓦ hotelplayacolibri.com. A good family choice offering spacious self-catering apartments (the largest sleep up to five, not including children) in a series of three-storey blocks laid out in a horseshoe around a central pool and tropical garden. Large rooms with full kitchens, cable TV and good-sized private balconies plus a decent stretch of beach across the road. Guarded parking at rear. A significant price hike at Christmas and Easter. US$89

El Rincón de Abi Emilio Prud'Homme ☎ 809 240 6639, ⓦ el-rincon-de-abi.com. A simple, clean and affordable B&B in the heart of the village, around 200m from the beach. Rooms are quite plain, whitewashed-stone affairs, but fairly large for the price and there's a small pool and bar. The French owners can arrange excursions including horseriding and jeep safaris. RD$1500

Villas Eva Luna Marico, off Francisco Caamaño Deno ☎ 809 978 5611, ⓦ villa-evaluna.com. The perfect couple's getaway, this is a haven of peace and quiet set back 300m from the western beach, away from the scooter and quad-bike bustle of central Las Terrenas. It boasts five stylish, Mexican-style villas that sleep two or four, with private terraces, kitchens and king-size beds, set around a small central pool and garden. Yoga, massage and aqua-gym are also on offer. Breakfast is included but it's still on the expensive side. US$130

EATING

Thanks to the large expat community, Las Terrenas has an excellent variety of **restaurants** – the majority lined up along the coastal road – from Spanish tapas, pizza and other Italian dishes, to gourmet French cuisine. Some of the best and most romantic are huddled together in the **Pueblo de los Pescadores** (ⓦ pueblo-de-los-pescadores.com) – the old fishermen's village – consisting of a row of refurbished beach shacks west of the main intersection, which are also the top spots for sunset drinking; just don't expect a quaint, rustic place as the refurbishment following a fire has created some pretty slick establishments. To escape the tourist scene, wander around the **Dominican barrio**, where you'll also find cheap *comida típica*.

Barrio Latino Libertad ☎ 809 240 6367. Simple, bustling café in the heart of the village with a large menu that takes in sandwiches, salads, burgers, pizzas and ice cream, but best of all are the breakfasts. Good for people watching, too. Mon–Sat 8am–9.30pm, Sun 8am–4pm.

La Boulangerie Française Plaza Taina ☎ 809 240 6751. This French café and bakery is just the place for a

continental breakfast – dunk your croissants in your *café au lait* like the expat regulars. Alternatively, stock up on some goodies for a beach picnic. Mon–Sat 7am–7.30pm, Sun 7am–7pm.

La Capannina Av. 27 Febrero 23 ☎ 809 886 2122. Decent Italian set under a thatched roof with a beach view, albeit across the road. Offers over twenty types of pizza (from RD$300) including a delicious special with salmon, bacon, caviar and rocket topping, as well as a few fancier offerings such as lobster and octopus. Daily noon–3pm & 6.30–11pm.

El Cayuco Pueblo de los Pescadores ☎809 240 6885, ⓦelcayucolasterrenas.com. Serves a bevy of good seafood dishes (US$390–750) including grilled langoustines and octopus carpaccio. Also a pretty hopping nightspot. Tues–Sun 11am–1pm.

La Cocinita Dominicana Duarte, next to the large branch of Banco Popular ☎829 433 8645. Dominican home cooking made with fresh ingredients and served on a pleasant terrace on the main road through town. You can eat good quality seafood and national meat-based dishes at considerably cheaper prices than you'll pay at most of the beachfront restaurants. If they're busy expect to wait a long time for your order. Daily until 11.30pm.

★**Mi Corazón** Duarte 7, at the corner with the Playa Bonita road ☎809 240 5329, ⓦmicorazon.com. This Swiss-owned establishment is undoubtedly the town's most elegant restaurant, set in a beautifully illuminated, colonial-style courtyard with an intimate bar area located on the balcony above. The menu changes frequently but expect creative dishes such as lemongrass soup with ginger and crab meat (starters from RD$500) or fish fillet in thyme and olive sauce (mains from RD$700). There's also a changing five-course set menu for RD$2150. May–Oct Tues–Sat from 7pm; Nov–April Tues–Sun from 7pm.

El Mocambo Duarte at the corner with the Playa Bonita road ☎809 240 5329. If dining at *Mi Corazón* is beyond your budget, enjoy the superb and surprisingly cheap pâtisserie of the restaurant's Parisian pastry chef in this sophisticated tearoom. The cakes and pastries will slip down at RD$150 while macaroons are just RD$40 – avoid

this place if you're on a diet. Daily 7.30am–7pm.

Pizza Coco Av. 27 Febrero ☎809 240 5250 or ☎809 499 6076. Reasonably priced pizzeria (RD$170–410 plus tax) with around forty different top-quality options. The candlelit outdoor seating area is better suited to groups than romantic couples – the kind of place you can pop into without any ceremony. Daily noon–midnight.

La Salsa Pueblo de los Pescadores ☎809 240 6805. Expensive but worthwhile seafood restaurant located at the western end of the refurbished row of old fishing shacks that cleverly incorporates half a dozen palm trees into the building architecture. Try the fish-of-the-day *ceviche* (RD$170) or the *cazoleta del pescador*, a kind of seafood hotpot (RD$490). Daily noon–3.30pm & 7–11pm; sometimes closed Sun.

La Terrasse Pueblo de los Pescadores ☎809 240 6730, ⓦlaterraserestaurante.com. The smartest restaurant in the old fishermen's village, this French affair offers a handsome dining space – linen tablecloths, ginger lilies in vases, waitresses in long white skirts – and top-notch, pricey cooking. Booking recommended. Daily noon–3.30pm & 7–11pm.

★**Le Thalassa** Francisco Caamaño Deno just before the Alisei hotel ☎809 902 6883 or ☎809 886 4161. Excellent French restaurant for fine dining at more affordable rates than others in town, drawing in tourists and expats alike. As the name suggests (Thalassa being a personification of the sea in Greek mythology), the restaurant specializes in seafood, and the seafaring theme informs the decor too, not least the porthole into the kitchen. Count on around RD$500 for mains such as *flambé* shrimp in pastis, and leave room for dessert – the mango and passion fruit crumble (RD$250) is exquisite. Tues–Sun 11am–3pm & 5.30–11pm.

DRINKING AND NIGHTLIFE

Las Terrenas has enough going on at night to keep the large numbers of independent travellers occupied through the early hours. The focal point is the **Pueblo de los Pescadores**, where there are several venues, and the action emanates out from here along Carmen and Libertad over to the collection of roadside bars and *La Bodega* at the main junction in town. The **dancehalls** typically don't get busy until late in the evening and the sex trade is relatively prominent in the **discos**, where you can expect to pay a cover. A memorable **night market** takes place from Friday to Sunday in the Dominican sea barrio directly south of the front and centred particularly on Carmen – locals sell food and booze from stalls and hang out along the road and play drums. The **Dominican barrio** also has several small shacks where locals hang out drinking rum but almost all the bona fide bars are aimed at the tourist market. Many of the **seafront restaurants** have bar counters and make good places for a drink too.

La Bodega Casa Linda, northern end of Duarte ☎809 787 1178. One of the biggest dancefloors in Las Terrenas hosts some of the rowdiest nightly parties – there is always plenty of action here, though things don't get going until after 11pm. There's no cover charge and the music is usually merengue, bachata and other Latin styles, making it popular with locals. It's a lot of fun but a shameless pick-up joint too. Daily 9pm–4am.

Clandestino Bar Pueblo de los Pescadores ☎809 703 2114. Tiny, casual, feel-good bar squeezed between restaurants with a mix of pop, funk and soul – enjoy the music from the casual beachfront seating, in the dinky upstairs lounge or on any improvised dancefloor that you can squeeze out of the tight space here. Daily 7pm–2am.

Coli Bar Playa Las Ballenas opposite Hotel Playa Colibrí ☎809 240 6434. This tiny beach bar, run for the benefit of

3

the clients at the hotel across the road but open to everyone, offers cocktails, beer and fresh fruit juices, right on the sand, often served to the sound of music, and can attract quite a crowd sometimes, especially at sunset. Daily 8am–7pm.

Gaia Pueblo de los Pescadores, opposite the refurbished fishing huts ☎ 809 914 1023. The town's hottest, slickest spot, a three-storey Miami-style nightclub with plenty of glitz. The ground floor plays mainly merengue and bachata; the first-floor techno and house; the open-air top deck more chilled lounge music. Expect wild weekends, with international DJs, dancing girls, fire-eaters and all-night-long action. Daily 7pm–5am.

★**La Luna** Mi Corazón building, Duarte 7 ☎ 809 240 5329. On the top floor of the vaulted building housing the most stylish restaurant in town is this comfy, chic lounge bar, one of most relaxing spots in Las Terrenas for a drink away from the beachfront. No local flavour but great if you just want to chat and chill and don't mind paying above average prices. Daily except Mon from 7pm; May–Oct also closed Sun.

★**Mojitos** Calle 27 de Febrero, Punta Popy ☎ 809 284 0337. Perched at the ocean edge on a beachfront verandah shaded by trees, this is as good as anywhere for sunset drinking when the serenity of the atmosphere and the view of the horizon are in perfect synch. There's a good cocktail menu and various versions of the eponymous Cuban classic. Simple and spot on. Daily 9am–10pm.

Paco Cabana Libertad, opposite Plaza El Paseo ☎ 809 240 5301. This luxury open-air beach bar and restaurant has loungers where you can relax with a cocktail watching the sunset as the oh-so-fashionable music wafts out from within. Not quite so glam in high season, when sweaty hordes turn up to dance on the sandy dancefloor. Wi-fi zone. Tues–Sun 10am–midnight.

Replay Pueblo de los Pescadores ☎ 829 717 1293. Cooler, clubbier and less casual than Clandestino, the other bar in the fisherman's village, the moody blue lighting and sleek decor are more appropriate later on, when the restaurants close and the place fills up with ravers – but it's too in-your-face for a sundowner. Daily 9pm–2am.

SHOPPING

There are four principal commercial plazas in town: three – **Plaza El Paseo**, **Casa Linda** and **Plaza Taína** – are huddled around the main intersection where Duarte meets Libertad while the other – **Beach Garden Plaza** – lies on Libertad near the corner of Carmen. All are very tourist-focused.

ART AND JEWELLERY

Haitian Caraibes Art Gallery Plaza Taína ☎ 809 240 6250. Offers one of the best selections of Haitian Naivist art and folk crafts outside of the capital. Mon–Sat 9am–1pm & 4–7.45pm.

Nativ'Arte Duarte 270 ☎ 829 262 3406. Selling a mix of Haitian and Dominican handmade arts and crafts, most of it commissioned specifically for this shop, there are all sorts of bits and pieces here, from imitation Taino sculptures, sarongs, candles and amber and larimar jewellery. Mon–Sat 9am–7pm, Sun 9am–noon.

Terrenas en Plata Plaza El Paseo ☎ 809 240 5359. The

best selection of jewellery in town, specializing in larimar and amber, with plenty of refreshingly original pieces displayed in their spacious, attractive shop, but steer clear of the endangered black coral pieces. Mon–Sat 9.30am–1pm & 3.30–8pm, Sun 10am–1pm.

FOOD

Supermercado Lindo Plaza Rosada, Duarte ☎ 809 240 6003. The largest and best stocked of the town's supermarkets with deli counters full of fresh meat, a reasonable choice of cheeses and a wide selection of wines. Mon–Sat 8.30am–1pm & 3–8pm, Sun 9am–1pm.

DIRECTORY

Banks and ATMs Banco Progreso in Plaza El Paseo and Banco Popular on Duarte between Av. 27 de Febrero and Salomé Ureña both have ATMs.

Exchange Fort Knox in Plaza El Paseo (Mon–Sat 8am–1pm & 4–8pm) gives competitive exchange rates and rents safe boxes.

Hospitals Las Terrenas Hospital is at 40 Ramón Matias Mella (☎ 809 240 6474 & ☎ 809 240 6725) while the Centro Galego Integral medical centre at 242 Duarte (☎ 809 240 6817) offers 24hr emergency attention.

Internet Mailboxes Etc at Plaza Rosada on Duarte and

Punto Clic in Plaza El Paseo provide reasonably fast access for RD$30 for 30min.

Laundry Lavanderia Las Terrenas (Mon–Fri 8am–7pm, Sat 8am–4pm, Sun 8am–noon; ☎ 809 240 5500) is between Flora Tours and Indrina Quad rentals on Duarte.

Mobile phones Claro on Duarte (Mon–Sat 8am–7pm) is located about 200m south of the main junction, where Duarte meets Av. 27 de Febrero.

Pharmacies The Farmacia Europea (Mon–Fri 8am–9pm, Sat 8am–noon & 1–7.30pm, Sun 8am–noon; ☎ 809 660 9037) on Duarte near the junction with Carmen is the largest and best stocked in town.

Police Ring ☎ 809 240 6022 or for the Tourist Police ring ☎ 809 240 6595.

Post office Head for the Casa de la Prensa (Mon–Sat

9am–7.30pm, Sun 9am–1pm) in Plaza El Paseo, which sells stamps, has a post box and also sells English-language newspapers and magazines.

Playa Bonita and around

Playa Bonita, 3km of uninterrupted beach that begins just west of Playa Las Ballenas in Las Terrenas, is a picturesque and tranquil strip of sand, backed by trimmed grass dotted with palm trees and an offshore reef that provides some of the best **snorkelling** on the peninsula. It's seen a fair bit of development over the past few years, but most of it has, thankfully, been discreet and tasteful – new hotels are set well back from the seafront, increasing the number of places to stay and eat without detracting too much from the unspoilt character. Stay the night and the sunset will leave you reeling, as will the canopy of stars.

Things are slightly less idyllic just inland where the **Las Terrenas Country Club** (ⓦlasterrenascountryclub.com), a golf club with adjoining luxury condominiums, has been built over the past few years in stop-start fashion as funding has ebbed and flowed. Just south of the golf club and standing in stark contrast to all the newly manufactured greenery, is a **thousand-year-old ceiba tree** (also known as a silk cotton tree), one of the largest and oldest documented trees on the island and an impressive gnarled giant.

Two kilometres around the headland from Playa Bonita, **Playa Cosón** is home to a small fishing community and an even more deserted 5km stretch of soft sand. However, development has begun to encroach even here, predominantly in the form of residential projects, many of which have stalled due to cash-flow difficulties. From Cosón the splendid beach continues west, uninterrupted for another 7km with no human outposts to speak of, before running smack into the **Cordillera Samaná**.

ARRIVAL AND INFORMATION   PLAYA BONITA AND AROUND

Entry to **Playa Bonita** begins at the *Coyamar* hotel, where a **paved brick path** provides access for motorbikes past the front of the hotels and along a progressively empty beach (where people sometimes take advantage of the isolation to swim or sunbathe nude). The beach track ends at *Hotel Atlantis*, though it is possible to **walk and scramble** 2km around the headland on an intermittent and indistinct path to **Playa Cosón**.

By car or quad bike From Las Terrenas seafront head south along Duarte pretty much to the end of the town where, just past the gas station, the right-hand turn at the crossroads takes you onto the Boulevard del Atlántico – from here it's 1km to the right-hand turnoff to Playa Bonita

and another 4km to the side road to Playa Cosón.
By taxi or motoconcho From the heart of Las Terrenas a taxi to Playa Bonita is US$15 and a *motoconcho* around RD$150; to Playa Cosón it's US$30 for a taxi and around RD$250 for a *motoconcho*.

ACCOMMODATION

There are several prime places to **stay** on Playa Bonita, most pretty good value given their scenic location. Each has a decent **restaurant** attached and if you're looking for natural beauty, peace and quiet, you're far better off staying here than in Las Terrenas.

PLAYA BONITA

★**Hotel Acaya** ☎809 240 6161, ⓦwww .acaya-hotel-fr.com. The most elegant hotel on the strip offers spacious tiled rooms, simply but tastefully furnished in wood and bamboo, with louvred doors and windows and an unpolished, less-than-perfect finish that distinguishes it from a more generic, chain-hotel experience. Each room has its own terrace or balcony; go

for those on the second floor, which are cooler and have better views. It also boasts a fabulous thatched lounge-restaurant in the garden with sea views and delicious food (mains RD$350–700). The Pura Vida surf school is also based here. Breakfast included. **US$90**
Hotel Atlantis ☎809 240 6111, ⓦatlantis-hotel .com.do. A whimsical, gleaming-white hotel, whose pretty rooms are palatial (the more expensive ones at

least), though one or two need a little touching up in places. Try to book either the "Jamaica" or the "El Paso" room, both of which offer panoramic views of the beach. Dining here is a must since the owner was the one-time chef of former French President François Mitterrand – at the very least try breakfast, as it's included in the price. **US$105**

Casa Grande ☎ 809 240 6349, ⓦ casagrandebeach hotel.com. This excellent-value hotel has ten fairly plain but good-size rooms in a large, handsome house set behind an expansive lawn. Together with the *Atlantis*, it serves the best food on Playa Bonita, with gourmet French meals in an elegant restaurant at the front. **US$99**

Coyamar ☎ 809 240 5130, ⓦ coyamar.com. Ten colourful, warmly decorated rooms with no frills (hot water but fans only), spread across two residential buildings, each with private balcony or terrace facing the beach and use of the small pool set back from the waterfront amid cheerful tropical gardens. The casual bar-restaurant serves a mix of moderately priced *criolla* and international dishes.

Breakfast included and room rates more negotiable than at many other places, especially for longer stays. **US$75**

PLAYA COSÓN

★**Casa Cosón** ☎ 809 853 8470, ⓦ casacoson.com. A gorgeous hotel comprising four rooms with sea view, two garden suites and three exquisitely and distinctively crafted villas with a large lawn stretching down to even vaster expanses of beach. Breakfast is included and dinner is a changing US$45 set menu (US$25 for under 12s). **US$150**

★**The Peninsula House** ☎ 809 962 7447, ⓦ thepeninsulahouse.com. In a class and price of its own, this Victorian-style mock plantation house is a regular in "best hotels in the world" lists – and it doesn't disappoint. The house is chock-full of antiques, original art and period furniture, with a billiard room, library, and a glorious swimming pool overlooking the grounds and the ocean. Guests in the handful of sumptuously decorated suites are thoroughly pampered by an army of staff dressed in white linen. During the day, you can decamp to the hotel beach house and matching, colonial-style *Beach Restaurant* (see below). Adults only. **US$580**

EATING

A number of the hotels at Playa Bonita, including those listed above, have beachfront **restaurants** open to non-guests and there are a handful of informal **beach shacks** on the sand, serving grilled, fresh-caught fish for a few pesos.

★**Beach Restaurant** Playa Cosón ☎ 809 962 7447. Enjoy refined yet relaxed dining at this superb plantation-style restaurant, which belongs to the luxurious *Peninsula House* hotel. Sheltered amid coconut palms, it offers a changing, creative menu of seafood-dominated dishes – just make sure you leave room for the exquisite desserts or home-made ice cream. Then enjoy a well-earned siesta in the hammock. Lunch only, closed Mon.

El Salto de Limón

The dusty village of **EL LIMÓN** – some 14km southeast of Las Terrenas – has limited appeal by itself, dominated as it is by a road junction and fading quickly into the surrounding woodlands, but it makes an ideal base for excursions to the magnificent waterfall **El Salto de Limón** 2km to the south. Buried in the forest and over 40m in height the waterfall is one of the most captivating natural sights on the peninsula and seeking it out is a great excuse to delve into the beautiful mountainous interior. Numerous operators, many of them based in Las Terrenas (see p.142), others more local, offer **horseback tours** to the falls. The path there from El Limón cuts across a broad **river** before climbing into the palm-thick **mountains**; as the waterfall comes into sight, the horses are tethered at a small waystation where you can have a drink before making the steep descent to the fall. The walk is well worth the effort to see the torrent of whitewater that drops precipitously off a sheer cliff in the middle of the wilderness, forming a **natural pool** at its base, where you can swim. You need to be in decent shape and well shod, especially after a lot of rain, when the boggy route can be treacherous. You'll also need to wear long trousers for the ride.

Within striking distance of El Limón are sibling beaches **Playa Limón** and **Playa Morón**. *Santi Rancho* (see box opposite) leads horseriding excursions to them, but it's also possible to walk from the village, setting off on the small path just east of the main crossroads. Playa Limón comes first, a beautiful, abandoned stretch of sand; then it's another 1km east along the shore to Playa Morón, which is even better – surrounded

EL SALTO DE LIMÓN TOURS AND OPERATORS

Upon arrival in Limón you'll be beset by several local *buscones* trying to steer you to one of the excursion outfits. Since several **scams** and various sub-standard operators exist, it's extremely important that you only sign up to go with a member of the local **ecotourism association** and it's best to book in advance. They all run *paradas* – small roadside restaurant-cum-tour offices, dotted among several hamlets in the locality, that act as base camps from where hikes and rides to the waterfall begin.

ESSENTIALS

Ecotourism association The local community-based ecotourism association, ACESAL (Asociación Comunitaria de Ecoturismo Salto El Limón; ☎ 809 360 9147) administers the dozen legitimate operators in the area and can provide advice on where the *paradas* are located – though you should be able to find most of them dotted along the Samaná–El Limón road, approaching the village from the south. Note that tour quality and the rates charged do vary among the providers, as does what is included.

Price and tipping Whether you come on a tour bus, or as an independent traveller, you should establish beforehand whether the price covers: transport to the *parada* (in the case of an organized tour); the park entry fee (RD$50); drinks and/or a meal; and the guide, who walks alongside you, describing the surrounding countryside, probably in Spanish. Many of the tour operators sub-contract the guides, who are local, self-employed men, making the question of who's paying who a little confusing. If the guide's tip is not included, find out from the operator (before you sign up) what the norm is. As a general rule you should aim to tip around US$10 but what a guide is and isn't happy with very much depends on the individual, and reports of guides expecting and in some cases demanding a minimum of US$20 are not uncommon.

RECOMMENDED OPERATORS

Parada La Manzana Arroyo Surdido, 4km south of El Limón ☎ 809 916 0892 or ☎ 829 931 6964, ✉ antoniadelanuez@yahoo.es. Highly recommended outfit, run by Antonia and Martín who, in addition to organizing a good trip, also prepare an excellent traditional lunch. RD$550 plus RD$50 for park entry fee.

Parada Ramona and Basilio El Café, 1km south of El Limón ☎ 809 956 5526 ✉ paradabasilioyramona @yahoo.es. The trail from this well-run *parada* to the waterfall is one of the longest and begins in the little hamlet of El Café where you can learn about their home-grown cocoa. RD$600 plus RD$50 for park entry fee.

Santi Rancho Just south of the intersection on the road to Samaná, ☎ 829 342 9976, ⓦ cascadalimonsamana.com. The pick of the bunch, and so preferred by a lot of the larger tour operators, is the combined ranch-restaurant *Santi Rancho* (see below). Their waterfall trip currently costs RD$750 per person, which includes the horse, guide and park fee; they also offer canyoning down Río El Limón.

---

by rocks, there's a large mountain cave on its eastern end into which the waves crash (safe to clamber around in at low tide).

ARRIVAL AND DEPARTURE   EL SALTO DE LIMÓN

To El Limón Getting to El Limón is fairly easy: during daylight hours, guaguas, usually pick-up trucks, shuttle between Las Terrenas and El Limón, and El Limón and Samaná (every 15min or so; both 45min; RD$60).

To the waterfall The waterfall is accessible by horse with any of the operators listed (see box above), as well

as several outfits in Las Terrenas (see box, p.142) and Samaná (see box, p.130) and takes roughly three hours as a round-trip from El Limón. You can also walk it but that's only advisable when it's very dry. If you want to avoid the tour-bus crowds, arrange an early morning or late afternoon visit.

ACCOMMODATION AND EATING

Santi Rancho Just south of the intersection on the road to Samaná ☎ 829 342 9976, ⓦ cascadalimonsamana.com. Four simple but clean cabins, with fan and mosquito net. Lunch at their restaurant (RD$300–500) is excellent quality – though

prices have risen as its popularity has increased – and offers greater variety than at most places, with goat, guinea fowl, fish in coconut milk and octopus featuring on the menu as well as the ubiquitous chicken, rice, beans and plantain. <u>RD$700</u>

3

West of the Samaná Peninsula

Just **west of the Samaná Peninsula**, the coast holds a series of excellent beaches, most of them surprisingly untouched by tourism. Here the road skirts the coast just a few metres from the sea in places, surrounded by forests of palm trees. There are two sizeable towns at either end of this strip, **Nagua** and **Cabrera**, the latter a focus of French Canadian tourism and the more diverting destination: just south of town are a waterfall, an eerie twilight meeting spot for thousands of egrets and a working coffee farm. Between the two, consider stopping at **Playa La Entrada**, a little-used strand of beach with the ruins of an abandoned village on its far end, and **Playa Diamante**, a turquoise inlet with views of the pounding surf just beyond its sheltering coral reef. More intriguing still is **Lago Dudú**, actually two freshwater lagoons favoured by divers, that makes for a popular local swimming spot.

Nagua

Below sea level and often stiflingly hot, **NAGUA** was once known as a bit of a political hotspot due to frequent labour strikes; it's peaceful enough these days although the workforce will never be slow to down tools if the need arises. Perhaps not surprisingly, few visitors stop in this industrial town, with its cement factory and federal penitentiary (the country's largest) providing a not-so-scenic backdrop. There's little to detain you in any case, the lone "sight" being the statue of **María Trinidad Sánchez** – who designed and sewed the first Dominican flag – in the Parque Central. The waterfront, north of the park, is fairly sedate, save for the annual **fiestas patronales** that take place January 14 to 21, in honour of the Virgin of Altagracia.

However, if you're travelling between any of the north-coast towns and the Samaná Peninsula, it's likely that you'll need to **change guaguas** here. An excellent road extends from Nagua inland to San Francisco de Macorís and the Cibao valley, quite scenic as it winds through the far end of the palm-covered Cordillera Septentrional, before plunging into some of the most verdant farmland in the world. Along the way you'll pass coffee, rice and cocoa **farms**, plus a number of small **pueblos** that see virtually no tourist traffic.

ARRIVAL AND DEPARTURE   NAGUA

By bus Caribe Tours is at Av. 27 de Febrero (☎ 809 584 4505). Destinations Río San Juan (6 daily; 1hr); Samaná (4 daily; 1hr); Sánchez (4 daily; 30min); Santo Domingo (10 daily; 3hr).

By guagua Guaguas leave from Parque María Trinidad Sánchez to San Francisco de Macorís (1hr 15min).

Playa La Entrada

Fifteen kilometres north of the Río Boba's mouth is **Playa La Entrada**, with a small, sparsely populated **town** of the same name perched at its northern end. From the entrance, at the corner of the C-5 and Calle Príncipe, roam 250m down to get to the picturesque mouth of the Río La Entrada. Just beyond you'll see a beautiful, **rocky island** in the water, though don't try to swim out to it – the water here is known for its rip-tides. From the mouth of the river, there's over 5km of sandy **beach** in each direction; indeed, the beach here continues eastward, uninterrupted, until Nagua. Walking the full length of the beach makes for a worthwhile but exhausting day.

El Dudú

1km north of La Entrada • Entrance RD$50 • Daily 9am–5pm

As you head north from Playa La Entrada, a sign on your left-hand side marks the entrance to **El Dudú**, two enchanting freshwater **lakes**, set in atmospheric **caves** with stalactites and lush overhanging foliage. When the sun is out the effect is truly magical; the brilliant, transparent blue water allows visibility of around 50m, making the place a major attraction for **divers**, who can explore the underwater tunnel that links the two caverns. The warm fish-filled spring water and Tarzan ropes that have been fixed up make it a popular place for swimming in at weekends.

Playa Diamante

North of Playa La Entrada, the rip-tide-laden waters are safe only for exceptionally strong swimmers until you reach **Playa Diamante**, 3km beyond La Entrada – you get to it via the dirt road off the C-5, which starts next to the *Diamante* restaurant. Expect a placid, blue beach cove sunk back from the ocean with a rock outcrop at its mouth. Several **hotel chains** are elbowing each other for permission to develop the site, but nothing has disturbed the surf yet.

Cabrera

CABRERA, 5km north of Playa Diamante, is the most visibly prosperous outpost along this part of the coastline – clean, uncongested and dotted with a number of attractive, pastel-coloured homes – but there's still very little to it. Its beach, **Playa Clara** at the north end of town, isn't bad, though it's no competition for playas Diamante or El Bretón, each within easy striking distance.

Better is the large **waterfall** just west of town, hidden off an unmarked dirt road across the C-5; the pool at its base is swimmable when the water level is high enough. Further into the mountains, a large tree, 3km west of the *La Catalina* hotel (see below) down a dirt road, serves as the nightly roosting site for thousands of **African egrets** that populate Dominican pastures. The birds arrive every night around 6pm without fail. Once the convocation is complete, the massive tree – identifiable by the enormous sheet of rock-hard guano that surrounds it – is abuzz with frenetic white motion and noise.

ARRIVAL AND DEPARTURE | CABRERA

By bus Caribe Tours runs through town and has an office at Lorenzo Alvarez 33, opposite the park (☎ 809 589 7212). Destinations Nagua (8 daily; 1hr 30min); Río San Juan (8 daily; 30min) San Francisco de Macorís (4 daily; 2hr 30min);

Santo Domingo (8 daily; 4hr).
By guagua Frequent guaguas to town along the north coast pass through Cabrera on Highway 5. You can flag them down anywhere en route.

ACCOMMODATION AND EATING

★**La Catalina** Head 3km west of Cabrera to a small pueblo, then south up a dirt road ☎ 809 589 7700, ⓦ lacatalina.com. A large country inn in lush, landscaped grounds perched atop a steep cliff that overlooks Cabrera and the sea. Choose from refined a/c hotel rooms or fan-ventilated one- or two-bedroom apartments. There are also two swimming pools and a terrace dining area, which serves excellent, pricey French cuisine (reservations necessary), though breakfast is included for hotel guests. Local tours, including horseriding or hiking excursions as well as golf or surfing can all be arranged. Double US$88, apartment US$118

The Silver Coast

MOUNT ISABEL DE TORRES CABLE CAR

The Silver Coast

The Dominican Republic's so-called Silver Coast, 300km of mostly prime waterfront property on the country's northern edge, hemmed in to the south by the Cordillera Septentrional mountain range, is one of the most popular tourist destinations in the Caribbean. With a seemingly unending supply of great beaches, such a designation is no surprise, though away from the heavy traffic of the resort towns – mostly around Puerto Plata and parts east – you may be surprised by the coast's unspoilt character and the diversity of its geography. The place has historical resonance as well, as the first shore that Columbus settled, though the Spanish colony later grew up around Santo Domingo on the island's south coast.

Columbus envisioned the area as a shipping point for vast deposits of **gold** that proved to be a product of his imagination; popular belief is that the sobriquet originated a few decades later when armadas bearing Mexican silver skirted the fortified shore to protect themselves from the pirates of the old **Cannibal Sea**. The word "cannibal" is a corruption of "Caribbean", after the Caribe Indians, who were reported practitioners of cannibalism. Indeed, sixteenth-century maps of the region invariably bore illustrations portraying natives roasting missionaries on spits.

A century after Columbus's "discovery", **Cuba** supplanted the north coast of the Dominican Republic as the favoured way station for Spanish booty plundered from Mexico and Peru. The region soon after began to rely on contraband trade with the very pirates it once fought, and the major settlements were razed to the ground by the Spanish Crown in 1605 as a punishment. The **Silver Coast**'s last four centuries have proceeded much as the first did, with periods of short-lived prosperity followed by long decades of subsistence. You'll see evidence of the occasional construction booms embedded in the major towns like geological strata.

Nowhere is this better seen than in **Puerto Plata**, a bustling, slightly down-at-heel city packed with atmospheric nineteenth-century architecture. Though it's an interesting place to explore, most visitors tend to bypass it entirely in favour of the calmer, more upmarket and more neatly manicured pleasures of **Playa Dorada** to the east, the largest all-inclusive resort complex in the world and home to a dizzying array of organized activities. Further east are more resort towns, linked by the coastal Carretera 5: chief among them are **Sosúa**, a former sex tourism centre that

Highlights

❶ Mount Isabela de Torres cable car, Puerto Plata There's no better way to view the north coast than from the summit of Mount Isabela de Torres – and no easier way to get there than on the Puerto Plata cable car. **See p.164**

❷ Río Damajagua waterfalls Climb, slide and swim your way past, through and over 27 waterfalls tumbling down a mountainous stretch of the Río Damajagua. **See p.166**

❸ Kiteboarding and windsurfing, Cabarete With warm water, near-perfect conditions and a huge choice of tuition and equipment, it's no wonder surfers and riders flock here from around the world. **See p.179**

❹ Blue Moon Retreat Exquisite Caribbean-Indian fusion food served on banana leaves in a tranquil mountain-top haven in the Cordillera Septentrional. **See p.183**

❺ Snorkelling near La Isabela Histórica Pristine coral, clear water and no crowds make this area off the north coast the best snorkelling spot on the island. **See p.190**

❻ Ecotourism in Río Limpio Tucked away in the mountains near the Haitian border, this beautiful and remote hamlet is a great place to experience *campesino* culture and embark on a trek to the little-visited Nalga de Maco national park. **See p.200**

HIGHLIGHTS ARE MARKED ON THE MAP ON PP.156–157

has – partly – cleaned up its image over recent years and features three separate beaches, plus an old Jewish quarter founded by World War II refugees; and **Cabarete**, the kiteboarding and windsurfing capital of the Americas, an internationally flavoured village erected over cattle pasture during the past twenty years. Even further east, things quieten down with no huge developments until you reach the Samaná Peninsula, although there are some interesting diversions along the way. The best of these is sleepy **Río San Juan**, a small town bordered by the thick mangrove swamps of **Laguna Gri-Gri** and a glorious 2km-long beach known as **Playa Grande**.

Some way west of Puerto Plata lie a series of remote pueblos where *campesinos* live in much the same way as they have for the last five centuries. Of interest here are **La Isabela Histórica**, the site of Columbus's first permanent settlement, which sits behind an immaculate bay with the best snorkelling on the island; the remote beaches **Playa Ensenada** and **Punta Rucia**, as beautiful as any on the island; and **Monte Cristi**, a remote, dusty border town flanked on both sides by a national park that protects a river delta, a collection of desert islands and a strip of cactus-laden mountain landscape.

South of Monte Cristi, most traffic heads for **Dajabón**, a trading post with an edgy frontier feel that comes alive twice a week with a bustling market. From there a magnificent road corkscrews up into the Cordillera affording stellar views across the border into Haiti and along the northern Dominican coastal plain, as well as the rural idyll of **Río Limpio**.

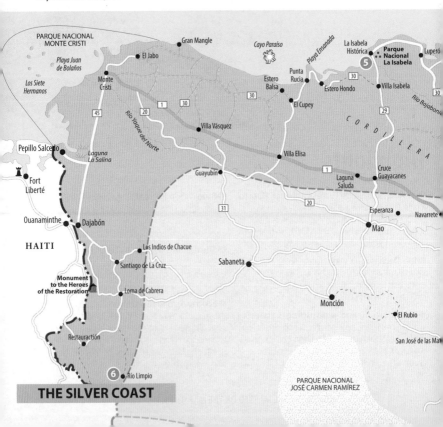

THE SILVER COAST

East of Puerto Plata The C-5 makes getting around easy, with plenty of guaguas and *públicos* shuttling between Puerto Plata and Río San Juan, with onward connections to the Samaná Peninsula. The country's major bus company, Caribe Tours, also links the region with the capital providing bus services from Santo Domingo to Sosúa via Puerto Plata and Santiago, while others link the capital to Río San Juan.

West of Puerto Plata Travelling west of Puerto Plata is more of a challenge (but not impossible) and only the most remote parts will need a 4WD. From the Carretera Puerto Plata (C-5), which heads south towards Santiago, you'll find a turnoff onto the C-30 just before Imbert. This road has turnoffs for the C-29 to Luperón and La Isabela and continues to Estero Hondo and Punta Rucia – rather rough roads for the most part, but slowly being paved. Beyond Punta Rucia are mule tracks; if you don't have an off-road vehicle, you'll have to head south to the Autopista Duarte (C-1), which stretches along the western Cibao valley, to reach Monte Cristi. From there, a surprisingly good tarred road sweeps up into the mountains as far as Restauración, 60km due south. After that, you'll need a 4WD as the road beyond is of variable quality and almost devoid of public transport.

Puerto Plata and around

PUERTO PLATA, the north coast's largest city, and its resort extension **PLAYA DORADA** are very different places. Playa Dorada is a walled-off holiday factory filled with immaculately tended all-inclusive resorts which between them host over half a million tourists a year. Puerto Plata, on the other hand, is a bustling, industrial city that often struggles to convince visitors of its merits. Indeed, the resort's success has contributed to the relative demise of Puerto Plata's own tourist industry, the city's tumbledown

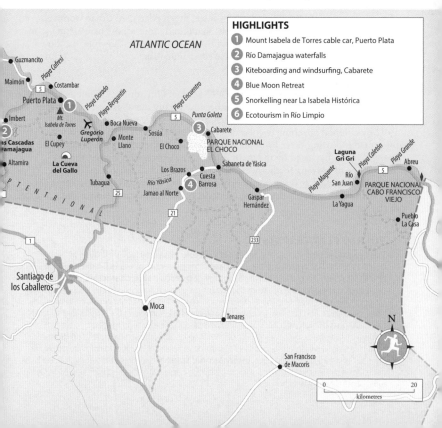

HIGHLIGHTS

1. Mount Isabela de Torres cable car, Puerto Plata
2. Río Damajagua waterfalls
3. Kiteboarding and windsurfing, Cabarete
4. Blue Moon Retreat
5. Snorkelling near La Isabela Histórica
6. Ecotourism in Río Limpio

ATLANTIC OCEAN

0   20
kilometres

streets and seedy bars struggling to compete with the all-inclusive hotels' air-conditioned charms. This loss of revenue has translated into a slight air of desperation, and your arrival is likely to attract the attention of touts trying (quite vehemently) to steer you in the direction of their services, be it a hotel, a guided tour or a visit to a cigar-making workshop. You'll need to be firm with your refusals.

There's much about Puerto Plata to enjoy, however – particularly its nightlife, with the city's famous **Malecón**, a 2km promenade bordering the Atlantic Ocean, best experienced on a weekend evening when its discos, outdoor bars and bonfire beach parties spring to life. Bordering the port is the urban core, the **Old City** (or **Zona Colonial**), a narrow grid of streets that was once the most stylish neighbourhood in the country. Highlights here include **Fortaleza San Felipe**, the only impressive vestige of colonial times in one of the oldest European settlements in the New World; the scores of often rather dilapidated Victorian **gingerbread mansions** that make an outdoor museum of the Old City; and the **Museo de Ámbar**, with its impressive display of prehistoric insects trapped in the translucent sap. Around the original town sprawls a patchwork maze of industrial zones and concrete barrios known as the **New City**, formed over the past century with the growth of the town's tobacco, sugar and rum industries. A little to the south lies the cable-car station for the ride to the summit of **Mount Isabela de Torres**, the flat-topped behemoth that lords over the city from the south.

Quieter than either the centre or Playa Dorada is the beach at **Costambar**, a peaceful but slightly insipid gated maze of townhouses and condos just a short *motoconcho* or taxi ride away from the Old City. A little further west you'll find the much livelier and pleasant-to-stay-in **Cofresí**, the site of the huge, much-advertised **Ocean World**, an aquamarine park home to dolphins, seals, sharks and more, whose new marina is one of the Caribbean's largest. Sited 15km southwest of the city, meanwhile, the **Río Damajagua waterfalls** offer an unmissable adrenaline rush.

Brief history

Sailing past the city's harbour on his 1492 voyage, **Christopher Columbus** gave it the name Puerto Plata de San Felipe – not because of any metallurgical associations, but because the waters had a silvery hue at sunset. The settlement established here in 1502 by colonial governor Nicolás de Ovando served for a time as a resupply point for armadas bearing silver from **Mexico** to **Spain**. As the sixteenth century wore on, though, it was bypassed by the main routes due to increasing piracy and the importance of Havana further west. It survived on illegal trade until the Spanish-controlled government in Santo Domingo destroyed all settlements along the north coast, forcibly deporting residents of Puerto Plata to **Monte Plata** just east of the capital.

PUERTO PLATA EXPATS

The worst questions you can ask an **expat** in Puerto Plata may include "Where are you from?" and "Why did you move here?" Milling among the tour operators, itinerant sailors, timeshare salesmen and retirees are a number of **questionable characters**, colourful in the extreme, many on the run from the law for tax evasion, insurance fraud and various other white-collar offences. The Caribbean adjuster for Lloyd's of London claims that at any given time you'll find some of Interpol's **most-wanted** wandering the streets, and a British crew filming a documentary on English expats said that every time they turned on the camera inside one popular watering hole, a half-dozen people ran for cover. The fugitives tend to attract a bewildering variety of law enforcement officials, including undercover FBI agents, Canadian Mounted Police, **international spies** and insurance detectives. It lends an eerie film-noir feel to the town, augmented by the narrow streets lined with slowly decaying nineteenth-century warehouses.

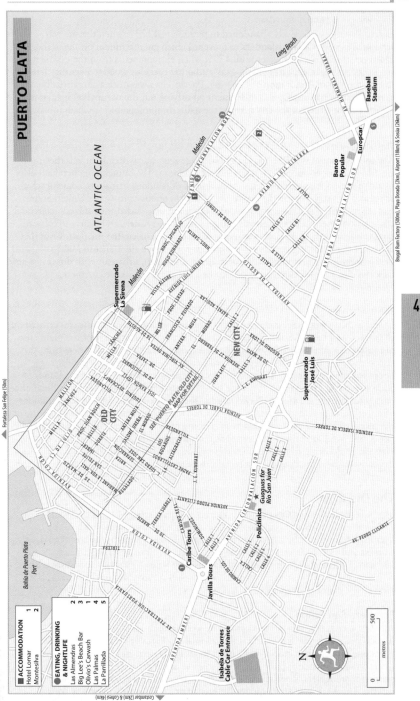

PUERTO PLATA

ATLANTIC OCEAN

Long Beach

Baseball Stadium

Malecón

Banco Popular

Europcar

Supermercado La Sirena

Malecón

NEW CITY

Supermercado José Luis

OLD CITY

SEE PUERTO PLATA: OLD CITY MAP FOR DETAIL

Guaguas for Río San Juan

Policlínica

Caribe Tours

Javilla Tours

Isabela de Torres Cable Car Entrance

Bahía de Puerto Plata Port

Fortaleza San Felipe (50m)

Costambar (2km) & Cofresi (4km)

Brugal Rum Factory (500m); Playa Dorada (2km); Airport (18km) & Sosúa (26km)

N

0   500
metres

■ ACCOMMODATION	
Hotel Lomar	1
Montesilva	2

● EATING, DRINKING & NIGHTLIFE	
Las Almendras	2
Big Lee's Beach Bar	3
Olivio's Carwash	1
Las Palmas	4
La Parrillada	5

4

Redevelopment and nationalism

Puerto Plata was effectively abandoned to pirates until 1737, when the site was repopulated with **Canary Islanders** to prevent French encroachment on the island. However, it stayed a backwater until 1751, when entrepreneurs from the capital rebuilt the port and began exporting mahogany and other precious woods. A century later during the **War of Restoration** of 1864–65, Puerto Plata was once again virtually demolished by nationalist guerrillas intent on driving out the occupying Spaniards. Quickly reconstructed, the city became the main shipping point for Cibao tobacco in the 1870s.

The boom years

The **tobacco boom** was Puerto Plata's golden age – for a few decades it was the wealthiest, most cosmopolitan town in the Caribbean. The burgeoning merchant class – many of them German exporters – built dozens of fabulous mansions, some of which remain to this day. But by the beginning of the twentieth century the United States had taken control of Dominican customs receipts and awarded themselves preferential trade status. Puerto Plata's German market shrunk and American barriers to tobacco sank the economy. In 1910 skyrocketing sugar prices resuscitated the port. Over the course of the following decade – a prosperous era dubbed the **Dance of Millions** (*Danza de los Millones*) – Puerto Plata took on more of a modern, urban air with dozens of new factories and a population explosion, snuffed out a few years later as America's Great Depression took its toll.

The modern era

Over his thirty-year rule, dictator **Trujillo**'s industrialization programme was centred on the capital and he did as much as he could to ruin Puerto Plata, one of the main areas of resistance against his dictatorship: he pulled up the **railway** that ran here from the Cibao and even filled in the deep **port** with concrete. In the 1960s, a smaller sugar boom led the government to revive the decrepit port, attracting tens of thousands of additional rural immigrants. A decade later, Puerto Plata was insulated from fluctuating crop prices by the creation of **Playa Dorada**. The resort complex has attracted millions of tourists and provided thousands of jobs, but the self-sustaining, walled-off nature of the place has prevented its success from rubbing off on the city. It is estimated that the new US$27 million cruise ship terminal and shopping plaza a few kilometres east at **Maimon** could bring the region an additional quarter of a million visitors annually – the consequences for Puerto Plata remain to be seen.

The Old City

The once-exclusive **Old City** of Puerto Plata, a compact area bounded by Avenida Colón, the Malecón and Calle José Ramón López, visually retains much of the Victorian splendour of its past, when it was populated by wealthy landowners, dock workers and European merchants who made their fortunes exporting tobacco, sugar and cocoa. The elaborate **gingerbread houses** they built – Victorian mansions with ornate exteriors and stilt-supported balconies – still survive, though time hasn't been kind to the majority of them.

Fortaleza San Felipe

Malecón, just west of Av. Colón • Tues–Sun 9am–4.45pm • RD$100 (includes audio guide) • ☎ 809 261 1911

A good place to begin wandering is the colonial-era **Fortaleza San Felipe**, a solid limestone fort perched atop a rocky outcrop at the western end of the Atlantic-facing Malecón. The Spaniards built it in 1540 to serve as a defence against corsairs and a prison for smugglers; when the city was torched in 1605, it was the lone structure to survive. There are now **audio guides** (in French or English) to accompany your

PUERTO PLATA: OLD CITY

ACCOMMODATION
Hotel Kevin 1
Victoriano 2

EATING & DRINKING
Aguaceros 2
Eskina 3
Mariposa 4
Nuevo Pola 5
Tam Tam 1

exploration of the towers and gun turrets or down into the old prison cells that were in use throughout the Trujillo era. Some of the most esteemed figures in Dominican history have been imprisoned here, including Father of the Country **Juan Pablo Duarte** (incarcerated in 1844 after a bungled attempt to declare himself president) and the husbands of national martyrs the Mirabal sisters, who were murdered by Trujillo's secret police after visiting their spouses in prison. The old prison houses a small **museum** with artefacts such as prisoners' shackles, cannonballs and coins.

Whether or not you go inside, you can't miss the views from this corner of the city. Bordering the fort is the seaside **Parque Luperón**, featuring a bronze equestrian statue of the general who ruled the country for a year from Puerto Plata. Cast your eyes towards town from here and atop a small hill you'll notice the impressively restored **lighthouse**, a rare cast-iron construction with an open spiral staircase dating to 1879. Unfortunately, it is not open to visitors.

Parque Central
Corner of Separación and Beller

The heart of the Victorian city is the recently remodelled **Parque Central**. The otherwise uninspiring paved plaza is enlivened by some smart palm trees interspersed with faux-colonial lamps. Its benches are arranged around a central two-storey **gazebo**, a 1960s replica of one that stood here a century earlier. Following hurricane and earthquake damage, **Catedral San Felipe Apóstol** at the plaza's south side has also undergone stop-start surgery over the last decade or so and now contains some splendid Italian stained-glass windows donated by local wealthy families.

The roads flanking the park boast some of the city's finest **Victorian architecture**, notably an impressive white gingerbread mansion on the northwest corner, which until recently served as a Pentecostal church. On the southeast corner, the pink gingerbread house at Separación 22, former home of a wealthy German merchant, is the city's **cultural centre** (Mon–Fri 9am–noon & 3–5pm; ☎809 261 2731) and houses occasional exhibitions by local artists. The old Moorish **town hall** next door, which still serves as the office of the mayor, is another striking building. Stroll down almost any nearby street to see more such buildings, though many are in partial or complete disrepair.

Plaza Arawak

San Felipe and Beller • Mon–Fri 8.30am–5pm • Free

Northwest of the central plaza, is **Plaza Arawak**, an office building with a pleasant central courtyard that displays a modest collection of stone **Taino** sculptures known as *cemis*, notable for their grimacing features and inward-spiralling eyes. Discovered just west of Puerto Plata and at Samaná's Cuevas de Agua, the artefacts are physical embodiments of the Taino gods that were used in ecstatic religious ceremonies.

Museo de Ámbar

Duarte 61, one block east of the Parque Central • Mon–Fri 8am–5pm, Sat 8am–noon • RD$50 • ☎ 809 586 2848, Ⓦ ambermuseum.com

The popular **Museo de Ámbar** comprises two floors of insects trapped in amber and various other amber-related exhibits in a renovated c.1900 mansion called Villa Bentz, built by one of the town's wealthiest German tobacco families. At the entrance, a few artefacts give you a sense of how the family lived. The first-floor museum, though, is the main draw: an amber collection culled from the mines in the Cordillera Septentrional south of Puerto Plata containing Jurassic and Triassic leaves, flowers, spiders, termites, wasps, ants and other insects, along with one small several-million-year-old lizard identical to those on the island today. There's also a **gift shop** with polished jewellery and chunks of raw amber for sale, but you'll get a better selection elsewhere.

Mercado Nuevo

Isabela de Torres and Villanueva • Daily 8am–9pm

Aimed mainly at tourists, the **Mercado Nuevo**, crammed with colourful, crowded stalls, is housed in a decaying, star-shaped concrete structure. Among the mass-produced Haitian paintings, T-shirts, lewd novelty items and maracas you'll find quality rums, Cuban cigars and some good wicker furniture, all fairly cheap if you're willing to haggle.

Mercado Viejo

Ureña and Separación • Daily 8am–6pm; prices not negotiable

The locally orientated **Mercado Viejo** spills onto the pavement from a series of former private homes. More utilitarian than the Mercado Nuevo, here you'll find hardware, furniture, lawn flamingos and a **botánica** (a shop dedicated to syncretist religious items) that is identifiable by the pictures and icons propped along the outside wall. This is as good as any place to learn about Dominican folk religion; ask and the owner will give you the address of one of the old-fashioned *brujos* – syncretist folk healers who are still a staple of rural Dominican life – who live in the outer barrios.

Avenida Colón

Avenida Colón marks the Old City's western boundary, with nothing too much of interest beyond it – just the port and the extremely poor barrio Agua Negra. Along Colón you'll find decrepit **Victorian warehouses** that once stored cargo waiting to be shipped to Europe. Despite thorough decay, much of their original ornamentation is still visible, including elegant, dangling icicle awnings on a few. At the corner of Colón and Duarte is the century-old **immigration centre building**. There's not much to see and you can't go in, but there is a railway car that stands on its front lawn as an informal monument to the long-gone railway that transported tobacco from the Cibao region.

The New City

Puerto Plata's **New City** spreads outward in three directions from the Old, roughly confined by Avenida Colón, Circunvalación Sur and Avenida Hermanas Mirabal, though further, less-developed barrios exist beyond this convenient circumscription. The majority of the area is taken up by **residential** neighbourhoods and heavy **industry**, and particular sights of interest are well spread out, so you'll need to take a *motoconcho* or taxi to get from place to place.

The Malecón

The centre of social life is the 2km-long **Malecón**, a spacious ocean promenade dotted with hotels and cafés that extends west from Avenida Colón and runs the entire length of the Old Town's seafront. During the day it's a fairly quiet spot to hang out or stroll on the beach but come weekend evenings a line of wooden bars opens up along the **Cosita Rica** beach and the whole place comes to life. If you're planning to make a night of it here, keep your wits about you as petty thievery, gay cruising and prostitution are rife.

Long Beach

At the Malecón's far eastern end is the town's former social fulcrum, **Long Beach**, which in 2006 was given a US$7 million facelift as part of a government scheme to improve the area. This involved shutting down and demolishing (with little warning) the collection of ramshackle bars there, replenishing the beach with sand brought in from Río San Juan, and replacing the open sewage outlet with a proper treatment works. Only the latter could be described as an unqualified success as the removal of the bars has drastically changed the character of the area, driving away much tourism. A few locals walk their dogs there in the morning, but otherwise the place is empty.

Brugal Rum bottling factory

Across from Plaza Turisol on Av. Manolo Tavarez Justo • Mon–Fri 8am–3.30pm • Free • ☎ 809 121 1888 ext 2223

From Long Beach, Avenida Hermanas Mirabal extends inland to Avenida Circunvalación; 500m to the east lies the large **Brugal Rum bottling factory**. Even if you haven't sampled its products you're likely to recognize the red, white and blue Brugal logo, as it appears on town signs sponsored by the company throughout the country. It's a popular stop-off for tour groups but individuals can just turn up and join one of

---

CLIMBING MOUNT ISABELA DE TORRES

If you want to tackle **Mount Isabela de Torres** solo rather than take the **cable car** (see p.164), look for the well-marked **path** that starts at the isolated pueblo of El Cupey, 10km by road and on the opposite side of the mountain from Puerto Plata. Head west on Av. Circunvalación Sur for 2km, then turn left down Calle los Rieles which wends its way around the mountain (deteriorating as it goes) till you reach El Cupey, which has few facilities, though a couple of local farmers rent out horses and guides for the ascent – a taxi there will cost in the region of US$25–30 each way from Puerto Plata. The ascent is an arduous **four-hour trek** up the 820m mountain through a canopy of rainforest; **start early** to maximize your chance of a clear view from the summit. If lucky you may catch sight of the endangered **Hispaniola parrot** or the red-tailed hawk. There's also a small system of **Taino caves** with petroglyphs near the summit, an hour's hike west off the main path – look for a guide in El Cupey if you want to see them (around RD$500).

Another great hike from the pueblo is the trail that leads away from Mount Isabela up to the Río Camú and **La Cueva del Gallo**, an underground river cave several hundred metres long that traverses the side of the mountain to the south of **El Cupey**. Just 3km from the pueblo, it's a less rugged hike than the Isabela trek and can be done in half a day without a guide.

Alternatively, Cabarete-based Iguana Mama (see p.181) runs twice-weekly **hiking excursions** to the top that take off from Puerto Plata (Mon & Fri 7.30am–3.30pm; US$88); you take the cable car back down.

PUERTO PLATA TOURS AND ACTIVITIES

The popularity of Playa Dorada has attracted professional **tour operators** offering a variety of interesting day-trips. As well as those listed below, check out Cabarete-based **Iguana Mama** (see p.181), which offers **mountain-bike trips** and the like in the mountains south of here, and the excellent, ethical **Monkey Jungle** (see box, p.177).

Fun City Action Park 2km east of the Playa Dorada complex ☏ 809 320 1031, ⓦ funcity-gokarts.com. If you're here with kids, this is a great place to distract them for an afternoon, with four separate go-kart tracks, plus bumper cars and a playground. Day passes (RD$450, RD$350 for kids 12 and under) get you unlimited rides, though food and drinks are not included. Daily 10am–6pm, Sat & Sun till 7pm.

Outback Safari Plaza Turisol, Avenida Luperón Km 2.5 ☏ 809 320 2525, ⓦ outbacksafari.com.do. The best of the adventure jeep tour outfits, with one option (Mon–Sat 9am–4pm; US$89) that includes swimming in a Cordillera Septentrional stream, boogie-boarding on a less popular north coast beach and popping in for coffee with a local family. There's always a bit of rum flowing so expect it to become quite lively as the day wears on.

Rancho Lorilar Calle 3 in Sabana Grande just below Mount Isabela ☏ 809 320 0498. The north coast's largest stable offers highly professional horseriding in small groups with excellent guides: two hours for US$45, and a full-day tour for US$95 (US$10 extra for a private outing); the latter includes lunch and a refreshing dip in a lagoon. Prices include hotel transfer.

Sea Pro Divers Plaza Playa Dorada ☏ 809 320 2567, ⓦ seaprodivers.com. By far the best scuba-diving shop in town with most of their local dives around Sosúa. A two-tank day-trip costs US$90 (equipment rental US$12; 10 percent discount if booked online); you can also sign up for an eight-dive package, spread out over several days for US$320.

Tip Top (no office) ☏ 809 710 0503, ⓦ catamarandomrep.com. Of the alcohol-soaked catamaran cruises that ply the coast – generally sailing to Sosúa and back, breaking for snorkelling and lunch in Sosúa bay – this is the top choice. Their tour (US$79) sails out of Maimón, west of Puerto Plata, alternating excursions to Sosúa with trips to Luperón.

the tours which are really little more than a PR exercise for the company – there's a brief video and a glance at the bottling and packing operations before some free rum-based margaritas are served up.

Mount Isabela cable car

Signposted just east of the Shell station on the Circunvalación Sur • Daily 8.30am–5pm; café Tues–Sun only • RD$350 • ☏ 809 970 0501 • A *motoconcho* to the entrance should cost RD$30, a taxi US$15

Puerto Plata's crowning attraction is the **Mount Isabela cable car**, which is not to be missed – the views of the city and coast on the ten-minute ride to the top of the 820m peak are stupendous. At the summit a statue of Christ the Redeemer with its arms spread out over the city (a slightly downsized version of the Río de Janeiro landmark) crowns a manicured lawn. Also on the grounds are a **botanical garden**, a small **cave**, a pricey **café**, and a **souvenir shop**. The mountain is now a protected national park, covered by rainforest on its far side and inhabited by 32 species of indigenous bird. But there's a more pressing reason to avoid wandering beyond the designated tourist area – the mountain is gradually **splitting**. The brown splotch on its face, visible from the city, is a landslide created by the process, and there are some deep fissures at the summit.

Playa Dorada

3km east of Puerto Plata on the C-5 • 15min by *motoconcho* from Parque Central

PLAYA DORADA lies just 3km east of Puerto Plata but is truly a world away – unless you can find the public entrance at the far west of the beach, you won't be allowed access from the main road without a resort wristband. Inside Playa Dorada's confines are **fourteen resorts**, each an entity unto itself, with restaurants, discos, swimming pools, hot tubs and an array of sports facilities. Meandering between them is a Robert

Trent Jones-designed **golf course**. Frequented by half a million package tourists per year, Playa Dorada is the perfect place to lie for a few days on a beach and be pampered, though those seeking more than a cruise ship on sand may find that its alluring promotion campaign – like the city of gold after which it was named – is mostly a mirage.

The **beach** is the main draw – 2km of golden sand from which you're treated to terrific views of Mount Isabela. The **hotels** offer a variety of activities that take up much of the beach space, including volleyball, merengue lessons, parasailing, group aerobics and spaghetti-eating contests. Factor in the numerous souvenir vendors, hair braiders and touts flogging timeshare apartments and you can picture the frenetic scene, but there are still places reserved for **tranquil** sun worship. If you do go walkabout, remember to remove your resort wristband as it will mark you out as an easy victim for shysters and criminals. Various **day passes** are available from most resorts, which entitle non-residents to use of their facilities.

Costambar

2km west of Puerto Plata on the C-5 • 10min by *motoconcho* (RD$50) from Parque Central, or take Javilla Tours' *corto* service which passes by on the highway (RD$25)

Costambar is a rambling settlement of townhouses and private homes, time-shared, rented or owned by expats and well-to-do Dominicans. Once you make your way through a spaghetti bowl of lanes, you'll find a lightly populated **beach** far better than the one in Puerto Plata, though there's little shade. It has a handful of restaurants right on the water offering pizza and sandwiches, and views across the harbour of the city lights are an added bonus at night.

Cofresí

5km west of Puerto Plata on the C-5 • 20min (RD$80) by *motoconcho* from Parque Central or take Javilla Tours' *corto* service which passes by on the highway (RD$25)

From Costambar, it's a further 3km to **Playa Cofresí**, named after infamous Puerto Rican pirate Roberto Cofresí (born Robert Kupferstein), though there's no documented link between them. Once home to a small fishing village, Cofresí's golden beach is now backed by a number of hotel and resort complexes. The ocean near here gets extremely choppy, better for bodysurfing and boogie-boarding than a pleasant swim. Along the beach you'll find a few beach shacks serving delicious fried fish with *tostones* and beer for as little as RD$350. There are also a couple of good restaurants nearby (see p.170) and it's a nicer and more sociable beach than Costambar.

Ocean World

Ocean World Far western end of Cofresí beach • Daily 9am–6pm • Admission including lunch US$69 (children and seniors US$54); swimming with dolphins US$109–199 depending on time (children and seniors US$89–169; day pass included); swimming with sea lions or nurse sharks and stingrays US$79 • ☎ 809 291 1000, ⓦ oceanworld.net • **Casino** Daily 4pm–3/4am • ☎ 829 237 1380, ⓦ oceanworldcasinos.com

Cofresí's impressive **Ocean World** is the premiere tourist attraction on the north coast, with its own casino and a marina that acts as a major port of entry to the country, welcoming fully laden cruise ships throughout the year. Modelled on Florida's SeaWorld, the ambitious US$25 million complex features massive artificial lagoons housing dolphins, nurse sharks, sea lions, stingrays, and even a tiger. You can snorkel over an **artificial reef** full of colourful tropical fish, view tanks of piranhas and aviaries filled with Hispaniolan parakeets, parrots and toucans. It doesn't come cheap, though, with a hefty admission charge – lunch is included, but the food is mediocre at best – and additional fees if you want to swim with dolphins (described rather awkwardly in the promotional blurb as "dolphin petting, feeding, kisses and hugs") or the other creatures.

The Río Damajagua waterfalls

Just outside Imbert, around 15km southwest of Puerto Plata • Daily 8.00am–3pm • RD$280–500, depending on number of waterfalls visited and including guide • ⓦ 27charcos.com • By car from Puerto Plata, head southwest along the C-5 until you see the Damajagua sign 3km south of the Imbert Texaco station; by bus, take one of the frequent Javilla Tours buses to Imbert (20min; RD$35) then hop on a *motoconcho*; alternatively a taxi will cost around US$60, with waiting time

Just outside the town of **Imbert** you can climb (and sometimes even slide down) a stunning series of **waterfalls** along the high, early course of the Río Damajagua. The 27 natural, boulder-strewn cascades carve through mountain wilderness, the water crashing down at breakneck speed. It's a wet, challenging and extremely rewarding hike up, with a great hilltop view at the end. If not part of an organized tour – most of the operators in Puerto Plata, Sosúa and Cabarete, such as Iguana Mama (see p.181) offer the trip – pack your swimsuit and make sure you're wearing robust **footwear**. You pay your admission fee, meet your guide and pick up the life jackets and mandatory safety helmets at the **visitor centre**, from where it's a twenty-minute hike to the falls. Each individual cascade has its own feature. Some have pools for **swimming** or ladders for climbing up, while others have natural chutes waiting to be slid down. The climbs can be pretty steep and the flow of water fierce at times, particularly after heavy rains, and you should exercise extreme caution at all times. **Children** under eight are only allowed to tackle the first cascade.

The visitor centre, which has an attached restaurant, is a sign of the site's growing popularity and importance to the local tourist industry. Now designated a national monument, the falls have become an almost obligatory stop-off for the region's all-inclusive tour operators. The revenue generated has allowed the authorities to upgrade the paths linking the falls, several of which have been turned into nature trails. The surrounding community has also benefited, with a percentage of each admission fee set aside for local development projects.

ARRIVAL AND DEPARTURE
PUERTO PLATA AND AROUND

BY PLANE
Aeropuerto Gregorio Luperón (ⓣ 809 291 0000), 18km east of Puerto Plata, is the main northern entry point into the country. It has no domestic connection services.

Facilities There is a Banco de Reservas ATM and currency exchange (Mon–Fri 9am–4pm) within the strip of shops lining the front of the airport, alongside a number of car rental offices, which have a better selection of vehicles than you'll find in the city (see opposite).

Getting into town Although most of the expensive hotels have shuttle buses waiting for their clients, *motoconchos* can also take you into town for RD$200, and there are plenty of taxis heading to points further out (US$40 to the city; US$25 to Sosúa). If those seem a little steep, note that less than a couple of hundred metres outside the terminal is the main coastal road, Carretera 5 (C-5), stretching from Puerto Plata all the way to Samaná. From the C-5 you can catch a guagua going in either direction; a trip to Puerto Plata or Sosúa should cost around RD$50.

BY CAR
If coming by car from Santiago you'll arrive via either the well-maintained and relatively flat C-5 or the C-25 (also known as the Carretera Turística) which, though it may look on maps like a quicker option, is a narrow, twisty, distressed mountain road, although you will be rewarded with stunning highland scenery. At Puerto Plata the C-5 becomes the extremely congested Avenida Circunvalación Sur, marking the city's southern border.

BY BUS OR GUAGUA
By bus The city is a major junction for Caribe Tours and Metro, whose buses arrive from Santo Domingo (14 daily 6am–7pm; 4hr; RD$330) via Santiago (1hr; RD$110). The terminal for Caribe Tours (ⓣ 809 586 4544, ⓦ caribetours.com.do) is on Camino Real at the junction with Eugenio Kunhardt; Metro's terminal (ⓣ 809 586 6062, ⓦ metroserviciosturisticos.com) is in the Old City on the corner of Beller and 16 de Agosto. If you're headed for the Samaná Peninsula contact Transporte Papagayo (ⓣ 809 749 6415; Spanish only). They run a daily bus service from Puerto Plata (4hr; RD$600), leaving at around 6.30/6.45am, and they can usually pick you up at your hotel. If you're coming to Puerto Plata, the bus leaves Samaná at around 2pm. Again, you can arrange a hotel pick-up.

By guagua Another transport option is Javilla Tours, located just off Avenida Circunvalación Sur at 30 de Marzo (ⓣ 809 970 2412, ⓦ javillatours.com.dr). They provide a regular guagua service to Santiago (1hr 30min; RD$120) via Imbert (RD$35) and Altamira (RD$65), so are useful for reaching the Damajagua waterfalls and further west along the coast.

The guaguas that travel the length of the coast, every 15min or so during daylight hours, all end up at the Parque Central, from where you can pick up a taxi or *motoconcho* if your hotel isn't within walking distance.

GETTING AROUND

By motoconcho The cheapest and fastest form of taxi, though not particularly safe – the official ones who wear coloured bibs are marginally better on that score. To get to any of the beaches should cost less than RD$150.

By public bus Cheaper than *motoconchos* but far slower are the public buses shuttling between Playa Dorada and Parque Central. The price is RD$30, but it can take up to 30min to get from one side of town to the other.

By taxi Taxis are relatively expensive and they'll ask US$15 to Playa Dorada from Parque Central, though it should be more like RD$300 (still a huge rip-off). It's best to pick them up at one of their main gathering points: Parque Central, Long Beach, the traffic circle at Circunvalación Sur and Colón, or the entrances to Playa Dorada and Costambar.

The cars don't have meters though the taxi offices have set fares – if catching a taxi in the street, settle on a fare before you get in and don't be afraid to bargain. To call ahead for a pick-up and get a quote (recommended), try Central de Taxi (☎ 809 586 7498).

By car If shuttling back and forth from Costambar or Playa Dorada, renting a car can spare you the hassles of public transport and expense of taxis. Reputable operators at the airport include Avis (☎ 809 586 4436, ⊛ avis.com), which also has an office on the main C-5 highway, opposite the entrance to El Pueblicito Plaza Commercial; Budget (☎ 809 586 0284, ⊛ budget.com), which is also in Playa Dorada (☎ 809 320 4888); Europcar (☎ 809 86 0215, ⊛ europcar. com); and Hertz (☎ 809 586 0200, ⊛ hertz.com).

INFORMATION

Local "guides" will likely pounce on you as you arrive, but it is not recommended that you use them to orient yourself or find accommodation. If you do take one on, make sure they have an official ID card; their services should cost around RD$500 a day, though they make more from commissions by dragging you round shops.

4

Tourist information The government tourist office (Mon–Fri 9am–5pm; ☎ 809 586 3676) on Calle José Carmen Ariza 45, just off the main square, can provide you with maps and several glossy brochures. However, the best source of information – unless you're staying in a resort – is probably The Meeting Place (Tues–Fri 11am–5pm, Sat 11am–3pm; ☎ 829 455 6110, ⊛ meetingplacepuertoplata.com), situated two blocks from the park at Juan Bosch 60, whose knowledgeable volunteers run an English-language bookshop and resource centre for expat travellers, as well as having a small exhibition of historic photographs of the city.

Newspapers and website The easiest way to find out information in English is the excellent and informative ⊛ popreport.com. The city also boasts a weekly rag in Spanish, *El Faro* (⊛ periodicoelfaro.com.do), which offers some listings and local news. Also worth a look is *The Costambar Monthly* (⊛ costambarmonthly.wordpress.com), which can be found in many expat haunts.

ACCOMMODATION

It's advisable to **book** your hotel before arrival if possible. **Rates** are often advertised in pesos, but you can also pay in US dollars and rates are increasingly negotiable in low season. The best luxury options are the all-inclusives east of town within **Playa Dorada** (prices given, except for *Casa Colonial*, are all-inclusive for two people sharing a double room); note, however, that the majority are aimed squarely at the mass market and may not always live up to the "luxury" or self-appointed "five-star" billing. Most of the handful of **downtown** options are at the basic, budget end of things, but are at least handy for nightlife. Other possibilities are **Cofresí**, which offers a couple of resorts and a few villas, and the less sociable **Costambar**, which predominantly provides condominiums. For the latter, if you haven't booked in advance online, the best way to find an apartment is to drive or walk around, peeking in the various places with "For Rent" signs out front. Set high up in the hills above Puerto Plata, **Tubagua Plantation Village**, meanwhile, is the perfect spot to escape the sultry climate.

PUERTO PLATA

Hotel Kevin Prof. Juan Bosch 41 ☎ 809 244 4159, ✉ hotel-kevin@hotmail.fr; map p.161 With more of a traveller feel than others in the city, this tropically decorated wooden guesthouse has some very nice, clean rooms (a/c RD$400 extra), all with hot water. It also has a pleasant and comfortable first-floor terrace, and serves good food and drink at the bar-*comedor* downstairs,

including a RD$200 *plato del día*. RD$800

Hotel Lomar Malecón, just west of Puerto Plata beach ☎ 809 320 8555; map p.159. Rooms are spacious and clean, with cable TV, wi-fi, mini-fridges and plenty of hot water, but many of the furnishings and fitments are looking distinctly careworn and a firm managerial hand is lacking. Good ocean views in some rooms since it's a stone's throw from the beach. RD$200 extra for a/c. RD$1200

★**Montesilva** La Estancia ☎809 320 0205; map p.159. Clean, simple and safe on a quiet backstreet, this is one of Puerto Plata's cheerier budget offerings with twelve rooms, all with cable TV and a/c, and a small swimming pool. Wi-fi in lobby only. RD$1200

Victoriano San Felipe 33 ☎809 586 9752; map p.161. Reasonable budget option in a nineteenth-century building, with friendly staff and clean, functional, rather dark rooms, with cable TV and fans. The better rooms for RD$200 more have a/c and hot water. Wi-fi available in the lobby. It can be noisy at night. RD$600

PLAYA DORADA

Barcelo Puerto Plata ☎809 320 5020, ⓦbarcelo .com. With the beach in front and the golf course behind, the *Barcelo* provides a perfect distillation of the Playa Dorada experience: blandly comfortable rooms with terrace/balcony, a handful of restaurants – both buffet and à la carte – plentiful sports facilities, including two swimming pools, tennis courts, golf and watersports, plus nightly entertainment, including a disco on the beach. Has a minimum-stay period of four days during peak seasons (mid-Dec to late April) US$240

★**Bluebay Villas Doradas** ☎809 320 3000, ⓦbluebayresorts.com. Right on the beach and offering a higher standard of accommodation than the Playa Dorada norm, the *Bluebay* has good-sized, neatly decorated rooms, three pools, tennis courts, a spa with hot tub and sauna plus above-average buffet fare and decent à la carte restaurants. With a warm, intimate atmosphere this adult-only resort is a good couple's choice. US$164

★**Casa Colonial** ☎809 320 3232, ⓦcasacolonialhotel .com. You won't get anything as commonplace as an all-inclusive package offered at the *Casa Colonial*, Playa Dorada's only true five-star luxury hotel. Small (just 50 suites) and awfully stylish, it boasts large, high-ceilinged rooms with every facility imaginable including a sumptuously elegant restaurant, the best spa facilities in the area, high-speed internet access in the rooms and 24hr room service. If you can afford it (and you'll need at least US$360 a night even in low season), this is the place to come. Two-night stay minimum. US$455

Celuisma Tropical Playa Dorada ☎809 320 6226, ⓦceluismacaribe.com. Towards the budget end of things so not the grandest of resorts, but the grounds are pleasant and the stretch of sand excellent, with funky four-poster beach beds. The rooms are large, too, decorated in minimalist-tropical style. US$157

Iberostar Costa Dorada ☎809 320 1550, ⓦiberostar .com. Just west of Playa Dorada on a stretch of coast known as Costa Dorada, this is one of the area's best hotels offering superior amenities, well-manicured gardens and comfortable rooms. The à la carte restaurants are above average. It is generally noisy and chaotic, though, so request a room in the 7000 block, which is shielded from the disco noise but still has good views from the balconies. Three-night stay minimum. US$296

COSTAMBAR

Residence La Gaviota On the left as you go down to the beach on Calle Principal de Costambar ☎809 970 7289. If you fancy something a little more homely and less touristic, this Italian-run and-owned guesthouse with just two rooms is just the ticket. Very nice little studios, with their own tiny kitchens, although you could treat yourself and eat at the on-site restaurant. RD$500 extra for a/c. RD$1300

Villas Jazmin Cristóbal Colón ☎809 970 7010, ⓦvillasjazmin.com. Operates several blocks of one- and two-bedroom apartments a few minutes from the beach, from the standard no-frills variety (though still with a/c, cable TV & hot water) to the more modern *Villas Jazmin Plus* (from US$200), boasting tasteful oak furnishings and top-notch electrical appliances. Wi-fi is available (extra charge) and there's a kids club, exercise room and tennis court. Huge discounts in low season. US$80

COFRESÍ

Be Live Carey Paradise Drive ☎809 970 3364, ⓦbelivecarey.com. Formerly *Sun Village Resorts*, this superior all-inclusive sprawls over the hillside behind the beach and next to Ocean World. It boasts numerous oceanfront rooms and suites, five restaurants and a full-service spa. Book well ahead. RD$206

Chris and Mady's Calle Cofresí ☎809 970 7502, ⓦchrisandmadys.com. Small new apartment block with plenty of natural light offering a couple of suites (one- and two-bedroom) with nice balconies and homely wicker furniture, or a much smaller studio flat. This is a good budget option, there's a decent restaurant attached and the owners are not only friendly but a good source of local info. US$40

Lifestyle Hacienda Resorts ☎809 586 1227, ⓦlhvresorts.com. A complex of three separate hotels; of these, *Crown Villas* is the best and by far the most expensive, comprising opulent villas, complete with private pool, grounds and a battalion of staff to pamper you for around US$5000 per night. *Tropical* has a better location, on the beach, better food, and is far easier on the wallet at US$114. US$114

TUBAGUA PLANTATION VILLAGE

Tubagua Plantation Village 30km along the mountain road to Santiago ☎809 970 7052, ⓦtubagua.com. With superlative views along the coast, this rustic eco-lodge offers wood-and-thatch dormitory or semi-open A-frame bungalow accommodation, cooled by the breeze and equipped with mosquito nets. The shared, solar-powered showers are fed by springs, and the communal dining area encourages socializing. Fresh food, much of it grown in their organic gardens, is cooked in a traditional open kitchen. Prices include a substantial breakfast and there is free wi-fi. **Dorm US$30, double US$50**

EATING

Puerto Plata has several decent **restaurants** – from rice-and-bean *comedores* to more upmarket places – and quite a few ordinary ones. Most are scattered within the **Old City** and along **the Malecón**. If staying at an all-inclusive at **Playa Dorada**, you'll be largely restricted to whatever is provided by your hotel, although there are a couple of independent restaurants if you fancy a change (and spending some money). The mid-range restaurants around **Costambar** and **Cofresí** are also a good option for dinner. If cooking for yourself, stock up on **groceries** at the Malecón's easy-to-spot La Sirena hypermarket (Mon–Sat 8am–10pm, Sun 9am–9pm), which also has a food court.

PUERTO PLATA & PLAYA DORADA

Aguaceros Malecón 32 ☎ 809 526 2796; map p.161. Tasty Mexican dishes served in a festive, oceanfront barn. Fajitas, and even better the massive burritos and quesadillas, come in at around RD$350 per piece. They also do potent cocktails and occasionally have Mama Juana. Daily 10am–11pm.

Las Almendras Malecón and Carolina ☎ 829 937 8012; map p.159. With tables set up beneath tall shady trees just across from the seafront, this is a nice spot to sit and watch the world go by. The limited menu sticks to the staples and the food, though decent, is rather overpriced at around RD$500 a head, though there is a pizza combo for RD$330. Daily 11am–11pm.

Eskina 12 Julio at Seperación ☎ 809 979 1950; map p.161. Open-sided Dominican restaurant under a coconut-leaf thatch serving very good *criolla* cooking to the local middle classes and the odd tourist. Does a very good *plato del día* for RD$250, while mains are mostly in the RD$250–350 range – the beef *carne ripiada* (shredded beef) is superb. Be warned, the service can be quite slow when it's busy. Daily 10am–midnight.

Lucia Casa Colonial, Playa Dorada ☎ 809 320 3232, ⓦ casacolonialhotel.com. Stylishly attired waiters attend to your every need in this beautiful, high-ceilinged dining room that's adorned with tasteful tropical blooms. In fact the service is even better than the expensive Caribbean-fusion cuisine, which can also be enjoyed outside on the patio. Mains start at around US$20. Daily 6.30–11pm.

★**La Parrillada** Circunvalación Sur ☎ 809 586 1414, ⓦ laparrilladasteakhouse.com; map p.159. One of the best steaks in town chargrilled Argentinean-style on a vast barbecue, along with sausages, chicken and other meats. A pleasant eating spot despite its proximity to the roundabout. You'll pay from RD$500 a head. Tues–Sun noon–11pm.

Mariposa Beller 38 ☎ 809 970 1785, ⓦ heladosmariposa.com; map p.161. Very well located right on the Parque Central, this old-school ice-cream parlour serves up an astonishing array of elaborate and delicious frozen goodies, as well as sweet pastries and coffee. All the products are made by the shop using natural ingredients, and prices start from around RD$80. Daily 8am–10pm.

Nuevo Pola Beller 60 ☎ 809 586 9174; map p.161. Beautifully decorated and housed in a charming old wooden colonial building, this place is one of the few international-style restaurants in the quarter, though the middling food is somewhat overpriced (mains run at around RD$450 and taxes are not included on the menu either). However, its location is sublime and there's an outside terrace to soak it up. Free internet. Mon–Sat 8am–10pm.

Las Palmas Luis Ginebra 47 ☎ 809 586 7065; map p.159. Upmarket Italian restaurant-café set on the wraparound balcony of a colonial mansion, partially sheltered from the street noise by its shady garden. It attracts a discerning clientele from as far away as Santiago with its wide-ranging menu, from the classic *Saltimbocca alla Romana* – veal with cured ham and sage – to imported Aberdeen Angus steaks (RD$900). Seafood mains from around RD$500, though pasta from RD$250. Daily except Tues noon–11pm.

4

PUERTO PLATA FESTIVALS

Puerto Plata holds the usual Dominican festivals: there's a July 5 **fiesta patronal** in honour of San Felipe, featuring large crowds drinking and dancing along the Malecón; and **Carnival**, in February, when hundreds of townspeople parade around in full regalia and thwack passers-by with inflated balloons. Better than either of these, though, is the renowned **Merengue Festival** – which typically sees parties right along the Malecón – that is usually held during the third week of October, though the exact timing varies slightly from year to year. There's also a **cultural festival** involving all sorts of music and dancing alongside art and craft exhibitions that takes place in the third week of June round the fort and central plaza.

Tam Tam Malecón ☎ 809 970 0903; map p.161. Small, open-front expat hangout, one of three almost identical places at the western end of the Malecón. The conversation tends to be better than the food, but it's a nice place for breakfast or to hang out with an afternoon beer. Daily 8am–4pm.

COSTAMBAR

El Carey Restaurant Costambar Beach ☎ 809 918 1484. Recently revamped, this bustling spot on the beach is good for burgers, soft-shell tacos and grilled fish – you can eat very well for around RD$500. Fridays are barbecue nights, with bonfires on the beach, while Sundays feature karaoke from 2pm. Daily 11am–midnight.

★ **Cenica** Costambar main entrance ☎ 809 970 7213. Formerly *El Portal*, this excellent and reasonably priced restaurant serves home-cooked Dominican grub in a thatch-roofed patio setting. The fish is tender and fresh, the *sancocho* and *mofongo* (on request), are delicious and the friendly owner serves *platos del día* for just RD$125. Daily 9am–10pm.

The Italian Way On the left as you go down to the beach on Calle Principal de Costambar ☎ 809 970 7289. Classic-style Italian restaurant, with outdoor tables and a convivial Italian host, that serves very good pastas and seafood (though not pizza) along with a small range of excellent Italian wines. The *linguini al scoglio* (RD$400) is excellent, as is the two-person seafood pasta dish (RD$1200). Daily 5–10pm.

COFRESÍ

Chris & Mady's Calle Cofresí ☎ 809 970 7052, ⓦ chrisandmadys.com. Relaxed open-air beachfront bar popular with expats and travellers alike, dishing up quality burgers, seafood and meat dishes. The grilled-fish *mahi-mahi* (RD$600) is a house speciality and the Sunday barbecue a draw. Main courses from RD$400, and breakfast bacon and eggs (RD$250) are available all day. Free wi-fi. Daily 7am–11pm.

Le Papillon Villas Cofresí ☎ 809 970 7640, ⓦ le-papillon.de. Long-standing fine dining favourite, this relatively formal German-owned (but French-leaning) restaurant is up a signposted dirt track across the highway from Playa Cofresí, and serves a host of terrific meat and seafood dishes (with mixed meat and seafood a speciality) and some vegetarian options. Mains from RD$600. Tues–Sun 6–11pm.

★ **Los Tres Cocos** Las Rocas ☎ 809 970 7627. Delightful Austrian restaurant with great service and a menu featuring schnitzel plus a host of other dishes (the coconut sea bass is recommended). The open-air setting is romantic, down a small street off the main road. Most mains are in the RD$300–800 range. Daily 5–10.30pm.

DRINKING, NIGHTLIFE AND ENTERTAINMENT

Fed by a metropolitan combination of dance-crazy Dominicans and vacationing foreigners, the **clubs** in Puerto Plata are crammed until dawn – be mindful of personal safety when leaving. You won't find a lot of local **live music**, but big-name **merengue** acts pass through the major venues on a regular basis. The **bar** scene is dominated by expat establishments – these can be fun places to meet some colourful characters. There is a lot of more laidback nightlife along the eastern end of Malecón by Cosita Beach where expats and locals drift from beach bar to beach bar or drink by their vehicles in the street. Although the Playa Dorada **resort discos** are open to all, the majority are pretty boring, expensive and half empty; those listed below do the best trade, more often than not crowded with a mix of foreign visitors and Dominicans. More sedentary entertainment options are provided by a few glitzy **casinos**, the best of which is at Ocean World (see p.165), and *The Meeting Place* (see p.167) which has a Saturday afternoon **movie club**, details of which are on the website. There are no big **cinemas** in Puerto Plata at present (though plans are always afoot).

SPORTS IN PUERTO PLATA

The annual festival aside (see box, p.32), Puerto Plata is no cultural centre, but there are plenty of diversions. The old José Brieño **baseball** stadium, just by the roundabout linking Circunvalación Sur with Avenida Hermanas Mirabal, occasionally stages exhibition games. However, the lack of a roof prevents it from hosting professional competitions during the winter season – the authorities fear that Puerto Plata's high rainfall would see too many games cancelled. Nonetheless, it still provides a venue for travelling circuses and revivalist religious meetings. There is also one *club gallístico* with regular **cockfighting** at Parque Duarte on Hernández (Tues & Sun 2–6pm; RD$50). If you don't want to be a spectator, **golf** is a popular option – Costambar has a modest nine-hole course, but virtually everyone goes to the magnificent Robert Trent Jones course at Playa Dorada (☎ 809 320 4262, ⓦ playadoradagolf.com), with its exquisitely maintained lawns and several links holes.

PUERTO PLATA

Big Lee's Beach Bar Casetta #8 on the Malecon ☎829 868 0017, ⓦbigleesbeachbar.com; map p.159. Friendly American-owned beach bar serving Stateside fried favourites such as burgers (under RD$240) as well as British fish 'n' chips (RD$200). Very cheap drinks on Tues and Thurs and live music at sunset on Fri, plus occasional karaoke. There are several other beach shack bars along here. Daily 9am–11pm (or later).

Olivio's Carwash Colón, just north of Circunvalación Sur; map p.159. Typical "car wash" style Dominican watering hole-cum-dance venue, frequented mostly by locals though it does see limited tourist traffic. Earplugs might be a good idea, but it gives you a great sense of what the local nightlife is all about and a big beer is just RD$100. Daily 10am–midnight (2am at weekends).

PLAYA DORADA

Coco Bongo Playa Dorada Plaza ☎809 320 2259. Small, dark nightclub attracting both tourists and Dominicans, mixing occasional merengue and salsa with a hefty dose of dance, reggaeton, hip-hop and house. Attracts a slightly younger crowd than most places on the beach. Daily 6pm–4am.

Hemingway's Café Playa Dorada Plaza ☎809 320 2230. Haven for boozy tourists intent on having a good time or watching sports on the big TV in – of course – nautically themed surroundings. Good-quality American comfort food – burgers, ribs and steaks – though at US prices, with mains around RD$450. Free wi-fi and no cover, except when big-name bands pass through. Daily 8am–midnight.

DIRECTORY

Ambulance Dial ☎911 in case of emergency.

Banks and currency exchange There are several banks with ATMs on and around the Parque Central and one in the La Sirena hypermarket on the Malecón.

Consulates Canadian Consulate, Calle Villanueva 8 (Mon–Fri 9am–1pm; ☎809 586 5761, ⓦcanadainternational.gc.ca); Honorary British Consulate, Beller 51 (Mon–Fri 9am–5pm; ☎809 586 4244, ⓦukinthedominicanrepublic.fco.gov.uk); US Consulate, Villanueva 8 (Mon–Fri 8.30am–12.30pm & 2–5pm; ☎809 586 4204, ⓦsantodomingo.usembassy.gov/ca_pp-e.html).

Dental Dr Freddy Lepe, corner of Duarte & Villanueva (☎809 586 6666).

Hospital Clínica Dr Brugal, Ariza 15 by Juan Bosch (☎809 586 2519) and Centro Médico Dr Bournigal at A Mota 1 (☎809 586 2342) both have 24hr emergency facilities, and there is a medical centre attached to the *Be Live Carey* resort in Cofresí.

Laundry Most hotels have laundry service; otherwise go to Lavendería Puerto Plata, Av. M.V. Justo 2 at Av. Circunvalación Sur (Mon–Sat 8am–6pm; ☎809 586 6125).

Pharmacy Of the numerous pharmacies scattered around town, Farmacia Socorro at Beller 41 (☎809 586 2252) is closest to the Old City while Farmacia Carmen at 12 de Julio 39 (☎809 586 2525) is the best stocked.

Police The main police station is next to the football stadium on Av. Luis Ginebra, near the Malecón (☎809 586 2331).

Post office Puerto Plata's efficient main post office (Mon–Fri 8.30am–5pm) is on the corner of 12 de Julio and Separación. EPS, a private postal service, is at Carretera 5 Km 3, Plaza Turisol.

Telephone and internet Codetel at Beller and Padre Castellanos (daily 8am–6pm) offers internet at RD$36/hr.

East of Puerto Plata

Resort development around Puerto Plata has gobbled up most of the prime beachfront **east** of the city; as such, you'll have to trawl the coast all the way to **Río San Juan**, some 70km away, to find anything approaching unspoilt coastline. If you're up for a bustling resort town offering plenty of adventure sports and some great nightlife, though, you couldn't do better than burgeoning **Cabarete**, a kiteboarding and windsurfing enclave with a decent nightlife. Just west of Cabarete, **Sosúa** has a different kind of appeal, offering more sheltered beaches, a plethora of hotels, restaurants and diving. Wherever you go, there are plenty of hidden pleasures in the **Cordillera Septentrional** bordering the coast, including a secluded gourmet Indian fusion restaurant and several ranches offering horseriding expeditions into mountain wilderness.

Sosúa

Set along a sheltered horseshoe inlet at the eastern end of the Bahía de Sosúa, the large resort town of **SOSÚA** is a long-popular holiday destination, but the tourists who come tend to be looking for quite distinct things: there are the sea-bound scuba divers;

families who return year after year to enjoy the busy, pretty beach; and, at the centre of the town, those seeking the remnants of its once-thriving sex industry – a side of Sosúa that is, thankfully, easy to avoid. Sosúa's **fiesta patronal**, in honour of San Antonio, is held on June 13 in the **Los Charamicos** barrio.

Brief history

Sosúa was created in the late nineteenth century by the **United Fruit Company**, which used it as a port for their extensive banana plantations along today's El Choco Road. In 1916, following a pattern that would be repeated throughout the Americas in the twentieth century, United Fruit abruptly abandoned their operations in the Dominican Republic, and Sosúa lay mostly derelict until 1938–39, when Trujillo provided refuge for several hundred Jews (see box below) fleeing from Nazi Germany, who settled just east of Playa Sosúa and created the barrio known as **El Batey**. Here, they formed a successful dairy cooperative – Productos Sosúa – which operates to this day.

Tourism – the good and the bad

The first stirrings of tourism came in the 1970s as wealthy Dominicans and retiring foreigners began building winter beach homes in the area. The explosion of **sex tourism** in the 1980s brought on the real boom, however, as young Dominican women from the outlying rural districts supported families back home by catering to the desires of tens of thousands of travellers. Large-scale **hotel development** ensued, and much of the traditional fishing and agriculture was abandoned – not surprising given that even today many farm workers earn just RD$150 a day. The wealthy retirees petitioned against this unsavoury atmosphere and, in 1996, finally convinced the government to act: over the course of a year, the national police **closed every bar** in Sosúa. With its controversial lifeblood squeezed dry, the local economy promptly collapsed, leaving an abundance of empty hotels and restaurants. Slowly but surely the town has risen from its ashes, helped in no small part by **low prices** but also because, quite simply, it is a pleasant little town with some great beaches. Nonetheless, although no longer the town's main attraction, the sex trade is still much more in evidence here than in any other resort along this stretch.

El Batey

The **El Batey** barrio maintains a bright and somewhat jovial disposition despite its dark past as a sex-tourism hotspot. The main epicentre stretches along Pedro Clisante between Dr Rosén and Duarte to the west, with most of the action focused on and around the junction. The surrounding streets are peaceful and tidy with well-established gardens, and in recent years malls have been going up in place of some of the town's oldest buildings. The major changes have included the demolition of the

---

TRUJILLO AND THE JEWS

You might wonder how it was that seven hundred and fifty **Jewish refugees** fleeing Nazi oppression in Germany were given refuge by one of the worst dictators in Latin America. Ironically, it came about as the result of Trujillo's massacre of 15,000 unarmed Haitians during **Operation Perejil** (see p.270), and his close relationship with the US government. In 1938 US President Franklin D. Roosevelt arranged a **global conference** in Évian, France, to try to organize a dispersal of Jews from Germany, perhaps from altruism, though more likely as a way to deflect criticism from the US government for its own restrictive immigration policies towards German Jewry. Unfortunately, the conference was a disaster and only one country ended up agreeing to take any refugees – the Dominican Republic. This was done partly as a sop to **US liberals** who were horrified by Operation Perejil and the US support of the dictator but also, as the ever-opportunistic Trujillo put it, to "whiten" the country – one of the reasons for the massacre in the first place.

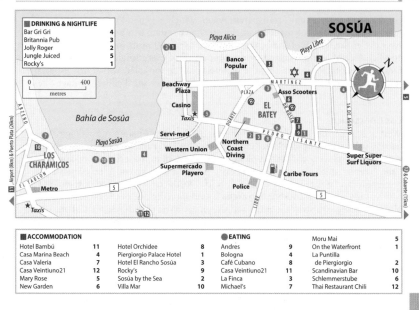

DRINKING & NIGHTLIFE	
Bar Gri Gri	4
Britannia Pub	3
Jolly Roger	2
Jungle Juiced	5
Rocky's	1

ACCOMMODATION				EATING			
Hotel Bambú	11	Hotel Orchidee	8	Andres	9	Moru Mai	5
Casa Marina Beach	4	Piergiorgio Palace Hotel	1	Bologna	4	On the Waterfront	1
Casa Valeria	7	Hotel El Rancho Sosúa	3	Café Cubano	8	La Puntilla	
Casa Veintiuno21	12	Rocky's	9	Casa Veintiuno21	11	de Piergiorgio	2
Mary Rose	5	Sosúa by the Sea	2	La Finca	3	Scandinavian Bar	10
New Garden	6	Villa Mar	10	Michael's	7	Schlemmerstube	6
						Thai Restaurant Chili	12

4

original **United Fruit Company warehouse**, at the western end of Duarte, and its replacement with banks and shops. The town's most unappealing addition is the unsightly **casino**, a vast monolith that lords over the main plaza. More positively, a small new beach has been formed, courtesy of Hurricane George, just east of the old barracks in front of the *On the Waterfront* restaurant (see p.176) – access to **Playa Alicia**'s soft sand is via the restaurant. Unlike Playa Sosúa, there is no natural shade, but you can rent umbrellas and enjoy a more peaceful environment, and the newly planted trees are growing quickly.

The synagogue

One block east of Duarte, on Martínez and Dr Rosén • Mon–Fri 9am–1pm & 2–4pm, Sat 9am–1pm • RD$150 • ☎ 829 729 5435

The Jewish legacy still remains in Sosúa, not least at the old **synagogue** – a simple wooden structure adorned with a fifty-year-old Star of David – that is still used by a number of Jewish-Dominican descendants of the settlers. The small attached museum, **El Museo de Sosúa**, recounts the early experiences of Jewish refugees and the development of their agricultural cooperative through photographs and a few of the settlers' personal effects. The settlers' enormous pasteurizing plant is still in operation at new, larger premises just down the road, and Productos Sosúa remains the largest dairy producer on the island.

Playa Libre

At the far eastern end of Calle Dr Rosén, a walkway leads to **Playa Libre** and its all-inclusive hotels. A several-hundred-metre sandy cove enclosed by a cliff, the beach has become a haven for tourists who want to avoid the hassles of Playa Sosúa. Atop the cliff is a large, communal **terrace**, which makes a pleasant place from which to admire the bay.

Playa Sosúa

Crescent-shaped and bounded by cliffs, 500m-long **Playa Sosúa** separates the town's two barrios, El Batey and Los Charamicos. The crowded stretch of sand is in stark contrast to the small bay's transparent water, which is generally completely placid; just behind it, a row of shaded bars, lobster-tank restaurants and souvenir shops runs the entire length of the beach (there are over 180 units in total and you stand a good chance of being accosted by the proprietor of every single one). Some stalls rent snorkelling equipment for the reef just outside the inlet, which isn't especially spectacular but does have some tropical fish. For better snorkelling, contact one of the dive shops (see box below).

Los Charamicos

West of Playa Sosúa spreads the Dominican barrio of **Los Charamicos**, a tangle of narrow streets lined by shacks selling food supplies and rum, *motoconchos* manoeuvring past stickball-playing children as older locals take it all in from their front-door steps. **Calle Arzeno**, which skirts the barrio's eastern edge, boasts several good open-air restaurants and great views of the beach below. At the far western end of town on Calle Morris Ling, the local **cockfighting arena** is undoubtedly one of the most authentic places to observe this violent ritual and the enthusiastic crowds it attracts. Four blocks west, a dirt road turns sharply down to rubbish-strewn **Playa Chiquita,** the locals' beach of choice, full of families and teens barbecuing pigs over bonfires and engaging in general merriment.

ARRIVAL AND DEPARTURE   SOSÚA

By plane Many who come here arrive directly from Puerto Plata's international airport, 12km west; a taxi into town should cost around US$25. You can also take a *motoconcho* for RD$200–250, or walk onto the C-5 and flag down a guagua for RD$35.

By bus Metro Tours buses (☎809 571 1324, ⓦmetroserviciosturisticos.com) serving Santo Domingo (5 daily in each direction 8.20am–5pm; RD$320), via Puerto Plata and Santiago, pick up and drop off passengers by the Texaco station on the C-5. Caribe Tours (☎809 571 3808, ⓦcaribetouts.com.do) has its office

further west along the main road at the entrance to Los Charamicos, and does the same trip (14 daily 5.20am–6.20pm; RD$330).

By guagua Guaguas stop on the C-5 at the town's two main entrances, from where it's a few minutes' walk to the centre, and shuttle constantly (around every 15min) between Río San Juan (RD$160) and Puerto Plata (RD$35). After nightfall you'll be reliant on *públicos*, which run until around 10pm and charge slightly more (RD$40–50); they leave from the local terminal across the road from the Texaco.

GETTING AROUND AND TOURS

By taxi The local taxi operator Sindicatos Chóferes Gregorio Luperón (☎809 571 2797) has several stands; the main one is by the casino in the main plaza with rates posted outside.

By car or scooter If you want to rent a car to explore further

afield, your best bet is one of the international companies located at the airport, although there are a few reliable agencies in town, including Freddy's (☎809 571 3146), 1km outside town towards Cabarete at the economical OK Motors

---

DIVING FROM SOSÚA

Sosúa is the best place on the north coast for **diving** and lays claim to one of the island's best outfits, **Northern Coast Divers**, located at Pedro Clisante 8 (☎809 571 1028, ⓦnortherncoastdiving.com). The multilingual staff run daily boat trips to several local hotspots, including the Airport Wall, a 33m wall dive with **tunnels**; and the Canyon, two walls formed by the splitting of the reef only 2m apart. They also head further afield to Paradise Island near Punta Rucia or the Caverns of Cabrera (otherwise known as El Lago Dudú). It used to be that boats would venture all the way to Río San Juan (whose corals are sadly now almost all destroyed), but recent marine conservation work has meant there are now sufficient good dive spots near Sosúa itself. **First-time** dives start from US$60, with 3-day PADI Open Water courses from US$400. The shop can also arrange **snorkelling** trips (1hr 30min across two locations; US$30) as well as pick-ups from nearby resorts. The European-run **Merlin Dive Centre** (☎809 571 2963, ⓦdivecentermerlin.com) on the beach road also has a good reputation and is slightly cheaper.

(☎809 571 1666, ⓦok-motors.com). For scooters, try the Italian-run Asso on Calle Dr Rosén (☎809 571 2588, @scooter-for-rent@hotmail.com) who have new scooters to rent for US$20 a day.

Tours Mel Tours in Beachway Plaza (☎809 571 4002, ⓦmel-tour.com) offers full-day catamaran tours of the coast (US$95 per person), half-day horseriding (US$45), river rafting (US$105), Puerto Plata city tours on Tues and Thurs (US$35), whale-watching on Mon, Wed and Fri (US$145) and more.

ACCOMMODATION

Sosúa has plenty of accommodation options; most hotels are in **El Batey**, but there are also a couple of budget options in **Los Charamicos**. In addition, there has been a major boom in private homes and gated condominium construction over the years, which means you can also rent an **entire house** or flat for a week or more for around what a luxury hotel room would cost.

EL BATEY

Casa Marina Beach Alejo Martínez ☎809 571 3690, ⓦcasamarinabeachhotel.com. This 330-room all-inclusive complex squeezed into a small beachfront plot, offers plenty of activities. Usual standard accommodations and a choice of Italian, seafood and Mexican restaurants as well as the ubiquitous buffet fare. RD$4790

★**Casa Valeria** Dr Rosén 28 ☎809 571 3565, ⓦhotelcasavaleria.com. An excellent mid-range choice, with a selection of rooms and apartments (sleeping up to four, with kitchens) set back from the road, surrounding a small pool and leafy garden. The quite plush terracotta-tiled rooms have TVs and a/c and are decorated in a comforting, homely style. There's also a good restaurant serving breakfast in the morning, plus a mix of Dominican and international dishes come evening. RD$2150

★**Casa Veintiuno21** Reparto Taváres and Piano 1, signposted just north of the highway ☎829 342 8089, ⓦcasaveintiuno.com. Deluxe, welcoming, Belgian-owned B&B situated a little inland on the hill in a gorgeous modern building with sleek, sophisticated furnishings. Also has a pool, gym and gourmet restaurant on site (see p.176). With only three rooms you can expect a personalized service. US$160

Mary Rose Alejo Martínez 33 ☎809 571 3428, ⓦmaryrosedr.com. Good-value modern one- and two-bedroom self-catering apartments set round a pleasant pool. Fully fitted kitchens, a/c, wi-fi and flat-screen cable TV. Excellent rates for longer rentals (US$275/week plus US$35 for cleaning) and they can pick you up at Puerto Plata Airport. US$325/week

New Garden Dr Rosén ☎809 571 1557, ⓦnewgardenhotel.net. Decent mid-range option on a quiet street, with spacious rooms in a large motel-like complex set around a central pool. It also boasts an Italian restaurant, wi-fi, and a welcoming garden. The price includes breakfast. US$75

Hotel Orchidee Dr Rosén 24 ☎829 380 0715, hotelorchidee.ch. Small, quiet, Swiss-run guesthouse with basic but comfortable one- and two-bedroom apartments as well as several double rooms, some with a/c (US$7 extra per night). So immaculately clean you would

gladly eat off the floors. Also has an excellent German/international restaurant (daily 6–11pm) and very good wi-fi. RD$1500

Piergiorgio Palace Hotel La Puntilla 1 ☎809 571 2626, ⓦhoteliergiorgio.com. The town's most glamorous choice, set in a faux-Victorian manor right on a rocky promontory. The high-standard rooms have balconies (some with sea vistas, though a set of newly erected condos have blighted the views somewhat) and all the amenities. Room rate includes a buffet breakfast and the excellent *La Puntilla* restaurant (see p.176). US$95

Hotel El Rancho Sosúa Dr Rosén 36 ☎809 571 4070, ⓦhotelelranchososua.com. Good-value rustic-style hotel with thatched roof, terracotta tiles and rough plastering set round a small pool and tropical garden frequented by hummingbirds. The seventeen small rooms, which all have fan, cable TV, fridge and wi-fi, are brightly painted with themed murals and matching bas-relief in the bathrooms; some have a kitchenette. The on-site café-bar serves tasty tapas. US$60

Rocky's Dr Rosén 22 ☎809 571 2951, ⓦrockysbar.com. Cheap rooms (especially for El Batey) that are a little spartan but do have satellite TV, ceiling fans, hot water & wi-fi; some have optional a/c. They're set at the back of the popular bar (see p.177), which means it doesn't get quiet until after midnight. US$29

Sosúa by the Sea B. Phillips at Martínez ☎809 571 3222, ⓦsosuabythesea.com. Very clean and tidy hotel that also offers all-inclusive deals – add US$20 a day per person. Staff are friendly and there's a decent strip of beach, swimming pool, a selection of airy a/c rooms, and a tour desk – but it can get crowded and noisy in the high season (mid-Dec to late April). Prices include breakfast but not 26 percent tax. US$70

LOS CHARAMICOS

Hotel Bambú Above Tienda Mery on El Tablón, the first road left as you enter Los Charamicos from the main road ☎809 865 3848. You may have to yell a bit before you can get any service, but these are the cheapest digs in town. The normal rooms are very dark, uncomfortable and small, so it's worth splashing out RD$500 for the big ones that have

4

balconies overlooking the boisterous street life – this is the area where the working girls and boys live (though not work), but is safe enough if you keep your wits about you. RD$250

★**Villa Mar** Arzeno, near the beach entrance ☎809 571 2256, ⊛villamarsosua.com. An old villa with a friendly atmosphere that offers double rooms or apartments (some with kitchens and sea-view balconies) that vary in size and price, sleeping up to six. All have fans, hot water, wi-fi, and a fridge. Good long-term rates are available. Double rooms US$23, apartments US$45

EATING

Sosúa has plenty of eating options, from the simple *pica pollo* joints and stand-up **cafeterias** of Los Charamicos to the elegant, waterfront seafood **restaurants** of El Batey. In between, Playa Sosúa boasts numerous (largely interchangeable) shack restaurants serving up fresh seafood right on the beach. **Prices** are fairly reasonable and **reservations** are rarely necessary, even in the best joints. The largest supermarket is El Batey's Supermercado Playero, on the C-5 at the eastern El Batey town entrance (daily 8.30am–6pm), but you'll find far cheaper **groceries** in the many small shops of Los Charamicos. Playero, which has a smaller branch on Pedro Clisante, also offers fresh French bread and various European delicacies aimed at the local expat community.

EL BATEY

Bologna Alejo Martínez 13 ☎809 571 1144. Locals and expats regularly return to this Italian restaurant for good, reasonably priced food in relaxed surroundings. The wood-fired oven pizzas (mostly RD$310–390) are delicious as is the beef and ricotta cannelloni (RD$380); they also offer delivery. Daily 8am–11.30pm.

Café Cubano Pedro Clisante 17 at the corner of Libre ☎829 921 1763, ⊛sosuacigars.com. This neat, nicely tiled café-bar, with just a handful of tables, provides a touch of sophistication along this often tacky strip. Breakfasts are great (RD$165–190) and they also serve decent sandwiches (RD$150–225), cakes (RD$45–125) and the like. Let the Cuban rum flow in the evening with cocktails from RD$70; they also sell premium cigars to round things off. Mon–Sat 8am–11pm.

Casa Veintiuno21 Reparto Taváres and Piano 1 ☎829 342 8089, ⊛casaveintiuno.com. One of the best restaurants in town, this place is 100m inland from El Batey in the plush barrio above town. French and tropically influenced food, including very good seafood, all served in their classy open-sided dining room that spreads out around the pool. Look at around RD$1000 per person (more if seafood). Wed–Sun 6–10pm.

La Finca Alejo Martínez 18 ☎809 571 3825. One of Sosúa's top gourmet choices with more than twenty years' experience, *La Finca* serves welcome variations on typical tropical cuisine – think stewed goat in rum sauce, tuna with lemongrass and capers, and grouper with saffron, with mains running RD$270–950. The elegant dining room is set in an antique building. Tues–Sun 5.30–11.30pm.

Moru Mai Pedro Clisante 5 ☎809 571 3682. Decent international food in a smartly decorated open-sided diner. The chic and convivial atmosphere makes it popular, although it's not cheap – expect to pay RD$495 for shrimp with saffron rice. Sumptuous breakfasts are available earlier in the day (8am–3pm) for around RD$175. Daily 8am–midnight.

★**On the Waterfront** Dr Rosén 1 ☎809 571 3024. Choose from fresh lobster, red snapper, sea bass, grouper or calamari while soaking up the view from the sweeping oceanfront patio at this terrific seafood restaurant. Not as pretentious as *La Puntilla* but just as good and one notch less expensive – try the *langosta al Pernod flambé* (RD$1000). Free wi-fi and live music on Saturday evenings. Daily noon–11pm.

La Puntilla de Piergiorgio La Puntilla 1. Sosúa's best-known restaurant, set along a series of grand waterfront patios with fountains, affords spectacular views across to Mount Isabela. Seafood dishes are usually the best choice, particularly the lobster, though there's a good range of salads and vegetarian options. It's the dearest place in town, averaging around RD$2000 per person for a meal with drinks. Daily noon–11pm.

Schlemmerstube Pedro Clisante, next to the Live Bar ☎829 891 9102. Some of the best German food in town, with sausages, hamburgers and grilled chicken (perfect hangover preventatives and cures, basically) all for under RD$200. As it's right at the heart of the night-time action, be warned that you may be party to a little dubious "business" being conducted out in the street. Daily 10am–2am.

Thai Restaurant Chili La Mulatta 2, 5km inland from town ☎809 913 2159, ⊛thairestaurantchili.com. Although the owner is German, the chef is Thai, and this is the best option for Asian cuisine in the area, served outside in a large tropical garden with a pool. Most mains are in the RD$300–600 range, and the green curry is recommended (as is making a reservation before you go). You'll need to take a taxi here. Wed–Sun 6–10pm.

LOS CHARAMICOS AND PLAYA SOSÚA

Andres Playa Sosúa ☎829 340 4296. At the western end of the beach, this relatively large venue cooks up great mounds of reasonably priced fish and seafood on a large open-air grill. The *salpicón de mariscos* (RD$2200) – seafood taster plate – is a good bet if you're in a group. Eat either standing at the bar or on the beach. Daily 7am–10pm.

Michael's Arzeno, at beach entrance ☎ 809 440 2868. This inexpensive seafood spot is frequented mostly by locals. Perched on a cliff top, it offers great views of the beach and a relaxed atmosphere. Fish-of-the-day specials are good value (RD$300–700) and the crab in *criolla* sauce is delicious for RD$300. Daily 10am–9pm.

Scandinavian Bar Playa Sosúa 152 ☎ 809 399 8321. One of the better open-air beach bar-restaurants, with a constant flow of rock'n'roll and inexpensive, well-prepared ribs, German sausages, and steaks, all cooked in front of you in its pristine kitchen. Also has a very wide selection of imported liquors, and free wi-fi. Daily 8am–6pm.

DRINKING AND NIGHTLIFE

Most of Sosúa's **nightlife**, from ear-throbbing clubs and open-air discos to replica British pubs, is aimed squarely at expats. Many also cater to male holiday-makers on the lookout for a little more than a drink and a dance. **Prostitution** is fairly mainstream in Sosúa, which at least makes it easy to spot the places you should avoid – particularly *D'Latin Drink* and the others along that strip of Clisante; do be aware, however, that it takes place in almost all of the city's nightspots to some extent, including the large **casino** adjoining the *Sosúa Bay Hotel* at the west end of Pedro Clisante. Although most of the businesses on **Playa Sosúa** are closed by 7pm, it's actually a very nice place to go later, when the small handful of bars still open are welcoming and convivial.

Bar Gri Gri Playa Sosúa ☎ 809 605 0973. A great little beach bar set amid a clutch of similar establishments in the centre of Playa Sosúa. A major meeting point, with shady seating under nearby trees, they do a nice line in piña coladas served in a pineapple. Daily 9am–7pm.

Britannia Pub Clisante and Libre ☎ 809 571 1959. Rowdy, narrow English pub catering to tourists – it's somewhat nondescript, but still a decent place for a few drinks. Living up to its name, it provides such British culinary delights as fish 'n' chips, and eggs, beans and chips for under RD$300. Daily 8am–11pm.

Jolly Roger Clisante 11 ☎ 809 571 4072, ⓦ jollyrogersosua.com. Catering unashamedly to the local resorts' knees-up crowds, this tacky pirate-themed bar has extended happy hours every day from noon–8pm

with darts, bingo, and karaoke on Thursdays. It's frequently swinging, and the pub grub sold for RD$100–250 helps absorb the booze. Wi-fi available. Daily 11am–2am.

Jungle Juiced Playa Sosúa 147 next to the showers. Nice Swedish-run outdoor bar/shack on the main beach with ice-cold beer and mixed drinks, including a tasty but incredibly strong rum punch that enhances the beach-going experience considerably. It's a great place to meet people, and you can order food from their restaurant next door. Daily 9am–7pm.

Rocky's Dr Rosén 22 ☎ 809 571 2951, ⓦ rockysbar.com. Friendly, jam-packed hangout popular with expats, dishing up great burgers, slabs of barbecued ribs (RD$320), good fried breakfasts and ice-cold beer. Mama Juana shots (a Dominican aphrodisiac) are offered to those hoping to really make a night of it. Daily 8am–midnight.

Cabarete and around

Stretched along the C-5 between the beach and lagoon that bear its name, **CABARETE** is a crowded international enclave that owes its existence almost entirely to **windsurfing** and **kiteboarding**. There was no town to speak of in 1984 when legendary windsurfer Jean

MONKEY JUNGLE

A popular addition to the activities on offer along the Silver Coast is the **Monkey Jungle** (daily 9am–4pm; ☎ 829 649 4555, ⓦ monkeyjungledr.com; cash only) which offers half-day tours of their impressive 300-acre compound 9km inland at the foot of the mountains along the Choco Road. Apart from interacting with and feeding the squirrel and capuchin monkeys (US$25), they also have an exhilarating 1441m-long **zipline** tour (US$50) with marvellous views of both mountains and sea. It's the longest in the Caribbean and includes an adrenaline-pumping 10m **fandescender** into a cave. They are also happy and able to take any physically disabled customers on the zipline, including paraplegics. Started by a charming (and no-nonsense) retired American couple, the **non-profit** attraction not only generates money to maintain a charitable free medical and dental clinic for the poor of the region, but also provides employment for more than forty locals in this economically deprived area. To get there you can either book a **tour** from more or less any accommodation or agent between Puerto Plata and Cabarete (US$80), or you can **make your own** way there – the turnoff from the C-5 is signposted between Sosúa and Cabarete, or take a taxi from Cabarete (US$25), Sosúa (US$20) or Puerto Plata (US$40–50).

Laporte discovered the area's near-perfect conditions. The town quickly became a haven for sculpted surf bums debating the nuances of surf gear in between death-defying feats, a scene that was augmented exponentially when **kiteboarding** became part of the mix in 2000 – it has now gone on to become the area's dominant watersport. The multicultural cross-section of aficionados of the two activities has led to a growing community of people from across the globe, which has in turn attracted hotel chains and an assortment of adventure sports outfits. In fact, it's hard for return visitors to believe how quickly Cabarete has blossomed.

Today "Cabarete" spans more than 4km of the highway, with no end to the expansion in sight. A spate of recently built **all-inclusives** has led to the growth of a more traditional brand of tourism, but the clients at these new hotels are generally younger, hipper and more interested in adventure sports than guests at more family-oriented complexes like Playa Dorada. And the open, accessible layout of the town prevents it from having the closed-off atmosphere of other Dominican tourist enclaves. Be warned that you will need to put on insect repellent towards sunset and at night due to the mosquitos from the lagoon.

The town

What there is of a **town** consists of the hectic and rapidly expanding strip of restaurants and hotels stretching out along the C-5 for well over 4km just behind the water. The main Dominican barrio is set back towards the lagoon, along the road to the national park, and on the eastern perimeters along a road known as **Pro-Cab**. As you'd expect from a town that grew up on surfing, the beach, **Playa Cabarete**, is where the real action is. Here, and at **Kite Beach**, 2km west of town, kitesurfers, windsurfers and

4

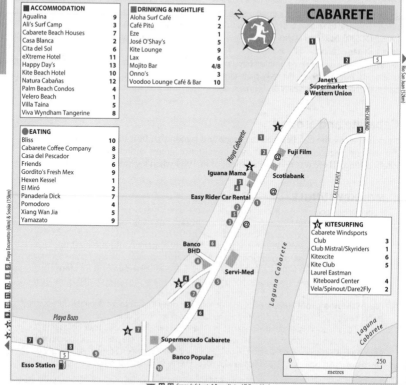

▣ ACCOMMODATION	
Agualina	9
Ali's Surf Camp	3
Cabarete Beach Houses	7
Casa Blanca	2
Cita del Sol	6
eXtreme Hotel	11
Happy Day's	13
Kite Beach Hotel	10
Natura Cabañas	12
Palm Beach Condos	4
Velero Beach	1
Villa Taina	5
Viva Wyndham Tangerine	8

● EATING	
Bliss	10
Cabarete Coffee Company	8
Casa del Pescador	3
Friends	6
Gordito's Fresh Mex	9
Hexen Kessel	1
El Miró	2
Panadería Dick	7
Pomodoro	4
Xiang Wan Jia	5
Yamazato	9

▣ DRINKING & NIGHTLIFE	
Aloha Surf Café	7
Café Pitú	2
Eze	1
José O'Shay's	5
Kite Lounge	9
Lax	6
Mojito Bar	4/8
Onno's	3
Voodoo Lounge Café & Bar	10

CABARETE

Janet's Supermarket & Western Union

PRO-CAB ROAD

Rio San Juan (32km)

Playa Cabarete

Fuji Film

Iguana Mama

Scotiabank

CALLE BAHIA

Easy Rider Car Rental

☆ KITESURFING	
Cabarete Windsports Club	3
Club Mistral/Skyriders	1
Kitexcite	6
Kite Club	5
Laurel Eastman Kiteboard Center	4
Vela/Spinout/Dare2Fly	2

Banco BHD

Servi-Med

Laguna Cabarete

Laguna Cabarete

Playa Bozo

Playa Encuentro (6km) & Sosúa (15km)

Supermercado Cabarete

Banco Popular

0 — 250 metres

Esso Station

13, **10**, Cuevas de Cabarete & Parque Nacional El Choco (1km)

sun-worshippers rule the shoreline. Between the two, and a little further out to the east, you'll find more peace and quiet.

El Choco National Park
1km south of the C-5 on Callejón de la Loma • Mon–Fri 8.30am–5.30pm • US$20 including guide in English

Behind the town to the south is **El Choco National Park**, a lush green wilderness that contains the lovely **Laguna Cabarete**, home to thousands of birds but surrounded by dense brush and somewhat hard to get around – indeed, most of it is fenced off as it's owned by a Brazilian rancher whose cattle roam the area. The park also holds the much easier access **Caves of Cabarete**, a set of holes around the lagoon that have been fenced off and illuminated with electric light. There's a park entrance down a well-marked turnoff just west of town, where you will be assigned a guide to the caves and lagoon. You'll see a few signs of Taino occupation (though twentieth-century graffiti is more prominent than any Taino art) and have the opportunity to swim in an underground pool.

Playa Encuentro
6km west of Cabarete on the C-5 • To get here from Cabarete, take a *motoconcho* (RD$60–80) or taxi (RD$250) direct, or take a guagua (RD$15) as far as the *Coconut Palms Resort*, then walk 1.5km down a paved road to the beach.

Undeveloped **Playa Encuentro** has massive waves – of the sort unseen in most of the

---

WINDSURFING AND KITEBOARDING IN CABARETE

The conditions for **windsurfing** in Cabarete are so perfect that the whole bay could have been designed specifically with this in mind. The **trade winds** normally blow from the east, meaning that they sweep across the bay from right to left allowing easy passage both out to the offshore reefs and back to the beach, and the water is always warm. Downwind, the waters lap onto the amusingly named **Bozo Beach**, which will catch anybody unfortunate enough to have a mishap. The offshore reef provides plenty of surf for the **experts** who ride the waves, performing tricks and some spectacular jumps. The reef also shelters the inshore waters so that on all but the roughest of winter days they remain calm. The morning winds are little more than a gentle breeze and this, coupled with the flat water, makes the bay ideal for **beginners**, especially in summer when the surface can resemble a mirror. Then, as the temperature rises, the trade winds kick in big-time and the real show starts with the highest winds between 3 and 4pm. Wind speeds are generally 16–30 knots in the summer, and slightly lower during the winter at 10–23 knots, although the waves are bigger then. Take some binoculars if you want to see the action out on the reef.

Two kilometres west of Playa Cabarete, hidden behind Punta Goleta, is the white-sand **Kite Beach** which has become a massive international hub for **kiteboarding**. In many ways similar to windsurfing, but using a much smaller, more manoeuvrable board and relying on a huge C-shaped kite to provide the power instead of a sail, kiteboarding requires less wind. As a result, the riders travel faster than their windsurfing counterparts, allowing them to perform huge jumps and tricks that would be impossible with a sail. Its spectacular nature has greatly boosted its popularity and in recent years kiteboarding has taken over from windsurfing as the pre-eminent watersport throughout Cabarete – everything between Kite Beach and Bozo Beach is now pretty much taken up by the sport. And in the last half of June, sponsorship permitting, Kite Beach is also one of the locations of the prestigious **Kiteboarding World Cup** (ⓦ prokitetour.com) – check website for details. Meanwhile, good old-fashioned **surfing** has become increasingly popular, especially along Playa Encuentro west of town (see p.180).

There are windsurf and kiteboard **schools** (see p.180) strung right along the beach. The schools have a confusing array of pricing structures but there's not really much difference between them. The choices come down to the make (rather than quality) of equipment, the level of technological aids used, the amount of gear in stock (important during busier times like Christmas–New Year and July–August), the launch position on the beach, and the languages spoken by the staff. Nonetheless, there can be differences in the weight and age of the boards, masts and booms, so if you haven't booked in advance you should check two or three out and see what equipment they have available, especially in high season.

4

ACTIVITIES AND OPERATORS AT PLAYA ENCUENTRO

For **surfing lessons** you'll pay around US$45 for a two-hour class and US$100–120 for a five-day camp, but check whether board rental is included, and ask around for who has the best instructors and rates. Surfboard **rental** costs US$20–25/day, or US$110–140/week. Below is a selection of the more established **surf schools**.

3-2-1 Take Off ☎809 963 7873, ⓦ321.takeoff .com. Long-standing surf school that runs lessons for all standards. Also organizes the Master of the Ocean Triathlon every February (a competition involving surfing, windsurfing and kiteboarding) and can find you private rooms for rent nearby (around US$35 a night).

Buena Onda ☎829 877 0768, ⓦcabaretebuenaonda .com. Fairly new outfit providing lessons and rental plus excursions to Playa Grande and Playa Preciosa (see p.186). Transport to and from the beach from Cabarete is an extra US$5.

Cabarete Surf Camp ☎809 571 0733, ⓦcabaretesurfcamp.com. The camp offers some of the cheapest rates and provides showers at the beach, transport to and from Cabarete (included in lesson prices) and offers weekly surf trips to other beaches. Their accommodation is at *Ali's Surf Camp* (see p.183) by the lagoon. Check out their website for their range of economical accommodation/food/surfing packages.

DR – which attract a good number of surfers and a handful of highly skilled, possibly suicidal **kitesurfers**. It's worth stopping off between 6am and 8am to watch the most daring of them ride atop 6m waves, execute 360-degree leaps and even ride within the curl of the waves on the rare occasions when the surf is large enough to allow it. Every March the **Encuentro Classic** takes place here, one of the top-rated surfing competitions in the world. If you fancy a go yourself, try one of the **surf schools** (see box above) that run out of small wooden huts variously serving as offices, repair workshops and snack bars. At weekends, it actually gets quite rowdy here, with many locals using this slightly less touristy beach for drinking and listening to deafening Latin music. In 2013, there was a fear that the seafront would be developed like Cabarete but, thanks to local opposition, the beach has been declared a **national ecotourism sport park** – it will continue to be a lovely spot for some time yet.

Sabaneta de Yásica and around

To get here take any guagua running along the highway

SABANETA DE YÁSICA, a few kilometres southeast of Cabarete, is a nondescript concrete town at the junction of the **Río Yásica** – a large river with little development along it – and the Atlantic. It's the starting point of a delightful excursion run by a local company (see p.181) up a tributary of the Yásica to the large **Laguna Islabón**, then back along the Yásica to the river's mouth, passing through otherwise impossible-to-access, dense **rainforest** and **mangrove swamp**, home to an enormous variety of orchids, tropical birds and reptiles.

South from Sabaneta de Yásica, the **Sabaneta–Moca road** winds through the heart of the Cordillera Septentrional past a number of relatively prosperous agricultural pueblos. One of them, pueblo **Los Brazos**, is an isolated mountaintop compound that, if you're looking for restful mountain scenery and amazing food, makes a great place to spend a few nights.

ARRIVAL AND DEPARTURE   CABARETE AND AROUND

Guaguas run regularly every 10–15min from Cabarete to Río San Juan, Sosúa, and Puerto Plata, which are all connected by bus to Santo Domingo and Santiago. These guaguas are also handy for Puerto Plata airport, where the terminal is just 400m away from the main road. A taxi from Puerto Plata airport to Cabarete should cost US$35. Samaná airport is 2hr 30min away by taxi (US$100–150), or multiple guagua rides (around RD$300), and many of the cheaper flights (especially from Canada) land there. A reliable taxi firm who serve all the airports is Cocotours (☎809 586 1311, ⓦcocotours.com); a Santo Domingo transfer would be US$109, for example.

GETTING AROUND

By taxi Taxis are not cheap along the Silver Coast but they are easy to find. Try Taxi Sosúa (☎ 809 571 0767), located right in the middle of Cabarete; it has a board outside the office indicating their fixed (and high) prices.

By motoconcho The exponential growth of visitors has led to hotels cropping up for over 1km around the main strip, the furthest ones being accessible via the cheap and omnipresent *motoconchos*. You should never have to pay more than RD$30 during the day to get from an outlying hotel to the main strip, RD$60 at night – note

that their first price may well be RD$50 and RD$100 respectively.

By car or motorcycle On the main road is German-run Easy Rider (☎ 809 571 0250), who are probably the best and most economical of the rental outfits, with a wide range of cars from US$39, and motorbikes from US$15 per day, with good non-deductible insurance provided for US$2–10 a day. The friendly owner, Josef, has been here well over two decades and is also a great source of information – he's happy to advise even non-customers.

ACTIVITES AND OPERATORS

While **windsurfing** and **kiteboarding** are for many visitors the whole point of coming to Cabarete, you can enjoy several other activities while you're here as well. One popular attraction in the surrounding countryside is the **mountain-biking trail** along the old El Choco road – once used to truck bananas from the countryside to the coast but now little more than a dirt path – that promises wonderful scenery and glimpses of rural life. Also along the Choco road you'll find the excellent, ethical **Monkey Jungle**, with the Caribbean's longest **zipline** (see box, p.177). A more leisurely way to appreciate and learn about the countryside and its population is to go **horseriding**, easily organized through several tour companies (Iguana Mama included) or your hotel, though you can also book directly with several local ranches such as **Rancho Veragua**; or by taking a **river trip** along the Río Yásica (see opposite). The website ⓦ activecabarete.com provides useful information and web links for the full range of Cabarete's outdoor activities.

KITESURF AND WINDSURF SCHOOLS AND EQUIPMENT RENTAL

Cabarete Windsports Club ☎ 809 571 0784, ⓦ cabaretewindsportsclub.com. A small and friendly centre just in front of the *Villa Taina*, with which it is affiliated. The clientele is mainly German, but English, French and Italian are spoken as well. Very personalized and good for families – they'll even take beginners onto a lagoon to start. US$150 for three sessions windsurfing (1.5–3hr depending on group size) on the water and US$360 for the same time kitesurfing; US$50 per day equipment rental.

Club Mistral/Skyriders Eastern end of Cabarete beach ☎ 809 571 979, Germany ☎ 49 881 925 4960, ⓦ clubmistral.com. A well-stocked centre with great staff for windsurfing, kiteboarding and surfing that benefits from being part of a large international company.

Kite Club Kite Beach ☎ 809 571 9748, ⓦ kiteclubcabarete.com. Well-organized IKO-affiliated club which also runs instructors' courses, and has a lively club (membership from US$15/week) and café on the beach. A three-day beginner's package costs US$438 (in a group of two). Also offer wakeboarding.

Kitexcite Kite Beach ☎ 809 571 9509, ⓦ kitexcite.com. Opened way back in 1999 and the original kiteboarding school on Kite Beach (part of the *Kite Beach Hotel*). The German owner claims to have trained or worked with almost all the other instructors on the beach. Staff can speak English, German, French or Spanish and the teaching is quite hi-tech with radio helmets to give instant feedback on your performance on the waves, and video feedback

after. Charges US$438 for a three-day beginner's course.

Laurel Eastman Kiteboard Center Millennium Hotel, Cabarete Beach ☎ 809 571 0564, ⓦ laureleastman .com. School founded by a legendary female kitesurfer who does a good job of training newbies, and uses video support. Four-day private courses for US$498 and four-day two-person lessons for US$438.

Vela/Spinout/Dare2Fly Cabarete Beach ☎ 809 571 0805, ⓦ velacabarete.com, ⓦ dare2fly.com. German-owned and the best-stocked of Cabarete's windsurf centres, with free daily clinics and a lively social scene at the adjoining bar. They charge US$415 for a week's kiteboarding equipment rental. Their Dare2Fly station on Kite Beach offers equipment rental and lessons daily, from US$420 for a three-day introductory course with equipment.

ADVENTURE TOUR OPERATORS

★**Iguana Mama** Carretera 5 ☎ 809 571 0908, ⓦ iguanamama.com. The very best of the country's adventure operators, with imaginative tours, friendly and well-trained staff, and an admirable ethical record. They offer a huge selection of half-day mountain-bike trips (US$65–110), suitable for all levels of rider and fitness, as well as week-long adventure tours of the island, hikes up Mount Isabela (US$95; see p.163) and multiday treks through the Cordillera Central to Pico Duarte (US$522). They also rent out quality mountain bikes for US$25/day and offer horseriding for US$55/half-day. Transport from your hotel is not necessarily included.

Islabón Jungle River Tours On the main road 3km from both Cabarete and Sabaneta de Yásica

4

(see opposite) ☎ 809 667 1960. Operates a rainforest tour (2hr 30min; US$45) up a tributary of the Río Yásica to Laguna Islabón, then turning back along the Yásica to the river's mouth. Phone first to make a reservation.

Kayak River Adventures Carretera 5, next to the Cabarete Coffee Company ☎ 829 305 6883, ⓦ kayakriveradventures.com. Relaxing half-day (US$59) or full-day (US$89) excursions down the Yásica, offering an opportunity to swim there too. Overnight camping can also be arranged as can two-day tours to Punta Rucia and whitewater rafting in Jarabacoa.

Laser Training Centre Cabarete Beach ☎ 809 571 0640, ⓦ caribwind.com. The place to learn to sail, boasting three Beijing Olympic medallists on the team. Beginner and intermediate sailors can have three two-hour sessions at US$360 for two people; US$300 for private tuition. Weekly and monthly packages are available for advanced sailors.

Rancho Veragua In Veragua, 12km south of Cabarete ☎ 203 228 3156, ⓦ ranchoveragua.com. Offers a choice of mountain-based or beach-based half-day horseriding tours (US$75), both including the chance to swim and with the option of enjoying a traditional Dominican lunch at the ranch for an extra US$5. They speak English and are very good with kids too.

ACCOMMODATION

Cabarete has a bewildering variety of accommodation, including small **pensiones**, several good mid-range choices, a number of apart-hotels and a few **all-inclusives**. Increasingly popular are the **condominium** rental complexes, particularly on the west side of town as many allow you to launch your kiteboard directly off the beachfront and the prices are still comparatively reasonable for the Caribbean. The oldest, most established hotels are in the **town centre** (which is also where you'll find the best restaurants and bars); a run of condos and newer all-inclusives line **Punta Goleta** at the western edge of the main strip; and another spate of new hotels has sprung up around **Kite Beach**, 2km west of town. Regardless of location, it's advisable to **book** ahead. If you'd like a more Dominican experience, try staying south of the centre down **Callejón de la Loma**: this is where the locals live and there are a couple of small, economical (but decent) hotels, and inexpensive *comedores*. Prices below are all nightly unless otherwise stated. Just outside of town, the **Blue Moon Retreat** is a must.

MAIN STRIP

Cita del Sol Carretera 5 ☎ 809 571 0720, ⓦ citadelsol .com. A hidden gem, far enough away from the road to cut out most of the chaos and yet near several restaurants. Good-sized, recently refurbished one-bedroom apartments with kitchens and a pleasant pool area for relaxing. US$420/week

Palm Beach Condos Carretera 5 ☎ 809 571 0758, ⓦ cabaretecondos.com. Right in the middle of the action on the beach, with full-service apartments sleeping four (private patios with sea views) and smaller (also cheaper) studios with kitchenettes. All tastefully furnished and with high-speed internet, set round a lovely tropical garden and pool. A minimum stay of a week is required during peak periods. Studio US$121

Villa Taina Carretera 5 ☎ 809 571 0722, ⓦ villataina .com. A restful choice, with helpful staff, great atmosphere and a selection of clean, tidy rooms, all with the usual mod cons (and some with balconies and sea views), plus a quiet beachside restaurant. Lots of activities, including canyoning, horseriding, sunset cruises and, of course, kiteboarding are offered. Rates include breakfast. US$127

WEST OF THE MAIN STRIP

Agualina Carretera 5 ☎ 809 571 0787, ⓦ agualina .com. Nice full-service apartments right on Kite Beach, with an in-house kiteboarding school, Dare2Fly (see p.181). Unlike similar places, the apartments are not only spacious (the biggest have three bedrooms and sleep up to six), they're also stylishly done and all have balconies and sea views. Highly recommended if you're going to spend most of your time on Kite Beach. Double US$100

Cabarete Beach Houses Carretera 5 ☎ 809 571 0744, ⓦ cabaretebeachhouses.com. Excellent-value high-end accommodation, especially if you're with a group – these two-storey apartments, 1km west of Cabarete's core, boast two huge bedrooms, a spacious lounge and well-equipped kitchens, but what makes them really stand out are the rooftop sundecks (with shower) affording great sea views. Located on a quiet section of beach with a private pool and a tennis court. US$105

★ **eXtreme Hotel** Carretera 5/Kite Beach ☎ 809 571 0330, ⓦ extremehotels.com. Canadian-run and eco-friendly (they recycle and are solar-powered), this is the pick of the adventure-sports hotels on Kite Beach, and noted for its lively atmosphere – hardly surprising as it's the site of the Caribbean's only underground skate park. Also boasts a circus, gym (yoga lessons available), pool, and Spanish language school. Rooms are fairly basic – most have no a/c – but have two to three beds to accommodate large groups. Minimum-stay two nights, with good rates for long-term stays. Wi-fi available. US$59

Happy Day's Entrada la Colonia El Alto Cabarete ☎ 809 571 9726. Right out south of the main road in the village (turn left from Callejón de la Loma at *Mary's Restaurant*), this small hotel has basic but comfortable rooms with fans and small balconies. Very good value for the money and, as it's mostly a residential street, is more of a Dominican experience (in other words, it's quite loud). RD$600

Kite Beach Hotel Carretera 5 at Kite Beach ☏ 809 571 0878, ⓦ kitebeachhotel.com. Large Kite Beach hotel with its own kiteboarding school, Kitexcite (see p.181). A mix of reasonably decorated rooms and apartments, all with a/c and cable TV. The older rooms are cheaper and there are big discounts for long-term stays. Double rooms U$$79

Natura Cabañas Carretera 5, 5km west of town within the Perla Marina gated community ☏ 809 571 1507, ⓦ naturacabana.com. Secluded complex with ten tastefully decorated bungalows (some with kitchens), crafted out of stone, wood and thatch, set among tropical gardens backing onto a private beach (though strong currents preclude swimming). On site there's a spa, yoga pavilion and excellent restaurant. The place markets itself as the "eco alternative", but in fact offers just a slightly more rustic (and pricier) version of what's available in Cabarete Town. Still, it's a great place to get away from it all. U$$155

Viva Wyndham Tangerine Carretera 5 ☏ 809 71-0402, ⓦ vivaresorts.com. One of the biggest and best all-inclusives here, following the standard *Viva* template with 273 large rooms (with minibars and terraces), buffet, Italian and Mexican restaurants, boundless activities and easy beach access. Per person U$$89

EAST OF THE MAIN STRIP

★**Ali's Surf Camp (Cabarete Surf Camp)** Pro-Cab Rd ☏ 829 548 6655, ⓦ cabaretesurfcamp.com. Friendly backpackers-style surf camp set on the lagoon (so be prepared for mosquitos when the wind drops) with its own surfing facilities on Encuentro Beach (see p.179). Lodgings are varied but all cheerily decorated, from simple, fan-ventilated rooms with mosquito nets, sinks, storage space and shared washing facilities to a fully equipped "Tarzan house" sleeping six (US$100) with rooms, studios and apartments in between (a/c costs US$15 extra per night). The lovely tropical grounds contain a small pool, sun loungers and a communal thatched bar-restaurant which provides set menus including vegetarian dishes and is a prime spot for meeting fellow travellers. Rates include breakfast and dinner. U$$40

Casa Blanca Carretera 5 ☏ 809 571 0934, ⓦ casablancacabarete.com. Solid mid-range option just off the beach, comprising nine studios with kitchenettes and seven spacious but sparse rooms with a few having TV and a/c (US$7 extra per night). You can use the communal kitchen and dining area for an extra US$3 per day and there's a modest but pleasant pool area where breakfast is served. Free gear storage and good kite- and windsurfing package deals available. Double U$$42

★**Velero Beach** Carretera 5 ☏ 809 571 9727, ⓦ velerobeach.com. The town's fanciest choice, the *Velero* is a very attractive hotel with large, luxuriously equipped rooms (all with oceanfront balconies and high-speed internet access), plus some even larger two-bedroom suites, which come with kitchens and can accommodate a family of six. Attentive service, a gorgeous pool area, top-notch restaurant and tropical gardens (with four-poster sun loungers) complete the picture. U$$169

BLUE MOON RETREAT

★**Blue Moon Retreat** Down a signposted track just before the village of Los Brazos on the C-21 to Moca ☏ 809 571 0614, ⓦ bluemoonretreat.net. Mountain-top accommodation in four brightly decorated cabins scattered around a swimming pool, with comfortable beds and clean bathrooms. Even more notable is their unique restaurant, which serves multiple courses of delicious gourmet Indian-Caribbean fusion food on banana leaves (US$20 a head). Diners sit cross-legged on the floor on mats and cushions under a coconut-thatch roof, and vegetarian food is available. Reservations usually have to be made at least three days in advance, and they only serve parties of eight or more people; if short of the requisite number, give them a call anyway, and see if you can piggyback onto another party. It's a twenty-minute drive from Cabarete (usually around US$20 each way by taxi); from Sabaneta there are *motoconchos* that can take you the 10km here for around RD$150. If staying the night here, the cabin price includes breakfast. Cabin U$$50

EATING

Cabarete has an array of good **dining** options, the impressive range thanks to the largely expat ownership. Indeed, outside of Santo Domingo and Las Terrenas, Cabarete may have the best French and Italian food available in the Dominican Republic. Even with all of these choices, though, a pilgrimage to the wonderful nearby Caribbean-Indian restaurant **Blue Moon Retreat** (see above) is a must when in town. Those with kitchenettes should head for **groceries** at the well-stocked Janet's Supermarket, which is next door to the *Casa Blanca* resort at the east end of the downtown strip. At night, the bars and restaurants spill out onto the sand, making for a superb dining scene at both Playa Cabarete and Kite Beach, where you can eat at a quality restaurant with sand between your toes. It also gets pretty lively later as many of the bars take on the role of discos and clubs.

Bliss Callejón de la Loma 5 ☏ 809 571 9721, ⓦ activecabarete.com/bliss. Tropical takes on Italian staples – such as gazpacho soup with tiger shrimps and avocado, or lobster with pastis – in a very elegant and stylish courtyard dining space next to a swimming pool,

just back from the road. Mains in the RD$300–600 range. Daily except Wed 6–10.30pm.

★**Cabarete Coffee Company** Carretera 5 ☏ 809 571 0919, ⓦ cabaretecoffeecompany.com. Inexpensive (all dishes under RD$200), no-frills café using locally grown or organic ingredients where possible. All-day breakfasts range from bowls of yoghurt, nuts and granola (RD$150) to the less healthy waffles with whipped cream (RD$250). Delicious, inventive salads and deli sandwiches are just the ticket for lunch with the peanut butter and jelly panini (RD$75) an improbable hit, and vegan and gluten-free food is available. Join one of their day-trips to the estates where they source their organic coffee and cocoa. Don't miss out on the fabulous mural in the toilet. Wi-fi available. Daily 7am–3pm.

Casa del Pescador Carretera 5 ☎809 571 9411. The best seafood in town, where you can pick the lobster of your choice from the pool at the front. The plastic chairs make it look cheaper than it is – expect to pay around RD$300–700 for mains. Surf and turf options also available. Daily 10.30am–11pm.

Friends Carretera 5 ☎809 571 9733. Next door to *Panadería Dick*, this nice breakfast (RD$100–250) and lunch spot serves hearty sandwiches, salads and fruit shakes. Also has more exotic fare such as the Canadian favourite *poutine*, and savoury French galettes, as well as free wi-fi. Daily 7am–4pm.

Gordito's Fresh Mex Plaza Ocean Dream ☎829 844 3434, ⓦgorditosfreshmex.com. Generally agreed to be the best Mexican food in town, this clean, very busy joint serves excellent, filling burritos (RD$120–200), tacos (RD$50–70) and salad bowls (RD$145–200) either inside or out on the patio to a largely North American crowd. The fish burrito is well worth a try and vegetarian options are available. Mon–Sat 11am–8pm.

Hexen Kessel Carretera 5 ☎809 571 9304. Restaurant-cum-meeting place, open 24hr, that's a little bit more rough and ready than its beachfront counterparts. You sit at picnic-style tables ordering from a long blackboard featuring German specials (such as schnitzel or sausages for around RD$450), as well as burgers (RD$180) and pizza (from RD$250). Open-sided, making it the best people-watching spot in town. Daily 24hr.

El Miró Playa Cabarete ☎809 853 6848. Excellent and authentic Spanish tapas and rices along with a few Moroccan and Japanese dishes (sushi roll two-for-one happy hour daily 5–6pm), served either on the beach or in the Miró-themed interior. The tapas (RD$150–495) are great, as are their range of wines, though it isn't cheap, with mains running RD$585–845, and the superb black paella coming in at RD$1450. Daily noon–midnight.

Panadería Dick Carretera 5 ☎809 571 0712. Just the smell of this place will give you a lift, with various gourmet breads for a few pesos, great Danishes and French-quality croissants. They also have fresh orange juice and "cappuccinos" that taste like French *café crème*. Daily 7am–5pm (closed Wed & Sun afternoon).

★**Pomodoro** Cabarete ☎809 571 0085. This is a very good pizzeria with a warm ambience, serving over thirty variations, from the RD$260 margherita to the RD$440 special (mozzarella, gorgonzola, parmesan and prosciutto) under an awning on the beach. Live jazz on Thurs. Daily 11am–11pm.

Xiang Wan Jia (El Chino) Carretera 5 ☎809 571 0972. Cabarete's only Chinese restaurant is a winner, with dim sum, prawn fried rice, chop suey and their excellent prawns in black bean sauce (mains RD$140–200) all served in informal surroundings. The food, healthier and less salty than you'll find elsewhere on the island, is better in the evening when the Chinese owners are there. Takeaway available. Daily 10am–10pm.

Yamazato Plaza Ocean Dream ☎809 571 0814, ⓦyamazato.com.do. The best Japanese food in Cabarete. This stylish restaurant serves a wide range of dishes from classic Japanese sushi and bento boxes to delicious Thai stir-fries. Mains run RD$450–600 while sashimi and sushi rolls are RD$215–300 – you can also eat more economically with one of their lunchtime specials (RD$140–250). Tues–Sun noon–2.30pm & 5.30–10pm.

DRINKING, NIGHTLIFE AND ENTERTAINMENT

As the sun starts to set, the happy-hour **bar crawls** begin. Cabarete is packed with **bars**, but only those with the prime beachfront locations garner the majority of the business. There's occasionally **live music** at various locations (though the standard is sometimes quite appalling), and every late October/early November Cabarete provides some of the venues for the annual **Dominican Republic Jazz Festival** (ⓦdrjazzfestival.com).

Aloha Surf Café Just off Playa Bozo, at the entrance to Ocean 1 ☎809 904 7281. As the name suggests, this is a laidback, popular watering hole for surfers, where the good food also attracts a fair number of residents from the nearby condos. Thursday is barbecue night with an all-you-can-eat buffet (US$8–15 depending on meat; reservation recommended) and on Friday there's live music. Wed–Sun 4pm–3am (or later).

Café Pitú Carretera 5/Playa Cabarete ☎809 601 3075. This relaxed, friendly beach café does a mean chicken

enchilada as well as pizzas (RD$230–350) and each night has a different theme: two-for-one pizzas on Tuesdays, for instance, and reggae nights on Thursdays (with "Rasta pasta" for RD$99). Daily 7.30am–1am.

Eze Playa Cabarete ☎809 571 0586. Mellow beachfront bar offering California wraps (RD$275–315), smoothies and fresh fruit juice in the day. When the sun goes down, it's time for the laidback nightlife to begin – grab a hammock. Daily 8am–2am.

José O'Shay's Playa Cabarete ☎809 571 0775.

Irish-themed bar that strains every sinew to get the party started. Events include live music, discos and its biggest draw – big-screen sports on the beach. Although it only has Guinness in cans, its range of liquors is quite good. Attracts a dedicated North American crowd. Daily 8am–2am.

Kite Lounge *Extreme Hotel*, Kite Beach ☎ 809 571 0330. Usually packed with kitesurfers chilling and watching other kitesurfers performing their tricks, while sipping a smoothie or a beer, or enjoying a game of table tennis. Inexpensive breakfasts and lunch served, though the cocktails are pricier. Daily 8am–7pm.

★ **Lax** Cabarete Beach ☎ 829 745 8811. Popular place to come both early evening, when it serves a pretty decent bar menu (various happy hours for different drinks), and later when there's often dancing. Relaxed and loaded with rows of couches under sail-like awnings on the sand looking out over the sea. Occasionally hosts live music. Daily 8am–midnight (later at weekends).

Mojito Bar Cabarete Beach and Kite Beach ☎ 829 298 0712. Currently the "it" place on the beach, this tiny Italian-run cocktail bar takes up just a sliver of the beach between two larger venues, but manages to be more popular than either. The mojitos (RD$140) are very good, as are the frozen cocktails, and they also do a pukka caipirinha (RD$180). If you need something to soak up the alcohol, try the delicious Italian sandwiches. There's a larger but not-quite-as-popular branch on Kite Beach. Daily except Tues 12.30pm–3am.

Onno's Cabarete Beach ☎ 809 571 0461, ⓦ onnosbar .com. Lively bar-restaurant on the beachfront in the centre of the strip. The small dance area gets going in the wee hours, playing mainly European and American hits. They also have pretty good food, including pizzas from RD$320, though it's cheaper (for various drinks too) during happy hour from 5–9pm. Daily 8am–3am.

Voodoo Lounge Café and Bar Entrada de Callejon de la Loma ☎ 809 924 8686. Smallish Italian-run bar in a coconut-leaf hut away from the beach that is a favourite of the younger expat community. The bar has a few German and Belgian beers as well as the usual suspects and the 24-hour café next door serves a small range of bready Italian snacks such as pizza, bruschetta and the house speciality *piadini* for RD$100–150. Open-mic on Wednesdays; live music or DJs at the weekend. Daily 5pm–1am.

4

Río San Juan and around

The small, friendly fishing village of **RÍO SAN JUAN**, 51km east of Cabarete, borders a large mangrove lagoon, **Laguna Gri-Gri**, as well as being in reach of several great **beaches**, including **Playa Caletón**, **Playa Grande** and **Playa Preciosa**. Although development has taken place around the village over the past decade, it has remained little changed: its tree-lined streets, easy-going atmosphere and simple reliance on boat building, fishing and dairy farming come as a welcome change from the resort bustle to the west.

Laguna Gri-Gri and maritime activities

Northernmost end of Duarte and down the steps • Boat tours (2–3hr; RD$1500 for 3 to 6 people and RD$250/person thereafter); snorkelling (2hr; US$40 per person); fishing (5–6hr; US$75 per person) • ☎ 809 589 2277

The town's main attraction is **Laguna Gri-Gri**, a magnificent mangrove reserve traversed by organized **boat tours** that you can arrange and board from a small quay at the end of Duarte. The tours head out of the lagoon through the mangroves; go early in the morning if you want to catch more of the birdlife. The boat then enters nearby **Cueva de la Golondrina** (Swallow's Cave) to admire the stalactites and stalagmites, before heading along the coast to **Playa Caletón**, where you get to swim. You can also arrange to go snorkelling or fishing trips here. To see the lagoon's birdlife **on foot**, walk east from the *Hotel Bahía Blanca* to the peninsular bird sanctuary that the tour skirts, which is at its most active just before dusk when hundreds of egrets return to roost. Alternatively take the dirt footpath to the left of the tours office.

The town beaches

Three tiny **beaches**, which pretty much disappear at high tide, are within a two-minute walk from town. Two are bisected by the *Hotel Bahía Blanca*: to the west, **Playa de Río San Juan**, the main town beach, and to the right, **Playa de la Guardia**, which has a volleyball court. If you follow a 50m track at the end of the sand you reach **Playa de los Muertos** (so named on account of its proximity to the cemetery). The best sands, however, lie a couple of kilometres east of town: **Playa Caletón**, a small cove surrounded by rocks and safe for swimming, is the closest and accessible via the marked turnoff along the C-5.

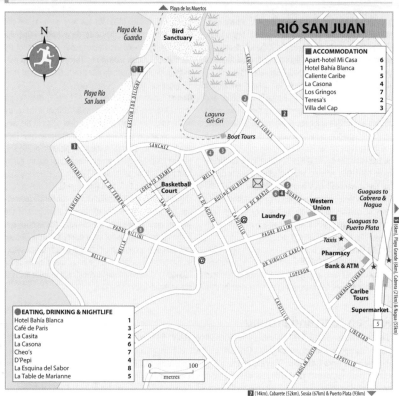

Playa Grande and Playa Preciosa

9km kilometres east of the town on the C-5 • **Playa Grande surf school** Daily 10am–6pm • 2hr 30min classes US$45, board rental only US$25 • ☎ 829 705 1416

Reached by a paved road leading off from the highway, **Playa Grande** is the area's most spectacular beach, a gorgeous and gently sloping stretch of golden sand splashed by green-blue waters and overlooked by swaying palms and cliffs. It's become increasingly popular in recent years, included on many package tour operators' itineraries, and the parking area is now home to several shack **restaurants** and vendor **stalls** that sell souvenirs and rum drinks from coconuts.

The cliffs to the west are topped by the Playa Grande **golf course** – neatly symbolizing encroaching development along this coast – while, to the east, a paved path by the toilets leads to the pristine sands of the somewhat smaller **Playa Preciosa** which, unless there are good waves for the surfers, you'll likely have to yourself. Be warned that both beaches are renowned for ferocious **rip-tides** (see box above), so take extra care when swimming. Playa Grande, which has a tiny **surf school** that also rents boards, often has a **lifeguard** (at its eastern end); Playa Preciosa does not.

Parque Nacional Cabo Francés Viejo

19km east of Río San Juan; look for a faded sign • Mon–Fri6am–7pm • Free

East of Río San Juan on the gradually deteriorating C-5, between the towns of Abreu and El Bretón, is **Parque Nacional Cabo Francés Viejo**, a small national park centred on a majestic cape, with the rather sad-looking ruins of a concrete lighthouse at its far end. If you're out this way it's a great place to take a stroll and look out over the ocean. East

RIP-TIDES

Common on beaches with high surf, **rip-tides** are dangerous ocean conveyor belts that funnel the water being smashed against the coast back to sea. Surfers and windsurfers actually find them desirable, as they pull you effortlessly out to the big waves, but they can pose a life-threatening problem for less experienced swimmers; indeed, at Playa Grande, a couple of people die each year in the tides. If you're not a **strong swimmer**, it's best to keep off beaches with high, crashing surf altogether. You can sometimes – but not always – identify rip-tides by sight as ribbons of sea that don't have any large waves travelling across their surface. At times they'll also have a different colour from the rest of the water. If you're caught in a rip-tide, do not attempt to swim against the powerful current. Instead, swim to the **right** or the **left** – and not directly back to the shore – until you are out of its grip.

of here there's little of interest besides some ruggedly beautiful beaches beneath high cliffs (especially **Playa El Bretón**, just below the entrance of the park) until you reach **Cabrera** (see p.151).

ARRIVAL AND GETTING AROUND

By bus or guagua The transport hub is around the Texaco station on the corner of the C-5 and Calle Duarte at the main entrance into town. Caribe Tours has an office here and operates both a stopping and an express service to and from Santo Domingo (8 daily; 6am–4pm; RD$320). The guagua stop for Nagua and Cabrera is on the east side of the highway by the town's main supermarket and transport passes frequently throughout the day. Guaguas bound for

RÍO SAN JUAN AND AROUND

Puerto Plata leave from the end of Calle Duarte just before the highway, travelling via Cabarete and Sosúa, and run until around 4.30pm for RS$125. *Públicos* do the same trip for the same price, but run until slightly later.

By taxi To book a taxi from town to the beaches and resorts, call Taxi Río San Juan (☎ 809 589 2501) – the office is on Duarte and has a list of destinations and prices in US dollars painted outside.

ACCOMMODATION

There are quite a few places to **stay** in town as well as a couple of resorts west along the coast, and three great foreign-run beach camps with swanky cabins and good food on Playa Magante, 14km west, which is a quite lovely and underused beach. The town lodgings, however, like everywhere else in Río San Juan, periodically suffer water and electricity cuts.

Apart-hotel Mi Casa Duarte 33 ☎ 829 221 0339. The cheapest place to stay in town providing dark, Spartan but clean en-suite rooms with serviceable beds, TV and fan. Still, it's nicely placed in the middle of town and the people who run it are very friendly, although don't speak any English. RD$500

★**Hotel Bahía Blanca** Deligne ☎ 809 589 2562, ✉ bahia.blanca.dr@codetel.net.do. The main hotel in town boasts an enviable location on a rocky promontory overlooking a small beach and attracts a good mixture of Dominican, European and North American guests. French-Canadian-run with an appealing yesteryear feel, its fan-ventilated rooms are large and simple (no a/c or TV though there is wi-fi) with faded furnishings but large windows, some offering great ocean views. The restaurant offers an international menu at reasonable prices and tours can be arranged. There are three cheaper more dingy rooms downstairs for RD$720, but they are often reserved. RD$1200

Caliente Caribe Abreu ☎ 809 696 3397, ✇ calienteresorts.com. Naturist and lifestyle-group resort

with a private beach and the usual all-inclusive amenities. The rooms and facilities are good but pricey, but if you want to go naked, this is the only place on the island to do it. All-inclusive day passes (9am–5pm; US$55) are also available to use the facilities on the 23-acre grounds that include tennis courts, hot tubs, volleyball and spa treatments. Usually couples only and price is based on two people sharing. US$290

Los Gringos Playa Magante ☎ 809 841 5606, ✇ losgringosdr.com. European-run beach camp with three faux-traditional cabins sporting thatch roofs, and hammocks on the porches, but very modern inside, slap-bang on this almost deserted yet lovely beach. Also has a restaurant and bar, serving very good global food with a European touch (as well as varied wines), and caters for vegetarians. US$80

Teresa's Miguel José Balbuena 14 ☎ 809 589 2789. Four rooms of varying prices (long-term rates negotiable) in a family home in a quiet residential street near the lagoon, ranging from a tiny double with shared bathroom and fan for RD$700 to a nicely decorated room with en-suite bathroom, a/c and satellite TV for RD$1200. Guests also

have access to a rooftop terrace and shared living space with a fridge. Wi-fi available on the ground floor, and occasionally upstairs if the wind's right. RD $700
Villa del Cap The end of 27 de Febrero ☎ 809 855 5733. Nicely located on the western point of the beach opposite *Hotel Bahía Blanca*, this place is slightly more in the twenty-first Century, with funky decor and modern art on the walls. Six comfortable ethnic-chic rooms, with the use of a shared kitchen and patio, overlooking the sea. No TV in the cheapest rooms, but there is a/c in all. US$50

EATING, DRINKING AND NIGHTLIFE

Hotel Bahía Blanca Deligne ☎ 809 589 2562. The best view of any restaurant in the town, with decent seafood and the usual international favourites served on a terrace overlooking the ocean. Count on paying RD$250 and above for mains. Daily 8am–11am & 7–10pm.

Café de Paris Sánchez, opposite the lagoon ☎ 809 778 0687, ⊚ cafedeparisriosanjuan.e-monsite.com. French satellite TV, sports and pop videos compete with *D' Pepi's* sound system in this café-bar – with the emphasis on "bar" given the dark interior. Enjoy croissants and coffee for breakfast, cocktails and tapas (for RD$150–200 each) in the evening. With an extensive wine list and free wi-fi. Daily 8am–midnight or later.

La Casita Sánchez opposite Las Flores. Cosy, open-sided thatched Italian-run restaurant serving a good range of pasta and large, excellent pizzas (most RD$300–450) though it is the beef fillet with mushroom sauce (RD$550) that garners the most support. It's by far the best Italian in town, and they have a good range of desserts and Italian liqueurs too. Daily 6pm–midnight or until the last customer leaves.

La Casona Duarte 6 ☎ 809 589 2597, ⊜ c_dolores_06 @hotmail.com. Traditional Dominican cafeteria with a long sit-down counter and a genial proprietor offering *comida rapida*. Make sure you sample the house speciality, one of their freshly made, crispy empanadas (RD$45–75) the crab one with vegetables and cheese is the best. They also have a couple of decent rooms for rent upstairs for RD$700/800. Daily 9am–10pm.

Cheo's Padre Billini 66 ☎ 809 589 2724. Pleasant Dominican café with square tables, tablecloths and artificial flowers serving a mix of local dishes – the *parillada de mariscos* (RD$1100 between two) is the chef d'oeuvre – and international staples which attracts both locals and tourists. Fish and meat mains from around RD$300–400. Daily 9am–10pm.

D' Pepi Sánchez and Capotillio (no phone). The roosting egrets in the bird sanctuary opposite have their ear drums sorely tested every night as *D' Pepi's* mega sound system blasts forth across the lagoon and the beer flows. The place to dance through the night at weekends, with live music Fri & Sun. Daily 3pm–midnight.

★ **La Esquina del Sabor** Mella, opposite the park ☎ 809 991 0561. Lively, corner patio restaurant, providing a great spot for people watching as the partying in the park gets going of a weekend. Excellent inexpensive food too: delicious *platos del día* and *mondongo* (both RD$150), or fresh fish 'n' chips for only RD$250. Also serves Mexican food. Daily 9am–11pm (closed Tues).

La Table de Marianne Duarte 15 ☎ 829 494 4445. Your best bet for breakfast, this Belgian-run café serves fantastic pastries, cakes, omelettes, and coffee amongst other things, as well as some good European mains (RD$180–500) such as steaks at lunchtime – they also serve decent wine by the glass (RD$130) to wash it down. The also serve superlative home-made ice cream, and you can enjoy them all on the tables overlooking the street. Mon–Fri 8am–5pm.

West of Puerto Plata

The contrast between east and **west of Puerto Plata** couldn't be more striking. In place of the paved highways, resort complexes and golf courses that prevail in much of the east, the west contains vast stretches of small family **farms** and untrammelled **wilderness** along rough dirt tracks, though some are slowly being converted into proper roads, as developments try to creep further along the coast. The view towards foreign visitors is different in the west, too: an old code of warm, formal manners prevails, and strangers will often go to great lengths to assist you out of sheer good nature.

One thing that doesn't change is the proliferation of lovely **beaches** – though these get far more use from locals than tourists. Most **coral reefs** along here are still intact, with the island's finest located between **Punta Rucia** and **Monte Cristi**. Fine coastal detours from the Carretera Luperón that heads west from just outside Puerto Plata include **Luperón** itself, a remote seaside village that has a dead resort but a pristine beach; **La Isabela Histórica**, a scenic fishing village that holds the remains of Columbus's first settlement; and the twin beaches **Playa Ensenada** and **Punta Rucia**,

DRIVING ROUTES WEST FROM PUERTO PLATA

Two **routes** lead from Puerto Plata to **Luperón** and **La Isabela**, the first – and quicker – being the Carretera Luperón (C-30), which you can pick up 1km north of **Imbert**, a town marked mainly by its large Texaco station. A word of warning: it's worth keeping an eye out for farm animals wandering along the curvy C-30, and indeed all the way to the border, as this is ranching country.

The **second route** from Puerto Plata to Luperón along the coastal road is a much rougher ride than the first, but offers better scenery and an intimate look at the lives of the DR's rural *campesinos* as you drive through a series of seaside *campos* (outposts so small they couldn't even be called pueblos), dotted with thatch huts, small vegetable gardens and freely roaming farm animals. From the Carretera Navarette Puerto Plata, take the northwest turnoff marked "Guzmancito", 13km beyond Puerto Plata and about 1km south of Maimón. Just after turning, you'll hit the small beach of **Playa Maimón**, typically frequented by a few locals. You're better off forging ahead to **Playa Guzmancito**, a gorgeous, mostly abandoned beach another 10km down the road near the tiny fishing *campo* of Cruce de Guzmán, where you can **camp** if you ask permission from the townsfolk first. A few kilometres further, you'll also find the tiny and idyllic **Playa Cambiaso** where the three local families can bring tables and fresh seafood (RD$200–500) onto the beach for you. From here the road passes through the foothills of the Cordillera Septentrional for 15km, affording occasional spectacular **ocean views** before ending at the Carretera Luperón, from where you can carry on to Luperón and La Isabela.

two of the most unspoilt stretches on the coast. At its westernmost point, towards frontier town **Monte Cristi**, the region's terrain becomes a cactus-dominated desert landscape. Inland a long, fertile strip of verdant **rice paddies** is set between imposing **mountain** ranges.

If you're driving out this way, keep a close eye on your fuel, as **petrol stations** are few and far between. If you do get low, look out for the occasional roadside house with beer bottles or demijohns propped on a table.

4

Luperón

Until recently, **LUPERÓN** was the most developed of the western beach towns, but since the death of the **resort** here – you can wander around its eerie, abandoned streets and apartments above the town's main beach, **Playa Grande** – it has returned to a dusty, low-key feel typical of this stretch of coast. The lovely beach, though clean and pristine, is more or less deserted, and only one erratically opening bar remains to serve the few locals who sometimes hang out down there. You can have the 1km of pearly sand lined with sea grapes and palms almost to yourself. Though a lovely setting, you need to watch out for sea urchins in the water. Other than kicking back on the beach, the only other things to do are hire a boat at the marina to take you out to the reefs, or take a day-trip to La Isabela (see below).

ARRIVAL AND GETTING AROUND   LUPERÓN

If you're not going by **car** (see box above), take a Javilla Tours **bus** (see p.166) from Puerto Plata to Imbert, where you can catch a **guagua** (RD$60) to Luperón. If you don't have your own transport and need a **taxi** to La Isabela Histórica or Punta Rucia from Luperón, try Nino's (☎ 809 493 6950), a reputable English-speaking operator.

ACCOMMODATION

Casa del Sol Carretera La Isabela ☎ 829 464 5155. This Canadian-Dominican-owned place, half a kilometre northwest of town on the beach road (a continuation of Av. 7 de Febrero), is the nicest option at present, with five decent, quite homely rooms above a good restaurant (daily 4–10pm) which is famous locally for its pepper

steak. The rooms are a fairly overpriced, but the location is quiet. RD$1200

El Paraiso At the junction of Av. 7 de Febrero and Calle 12 de Octubre ☎ 809 571 8823. The rooms in this centrally located budget hotel are fantastic value for money with a/c, cable, comfortable beds and a balcony

---

LUPERÓN'S MARITIME EXPATS AND REEF TRIPS

At the northern end of Av. Duarte is the slightly grubby **Puerto Blanca Marina** (☎ 809 571 8644). The bay here is the best place to rest from the **trade winds**, offering ample protection from hurricanes and tropical storms – even Columbus is said to have taken shelter here. It's also an inexpensive **mooring** spot, meaning that the marina is usually bustling with world-travelling vagabonds (and a few ne'er-do-wells) and the area around has become a **social centre** for expats in the area, since most are staying on boats. It's normally easy to find someone at the marina willing to take you, for around US$120, on a sailing day-trip to the hard-to-reach **reefs** around La Isabela Histórica and Punta Rucia. Ask around the bars for recommendations and make sure that your prospective captain has radar, radio, life jackets and an emergency life raft. A second smaller and newer marina, the **Luperón Marina Yacht Club** (☎ 809 571 8606), lies east of the original.

---

overlooking the street. They don't speak English, and there's no restaurant or wi-fi, though there is an internet café downstairs which charges RD$50/day for wi-fi. **RD$700**

EATING AND NIGHTLIFE

Luperón isn't very exciting by night, though **locals** do gather along Av. Duarte and at the park to listen to music streaming from a dozen different car radios. Otherwise, there's the mostly nautical **expat scene** near the marina, also on Av. Duarte, where you'll find a sometimes interesting mix of retirees and sailing folk.

★ **Lotty Restaurant** Corner of Av. Duarte and Av. 7 de Febrero ☎ 829 401 6921. Reliable, no-frills Dominican restaurant that attracts both locals and foreigners alike with its excellent and well-priced seafood (RD$250–270), meat (RD$100–300) and filling, tasty *platos del día* (RD$125). Mon–Sat 8am–10pm.
Wendy's Bar Av. Duarte where it meets Calle Independecia ☎ 809 571 8618. Wendy is a great host and has made her bar the centre of expat social life, serving American comfort food (RD$200–350) and a wide range of drinks (including the recommended mango margaritas) either inside at the bar or outside on the nice terrace. Mondays and Tuesdays are hotdog and movie nights (hotdogs RD$20) with karaoke on Fridays. Daily 9am–midnight (or later).

La Isabela Histórica (El Castillo) and around

13km west of Luperón • Three guaguas leave from Luperón (9am, noon and 3pm; 20min; RD$50), returning as soon as they arrive

The Carretera de las Américas heads west from Luperón to sleepy **LA ISABELA HISTÓRICA**, a seaside village (also known locally as El Castillo) located on the site of Columbus's first permanent settlement, La Isabela, the remains of which are now nestled inside the small **Parque Nacional La Isabela**, just east of the village. The scenery itself makes the trip worthwhile, with prosperous plantations, rolling hills and breathtaking views of the sea. Still, the best ocean vistas are reserved for the village, which is set on a splendid bay of tranquil blue water with a solid wall of imposing peaks stretching in both directions.

The village itself is just a few houses scattered around a grid of tiny dirt roads on a steep hill. The village beach, **Playa Isabela**, attracts few visitors and is marked mainly by the small wooden boats moored just offshore and children fishing at the water's edge, with three shacks serving food and drinks. A kilometre out to sea from La Isabela Histórica is an intact, living **coral reef** – rare on this island – where you'll see a healthy, multicoloured home to thousands of tropical fish and sea creatures. *Rancho del Sol* (see opposite) can arrange regular scuba and snorkelling trips, and can also take you to other remote reefs west of Punta Rucia.

ACCOMMODATION AND EATING   LA ISABELA HISTÓRICA

Cafétéria Piez de Colon Playa Isabela. If you don't fancy either of the small *comedores* in the village, this is your best bet. Seafood and fish (RD250–600) are served on the beach under a coconut-leaf roof, along with simple pasta dishes (from RD$170) and cocktails (from RD$130). Mon–Sat 9am–10pm.

Rancho del Sol Carretera de las Américas, at the turnoff for the park ☎ 849 250 6430. The only formal accommodation in town, this has eight simple but well-maintained doubles and twins with a/c, cable, and hot water. All are historically furnished and have balconies with rocking chairs overlooking the sea. No internet, but there is an internet café on the road to the beach. <u>RD$1050</u>

Parque Nacional La Isabela

Off the main highway, just east of El Castillo • Daily 9am–5.30pm • RD$100; Spanish-speaking guide free but tips welcome

Parque Nacional La Isabela takes up much of La Isabela Histórica's shoreline and preserves the ruins of **La Isabela** (see box below), the second oldest European town in the New World built after the short-lived La Navidad (now in present-day Haiti) was burned to the ground by the locals after just one year. Centred on the private home of Columbus himself, which boasts a splendid view of the bay, the park also encompasses the excavated stone **foundations** of the town and a small museum – a local guide from the main park office will take you around. Presumably there were far more extensive ruins up until 1960, when Trujillo bulldozed the site in order to turn it into a military fort to defend against sea invasion by insurgents linked to Cuba's Fidel Castro. But you'll still see the remnants of two large warehouses, a sentry tower, a chapel, what some assert was a clinic, and **Columbus's house**, which retains a good portion of its walls intact. A number of skeletons have been unearthed from the chapel's cemetery; one – a Catalan who died of malaria – is rather unceremoniously on display in a box near the museum. Two ancillary sites have been uncovered outside the park, both rather uninspiring and not really worth the time.

The museum

The park **museum** offers an account (in Spanish) of the cultures of both Spaniards and Tainos at the time of their first encounter. Better than the solemn recitations by the

4

THE BEGINNING AND END OF LA ISABELA

Founded in 1493 by Christopher Columbus and some 1500 Spanish settlers under his command, **La Isabela** was strategically located on a defensible ocean bluff but far from fresh water and fertile soil – oversights that led to its abandonment in favour of Santo Domingo after only four years. Columbus intended that it would become the **gold-bearing capital** of Spain's empire, organizing it according to the *factoria* system of Portugal's colonies along the northwest coast of Africa: in these, a small group of entrepreneurial partners forced natives to hand over a valuable local commodity (in this case, gold), either as tribute or in exchange for European goods at a ridiculously low rate.

However, it soon became evident that there was not much gold to be had and, after **yellow fever** and **malaria** killed half of the original settlers, the rest became increasingly disenchanted. A further sticking point was the Spanish tradition of Christian conquest, which allowed soldiers to enslave the people of conquered lands. At first Columbus opposed transplanting **slavery** here – as hardships mounted he demanded that colonists perform manual labour regardless of rank. This alienated the **nobility** and, after a failed coup attempt, several of them stole one of his boats and set off for Spain to complain of the goings-on. In mid-1494, Columbus, perhaps realizing that he was in danger of losing the faith of his men, waged two military campaigns to **capture Tainos**, allotting slaves to his men in lieu of monthly wages. The Indians were to work the surrounding fields, though many were able to escape.

Two years later Columbus sailed to Spain to request more settlers, leaving his brother **Bartolomé** in charge of La Isabela. On his departure, a group of colonists led by Columbus's personal servant Francisco Roldán revolted and went to settle in the outlying countryside. Bartolomé abandoned La Isabela in 1497 with his few remaining men for the site of Santo Domingo, where one Spaniard had found a large gold nugget. On Columbus's return in 1498, his town lay **abandoned**; two years later, he was removed from command in Santo Domingo and sent back to Spain in disgrace.

guide are the hundreds of excavated artefacts, including a pottery oven, a kiln and several containers that still held mercury (used to purify gold) when they were unearthed, along with smaller items such as a tiny sixteenth-century crucifix, unglazed Moorish-style pottery shards and several Taino religious icons. Just outside the building are small plots where local anthropologists use traditional agricultural methods practised by the Taino and the colonists.

Templo de las Américas

Just east of El Castillo, across the highway from Parque Nacional La Isabela • Daily 8.30am–5pm • Free

The **Templo de las Américas**, a spotless neo-colonial church topped by a high central dome, merits a quick look round after a visit to Parque Nacional La Isabela. It was constructed for pope John Paul II's visit to La Isabela in 1992 for the Columbus Centenary, the pope giving Mass there on the anniversary of the admiral's landing; a plaque on the outside commemorates the visit. The interior is simple but striking, with some interesting modernist stained-glass windows; even better is the elevated vista of Bahía de Isabela from the top of the steps.

Laguna Estero Hondo

Around 10km west of La Isabela Histórica • Boat tours can be arranged through *Rancho del Sol* in Isabela Histórica (RD$6000 for up to 4 people), *Manatee Bay Restaurant* on Playa El Pato (see opposite), or El Paraíso Tours in Punta Rucia (☎ 809 320 7606, ⓦ cayoparaisord.com)

Around 10km west of La Isabela Histórica is **Laguna Estero Hondo**, one of the last remaining Dominican homes of the **manatee**, which had been killed off in droves in recent decades, largely in speedboat accidents, though conservation efforts seem to be working and the population is now recovering. You can explore the lagoon on **boat excursions**, though manatee sightings are not guaranteed – it is estimated that there are only around four dozen individuals left at most – but you will see a gorgeous **mangrove reserve** that serves as a haven for **tropical birds**, such as egret, wood stork and roseate spoonbill.

West to Playa Ensenada

From La Isabela a road to Punta Rucia extends west around the lagoon and heads through increasingly arid scrubland to a series of **beaches** that relatively few foreign visitors make it to. The road is mainly dirt and there are two shallow **rivers** for which bridges have yet to be re-built. If it hasn't been raining, it's usually possible to drive through these (both are normally under 30cm deep) and there's never a shortage of locals loitering nearby to assist if you're not confident – deep breath, slow constant speed, and only accelerate if you start to slow, as stopping at any point is usually a bad idea. Be aware, though, they'll want a good tip. After around 5km, the road improves and a turnoff north of **Villa Isabela** heads west to pueblo **Estero Hondo**, a village with few tourist facilities but set in a river delta replete with birdlife and mosquitoes.

Four kilometres further west is **Playa El Pato**, a small cove protected by a giant reef that turns it into a large natural swimming pool, which is rather sparsely populated, with just one restaurant and a hotel on the hill above (see opposite). This is surprising as it is possibly one of the prettiest spots on the Silver Coast and certainly more so than the busier **Playa Ensenada**, 1km further west, where many Dominican families come to take advantage of the shallow waters. The western end of the 1km-long Playa Ensenada, in front of the *Punta Rucia Lodge*, is quieter, with stunning white sand, gently lapping turquoise water and a few small boats bobbing just offshore with the mountains as a background. Turn right to the eastern end of the beach for a totally different cultural experience with radios blasting the sounds of bachata and a line of restaurants selling seafood, pizza, and rum – the food's usually excellent and the rum's always cheap.

★**Manatee Bay Restaurant/Villa Manatee Hotel** Playa El Pato, signposted off the C-30 4.5km north of Estero Hondo ☎ 849 862 9565, ✉ vacamarina@hotmail.com. Tucked away behind a usually deserted beach, this restaurant (daily 6am–6pm) serves very good *criolla*-style seafood dishes (from RD$250), as well as a good *plato del* *día* for RD$250, all served in its smart Taino-themed interior. They also arrange snorkelling and manatee-watching trips to Cayo Arena. You can also book rooms here for the breezy *Villa Manatee Hotel* whose rooms, although very basic and way overpriced, have possibly the best views of any hotel on the Silver Coast. RD$1500

Punta Rucia and around

Just around the point from Playa Ensenada, **Punta Rucia** is arguably the most beautiful beach on the north coast, with its ivory sand and great mountain views. It attracts fewer people than Ensenada but has several informal local places to stop for lunch or a beer, some with live music. The small point that separates the two beaches is bordered by a thriving **coral reef**, which provides good snorkelling.

The only **paved route** to Punta Rucia is along the C-29, a road that leads north from the Santiago–Monte Cristi Carretera (C-1) at Cruce De Guayacanes, via Villa Isabela (where there is also one daily **guagua** service up to Punta Rucia) where the well-paved C-30 leads west along the coast through Estero Hondo. The C-30 then carries on south for 14km to Villa Elisa on the C-1, though the money ran out before they could tarmac it so it's fairly rough going, but a much shorter route than coming via the C-29 if you don't mind a bumpy ride.

ACCOMMODATION AND EATING

4

There are a few Dominican **seafood restaurants** along the beach while all along both Punta Rucia and Playa Ensenada vendors sell fresh **oysters** culled the same day from the nearby river's mouth. The following are the best places to stay in the village, although there are three places which rent out very basic rooms for RD$500–600 and advertise on the main street, such as *Mini-Hotel Kenia* (☎ 829 573 2626).

★**Punta Rucia Lodge** Between Punta Rucia and Playa Ensenada ☎ 849 858 8400, ⊛ puntarucialodge.com. One of the prettiest hotels on the Silver Coast, this high-end Belgian-run resort rents just six luxurious, Indonesian-style huts, all spotlessly clean, comfortable and a mere stone's throw from a pristine beach. Service is impeccable and prices includes breakfast and à la carte dinner at their excellent restaurant (open to non-guests) which overlooks the pool. Pick–up from Puerto Plata available. US$137/person

Villa Playa Punta Rucia seafront ⊛ villaplaya.com. Gorgeous two-storey beach house right on the front with two large mahogany rooms, sea-facing balconies, a fully equipped kitchen, maid/cooking service, kayaks and even a fishing boat for guests' use (at an extra charge). Rate is per week (the minimum) for four or five guests. US$1950/week

Villa Rosa Punta Rucia seafront ☎ 809 801 8160, ⊛ lavilla-rosa.com. Situated right in the middle of the bay, this tiny French-run bistro also has three guestrooms surrounding a lovely garden and small swimming-pool out the back. Serves great continental breakfasts (RD$150) as well as one (usually French) dish per day (RD$600–800) for lunch and dinner which will be written on the board outside. Very good food using excellent (and often home-made) ingredients, and the best wi-fi in town. Price includes breakfast. €36/US$48

Cayo Paraíso (Cayo Arena)

7km west of Punta Rucia • **Boat tours** Run twice daily from Punta Rucia with El Paraíso Tours (☎ 809 320 7606, ⊛ cayoparaisord.com) • US$40 with lunch and drinks included

From Punta Rucia (and with almost every tour operator and many hotels along the coast) you can pick up a boat tour to **Cayo Paraíso**, also known as Cayo Arena, a small, perfectly circular desert island surrounded by thriving coral and sea life, and with a handful of palm-thatched tourist amenities in the centre. Unfortunately, when tour groups from Playa Dorada pour in during peak season and at weekends, the tiny sandbar can be rather crowded; you should also note that the only toilet facilities are on the mainland. The boat trips generally include snorkelling around the island plus a large lunch, before returning via dense snarls of mangroves in **Monte Cristi national park**.

West to Monte Cristi

The condition of the dirt road west deteriorates beyond Punta Rucia, so if you want to head **west to Monte Cristi**, you'll have a tough, though likely rewarding, time of it. It's not too bad to pueblo **El Cupey**, where the main road continues south to meet up with the **Carretera Duarte**, but west of this is the arid **La Costa de Buen Hombre**, a long stretch of desert terrain dominated by scrub brush, which you'll need an off-road vehicle to traverse. The main trail soon dissolves into a narrow **mule track**, intersected at random by others that are equally narrow and badly surfaced – maps of the area don't do it justice, so be prepared to ask directions from the mule teams you'll encounter along the way. Stick to the coast and you'll find a modest sign marking the turnoff to **Gran Mangle**, one of the most isolated fishing villages in the country. Set on a small, dramatic point, Gran Mangle is mostly rocky coast, but there are a few patches of beach here and there along with an intact coral **reef**. A mule trail continues in a similar vein for around 20km, leading to the pueblo **El Jabo**, near the base of the towering **El Morro mesa** (see p.196). From here you'll navigate around El Morro through the weeds, avoiding the mesa's soggy moat, to get to **Playa Juan de Bolaños** and **Monte Cristi**, at the country's northwestern tip.

The Carretera Duarte (C-1)

Bordering the Cordillera Septentrional to the south is the **Carretera Duarte** (an extension of the Autopista Duarte, which stretches between Santiago and Santo Domingo), a road that provides a far easier way to get to Monte Cristi than the coastal mule tracks. The well-paved freeway stretches from Santiago to Monte Cristi, intersecting the Carretera Puerto Plata at **Navarrete**, a major tobacco centre. As you move west, tobacco fields quickly give way to banana trees and rice paddies and then, at **Villa Elisa**, the land quite suddenly becomes arid, transforming into a cactus-dominated desert teeming with goats. If driving, you should be careful of the fierce crosswinds that blow across the highway, especially if you're on a motorcycle. The **towns** that line the road are all fairly basic, with at most a couple of *colmados* and the occasional cockfighting arena. As far as basic necessities along the way go, petrol stations are, mercifully, posted every 20km or so, and the best place to eat along the way is *Parada Jennifer,* recommended for its goat dishes, which is at the Punta Rucia turnoff in Villa Elisa.

Monte Cristi and around

MONTE CRISTI has the feel of the mythic Wild West, a dusty frontier town bearing the occasional tarnished remnant of its opulent past along wide, American-style boulevards that the sand incessantly tries to reclaim. Most people use Monte Cristi as a base from which to explore the local **beaches** and the **Parque Nacional Monte Cristi**. The latter protects a towering mesa named **El Morro**, an enormous river **delta** region with a wildlife-filled mangrove coast and a series of seven tiny **sandy islets**, encircled by coral, where sea turtles and migratory sea birds lay their eggs.

Brief history

Among the very oldest European cities in the New World, Monte Cristi was founded in 1501 and became one of the country's most important ports in the eighteenth century, when it shipped out vast quantities of mahogany. The next century saw the port, like Puerto Plata to the east, benefit greatly from the **tobacco boom**, but its prosperity came to an abrupt end during the era of Trujillo, who shut down its shipping in retribution for local resistance to his rule. The town has never fully recovered, and the only industry of note comes from the large Morton **saltpans** – rectangular pools of the salty local water that are filled from a canal and then harvested by allowing the water to evaporate – just north and south of the city, which supply much of North America's table salt.

CARNIVAL IN MONTE CRISTI

Monte Cristi is somewhat infamous for its peculiarly violent **Carnival celebrations**. Each Sunday in February, the locals split into two groups: the Toros, who dress in stylized Carnival bull masks and bright cloth outfits decorated with mirrors, whistles and other miscellaneous bangles, and the unadorned Civilis. Both parties protect themselves by putting on four or five layers of clothing, including winter coats, then proceed to attack each other in the streets with **bullwhips**. Police measure the whips beforehand to ensure that they do not exceed a certain length, and combatants are not supposed to hit anyone in the face, though these safety measures don't eliminate the danger. **Onlookers** are supposed to be safe from the proceedings, but with hundreds of people whizzing deadly weapons through the air, you're better off watching the "festivities" from the first-floor balcony of the *Hotel Chic* restaurant, conveniently located at the centre of the action.

Parque Central

The town focus is the charming **Parque Central** with its Eiffel-style **clock tower**, imported from France in 1895. Local legend has it that Cuban revolutionary José Martí said of it before setting out to Cuba. "this clock will very soon ring the hour of Cuba's liberation". Other than **Villa Doña Emilia Jiménez**, there's a pleasant 1920s faux-colonial church at the south of the park and, at the eastern side on Duarte, **El Museo de Montecristi** (ⓦmontecristi.org), which was not yet opened at the time of writing but is set to contain locally found, mainly pre-Columbian Taino artefacts, plus a smaller exhibition of objects salvaged from the many European shipwrecks along this treacherous stretch of coast.

Villa Doña Emilia Jiménez

North side of Parque Central • Sat & Sun 9am–5pm • ⓣ 809 579 2452, ⓔ moreca@codetel.do

A palatial old wooden building, the Victorian-age **Villa Doña Emilia Jiménez** was the family residence of the businesswoman and sister of early Dominican president Juan Isidro Jiménez. This extraordinary woman, from one of the richest families on the island, not only imported the building wholesale from France but was also opposed to Trujillo – she **hid Haitians** in the cellar here during Operación Perejil (see p.270) and once publicly snubbed Trujillo's amorous advances. The building has been under restoration since 1990 and is still a work in progress, though inside you'll find a tiny **tourist office**, currently only open at weekends, which can supply you with a map and guide of the nineteenth-century **gingerbread mansions** around the park and elsewhere in town. They also have a small collection of historical photos and sell some local, artisan-made produce – the tropical fruit wines are inexpensive and delicious.

El Museo Máximo Gómez

Five blocks east of Parque Central at Calle Mella 29 • Officially Mon–Fri 9am–noon & 2–5pm but keeps unreliable hours • Free • ⓣ 809 579 2474

Housed in a pretty gingerbread mansion once owned by the Cuban liberator, **El Museo Máximo Gómez** is a small museum set in a nice garden, with period furnishings, personal mementos, and an account of his fight for the liberation of both Cuba and the Dominican Republic from Spain. It was in this building that José Martí and Máximo Gómez wrote and signed the Manifesto de Montecristi, outlining their revolutionary goals and plans, and a bronze bust of each of them stand outside. Unfortunately, the museum is rarely open.

The beaches

Playa Juan de Bolaños 2km up Calle Bolaños past the saltpans • Playa de los Muertos By car, drive south of town on Carretera 45 until you arrive at the first bridge; from there take a right, and the road will lead you straight to the beach

Playa Juan de Bolaños is the area's most popular beach, though it's pretty unremarkable. At its entrance you'll find a cluster of hotels and a restaurant; elsewhere it's less

4

populated. As you head east, the beach road passes numerous small fishing boats and the large Club Nautico Marina before arriving at the entrance to the eastern half of **Parque Nacional Monte Cristi**. Five hundred metres to the west is a river you'll have to ford by foot to reach the beach known locally as **Playa de los Muertos** (Beach of the Dead) for the corpses that washed up here from hurricane-sunk Spanish galleons in the early sixteenth century; its most notable feature today is the palm trees that have been uprooted and deposited here by tide and tropical storms.

Parque Nacional Monte Cristi

Park office located at far eastern end of Playa Bolaños • Office open daily 8am–5pm • Free

The **Parque Nacional Monte Cristi** covers around 1100 square kilometres surrounding Monte Cristi – it is separated into two halves by the town and also stretches out to sea. Much of it is only possible to visit by **boat**, but you can easily rent one near the beach or through your accommodation.

The eastern section

The park's **eastern section** is often referred to as **Parque El Morro**, after the flat-topped 200m-high mesa (tableland), El Morro, that takes up a good chunk of it. Climbing the mesa is reasonably straightforward: a set of steps leads up from the highest point on Carretera del Morro, just past *Hotel El Morro* and near the park office. At the foot of El Morro's eastern slope is the lovely and unpopulated **Playa de Morro**, though it only exists from around February to August and loses the sun at around 4pm. To gain access, park at the end of the same road and continue down on foot. From there you can swim out to **Isla Cabrita**, a large island punctuated by a lighthouse, some 300m offshore. The waters surrounding the park contain several **shipwrecks**, two of them colonial-era galleons – long plundered – that sought safe harbour from storm in the Bahía Manzanillo just west of here and didn't make it.

The western section

The much larger **western section** of the national park encompasses an inland swath of arid **desert** environment and a dense coastal **mangrove swamp** dotted with small lagoons, which is home to innumerable orchids, ibises, egrets, pelicans and a host of other birds. The alluring mangrove coast is accessible only by **boat**; on the trips you'll see several river deltas thick with mangroves and perhaps a couple of crocodiles, as well as tour groups from further east, who visit the mangroves as part of a trip out to **Cayo Paraíso** (see p.193).

The protected area also stretches out to sea in the west, taking in **Los Siete Hermanos**, seven tiny islands 1km offshore, with arid vegetation and desolate beaches, which host thousands of nesting terns, noddies and sea turtles. By far the most beautiful of the islands is known as "**Tuna**", in honour of the gorgeous, white-flowering tuna cacti that grow here.

ARRIVAL AND DEPARTURE
MONTE CRISTI

By guagua Monte Cristi is fairly well served by public transport. Frequent guaguas run here from both Dajabón (every 20min until 10pm; 40min) and Santiago (every 20min until 5pm; 2hr 15min) via Santo Domingo (5hr). The guagua station is at the top end of Calle Duarte, near the Shell petrol station. From here it's a 5min walk to the centre of town or a RD$80 *motoconcho* ride down to the accommodation at the beach.

By bus Offering a greater degree of comfort to the guaguas for about the same price, Caribe Tours (☏ 809 579 2129) runs a bus service to and from Santo Domingo (6 daily 7.30am–4pm; 4hr 30min; RD$350) via Santiago (2hr; RD$190). Their office is a couple of blocks further into town from the guagua station, just off the main intersection between Duarte and Av Mella.

INFORMATION AND TOURS

Information The only place to seek out local information is the tourist office open at weekends in Villa Doña Emilia Jiménez.

Tours The most economical tours are available from the Spanish-speaking Soraya & Santos Tours (☏ 809 961 6343) who are on Bolaños. They cost around RD$2000 to and from

Isla Cabrita, RD$4000 for a couple of hours exploring the mangroves, and RD$12000 for a trip to three of the islands at Los Siete Hermanos – make sure both parties are agreed on price, timings, and what is included before setting off and pay no more than half upfront. Pricier tours in English can often be booked through your hotel, or with Paraíso Tours in Punta Rucia (see p.193). The same agents can arrange trips to an area called the Cordillera, possibly the best fishing ground on the Dominican coast; this will cost from around US$75 for a half-day.

ACCOMMODATION

Cayo Arena Playa Juan de Bolaños, 250m west of the beach entrance ☎809 579 3145, ⓦcayoarena.com. Decent-sized two-bedroom apartments on the beach, with ocean-view balconies (some better than others), a/c, hot water, and kitchenettes. They sleep six and so are ideal for families. They also run tours to Haiti. RD$3840

Chic Hotel Corner of Monción and Duarte ☎809 579 2316, ⓦchichotel.info. The best budget option in the town centre offers good value, though rooms and bathrooms are small and upstairs ceilings are low. The basic rooms have fans (an extra RD$400 for a/c) and some have hot water. There's an attached restaurant and a bar, the latter better than the former. Wi-fi in the lobby. RD$650

Los Jardines Playa Juan de Bolaños, 300m west of the beach entrance ☎809 579 2091. These four simple cabin-rooms with cold-water showers and fans are set in a small manicured garden – a nice spot but slightly overpriced. The place also rents out rowing boats and jeeps, and they can organize tours to Haiti. You'll pay RD$200 extra for a/c. RD$1600

Hotel Montechico Bolaños, by the sea ☎809 579 315. The fabulous location over the water – you can hear the waves lapping – and smartly painted exterior promise much though the rooms themselves are merely adequate. Nonetheless, they're clean, with decent beds, a fan (a/c is extra) and a fridge. Also has a good restaurant on the terrace overlooking the water, and even its own small disco. RD$1200

Hotel El Morro Carretera del Morro ☎849 886 1605, ⓦelmorro.com.do. Recently renovated and located off the water at the base of El Morro in quiet, peaceful surroundings, this luxury resort is the best accommodation in town. Modern, stylish rooms, attentive service and a pleasant pool overlooking the sea justify the price. US$115

EATING AND DRINKING

Monte Cristi is not a great place for **nightlife**, but there are a couple of spots in town, including a disco attached to the *Hotel Montechico* and a decent bar at *Chic Hotel* near the Parque Central.

★**Bar-restaurant Doña Ana** Altagracia 75, opposite the baseball field ☎809 733 0262. The place to go for the town's best Dominican cuisine at modest prices: chicken, fish, beans and especially the local goat speciality *chivo picante* (RD$290), washed down with ice-cold beer. Located about 1km to the south of Duarte in a quiet suburb. Daily 9am–11pm.

Cocomar Bolaños, on the beach ☎809 579 3354. Offering spectacular sunset views over the water, this recently renovated place has a somewhat kitsch nautical style with plastic boats, nets and fish aplenty. But the staff are friendly and the seafood comes by the mound, albeit at tourist prices. Try the crab (RD$455) or various fish (from RD$360). Daily 8am–10pm.

Pizzeria Paolo Bolaños, just as you leave the town ☎809 931 0911. A hole-in-the-wall place with tables in the street offering large thin-crust pizzas made by the Italian owner-chef, ranging from simple cheese (RD$250) to the tinned-mushroom-topped "Super Hongos" (RD$400). Half-pizzas also sold. Daily 4–11pm.

Terraza Fedora Bolaños 12, just as you leave the town ☎809 579 2843. For something a bit more typically Dominican, try this open-sided, coconut thatch-roofed dancehall which isn't hard to find as it's perpetually blasting out merengue and bachata at top volume. It's always lively, and you can soak up the booze – ice-cold beer a speciality – with pizza from *Pizzeria Paolo* next door. Mon–Fri noon–10pm, Sat & Sun 9am–10pm (or later).

The northern Haitian border

From Monte Cristi a fairly good road heads almost due south, skirting the protected mangrove forest lining the **Bahía de Manzanillo**, before hitting the Haitian border 34km later at the edgy frontier town of **Dajabón**. Few travellers venture further, but those who do are rewarded with splendid mountain scenery and spectacular views as the road spirals up into the Cordillera Central, hugging the border, as far as the remote hillside town of **Restauración**. From here, you can gain access to a little-visited national park, the **Parque Nacional Nalga de Maco**.

Dajabón and around

DAJABÓN, 34km due south of Monte Cristi, is the biggest of the border towns; it holds the largest formal **border crossing** (see box below) and best regional market. The Spanish had a fort here from the mid-sixteenth century, but it was little more than a collection of small farms until 1794, when Touissant L'Ouverture slaughtered most of the locals and resettled the spot with Haitians (the river that flows along the border here has been called **the Massacre** ever since).

The market

Covers the eight square blocks bordering the bridge • Mon–Fri 9am–4pm

Dajabón is now firmly Dominican, but hundreds of Haitians pour into town on **market days**. Freelance Dominican entrepreneurs – who come from as far away as Santo Domingo – buy bulk quantities of grain and produce from Dominican farmers, swapping them with Haitians for UN-donated or Haitian-made clothing and household goods and then selling the Haitian wares to individual clothing and department stores in the major cities; many of the "designer" labels that you'll find on the streets of Santo Domingo are actually Haitian counterfeits. The Haitians come across the "**Friendship Bridge**" at the western end of town – the women balancing huge bushels crammed with gym shoes on their heads while the men lift impossibly loaded wheelbarrows – and claim small patches of pavement for their impromptu shops.

ARRIVAL AND DEPARTURE
DAJABÓN

By bus or guagua Guaguas arrive and depart from near the arch at the entrance to town and shuttle between Monte Cristi (every 20min; 30–40min; RD$50) or Santiago (2hr 30min; RD$200), with last departures from Dajabón around 6pm and 4pm respectively. Less frequent services head south to Loma de Cabrera (40min; RD$60) where you can change for onward transport to Restauracion or Río Limpio. Caribe Tours is a block west on Marcelo Carrasco and has buses running to and from the capital (6 daily 6.45am–3.15pm; 5hr; RD$350).

By car You're not allowed to drive a rental car into Haiti, and the bridge in Dajabón isn't wide enough for vehicular traffic in any event.

ACCOMMODATION AND EATING

Gran Hotel Raydan Pablo Reyes, on the corner with Gastón F. Delingne ☎ 809 579 7366. Located on the main road coming into town, this is Dajabón's best hotel by far. Rooms are comfortable and clean with cable TV and fan or a/c. The cheaper ones are in another building across the road and don't have wi-fi, hot water or a/c. The hotel also has a restaurant serving the usual range of Dominican and international dishes – it's only a block from the arch of the town gate, location of the informal guagua station. RD$1300/500

CROSSING THE BORDER INTO HAITI

Normally, the border is **open** daily 9am to 5pm (8am–4pm in Haiti as they are one hour behind). Once onto the bridge, you'll be swamped by touts trying to get you on their *motoconcho* or "help" process your visa. Be firm – a polite but insistent "thanks, but no thanks" will deter them eventually. The border **formalities** are fairly straightforward and **moneychangers**, who sit outside the immigration office, will give you one-to-one on Dominican pesos for Haitian gourdes – about the same as the bank rate.

COSTS

Crossing into Haiti at Dajabón for a day-trip to Fort Liberté isn't cheap; you'll pay a US$20 departure tax to the Dominicans, then stop off at the Haitian outpost on the other side and pay US$5 "charge", then on your return, the Haitian side will take another US$20 departure tax (with receipt), while the Dominicans will take another US$10 for a new Tourist Card. Factor in the *motoconcho* from the border to the fort and you're looking at least US$62.

THE HAITI EARTHQUAKE

In January 2010, measuring 7.0 on the Richter Scale, the most powerful **earthquake** to hit Haiti in two centuries caused unprecedented devastation on the western side of Hispaniola, killing almost 300,000 people, injuring as many, and leaving an estimated 1.5 million homeless. The epicentre was located close to the capital, **Port-au Prince**, reducing entire urban areas to rubble. The fact that 25 percent of Haiti's civil service was wiped out in the disaster, combined with the country's already fragile physical and social infrastructure, added to the usual panoply of problems that beleaguer large-scale relief efforts. Despite the Dominican Republic's perennially acrimonious relations with its poorer neighbour, **President Fernández** garnered international plaudits for his immediate response to the earthquake, supplying medical services, volunteers and pledging vast sums of aid, including $40 million for a new university. He also championed the right of the Haitian government to maintain control of the aid efforts, while facilitating the arrival of supplies and relief personnel through the DR. Another positive outcome was that the disaster jolted the Dominican-Haitian Mixed Bilateral Commission out of its torpor as it met for the first time since 2000 to address issues of mutual concern.

However, although the anticipated mass influx of **refugees** across the border into the DR did not occur in the initial aftermath of the quake, over the next twelve months around a million people were thought to have entered the country despite the sustained relief efforts. This increase in migration has put a strain on the countries' precarious new relationship, as thousands of Haitians deemed to be in the DR illegally are being **deported** back over the border on a scale unprecedented in recent years. In 2013, the Dominican Republic's high court also ruled that citizenship could be granted only to those born to one Dominican parent since 1929, legalizing retroactive denial of citizenship – not only for Haitians, though they make up the majority, but also for many Dominicans of European or Chinese descent. This act, which would leave tens of thousands of people of Haitian-descent effectively stateless, many of whom speak only Spanish, caused widespread **international condemnation**, prompting furious back-peddling by the government. It's a thorny issue, especially as the Dominican Republic's sugar and construction industries rely on Haitian migrant labour, and one that seems unlikely to be resolved quickly or easily.

4

Haiti: Fort Liberté

100m west of the town of Fort Liberté • It takes around half an hour and 150 Haitian gourdes each way from the border by *motoconcho* via the Haitian town of Ouanaminthe (referred to by Dominicans as Juana Méndez)

Dajabón is usually the busiest overland point of entry, partially because it's within striking distance of **Fort Liberté**, the most interesting site along the border. One of the oldest and best preserved French forts in the New World, it lies in ruins along the **Bay of Dauphin**, a perfectly round body of deep-blue water with a bottleneck opening to the Atlantic visible in the distance. Called Fort Dauphin during French rule, it was constructed to defend the strategic bay and large French fleet that the waters harboured. The **eastern wall** is in rubble at several points, but the bulk of the fortress is intact, its armoury now inhabited by stray goats, and with several passageways leading through the chambers of the large, central building. You can still see the plaza's irrigation system that fed fresh water into a central fountain; the two large holes in the ground nearby led to the prison. The **western wall** is intact as well, with a narrow, coral walkway from which to peer at the spectacular bay views – on the water you'll see wooden fishing boats with home-made sails, and birds diving into the water for fish.

The **town** of Fort Liberté merits only a quick look; check out the market, with stalls hawking produce, live chickens, fried johnnycakes and various household wares. It's fairly poor, however, and not only will you be asked by random passers-by for "un dollar américain" (they're not persistent about it) but there are no restaurants, so make sure you eat before you come.

Loma de Cabrera and around

The beautiful, pine-dominated Cordillera Central begins as you approach **LOMA DE CABRERA**, a mellow frontier town named after Restoration General José Cabrera, sited 20km south of Dajabón. This ribbon of dusty shacks lines the main road from the north for approximately 1km and then splits at a congested junction, where the road south to Restauración bears right. The only feature of interest to tourists within the town itself is the **Haitian market** held on Tuesday mornings. Just east of town, though, you'll find a popular free **balneario** on Calle María Trinidad Sánchez – a pleasant enough place to visit, though it's crowded on weekends and noisy thanks to a disco nearby. The grounds surrounding it are rubbish-strewn, but the *balneario* itself has clean mountain water and is set beneath a picturesque cascade.

Monument to the Heroes of the Restoration of the Republic

9km west of Loma de Cabrera, just north of the village of Capillo • Daily 9am–6pm • Free • *motoconcho* from Lomo de Cabrera RD$50–80

The **Monument to the Heroes of the Restoration of the Republic**, referred to more commonly as the "Monumento de Capotillo", is a stylish twentieth-century tribute to the renewal of Dominican independence, set on the spot where General Cabrera crossed over the border with his rebel troops and began the war against the occupying Spaniards. Designed by Dominican architect **Rafael Calventi** and completed in 1983, the complex – a series of broad steps rising up to a large building that holds several sculptures, all of it fashioned from Italian marble – has the feel more of abandoned ruins than contemporary civic monument, acknowledged and accented by Calventi through the use of a field of mock pillars scattered along the expansive marble steps, cleanly sliced off at various points to suggest an ancient city gone to rubble. On the elevated **central plaza** are two structures shaped in the form of stylized axe heads, the larger of which holds six social-realist murals depicting the conflict. Rising up from a hole in the building's floor is Ranico Matos' *The Flame of Liberty*, a brilliantly contrived sculpture that imparts the hypnotic motion of flame through spiralled steel. Behind the monument a small path leads to a **hill** marked with a Dominican flag – walk up for terrific views of the Haitian countryside.

ARRIVAL AND DEPARTURE   LOMA DE CABRERA

By bus or guagua Caribe Tours has an office on the left as you enter the town from Dajabón. The last departure for buses to Santo Domingo (3 daily; 4hr; RD$350) via Santiago (2hr 30min; RD$200) is at 3pm. Frequent guaguas from Dajabón (40min; RD$60) deposit passengers at the main crossroads; those wanting to travel on to Río Limpio (last departure at 2pm; 1hr 30min–2hr; RD$150) or Restauración (30–45min; RD$70) should walk round the corner to the Cooperativa and wait for a less frequent *público* (usually a pick-up truck) to fill.

ACCOMMODATION AND EATING

D'Carmen Buffet 100m south of the Caribe Tours station at Av. Duarte 118 ☎ 809 579 4338. The best of the town's meagre offerings, this place serves pretty tasty *criolla* cooking in a proper sit-down environment at a good price, with the filling *plato del día* for RD$150, and the evening buffet RD$120–200 (7.30–10pm). There's another decent restaurant inside the Caribe Tours station, which is almost as good. Daily 8am–11pm.

Santa Clara Av. Duarte 89 ☎ 809 579 4281. Accommodation is basic in Loma de Cabrera, and the *Santa Clara* is your best bet, with very clean rooms and private cold-water baths. Really, though, you're better off staying at the Río Limpio cabañas (see opposite) if you can get there. RD$350

Río Limpio and around

If peace and quiet are what you're looking for, you'll find the mountain hamlet of **RÍO LIMPIO**, 22km south of Lomo de Cabrera, to be easily the most idyllic spot along the entire border; it's also the nearest point to the **Parque Nacional Nalga de Maco**. As you

PARQUE NACIONAL NALGA DE MACO PRACTICALITIES

To visit Nalga de Maco you can get a **permit** from the **forestry supervisor** in Río Limpio, whose office is on the main street and on the right as you come down the hill. He is familiar with the caves and can help find a good local **guide** (RD$1000/day) and **mules** (RD$500/day). If you have more than one mule, you'll also need a **muleteer** who will cost more than a mule but less than a guide. Pack food, camping equipment, torches or headlamps, insect repellent and lots of water. The entire trip lasts **three days**, one day to get there, one day exploring the cave, and then one day to return.

head off the highway 10km south of Lomo, a rough dirt road leads 12km up the mountains through tiny villages and *campos* to where it sits majestically at 668m on the banks of **Río Artibonite**, with spectacular views of the surrounding mountains and valley. While the tiny village doesn't hold any major sights, it's a relaxing spot to unwind – you can swim in the local river, or do some lovely hikes or horseriding to the waterfalls nearby such as the gorgeous **Cascada de Río Bonito**.

The hamlet is also a hub of **ecological and development projects**, organized by community-run Servicio Dominicano de Desarrollo Integral y Ecoturístico Local (SEDDIEL), the main centre being at the **Centro Ecoturístico Río Limpio** in the village, while a less bureaucratic offshoot lies a little way out of town at the **Centro Verde de Río Limpio** (see below). Both are run in conjunction with Belgian and Scandinavian volunteers and funding. Ask at either about cultural events (local musicians sometimes play), or tours of the rice factory, coffee-processing plant, craft workshops or organic farms.

Parque Nacional Nalga de Maco

The little-visited national park of **Nalga de Maco** is named after the twin peak at the heart of the park whose name literally means "Frog's Butt", because the shape resembles a colossal frog that has fallen out of the sky and landed bottom-up. The main reason for coming here (apart from the stunning scenery) is to visit the **Cueva Nalga de Maco**. Though it involves a three-day trip, trekking there and back, and you'll need a guide (see box above), the cave itself is quite accessible, and you can see 250m worth of passages without crawling through guano or going underwater. You enter the cave system via a canyon set between the two peaks – if the peaks are the frog's buttocks, you can probably guess what they call the cave entrance. At the entrance stands a large stalagmite that has been dressed up as a *Vodú* representation of the Virgin of Altagracia, while inside are several Taino pictographs, including a remarkably beautiful hummingbird.

ARRIVAL AND INFORMATION   RÍO LIMPIO

Although the road is quite rough, *públicos* run around to Río Limpio from the Cooperativa in Lomo de Cabrera (5–6 daily until around 2pm; 1hr 30min–2hrs; RD$150). Most cars can make the trip, though you'd be better off in something with a high wheel arch unless you want to drive very slowly as you may well damage your car.

ACCOMMODATION

Centro Verde de Río Limpio 300m southwest of Río Limpio ☎829 577 7119, ⓦriolimpio.info. Although there are also cabañas (as well as camping facilities and a restaurant) down in the village at Centro Ecoturístico Río Limpio (☎809 984 5426) this place is much more laid-back and homely. Its basic wooden cabins all overlook the jungle and the more expensive ones (RD$800) also have their own bathrooms, though none have electricity at present. An internet connection of sorts is available in the office, and very good home-cooked meals (RD$150–200) are served in the dining hut on request. Reservation is recommended at either centre as both are often fully booked with groups – expect to wait a while for a reply. **RD$500**

The Cibao

CIGAR FACTORY

5

The Cibao

Cibao (rocky land) is the word Tainos used to describe the Cordillera Central mountain range that takes up much of the Dominican Republic's central interior, ploughing its way westward through Haiti (where it's called the Massif du Nord) and then popping up again in Cuba and Central America. The Dominican section of these mountains has by far the highest peaks in the Caribbean; indeed, they're higher even than North America's Appalachians, with some mountains over 3000m, including Pico Duarte, the Caribbean's loftiest at 3087m. Today the heart of the range is protected as Parques Nacionales Bermúdez y Ramírez and Reserva Científica Valle Nuevo, three national parks inaugurated between the 1950s and 1970s to preserve the remaining virgin pine forest and cloudforest, as well as the many rivers that begin in these parts and provide ninety percent of the DR's fresh water, plus a third of its electricity.

Today, though, Dominicans use the term Cibao more to describe the fertile **Cibao valley** – the island's breadbasket since pre-Columbian times – that lies between the **Cordillera Central** to the south and west and the **Cordillera Septentrional**, the mountain range to the north. This valley can be neatly divided into two sections: the **western Cibao**, a ribbon of farmland north of the central mountains, increasingly arid as it approaches the Haitian border, with some beautiful highland scenery around **San José de las Matas** and **Monción**; and the prosperous **Vega Real**, a triangle of alluvial plain between **Santiago**, **Cotuí** and **San Francisco de Macorís**, which contains some of the deepest topsoil in the world. During the nineteenth century the Vega Real's agricultural middle classes were the country's primary exponents of democracy and engaged in a century-long struggle for power with the demagogic cattle ranchers of the southeast.

The appeal of the Cibao is not as obvious as that of the coastal resorts, but you'll still find plenty to do, especially in **Santiago**, the country's second largest city after Santo Domingo. Besides its legendary nightlife, Santiago is well positioned for short excursions into the neighbouring farmland, which produces some of the world's best **cigars** – you can easily see the process first-hand. South of Santiago, en route to Santo Domingo, is a chain of Cibao towns that Columbus founded as gold-mining outposts. Of these, **La Vega** is a choice stop, holding the DR's largest **Carnival** celebration and the ruins of Columbus's colony La Vega Vieja, just northeast of the present-day city.

For most, however, the first priority is the **mountains**. Surrounded by picturesque scenery, the small but bubbly town of **Jarabacoa** is best set up for tourism, with a tidy array of hotels and restaurants, plus plenty of adventure-tour outfits offering everything from whitewater rafting, kayaking and cascading to three-day (or more)

CARNIVAL

Highlights

❶ Centro León Explore the history and culture of the Dominican Republic, from Taino petroglyphs to contemporary art and merengue, at Santiago's world-class cultural centre. **See p.210**

❷ La Vega Carnival A massive street party in February with platoons of rowdy participants roaming the streets in expertly hand-crafted masks. **See p.220**

❸ Higher Salto Jimenoa The biggest and very best of Jarabacoa's many thundering waterfalls, used as a backdrop for the opening scene of *Jurassic Park*. **See p.222**

❹ Whitewater rafting, Jarabacoa The Río Yaque del Norte plays host to a number of intense whitewater adventures as well as many other outdoor activities. **See p.222**

❺ Pico Duarte Five strenuous treks lead up to the summit of the Caribbean's tallest peak, a can't-miss adventure for all outdoor enthusiasts. **See p.226**

❻ Constanza Relax in this lush, circular Shangri-La valley in the Cordillera Central which offers waterfalls, excellent hiking and a Taino site. **See p.228**

HIGHLIGHTS ARE MARKED ON THE MAP ON P.206

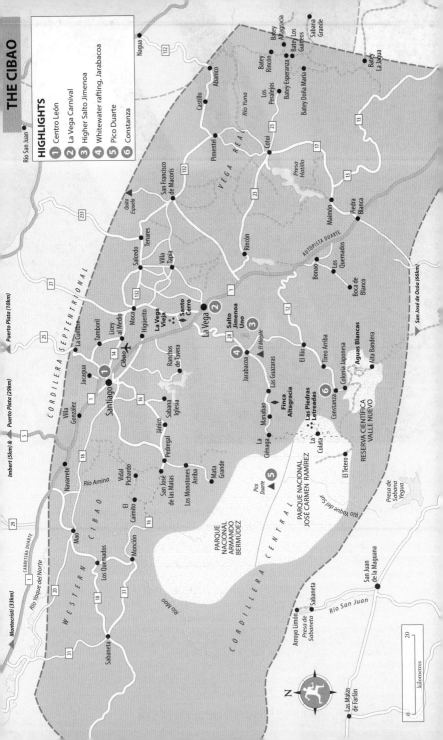

5

CIBAO TOBACCO

Tobacco was first cultivated (and given its name) by the Tainos, who pressed the leafy plant into a rock-hard substance to be smoked in pipes. Many Cibao peasants still make this form of tobacco – called *andullo* – which you can find if you ask around in Tamboril, Navarrete or Villa González (see box, p.217); it's sometimes even for sale in local *colmados*. **Export** began in 1679, when Cibao farmers started growing it for the French colony on the western side of the island. For two centuries, Dominican tobacco was widely praised as top quality, but when large-scale export to Germany for cigarette filler began in the mid-nineteenth century, that quality soon began to erode.

Tobacco was traditionally farmed by local peasants, who grew small plots of it alongside their vegetable gardens and sold the dried leaves to local middlemen for cash, who then transported it to Puerto Plata and sold it at a profit to large German export firms. When the US took over customs receipts in 1907, the Germans imposed tariffs that eradicated the old market, and many of the former middlemen opened **cigar factories** for export to the US. Cigar quality wasn't first-rate, though, until the Cuban revolution sent many prominent Havana tobacco men to the Cibao, where they developed an industry that today sells more cigars than Cuba's, and of the same high quality. During the 1990s, many small-scale businessmen tried to take advantage of the high profile of Dominican cigars by opening up factories of their own, but they had a hard time matching the quality of more established firms and most have now gone out of business.

If you're in the region to **purchase cigars**, don't be surprised to find that many of the best-known DR brands are not readily available locally – companies dedicated to export are usually not interested in regional distribution. While this puts the visitor in the difficult position of appraising quality without the benefit of recognizable brand names, the good news is that regional product is often as good or even better – and usually much cheaper. If you're not a connoisseur, though, and are looking to buy cigars without first smoking a tester, there are two nationally available brands that shouldn't let you down: **Carbonell** and **León Jimenes**. The latter also markets **Aurora**, a secondary quality brand that is widely available.

treks up bald-headed **Pico Duarte**. Another Pico Duarte trail begins near **San José de las Matas**, a mellow mountain village that makes a pleasant day-trip from Santiago. One of the most difficult trails, meanwhile – a gruelling five-day trek – sets off from **Constanza**, a circular utopian valley in the heart of the highest part of the range. Aside from the isolation and fresh air, Constanza's attractions include several hiking trails, an impressive waterfall and a jagged but scenic road that leads south through the **Reserva Científica Valle Nuevo** to **San José de Ocóa** at the southern end of the range. Wherever you choose to explore, remember that these are substantial mountains and should be explored only with hiking boots, warm clothing and decent waterproofs.

If you really want to get away from other tourists, look no further than the farming towns in the Vega Real: **Moca**, **San Francisco de Macorís,** and the delightful **Salcedo**, a small, laidback town with a vibrant nightlife.

Santiago and around

For five centuries **SANTIAGO** (or Santiago de los 30 Caballeros, to give it its full name) has been the main transport point for Cibao tobacco, bananas, coffee and chocolate; farmers still truck the lion's share of their produce here before it is transported to Puerto Plata and Santo Domingo for export. Set at the intersection of the western Cibao and the Vega Real, and with easy access to the country's two major ports, its prime location has brought settlers back time and again (Santiago's population of just under a million trails only that of Santo Domingo) even after destruction by various earthquakes, invading armies and fires.

5

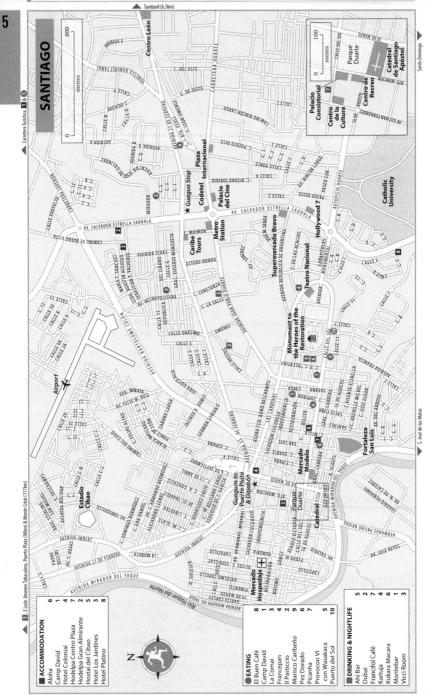

SANTIAGO

■ ACCOMMODATION

Aloha	6
Camp David	1
Hotel Colonial	4
Hodelpa Centro Plaza	7
Hodelpa Gran Almirante	2
Hostal del Cibao	5
Hotel Los Jardines	3
Hotel Platino	8

● EATING

El Buen Café	8
Camp David	1
La Comai	3
Francepan	4
Il Pasticcio	2
Marisco Caribeño	9
Pez Dorado	6
Picanha	7
Provocon VI con Wasakaca	5
Puerto del Sol	10

■ DRINKING & NIGHTLIFE

Ahi Bar	5
Dubai	2
Francfol Café	7
Kartuja	4
Kukara Macara	6
Montebar	1
Vicci Room	3

5

The city has a few traditional sights worth visiting, but it's also a good place to discover some of the crafts and culture for which the Dominican Republic is famous – particularly cigar-making and music. As the birthplace of *merengue périco ripao*, there's a good club scene here based mostly around this indigenous style – a blend of accordion, *tambora* and *güira* – with the city having produced many of the DR's top musicians.

Otherwise, it's worth spending a few days browsing **downtown Santiago** and its surrounding barrios. On the edge of the city centre looms the mighty **Monumento a los Héroes de la Restauración**, visible from pretty much anywhere in the city. Nearby lies one of the country's biggest and best cultural centres, **Centro Léon,** which is worth an afternoon's visit in itself. Calle del Sol, meanwhile, which runs west between the monument and the Parque Duarte, is the city's major **shopping district** and the heart of downtown activity. Further out, you can opt for a few nice factory tours, either to check out the local **tobacco** product or to see how **rum** is made.

Brief history

Originally founded in 1495 at Jacagua, 11km to the north, by one of the Columbus brothers (nobody is sure which), the city was rebuilt on its present site two years after a devastating earthquake in 1504, before being destroyed again by another earthquake in 1562. Santiago has been associated with **tobacco** since it was introduced for export to the French in 1679 and its economic significance is possibly why the Haitian army invaded in 1805, slaughtering most residents. But the city was again rebuilt and served for the rest of the century as transport hub for tobacco destined for Puerto Plata and Germany, and has even served as the nation's **capital** at various times. Incidentally, the "30 Caballeros" of the city's name come from the thirty knights transferred here from nearby La Isabela in 1504. Upon arrival, their arms and horses were taken from them, and they were set to work in the fields – this caused no small controversy when they returned to Spain, and the city was named after the ignominious incident.

Monumento a los Héroes de la Restauración

Eastern end of Calle del Sol • Tues–Sun 9am–noon & 2–6pm • RD$60 to climb to the top • ☎ 809 241 1391

Defining the eastern boundary of downtown is the gleaming white **Monumento a los Héroes de la Restauración**, Santiago's most impressive sight. Built by Trujillo in 1944 in honour of himself, it was quickly rededicated on his death to the soldiers who lost their lives in the Dominican Restoration War with Spain from 1863–65 (see p.266), and the statue of the dictator at its base hastily removed. Another statue, personifying Victory as a woman, sits atop its 70m pillar, her arms extended martially towards the sky. The monument is perched on top of a hill, making it visible from most of the city, which locals say was originally intended to symbolize the omnipresence of the secret police.

The area surrounding the monument used to be rather rowdy, particularly after dark, but following a thorough refurbishment and general sprucing up in 2007, it's much more welcoming. The monument can be reached via a new stairway – lined with palm trees – or a wheelchair-accessible ramp, and around it are three small plazas dedicated to Santiago's traditions, writers and baseball team. Come nightfall

---

STAYING SAFE IN SANTIAGO

Like all the country's big cities, the centre of Santiago is perfectly safe during the day, but at night it is probably safer to stick to the main streets, and taking a taxi is highly advised, especially if you're on your own. Santiago's **outer barrios** are an uneven mix of heavy industry and residential neighbourhoods; with the exception of wealthy Los Jardines, home to the *Hodelpa Gran Almirante* hotel (see p.213), they should be explored exclusively during the **daytime**, even the main roads.

5

the area becomes a popular meeting point and the tower is illuminated, while a few snack bars open at its base.

During the day, it's possible to climb the stairs to the top of the monument to take in the breathtaking **panorama** of Santiago and the surrounding valley and mountains. The inside is given over to a small museum of the Restoration War and a large **mural** by Vela Zanetti, a social-realist influenced by Diego Rivera, who was forced to leave the country after ignoring Trujillo's request that his painting be a direct tribute to the dictator. The mural depicts Dominican peasants, labourers and soldiers winding up the monument's circular stairway in arduous pursuit of liberty; though much of it is covered to prevent further deterioration, you can see portions of it as you clamber to the top.

Centro León

27 de Febrero 146 • Tues–Sun 10am–7pm • RD$100, Tues free • ☎ 809 582 2315, ⓦ centroleon.org.do

The most compelling attraction in the area around the monument – and in all of Santiago for that matter – is the **Centro León**. Opened in 2003, this outstanding, multifaceted cultural centre is housed in an ostentatiously postmodern building – all concrete, glass and angles – surrounded by neat gardens dotted with palms. It's a huge place, divided into four large sections. In addition, the centre is home to a good **café**, pleasant gardens adorned with statues, and a **gift shop** where you can buy replica Taino artefacts and, of course, cigars. You can also come for concerts and performances, some featuring the city's renowned **merengue** music. Note that written information at the centre is currently in Spanish only.

Section one

Section one is home to a museum of history and anthropology detailing the story of the Dominican peoples, examining the population's various conflicts, ethnic diversity and growing sense of national identity, as well as the impact people have had on the country's ecosystems and natural resources. The highlight is the remarkable collection of **Taino artefacts**, including a host of intact aboriginal necklaces, *cemi* statuettes, decorated pots, daggers, axe-heads and vomit sticks, used to induce vomiting after a large banquet.

Section two

Section two is devoted to a superb Dominican **art collection**. Notable works include local modernist masterpieces like Jaime Colson's folk-Cubist *Hombre con Pipa* and Celeste Woss y Gil's imposing self-portrait *Autorretrato con Cigarillo*, as well as more abstract works such as Paul Guidicelli's Expressionist depiction of a *Vodú* priest sacrificing a chicken, *Brujo Disfrazado de Pájaro*.

Sections three and four

The **third section** is set aside for temporary exhibitions, concerts (including merengue) and film screenings – check the website for details. The **fourth** is devoted to a display on the lives of the León Jimenes family, whose tobacco and alcohol wealth paid for the centre – they're the owners of Aurora cigars and Presidente beer.

Parque Duarte

A fine tree-covered square at the heart of the city, **Parque Duarte** tends to be crowded with people throughout the day – shoppers, shoeshine boys, "guides" who'll start telling you about the city and implore you to follow them (be polite but firm with your refusals) and the unemployed, who often wait here en masse to be picked up by one of the local building contractors when work becomes available.

5

Catedral de Santiago Apóstol

At the park's southern end • Open to visitors Mon–Sat 5–6pm, with Mass at 6pm

The **Catedral de Santiago Apóstol** is a cream-coloured, concrete building completed in 1895 with intricate carvings on its mahogany portals and stained-glass windows by contemporary Dominican artist Rincón Mora. The marble tomb of nineteenth-century dictator Ulises Heureaux is in the sanctuary.

Centro de Recreo

West side of the park • No formal opening hours, door often left open • Tip around RD$150 for tour

The **Centro de Recreo**, where Trujillo based himself while in town, is an ornate Moorish-style mansion built in 1894. One of the English-speaking "guides" who hang out in the park will show you around (usually asking for a tip that they'll describe as "a donation for the orphanage"). You can sit in the dictator's shoeshine seat, see his offices, and wander upstairs to the small ballroom where he danced merengue; it's currently used as a practice hall by ballet students.

Palacio Consistorial

West side of the park • Tues–Fri 10am–noon & 2–5.30pm • Free

The **Palacio Consistorial**, a Neoclassical palace built in 1895, was once the city hall but now hosts a small **museum** documenting Santiago's history, mostly through photographs, and an exhibition of Carnival masks. It was designed by a Belgian architect and set the tone for many of the buildings in the downtown area, whose grand designs marked Santiago's growing wealth and prosperity.

Mercado Modelo

Calle del Sol • Daily 9am–7.30pm

To the east of Parque Duarte, narrow pedestrianized **Gral Cabrera**, packed with stalls overflowing with cheap clothes, shoes and toiletries, leads 100m to the **Mercado Modelo**, a covered market with its main entrance on Calle del Sol. Inside are stalls selling tourist tat, cigars, amber and larimar jewellery, and bottles of Mama Juana, the country's famed aphrodisiac-cum-cure-all. A bustling maze of colours with both interesting and mundane wares on offer, it's a great place to wander and buy souvenirs, but be prepared to haggle.

Mercado Hospedaje

Corner of 16 de Agosto and Espaillat • Mon–Sat 6.30am–6pm

Taking up most of the western end of downtown is the enormous outdoor **Mercado Hospedaje**, the city's largest agricultural market and a fascinating place to wander around, although the appeal may not be that obvious at first. The roads leading in are lined with huge bins of beans, corn, bananas, tobacco, oregano, garlic and cassava, but these everyday items do little to foreshadow the atmosphere inside, which has an almost timeless, otherwordly feel to it – within the market, the local **botánica** sells

---

ESTADIO CIBAO

Just north of the centre in the Pueblo Nuevo barrio lies **Estadio Cibao** (Av. Imbert and Domingo Bermúdez), the largest professional baseball stadium in the country. The winter season lasts from mid-November to early February and it's best to book tickets (RD$75–350) in advance on ☎809 575 1810, as the bigger games can sell out – check local newspapers for schedules. There are a few much more low-key games in the summer season which runs from June to August. Day or night, take a taxi to and around Pueblo Nuevo – it's not the safest of places.

5

portraits of *Santería* (*Vodú*) saints, potions are whipped up on the spot for every conceivable malady, while in hidden back rooms it's possible to get your **tarot cards** read for a small fee.

ARRIVAL AND DEPARTURE

SANTIAGO

BY PLANE

Cibao International Airport (☎ 809 233 8000) is around 15km southwest of the city and the airport taxi drivers charge about DR$700 to the downtown area – if you walk a few hundred metres to the main road, however, a regular city taxi will cost only RD$250–300 and a *público* even less. There are no domestic flights from this airport.

BY CAR

All three highway entrances to town – the Autopista Duarte, the Carretera Duarte and the Carretera Turística – lead directly to the city centre. All the hotels listed below have secure parking.

BY BUS

Stations The two main bus companies have bases in Santiago. Caribe Tours has two stations: one (☎ 809 576 0790, ⓦ caribetours.com.do) lies at the northwest end of town on 27 de Febrero and Las Américas, in the barrio of Las Colinas; the other (☎ 809 241 1414) is further east along 27 de Febrero, in Los Jardines, round the corner from the Metro Tours' station on J P Duarte and Maimón (☎ 809 227 0101, ⓦ metroserviciosturisticos.com). From these locations you can (and should if it's after dark) take a taxi to the city centre for around RD$150.

Services Both companies have numerous daily departures north to Puerto Plata and south to Santo Domingo. The Caribe Tours service from Santo Domingo to Dajabón (6 daily; RD$200) via Monte Cristi (RD$190) also picks up and drops off passengers in Santiago. To reach Samaná you'll first need to get to San Francisco de Macorís by guagua to connect with one of the Caribe Tours buses (4 daily; 2hr; RD$140) to the peninsula, or take guaguas the rest of the way from there.

Destinations La Vega (21 daily; 45min); Monte Cristi (6 daily; 1hr 45min); Puerto Plata (20 daily; 1hr 15min); Santo Domingo (every 15–30min; 1hr); Sosúa (17 daily; 2hr).

BY GUAGUA

For Puerto Plata (every 30min until 7pm), Dajabón via Monte Cristi (hourly until 8pm) and Monción via Mao (every 30–45min until 7pm), head for the guagua station on the corner of 30 de Marzo and Cucurullo (near *Hotel Colonial*). For San José de las Matas use the station on Calle Valerio a block west of Parque Valerio. Guaguas to and from La Vega, Moca, Tamboril, San Francisco de Macorís and Salcedo mostly leave from near the bus stations on 27 de Febrero at the junction with Av. Estrella Sadhalá or at the park on the corner of Sabana Large and Restauración.

GETTING AROUND

By carro público *Públicos* cover most city transport needs; a one-way ride should cost around RD$20–30. They are recognizable by the large letter on the windscreen, with Route A probably the most useful one, passing by Parque Duarte, running up Calle del Sol and then along Av. 27 de Febrero.

By taxi Private taxis wait at the city parks, though it's better to call directly for a pick-up at night: reliable operators include Camino (☎ 809 971 7788) and Servi (☎ 809 971 6737). You shouldn't need to pay more than RD$150 for anywhere fairly central. Taxis are definitely

advisable at night, especially if you're on your own; be careful if approached by unlicensed drivers (*pirates*) who often work at night, though it might be worth the risk if you've somehow wound up in a bad neighbourhood.

By car If you intend to explore the surrounding countryside, consider renting a car. Established firms include Adventure, at the airport (☎ 809 612 5494, ⓦ adventurerentcar.com); Budget, at the airport (☎ 809 233 8230, ⓦ budget.com); and Nelly, Av. JP Duarte (☎ 809 582 7997, ⓦ nellyrac.com) or at the airport (☎ 809 233 8177).

INFORMATION AND TOURS

Tourist information Apart from the fairly useless information desk at the airport, the best place for hard facts are from the English-speaking staff at the Monumento a los Héroes de la Restauración.

Tours Horse-and-carriage rides run from Parque Duarte up to the monument and back; the price is negotiable, but

expect to pay around RD$600 return, depending on your route and how many of you there are.

Travel agents Abby Tours at Sabana Larga 117 (☎ 809 971 7045, ⓦ emelytours.com.do); Gómez Tours at 27 de Febrero (☎ 809 576 4673).

ACCOMMODATION

Given that Santiago is the country's second city, the place is not as well set up for **accommodation** as you might expect. Though there is good choice at the higher end of the scale, with a range of comfortable business hotels, mid-range options are lacking and the two budget establishments listed below are not ideal though they are the best available. They are also both located in a neighbourhood where caution should be exercised at night.

Aloha Sol Calle Del Sol 50 ☎ 809 583 0090, ⓦ alohasol .com. Modern hotel with a/c, cable TV, free wi-fi, breakfast included and great hot showers, although the rooms are quite small; it's worth paying the extra RD$150 for a larger "executive superior" room. It's right in the centre of the shopping district and is a good alternative for those who want comfortable accommodation but can't afford the *Hodelpa Gran Almirante*. US$86

Camp David Carretera Turística Km 12 ☎ 809 276 6400, ⓦ campdavidranch.com. A one-time Trujillo mountain home turned hotel and restaurant that's popular with wealthy Dominicans and a top choice for those who want to stay outside of the city centre. Many of the large, restful rooms have balconies with stunning views over the city. A museum on site houses many of the former dictator's cars, including the one in which he was assassinated. It can get chilly at night, so bring extra layers. Look for the turnoff east on the Carretera Turística, then drive up a winding road for 2km. RD$4650

Hotel Colonial Cucurullo 109 ☎ 809 247 3122, ⓔ colonialdeluxe@yahoo.com. The good-value rooms are clean, with TV and a/c, albeit a bit small and dark. It's central too, and even though the hotel's rowdy environs are unnerving to some its location near a main road actually makes it safer as there are always people around. The newer, ambitiously named *Colonial Deluxe* wing next door has slightly nicer rooms for a little extra. The rooms at the front of both pick up the wi-fi from the lobby. RD$900

Hodelpa Centro Plaza Mella 54 ☎ 809 581 7000, ⓦ hodelpa.com. Recently renovated, this spacious hotel enjoys an ideal central location, with huge rooms and all the amenities you could wish for including an airport shuttle bus, gym, excellent top-floor restaurant (great views) and even a casino. Large buffet breakfast included. Regular special offers make it even more attractive. US$142

Hodelpa Gran Almirante Av. Estrella Sadhalá and Calle 10 ☎ 809 580 1992, ⓦ hodelpa.com. Despite its rather bland exterior, this is terribly elegant inside with a huge, white marble-clad lobby. Set in a wealthy northeastern suburb, the hotel boasts two excellent restaurants and a large adjoining casino. Best of all it has a fabulous rooftop sundeck complete with a decent-sized infinity pool, hot tub and bar, offering superlative city and mountain views. If you've got the money, this is the place to stay. US$218

Hostal del Cibao Monción 40 ☎ 809 581 7775. The central location is a selling point, but this inexpensive, modest hostel could do with a lick of paint. Rooms are fairly gloomy but generally clean with fan, TV and tepid showers, but no wi-fi. Note that the place is locked tight most of the day and always at night (it's on a fairly deserted street, in a fairly bad neighbourhood) though you should be able to reach a caretaker by ringing the doorbell, which is tucked just inside the gate. RD$600

★ **Hotel Los Jardines** Av. Texas and Calle 10 ☎ 809 276 8222, ⓦ hotellosjardinesrd.com. Located at a peaceful spot in the posh Los Jardines area, this is by far the pick of the mid-range options, and although the cheapest rooms are pretty small they have great beds and the usual business trimmings – minibar, wi-fi, and safe. Breakfast is included and there's a roof terrace. RD$2200

Hotel Platino Av. Estrella Sadhalá ☎ 809 724 7576, ⓦ hotelplatinord.com. If *Los Jardines* is full, this is your next mid-range choice. The rooms are pleasantly furnished (though the cheaper ones are rather small) with a/c, minibar and TV. There's a cosy restaurant, internet access and a garden round the back. RD$2383

EATING

There are lots of moderately priced **restaurants** near the monument and Catholic University. For **groceries**, try Supermercado Bravo (daily 7.30am–10pm) at Av. Republica de Argentina and Av. Estrella Sadhalá.

El Buen Café San Luis 40, just off Calle del Sol ☎ 809 582 6755. This small, friendly café is about the only budget place in the city centre that will serve you breakfast – fresh juices, omelettes, sandwiches, coffee and toast – with fajitas, burritos and other simple dishes on the lunch menu, all for under RD$200. If you don't want your sandwich smothered in ketchup, let them know first. Mon–Sat 7.30am–7pm.

Camp David Carretera Turística Km 12 ☎ 809 223 0666, ⓦ campdavidranch.com. Former Trujillo mountain home, now converted into a gourmet restaurant and hostelry (see above) that offers a long list of choice seafood dishes and steaks (mains from RD$600) and some fantastic views. Can get a little chilly at night. Daily noon–11pm.

La Comai Metropolitana and Republica Del Libano ☎ 829 253 8810. Cosy, stylish mid-range restaurant with a small plant-filled patio, wooden furniture and a brightly painted horse trap as a sign. Serves very good mid-priced authentic Dominican food and a DR$200 weekday lunchtime buffet. Daily 11am–3pm & 7pm–midnight.

Francepan Av. 27 de Febrero 33 ☎ 809 971 0050. Pleasant café set back from the road, with a tiled, open-sided patio offering delicious soups, salads, classic meat dishes, deli-style sandwiches and burgers plus all the goodies from the on-site bakery. Mains start at around DR$250. Popular

5

with middle-class families, drawn by the kids' menu and convenient parking. Daily 8am–midnight.

★ **Il Pasticcio** Av. El Llano at C 3 ☎ 809 582 6061, ⊚ ilpasticcio.net. Home-made pasta (RD$230–420) reigns supreme in this classy Italian restaurant which is filled with original artworks – even on the ceiling. Porcini mushrooms are among the hard-to-find delicacies on offer. Don't forget to leave room for the divine tiramisu. Tues–Sun noon–3pm & 7–11pm.

Marisco Caribeño Calle Del Sol 1 ☎ 809 971 9710. Slightly overpriced but decent fish restaurant tucked away just down from the monument, with a nice terrace and congenial atmosphere, especially on weekday lunchtimes when they have great-value *plato del día* for DR$127. Ordering à la carte, you'll spend around DR$500 a head – try the *delicias de los 7 mares*, a mix of seafoods served in a carved pumpkin (RD$420). Daily 11am–midnight.

Pez Dorado Calle Del Sol 43 at Parque Altagracia ☎ 809 582 4051. The granddaddy of elite Santiago dining, this institution has been around since 1964. High-end, expensive *comida criolla* in a dark, formal environment, including such tasty dishes as chicken with garlic, cilantro and olives, octopus, sea bass and also excellent Chinese offerings and an extensive wine list. Mains mostly RD$625–850. Daily noon–11pm.

Picanha Del Sol 13 ☎ 809 775 0786, ⊚ picanha .com.do. Strictly for meat-lovers, this friendly Brazilian *churrasqueria* serves barbecued meats, carved at the table, on an all-you-can-eat basis (RD$800 /person including side dishes). Morsels include parmesan pork, filet mignon, spare ribs, and chicken breast. Mon–Sat 6pm–midnight, Sunday noon–midnight.

Provocon VI con Wasakaca Sabana Larga 39 at Restauración ☎ 809 276 8111. Just about the best *pollo al carbon* you'll find anywhere, served in basic surroundings at a good price. Marinated in lemon, garlic and herb "wasakaca" sauce, the chickens are then roasted on rapidly revolving spits, cooking them to crispy-moist perfection, and served with a small choice of Dominican sides – all for under RD$200 per person. They also have a branch on the Autopista Duarte in the Plaza Domyn Mall, and another in Moca. Open 24hr.

★ **Puerto del Sol** Del Sol 1 at the monument ☎ 809 947 1414. Comfy lounge sofas and a wall of sports screens, plus a tasty, wide-ranging menu (everything from salads to sushi) and very cold beer. The crowded open-air patio affords a superb view of the monument and promises great people-watching. There's no Presidente beer as it's owned by a rival beer distributor. Daily 11am–2am.

DRINKING AND NIGHTLIFE

Santiago's **nightlife** is rowdy and diverse, with the bars around the monument popular until 11pm, when the crowds move to alternative venues. Most other places don't get going till at least this time, and the party usually goes on till at least midnight during the week and 4am or later at weekends. Clubs, from cavernous to cramped, fill the city, offering a steady stream of **live music**. Most clubs and bars lie within a reasonable distance of one another, making it easy to hit two or three in a night, though walking is not advised, even for short distances. Be aware that prostitution is rife in several places – the aptly named *Passions* is probably one to steer clear of.

Ahí Bar Restauración 71 ☎ 809 581 4461, ⊚ ahi-bar .com. Attracting a smart clientele, this lively bar just west of the monument with a tree-shaded outdoor terrace is a fine place to wind down at the end of the day. It's also a good place to grab food as it offers a reasonable menu of Mexican and *criolla* staples starting at DR$345 for mains. Daily 4pm–2am, Fri & Sat until 4am.

★ **Dubai** Plaza Zona Rosa, Calle Salle ☎ 809 226 3372. There's a young, hip crowd here, drawn by a playlist that alternates English-language hits with intense bursts of merengue, salsa, hip-hop and reggaeton. Also popular with the international students from the university, especially on Wednesdays when women drink for free. Wed–Sun 8pm–4am, later Fri & Sat.

Francifol Café Del Sol 127 at Parque Duarte ☎ 809 226 3372. A classy bar in a busy downtown area with some of the coldest beer around. Looks more like a nightclub, but it is an excellent place for drinks and conversation. Plays mainly anglophone pop, rock and electronica. Wed–Sun 8pm–4am.

Kartuja Matúm Hotel, Las Carreras 1 ☎ 809 724 4671. Perennially popular as its hotel location seems to exempt it from the weekend licensing laws that apply to private clubs and bars – in theory this means it never has to shut. The crowd is older and less self-consciously stylish than at *Dubai* or *Vicci Room*. Open 24hr.

Kukara Macara Av. Francia west of the monument ☎ 809 241 3143, ⊚ kukaramacara.net. A camp classic with its giant cacti, waiters in full cowboy regalia and brightly lit replica stagecoach above the door, this club clearly takes its Wild West theme very seriously. It's a lot of fun, with two open-air floors, plus great Mexican food and even better breakfasts. Daily 8am–1am.

Montebar Av. 27 de Febrero ☎ 809 575 0300, ⊚ tipicomontebar.com. A heaving *típico* disco with tables surrounding a central dancefloor, this is the place to hear genuine merengue and bachata, especially when the live bands start playing after midnight. You'll need a taxi to get you there and back. Fri–Sun 9pm–4am.

5

SANTIAGO FESTIVALS

Santiago is one of the country's prime places to celebrate **Carnival**. Festivities take place every Sunday in February at the monument with throngs of costumed participants wearing colourful papier-mâché demon masks (*caretos*) and assaulting each other with inflated sheep bladders – don't wear anything that you feel too precious about. Things culminate on **Independence Day** (February 27), when the entire city comes out for a parade around the monument, accompanied by mobile freak shows, home-made floats and Haitian *gagá* bands. If the local baseball team wins the Caribbean Series Championship, the partying lasts for another week. More information is available in Spanish at ⓦ carnavaldesantiago.org. The local **fiesta patronal**, in honour of patron saint Santiago Apóstol, is held on July 22 and features dancing, drinking and a display of horseriding beside the monument.

If you're interested in getting behind the scenes of Carnival, head for **Pueblo Nuevo**, otherwise of interest primarily to baseball fans (see box, p.211). The barrio is home to Santiago's most esteemed **mask maker** (*caretero*) Angelo Leonardo Cabrera ("El Mambo"), whose family have been making masks for five generations. Phone ahead (☎ 809 790 9005) and he will gladly show you around his tiny but colourful workshop at Dr. Janus 104, explaining the significance of the masks, and how it's possible to tell – to the barrio – where a mask was made. You can purchase one for the relatively cheap price of RD$1000–1500; he also runs two-day courses (US$50) in how to make them using papier-mâché or clay. Be sure to take a taxi and ask it to wait for you during your visit as the neighbourhood is more than a little edgy – Angelo can arrange the cab when you call him and you'll be perfectly safe with him.

Vicci Room M. Alvarez 8 ☎829 712 6633. Swanky nightclub geared toward the wealthy young college crowd, with local and international DJs playing pumping dance music till late, with a very nice chill-out terrace for when you need a rest. Also has occasional midweek all-you-can-drink specials (men DR$600, women RD$300). Daily 8pm–midnight, until 2am or later Fri & Sat.

ENTERTAINMENT

For those after more highbrow entertainment, the city offers a modest programme of **theatre** and **classical music**. For a low-key night out there are several multiscreen **cinemas** – some films are in Spanish, but many more are in English with subtitles. The hotels *Centro Plaza*, *Gran Almirante*, *Aloha Sol* and *Hotel Matúm* all have **casinos**. Santiago's major daily **newspaper**, La Información (ⓦ lainformacion.com.do), contains listings of events and a cinema schedule.

Centro de la Cultura Calle del Sol and Monción ☎809 226 5222. As well as being the home of the highly regarded School of Fine Arts, regular opera, theatre and chamber music productions are hosted in the auditorium here. Phone or check La Información's website for what's on.

Gran Teatro del Cibao Av. Las Carreras 1 ☎809 583 1150, ✉ teatrodelcibao@hotmail.com. This palatial slab of Italian marble with near-perfect acoustics hosts a couple of opera productions per year, with occasional merengue concerts, chamber music and theatre in the smaller concert hall. For big-name acts and shows, tickets start at around RD$2500.

Hollywood 7 Av. Estrella Sadhalá ☎809 971 4880. Relatively inexpensive multiplex cinema, with tickets at RD$125 (Tues & Wed RD$50) with English films either dubbed, or less often subtitled.

Palacio del Cine Plaza Bella Terra Mall on Av. JP Duarte ☎809 226 3228, ⓦ palaciodelcine.com.do. This newer and rather swanky cinema has tickets from RD$100, as well as RD$250 VIP screenings that have reclining leather seats and waiter service.

DIRECTORY

Banks and currency exchange There are several banks on Calle del Sol with 24hr ATMs, including Banco Popular, Del Sol and Sánchez, and Scotia Bank.

Hospital If you have a medical emergency, head to Centro Médico Cibao at Av. JP Duarte 64 (☎809 582 6661), just west of Las Carreras, or Clínica Corominas at Restauración 57 (☎809 580 1171, ⓦ corominas.com.do). Call ☎911 for other emergencies.

Internet There are numerous internet cafés around town: Internet Yudith, who also do photocopies and printing, at Calle 16 de Agosto; a place next door to the *Hostal del Cibao*, which you can also make calls from; and *Café Decano* at Av. Estrella Sadhalá by the *Platino* hotel. Most of the city's hotels, restaurants and shopping plazas now offer free wi-fi access.

Laundry Joseph Cleaners at Las Carreras 29 at JP Duarte (☎809 583 4880).

Pharmacy Farmacia Carol at Av. Estrella Sadhalá 29 (☎ 809 241 0000) is open 24hr; another good central option is Farmacia San Luis at San Luis 61 at Independencia (Mon–Sat 7.30am–9pm, Sun 9am–6pm; ☎ 809 247 6494).

Police Main office is at Sabana Larga and Calle del Sol (☎ 809 582 2331). Call ☎ 911 for emergencies.

Post office Main office is at Calle del Sol and San Luis. There's an EPS at Hostos 3 and Ulises Franco Bidó (Mon–Fri 9am–5pm, Sat 9am–noon; ☎ 809 581 1912).

Around Santiago

In Santiago's immediate vicinity, the urban sprawl quickly peters out into tobacco farmland, and the villages that exist to support this agriculture are neither set up for tourists nor worth your time. That said, the **cigar factories** (see box opposite) in Tamboril that process the weed certainly merit a visit, as do the **La Cumbre amber mines**, a short trip along the Carretera Turística, an incredibly scenic but potholed route that weaves its narrow way up into the lush, rolling mountains of the Cordillera Septentrional. West of Santiago are **San José de las Matas** and **Moncíon** which are highland highlights.

La Cumbre amber mines

The mines lie 4.5km from La Cumbre at the tiny village of La Tierra de Lominero • By car, take the turnoff at the centre of La Cumbre marked "La Cumbre de Juan Vegas" and continue west for 3km along a rough track where a left turn heads north uphill for 1km, from where it's another 500m down to the village; by public transport from Santiago take a guagua heading north to Sosúa and get it to drop you in La Cumbre, from where you can either walk or take a *motorconcho* (RD\$150).

A short journey north along the potholed but scenic Carretera Turística that winds its narrow way up into the lush mountains of the Cordillera Septentrional lie the **La Cumbre amber mines** – the largest in the world and a setting (and inspiration) for the movie *Jurassic Park*. Despite the glamorous connotations the mines are extremely basic: these 10–18m deep holes in the ground are supported by rickety wooden frames and covered with blue plastic sheeting with an extensive network of tunnels spreading out under the mountain from the bottom of the pits. The miners, who work by candlelight, will sell you chunks of amber at a very good price – be aware that this is technically illegal. It is not possible (or desirable) to go down one of the mines and after heavy rains they will often be closed. If you walk back up the hill and turn right, you can reach the top of the ridge, from where you can see the entire Cibao valley and – far in the distance – a slice of the Atlantic Ocean.

San José de las Matas

La Toma del Río Antonsape *balneario* lies 15km out of town along a rough road • Taxi RD\$1500 • 45min each way

The easiest excursion into the mountains from Santiago is **SAN JOSÉ DE LAS MATAS**, a sleepy hill station looking out over the northern Cordillera Central, here packed with palm trees and coffee plantations. In part it's so quiet because the town has the country's highest per capita rate of immigration to the US; many of those who stay at home are supported by relatives in New York. San José is a great starting-off point for several day-hikes and an arduous five-day round-trip trail to **Pico Duarte** (see p.226), and is particularly interesting during the **fiesta patronal** – held during the first week of August – when hundreds of relatives return from the States for the festivities, and during Christmas, when there's a candlelit procession on horseback at night.

There's little to do within town except take a leisurely walk and admire the views: for one such lookout, take the dirt path behind the post office, on 30 de Marzo, to a **cliff-top park** with a good vantage point over the neighbouring mountains. Most viewpoints and some natural swimming holes lie several kilometres outside San José, with the best *balneario*, La Toma del Río Antonsape, a robust taxi ride away at **Mata Grande**, a pueblo that is also the starting point for the Pico Duarte trek (see p.226).

5

CIGAR FACTORIES

The fertile soils of the Cibao valley yield some of the world's finest tobacco (see box, p.207). Whether you're a cigar aficionado or simply interested in watching the process, consider a trip to one of the **cigar factories** around Santiago. Visits generally start at the warehouse where you can see the large bales of tobacco being brought in from the farms, then the leaves getting stripped and sorted into different grades before being taken to the *sala de tabaqueros*. Here the *tabaqueros* mix different leaves at wooden desks before rolling them into cigars, usually while puffing on a large stogie themselves. You'll probably be offered a fresh cigar at some point of the tour, and also the opportunity to buy at a good price – from around RD$20 per large cigar.

GUAZUMAL

The suburb of Guazumal lies around 5km northwest of central Santiago and is easily accessible as it's at the western end of *público* route A from Calle Sol or 27 de Febrero; a taxi will cost around RD$150–200.

E. León Jimenes Tabacalera Parque Industrial Tamboril, Av. Tamboril ☎809 734 2563, ⓦlaaurora .com.do. This is the new home of the Aurora brand, who've been making cigars in Santiago since 1903. Guides speak English and after the free tour you're escorted to a deluxe smoking room to receive a free cigar, accompanied by free Presidente on tap (the company also owns the ubiquitous beer brand). Mon–Sat 9.30am–5pm.

TAMBORIL

Tamboril, 6km east of Santiago (though more or less a suburb of it) is one of the world's most famous cigar towns. Santiago's 27 de Febrero becomes Calle Real in Tamboril – take one of the many guaguas (25min; RD$50) that head in this direction, as both of the factories below are located along this route – you can easily ask the driver to drop you off.

El Artista Av. Presidente Calle Vasquez ☎809 580 5282. Not the biggest operation nor the best cigars, but they are the friendliest and the guide Orlando speaks excellent English. Founded in 1956, the company is called El Artista because the *tabaqueros* often sing while they work. Tours are free. Mon–Fri 8am–5pm.

Flor Dominicana Calle Real ☎809 580 5139, ⓦlaflordominicana.com. The largest operation in town and one of the most famous brands. They aren't quite so welcoming and this one's more for those who want to buy quality cigars rather than just enjoy the factory experience. Tours are free but phone ahead. Mon–Fri 8am–5pm.

SAN JOSÉ DE LAS MATAS

ARRIVAL AND DEPARTURE

By guagua Guaguas arriving in San José from Santiago (every 35–45min 6am–7pm; 1hr; RD$100) pull in at the Texaco on the eastern side of town, from where you can also catch a much less frequent guagua west to El Rubio (6am–5pm; 20min; RD$50) where the road deteriorates considerably and you'll have to change to a *público* to get to Monción, which leave when full.

By car From Santiago, head west on Calle 30 de Marzo, cross the Hermanos Patiño Bridge and continue west for 28km. The road isn't bad – it usually takes around 40min. If you're driving further west, note that the road between El Rubio and Monción is fairly bumpy.

ACCOMMODATION AND EATING

Most visitors choose to make a **day-trip** of the town, but those looking to stay the night will find a couple of simple hotels, as well as one splendid mountain retreat. There are a few **cabañas** and **hotel-restaurants** on the road coming into town from Santiago, which are bearable but noisy.

Hotel Familial 16 de Agosto 17 ☎809 579 0657. Of San José's two budget hotels (which face each other along the street north of the Parque Central), this one, housed in an orange building, is the better choice. Rooms are shabby and basic but clean, with hot water, ceiling fans, and rocking chairs outside the door. RD$400

Hotel La Mansión 2km north of town at Av. La Mansión 56 ☎809 571 6633, ⓦhotellamansionsajoma.com. The plushest hotel (and restaurant) in town is perched among the pines in the hills just north of town inside a gated community. Many of the luxurious rooms have fantastic views of the mountain, as does the pool and terrace. Also does an all-inclusive RD$5500 deal (dining à la carte at their excellent *Las Pinas* restaurant) based on two people sharing. RD$2250

Tropicaribe Mella 6 ☎809 578 8234. Inexpensive restaurant with an outdoor patio where you can enjoy a

5

fairly standard range of Dominican dishes. It's a good place to try *mondongo* (tripe), but if you're not feeling adventurous go for their very nice *plato del día* for RD$120. Most dishes cost under RD$300. Daily 9am–11pm (Tues from 2pm).

Monción

26km west of San José • **Casabe Doña Mechi** 3km north of Monción in Los Piños • Mon–Fri 7am–8pm • ☎ 809 572 2682

A scenic but badly deteriorated road leads from San José to sleepy **MONCIÓN**, a pretty mountain town unremarkable but for a nearby riverside site, **Los Charcos de los Indios**, that locals claim is of Taino origins. You can arrange tours of the site at **Casabe Doña Mechi**, a tiny, family-run cassava bread factory (see box below) situated a little north of town. While you're there, it's worth asking to be shown around – you'll see the various elaborate contraptions for scraping, washing and grinding the tubers and the enormous ovens in which they are baked into bread. On the face of it Monción itself hardly justifies more than a day-trip, but you'll find the locals – who are unused to tourists – extremely hospitable, and one of the country's best restaurants is nearby too.

Los Charcos de los Indios

3km north of Monción • Tours arranged at Casabe Doña Mechi for a negotiable fee: expect to pay RD$5800 each for fewer than four people • Bring swimwear

Los Charcos de los Indios is an eye-popping Taino site that sees precious few visitors. The difficulty of finding it largely explains that – from the cassava factory, it's first a ten-minute drive and then a thirty-minute **hike** along a boulder-strewn river to a breathtaking double waterfall (though not in dry season) with a large, clear swimming hole. Venture another 300m and you'll be rewarded by the Charcos **site** itself – yet another double waterfall with a huge, deep swimming pool and high rocks from which local children dive. Towering above the swimming hole is what appears to be a 30m-high totem of a Taino face carved out of the rock. The site has yet to be officially authenticated by Dominican archeologists, since it could possibly be a natural rock formation, though the locals are convinced of its Taino provenance, claiming that the site used to be littered with the remains of a native settlement. If genuine it would be the largest indigenous artefact in the Caribbean.

ARRIVAL AND DEPARTURE
MONCIÓN

By guagua If you're coming here from San José, you'll need to change at El Rubio and get a *público*.

By car If you're not visiting San José first, the easiest way to get to Monción is via the paved road that leads from Mao – which is the route guaguas from Santiago take – twice the length of the San José road, but just as fast and a much smoother ride.

ACCOMMODATION AND EATING

Las Américas Calle Duarte 88 ☎ 809 579 0065, ✉ clamorel81@hotmail.com. Monción's main hotel is a definite step up from the usual small and dingy rural establishments, with decent-sized, well-decorated rooms,

---

CASSAVA BREAD

Still a staple Dominican food, **cassava bread** dates back to the Tainos. Low in fat and protein but high in carbohydrate, it's baked from a flour produced by grating, draining and then drying the tube-like roots of the bitter **yuca** plant. Traces of ancient cassava bread production have been found across the Caribbean and it probably owes its success to the fact that the mother plant, yuca (also known as cassava and manioc), grows easily in poor soil and is hardy enough to withstand both drought and hurricanes. The roots are ready to **harvest** after only ten months but remain useful for up to two years, and the bread, once baked, can be **stored indefinitely**. Resembling a cracker more than traditionally baked bread, it has little taste of its own but makes a great side dish with traditional Dominican stews and is delicious served with avocado and salt.

balconies and comfortable beds. RD$1200

D'Amigos Café Duarte 42 ☎ 809 579 0812. This friendly place does deliciously spiced grilled chicken wings, plus pizzas, seafood and an immensely popular Sunday lunch buffet (11.30am–3pm). Most mains are upwards of RD$250. The owner speaks English well. Daily 8am–midnight.

★**Restaurante Cacique** Cacique, 8km north of Monción on Highway 16. One of the country's pre-eminent restaurants for goat and lamb dishes, all served with the local cassava bread, and very reasonably priced at around RD$200–250 for a main. It's set on an outdoor patio and is open daily for lunch, though there are usually only three items on the menu board. Daily 10am–4pm.

The Cordillera Central

The mighty **CORDILLERA CENTRAL**, slicing through the Dominican Republic's heart, was sparsely populated during colonial times by communities of slaves in hiding, known as *cimarrones*; as the centuries wore on, the ex-slaves were joined by Cibao valley peasants pushed out of the Vega Real by large landowners. These settlers would cut sections of forest and fence off small agricultural settlements called *conucos*, moving on to another plot once the topsoil had been washed down the side of the hill. This practice carried on into the twentieth century until the national government put a stop to it by setting up three national parks within which farming is illegal, and these are now growing centres of ecotourism. Most of the old *conucos* are returning to wilderness, though a couple have evolved into thriving towns.

For the most part, the mountain roads are horrific, and to head deeper into the range you'll need a **donkey**; blazed trails lead to **Pico Duarte** from five separate points, with stops in secluded alpine valleys Tétero and Bao. On the eastern edge of the valley, the towns of **La Vega** and **Bonao**, both founded by Christopher Columbus, are mid-sized industrial centres with little of interest to visitors most of the year, though La Vega's Carnival is the country's best.

La Vega and around

La Concepción de la Vega, more commonly referred to as **LA VEGA**, just 30km southeast of Santiago, started out as one of Columbus's gold-mining towns, only to be levelled in a sixteenth-century earthquake and rebuilt as a farming community. Aside from the ruins of this old settlement, known as **La Vega Vieja**, there's little in today's noisy, concrete city to hold your attention. However, La Vega's **Carnival** celebrations in February (see box, p.220) are generally acknowledged to be among the most boisterous and authentic – as well as the oldest – in the country.

Catedral de la Concepción de La Vega

Calle Mella at Parque Central • Daily 6am–noon & 3–6pm • ☎ 809 573 4613

La Vega's fascinating **Catedral de la Concepción de La Vega** is surely the most subversive piece of architecture in the country, and considered something of a national embarrassment by many. Its team of architects envisioned a people's church built in the same concrete-box mode as most urban dwellings, reflective of the bleak poverty of most of its parishioners. The convoluted main structure is divided into a dozen towers with Gothic portals – note the central cross, fabricated from threaded pipes, and the industrial ornamentation of the facade. There are a few out-of-place colonial elements to the building as well, as it was initially intended as a celebration of the Columbus Centenary, to include brick gun turrets on all sides; the idea was subsequently abondoned.

Under the auspices of the cathedral, the **Museo de Vega** is set to open in late 2014 just across the park from the cathedral, next to the Casa de Cultura on Prof. Juan Bosch and will contain various Taino artefacts found in the region as well as a display of carnival masks.

5

CARNIVAL IN LA VEGA

Archeological evidence from La Vega Vieja indicates that **Carnival** has been celebrated in the area since the mid-1500s – and in the intervening period they've got really quite good at it. A twenty-block promenade is set up between the two main parks, along which parade platoons of demons in impressively horrific **masks**, the making of which is something of a local specialized craft. Many city dwellers who spend their days as hotel clerks, bankers or auto mechanics use much of their free time perfecting mask making; in addition to papier-mâché, they often use materials like bull horns, bone and sharpened dogs' teeth. If you'd like to **buy** one, try asking at *Hotel Rey* or in the new **Museo de Vega**; expect to pay at least RD$1000, depending on how elaborate the design is. Better still, head to Santiago and visit "El Mambo" (see p.215). Accompanying the **parades** are blaring loudspeakers and food and liquor vendors that animate and feed the crowds, which average up to seventy thousand each afternoon – many of them watching from rooftops.

Santo Cerro

5km north of La Vega, off Autopista Duarte or the Moca road

North of town is **Santo Cerro** (Holy Hill), the site of an important 1494 battle between the Tainos and Columbus, who was leading an inland expedition to round up natives as slaves. A large company of Tainos from the valley below attacked his troops here and, so legend has it, were getting the better of the invaders until Columbus raised a large, wooden cross on the hill – at this, an apparition of the Virgin perched atop it, and the emboldened Europeans slaughtered the enemy. It's hard to imagine a more peaceful spot today, crowned by a beautiful brick **church** and an unbelievable view of the Vega Real. Within the sanctuary is an imprint purported to be the place where Columbus planted the cross.

La Vega Vieja

9km north of Vega on the Moca road • Mon–Sat 9am–noon & 2–5pm • RD$100 • No phone

On the western side of the road to Moca are the ruins of Columbus's original city **La Vega Vieja**, founded in 1494 after the nearby Santo Cerro battle. It went on to become one of the colony's most important mining outposts before the 1562 earthquake. Though protected as a national park, the foundations on display – the fortress, a church, portions of the aqueduct and a few stone houses – make up only a tenth of the original city and are, for the most part, exceedingly overgrown. The **fort** is the most extensive ruin, with most of its walls intact; colonists plundered much more of the stone in the nineteenth century to build the church at Santo Cerro. The ruins are guarded by a lone soldier, who will show you around and can unlock the small **museum** which contains some badly maintained but interesting artefacts dug up on site, such as swords, pots, and coins plus – for some reason – a rusty sewing machine that is obviously not from Columbus's era.

ARRIVAL AND DEPARTURE   LA VEGA

By bus or guagua Caribe Tours (☎ 809 573 6806) connects with Santo Domingo (28 daily 6am–8pm; 1hr 30min; DR$210) and has a terminal a few kilometres from the centre on Av. Rivas, just off the Autopista Duarte. In the town centre, on Pedro Rivera (close to where it intersects with Av. Rivas), lies the bus station for Expreso Vegano (☎ 809 573 4613), which runs an almost identical service to and from Santo Domingo. Although Caribe Tours also operates four buses a day from Santo Domingo to Jarabacoa, which stop off at La Vega, more frequent guaguas (every 30min 7am–6pm; RD$70) set off from the corner of 27 de Febrero and Calle Don Antonio Guzmán to Santiago, Asotraevesa (☎ 809 242 3474) runs regular guaguas (every 30min 6am–8pm; 40min; RD$80) from their station just north of the park on Calle Don Antonio Guzmán – these serve their station at the Parque de los Chachases in Santiago.

By taxi Taxis across town or between bus terminals cost RD$150, or RD$100 by motorcycle. Try Taxi del Valle (☎ 809 573 1313).

ACCOMMODATION AND EATING

For a city of La Vega's size, decent **hotels** are in short supply; many lack even the most basic amenities like a toilet seat, mosquito net or hot water.

Engini Pizza Calle Don Antonio Guzmán 1 ☎ 809 573 2750. This place has a child-friendly pizza parlour by the road; the adults head to the restaurant and bar at the back, with its stylish, Art Deco interiors, fun crowd and massive karaoke sound system. Specialities include shrimp and *lambí*; portions are generous, with mains starting at around DR$250. Daily 7am–11pm (later at weekends).

Hotel Rey Calle Don Antonio Guzmán 3 ☎ 809 573 9797, ✉ hotelrey97@hotmail.com. By far the best option in town – the rooms are clean and comfortable,

with a/c and cable TV, staff are friendly, and there's a decent on-site restaurant dishing up *comida típica*. Book ahead. RD$2092

Zitro Hotel Calle Don Antonio Guzmán 3 ☎ 809 573 7731, ✉ jerryortiz@gmail.com. Brand new, and just across the road from the *Hotel Rey*, this is by far the best of the budget options, with large, brand-spanking-new rooms, though they do lack a/c. Be warned, however – the rooms by the road can be a little noisy, and there's a bar right next door. DR$600

Jarabacoa

JARABACOA, a mountain resort peppered with coffee plantations, is popular with wealthy Dominicans for its cooler climate and is also one of the island's adventure sports hubs, with trekking, whitewater rafting, paragliding, canoeing and horseriding all easy to arrange. The pine-dominated mountains that surround the town – dubbed rather inanely "The Dominican Alps" – hold four large **waterfalls** (*saltos*), several rugged **trails** fit for day-hikes, three **rivers** used for whitewater rafting and the busiest starting point for treks up Pico Duarte.

The town's tiny but expanding grid runs right alongside the pretty **Río Yaque del Norte** and the area surrounding the town has seen a good deal of development in recent years as a number of new residential communities have been created, both for expats and wealthy Dominicans looking for a mountain retreat.

Salto de Baiguate

Around 5.5km south of town off the road to Constanza: getting there is fairly straightforward as it's signposted just outside town on Av. Pedregal, at the end of the usefully named Calle Baguate • Daily 8.30am–6pm • Free

The least-visited falls near town is **Salto de Baiguate** which, at 60m, is a bit higher than (Lower) Salto Jimenoa. While not as pretty as the others, it has a large cave and a very good swimming hole at its base, which is why it's also where canoeing trips end –

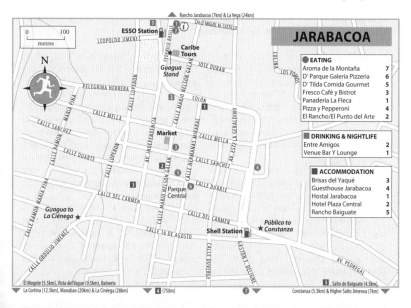

JARABACOA

● EATING
Aroma de la Montaña	7
D' Parque Galeria Pizzeria	6
D' Tilda Comida Gourmet	5
Fresco Café y Bistrot	3
Panadería La Fleca	1
Pizza y Pepperoni	4
El Rancho/El Punto del Arte	2

■ DRINKING & NIGHTLIFE
Entre Amigos	2
Venue Bar Y Lounge	1

■ ACCOMMODATION
Brisas del Yaqué	3
Guesthouse Jarabacoa	4
Hostal Jarabacoa	1
Hotel Plaza Central	2
Rancho Baiguate	5

5

other than these visitors, hardly anyone comes here and chances are you'll be able to enjoy it alone.

Lower Salto Jimenoa

Signposted 2km north of town off Carretera Jarabacoa from where it's a further 6km and past the golf course • Daily 8.30am–7pm • RD$100

The most popular of Jarabacoa's falls is the crashing 40m **Lower Salto Jimenoa** or **Salto Jimenoa Dos** which boasts a deep pool good for swimming, staffed by a lifeguard, and surrounded by lush vegetation. It's accessible on foot via a rickety suspension bridge, rebuilt after Tropical Storm Olga raged through the area in late 2007.

Higher Salto Jimenoa

7km along the Constanza road: head for 7km until you reach a small pueblo, where there's a large sign on the left indicating the waterfall • Daily 8am–6pm • RD$100

The most impressive Jarabacoa waterfall by far is the **Higher Salto Jimenoa**, or **Salto Jimenoa Uno**, as it's often called. This is a tougher proposition as it involves a fifteen-minute descent down a steep path into a ravine and therefore a longer, tougher climb back out. It's quite a sight as the water drops 60m from a hidden lake above and thunders into a huge pool at its base. The spray creates delightful rainbow patterns on the rocky walls and it's easy to see why this was chosen as a setting for a scene in *Jurassic Park*. It's certainly worth the effort of getting here and you'll probably have the place to yourself.

ACTIVITIES AROUND JARABACOA AND THE CORDILLERA CENTRAL

The **Río Yaque del Norte**, a beautifully blue, fast-flowing mountain stream that rises up in the very heart of the Cordillera Central mountain range, plays host to a number of different whitewater adventures. The lower sections are used by several **rafting** operators and offer some exciting drops up to grade IV. The nearby **Jimenoa and Yásica rivers** offer even more severe challenges, but these are only accessible to experienced kayakers; note that none of the whitewater rafting trips are available to children under 12. Many of Jarabacoa's rivers and waterfalls can also be enjoyed firsthand by taking a **canyoning** trip with one of the local tour operators. Accompanied by an experienced guide, you'll make your way downstream using a combination of swimming, jumping, walking and rappelling. Previous experience isn't necessary and it's a breathtaking way to see some unspoiled countryside. Other local outdoor options include **hiking**, **biking** and **horseriding**.

Iguana Mama. C-5 in the centre of Cabarete ☎ 809 571 0908, ⊕ iguanamama.com. Although based on the coast, Iguana Mama – the best (but among the priciest) of all the island's adventure specialists with impeccable ethics – offers many excursions in the Cordillera Central, including multi-day mountain-bike odysseys across the range, whitewater rafting (US$100) and three-day hikes of Pico Duarte (US$520).

Rancho Baiguate A marked turnoff about 1.5km out on the road from Jarabacoa to Constanza leads another 1km to the resort ☎ 809 574 6890, ⊕ ranchobaiguate.com.do. One of the island's biggest, best-organized and most expensive tour operators, with most of their clients coming from the all-inclusives on the north coast. They run a wide range of adventure tours, including whitewater rafting (US$50) and canyoning (US$50). Other excursions include hiking to

the falls (US$25–50), mountain biking (US$25–40) and short horseriding trips (US$9–11). Longer trips include a guided three-day hike to Pico Duarte (US$255–560), the same hike taking a more leisurely four days (US$325–850), and a five-day hike, which takes in the peak and Valle del Tétero (US$415–1050). The lower prices are for five or more people, while the highest is for one person alone, and includes all transport, camping equipment, food, guides and mules. One of the English-speaking guides here also privately runs a paragliding outfit (⊕ paraglidingtonydominicanrepublic.com; RD$25000).

Rancho Jarabacoa Signposted 2km north of Jarabacoa, from where it's another 5km ☎ 809 222 3202, ⊕ ranchojarabacoa.com. Offers rafting (US$50), canoeing (US$50), three-day treks to Pico Duarte (US$300) and horseriding (US$10) in the nearby pueblo of Sabaneta. Slightly less expensive option than Rancho Baiguate for some activities.

El Mogote

5.5km southwest of Jarabacoa on the road to Manaboa • Monastery ☎ 809 866 0591

A couple of kilometres west of Jarabacoa on the road to Manabao you'll see a marked turnoff for **El Mogote**, a 1525m-high mountain with a **trail** (best of the local day-hikes) that can be done in a five-hour round-trip; make sure to bring food and plenty of water, as the last stretch is extremely steep. There's also a white, modern-looking Cistercian monastery, **Santa Maria del Evangelio**, a few metres up the trail, where many of the monks have taken a vow of silence – if you would seriously like to retreat, they can arrange a cell for you at a small cost.

Vista del Yaque and Salto Las Guázaras

9.5km west of Jarabacoa on the road to Manabao • No opening hours; bar open daily 9am–11pm • Free

Continuing west along the road to Manabao, a further 4km beyond the turnoff to El Mogote, brings you to **Vista del Yaque** – here you'll find a pool that's ideal for swimming, with small rapids and a shaded outdoor bar looking out over the mountains. From here, a 1km trail leads south to the waterfall **Salto La Guázaras**, a 62m cascade that gets few visitors.

La Cortina and Los Dajaos

12.5km west of Jarabacoa on the road to Manaboa • No opening hours • Free

Just 3km west of Vista del Yaque lies **La Cortina**, yet another *balneario* – this one set on the edge of a cliff, with a cemented swimming pool and, of course, a bar. It's also the setting-off point for a four-hour hiking trail called **Los Dajaos**, which ploughs south through the mountains towards Constanza before looping back to the highway and the tiny pueblo of Manabao.

ARRIVAL AND GETTING AROUND   JARABACOA

By bus or guagua Caribe Tours (☎ 809 574 4796) runs buses to and from Santo Domingo via La Vega and Bonao (4 daily 7am–4.30pm; 3hr; RD$280) from the back of the Esso station on Federico Basilis at the town's northern entrance, which also functions as the guagua depot. Guaguas shuttle to and from La Vega (at least every 30min; 40min; RD$75), while *públicos* (generally pick-up trucks) bound for Constanza (around 6 daily; 1hr 30min; RD$175) leave from Paseo de los Maestros, diagonally opposite the Shell station. All public transport stops at 6pm.

By taxi For a taxi, call Jaraba Taxi (☎ 809 574 4640), located next to the Caribe Tours office.

By motoconcho Not difficult to find as they cruise in town – they can take you around the surrounding areas for cheaper than a taxi; count on around RD$20–30/km, and add what you feel appropriate for waiting time.

INFORMATION

Tourist office The private tourist office (daily 8am–1pm & 3–7pm) is run by *Rancho Baiguate* and is located just at the entrance to town at Independecia 16; it is part of *El* *Rancho* restaurant. They can help you with any problems (in English) and supply a decent map of the area (RD$125) as well as telling you about their tours.

ACCOMMODATION

With the recent increase in visitor numbers, Jarabacoa's **accommodation** options have seen steady improvement over the last decade though none really stand out.

Brisas de Los Alpes C-28, halfway between Jarabacoa and La Vega ☎ 829 470 6533, ⓦ brisasdellosalpesresort .com. Set high in the mountains and surrounded by pine trees, this faux-alpine lodge complex, which includes a decent-sized pool, offers a range of very comfortable apartments and two- and four- person self-catering villas, all with kitchens, cable TV and living rooms. Tours of the area are also offered. RD$1500

Brisas del Yaqué Independencia 13 ☎ 809 574 2100, ⓔ hotelbrisasdelyaque@hotmail.com. Large, modern rooms but many overlook the market so are noisy early in the morning; the quieter ones face the car park. Free wi-fi and friendly staff. Also has a good mid-price restaurant on site. RD$2000

★ **Guesthouse Jarabacoa** Casa 8, Calle 7, Medina ☎ 809 365 9102, ⓦ guesthouse-jarabacoa.com. Two-storey German-run guesthouse set in its own walled grounds in a quiet Jarabacoa suburb, eight blocks

5

(around a 10min walk) from the centre. Rooms are clean and cosy, and the friendly owners can help organize tours of the area. They serve a mean continental breakfast for RD$250, and also have new one- and two-bedroom self-catering apartments for rent from US$250/month. **RD$1500**

Hostal Jarabacoa Hermanas Mirabel at Colón ☎ 809 574 4108. One of the least expensive mid-price places in town, it's close to the bus stops and is easy to find on arrival. Although the rooms are a tad small, they're very clean and have a/c and cable – a good choice if you plan to be mostly out and about. **RD$1500**

Mi Vista C-28, 3km outside Jarabacoa ☎ 809 344 4809, ⊕ mi-vista.com. Good-value mountain resort with five large, pleasant two-bedroom bungalows, with patio views and several cheaper two-person cabañas. There's a swimming pool, a lovely open-air terrace restaurant and a whole raft of tours on offer, including horseriding and mountain biking. **US$70/person**

Hotel Plaza Central Mario N. Galán by the Parque Central ☎ 809 574 7768. The town's budget option – rooms are clean enough, with fans and showers, but otherwise extremely basic (as you'd expect for the price) and being next to the park means it's noisy until late. Wi-fi in the lobby and surrounding rooms. **RD$500**

Rancho Baiguate (see p.222) ☎ 809 574 6890, ⊕ ranchobaiguate.com. Sprawling ranch in woodland surroundings with basic rooms, plus a softball field, basketball court, table tennis, swimming pool, fishing pond and organized excursions. It is a little overpriced, though – rates are per person and include three (very mediocre) buffet meals. **US$60**

EATING

Long before Jarabacoa became an adventure sports hub, it was the favoured summer retreat of Santo Domingo and Santiago's upper classes. Though most foreign visitors arrive by the busload on day-trips from their beach hotel, those staying the night will find several **restaurants** to choose from, mostly catering to these Dominican weekenders. Also look out for the super-cheap local snack foods sold from carts around Parque Central.

Aroma de la Montaña Jamaca de Dios, 2km south of town ☎ 829 452 6879, ⊕ aromadelamontana.com. Fine dining at this exclusive residential complex high in the mountains above Jarabacoa – it's worth coming up here for the views alone and the rotating floor means you won't miss a thing. Though there's the odd nod to Dominican cuisine – goat in red wine, for example – the influence is more North American, with plenty of beef and chicken dishes from around RD$550, and even ribs at weekends. Daily 11am–10pm, Fri & Sat until 11pm.

D'Parque Galeria Pizzeria Duarte at Parque Central ☎ 809 574 4769. Inexpensive and fun, this outdoor pasta and pizza joint is decorated in an ethnic style with lots of bamboo furniture. The pizzas are excellent, they have some vegetarian options and they also do some good *criolla* dishes such as guinea fowl. Mains and pizzas start at around RD$200. Daily 11.30am–10.30pm, until midnight at weekends.

★ **D'Tilda Comida Gourmet** At the north of the Parque Central at Duarte 44 ☎ 809 574 4181. It might not be "gourmet" but this basic buffet restaurant serves up high-quality, typically Dominican grub in large quantities at a great price, with a substantial plate of food just RD$125. Only open at lunchtime, it's immensely popular and so has a ticket system – take a number as soon as you arrive. Mon–Fri 11.30am–3pm.

Fresco Café y Bistrot Mario N. Galán opposite the market ☎ 809 574 7744. Very clean, modern and stylish café that serves delicious and healthy breakfasts (RD$60–140) as well as European-style salads, burgers, pasta and meats and a few Mexican dishes with mains starting at around RD$250. Also does great coffee, hot chocolate and has a wide range of teas. Daily 8am–11pm.

Panadería La Fleca Independencia 1. Located right next to La Vega guagua station and Caribe Tours, this bakery-cum-café is a great place to get your bearings. They serve fantastic sweet and savoury breads and pastries, good coffee and a small selection of hot dishes for around RD$200. Attached to *El Rancho*, and has free wi-fi. Daily 7am–10pm.

Pizza y Pepperoni Paseo de los Maestros ☎ 809 574 4348. Simple restaurant dishing up reasonable pizzas in three sizes (from RD$200) to eat in or take away. Popular with families, the place has a play area and four flat-screen TVs, usually showing sports. Daily 11am–11pm.

El Rancho/El Punto del Arte Main crossroads at town entrance ☎ 809 574 6451. Another part of the *Rancho Baiguate* empire, this excellent restaurant serves pizza plus specialities like baked chicken stuffed with banana, garlic soup, crepes, seafood and steaks – mains are around RD$200–800. There's a nice ambience, too – the walls are adorned with art by top Dominican and international painters. Daily 7am–2am.

NIGHTLIFE AND ENTERTAINMENT

You'd be mad to miss the free **baseball** games during the season at the field on Calle La Confluencia, just west of the crossroads, where games are played nightly at 7pm. In addition to the spirited play on the field, there's a **bar** in the dugout and the outfield abuts an outdoor **pool hall** – all in all, a great way to spend an evening relaxing and getting to know some locals. For the latest info on other nightlife go to ⓦ bonchejarabacoa.com.

5

Entre Amigos Above Supermercado El Cofre at Colón 182 ☏ 809 574 4701. This is the most established dance venue and ever popular with an energetic young crowd, with DJs every weekend and karaoke before 11pm. Very popular and very crowded at weekends. Daily 9pm–2am (later at weekends).

Venue Bar Y Lounge ☏ 809 669 0331. There are plenty of bars in town, with a particularly large congregation lining Parque Central and the main crossroads, both of which turn into serious party zones at weekends. This is the current choice for the smartly dressed and slightly older. "Ladies night" is every Friday when said ladies drink for free. Daily 6pm–1am.

Parques Nacionales Bermúdez y Ramírez

Two national parks protect much of the mountains, cloudforests and pines present in the Cordillera Central, **BERMÚDEZ** and **RAMÍREZ**, each encompassing over seven hundred square kilometres that really need to be explored on an organized trek up **Pico Duarte**, the highest mountain in the Caribbean. At the very least, you'll need to check in with a ranger and be accompanied by a guide for whatever trip you take into the parks.

Once in, you'll see no small array of **flora**, though the endemic Creole pine tends to proliferate. Reforested Caribbean pines have been planted in places where there was once agriculture, and scattered palm trees dot the fringes. You'll also spot many orchids and bromeliads, along with Spanish moss and parasites known as The Count of Pines, their branches winding up the trunks of other trees and slowly strangulating them. There aren't many large **animals** in the mountains – persistent rumours of wild pigs aside – but you'll notice a number of lizards and even Coquí frogs near the summit of Duarte; the relatively rare tarantula or non-poisonous snake is also known to make an occasional appearance. There are plenty of **birds**, too, especially Hispaniolan parrots, hummingbirds and woodpeckers; you'll hear a raucous population of white-tailed crows near the summit.

Signs of **agriculture** are visible in the small valleys along the southern half of Ramírez, though the traditional slash-and-burn farming has been banned. Local folklore has it

---

TREKKING PRACTICALITIES

You can trek up Pico Duarte at any time of year, but most people choose to ascend **between November and March**, when there's less chance of heavy rain. Regardless, you should never attempt the hike without a long waterproof coat with a hood, winter clothing (at night the temperature can reach freezing), a sleeping bag (these can often be rented locally too) and good hiking boots. Whichever of the trails you choose, you are required to register in the park office at the head of the trail. If not part of an organized tour (see box, p.222), you'll need to pay the RD$200 **park entrance** as well as hiring at least one **guide** for every five people (RD$1000–1500/day plus meals). It's also a good idea to rent at least one **mule** (RD$500/day) as it'll make your trekking less of a chore – the chances are that the guide will insist on it anyway, to carry water and food as well as to get you down safely if things go wrong. If you have more than one, you'll need a muleteer too (RD$500–800/day plus meals). You'll also need to purchase enough **food** for yourself and the guide, plus supplies for an extra day and a half in case of emergency. Stock up on **water** as well, and bring purification tablets or a filter for any river water you might drink. There are several very basic **cabins** with wood-burning stoves (but little else) in which to sleep along the routes, but a couple of the treks will require **tent camping** for one night. Cabins and campsites are situated together within the park and are free, with tents usually provided by the guide or tour operator, though it's best to check before you book, or bring your own – the cabins can be rather unsavoury and having a tent is generally preferable. On any of the five trails described below, you'll spend the night before or after your Duarte ascent at the nearby **La Compartición** cabins, for which there is a RD$500 charge.

5

that small bands of Tainos are still holed up in the deepest mountains waiting for the Spaniards to depart, and that the trails are haunted by **ciguapas** – mythical blue-skinned women with their feet back-to-front who seduce young men at night and lure them to their deaths at the bottoms of streams.

Pico Duarte

Five strenuous treks lead up to 3087m **Pico Duarte**, which towers over the centre of the mountain range alongside its sibling peak La Pelona ("Baldy"; before 1930 they were known as Pelona Grande and Pelona Chica). The lack of fresh water on the mountain has left it uninhabited through the centuries – though Tainos once lived in the nearby **Valle del Tétero** – and the first recorded ascent was only in 1944.

Climbing to the very top of the Caribbean's highest mountain holds definite cachet, and the view from the treeless peak is magnificent (though even here you can't quite escape from it all – Duarte's face is sculpted onto one of the rocks). If you've come this far, think seriously about extending your trek to include Valle del Tétero – a broad savannah with roaring mountain rivers, wild horses and Taino petroglyphs. This can be done by adding a two-day loop onto the La Ciénega trek or by following one of the trails that crosses the valley on the approach to the peak. Unless you're a seasoned trekker, you'll do well to stick to the La Ciénega route.

La Ciénega trail

La Compartición cabin RD$500 • Guaguas for La Ciénega (every 2hr until 6pm; 1hr 30min; RD$100) leave from the south of Jarabacoa on Calle Obdulio Jímenez

The most popular trip up the mountain starts from the tiny pueblo of **La Ciénega**, 25km southwest of Jarabacoa, where you'll need to register for the 46km round-trip at the office by the park's entrance on the far side of the village. It's advisable to arrive in the afternoon, sort out the formalities and then camp down in the village with a view to starting out early the next morning.

The first leg is little more than a comfortable 4km riverside stroll to a bridge across the river at **Los Tablones**. Once over the river, however, the climbing starts in earnest and you'll gain over 2000m in the next 14km, mostly on a badly eroded track that wends its way through some wonderfully wild woodland. Regular stops at official picnic sites allow you to get your breath back and to peep out through the canopy for a glimpse of the totally pristine wilderness that surrounds you.

You'll spend the night in a ramshackle cabin at **La Compartición** and then scramble up the last 5km at around 4.30am to be on the bare rocky summit for sunrise. It's quite a stirring sight to watch the sun creep over the horizon, casting a bright-red hue on the banks of cloud beneath your feet. You'll then backtrack to collect your belongings at the cabin and start the long descent back down to the village.

Mata Grande trail

A taxi (45min) to Mata Grande from San José de las Matas costs RD$1500

Allow five days for this 90km round-trip trek with elevation going from 850m to 3087m. To get there from **San José de las Matas** (see p.216) go 5km east on the road to Santiago, take the marked turnoff at the town of Pedegral and head 15km south to the park station at pueblo **Mata Grande**, where you can register and hire a guide and mules. The first day of the trip is 20km past abandoned farming towns and sweeping views of Santiago and the Vega Real to the cabin at **Río La Guácara**. A good spot to stop and unpack lunch is 8km south of Mata Grande at the Arroyo Las Lagunas cabin, where you should also load up on water. The second day follows the cloudforest of the Río Bao 12km to the gorgeous **Valle del Bao**, a stunning, elevated plain bereft of trees with high grass and wild horses, a large cabin and a view of La Pelona. On the third day, 10km in total, you'll ascend La Pelona, then join up with the Sabaneta trail to hit the top of Pico Duarte.

Sabaneta trail

Erratic and infrequent guaguas head to Presa Sabaneta from the corner of Carretera Sanchez and Pedro J Heyaime in San Juan de la Maguana, so the best way is by taxi (around RD$1200)

This trail was supposedly blazed by local messiah **Liborio**, who ducked the American Marines for several years in these mountains (see p.246). You'll need six days to do this 96km round-trip journey, spanning from 600m to 3087m in elevation. This trek is much harder than La Ciénega and Mata Grande, and you'll encounter few (if any) fellow travellers along the way. To get there from **San Juan de la Maguana** (see p.245), take the paved road north from the city's Rotunda Anacaona for 20km to the enormous dam, **Presa Sabaneta**. A few hundred metres in front of the dam you'll find a car park and the park station, where you can secure a guide and mules, and camp for the night before setting off.

The first day is not particularly long but quite steep, 12km to the cabin at **Alto de la Rosa**, a 1600m peak. Along the way you'll pass abandoned banana plantations and farms, many of which were blasted hard by Hurricane Georges. The second day is a slow 22km slog through dense vegetation to the **Macutico** cabin in the 2200m high Río Blanco valley, where you can stock up on water. The third day is the toughest, climbing Pico Barraco before joining up with the Mata Grande trail at the top of La Pelona and continuing on to Pico Duarte and the cabin at Compartición.

Las Lagunas trail

For guides, further details and reservations contact the Asociación de Guias de Montana La Reservadora Ambiental de Padre Las Casas (AGUIMORA) on ☎ 809 488 0405 • A guagua service runs from Azua (see p.244) every couple of hours 7am–5pm; you can also pick it up on the Carretera Sanchez at Cruce de las Yayas if coming from San Juan de la Maguana

Another strenuous six-day trek, this round trip of 108km is even more difficult than the Sabaneta trail. To get there from **San Juan de la Maguana**, take the Carretera Sánchez east and take a left at the signposted Cruce de las Yayas, 9km north to Padre Las Casas. At the town's main crossroads take a left and 100m further on you'll find the **Las Lagunas** park station, where you can hire a guide and mules. They don't get much traffic on this route, so you may have to offer the park officer a few hundred extra pesos to get permission to use the trail. The first day goes through palm and deciduous forest dotted with lagoons and small subsistence farms. Convenient markers along the way are riverside El Limón at 3km; El Botoncillo 2km further; Las Cañitas (a military outpost with camping and a hilltop panorama) 2km beyond that; and **El Tétero** – a traditional cattle-raising *campo* where you should camp for the night – 3km further still.

The second day takes you 4km north past numerous farming shacks before joining up with the Constanza trail at Sabana Andrés; from here it's another 4km of small farming *campos* and 6km of dense, unpopulated pine forest to the top of 2100m Alto del Valle, then 4km almost straight down to 1500m-high **Valle del Tétero**. The peaceful valley holds a pine forest adorned with thick cobwebs of Spanish moss, a large cabin, dozens of wild horses, two freezing-cold rivers and – at its eastern end – a number of Taino petroglyphs that archeologists believe denoted an island-wide peace treaty between *caciques*; ask at the park station for directions to these ancient markings. From here it's 5km to El Cruce and up the La Ciénega road to Pico Duarte. Accommodation along the way is either camping, or AGUIMORA can organize homestays in villages for a few hundred pesos.

Los Corralitos trail

Ministerio de Medio Ambiente Mon–Fri 8.30am–5pm • ☎ 809 539 1212

At 86km and six days round trip, it's not the longest but is easily the steepest and toughest of the Pico Duarte trails, and for this reason rarely used; you'll also need to seek a free permit from the Ministerio de Medio Ambiente, located just east of central **Constanza** on Av. Gen. Luperón. From Constanza take a taxi (it'll have to be something with a high wheel arch) 8km west to **Los Corralitos**, where you can acquire a guide and mules. If you'd

5

like, you can drive another 8km to the cabin at Los Cayetanos, which will cut three hours off your travel time. From here it's three more hours past sadly deforested mountainside to the confluence of the rivers Grande and Yaquesillo – the border of Parque Nacional Ramírez – and another 7km through a small valley and over several hills to the **Los Rodríguez** cabin, where two park employees are stationed. The second day is sixteen extremely steep kilometres to the **Valle del Tétero**. Four kilometres along the way, the path intersects with the Las Lagunas trail at Sabana Andres; you'll reach the valley and its park cabin 14km further on. The third day goes 5km to El Cruce and then up to Pico Duarte.

Constanza and around

Created millennia ago by a crashing meteor, **CONSTANZA** is a drop-dead gorgeous, circular valley set deep in the mountains at an altitude of 1300m. It has been populated and farmed since the Taino era but had virtually no contact with the outside world until the end of the nineteenth century, when a decent dirt road was finally laid down. Later development occurred when Trujillo trucked in some two hundred Japanese families in the 1950s to introduce their farming methods. The **Colonia Japonesa** still exists just south of the town on Avenida Gral. Duverge, and all manner of non-tropical crops are grown on the farms today, including strawberries, raspberries, apples, garlic and roses.

As you first pass over the lip of the crater you'll be stunned by the fertile, flat valley, which is irrigated by thousands of sprinklers and hemmed in on all sides by jagged peaks. The **town** itself, taking up the western quarter of the valley, is mostly residential and fairly compact. The hub of activity is the **farmers' market** just north of Calle Luperón – the main thoroughfare – where truckloads of goods are loaded up and shipped to Santiago, Santo Domingo and beyond. If you stay the night, it's worth heading out to the eastern lip of the valley crater on a clear day, to check out the unbelievable **sunset**. Less inviting is the town's **military base**, which has been a permanent presence since Castro attempted a Communist takeover here in 1959. At the south end of town sits the decaying **Nueva Suiza**, an abandoned Trujillo manor that was used for a time as a resort spa but is now fenced off and boarded up.

Be sure to bring plenty of **warm clothing**: Constanza can get very cold all year round, particularly at night in winter when frost on the ground is not uncommon. It's one of the few Dominican towns where you'll regularly see the residents wrapped up in thick coats and woollen scarves and hats. The **fiestas patronales** are in late September but there are periodically major cycling and motocross competitions that enliven proceedings.

Aguas Blancas

14km south of Constanza town along Av. Gral. Duverge • You should be able to arrange a bumpy *motoconcho* ride for around RD$300–400, including waiting time (allow 2hr); most hotels in town can organize a suitable vehicle for you for around RD$1500, while Safari Constanza also offer a tour

---

HIKING IN CONSTANZA

As you'd expect among such dazzling scenery, the Constanza valley boasts several of the DR's finest **hiking trails**. One three-hour trip sets off from *Rancho Constanza* – from the hotel, take the dirt road north until you reach a white house at the top of the hill, the starting point of a trail that leads into the thick of the alpine forest. You can also set off 5km east of Constanza, via the Carretera Constanza, to the adjoining valley of **Tireo Arriba**, which holds a smaller farming pueblo worth exploring for a look at the local way of life. If you have your own transport, keep going 8km further east to pueblo **La Parma** – just before you reach the road to Jarabacoa – for a hike along the **Río Arroyazo**. Ask locals to direct you to the riverside walking path, from where it's a 45-minute hike to an unspoiled wilderness *balneario*, with small cascades along the river giving way to a large pool partially enclosed by boulders.

SOUTH FROM CONSTANZA TO SAN JOSÉ DE OCÓA

The gutted, sky-high **road** that leads 90km south from Constanza to San José de Ocóa (see p.243) is considered by many to be the country's worst, and it offers an adventure, however hazardous, that you're not likely to forget soon. Do not attempt it unless you have an excellent 4WD and are an experienced mountain driver. Allow five hours and be sure to bring two spare tyres, winter clothing and emergency supplies. The road runs south past the turnoff to Aguas Blancas from where it's 4km before you reach the entrance to the national forest reserve known as **Reserva Científica Valle Nuevo**. In this steep alpine wilderness that has at least six distinct ecosystems, the views extend across a large chunk of the Cordillera Central, and for much of the trip you'll be skirting the edge of a cliff far above the clouds. If you wish to explore the park, the best way is through *Villa Pajón* (see below) who can organize various activities. If you have time, stop 30km south of Constanza, where you can get a glimpse of a concrete split pyramid, **Las Pirámides**, built in 1957 by Trujillo to mark the exact centre of the island. There are also basic, free **camping** facilities next to the monument, ideally placed on the grassy plain and surrounded by *piñones* (pine trees).

★**Villa Pajón** 20km south of Constanza and signposted along the way ☎809 334 6935, ⓦvillapajon.do. Relax in luxury amid remote mountain wilderness at this set of lovely cabins built on the site of an old saw mill. Each cabin has its own fireplace, kitchen, bath, outdoor barbecue and multiple bedrooms. There is electricity (solar-powered) only in one of the larger cabins but kerosene lamps are provided. Bring your own food with you; otherwise you can arrange in advance to have someone cook and perform housekeeping. Outdoor activities abound, including unbelievable hiking and horseriding into the surrounding mountains. RD$2600

A decent dirt road leads south of town to the area's major sight, **Aguas Blancas**, a torrential, 83m **waterfall** in three sections with a large pool at the base. The scenery alone is worth the somewhat difficult journey out here – towering 2000m mountains veined with cavernous valley ribbons, half of it virgin pine forest and half terraced agriculture. Farms teeter on mountain tops so inaccessible you'll wonder how the building materials ever got there; look also for the many cattle that graze precariously along zigzagging paths worn into the steep mountainside. The path to the falls is signposted from the main road, a couple of kilometres beyond the bridge south of the village of **El Convento**, where you could enquire about guides at *La Perla* restaurant (see p.231).

Las Piedras Letreadas

30km northwest of Constanza town • The only way to get here is with a 4WD via the village of Culeta, where the paved road runs out and you should ask for directions to the track that leads to the site; Safari Constanza do a tour here

North of Constanza, in the lofty Valle de la Culata just inside the boundary of the Parque Nacional Bermúdez (see p.225), lie **Las Piedras Letreadas**, an impressive collection of Taino pictograms and petroglyphs. This shallow cave, where many stick figures and animals are chiselled into the walls is claimed to be the biggest Taino monument in the Antilles, and it's well worth the difficulty of reaching. There are various theories which postulate it was a temple or sanctuary, with one even claiming the Taino considered this place the centre of the island. Since the road continues north from Culata to La Ciénega it would make an interesting alternative route there or to Jarabacoa.

ARRIVAL AND DEPARTURE
CONSTANZA

By guagua Guaguas drop off and pick up at their stop at the entrance to Constanza town on Calle Luperón, just before the Banco Popular. Guaguas for the north–south Autopista Duarte (7am–8pm; 1hr 10min; RD$200) run up the smooth yet twisting paved road that begins 6km north of Bonao.

By público *Públicos* (generally pick-up trucks) bound for Jarabacoa (around 6 daily; 1hr 30min; RD$175) leave from the same place as the guaguas.

5

INFORMATION AND TOURS

Tourist office There's a helpful semi-private tourist office with no sign next to Ciber Shop at Duarte 17 (Mon–Fri 9am–noon & 2–6pm; ☎ 809 539 2900). They are very knowledgeable and can provide you with detailed information on tours and hikes, a useful free map of the town and surrounding region and direct you to a hotel.

Tours The biggest outfit in town is Safari Constanza (☎ 809 539 2554, ✉ safari.constanza@hotmail.com or contact through the tourist office) who organize day-trips to Aguas Blancas (RD$700), Las Piedras Letreadas (RD$700) and Las Pirámides via Aguas Blancas (see box, p.229; RD$1500); prices are per person for a minimum of four and don't include the RD$100 park entrance fee. Cluster Ecoturístico Constanza, located by the airport on the road into town (daily 9am–1pm & 2–6pm; ☎ 809 539 1022, ⊛ constanza.com.do) are a more community-based operation, running a range of excursions from mountain hikes and local sightseeing to fruit farm visits.

ACCOMMODATION

There's a modest selection of **accommodation** comprising a handful of small budget hotels within Constanza town, which all provide hot water, and a couple of much more spacious and holiday-oriented establishments up on the hillside 2km east of town, which draws many families from Santo Domingo at weekends.

★**Altocerro** 1.5km east of town centre and signposted north at Guarocuya 461 ☎ 809 530 6192, ⊛ altocerro.com. Comfort and sophistication in an idyllic mountain setting where guests can choose from villas that accommodate up to seven people, hotel rooms or suites; there's even camping in a lovely wooded area at the back, with barbecues and campfire pits. The villas – which come with fireplaces for chilly nights – and all hotel rooms have balconies affording fabulous mountain views, while the main block has a good restaurant and mini-mart. Breakfast is included in the rates, which are cheaper midweek. Quad rental (RD$600/hr) and horseriding (RD$225/hr) can also be arranged. **RD$2500**, camping **RD$250**/person

Hotel Dilania Gastón Fernando Deligne 7, half a block behind the Banco Popular ☎ 809 531 2213. This pleasantly quiet hotel comprises a dozen spotless but spartan en-suite rooms (hot water and cable TV) with comfy beds, and is set round a small garden. The on-site restaurant serves good food but expect leisurely service; don't miss the home-made strawberry juice. **RD$800**

Mi Casa Sánchez at Luperón ☎ 809 539 2764. Central location with simple, clean rooms (cable TV and hot water), though a little dark, and decent beds. It also has a good restaurant where you can eat breakfast for RD$200 extra. **RD$1300**

Rancho Constanza 2km east of town centre, where it's signposted, and about 2km north ☎ 809 682 2410, ⊛ ranchoconstanza.tripod.com. More rustic and rough-and-ready than *Altocerro*, this hillside resort consists of spacious, though dark, self-catering villas or hotel rooms and suites, which additionally offer free wi-fi. Breakfast is included and they also have a lunch/dinner buffet (RD$500). **RD$3000**

Hotel Valle Nuevo In the south of town at Gratereaux 99 at Antonio Cabral ☎ 809 539 1144. Ignore the tacky furnishings – murals above the bed, frilly toilet covers and faux curtain tassels – as this place offers the best value in town. Rooms are comfortable, with fridges, and a couple of communal balconies offer fine mountain views. **RD$1300**

EATING AND DRINKING

Wherever you eat in Constanza, you're likely to get a good sampling of the **local produce**, often plucked from the fields the same day.

Altocerro 1.5km east of town centre and signposted north at Guarocuya 461 ☎ 809 530 6192, ⊛ altocerro.com. Expect tourist prices here but the view alone from the first-floor terrace restaurant makes a visit worthwhile. That said, the food is satisfying too, particularly the meat accompanied by locally produced veg. Mains generally RD$350–1000. Daily 8–10am & noon–10pm.

★**Comedor Luisa** Antonio Mario García 40 at Matilde Viñas ☎ 809 539 2174. This cosy restaurant next to the baseball pitch, is the best place for authentic, tasty Dominican food, with the beef dishes being particularly good – expect to pay RD$200–300 for a meal. Mon–Sat 12.30–10pm.

Lorenzo's Luperón 83 ☎ 809 539 2001. Hardly a buzzing atmosphere, and the elevator music can grate, but the menu is extensive – sweet and sour pork fillet, guinea fowl and rabbit, plus the usual pastas and pizzas – and the food is generally good. Most mains are RD$190–350. Daily 8.30am–11.30pm.

Mi Casa Sánchez at Luperón. Service can be lacking but the Dominican specialities, such as goat, rabbit and guinea fowl, are consistently good. There are also the usual chicken, fish and pasta dishes, while the *lomito saltado* (a Peruvian dish of spicy beef with rice) is very tasty. Most mains RD$190–310. Daily 7.30am–10pm.

★**La Perla de Aguas Blancas** El Convento village, 10km south of town ☎ 809 991 5530, ⓦ laperla-bar .com. Within striking distance of the falls, this charming, rustic bar complete with Japanese garden is set in wooded surroundings populated by parrots. A great place to reward yourself with some *comida típica* after a walk to the falls, or to just chill with a beer. Also offers camping space. Phoning before making the journey is advised. Mon–Thurs on request, Fri–Sun from 10am–midnight (or later).

5

The Vega Real

East of Santiago, the **VEGA REAL**, an unbroken expanse of farmland bounded by a triangle of Cibao farming towns, is responsible for a phenomenal amount of agricultural produce and tobacco, but it's not exactly high on tourist appeal, lacking any really compelling sights or activities. If you feel like getting lost for a few days, though, you'll likely find its towns more pleasant than those on the over-industrialized Autopista Duarte. **Moca** is an easy enough day-trip from Santiago while **San Francisco de Macorís** – from where you can make a splendid mountain hike into the Cordillera Septentrional – requires a bit more effort. In between is **Salcedo** which is much more accessible, and feels a bit like Bedford Falls from *It's a Wonderful Life*, except with colourful murals on many of the buildings and thumping merengue in the air.

Moca

MOCA, a sizeable farming depot 16km east of Santiago, is set amid some of the most fertile land in the valley. It's better known, though, for two episodes from Dominican history – as the birthplace of the 1842 **Moca Constitution**, which set democratic standards for government that have rarely been adhered to, and as the site of nineteenth-century despot Ulises Heureaux's assassination. There's nothing here to commemorate the former, but the latter event is celebrated in downtown Moca at a small park on Calle Vasquez, where you'll find the **Monument to the Tyrant Killers**, a small Art Deco sculpture honouring assassins José Contreras and José Inocencio, erected right on the spot where Heureaux was shot. The main reason to come here, however, is the lovely **Iglesia de Corazón de Jesús**.

Although the town is safe during the day, you'll notice that the streets in the centre are patrolled by pairs of armed **soldiers** in an attempt to control the crime-wave and political unrest that has hit the town in recent years. It is not advisable to spend the night here, and you should be vigilant of your possessions at all times.

Iglesia de Corazón de Jesús

Corner of Sánchez and Corazón de Jesús • Mon–Fri 9am–5pm, Sat 3–6pm, Sun for Masses • ☎ 809 578 2683

Nicer than anything in the workaday downtown district, the nineteenth-century **Iglesia de Corazón de Jesús** sports a neo-Plateresque facade and a prominent clock tower. The spacious interior floods with coloured light through its beautiful imported Italian stained-glass windows and it boasts an impressive pipe organ.

ARRIVAL AND DEPARTURE   **MOCA**

By guagua Guaguas to Moca from Santiago mostly leave from near the bus stations on 27 de Febrero at the junction with Av. Estrella Sadhalá or at the park on the corner of Sabana Large and Restauración. There are also frequent guaguas to and from la Vega at least every 30min during daylight hours (45min; RD$60).

Salcedo

A tiny, friendly city midway between Moca and San Francisco, **SALCEDO** is one of the nicest towns in the region and one of the best and safest places to experience Dominican small-town life. It is also very pretty, mostly because many of its buildings are covered with colourful **murals**, for which Salcedo is becoming renowned – you can easily spend an afternoon just strolling round the streets to see

5

them all. A couple of good ones are the ballet dancers on the wall of the sports hall, and another, next to the police station, of the **Mirabal sisters**, who were local martyred victims of Trujillo. Just north of the **Parque Central** lies the **Kansas City Royals Baseball Academy**, which is worth a visit during the summer when free home games of the Salcedo Royals are scheduled.

Museo Hermanas Mirabal

Daily 9am–5pm • RD$100 • ☎ 809 587 8530

The house that the Mirabel sisters grew up in, 4km east of Salcedo's centre, is now the **Museo Hermanas Mirabal** and provided the setting for much of Julia Álvarez's best-selling novel *In the Time of the Butterflies*. Unfortunately, its tacky period furnishings and cordoned-off bath towels stencilled with the sisters' names will only engage aficionados of Mirabal lore.

ARRIVAL AND DEPARTURE   **SALCEDO**

By bus Caribe Tours has an office in the south of town just off Colón at Bobby Dhos 19, from where there are daily departures to Santo Domingo (4 daily; 2hr 15min; RD$230) via La Vega (45min; RD$60).

By guagua Regular guaguas bound for Santiago, Moca or San Francisco de Macorís leave from different spots close to the park.

ACCOMMODATION, EATING AND NIGHTLIFE

El Carnero Av. Doroteo Tapia 30 ☎ 809 577 4070. One of the better options along this street, this ranch-style place serves a good-value range of Dominican dishes such as their excellent *mofongos* as well as meats, fish, pizzas, and a couple of Mexican favourites – you can easily eat for under RD$200. Daily 9am–5am.

La Casona/Gran Imperial A block from the park at FR Mollins 51 just off Av. Doroteo Tapia ☎ 809 577 4468. There are clean, basic rooms here, with hot water, a/c and cable TV. The optimistically named *Gran Imperial* half of the hotel has rooms for RD$1000 which are bigger, nicer, and

slightly further away from the loud bars round the corner. **RD$800**

Orlando Car Wash 1km from the centre on the road to San Francisco de Macorís ☎ 809 577 2367. Salcedo is a great place to experience Dominican nightlife as it's not only lively, but is much safer than nearby towns and cities. If the many crowded bars on Av. Doroteo Tapia by the hotel are a bit hectic, try this place just outside of town. It has a pleasant open-sided dancefloor surrounded by tables, with pounding merengue, to which mature couples dance all night. Daily 7pm–2am (4am at weekends).

San Francisco de Macorís

The farming city of **SAN FRANCISCO DE MACORÍS**, with a 200,000-strong population in the heart of the Vega Real, owes its prosperity to the **cocoa industry** – the business lies behind what few major sights there are in town. Chocolate is not the only money-making product here, though: in recent years, the city has served as a laundering point for **cocaine** profits, a far cry from its **tobacco-producing** heyday in the nineteenth century.

The compact **downtown** holds most of the major office buildings, restaurants and discos – the latter supplies San Francisco with some of the DR's best nightlife, though be careful if you're on your own. It's also worth checking out the large **Mercado Modelo** (at Sánchez and Castillo), an enormous produce and cocoa depot where peasants from the surrounding countryside come with pack animals to sell their goods during the day. There's not much else in the way of entertainment, though you should check out a **baseball game** in the winter at the Estadio Julián Javier stadium just east of town on Highway 122 (☎ 809 566 4882, ⊚ gigantessfm.com).

Reserva Científica Loma Quita Espuela

15km north of San Francisco on Calle Manuel Maria Castillo, then 1.5km north on a track following the signpost to Rancho Don Lulú • RD$50 entrance; guide RD$100 per person, with a minimum spend of RD$500 daily; mule RD$300/day • ☎ 809 588 4156, ⊚ flqe.org.do

• During daylight hours take a *público* (hourly; 25min; RD$50) from outside the small market on the corner of Manuel Maria Cartillo and Libertat in San Francisco, and ask to be dropped off at the turnoff

More diverting than the scant city sights is a day-trip (or even better, combine your visit with a short stay at *Rancho Don Lulú*) up to the **Reserva Científica Loma Quita Espuela**, a virgin rainforest reserve set on the side of a high Cordillera Septentrional mountain. It is managed by a local NGO that offers a guided hike (in Spanish) up Quita Espuela, explaining about the flora and fauna; what's more the views over the Cibao from the observation tower on the **summit** are stunning. A shorter, less demanding trek through coffee and cocoa farms, ending at a waterfall with a **swimming hole**, is also available. Longer expeditions of two days or more can be arranged with a **guide** on request though you'll need to bring your own camping gear, food, and probably hire a mule. If you can't find the park ranger at the office, go back down the track and knock at the house that's often playing stunningly loud merengue.

ARRIVAL AND DEPARTURE   SAN FRANCISCO DE MACORÍS

By bus and guagua Caribe Tours (☎809 588 2221) offers bus services to and from Santo Domingo (13 daily; 2hr 30min; RD$260) and Samaná (4 daily; 2hr 30min; RD$140), dropping off and picking up four blocks southeast of the Parque Central on the corner of Manuel Maria Castillo and Gaspar Hernandez. Guaguas run to Nagua, and La Vega via Salcedo from Av. Libertad and Duarte.

By taxi Private taxis are plentiful, with a minimum usually set at RD$150; taking one to Loma Quita Espuela will cost around RD$800. Try Jaya Taxi at S. Ureña 10 (☎809 244 2555).

ACCOMMODATION AND EATING

San Francisco doesn't offer too much in the way of **hotels** or **restaurants**, but **nightlife** is pretty vibrant here as the town's discos get more than their fair share of big-name merengue and bachata acts – hand-painted advertisements posted throughout the city will keep you up to date on who's playing and where.

De Moya Ananda 27 de Febrero at Papi Olivier ☎809 588 0669. This is the favourite haunt of San Francisco's middle classes for its good, well-priced buffet food in pleasant, stylish surroundings – the spread after 11.30am costs RD$95–300, depending on your choices. It's also a fine choice for breakfast as it has an attached bakery that serves great coffee. Daily 6.30am–10pm.

Hotel Libano Restauración 17 at Parque Central ☎809 588 2419, ✉hotellibanosfm@hotmail.com. If you can't make it to *Don Lulú*, try this decent mid-range choice in town which overlooks the park and is close to all amenities. All the clean, nicely decorated rooms have a/c, cable TV, wi-fi, very comfortable beds and hot water. RD$1180

★**Rancho Don Lulú** Entrance to Pico Quita Espuela ☎809 290 7995, ⓦranchodonlulu.com. Situated about a kilometre off the road down the track to Pico Quita Espuela, this friendly, family-run ranch has four basic doubles and six-person dormitories set amid the peaceful, verdant mountains. Price is per person (whether in a room or dorm) and includes three home-cooked *criolla*-style meals served in a gazebo by the naturally fed swimming pool. RD$1000

Restaurante Dorado El Carmen 55 at Restauración ☎809 588 5991, ⓦrestaurantdorado.com. A relatively formal place with decent Chinese, *criolla* and international dishes (mains from around RD$250) – the RD$450 seafood paella is very good. Bottles of wine from RD$320. Daily 10am–midnight.

The southwest

SAN RAFAEL

The southwest

The coast west of Santo Domingo grows more beautiful the further out you go. While you may find the cities immediately west of the capital to be sprawling and none too attractive, the majestic beauty of the mountainous coastal road between Barahona and the Haitian border is simply jaw-dropping. Thanks to the lack of mass tourism, you'll find the area particularly unspoiled and suitable for independent exploration. Further inland, the region's diverse range of landscapes and natural attractions – from a salt-water lake set in the desert to expanses of wild, seemingly endless cloud forest – are collectively famous for the rich birdlife they hold.

Once the focus of Trujillo's personal sugar empire, the area is now better known as one of the country's poorest regions as a result of its over-dependence on the crop, its economy collapsing when sugar prices took a nosedive back in the 1960s. It is nonetheless rich in heritage: north of San Cristóbal, the caves of **El Pomier** hold some excellent **Taino rock art**, while the town of **San Juan de la Maguana**, north of Azua, is famed for its **religious festivals**.

To the west of the capital, the countryside devolves into arid semi-desert, punctuated by large, industrial cities of interest only for their own nearby beaches. **San Cristóbal**, **Baní** and **Azua** have tried to emulate the success of the Dominican Republic's other major sugar zone, the southeast, by attracting all-inclusive hotel developers to the many **pretty beaches** that run from San Cristóbal all the way to the border, but their efforts have so far been unsuccessful – perhaps because the beaches, however attractive, are mostly gravel or pebble. The one main exception are the fine, underdeveloped sands at **Las Salinas**, where the strong winds have created the giant dunes of **Las Dunas de Baní**.

Most travellers choose instead to head to the region's nominal centre **Barahona**, an old sugar-processing capital that has seen better days, thanks to the closing of its mill. Inland from Barahona vast tracts of sugar cane take over, while southwest along the coast you'll find several inviting rural fishing villages such as **Baoruco** and **La Ciénega** between the Caribbean Sea and the southern peaks of the **Sierra Bahoruco**, the island's second largest range after the Cordillera Central, which is covered with rainforest and boasts steep slopes that drop off abruptly at the coast. **Paraíso** – a pleasant town with a long gravel beach – is one of the prime spots along this stretch, while **San Rafael** and **Los Patos** both have rainforest waterfalls that tumble down from the mountains, forming freshwater pools before meeting the sea.

The flint-shaped peninsula in the far southwestern part of the country is taken up by **Parque Nacional Jaragua**; here the mountains retreat a little and lush greenery becomes stark desert. On the peninsula's sharp edge lies the beautiful **Bahía de las Águilas**, 8km of protected beach wilderness with no development or human inhabitants – an idyllic retreat, if a little tricky to get to. The government has made sporadic efforts to colonize this area with tourist infrastructure but, perhaps due to its remoteness, there has been little progress. Environmentalists are lobbying hard to stop any large-scale development and the good news is that a crop of small, eco-friendly tourism operations have sprouted in the past decade, both along the coast and in the densely forested mountains to the north.

ISLA CABRITOS, LAGO ENRIQUILLO

Highlights

❶ El Pomier caves A set of remote caves protected as a national park, adorned with thousands of Taino pictographs. **See p.241**

❷ Las Salinas A windswept village with the nicest bit of good sand near Santo Domingo and the gargantuan dunes of Las Dunas de Baní. **See p.242**

❸ Hiking around San José de Ocóa This quiet mountain town gets few foreign visitors, but the hiking trails that fan out across the spectacular southern mountains merit a few days' exploration. **See p.244**

❹ San Rafael and Los Patos Two beautiful beaches with pounding surf and waterfalls that thrum down from the rainforest-draped mountains and pour into the sea. **See p.252 & p.253**

❺ Bahía de las Águilas Arguably the best beach in the Dominican Republic, this 8km stretch of idyllic tropical paradise within Parque Nacional Jaragua is hard to get to and has no facilities – precisely why it's still perfect. **See p.255**

❻ Lago Enriquillo This Manhattan-sized salt-water lake features alligators, tens of thousands of tropical birds and rhinoceros-iguana-populated Isla Cabritos. **See p.258**

HIGHLIGHTS ARE MARKED ON THE MAP ON PP.238–239

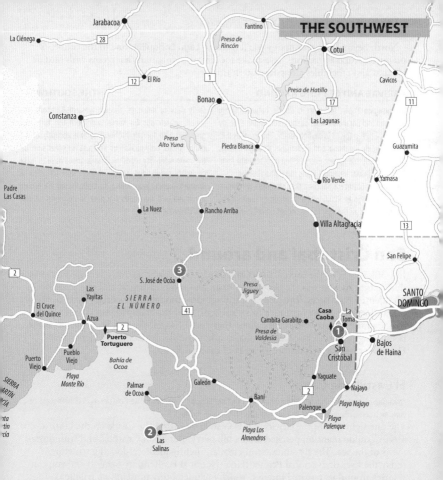

La Ciénega

Jarabacoa

Fantino

Cotui

28

Cavicos

Presa de Rincón

11

El Río

12

1

Presa de Hatillo

Bonao

17

Guazumita

Constanza

Las Lagunas

Presa Alto Yuna

Piedra Blanca

Río Verde

Yamasa

Padre Las Casas

13

La Nuez

Rancho Arriba

Villa Altagracia

San Felipe

2

SANTO DOMINGO

S. José de Ocóa

Las Yayitas

SIERRA EL NÚMERO

Presa Jiguey

Cambita Garabito

Casa Caoba

La Toma

El Cruce del Quince

Azua

41

Presa de Valdesia

San Cristóbal

Bajos de Haina

Puerto Tortuguero

2

SIERRA ARTIN RCÍA

Pueblo Viejo

Bahía de Ocoa

Galeón

Yaguate

Puerto Viejo

Playa Monte Río

Palmar de Ocoa

Baní

Najayo

Playa Najayo

Palenque

nta tín rcía

Las Salinas

Playa Los Almendros

Playa Palenque

C A R I B B E A N   S E A

HIGHLIGHTS

1 El Pomier caves

2 Las Salinas

3 Hiking around San José de Ocóa

4 San Rafael and Los Patos

5 Bahía de las Águilas

6 Lago Enriquillo

North beyond the mountains you'll come to **Lago Enriquillo**, one of the country's premier natural attractions, a vast lake the size of Manhattan that teems with birdlife, iguanas and crocodiles along its eastern tip.

ARRIVAL AND GETTING AROUND THE SOUTHWEST

By guagua Public transport is simple between Santo Domingo and Barahona, with guaguas running in a steady stream between towns in daylight hours. The guaguas thin out between Barahona and Pedernales through Oviedo, though you'll still get one every fifteen minutes until 3pm. There is no public transport along the Haitian border.

By car The Carretera Sánchez that stretches west from Santo Domingo to Azua, where it becomes Highway 44 and continues all the way to the border, is well paved and

fairly easy to navigate, though west of Barahona you should watch out for some tricky cliff-top turns. Be prepared also for the highway to end abruptly at the major towns, only picking up again at the other side. Off the main inter-city roads you'll sometimes have to make do with rough dirt roads, though the situation is improving every year. Along the border itself the terrain is rugged and the roads are poor to non-existent and you'll need a 4WD.

San Cristóbal and around

Just 30km west of the capital, **SAN CRISTÓBAL**, Trujillo's home town, enjoyed its heyday during his rule and was the beneficiary of an enormous cathedral and two palatial presidential residences. The cathedral still stands – though there's little reason to visit it – as does one of the mansions (now a school), and the cramped, asphalt city qualifies as one of the country's least appealing. That said, it is well situated for exploring some fascinating nearby sights: Casa Caoba, another Trujillo mansion, now derelict; and **El Pomier caves**, which feature an array of cave paintings.

El Castillo de Cerro

Prolongacion Luperón; from concrete Parque Central take Calle Padre Borbón (the road to Baní) west and turn south at the Isla Gasolina down Av. Luperón, where it's on the left • Daily 9am–5pm • Free • ☎ 809 480 8633

The one sight within the city itself is **El Castillo de Cerro** (The Castle on the Hill), a 1940s Trujillo mansion perched atop a hill overlooking San Cristóbal and with distant views of the sea. The six-storey, semi-circular, slightly medieval-looking structure is today the Escuela Nacional Penitenciaria (National Penitentiary School) and you can wander around its restored interior, which includes a tiny museum of Trujillo's misdeeds, as demonstrated by a small range of torture implements. Although it lacks the atmospheric quality of the abandoned **Casa Caoba** (see opposite) – as he never actually stayed here – the views are excellent and its high-ceilinged rooms impressive. If you visit, remember it is a formal educational environment and dress appropriately.

ARRIVAL AND DEPARTURE SAN CRISTÓBAL

By guagua Guaguas heading east and west along the highway, as well as north to La Toma, take off from where Av. Constitución crosses the highway, with frequent departures until early evening to Baní (30min), Barahona (3hr) and Santo Domingo (45min). During the

day you can also catch a guagua every hour or so from the market further south on Av. Constitucion to Najayo or Palenque.

By taxi A reliable taxi firm is Taxi Constitucion (☎ 809 478 3353).

ACCOMMODATION AND EATING

Aparta-Hotel Ayala Padre Ayala 110 ☎ 809 528 3040. The only good hotel in San Cristóbal, this basic but clean establishment is located on the street parallel to and east of Av. Constitución. The manager is a bit grumpy but the rest of the staff are lovely. Paying RD$100 extra will get you a room with a/c. **RD$650**

Restaurant Vagos Av. Constitución at Padre Borbón ☎ 809 528 5400. Handily just round the corner from *Aparta-Hotel Ayala*, this mid-price restaurant does a variety of good Dominican and European dishes (around RD$250 and upwards for mains) in a clean, smart environment – the *moro de guandules* rice is good. Daily noon–midnight.

Casa Caoba

Around 5km north of the centre off Carretera Medina, up an unmarked track on the west side of the road before the fork to La Toma and Pomier (ask in the village) • No opening times • Free; RD$100 tip for guard's tour in Spanish

Up in the mountains north of San Cristóbal sits **Casa Caoba**, another one of Trujillo's old mansions, and probably the most atmospheric of them all as it has been abandoned to the elements, more or less, since his death. A stylish building originally constructed entirely out of mahogany in 1938, with clean, stylized angles reminiscent of Frank Lloyd Wright, the mansion was Trujillo's favourite. It was surrounded by manicured Japanese gardens that are now going to weed and most of the walls have been scrawled with graffiti by the young people of the area who seem to be the only ones who visit. Though plans to convert it into a historical attraction have been hyped for years, only modest renovation has been completed and you'll have to make do with the guard's informal tour in Spanish, which navigates through the various rooms, including a secret chamber through which the dictator's mistresses were conducted to his bedroom, and a look at the intricately crafted woodwork still waiting to be cleaned up. If you can't find the guard, which is quite likely, you can wander the mansion by yourself by popping in through the gap in the fence to the left of the gate. Take good care as some parts don't look very safe, especially on the upper levels.

La Toma

7km north of central San Cristóbal; follow Carretera Medina north for 6km then turn right at the fork and continue for 1km • Daily 8.30am–7.30pm • RD$10; parking RD$50 • Guaguas arrive here from San Cristóbal's Parque Central (RD$40)

Extremely popular with locals at weekends, **La Toma** consists of a series of large cemented pools supplied with fresh water from the Río Haina. It's a nice place to swim under the shade of the trees and you can enjoy a cold beer and fried fish (RD$250) from one of the many stands just outside the car park on the main road.

Reserva Arqeológica El Pomier

Pomier, 11km north of central San Cristóbal • Daily 8am–4pm • RD$100 for park entrance, plus RD$300–1000 for a guide depending on number of caves visited (tours last 45min–2.5hr)

The **Reserva Arqeológica El Pomier** protects the most extensive collection of **cave pictographs** in the Caribbean – some as many as 2000 years old – though this claim to fame draws strangely few visitors. There are three major sets of caves, the other two being nearby Borbón and Santa María, but El Pomier is the only one open to the public. Upon arrival, you'll be assigned a park guide (Spanish only) who will take you to the first of four enormous, easily accessible chambers, two of which hold a variety of Taino pictographs – wear boots and bring a torch as the ones on the helmets aren't very good. In addition to scattered depictions of various birds and animals (which were once used for religious rituals) there are a number of interesting geological formations and one cave filled with thousands of **bats**. If you want to see the best petroglyphs, though, you're in for a bit of an adventure, including going down some steep cave walls using ropes.

ARRIVAL AND TOURS

RESERVA ARQEOLÓGICA EL POMIER

Getting there A *motoconcho* from San Cristóbal market costs RD$100; a taxi would be RD$400; or take one of the pick-ups stationed by the market on Calle Juanto María and Francisco Peynado for RD$30. By car, head 6km north on Carretera Medina and turn left at the fork following the signpost for "Cuevas de Pomier" for a further 5km; in Pomier another signpost directs you through a working

quarry before a track leads up to the caves

Tours Domingo Abreu (**☎**809 682 1577, **✉**domingoespele87@hotmail.com) runs regular trips to El Pomier which take in the more spectacular, somewhat inaccessible caves. He is the foremost expert on the caves, and in recent years has been at the forefront of protecting the caves from destruction by mining companies.

Najayo and Palenque

Najayo lies 14km south of San Cristóbal on the Carretera Palenque; Palenque is 6km further along the highway

San Cristóbal is close to a couple of terrific beaches, probably the only decent sand until Barahona: **Najayo**, which has an attractive strip of coarse beige sand, though does get rough waves; and the slightly more crowded **Palenque**. Named for a *cimarrón* encampment that survived here until the late eighteenth century, the beach at Palenque town's western end has remarkably calm waters, perfect for lazing about, but be prepared to be joined by plenty of others, especially at weekends. If you're here for longer than a day-trip, you can also check out the baseball camp of the San Diego Padres, which trains recruits year-round – look for the Padres sign on the road between Najayo and Palenque.

ARRIVAL AND DEPARTURE   NAJAYO AND PALENQUE

By guagua You can get dropped off next to the sand by guagua at Najayo (30min; RD$50) and 2km (a RD$50 *motoconcho* ride) from the beach in Palenque town (45min; RD$75); departures are every 30min until 6pm.

By motoconcho or taxi A *motoconcho* to Najayo/Palenque from San Cristóbal will cost around RD$200/300, while a taxi is around RD$800/1200.

ACCOMMODATION AND EATING

For the best places to eat on the beach, head 100m west from the turning to Palenque to the Cocolandia area where there's a line of decent and not too expensive seafood restaurants under the palms. If you're looking for budget accommodation, you'll find a couple of cheaper (but noisy) places in town for under RD$800, such as the *Mid-Caribbean Tropical Club*.

Najayo Beach Hotel Najayo beach ☎809 374 4011, ✉ hotelnajayo@yahoo.com. The only accommodation at the beach, this mid-price Art Deco-style hotel has a Mediterranean feel, with bright rooms and a lovely shady garden between it and the sand. Also has a fairly good restaurant specializing in seafood (mains from RD$350). **RD$1500**

Hotel Playa Palenque Palenque Beach ☎809 243 2525, ⊛hotel-playa-palenque.net. The best place near the beach, with large, airy, kitchen-equipped rooms that feature terraces overlooking a peaceful pool

and walled garden. They also serve good *criolla* food. **RD$1400**

★**Rancho Campeche** Just off the Carreter Sanchez (C-5) between San Cristóbal and Nizao near the village of Yaguate, around 15km north of the beaches ☎809 686 1053, ⊛ranchocampeche.com. This eco-lodge and campsite is a lovely, rural facility in the woods that offers three meals and a cabin room or a tent in the forest – it's a little hard to find, so call ahead for directions. They also arrange horseriding and tours to various local sites. **Cabin RD$1500, camping RD$1000**

Las Salinas

16km southwest of Baní at the end of the Carretera Las Calderas

For remote and windswept beauty try **LAS SALINAS**, a small town consisting of little more than a few dozen houses scattered about a curved peninsular, where vast salt pans are surrounded by beaches and a vivid blue sea. Salt is the big industry in the village; the fierce sun and winds here make a perfect place to evaporate it out of the water, and you'll pass vast mounds of the stuff if you head for the beach.

The beaches either side of the peninsular are pleasantly underused, though you'll have to search a little for the best spots – the most easily reached, east-facing **Playa Salinas**, comprises disappointingly compacted brown sand and is completely unprotected from the strong east–west winds. For a better beach, head to where there is a restaurant and bar at the end of the peninsular (and road). From its car park push west into the small dunes along a small track to where the sand is whiter and fine and you won't feel like you're sitting in a wind tunnel.

Even better, try searching out the south-facing **Dunas de Baní** whose fine white sand is blown into enormous dunes by the strong winds, and extend 15km west to the village of Matanzas (via Las Calderos) where you can access them by road – otherwise, just take any path south a couple of kilometres from Las Salinas. Although it's not a recreational beach (because of the wind), the dunes really are quite impressive and the sunset over the water from here is gorgeous.

Las Salinas is also a great place for **windsurfing** and the small resort *Hotel Salinas* (see below) serves as an informal windsurfing club at weekends, though you'll have to bring your own equipment.

ARRIVAL AND DEPARTURE   LAS SALINAS

By guagua Frequent guaguas (every 30min 7am–7pm; 40min; RD$55) link Las Salinas with Baní.

6

ACCOMMODATION

Hotel La Base Signposted from where the road turns north at the end of the village ☏ 809 603 3365. If you can't afford *Hotel Salinas*, the only other option is this small hotel housed in the tall yellow building (no sign on the building itself), whose handful of very basic rooms are pretty poor value, with hard beds and neither a/c nor hot water. On the plus side, it's very peaceful, gets a constant breeze and the upstairs views are good. RD$1100

Hotel Salinas Puerto Hermosa 7 ☏ 809 866 8141, ✉ hotel_salina@hotmail.com. Catering mostly to

wealthy Dominicans, this small resort on the main road in the centre of town has garishly painted but modern and comfortable rooms with good water pressure (a rarity in these parts) and also a pool, bar and disco. The setting is beautiful – the restaurant overlooks the town's small marina and serves the best seafood in the area – try the house speciality, lobster *criolla* (it's not on the menu) or the *lambí*; you can expect to spend around US$15–20 for a meal. They also do all-inclusive deals for RD$3500 per person (excluding alcohol). RD$3500

San José de Ocóa

25km north of the Carretera Sánchez along Highway 41

Tucked away in the mountains along the Río Nizao, the mountain hamlet of **SAN JOSÉ DE OCÓA** attracts weekenders from across the country, though few foreign visitors. Most come in the summer months, when temperatures in the valley below can be sweltering, to visit the river and take advantage of the lovely, sometimes rugged, mountain landscape that surrounds the town. San José itself is an easy-going and fairly modest place, consisting mostly of clapboard shacks – but there's no denying the majestic setting, with the town perched atop a high hill and offering views that stretch across the southern Cordillera Central.

ARRIVAL AND DEPARTURE   SAN JOSÉ DE OCÓA

By guagua Guaguas arrive and depart every hour or so during daylight hours from and to Santo Domingo (every

15min; 1hr 30min; RD$160) via San Cristóbal and Baní; they use the south end of the town's Parque Central.

ACCOMMODATION, EATING AND NIGHTLIFE

★ **Baco** Half a block west of the Parque Central at Duverge and 16 de Agosto ☏ 809 558 2368. Very good *pica pollo*-style restaurant with a choice of meats and fish served with potatoes or plantain for RD$150–200. The regulars tend to be solitary middle-aged males who obviously enjoy their food. Also has a few basic rooms for rent for around RD$700. Daily 7am–midnight.

Casa Conrado Guest House Rancho Arriba ☏ 829 392 0765, ✇ dominicanoutdoors.com. In Rancho Arriba, a small village a 30min drive north of San José and 50m off the main road, this remote, foreigner-run guesthouse has clean, fairly basic rooms and a comfortable terrace (with hammocks) overlooking the mountains. They organize various activities in the area (see box, p.244) and serve

meals for between RD$100–200, or you can use their kitchen to cook for yourself. Wi-fi for guest use. US$28

Pensión San Francisco Andres Pimentel 37 ☏ 809 558 2741. Probably the quietest and most peaceful of the town's accommodation options, this place is at the northern, residential end of the street. Rooms are small but clean and have a/c and cable TV but no wi-fi. Unlike the other hotels there's no restaurant or bar. RD$700

Rancho Francisco 2km south of town on the main highway ☏ 809 558 4099. This place rents out large, plush cabins with a/c, cable TV and small balconies. It's well-situated next to the river (though there's also a pool) and is far enough from the adjoining dancehall and restaurant that you can get a good night's sleep. Wi-fi is available in

6

ACTIVITES AROUND SAN JOSÉ DE OCÓA

Hiking trails abound in the countryside around San José de Ocóa; the easiest option is simply to set off on one of the dirt paths spiralling away from the town into the hills, or try one of the suggestions below.

PRESA JIGUEY

A good trip is to the scenic Presa Jiguey, a remote **dam and lake** 15km northeast of town by rough dirt road. Unless you walk it, you'll need your own off-road transport to get there; turn right at the fork in the road just north of town, and another right 5km further on – ask for directions from anyone you meet as there are several different routes around the area.

SAN JOSÉ–CONSTANZA ROAD

A more adventurous option is to drive the stunning but extremely rough San José–Constanza road, leading north of town right into the heart of the **Cordillera Central**; the road is not that bad up to the sleepy village of Sabana Larga, but from there to Constanza (see p.228) it gradually deteriorates into a very rocky track and you'll need a good **4WD**, spare tires and emergency supplies.

RANCHO ARRIBA

Take the northeast (and fairly decent) road along the other fork from Sabana Larga towards Piedra Blanca and after 26km you'll get to the more remote and rustic **pueblo** of Rancho Arriba. This is another great place for getting to know the mountains, and *Casa Conrado Guest House* (see p.243) can organize various activities in the area including horseriding (3–4hr; US$29), river-hiking to waterfalls (3hr; US$22), mountain biking, as well as off-road quad and 4WD tours.

the restaurant. The dancehall offers the best nightlife around, too, with good Dominican live acts and DJs at weekends. RD$1000

★ **Hotel Restaurant Marien** On the western side of the Parque Libertad on Andres Pimental ☏ 829 663 9067.

Most central of all the hotels, this well-run place also has one of the nicest bars. Although you'll be at the centre of the night-time action, most of their well-sized, clean rooms (with very funkily decorated bathrooms) are quite far from the street noise and boast a/c, cable TV and wi-fi. RD$500

Azua

Established in 1504 by the future conqueror of Cuba Diego Velázquez, **AZUA** is among the oldest cities in the New World. In the early sixteenth century, Mexico conquistador Hernán Cortes served as its mayor, but despite this lofty history there's nothing left of the original city, which was demolished by an earthquake in 1751. On top of that, Haitian armies occupied Azua multiple different times in the nineteenth century and, despite being repelled in the El Número mountain passes to the east, left the village virtually sacked. Although a celebration is held on 19 March every year to commemorate an 1844 battle that resulted in victory over the Haitians, the town's **Pueblo Viejo** holds no colonial ruins, and **Puerto Viejo** – the old port – is merely an industrial site for the extraction of natural gas. If you are travelling between Lago Enriquillo and San Juan de la Managua, you will have to change guaguas here. Although most travellers rush through, Azua does boast a couple of reasonable **beaches** and serves as a base for the Las Lagunas trail up **Pico Duarte** (see p.226).

The beaches

Playa Monte Río lies 3km south of town (to reach the waterfront, take the marked turnoff down Av. Sergio C. Vilchez by the motorbike store on Carretera Sánchez at Azua's eastern edge)

Azua's **beaches** are used almost exclusively by locals, and there are a couple of fairly respectable ones, including the compacted brown sand beach **Playa Monte Río.** Here fishing boats bob on calm waters and a few locally run outdoor restaurants serve grilled fresh fish with the requisite accompaniments of plantains, rice and beans. Some 500m west of these establishments is the much smaller and prettier **Playa Blanca**, which is secluded, though has much coarser sand – this placid turquoise cove is more popular as a swimming spot among the town's youth. If you keep heading west along the rough track that follows the coast, you'll end up on a high headland affording great **views** both along the coast towards Salinas and also inland to the mountains.

ARRIVAL AND DEPARTURE

AZUA

By guagua The main guagua station is near Parque Central on the corner of Calle Duarte and Garrido; during the day regular guaguas head east to Santo Domingo (every 10min 6am–6pm; 2hr; RD$150), although every hour or so there will be an "express" guagua which is fractionally more expensive and only fractionally faster. If you're going west to either Barahona (every 30min 6am–5pm; 1hr 30min; RD$200) or San Juan de la Maguana (every 15min 6am–7pm; 1hr 30min; RD$120) you'll need the Asodumas

guagua station which lies a further three streets west on the northwest corner of the Parque 19 de Marzo.

By bus The Caribe Tours station is right around the corner from Parque Central on Calle Fátima and runs services between here and Santo Domingo (8 daily 7.15am–6.15pm; 1hr 45min; RD$190). From Azua four of these services go on to Barahona (1hr 15min; RD$125) and four go to San Juan de la Maguana (1hr 15min; RD$130).

ACCOMMODATION AND EATING

San Ramon Carretera Sánchez at the town's eastern entrance ☎ 809 490 6079. If you do end up having to stay the night, you'll find this the cleanest hotel of a very basic bunch. For RD$400 more than the standard room, you can get a slightly bigger, less shabby room with a/c. <u>RD$600</u>

Francia Carretera Sánchez at the eastern end of town ☎ 809 521 2900. Homely restaurant 200m from the *San Ramon*, serving a variety of traditional Dominican dishes, such as garlic shrimp or chicken with rice, from a modest menu of two or three options that varies nightly. Mains in the RD$200–350 range. Daily 8am–9pm.

San Juan de la Maguana and around

Eighty kilometres northwest of Azua and fifty largely impassable, mountainous kilometres north of Lago Enriquillo, **SAN JUAN DE LA MAGUANA** is a major hub of agricultural transport for the surrounding valley. There's not much to draw you to this area apart from the colourful **religious festivals** held throughout the year, including a giant Altagracia procession on January 21; the *fiesta patronal* for San Juan from June 15 to 24, which features a full week of big-name live bands playing in the Parque Central; Semana Santa (Holy Week), when you'll see processions with large Haitian-style *gagá* bands and the crowning of a city queen; and **Espíritu Santo**, seven weeks after Semana Santa. The last-named is the most fascinating – festivities begin in the small town of El Batey, 18km northeast of San Juan, with an all-day procession in which a porcelain statuette draped in a white cape is carried to the big city. Along the way, many marchers become possessed by the Holy Spirit, Liborio (see box, p.246) and various Taino ghosts; these "horses" – as the possessed are known – behave in all sorts of ways: collapsing to the ground in a trance-like state, speaking in tongues, or prancing about like coquettish young girls.

The mountainous area **north of San Juan** was long inhabited by escaped slaves who established *cimarrón* settlements throughout the Hispaniola mountains. Their religious traditions have been transformed over the last century by the veneration of **Liborio**, who is still considered a living messiah by many here. If you're trekking up **Pico Duarte** (see p.226) on the Las Lagunas or the Sabaneta trail, note that they both start from north of here.

ARRIVAL AND DEPARTURE

SAN JUAN DE LA MAGUANA

By bus or guagua San Juan is the terminus for many bus routes that head west from Santo Domingo. Caribe Tours, whose terminal is round the corner from the *Hotel Maguana*

on Calle Dr Cabral, runs services to Santo Domingo via Azua (4 daily 6.30am–5.30pm; 2hr 30min; RD$270), while Transport del Valle, whose station is at Duarte 40 near

Independencia, also serves the capital (every 30min 6.30am–6pm; RD$270). You'll need to use guaguas to get to Las Matas de Farfán (every 25min 6am–6pm; 30min; RD$80) and onward to the Haitian border at Elias Piña (aka Comendador) – catch them either at Parque Central or the town's western gate.

ACCOMMODATION AND EATING

Hotel Maguana Av Independencia 72 ☎ 809 557 9293. Built in 1947 at the behest of Trujillo (his suite is still available for RD$2800 a night), this grand-looking building is by far the nicest place in town. Centrally located, overlooking Parque Duarte, the hotel's rooms are a little small but very reasonably priced and all have a/c, cable TV and wi-fi. Also has a very good restaurant (daily 8am–11pm), with mains running from RD$300. **RD$1300**

Rincón Mexicano 27 de Febrero 28 and Capotillo ☎ 809 577 3713. Very tasty Mexican food in clean, brightly coloured surroundings with good soft-shell tacos, fajitas, enchiladas and other Mexican favourites from RD$100–600. The *Chicanas* are especially good, but go easy on the salsa whatever you order as it's mighty hot. Also serves cold Coronas and excellent frozen cocktails. Daily 8am–midnight.

Las Matas de Farfán

Founded in 1780, laidback **LAS MATAS DE FARFÁN** was named for an eighteenth-century Azua merchant who would stop here for the night on his way to the border, to sleep beneath an enormous tamarind tree by the side of the local river. At Las Matas' heart is its **Parque Central**, thought by some to be the most beautiful in the nation, with a lovely gazebo standing in the middle of a densely wooded area of different species of trees. Every Sunday at 8pm the local symphonic band plays under the gazebo as the whole town comes out to watch. Wednesday and Saturday are **market days**, when hundreds of *campesinos* from the surrounding countryside come into town to sell their produce along Calle Independencia. There is also a similar smaller daily market along Santa Lucia (7am–6pm), with many stalls selling UN-donated clothing from Haiti. If you want more of a Haitian experience, take a guagua fifteen minutes west to the border town of **Elias Piña** (also called Comendador), where a chaotic cross-border market is held every Monday and Thursday.

THE LIBORISTA MASSACRE

At the beginning of the twentieth century, a charismatic faith healer named **Liborio** established a self-reliant commune in the mountains north of San Juan de la Maguana that attracted thousands of followers. Local peasants considered him a reincarnation of Jesus and worshipped him as such, though detractors maintained that he planned to march on Santo Domingo and set up a **Voodoo theocracy** with himself as high priest. He was branded a bandit by the American army during their occupation of the 1910s and 1920s; seeing his populist commune as a threat to their rule, they put a bounty on his head and sent out regular patrols to hunt him down. For six years he evaded capture by hiding out in the heart of the Cordillera Central with a handful of followers. When he was finally caught and murdered by American troops in 1922, rumours quickly spread through San Juan and Las Matas that Liborio had **risen from the dead**, and the soldiers had to dig up his corpse, drive it through the streets of San Juan in the back of a truck and display it in the Parque Central to prove otherwise.

The movement he founded, though, continued, with several local *brujos* claiming to have had direct spiritual contact with Liborio. In the early 1960s a group called **Palma Sola**, run by two peasant priests known as The Twins, set up a 1200-member utopian Liborista commune in the fields just west of Las Matas, by all accounts peaceful but deemed subversive enough to the government that on December 11, 1962, the military dropped **napalm** on them from airplanes – burning six hundred people to death and sending the rest scattering back to their villages. The fields outside Las Matas bear no marker to indicate that the commune members died here, but the Liboristas still dwell in the mountains around San Juan.

ARRIVAL AND DEPARTURE

LAS MATAS DE FARFÁN

By guagua Guaguas to Santo Domingo (hourly 7am–4pm; 3hr 30min; RD$350) stop at the corner of Independencia and 19 de Marzo and stop off in San Juan along the way, and westward services to the border at Elias

Piña (every 25min 7am–5pm; 15min; RD$50) leave from the same place. A more regular service to San Juan leaves from the station at the east entrance of town on the main road (every 25min 6am–6pm; 30min; RD$80).

ACCOMMODATION AND EATING

Independencia Calle Independencia 172 ☎ 809 527 5698. The best the town has to offer, though it's not particularly good value: if you want a/c, cable, space and light you'll need the superior rooms which are RD$200 more expensive. Still, it does have an attached *comedor* and café. **RD$1200**

Santa Lucia Southeast corner of the Parque Central ☎ 809 527 5277. Old-school *comedor* serving good-value Dominican food in its slightly worn interior, or outside overlooking the park. Most dishes are in the RD$160–250 range with the *chivo* (goat) being particularly good. Daily 8am–4pm & 7–10pm.

Barahona and around

The city of **BARAHONA** was founded by Haitian General Touissant L'Ouverture in 1802 as an alternate port to Santo Domingo. Once the informal capital of Trujillo's multimillion-dollar sugar industry, it has fallen on hard times due to the low price of sugar globally and the transition in the US from sugar to corn syrup in all manner of products. This is one of the reasons for the high crime rate in the town – while

BARAHONA

EATING & DRINKING
Brisas del Caribe	1
Melo's Cafe	3
La Pompa	2

ACCOMMODATION
Cacique	1
Hotel Costa Larimar	3
Gran Hotel Barahona	2
Guarocuya	5
Los Hijos de Dindo	4

6

perfectly safe during the day, it's not advisable to wander away from the **Malecón** or main streets after dark, especially if alone.

Nevertheless, it's quite a pleasant place in itself, and the town has a number of hotels, so many travellers use it as a base from which to roam the magnificent coastline that runs west of town all the way to **Parque Nacional Jaragua**. Most memorable along this stretch are the *balnearios* at **San Rafael** and **Los Patos**, long popular with locals but undiscovered by the outside world. Away from the coastline, the **Sierra Bahoruco** mountain range offers real wilderness hiking, while a boat trip on the **Laguna Cabral** is an idyllic birdwatching opportunity.

In town, the Malecón (officially Avenida Enriquillo) is a fun place to pass an evening as it gets crowded with food stands and partying locals at night. Its major landmark is the **Parque de la Ciencia** (science park) at the end of Calle J.F.C. Gómez where kids enjoy a solar-system-themed slide. West of the park, past a series of *super-fría* (cold beer) shacks, is a modest stretch of lovely sand bordered by mangroves; although the best part is in front of (and maintained by) the *Hotel Costa Larimar*, it is actually part of the public beach so feel free to use it. The town's most popular beach, however, is **Playa El Cayo**, a long stretch of less-inviting sand that lies at the opposite end of the boardwalk beyond **Ingenio Barahona**, which used to be the country's largest sugar mill but is now closed. The beach is typically crowded during the day with locals and vendors selling grilled fish.

ARRIVAL AND DEPARTURE   BARAHONA

By guagua All guaguas except the ones to and from Santo Domingo pick up and drop off at the old *mercado* (market) two blocks north of the Malecón at the corner of Calle Padre Bellini and Av. Luis E. del Monte, with vans departing every 15min southwest down the coast to Pedernales and northwest to Jimaní via Duvergé (every 45min; 2hr; RD$190) or Neiba (and onwards to Descubierto; every 30min; 1hr; RD$200). Santo Domingo guaguas arrive and depart (hourly; 3hr 30min; RD$250) at the Sinchomiba terminal at the northern entrance to the town on Av. Cassandra Damirón, with a few

continuing down the coast towards Pedernales also. Guaguas do not run after dark, so last departures are typically 3–4pm.

By bus Caribe Tours has a bus station near the Malecón on J.F.C. Gómez and runs services to and from Santo Domingo (4 daily; 3hr; RD$270).

By car Coastal Highway 44 connects the city with Azua, Baní and Santo Domingo to the east before continuing west all the way to the border, and a well-marked turnoff 11km east of town leads northwest to San Juan de la Maguana, Las Matas de Farfán and Elias Piña.

ACCOMMODATION

Barahona has a wider range of hotels than you'll find elsewhere in the southwest. Most accommodation is within a couple of blocks of the open seaside **Malecón**, four blocks south of the Parque Central.

Cacique J.F.C. Gómez 2 behind the Parque Infantil, Malecón ☎ 809 524 4620. One of the cleanest rock-bottom options and ideally located just a block from the waterfront. The rooms are fairly basic but do have fans and the wi-fi reaches most. Also has a nice rooftop area. RD$500

★**Hotel Costa Larimar** ☎ 809 524 5111, ⓦ hotelcostalarimar.com. A "resort" that never quite took off, this is still the best hotel in town, and offers majestic views of both the sea and the mountains. The rooms are clean, and have a/c, television, and slightly patchy wi-fi, and there's a nice pool too. It's not worth going all-inclusive, as the mediocre meals add RD$540 a night per person. Price is per person and includes breakfast. RD$1950

Gran Hotel Barahona Jaime Mota 5 ☎ 809 524 3442. A nice hotel, though away from the waterfront.

Service is commendable and the rooms are clean and comfortable, with a/c, TV, phone and hot water. Also has excellent wi-fi in all the rooms and a rooftop restaurant. RD$1170

Guarocuya Malecón 15 ☎ 5809 524 4121. If you want to be by the sea but can't quite afford *Hotel Costa Larimar*, try this boardwalk hotel, the views of the beach are great though the wi-fi and the hot showers are limited. Rooms are clean and bright, even If the bathrooms are little tatty. RD$1300

Los Hijos de Dindo 30 de Mayo 39 ☎ 809 524 5510. If you're on a very tight budget and the *Cacique* is full, this is the place for you. They keep the place clean, it's quiet, and you get a private, cold-water bathroom. It's not a great neighbourhood, however – exercise caution when returning home after dark. RD$600

EATING

For **cheap eats** you'll find the usual array of fast food, *pollo carbon* and pizza vendors in the Parque Central and along the Malecón.

Brisas del Caribe Eastern end of the Malecón ☎ 809 524 2794. This smart seafood restaurant offers impeccable service, a nice view over the water and a slew of great menu offerings, including grilled lobster, garlic shrimp and an amazing kingfish steak. It's also the only place on the island where you're likely to be served a large Presidente bottle in a champagne ice bucket. Expect to pay around US$25 for a meal. Daily 8am–midnight.

★**Melo's Café** Anacaona 12 ☎ 809 524 5437. The best in town: an unpretentious little diner with delicious American breakfasts (RD$125), as well as oatmeal and pancakes, and amazing French toast. Also serves up an outstanding *plato del día* (RD$200). Mon–Sat 8am–2pm; Mon–Wed also 6–9pm.

DRINKING AND NIGHTLIFE

Barahona's nightlife has been slightly curtailed by the soaring **crime rate**, though it's quite safe to enjoy the Malecón's line of small bars and restaurants that play high-octane **merengue** till late. Don't risk the discos near the **Parque Central** as they're not safe (and more or less centres of prostitution), though there are a couple of slightly less dodgy venues for dancing at the far western end of the Malecón – ask in town for up-to-date advice.

La Pompa Malecón, at the corner with Jaime Mota ☎ 809 524 1629. A fun outdoor bar, and a bit more upmarket than most along the Malecón, this stylish place, just across from the water, has wrought-iron furniture laid out under the trees. Very popular, especially when they're showing sports on the big TV. Daily 10am–midnight, until 2am Fri & Sat.

Cabral

15km northwest of Barahona • The two- to three-hour boat tour leaves from the park station (daily 8am–4pm; ☎ 829 479 9082; RD$700 per person, plus RD$100 park entrance) at the north end of town along Dr Feris Olivero

The small town of **CABRAL** sits on the eastern edge of the **Parque Nacional Bahoruco** (see p.257), though you'll still have to go some distance before entering the park itself. Cabral is home to the serene **Laguna Cabral**, a lovely expanse of water that provides habitat for numerous birds, including Criollo and Florida ducks, flamingos, ibises and herons – you can see the lagoon on a **tour**. Otherwise, the only reason for coming to Cabral is if you're around during Semana Santa, when the **Carnival Cimarrón** is held, a week of exuberant celebrations in which participants don devil masks (*diablos cojuelos*) and ornate costumes, and carry bullwhips. You can purchase a mask, if you like, by asking around at the park station at any time of year.

North on Highway 48, which picks up just past El Peñon, begins some of the densest and most primitive **sugar-cane** farming areas in the country. Along the road you'll see Haitian *bateyes* (see box, p.250) and the ruins of the old railroad that Trujillo built to ship the cane harvested here to the Barahona mill.

ARRIVAL AND DEPARTURE   CABRAL

By guagua Guaguas depart from near Barahona's municipal market (hourly 7am–6pm; 30min; RD$50), stopping briefly almost outside the park office during the day. The park itself is accessed by taking Dr Feris Olivero north at the central crossroads in town.

POLO MAGNÉTICO

About 10km south of Cabral along the Carretera Polo is the **Polo Magnético**, the stuff of rural legend – a place where the law of gravity is apparently defied. At an upward incline in the highway, marked by a roadside billboard, you can pull off on the right-hand fork and put your car in neutral; it will seem to be slowly pulled up the hill, as will any round object that you place on the pavement. A group of student surveyors from Santo Domingo's Catholic University established that the "pole" is an **optical illusion**, but many locals believe that the miracle results from the presence of magnetically charged ore beneath the road's surface.

6

HAITIAN BATEYES

For most of the twentieth century, the Dominican economy revolved around **sugar**. Though tourism recently replaced it as the top source of foreign currency, sugar plantations still exist all along the southern half of the island, their vast expanses of cane harvested by migrant Haitian labourers who live in meagre company barracks known as *bateyes*.

As early as the late nineteenth century, depressed sugar prices made Dominican labour too expensive for the sugar companies, and masses of **migrant workers** were imported from the British Antilles to fill the void. During the Great Depression of the 1930s, even this labour became too expensive, and formal agreements were reached that paid the Haitian government to recruit and export tens of thousands of cane cutters each year. The *batey* workers came from the poorest rural parts of Haiti, encouraged by the opportunity to save US$30–50 over the course of a season – in four or five years that would be enough to build a modest house and work a small subsistence farm back in their home country. Many, however, have come back empty-handed or, worse, never left at all.

The formal agreement has dissolved, and Haitians who cross into the Dominican Republic to work in the sugar fields do so *âba fil* (under the fence). After the earthquake in 2010, thousands more Haitians poured over the border in desperation for work, making the *bateyes* more crowded and wages even lower.

Batey **life** involves horribly substandard conditions. Manually cutting cane with machetes is backbreaking work, and the labourers are paid as little as US$5 per day. They have to work at least fourteen hours a day in order to feed themselves, pay bribes to police officers and company officials, and save a few pesos for the return to Haiti. Most *bateyes* have no bathrooms or running water, and workers must walk a kilometre or more for water and sleep five or six to a small room. Every year thousands of Haitians fail to earn enough for the **journey home**, and are forced to stay in the *batey* during the dead season, when there's little work available. The inhuman conditions have led various international human rights groups to declare the situation tantamount to slavery, but there has been little in the way of reform to date.

ACCOMMODATION

Hotel K'Nero International On the highway at the eastern edge of town ☎ 829 876 4767. The better of the town's two options, the rooms here are clean, comfortable and pretty good value. There's also an attached restaurant that does nice fish (which are sometimes taken from the small lagoon next door). For an extra RD$150 you can get a/c and a slightly larger room. <u>RD$650</u>

South of Barahona

The gorgeous coastline south of Barahona is the region's premier attraction, yet it remains virtually undiscovered by outsiders. Traverse the length of it, which takes roughly half a day even by public transport, and you'll find innumerable pretty coves tucked between high oceanfront cliffs. The first beaches to head for are **San Rafael**, **Paraíso** and **Los Patos** – just don't expect fine white sand, as most are of pebbles or gravel. Also worth a visit are the **larimar mines** north of Arroyo. The absolute highlights of the entire coast, however, are the flamingo-inhabited and little-visited **Laguna Oviedo**; and the remote paradise of **Bahía de las Águilas**, which has to be up there with the most beautiful beaches in the country.

GETTING AROUND   SOUTH OF BARAHONA

By guagua Guaguas run from Barahona all the way to Pedernales (every 15min 6am–3pm; there may be a couple of later departures as far as Paraíso) and pick up and drop off at various points along the highway. No guaguas run after dark.

Destinations Quemaito (15–20min; RD$30); Baoruco (20–30min; RD$50); San Rafael (30–40min; RD$75); Paraíso (40–50min; RD$90); Los Patos (50min–1hr; RD$100); Enriquillo (1hr; RD$150); Oviedo (1hr 30min; RD$200); Pedernales (3hr; RD$300).

Quemaito

6km south of Barahona

Quemaito, home to a couple of secluded hotels, is a beautiful little stretch of gravel that gets only moderate traffic, though it now has a small beach restaurant and looks set to be further developed in the near future. Three kilometres before Quemaito is **Playa Saladilla**, a little pebble cove protected by a reef, with shallow, calm water for swimming.

ACCOMMODATION QUEMAITO

★ **Casablanca** Down a rocky track, signposted at the north end of the village ☏ 829 740 1230, ⓦ hotelcasablanca.com.do. Boasting both natural beauty and gourmet cuisine, the singular *Casablanca* is set along rambling rural grounds perched on a cliff over the beach with nothing to disturb the silence except the constant wash of the waves, and gentle "biff, baff, boff" of the mainly French-speaking clientele. The rooms boast few amenities but are charming nonetheless, with private cold-water bath and fan. What draws people here is the food, prepared by the proprietor, a gourmet Swiss chef. A three- to five-course dinner, which will cost you RD$1300 upwards (depending on dishes), is served according to the French table d'hôte tradition, by which customers, after reaching a consensus, tell the chef what they want for dinner in the morning, she goes to the market and buys everything fresh, prepares it, and everyone sits together for the evening meal. Price includes breakfast. <u>US$65</u>

Playazul On the main highway 7km south of Barahona and 3km north of Quemaito ☏ 809 429 5375, ⓦ playazulbarahona.com. This majestically set hotel has well-maintained standard a/c rooms with twin beds, plus a nice little restaurant serving Franco-Dominican food, from around RD$500 per person, with excellent fresh fish (and good wines) and spectacular bird's-eye views of the coast from its perch atop a treeless seaside hill. Price includes breakfast. <u>RD$2500</u>

Arroyo and the larimar mines

5km south of Quemaito

South of Quemaito, the rainforested Sierra Bahoruco (see p.257) rises above the shore, dropping off precipitously at the water's edge. This is the landscape that surrounds the pueblo **ARROYO**, a tiny town with a dirt road turnoff that leads through the mountains to the local **larimar mines**. Along the road you'll see several stands where locals sell lumps of larimar for US$5–15, depending on size and quality. The main set of mines are little more than deep holes in the ground supported by wooden frames, but it's fascinating to watch local **miners** clamber acrobatically up and down them; they'll also sell you raw chunks of the stones. A hundred metres down the road, a large river with small **cascades** makes a good spot to cool off after the dusty journey.

ARRIVAL AND DEPARTURE ARROYO AND THE LARIMAR MINES

By car To get to the larimar mines from Arroyo, take the dirt turnoff at the cockfighting arena and head 8km through lush rainforest and past small mountain *campos*, then walk up the hill from the road. Bear in mind, though, that the road is quite bad, and you're in danger of losing a tyre if you are not in a 4WD.

By motoconcho It's possible to ask around in Arroyo for a *motoconcho* that will take you up to the mines for RD$150 each way (plus waiting time).

Tours The cheapest way to visit the mines is through Larimar Solidario (☏ 809 713 0974, ⓦ larimarsolidario.com), a local cooperative that only employs the physically handicapped and those marginalized by society. Their tours are in Spanish only at present, though they cost just RD$1000 per person; if you buy jewellery off them at their shop, you know your money's going to a good cause. Alternatively, most accommodations along the coast will offer to book a tour of the mines though Paraíso-based Eco Tour Barahona (☏ 809 243 1190, ⓦ ecotour-repdom.com; US$99 per person) who run day-trips in English to the mines. Book with them direct, however, and you'll save yourself around US$20–30 per person.

ACCOMMODATION

Aparta Hotel Pontevedra On the main road ☏ 809 341 8462, ⓦ pontevedracaribe.com. If you're interested in staying the night in Arroyo, the only option at present is these largely characterless concrete apartments with kitchens (though the price includes breakfast and dinner) that have easy access to the pebbly beach. There's also a pool for guest use. <u>RD$3000</u>

6

Baoruco, La Ciénaga and around

5km south of Arroyo, down a small road off the highway

BAORUCO and the much nicer **LA CIENAGA** are tiny adjoining fishing villages with a very pretty beach and a couple of small, new resorts. Aside from these, it's a sleepy little part of the coast, and the only activity you'll find is at the beach bars set up along the north end of the waterfront in La Ciénaga.

ACCOMMODATION   BAORUCO AND LA CIÉNAGA

Casa Bonita Baoruco ☎ 809 540 5908, ⓦ casabonitadr .com. Set on a hilltop above the highway, this place caters to both wealthy Dominicans and foreigners, and offers a bird's-eye view of the ocean, plus a swimming pool and an elegant restaurant; non-guests can have dinner on the patio for around RD$700. Don't expect 24hr service, though, as most of the hotel staff go home at 10.30pm. **US$217**

★ **Casa de Tarzan** 3km inland from Casa Bonita in Baoruco ☎ 809 977 4280, ⓔ casadetarzan@gmail. com. This rambling country manor-cum-mountain hideaway is set beside a waterfall and though it's hard to access it's certainly worth the trouble. You're likely to have the entire place to yourself, for starters, along with half a dozen hiking trails and a waterfront *balneario*. They don't have a restaurant but they do have a full kitchen for guests to use (bring your own supplies) and also rent bicycles and horses. The rough dirt approach road, which twice crosses a river, is tough without a 4WD but they can pick you up on the coast. Be sure to give at least a week's notice before you expect to arrive. **US$100**

Cachote

Microempresa Ecoturística Cachote ☎ 809 899 4702, ⓔ ecoturismocomunitariocachote@yahoo.com • A visit can be done either as a day-trip or an overnight stay in their clean but extremely rustic cabins and costs RD$1200 per person all-inclusive

A marked dirt road from La Ciénaga leads twenty gruelling kilometres into the mountains, crossing back and forth over a winding river before finally arriving at **CACHOTE**, an isolated mountain outpost set squarely in the middle of a large cloud forest. It's a rough trip, but once here your reward is the chance to interact with locals and learn about *campesino* culture – including folk medicine practices – in a really magical spot, thanks to the town's community-run **ecotourism** outfit, Microempresa Ecoturística Cachote, who can bring you here from the coast if you contact them in advance. You'll also get the chance to ride mules across mountain passes and hike one of their eight major **trails**. It's the best opportunity on the island to get an up-close look at life in the Dominican *campos*.

San Rafael

Five kilometres south of Baoruco

The pueblo **SAN RAFAEL** has an enticing beach – albeit one with a strong, crashing surf – and is crowded with Dominicans at weekends but only moderately populated the rest of the week. Fortunately, a **waterfall** thrums down the nearby mountains and forms a natural swimming pool at the beach entrance, with an unobtrusive artificial barrier walling it in so that water slowly pours over the edge into the sea. The area around here is a popular **camping spot**, complete with public shower and bathroom facilities, and some shacks nearby sell excellent, and reasonably priced grilled lobster and fresh fish. You can **hike** along the river's cascades into the mountains, or head up a turnoff just west of the beach, which leads to a spot with panoramic views atop a high cape.

ACCOMMODATION   SAN RAFAEL

Hotel San Rafael On the hill south of the beach ☎ 809 936 8434. One of the best-value options along the coast, this tiny hotel has just three rooms in a house next to the owner's and is perched atop the cliffs offering spectacular views from the balcony down onto the beach and along the coast. Rooms are fairly basic but clean, with a shared bathroom, and you also have use of an equipped kitchen. **RD$800**

Paraíso

PARAÍSO, sandwiched between San Rafael and Los Patos, is the "big town" along this stretch, where locals go for fiestas and weekend nightlife – it's also where you'll need to go for ATMs, pharmacies and internet cafés. But it still doesn't boast much in the way of hotels, and its restaurants are typical *comedores*. It does have a long strand of fairly sandy **beach** that can get brutally hot at midday due to the lack of shade.

ACCOMMODATION AND EATING   PARAÍSO

There are over a dozen different *comedores* and street vendors within town offering pulled beef and pork, fried *chicharrones* and the like.

La Morena Arz. Noel 19 ☎809 243 1343. Good home-style Dominican cooking at this tiny restaurant housed in an orange clapboard shack just south of the Parque Central. Fine *criolla*-style seafood dishes from RD$250 upwards, and if you fancy something meaty try the steak with onion and vinegar topping. Daily 7am–midnight.

Hotel Paraíso Av. Luperón at the western end of beach ☎809 243 1080, ✉dojasa_js@hotmail.com. The best rooms within the town and its location close to the water make this a decent enough place to stay for the night, with a/c or fan, cable TV and a fresh seafood restaurant. RD$1200

Rancho Platón 7km inland from Paraíso up a signposted track ☎809 561 1555, ⚲ranchoplaton .com. For a change of scenery from the coast, you could head into the mountains to this riverside *finca* deep in the Sierra Bahoruco. It offers five guest rooms, each with private bath, and a natural swimming pool made from the channelled waters of the neighbouring waterfall. The proprietors can also arrange sightseeing and horseriding excursions but you need to reserve at least a week in advance. Price is for two people sharing and includes breakfast; full board is available for an extra US$32 per person per night. If necessary, they can pick you up from Paraíso on request. US$216

Los Patos

Another stunning gravel beach lies 5km further west along the coast beyond Paraíso in **LOS PATOS**, where the ocean is again joined by a river descending from the mountains to form a freshwater swimming pool. The beach, surrounded by dense mangroves, is pretty lively throughout the week, with vendors lining it to take care of most visitors' culinary and souvenir needs.

ACCOMMODATION AND EATING   LOS PATOS

★**Oasi Italiano** Entrance at the end of a dirt road, at the back of town ☎829 926 9796, ⚲lospatos.it. Considering the setting, this is a surprisingly modern hotel with comfortable hot-water rooms. There's a swimming pool on site, plus a late-opening, sociable bar and an excellent and not too expensive Italian restaurant (daily 7.30–10am & 7–9pm) that is open to non-guests and offers the best dining around. RD$1300

Pula On the highway across from Iglesia San Miguel ☎849 815 7109. This excellent but basic restaurant serves up fresh seafood cooked either Italian- or criolla-style – try the *pescado con coco*, grilled lobster, or opt for the RD$150 *plato del día*. They also play great old golden age Latin music straight out of the 1940s. Daily 7am–10pm

Virginia Calle Peatonal behind the main road ☎829 279 8389. For the true "roughing it" experience check into this basic establishment. They offer all the mod cons – private cold-water bath, mosquito net and no toilet seats. At least it'll encourage you to spend more time out of your hotel room. RD$500

Enriquillo

The beachfront remains uninterrupted for 11km beyond Los Patos, punctuated by a number of small pueblos such as **Los Blancos**, where beneath a series of high, wide cliffs you can have the pebbly beach pretty much to yourself. The first town of any real size is **ENRIQUILLO**, majestically set over a jagged limestone precipice. A broad beach stretches to the west, but there are no trees along it and thus little respite from the sun. For seclusion head a few kilometres east of town and look for the extremely steep dirt road that leads down to a pebble beach cove. If you're so inclined, you can visit the most scenically sited *club gallístico* in the country, perched at the edge of a sheer cliff above the beach closest to town – entry to the Saturday **cockfights** costs RD$50.

If you're driving further west, fill up first at the **petrol station** in Enriquillo – it's the last chance for petrol out of a pump until **Pedernales**, 60km away, though you can still buy bottles by the side of the road in the few villages strung along the highway until **Oviedo**. There is also an **ATM** behind the station, though it isn't very reliable. Note that from Oviedo to Pedernales, there is no human habitation or facilities of any kind along the 38km (of actually quite good) road and it is therefore advised that you do not attempt to make this trip in the dark – guaguas certainly don't.

ACCOMMODATION AND EATING   ENRIQUILLO

Hotel Dayira On the highway in the centre of town ☎ 809 524 8135. This is the nicest of the very basic local accommodation and it's not too bad considering the price, offering very clean rooms with mosquito nets (you'll need them) and TV. There's also a lovely first-floor balcony with a sea view. **RD$500**

D'Maria Behind the petrol station on Calle Mirabel ☎ 809 524 8243. Clean and airy first-floor restaurant serving Dominican cuisine and, like most places in the area, specializing in seafood (mains RD$250 upwards) –the *criolla* lobster is great. They also do cheaper meat dishes and *platos del día* from RD$150. Daily 8am–9pm.

Parque Nacional Jaragua

Stretching from **Oviedo** in the east, almost to the Haitian border at **Pedernales** in the west, this must rate as one of the country's least-visited, yet most beautiful national parks, and includes fine opportunities for **bird-** and **animal-watching**, as well as being possibly the best part of the DR to enjoy pristine and unspoiled **beaches**. To get the most out of it, you'll need your own transport or to join a tour (see box opposite) – in some cases, both are required.

Laguna Oviedo

Lying at the park's eastern entrance, near the otherwise unremarkable village of **Oviedo**, is scenic **Laguna Oviedo**. The lake is often white with salt and features a wealth of **birdlife** on its shores, including many pink flamingos who flock here between February and August. There are also precious few visitors here, which makes it all the more pleasant.

To get onto the lake you'll need to take an organized **boat tour** (see box opposite), on which it is possible to visit one of the 24 islands that lie within the park, a number of which are inhabited by **iguanas**. However, if you just want to wander along Laguna Oviedo's shore, simply turn up at the park entrance at the east end of Oviedo – pay your entrance fee (see box opposite) and take the left fork in the road for the best birdwatching.

The coast

The park's **coast** is endowed with a wealth of beautiful beaches and islands. In the **western** section of the park, the flint-shaped Jaragua peninsula features several lovely stretches of sand, accessible via a well-marked turnoff 11km east of Pedernales (see p.256). Five kilometres in, keep an eye out for **Cabo Rojo**, a pretty beach near the bauxite plant that is popular with local kids as well as pelicans – just try not to look at the small port where the bauxite is loaded. From Cabo Rojo the road devolves into dirt past a series of meagre Haitian beach shacks, eventually leading to the tiny seaside cave settlement known as **Las Cuevas**, from where boats can be hired from local fishermen to **Bahía de las Águilas** and **Isla Beata**. Even if you don't want to head out that far the beach here is pretty magnificent itself, and away from the lone restaurant you're

ENTERING AND EXPLORING PARQUE NACIONAL JARAGUA

There are two **entrances** to the national park where visitors are required to pay a RD$100 park entrance fee. The eastern entrance, by **Laguna Oviedo**, is on the eastern edge of the town of Oviedo, which is served by guaguas travelling between Barahona and Pedernales. The **Bahía de las Águilas** entrance (a small hut) is in the village of Las Cuevas, which is accessed and signposted from the main coastal highway 11km east of Pedernales. There is no public transport here and you'll either have to come on a tour, with your own transport, or hire a taxi from Pedernales (Taxi Auto ☎829 240 8249; RD$1500). From the highway, take the wide red road heading south which leads 5km to the **port** (be very careful of the speeding trucks coming from the bauxite mine 20km north). The road deteriorates to a gravel track and passes **Cabo Rojo** beach where it then heads left, deteriorates further, and continues another 5km to **Las Cuevas**. From the park entrance, a rocky track leads 6km to the beach, though it is really rough going and a couple of stretches are quite steep – if you don't walk it (about an hour and a half) you'll need a **4WD** or decent **motorbike**. An easier way to get here, though, is on a **boat trip** from Las Cuevas, which you can either book through English-speaking *Rancho Típico*, or save yourself RD$200–400 by negotiating in Spanish with the fishermen by the park entrance.

Eco-Tour Barahona Paraíso ☎809 243 1190, ⓦecotourbarahona.com. Offer boat tours to Bahía de las Águilas and Las Cuevas (US$119/person with at least two people), and also Laguna Oviedo (same cost). Prices include pick-up from anywhere along the coast, English-speaking guide, lunch and soft drinks, park entrance fees and boat. Can include Isla Beata on request at little or no extra charge.

Jopaka Tours Pedernales ☎809 524 0332, ⓦjopakatours.blogspot.com, ⓔmarinojos@yahoo .com. A less expensive operator which specializes in overland tours to both Bahía de las Águilas and Hoyo de Pelempito (see p.258) together in a one-day trip

(RD$1800). Note that they don't speak English.

Rancho Típico Las Cuevas ☎809 753 8058, ⓔrodriguezsantiago33@hotmail.com. As well as organizing return boat trips to Bahía de las Águilas (15min each way; RD$2000 for a return boat for up to six people including snorkelling gear), they also offer a trip-of-a-lifetime one-day tour of the coast between Las Cuevas and Isla Beata (RD$18,000 with all food, drink, and snorkelling gear) which stops at fourteen different locations along the coast and includes birdwatching, snorkelling, several beach stops, picturesque fishing villages, and a lobster lunch on Isla Beata. They speak Spanish, English and French.

unlikely to encounter another soul. The entire coast east from Bahía de las Águilas to Laguna Oviedo is eye-wateringly gorgeous and includes a host of tiny fishing pueblos, beaches such as the 27km long Playa Blanca, coves, headlands, and a handful of islands, of which the highlight is palm-tree-studded **Isla Beata**.

Bahía de las Águilas

Splendid **Bahía de las Águilas** is the crown jewel of beaches on the Jaragua peninsula, and possibly in the country. It is spectacular, unspoiled and seemingly endless, in large part because it's smack-bang in the middle of the most inaccessible national park in the country. Pure white sand with the consistency of flour stretches for over 8km with a brilliantly azure sea in front and a dramatic rocky karst landscape behind. Even with the available boat services and tours (see above), there's typically no more than a handful of people for each of those kilometres and the experience is simply breathtaking – the Caribbean tropical paradise of your dreams. There are many good spots for **snorkelling** too, so bring your gear (or rent at exorbitant prices in Las Cuevas). As there's very little **shade** it's advisable to bring an umbrella or something comparable, and you'll need to carry lots of water and your own food as there are no facilities except a toilet.

Isla Beata

Trimmed with white-sand beaches, **Isla Beata** is the only one of the park's islands to be visited regularly, since the others are heavily populated with birds who have deposited thick layers of smelly *guano*. Its human inhabitants number just a few families of local

6

lobster fishermen but you won't be alone – enormous numbers of **rhinoceros iguanas** swarm across the rocks here and represent the only substantial and stable colony of these big reptiles in the world. Reaching up to a metre in length, they have no natural predators and you can approach them quite easily – should you so wish.

There's no way to get here on your own, but you can arrange a **boat trip** with the fishermen in Las Cuevas (see box, p.255), most of the tour operators in Pedernales, *Rancho Tipico* (see p.256), who include it as part of their superlative one-day boat tour of the park, or Eco Tour Barahona (see p.255).

ACCOMMODATION AND EATING

The National Park Visitors Centre Oviedo ☎ 829 305 1686. The park office rents out three basic double rooms overlooking the lake for RD$700 which are actually quite good value considering the stunning location, and it also has a campsite with basic facilities for RD$500 a tent per night. **RD$700**

Rancho Tipico (aka Rancho Bahía de las Águilas) Las Cuevas ☎ 809 753 8058, ✉ rodriguezsantiago33 @hotmail.com. Located next to a beach almost as lovely

as Bahía de las Águilas, this tropical restaurant serves very fresh seafood under a coconut-leaf roof, while the waves gently lap against fine white sand. Try the "Bahíafongos" (a seafood *mofongo*) or whatever the fishermen have just brought in, with mains around RD$400–600, though meat dishes are cheaper. They also rent tents on the beach at RD$400 for a two-person tent. Oddly, this place has a helicopter pad but no electricity. Daily 6am–midnight. **RD$400**

Pedernales

A dusty fishing town with a beautiful beach, **PEDERNALES** sits on the Haitian border and is in close proximity to some of the most remote and beautiful of the Dominican Republic's protected land in **Parque Nacional Jaragua**, as well as offering access to **Hoyo de Pelempito** (see p.258) at the southern edge of the Sierra Bahoruco.

In town, the logical spot to head for is **Playa Pedernales**, at the end of Avenida Duarte. Its uncrowded white-sand beach, strewn with eroded conch shells, offers a good view of the **Jaragua peninsula** to the east, as well as being a great place to watch the sunset over the water to the west. It's possible to walk along the waterfront here for several kilometres almost all the way into the national park, and since it's only used by dog walkers and kids most of the time, you can more or less have the beach to yourself. There's also a Haitian **market** held on Monday and Friday in the stretch of *territoria de nadie* (no man's land) just beyond the Dominican border outpost, featuring fake designer labels and housewares traded in exchange for foodstuffs. It is fairly straightforward to **cross the border** to Anse-a-Pitres in Haiti, and will cost you US$25 (US$30 to come back), here though getting anywhere further into Haiti is difficult and/or dangerous as there is hardly any transport infrastructure.

ARRIVAL AND DEPARTURE   PEDERNALES

By guagua You can get to Pedernales (every 15min 6am–3pm) via the guaguas that ply the route from Barahona, though in a few cases you'll need to switch vehicles at Paraíso. Guaguas pick up and drop off at the

Shell station at Pedernales' entrance. It takes around 3 hours from Barahona if the driver doesn't dawdle for too many snack-breaks.

ACCOMMODATION AND EATING

Within town there's a collection of evening-time **shacks** set up at the beach's car park at the end of Av. Duarte; this is a popular place to enjoy a **beer** and a snack (and deafening music) while watching the sunset. There are also a number of *bodegas* in town where you can stock up on **provisions** before taking off to Parque Nacional Jaragua.

Bahía de las Águilas Calle Villas Del Mar, a side street just west off Calle Caracol ☎ 829 630 6895. One of the best Italian restaurants in the southwest, this Italian-run

restaurant does extremely good pizzas (RD$350–500), as well as pastas, meat and seafood dishes – the baked lobster (RD$500) is sublime. It's a little pricey but well worth it, and the food is served in a pretty garden under a coconut-leaf roof. Daily 4–11pm.

Hotel Caracol Calle Caracol 13 ☎809 524 0516, ✉hotelcaracol01@gmail.com. The rooms here are of a similar quality (albeit less cosy) to those at the *Hostal D'Oleo Mendez*, but it has the advantage of being in a quieter area and is much closer to the beach. It's just round the corner from *Bahía de las Águilas*, too. RD$1000

Hostal D'Oleo Mendez Calle Antonio Duvergé 9 ☎809 524 0416. With its rooms surrounding an inner courtyard and restaurant, this very homely place has clean, comfortable and well-equipped rooms, despite the feeling you've travelled back in time somewhat. All rooms have a/c and wi-fi, and the restaurant serves up decent Spanish food from RD$150 upwards. RD$900

6

Sierra Bahoruco

The best way to experience the pristine wilderness of the **SIERRA BAHORUCO** mountain range is along the border with Haiti from the north, via the gravel track that begins at **Duvergé**, 38km west of Cabral, and passes through its largest village, **Puerto Escondido**. Protected by the government as **Parque Nacional Bahoruco**, the mountain range contains a variety of ecosystems – including a vast stretch of pine forest that rivals the Cordillera Central in scope, large swathes of virgin rainforest, and limestone desert in the foothills – which makes the park very popular with birdwatchers and hikers alike. Highlights include the cloudforests on **Loma del Toro**, the tallest mountain in the range; and, on the southern side of the park near Pedernales, the massive **Hoyo de Pelempito** depression, which allows visitors to peer down 700m through eight different climate zones.

Duvergé to Loma del Toro

The ascent from **Duvergé** to **Puerto Escondido**, a village of shacks perched atop the mountain 14km along the way, is easily the range's bleakest stretch of country, a landscape of parched mountainside bereft of vegetation, although the road isn't too bad and normal vehicles can manage it. However, at the village the scenery becomes greener and the road veers sharply west, deteriorating to a track only traversable with an off-road vehicle. Visitors should stop at the **park office** (see p.258) on the right to pay the entrance fee – there is also, should you wish to stay, an eco-lodge in the village called *Villa Barrancoli* (see p.258) which is very popular with twitchers – in theory, and with enormous luck, you can see all but two of the 32 bird species endemic to Hispaniola in these parts. From Puerto Escondido the ecology gradually transforms into rainforest mixed with ferns and pine and the route continues west through a deep valley dominated by avocado plantations. The road then goes north up a dry riverbed, rising steeply until it reaches the tiny hamlet of **El Naranjo**, 12km further on. Here it forks, and the left-hand turn heads 8km further up into the mountains to the village of **El Aguacate**, a small military outpost on the border which marks the beginning of the cloudforest zone. From here the road leads south and steeply upward again to **Loma del Toro**, the mountain range's highest point at 2367m. At this point the path reaches primary-growth rainforest, dotted with orchids and wild strawberries, and clouds pass below the road, while several spots offer spectacular views of **Lago Enriquillo** (see p.258). To return, backtrack to El Naranjo where the other road leads 13km north to the village of **La Florida** on the C-46, which heads east to Duvergé and Barahona, and west to the **Haitian border** at Jimaní. There is also a track south from Loma del Toro that follows the border 59km down to **Pedernales**, but it is long and arduous (though pretty), and you would need sufficient fuel and spare tyres as they are both unavailable in this remote area – it takes around 5 hours.

The potato market

5km south of Aguacate • Daily 6am–5pm

It might sound a bit dull but the daily **potato market** that takes place near **El Aguacate** is very much worth a stop. Taking place in a series of tents in the middle of the wilderness, locals from both sides of the border swap potatoes for clothing and Haitian *gourdes*. When they're not hard at work trading you'll see them playing poker beneath the central tent or cooking beans over a campfire, while their mules graze nearby.

Hoyo de Pelempito

38km northeast of Pedernales • Daily 9am–4.30pm • Park entrance RD$100, payable at the ranger station just before Las Mercedes (daily 9am–4.30pm)

Unique **Hoyo de Pelempito** is considered by many to be one of the natural wonders of the Caribbean. This 2.5km-wide and 7km-long triangular depression plunges down an incredible 700m and forms an autonomous microclimate of eight different life zones, its steep sides densely wooded and inhabited with an enormous variety of **birdlife** and **animals**. There is a modern wooden visitors centre and viewing platform at the top, from where you can clearly see the vegetation change from subtropical dry forest at the bottom, gradually evolving through another six life zones before becoming cloudforest at the top. There are bathroom facilities and a picnic area at the visitors centre as well as half a dozen great **hiking** trails, which are signposted and have information boards indicating the types of flora and fauna in the area. Unfortunately, a massive fire in the summer of 2013 destroyed great swathes of the area, so be aware that there may still be some scars on the landscape.

There is no public transport here and unless you take a tour from Pedernales with Jopaka Tours (see box, p.255) you'll need your own transport. About 11km east of Pedernales there is a road signposted south to Bahía de las Águilas and north to Hoyo de Pelempito. The road north is great for 14km till it gets past the bauxite mine, shortly after which you'll find a ranger station where you should buy your park ticket. From there the slightly less well-paved road winds its way up the mountains for another 6km until Las Mercedes where it deteriorates rapidly to a rocky track, only traversable with a 4WD, arriving at the visitors centre 7km later – if you don't have an off-road vehicle you could just walk from Las Mercedes.

ARRIVAL AND INFORMATION
SIERRA BAHORUCO

Getting to the park Getting to and from the national park involves either renting a 4WD from a big town such as Barahona or arranging for *Villa Barrancoli* to pick you up from Duvergé, the nearest point on the main road. Guaguas run every 30min or so to and from Duvergé on the routes between Azua and Barahona, and Jimaní.

Park entrance Entry to the park costs foreigners RD$100 (Dominicans RD$50) and should be paid either in Puerto Escondido at the park office on the right as you enter the village, or at the ranger station just before Las Mercedes on the way to Hoyo de Pelempito (both daily 9am–4.30pm).

ACCOMMODATION

Villa Barrancoli Puerto Escondido, on the Rabo de Gato trail ⓦ sites.google.com/site/puertoescondidotourism, ⓔ puertoescondido.turismo@gmail.com. The park is prime birdwatching territory; for those who fancy a stay in the wilderness, there's an appealing cabin complex just outside the park entrance on the Rabo de Gato trail. Huts are very basic, there is space for camping (with all equipment supplied) and meals are available on request for RD$250. They can pick you up from Duvergé, too. The lodge is located a little way up the trail, a well-marked 1–2 hour trek into the mountains. RD$800, camping RD$400

Lago Enriquillo and around

Habitat for tens of thousands of tropical birds and protected as Parque Nacional Isla Cabritos, **Lago Enriquillo** is an enormous 42km-long salt-water lake that is slightly larger than Manhattan island. Sitting at the southern base of the **Sierra Neiba**, the lake is the lowest point in the Caribbean, a full 46m below sea level. Many Dominicans spend an afternoon circling the lake, though it's hard to understand why – although the northern shore is lush and green, the area to the south beyond **Jimaní** is a barren limestone desert, and the C-46 runs well away from the water through an arid wasteland east until it reaches the greenery of **Cabral**. Better by far are the **boat tours** (see below) that take you to an enormous bird sanctuary filled with flamingos and hundreds of other **tropical birds**, which collectively form an unforgettable, multicoloured spectacle. Also a hit are the **American crocodiles** that inhabit this part of the lake, though you should take one of the morning tours if you want to see them – guides get into the water and steer them past the boat to give tourists a closer view. From there, the tours pass on to the arid, rhinoceros iguana-infested **Isla Cabritos** in the lake's centre, a sandy island covered with cacti where the half-tame reptiles crowd around you in the hope of being fed.

Getting to the **park entrance** – 4km east of **La Descubierta** – along the north shore of the lake is a lovely journey; there's a thick band of lush vegetation between the water and the arid mountains from **Neiba** (sometimes written Neyba) westwards. Neiba is the last town of any size, so if you need an ATM, decent pharmacy or supermarket, then you should stop off here. The plentiful streams that run into the lake make the region ideal for growing bananas and tomatoes – you'll know you're on the right track when you spot the red trail that overladen trucks leave behind by the side of the road.

La Descubierta

Northwest of the lake • **Las Barías** No opening times • Free

LA DESCUBIERTA is a rather charming and sleepy outpost in the wilderness that contains very little apart from a quite lovely central park and, a little south of there, **Las Barías**, an oak-tree-shaded *balneario* with a small swimming pool fed by two streams. It's great for a swim, and there are also a couple of open-air restaurants and a bar, which make it something of a night-time hangout.

Cueva de las Caritas

Entrance 5km east of town along the Carretera Enriquillo, 1km east from the park's boat-tour entrance • No opening times • Free

The **Cueva de las Caritas** is a nearby cave that holds dozens of chiselled pre-Taíno petroglyphs which look remarkably like acid house-style smiley faces. It's also one of the best places to watch the sunset over the lake – the angled rock is worn smooth below the carvings and forms a natural rock sofa, an ideal spot from which to appreciate it.

ARRIVAL AND TOURS

LAGO ENRIQUILLO AND AROUND

By guagua The only public transport to La Descubierta is by guagua from the fairly large town of Neiba (every 30min 7am–4pm; 30min; RD$100). Neiba is connected by guagua to both Azua (every 15min 7am–6pm; 1hr 30min; RD$300) and Barahona (every 30min 7am–6pm; 1hr; RD$200). The park entrance is 4km east of La Descubierta and the driver will let you off there if asked, going in either direction.

Park entrance and tours Boat tours (daily 7am–2pm; RD$3500 for 1–12 people) leave from the park entrance, 4km east of La Descubierta. The park entrance fee is RD$100 per person.

ACCOMMODATION AND EATING

La Descubierta has only three **hotels**, and just a couple of basic *comedores*, though there is also a *pica pollo* in the *balneario* which serves food until about 7pm, and the **bar** by the pool serves cold beers till late.

Hotel Iguana Av. Joaquin Aybar ☏ 809 958 7636. The rooms might be slightly crumbling and worn but they're immaculately clean and the welcome is heart-warmingly friendly. Home-style food can be provided on request (RD$100–200 per meal), but what really makes this place most recommendable is its rustic charm, with chickens out the back and a small group of cats that live in the dining area. **RD$400**

6

TRADITIONAL MERENGUE BAND

Contexts

History

For a brief moment at the end of the fifteenth century, when Christopher Columbus "discovered" the New World and Spain set up its first colony here, the Dominican Republic took centre stage in world politics, only to be quickly shunted to the periphery of the Spanish Empire. It has since endured centuries of struggle for independence, having been occupied by France and Haiti and even Spain again for a time. After winning its freedom, the nation was kept in chaos by competing regional strongmen, an early twentieth-century occupation by the United States and then the iron fist of a despot. Most recently, however, the country has witnessed four consecutive free and largely fair elections for the first time in the nation's history and a stable democracy has taken root.

Early settlers

Precious little is known about the **Arawaks**, the Dominican Republic's first inhabitants, who arrived in four distinct waves from the Orinoco and Amazon river basins in present-day Guyana and Venezuela, beginning around 3000 BC with the **Ciboneys**, nomads who moved among the island's caves, living and fishing along the rivers. Around 100 BC the Ciboneys were displaced by the more advanced **Igneri** Arawak culture, who left behind superb ceramics featuring geometric designs. In 600 AD the Igneri were in turn absorbed by the **Tainos** (see box, p.262), a late Stone Age culture. The final Arawak migrants were the warlike **Caribes**, who began moving up the Antilles in 1100 AD and were making regular raiding forays along the eastern coast of Hispaniola when Columbus arrived.

The arrival of Columbus

Christopher Columbus was a member of the Genoese sailor and merchant community that came to dominate seafaring trade in Europe in the fifteenth century and, in the service of the Portuguese Crown, established fortified trading outposts along the northwestern coast of Africa. His purpose in crossing the Atlantic was both material and spiritual: he hoped to find an easy **waterway to China and Japan**, where he would sign an exclusive agreement to export Asian goods for gold and to find the mythical realm of the Christian king **Prester John**, which was believed to lie somewhere in Asia, cut off from the rest of Christianity by the Islamic empire. King John II of Portugal wasn't impressed with Columbus's scheme when it was put to him in 1485; his scientific advisers told him that, while the Earth was indeed round, Columbus had radically underestimated its size. Nor did Spain's **Ferdinand and Isabella** immediately

c.3000 BC	100 BC	600 AD	1100 AD
Ciboneys, Dominican Republic's first inhabitants, settle on Hispaniola	Ciboneys displaced by Igneri Arawaks	Tainos become dominant culture in DR	Caribes reach the Antilles

TAINO CULTURE

Much of what we know today about **Taino culture** comes from excavated shards of their beautiful ceramics and the rock art they left in the many cave systems of the Greater Antilles, though first-hand accounts from the Spanish invaders add valuable context. The Spaniards reported that the Tainos tied two boards tightly to the heads of their newborn infants and left the heads bound for the first three years of life, resulting in an artificially flat, narrow forehead. Communal parties were held on feast days – which, as in today's Dominican Republic, occurred with astonishing frequency – where villages would gather to sing narrative **areito** songs, dance to drum-based music and get riotously drunk. Another major pastime during leisure hours was the **pelota** games (similar to football) held in large stone circles that can still be seen across the island. After the Taino evening meal, it was considered beneficial to head to the nearest river and induce vomiting as a means of cleansing the body.

Taino **religion** was based on agriculture, honouring two major gods and a plethora of lesser deities. Most important were **Yocahú** – an immanent life guru of sorts, responsible for the growth of crops and animal reproduction – and the evil but incredibly powerful **Huracán**, who wreaked havoc on Taino society with (unsurprisingly) hurricanes and earthquakes when not properly appeased.

The Tainos developed a remarkable system of **agriculture** in which large mounds of mulch were sprinkled with seed, producing enough food for the entire community with very little labour. Staple crops grown in this way included yuca, peanuts, pumpkins and corn. Their **economy** was founded on subsistence barter and the concept of feudal labour was completely alien, making the Taino ill-prepared for the changes of the late fifteenth century.

bite; only after they had won the historic surrender of Granada from the Moors in 1492 did they feel confident enough to devote resources to this decidedly risky project.

On the strength of a large royal loan, Columbus outfitted three ships with ninety of the most experienced sailors he could find. He set off from the Canary Islands on September 9, 1492 and spent a troubling month at sea without spotting a shred of land. Then, on October 12, with his crew growing increasingly restless, the ships sighted the tiny Bahamian island that Columbus named **San Salvador**. Seeing nothing there of any value, they hurried on westward to Cuba, which was also quickly abandoned when it became clear that it wasn't Japan. From here the ships headed east to a large island that resembled Spain in shape. Naming it **Hispaniola**, Columbus skirted its northern coast, encountering Tainos adorned with gold jewellery, who told him of a mountain range further south called Cibao, which he optimistically assumed to be Cipango, then the European name for Japan. In an attempt to circle the island from the west, the *Santa María* grounded on a coral reef off the coast of modern-day Haiti on December 25 and had to be abandoned. Taking this as a sign from God, Columbus set up a small fort there, which he named **La Navidad** in honour of the date, left 25 men to guard it and headed back to Spain with his two remaining ships.

Upon returning with a new expedition of 1500 men – mercenaries from the Moorish wars along with a sprinkling of Spanish nobility – in late 1493, Columbus found that La Navidad had been burned to the ground by the Tainos and all of its settlers killed. Only a short distance to the east, a scenic, defensible cape was chosen as the site for the first small colony, **La Isabela**. He turned his energies to establishing a trading settlement

1492	1493	1496
Columbus arrives on the island and names it Hispaniola	Columbus returns to the island on second expedition and sets up first colony at La Isabela	Columbus returns to Spain, leaving his brother Bartolomé in charge of the colony

where he hoped to sell cheap European goods to the natives in return for large quantities of **gold**, a new source of which was highly sought after in Europe.

Unfortunately for Columbus, gold had no real value for the Tainos and they proved singularly unwilling to exert much effort mining it. This meant he would have to set up a far more complicated operation to make the colony profitable, with the Tainos enslaved and forced to work the gold mines. But even before Columbus ventured off on his first slave-taking forays into the Cibao, La Isabela's settlers began dying in the hundreds from **malaria and yellow fever**. Panic and dissent swept through the colony and a petty noble took the opportunity to hijack one of the ships with a half-dozen others and headed back to Spain to complain of his treatment. Columbus returned to Spain in 1496 to defend himself against these charges, leaving his brother Bartolomé in charge of the colony. Bartolomé had even less control over the colonists and a revolt erupted. The rebel colonists abandoned La Isabela and Bartolomé and the few remaining loyal settlers moved to establish a new outpost at **Santo Domingo**. Columbus returned in 1498, but the Spanish settlers refused to obey his orders because they considered him a foreigner. Reports of unrest filtered back to the Spanish court and in 1500 bureaucrat **Francisco Bobadilla** was sent to the new colony to investigate the civil strife. Bobadilla quickly appointed himself the new governor and sent Columbus back to Spain in chains.

Genocide and gold

Spain's King Fernando replaced Bobadilla in 1501 with **Nicolás de Ovando**, a seasoned administrator of conquered Muslim lands in Andalucía, with instructions to impose order on the ever-unruly colony. Ovando instigated the monumental construction work that was to turn Santo Domingo into Spain's capital in the New World and expanded Columbus's system of **Taino slavery**. To this end, he waged several campaigns of conquest against the country's five large *caciques* – local communities responsible for great swathes of land – executing the leaders and herding the rest into the mines. At this time, the **Catholic Church** was at the height of its power and was looking towards the New World for expansion opportunities. The Vatican thus decided to turn Santo Domingo into a regional base for Christianity, sending successive waves of missionaries to construct a cathedral, several churches, monasteries and convents from which priests would depart to the American mainland and **proselytize**. For their part the colonists were eager to soften their enslavement of the local population with a veneer of piety and set up a new system, called **encomienda**, by which the Tainos' souls would ostensibly be saved in return for their slave labour. The Taino population quickly dwindled over the next twenty years. By 1514 only 11,000 remained in Spanish control out of a number once estimated at between 500,000 and two million.

To make up for the steep decline in the number of Tainos, the Spaniards embarked in 1505 on their first **slaving expeditions** in the Antilles and along the coast of Central America. Some entrepreneurs set up small forts from which regular forays could be made into the interior, thus laying the foundations for future Spanish colonies, such as Ponce de León in Puerto Rico and Juan de Esquival in Jamaica. Meanwhile, the Columbus family's tireless petitioning of the Spanish court for the return of their rights to the New World at last brought success and Christopher's son **Diego Columbus** was

1498	1500	1501
Columbus returns but has lost control of Spanish settlers	Francisco Bobadilla sent to island to regain control and Columbus sent back to Spain	Bobadilla replaced by Nicolás de Ovando as governor who builds much of what is today's Zona Colonial in Santo Domingo

appointed Ovando's successor in 1509. Diego began by immediately reapportioning most of the enslaved Tainos to himself and a few allies. This caused uproar among the colonists and King Fernando was forced to appoint the **Real Audencia**, a royal court of appeals that would check the governor's power. The Audencia did serve to control Diego's abuses and by the 1520s it had been taken over by corrupt local sugar barons who used it mainly to collect graft. The king also promulgated a series of laws that ordered the colonists to pay the Tainos fair wages for their labour and give them decent housing, but the decrees were ignored.

Back in Spain, a conquistador-turned-priest named **Bartolomé de las Casas** had been petitioning the court on behalf of the Tainos for several years, with limited success. When, in 1514, Fernando died and Cardinal Cisneros was appointed regent, Las Casas found he had a powerful new ally. One of the cardinal's first acts was to send Las Casas and three Jeronymite priests to Santo Domingo along with a squadron of troops, instructing them to free the Tainos and **resettle** them in several new *caciques*. However, as soon as the Tainos had been moved to their new homes, a smallpox epidemic broke out – brought over by the Europeans – killing all but 3000 of the remaining 11,000 enslaved natives. The Jeronymites took this as a divine signal that the Tainos should never have been freed and sent the survivors to work in the new sugar mills that were being built around Santo Domingo. Las Casas, though, continued to petition on behalf of the Tainos; in 1515 the cardinal accepted las Casas' suggestion that the sugar mills substitute **African slave labour**, which was used successfully in Portugal's West African colonies, setting in motion the African slave trade that was to dominate the New World economy for the next four centuries.

Sugar, slaves and pirates

As the gold economy ground to a halt, sugar swiftly filled the gap as the island's primary source of income. Numerous rural **sugar mills** sprouted up in the 1520s, leading to an exponential increase in the importation of slaves. The mill owners quickly formed a new colonial upper class and increased Spain's earnings on the island a hundredfold. Less wealthy colonists were forced to subsist by hunting the herds of wild livestock that roamed throughout the island, descended from the cattle brought over by Columbus and Ovando. Meanwhile, the several hundred remaining Tainos came together under the banner of a bandit named **Enriquillo** in 1526 and took to raiding the plantations from their base in the Sierra Bahoruco. As a matter of policy they would free any slaves they discovered, who joined the growing bands of escaped African slaves known as **cimarrones** – literally, "wild animals" – who were colonizing the island's nearly impassable mountain ranges. *Cimarrón* ranks expanded to such an extent that by the 1530s the Spaniards would only travel outside their plantations in large, armed groups.

The Spaniards also began to run into trouble with **piracy** in the 1540s. For most of the sixteenth century, Spain was at war with both the British and the Dutch and as part of their tactics these nations commissioned **privateers** – royally sanctioned and funded pirates – to infest Caribbean waters, boarding stray Spanish ships and absconding with their cargo, or raiding and torching isolated plantations. Havana was subsequently chosen by the Spanish as the designated stopping point between Spain and the silver

1509	1516	1518	1568
Diego Columbus succeeds Ovando as Governor	The sugar industry is launched in earnest	First licences granted to bring slaves directly from Africa specifically to work on sugar plantations	The number of enslaved Africans reaches 20,000

mines of Mexico and Peru. Ships headed for Santo Domingo or Puerto Plata had to break off from the fleet upon arrival in the Caribbean and brave the pirate-choked waters alone, which discouraged most merchants from doing business here. Aside from Santo Domingo, which managed to maintain some legal exports, Dominican ports were forced to rely on **contraband** trade with foreigners. By the 1550s this was the sole engine of the local economy.

Colonial decline and French encroachment

After fifty years of futile attempts to force towns along the northern and western coasts of Hispaniola to cease their contraband trade, the Crown decided to wipe them out. In 1605 Governor Antonio de Osorio was ordered to burn the colony's outer towns to the ground and forcibly resettle their residents in the countryside surrounding Santo Domingo. This disastrous action, known ever since as the **devastaciones**, permanently crippled the island's economy.

French and British adventurers took advantage of Spain's sudden retreat into a corner of Hispaniola to colonize the island of **Tortuga**, just off the northwestern coast, in 1629. Despite periodic Spanish raids, the new colony, whose inhabitants survived by pirating, growing tobacco and buccaneering (the hunting of wild livestock on Hispaniola), continued to prosper.

In 1640 the **French** kicked the British out and organized the notoriously unruly outpost into an official colony, from which they expanded onto the northern coast of present-day Haiti. Years of ferocious cat-and-mouse fighting ensued between the two remaining powers until, in 1697, the **Treaty of Ryswyck** was signed, establishing the borders as they are today at the north and south coasts, but leaving open the question of rights to the interior as a large chunk of it continued to be claimed by both countries. The French were gradually outdoing the Spaniards, however, and by 1725 the French colony **St-Domingue** (modern-day Haiti) had become the most prosperous colony in the Caribbean.

The Haitian revolution and occupation

French St-Domingue's unparalleled commercial success relied entirely on the mass importation of African slaves – during the eighteenth century slaves outnumbered Europeans and mulattos by more than ten to one. This unstable situation was made worse by the persecution by whites of the growing **mulatto** class. As the mulattos began arming themselves in the eighteenth century in order to win back rights that were increasingly denied them, the **white planters** meanwhile fashioned themselves as democrats in the style of Thomas Jefferson and plotted a revolution in which they would continue the slave system but end the burdensome tax demands of France. Of course, **African slaves** had the most to complain about, being forced to work twenty-hour days of backbreaking labour and subjected to all manner of hideous tortures and abuses.

On August 14, 1791, a Voodoo priest named **Boukman** held a secret convocation of hundreds of slaves from plantations across the colony, declared the independence of the new black republic called "**Haiti**" – the Taino word for the island – and sparked a

1586	1629	1640	1697
Francis Drake occupies and sacks Santo Domingo	The French and British colonize Isla Tortuga	The French oust the British, take control of Tortuga and expand their territory on Hispaniola	Island officially divided into Spanish and French halves

colony-wide revolution in which half of the plantations were burned to the ground within three months. Boukman was killed in the initial fighting, but **Touissant L'Ouverture**, a black slave who had served in the colony's French militia, quickly took over leadership of the revolt, which led to three decades of intense military activity along the Dominican border.

Spain saw the revolt as a perfect opportunity to gain control of the entire island. By promising freedom to all St-Domingue's slaves, they won the allegiance of L'Ouverture and his troops and soon conquered much of France's inland territory; after the bloody defeat of the British, they seemed set to take over the rest of the island. However, when the French responded by freeing the slaves, Touissant abruptly switched sides and his army forced Spain back to its old borders. In 1800 Napoleon rescinded the emancipation, provoking Touissant into declaring independence, formally setting up a Haitian constitution and government, and, in 1801, invading the Spanish colony to protect his eastern flank. This was the first of several invasions that would set the tone for Dominican attitudes toward Haitians into the twenty-first century. They included a 23-year occupation starting in 1822 during which the slaves were freed and major, highly chaotic land redistribution took place.

In the context of the unrest caused by the Haitian occupation, a number of white intellectuals in Santo Domingo formed the **Trinitarian movement** in 1838 under the leadership of **Juan Pablo Duarte**, a merchant whose business had been ruined by Haitian reforms. The Trinitarians plotted with dissatisfied Haitian army officers, wealthy mahogany exporter **Buenaventura Báez** and rich cattle rancher **Pedro Santana** in coordinating a **military coup** in February 1844.

For the rest of the nineteenth century the new Dominican state would be plagued by incessant internal strife. This was the era of the **caudillos**, strongmen based in every region of the country who commanded large armies of local peasants and who were usually far more interested in lining their own pockets than running the country. In large part, *caudillo* power was made possible by the constant fear of **Haitian invasions**, which occurred periodically and necessitated large armies to repel them. Once the Haitian army was dealt with, the *caudillo* forces would generally march on Santo Domingo and place their leader in power, a pattern that began at the very outset of Dominican independence. Both Báez and Santana were venal and corrupt and collectively flushed the Dominican economy down the toilet. In 1861 Santana went as far as betraying the country by selling it back to Spain in exchange for a large sum of money.

Spanish annexation and the Restoration

Under the terms of the **Spanish annexation**, finalized in 1861, General Santana retained military command of the new Spanish province but it quickly became apparent that the Spaniards planned to remove him from power; he had been deposed by mid-1862. The new Spanish authorities managed to efficiently alienate the Dominican populace through **discrimination** against the mulatto majority, who were constantly reminded that they would have been slaves in the neighbouring Spanish colonies of Cuba and Puerto Rico.

Having had their rights gradually eroded for two years, several hundred Dominicans rebelled at Santiago in February 1863, initiating the **War of Restoration**. Spanish soldiers

1791	1801	1822
Following a slave revolt in the French half of the island, the independent black republic of Haiti is declared	Haitian leader Touissant L'Ouverture invades the Spanish half of the island	Haitians invade and take control of the Spanish colony, beginning a 22-year occupation

marched on the city and dispersed the rebels quickly, but most fled into the mountains along the border – under the protection of the Haitian government – and engaged in **guerrilla raids** on Spanish targets. In August of the same year, the rebels launched an offensive and took control of the Cibao, burning Santiago to the ground in September in order to supplant the Spanish troops there. The Spaniards lost far more soldiers, though, to tropical disease; by the end of their occupation over 12,000 of their troops were dead from yellow fever. Realizing the futility of the war and not willing to sacrifice thousands more ground forces, the Spaniards began **negotiations** with the rebels, who were themselves in political disarray, and finally left unconditionally in July 1867.

Chaos and caudillos

The overthrow of Dominican rebel leaders during the War of Restoration presaged the most **chaotic period** in Dominican politics by far. By the time the Spaniards departed, the main towns were in ruins and across the island dozens of *caudillos* were fighting among each other for power. Guerrilla general **José María Cabral**, for example, had control over most of Barahona and the southwest during the war, but was in a precarious position because he relied on financial support from Buenaventura Báez's old mahogany-exporting partners in Azua. In Santana's old stomping ground, the southeast, cattle rancher **Caesario Guillermo** had cobbled together a coalition of former *Santanistas* that gave him regional ascendancy, while wealthy Puerto Plata tobacco exporter **Gregorio Luperón** had a firm hold of the north coast. The rest of the nineteenth century featured a dizzying series of military coups that left the nation in tatters. By the time military strongman **Ulises Heureaux** was **assassinated** in Moca in 1899 by the Cibao tobacco merchants he had been begging for a loan, the country's debt was over 35 million pesos, fifteen times the annual budget – and all revenues were administered by an American company that was entitled to take one-third for themselves.

The American occupation

The twentieth century began with the election of two Cibao politicians who promised to end the cycle of *caudillismo*, president **Juan Isidro Jimenes** and vice president **Horacio Vásquez**. This promise went unfulfilled, though, as by 1902 the two had fallen out over the division of patronage to their respective supporters, and their personal rivalry, and that of their followers, dominated the next decade. As civil war between various permutations of *Jimenistas* and *Horacistas* raged on (and on and on), the United States had become increasingly concerned that this endemic chaos would harm their military interests. Of particular concern were the massive debts that had accrued to European banks and the fact that, since the start of the twentieth century, various European powers had been sending naval warships to Santo Domingo in an effort to intimidate the Dominican government into honouring its financial commitments. The Americans were increasingly active in their defence of the **Monroe Doctrine**, which gave them the self-ordained power to dominate the hemisphere without the interference of Europe, and feared that the Germans might use the Dominicans' failure to pay their debts as a pretext to invade and set up a naval base at Samaná. To preclude this they insinuated

1844	1861	1863	1865
Independence is won and the Dominican Republic is founded	Spain annexes Dominican Republic	War of Restoration	The Dominican Republic wins independence for a second time

themselves further and further into the country's governance. When Cáceres was murdered by soldiers loyal to **Desiderio Arias**, a token *Jimenista* in the Cáceres cabinet, thereby launching the bloodiest period of civil war in the nation's history, the Americans sent a **Pacification Committee** to negotiate an end to the strife, nominating neutral Archbishop Alejandro Nouel to be the new president.

However, no sooner had the archbishop assumed office than Arias began another military coup that occupied the presidential offices. The Americans sent another commission suggesting the election of a *Horacista*, Congressman **José Bordas Valdez**, who was accepted by all parties as a temporary solution until democratic elections could be held. But Bordas quickly manoeuvred to stay in power, aligning with the *Jimenistas* and naming Arias his secretary of defence. When Bordas sold the Cibao railroad in 1913 to *Jimenista* interests, the *Horacistas* revolted, which brought yet another American commission that promised democratic elections in return for peace. Despite their assurances, the **January 1914 elections** were rigged by Bordas, who got a new million-dollar loan and kept the support of the increasingly intrusive Americans by agreeing to the direct US control of public expenditure.

Through his concessions to the Americans, Bordas alienated both Dominican parties and the *Jimenistas* and *Horacistas* combined in a new revolt to remove him from power. US President Woodrow Wilson responded in June 1914 with the **Wilson Plan**, which gave the Dominicans three months to end hostilities and choose a president, after which time the US Marines would intervene and impose a government on them. **Jimenes** beat Vásquez by a wide margin in the October elections and reinstated Arias as secretary of defence. From the start, he came into conflict with the Americans by refusing to recognize the American comptroller – who still controlled public expenditures – and rebuffed US demands that a **national police** be created under direct American command. The US meanwhile **occupied Haiti** in July 1915, with the implicit threat that the Dominican Republic might be next. The pretext came when Arias staged a military coup in April 1916. US Marines were sent into Santo Domingo to "protect the lives of resident foreigners"; by May they had taken control of the capital and were steadily expanding into the rest of the country. When a new government refused American demands in November, President Wilson announced a formal **military occupation**.

From 1916 to 1924 the **US Navy** administered the Dominican Republic from its base in Santo Domingo. While in power, the Americans reorganized the tax system, accounting and administration, built a new system of highways and improved primary education. They also allowed American products to flow into the country without taxation, censored the press, banned firearms and constructed a repressive **National Police Force** with which they battled and tortured various **guerrilla factions** that staged raids on US targets from the mountains. In the east, the highly organized **Gavilleros** bandits, operating in groups of thirty, harassed the invaders for the duration of their stay. Nevertheless, this was an economic boom time for the nation, largely due to the destruction of sugar beet farms in France during World War I, which led to skyrocketing sugar prices and produced the prosperous era known as the **Dance of Millions**, when old fishing villages like San Pedro and La Romana were transformed into more cosmopolitan port cities – though they were not to stay that way. In 1921 Warren Harding replaced Wilson as US president; having attacked Wilson during the

1879	1906	1916	1924
Gregorio Luperón seizes power, becoming the 20th official president of the republic, the 12th since 1865	The US assumes control of the Dominican Republic's customs department	US occupation begins	US occupation ends

campaign for the continued, in his view immoral, American presence in Hispaniola, Harding demanded a quick withdrawal from the island upon taking office. The Americans' initial demands to keep control of the National Police were refused and they left in 1924 with only customs still under their control.

The Trujillo era

The most devastating consequence of the US occupation was the formation of a National Police trained in the repressive techniques of an occupying force. The Americans had thought that this would end the power of the *caudillos*, but the new order produced instead a super-*caudillo*, **Rafael Leonidas Trujillo**, who was to maintain totalitarian control over the Dominican Republic for three decades. When the Americans left, Horacio Vásquez became the new Dominican president and appointed Trujillo chief of the National Police in recognition of his loyalty. In 1930, though, with Vásquez desperately ill, Trujillo staged a military coup that forced his former boss from the country. Sham elections were held later that year: Trujillo's police shot several other candidates and broke up all opposition rallies and the vote was rigged to ensure his success.

Over the next 31 years, Trujillo transformed the entire country into his **personal corporation** and appointed family members to the highest positions in the government. He operated monopolies in sugar, salt, rice, beef, milk, cement, cigarettes and insurance; he deducted ten percent of all public employees' salaries (which ostensibly went to his political party); operated two large banks; and received a percentage of all prostitution revenues. By the end of his regime, he directly employed sixty percent of the Dominican workforce. To this end he transformed **Santo Domingo** from a mere administrative capital to the centre of the nation's industry, initiating the urban expansion that continues to this day.

Trujillo's regime was one of the most astonishingly intrusive and **oppressive** in Latin American history. All citizens were required to carry identification cards that identified them by number; if they couldn't provide the police with a good reason for why they were walking the streets at a certain time, they were arrested. Real and suspected political opponents were imprisoned, tortured and assassinated by the thousands. But his most horrific accomplishment was manifested in **Operación Perejil** (see box, p.270), in which between 20,000 and 25,000 Haitian peasants, who had been farming on the Dominican side of the border, were exterminated.

Trujillo styled himself as a major player on the international scene, if one with little to no consistency, professing admiration for Hitler while at the same time accepting thousands of German Jewish refugees during World War II; taking a strong anti-Communist stance during the Cold War; murdering exiled Dominican scholars who spoke out against his regime in the United States; and even attempting the assassination of Venezuelan president Rómulo Betancourt in 1959. For most of his rule, Trujillo was actively supported by the **United States** because of his professed anti-Communism. President Franklin D. Roosevelt's classic line describing American policy in Latin America during the Cold War was made in reference to Trujillo: "He may be an SOB, but he's *our* SOB." In the late 1950s, though, Cuba's Fidel Castro took an interest in overthrowing the dictator and concerns about a possible

1930	1937	1940
The chief of the National Police, Rafael Trujillo, stages a military coup and takes control of the country	Under Trujillo, Dominican army massacres over 20,000 Haitian peasants farming on Dominican side of border	US signs treaty with Trujillo, handing back control of customs department

OPERACIÓN PEREJIL

The **genocide** began on the night of October 3, 1937, when hundreds of soldiers ambushed a religious procession outside Bánica and killed several hundred Haitians who had crossed the border to worship. For the next two months soldiers singled out and murdered as many **Haitians** as they could identify living in the Dominican Republic. The police distinguished the Haitians from the Dominicans by inducing them to say the word *perejil* ("parsley"), which native Kreyol-speakers tend not to be able to enunciate properly, lisping the letter "r". The captives were then sent to **"deportation" centres**, where they were processed (so that it seemed they had been deported), and subsequently taken out at night in small groups and hacked to death with machetes; their bodies were fed to the sharks in the Bahía de Manzanillo.

Communist takeover prompted the CIA to train a group of Dominican dissidents, who **assassinated** Trujillo in a dramatic car chase on the highway between Santo Domingo and San Cristóbal on May 30, 1961.

Fledgling democracy and American intervention

Upon Trujillo's death, vice-president **Joaquín Balaguer** rose to power under the tutelage of the Trujillo family, who had responded to the dictator's murder with multiple arrests, tortures and murders of political opponents, both real and imagined. A series of new opposition political parties was formed despite this repression, most notably writer **Juan Bosch**'s Partido Revolucionario Dominicano (PRD), which banded together with reform-minded military officers and threw the entire Trujillo family out of the country in 1961 – but not before the Trujillos absconded with over US$100 million of government money. The following year, Balaguer was forced into exile as well thanks to a nationwide strike that paralyzed the country for three months. **Democratic elections** were held in December of 1962, which were won in a landslide by Bosch. The PRD set out to re-establish **civil liberties**, ending the system of identification cards and lending funds to new, independent newspapers and radio stations. Bosch had few friends in the military, however (he had mistakenly been labelled a Communist) and in September 1963 a military junta deposed him. This military council was extremely unpopular and for the next two years the opposition parties of Bosch and Balaguer joined forces with a minority of the military officers. On April 24, 1965, the PRD's communications director, **José Francisco Peña Gómez**, announced over the radio that the revolution had begun and tens of thousands of people took to the streets in the capital. The **popular uprising** took control of the entire city and was preparing to launch a strike on the San Isidro Air Force Base east of the city – the military's last stronghold – when US president **Lyndon Johnson**, under the mistaken belief that the uprising was a Communist takeover that would create "another Cuba", sent 45,000 troops into the capital on April 28 and installed a temporary military junta composed of officers from San Isidro; the possibility of a more democratic, peaceful regime was therefore thwarted by American paranoia. A new election was called for June 1966, with Balaguer and Bosch the main candidates, but Balaguer's troops, a holdover from the Trujillo forces, assassinated and intimidated hundreds of PRD supporters and placed

1960	1961	1962	1963
Organization of American States imposes diplomatic sanctions on DR	Trujillo assassinated	Juan Bosch and the Partido Revolucionario Dominicano win general election	Bosch deposed by a military junta

Bosch under house arrest. As a result, Balaguer won the election by a slim margin and was installed as president for the next twelve years.

The Balaguer era

Balaguer began his regime in 1966 by founding a secret police unit called **La Banda**, which carried out the assassination of hundreds of his political enemies under the auspices of an "anti-Communist" campaign and clamped down on newspaper and television stations that were critical of him. He did, however, continue the programme of **industrialization** begun under Trujillo, this time funded by foreign investment. Much of the government's budget was provided by assistance from USAID, the IMF and the World Bank; a sugar quota was established with the United States that insulated the sugar mills somewhat from world price fluctuations; and plans to turn the country into a centre for tourism were developed. Political opposition was restricted to PRD members, many of whom were in exile in the United States, including Bosch in New York City, who felt that the PRD had moved too far to the right and so formed a new party, the **Partido de la Liberación Dominicana (PLD)**, leaving **Peña Gómez** to assume command of the PRD. By cultivating the endorsement of the rural peasants and urban poor throughout the 1970s, Peña Gómez became something of a national hero, though for a long while he was prevented from running for public office by La Banda's terrorist activities.

Despite Balaguer's violence against the citizenry and the widespread **corruption** of his government, he enjoyed US political and financial support until the election of **Jimmy Carter** in 1976. Under US pressure, La Banda was disbanded and elections were held in May 1978. Upon PRD presidential candidate **Antonio Guzmán**'s resounding victory, Balaguer's troops turned off all electricity throughout the country, stormed the election centre, beat the polling officers and burned many of the ballot boxes, declaring themselves the victors the next day. Carter refused to recognize the election and pressured the Organization of American States to follow suit. When it was clear that no further economic aid was coming and that the sugar quota was about to be suspended, Balaguer gave up and stood down in favour of Guzmán.

Guzmán fired Balaguer's cronies in the military and reinstated freedom of the press, but he also set about transforming himself into a new *caudillo*. His children, relatives and friends took all the country's key posts and millions of pesos were printed, wrecking the economy, so that he could hire hundreds of PRD members to newly created government jobs. Despite this attempt to buy them off, the PRD leadership denounced him for betraying the party's ideals and nominated **Salvador Jorge Blanco** for the next presidential election in 1982. Guzmán tried to convince the military to have Blanco assassinated before the election, but they would have none of it. When Blanco defeated Balaguer in the election and took office in May 1982, Guzmán became increasingly depressed and in July he committed suicide. Faced with the economic crisis created by his predecessor, Blanco was forced to negotiate an austerity package with the **International Monetary Fund** that cut salaries, raised prices and put restrictions on imports. So that he wouldn't be associated with these unpopular moves, Blanco initiated a propaganda campaign against the IMF even as he was negotiating a deal with them. This proved to be a fatal blunder, for when he implemented the Fund's

1965	1966	1978
US troops occupy DR	Joaquín Balaguer, a Trujillo protégé, wins presidency after a campaign of intimidation	Antonio Guzmán wins election after 12 years of Balaguer rule

reforms in April 1984, a massive three-day riot broke out in the capital that was quelled only after the army had killed dozens of protesters. Once implemented, though, the reforms worked, stimulating agriculture, strengthening the peso and creating growth. The unpopularity of the package nevertheless carried serious political consequences and Balaguer forced Blanco out of office in the election of 1986.

Balaguer's first priority was the **persecution of Blanco** so that he would never challenge for the presidency again. For an entire year, Balaguer staged weekly television broadcasts in which he denounced Blanco's administration as thoroughly corrupt and tore apart the former president's reputation. Blanco remained silent under the weight of these attacks and before long public opinion was firmly against him. He was finally arrested and imprisoned in April 1987, upon which he had a heart attack and was released for medical treatment in the United States. Though he was tried in absentia, found guilty and sentenced to 25 years, in the early 1990s he returned to the country and appealed the decision – Balaguer dropped the case in exchange for Blanco's promise to never enter politics again.

On the economic front, Balaguer dedicated himself to the total **reversal of the IMF austerity plan.** He set the official rate of exchange between pesos and US dollars at a ridiculously high rate, forbade public transactions in foreign currency and forced all businesses and tourists to convert their hard currency at the government's Central Bank at the artificial exchange rate. He also printed millions of new pesos without backing, a move that resulted in high inflation and an economic recession. In 1989 Balaguer exacerbated his problems by refusing to pay back the country's debts to foreign banks. Credit was cut off and access to essential goods – including medicine, electricity and oil – were shut down, creating the worst economic crisis of the century. Regardless, Balaguer managed to edge Bosch and Peña Gómez out in the **election of 1990**, though each got approximately a third of the vote, through a fraud that took thousands of Peña Gómez's rural supporters off the rolls and a virulent campaign that depicted Bosch as a corrupt Communist and Peña Gómez as a Voodoo priest.

Recession and power blackouts dominated the next four years, though Balaguer heaped hundreds of millions of dollars on extravagances like El Faro (see p.67) and the Gran Teatro del Cibao (see p.215). His popularity had waned to such an extent by the **election of 1994** that his only hope was a systematic, nationwide vote fraud. The same tired faces reappeared for this presidential contest: 84-year-old Balaguer, 82-year-old Bosch and 74-year-old Peña Gómez. Of these, only Peña Gómez generated much enthusiasm from his traditional constituency and all the polls had him ahead by a wide margin. But in his usual fashion Balaguer managed to destroy tens of thousands of his opponents' votes after a count that took three months to complete. Election monitors led by former US President Carter documented hundreds of irregularities by Balaguer supporters and to quell another **nationwide strike**, Balaguer agreed to reduce his new term to two years.

Hurricane Hipólito

Peña Gómez was the only one of the three latter-day *caudillos* to take part in the 1996 election: Balaguer didn't run as part of his 1994 deal and Bosch decided to make way for his young protégé **Leonel Fernández**, who edged Peña Gómez by a few thousand

1984	1986	1996
In the face of an economic crisis, IMF austerity measures implemented	Balaguer is re-elected president	Two years into his sixth term as president, Balaguer is forced to step down after irrefutable accusations of election fraud

votes. The **rapid growth in tourism** and the end of Balaguer's restrictions on hard currency helped pull the country out of its decade-long recession and Fernández's first term in office is remembered for giving the Dominican Republic the fastest-growing economy in the entire hemisphere for four straight years, though little actual legislation changed with the turnover in power thanks to a strong majority for Balaguer's party, the PRSC, in both houses of Congress.

The 1998 **local and congressional campaigns** were the freest in the nation's history, with no restrictions on campaigns and rallies and with independent monitors to verify a lack of corruption in the vote count. Peña Gómez ran for mayor of Santo Domingo, but died of cancer a month before the vote. As a result, a tremendous wave of nostalgic fervour for the man who had championed the poor swept the country and his party, the PRD, took a **majority in Congress**. In 2000 the PRD built on this momentum when **Hipólito Mejia** was named the nation's president, succeeding Fernández.

The Mejia administration was an unmitigated financial disaster for the Dominican Republic. Abject incompetence in the handling of the Dominican economy led to a huge recession, near-constant blackouts and spiralling inflation that knocked two-thirds off the value of the Dominican peso. Job growth was nil and government debt climbed out of control as Mejia appointed tens of thousands of PRD political apparatchiks to unnecessary government jobs. Even worse, a massive bank scandal robbed the Dominican economy of billions of dollars. **Hipólito**, as Mejia is unaffectionately known, was voted out by a landslide in 2004, in favour of a resurgent Fernández, who was able to bring government spending under control and begin work to stabilize the peso.

Stability and modest growth

Fernández was re-elected in 2008, which was a testament to the kudos he had earned – both at home and internationally – for his handling of the **economy**. Having served his maximum two terms, he could not run in the 2012 election, but relative political and economic continuity was ensured when fellow PLD candidate **Danilo Medina** was elected, defeating Hipólito Mejia and consolidating the party's power, with the PLD controlling both houses of Congress.

Under the PLD, **inflation**, which once threatened to spiral out of control, has been largely tamed and there have been some significant large-scale public works projects, including the ambitious programme to build a six-line **subway system** in Santo Domingo, the first two lines of which are already complete, and the expansion of the interprovincial road network. Despite this public spending, however, unemployment and poverty rates remain high.

The Dominican Republic today

Despite recent economic growth, glaring **social inequities** remain entrenched – and the jobs being created often don't pay enough to pull workers above the poverty line. The good news is that the **sugar monoculture** that existed for most of the twentieth century is slowly being replaced by a broader economy based on tourism, agriculture and industrial piecework, the last a result of the tax-free **industrial "free" zones** that have

1998	2000	2004
Hurricane George causes widespread devastation, leaving hundreds dead	After four years of economic growth under president Leonel Fernández, a new president, Hipólito Mejia, wins election	Fernández re-elected in landslide victory after economically disastrous presidential term of Mejia

been instituted across the island. These sectors cover land set aside for the construction of factories where the **minimum wage is suspended** and companies don't have to pay taxes to the Dominican government. The reality of this isn't great for most workers, although the zones have made for a marked increase in wage labour for **women**.

All-inclusive tourism constitutes an even bigger chunk of the economy but, as with the free zones, wages are low and hours long. Another downside is that government officials often seem unconcerned about the **environmental damage** that many resorts inflict on coastal mangroves and the wildlife habitat.

Money also comes from the hard currency poured into the economy by the million-strong **Dominican–American immigrant community** in New York City, which sends more than a billion dollars annually to relatives back home.

2008	2012
Fernández wins third term as president	Danilo Medina narrowly defeats Mejia in presidential election, ensuring at least 12 years of PLD rule

Environment and wildlife

The Dominican Republic occupies the eastern half of the most ecologically diverse island in the Caribbean, one that features more than six thousand indigenous flowering plants, a vast array of birdlife and ecosystems ranging from arid desert and tropical rainforest to dense mangrove swamps and towering, pine-covered mountain ranges. Much of this flora and fauna is found exclusively in the DR and nearly all is fairly easy to see – you'll find a wealth of tours focused purely on getting close to nature.

Specific highlights include: the **humpback whale nursing and mating grounds** in the Bahía de Samaná and within the Silver Banks Marine Sanctuary just north of the Samaná Peninsula; the mammoth **mangrove swamps** of Parque Nacional Los Haitises along the southern end of the Bahía de Samaná; the tall **pine forests** – interspersed with ribbons of deciduous **cloudforest** – and wilderness hiking trails of the sky-high Cordillera Central mountains; the thousands of flamingos and other tropical birds present around the Dominican Republic's many **lagoons**, especially Lago Enriquillo, where you'll also find American crocodiles and rhinoceros iguanas; the arid **desert** plains of both the southwestern and northwestern sections of the country and their diverse collection of cacti; the **virgin rainforest** in sections of the Sierra Neiba and Bahoruco mountain ranges in the southwest; the many large **cave systems** carved from porous limestone rock throughout the country; and the intact **coral reefs** along the far northwest coast, inhabited by brilliantly coloured fish.

Flora

Long-term **deforestation** from both commercial timbering and slash-and-burn subsistence agriculture has taken its toll on the Dominican Republic's once extensive forests, but several reforestation projects in parts of the Cordillera Central are beginning to repair some of the damage. Those willing to head a bit off the beaten path will still be able to find a wide variety of forest types within the DR, a small handful of them **intact virgin ecosystems**. The mountain ranges still contain hundreds of square kilometres of pine forest, along with scattered cloudforests, a few stretches of rainforest and dry forest mixing deciduous with ferns, palms and pines. At lower altitudes you'll find everything from mangrove swamps and wetlands to grassy, cultivated savannahs, arid deserts, and vast tracts of irrigated land denuded of its original vegetation and given over entirely to sugar cane.

Trees and shrubs

The DR is home to a wide array of **trees**, many of them endemic. Of special import to the local economy have been the precious woods that have been logged for centuries, particularly the **Hispaniolan mahogany**, which can still be seen in parts of the Cordillera Central, Sierra Bahoruco and Parque Nacional del Este. **Calabash** was used for gourds first by the Tainos and later by colonial *cimarrones* and today's rural farmers, while the **piñon**, known to the outside world as Mother-of-Cocoa, takes on enormous significance, both practical and religious. Known for its miraculous ability to grow back from a single branch, it is used by farmers for fencing off their land and for an easily replenished source of firewood. Meanwhile, it holds mystical significance for devotees of Dominican *Vodú*, in part because it "bleeds" red sap during the weeks leading up to Semana Santa. The sap is also a powerful poison used in local folk medicines and branches of the tree are used as staffs by rural faith healers.

The dominant tree in the pine forests, meanwhile, is the **Creolean pine**, another endemic species. Cedars, copeys, myrtle, laurel, cherry, wild sumac, juniper, walnut and cashew trees also proliferate in the mountains, whereas the deserts are dominated by a profusion of acacias, copeys, gumbo-limbos, frangipanis, mesquite, lignum vitae, poisonwood and sage. The deserts are also home to several varieties of cacti, some of them quite beautiful – particularly the **prickly pear cactus**, known locally as "Tuna", which bears beautiful white flowers and a fruit that's consumed raw by denizens of the Dominican Republic's southwest.

Of the sixty different types of palm tree spread across the island – most densely along the Samaná Peninsula – the graceful **Hispaniolan royal palm** is one of only a few thought to be indigenous; climbing to twenty metres or more in height, its leaves are used for rural roofing, the trunk for walls and the nuts for feeding livestock. The tightly bunched leaves of the **Hispaniolan hat palm** convey the illusion of a dark-green, frazzled wig high atop their fifteen-metre or higher trunks and are found most plentifully around Punta Cana. The classic **coconut palm** can be found there as well and along the beaches of Samaná; every part of their fruit is used for something or other, be it food or floor mats. On other parts of the Dominican coast you'll see lots of **sea grape**, a small gnarled tree with fan-shaped leaves, named for the extremely sour fruit that hangs from its branches; or the swamp-dwelling **gri gri** that are remarkably resistant to tropical storms and hurricanes and can be found along the island's lagoons and mangrove estuaries. Even more prevalent are **red mangroves**, though you'll also find **button mangroves** in the Bahía de Manzanillo and **white mangroves** in Parque Nacional Los Haitises. All the mangroves are central to the health of coastal ecosystems, affording protection from hurricane surges and providing a protected nursery for an array of sea creatures and birds.

Flowers

Flower farming and export is becoming a major business in the DR, largely because of the wide array of beautiful **tropical flowers** that are endemic here, including four hundred different types of **orchid**, over half of which grow in the Sierra Bahoruco. Also found throughout the island in abundance are **heliconias** and **bromeliads**, while **bougainvillea** can be seen along the coast west of Barahona, **hortensias** in the area surrounding Bonao, **frangipani** in the arid regions and **roses** in the flower farms of Constanza.

Fauna

Though not as diverse as the vegetation on the island, thanks in part to the number of species that have become **extinct** since humans have settled on Hispaniola, the animal kingdom in the Dominican Republic still has a colourful and vital presence, if often confined to habitats that are, out of necessity, cordoned off for preservation and run by the national government.

Marine life

Much of the **coral reef** – astonishingly complex ecosystems that support diverse marine life, from various algae to tiny crabs and eels, not to mention brilliantly coloured coral itself – that once ringed the entire island of Hispaniola has been destroyed by pollution, development and the careless practice of some subsistence fishermen, who make a habit of dropping anchor over the reef when they fish. The only place where you'll find a substantial stretch of intact reef – with an accompanying spectacular array of colourful sea life – is along the **northern coast west of Luperón**. Here in the reefs live a broad array of tropical fish, anemones, sponges and the like. Smaller, but quite beautiful, sections of the original reef survive at the eastern tip of the Samaná Peninsula, around Islas Saona and Catalina in the Parque Nacional del Este and at some points surrounding Parque Nacional Jaragua. Forty kilometres further out from the island's north coast, the rocky shelf that supports the island gives way abruptly to the 9000-metre **Brownson Trough**, one of the deepest underwater pits in the world and entirely unexplored. Along the edge of the trough north of the Samaná Peninsula sits another, largely unspoiled reef, protected by the Dominican government as the **Silver Banks Marine Sanctuary**, which also serves as feeding ground for large schools of dolphin and big fish and winter mating ground for thousands of humpback whales.

The **whales** are the single most spectacular marine animal inhabiting the surrounding waters and if you're not up for a week-long boat excursion to Silver Banks, you'll find plenty of day-trip boats to take you out to see them in the Bahía de Samaná every January and February. Other marine mammal life close to Dominican shores includes the highly endangered **manatee**, a famously gentle relative of the seal that ancient mariners may have mistaken for mermaids. More commercial species include **big fish** like marlin, swordfish, sea bass, snapper, mackerel, tuna and kingfish and **crustaceans** such as spiny lobsters, shrimp, crabs and sea urchins – the latter are shipped off en masse to Japan's restaurants.

Amphibians, reptiles and insects

Large **reptiles** are among the DR's most spectacular wildlife species, especially the **American crocodiles**, which grow up to nearly 5m in length and inhabit Lago Enriquillo, Parque Nacional Monte Cristi and Laguna Gri-Gri, as well as the salt-water Étang Saumatre just across the border in Haiti. Also evident in Lago Enriquillo, the northwest and the southwest are **rhinoceros iguanas**, which grow to 2m in length – at Isla Cabritos in Lago Enriquillo they are tame enough to feed and have begun to prefer sweet cakes over the cactus flower that was once their native food. A variety of smaller **lizards** inhabit virtually every corner of the island, including the **world's smallest reptile**, *Sphaerodactylus ariasae*, a miniature gecko discovered on Alto Velo in the nation's southwest that measures a mere 1.6 centimetres in length.

The tens of thousands of enormous **sea turtles** that laid their eggs on Hispaniolan shores during the time of Columbus are mostly a thing of the past, but some can still be found in the islands called Los Siete Hermanos outside Monte Cristi, along Playa Limón just east of Miches, and in parques nacionales Jaragua and del Este, along with Isla Tortuga off the northern coast of Haiti. Unfortunately, local hunting threatens to drive them to total extinction; turtle meat is used in soups, intact shells can fetch a high price and bits of shells are sometimes used as protective covers for roosters' claws in cockfights. The largest of the sea turtles is the appropriately named **leatherback**, which bears a thick, tough hide in place of a hard shell. Other species that inhabit the island are the **hawksbill**, extremely rare because its shell fetches such a high price on the black market; the stocky, small-headed **loggerhead**; and the vegetarian **green turtles** that lay their eggs en masse along the shores of Los Siete Hermanos. Tiny freshwater **slider turtles** can be found in the Laguna Cabral just north of Barahona. Further inland, the island is home to a number of small **tree frogs**, including – in a small zone of the Cordillera Central right around Pico Duarte – the astonishingly loud **coqui frogs** that were once thought only to live on Puerto Rico.

Insect life is abundant throughout the DR but numbers and diversity reach their peak in the mangrove estuaries and lagoons, particularly Parque Nacional Los Haitises. The arid country west of Barahona, though, is the best place for **butterflies**, and lepidopterists come to study the many varieties of swallowtail, monarch and flambeaus. Elsewhere, insect life makes itself known mainly through the variety of bites and sores incurred; **mosquitoes** are particular pests and can sometimes spread malaria and dengue fever, while **sand fleas** are a major problem along some of the island's beaches, particularly Punta Rucia, Playa Limón and Playa Monte Río.

THREATS AND RESTRICTIONS

Much of the Dominican Republic's natural beauty is **under threat** from the ongoing effects of deforestation and development. The government has been working hard to protect what remains of its wilderness by creating a series of **national parks and scientific reserves**, but their limited resources mean that upkeep of these areas is often less than perfect. Paying tourists play a vital role in the potential success of these projects and much relies on the willingness of visitors to be responsible and endeavour to support the vital educational programmes that seek to preserve these remnants.

It is **illegal** to buy most items that involve the use of wild animals or flowers in their production, though there is some trade in these products. This applies specifically to tortoiseshell, black coral, various species of butterfly, products made from crocodile skin and turtle shells. Trade in **living animals**, including tortoises, iguanas and parrots (often sold as nestlings) is also illegal. **Mahogany** once proliferated in Dominican forests but is now endangered. While the cutting of mahogany is restricted in the country today, the sale of mahogany products is still technically legal and the threat to its existence will doubtless intensify if people continue to buy it.

Birds

Some three hundred **bird** species make the DR their year-round home, including 27 **endemic species**. The endemics are a major draw for independent tour expeditions – including one that recently drew former US president and life-long birdwatcher Jimmy Carter to tour the Dominican outback. Among the endemics are the ridgeway hawk, narrow-billed tody, broad-billed tody, Hispaniolan parakeet, Hispaniolan parrot, Hispaniolan woodpecker, ashy-faced owl, black-crowned palm tanager, green-tailed warbler, white-necked crow, bay-breasted cuckoo and more. The **southwest** is of special interest for birders, with four large lagoons, two offshore islands, the Jaragua Peninsula and the Sierra Bahoruco holding a near limitless spectrum of birdlife.

The DR's many **lagoons and mangrove estuaries** have the widest variety of birdlife on offer, inhabited not only by thousands of **flamingos**, the most ostentatiously beautiful of the lagoon birds, but also herons, egrets, ibises, roseate spoonbills, cuckoos, black-cowled orioles and village weavers, the last an African import. The **freshwater lagoons** are also inhabited by eleven varieties of duck, alongside rails, jacanas and grebes, while the **mangrove coasts** add a number of seafaring birds, especially the entertaining brown pelicans, boobies, frigate birds, cave swallows and terns. Predatory birds in these areas include the occasional osprey and peregrine falcon.

In the **mountains** you'll find some of the most interesting native birds, including the endemic **Hispaniolan woodpecker**, a menace to local trees – and thus despised by *campesinos* – along with narrow-billed todies, red-tailed hawks, white-necked crows, thrushes, tanagers and siskins. The rare **Hispaniolan parakeet**, known locally as the *perico*, dwells in the Cordillera Central and sections of the Neiba and Sierra Bahoruco, while the endemic **Hispaniolan emerald hummingbird** – which you'll often see along the Pico Duarte hiking trails – is still widespread in the Cordillera Central and is occasionally found elsewhere on the island. Many mountain-dwelling birds have recently been placed at risk due to changes in coffee-growing practices. As much of the original tree canopy of the mountain ranges was destroyed over the last century, migratory songbirds adapted by nesting in the shade overstories that were traditionally used by coffee growers. The increasing popularity of espresso beans has caused farmers to do away with shade cultivation in favour of an open-air method that produces a stronger coffee, thereby destroying an important bird habitat. Happily, many of the **cooperative coffee plantations** that have recently sprung up around Jarabacoa stick to the old shade method, but species numbers are still plummeting.

Along the **open country** you'll find an enormous range of birds, though the most commonly espied are the **cattle egrets** that pick off insects stirred up by local herds and gather at dusk by the hundreds at a few select sites. Also around Bonao are the large **turkey vultures** that you'll see circling the countryside from high above; you may also catch a glimpse of the island's various warblers, honeycreepers, grackles, palmchats and terns. The yellow-black **village weavers** can be found seasonally in the western Cibao's rice fields, while caves, ruins and dense woodlands across the country are home to numerous **barn owls**. The **predatory birds** that dominate the flatlands are the endemic Ridgeway's hawk and the small, lizard-eating falcon known as the American kestrel. Today the **Hispaniolan parrot**, locally known as the *cottora*, is quite rare, its plumage all emerald but for a small spot of white on the forehead.

Land mammals

There are few **land mammals** in the Dominican Republic aside from pack animals and the dogs and rats brought over early on by the European colonists and still common denizens of city streets. Aside from a dozen different species of **bat**, which can be seen in the island's many caves, the only mammals native to the island are highly endangered and your only real hope of seeing them is at Santo Domingo's zoo. Of particular interest among these are the **solenodon**, a primitive nocturnal anteater with a comically long snout and the only insect-eating mammal native to the Caribbean; and the **hutia**, a one-foot-long, tree-climbing herbivore. Both also live in small numbers in parques nacionales del Este and Los Haitises.

Music: merengue, bachata and beyond

As its home turf, the Dominican Republic positively pulsates to the sound of merengue. It pours out of passing cars, thrums from boom boxes and blares from every shop front. And in the countless rural taverns and high-tech dance clubs that dot the island, merengue is the main item on every menu.

No wonder then that merengue's explosion onto the New York scene in the 1980s and ensuing dissemination across the globe is a source of intense pride for all Dominicans. The music is so closely identified with the local character that, for them, to love merengue is to love the island itself and the people who inhabit it. The 1970s icon **Johnny Ventura** has now returned home to become a major political figure. And multi-platinum Latin superstar **Juan Luís Guerra**'s (see box, p.284) conquest of the world, topping even the sales of crooner Julio Iglesias and winning multiple Latin Grammys in 2007, is an unparalleled national success story.

Certainly not all have caught the fever and public perception of merengue often involves the vision of Vegas-style performers lip-synching on a Spanish-language cable network. Let that not be your lasting vision, however; this ever-evolving musical style is just now coming into its own.

Roll call

As with all Afro-Caribbean genres, merengue is easily identified by its omnipresent **beat pattern**. When compared to salsa or calypso, the merengue pattern seems aggressively unsyncopated, its souped-up military rat-a-tat landing squarely on 1 and 3. But one of several interlocking patterns rattles through the rhythm section over this signature on-the-beat thump the way a city seethes around its neatly numbered grid.

The **instrumentation** is a blend of traditional rural orchestration with contemporary electronics and strong, salsa-influenced horn sections. **Saxophones** and **trumpets** are always present in contemporary bands, with a trombone occasionally added. The main purpose of the horns is to rip off a series of crisp, pyrotechnic riffs. The **bass** never strays far from thumbing out the underlying groove. The **piano** underlines the harmony with arpeggios and syncopated chord movement and is often electric. And that quintessential old-time instrument, the **accordion**, still makes an appearance in a few modern bands.

The **percussion section** is the backbone. The **congas** slap out a series of African beats that provide the primary fire and groove. The **tambora** is a two-headed lap drum that is anchored by a hand at one end and rapped with a stick at the other. Often a **bass drum** is used, an innovation that began as Dominican performers incorporated disco elements into their repertoire during the 1970s in order to stave off bankruptcy in the face of the Bee Gees. And always beneath its more ostentatious neighbours is the incessant scrape of the **güira** – traditionally fashioned from a kitchen utensil – a cultural inheritance of the Tainos who inhabited the island before Columbus, its tireless hoarse rasping like that of a dying man begging to be remembered.

Let us not forget those who skim the cream off this rich cross-cultural blend, getting most of the credit and all the wanton glances – the **singers**. The most traditional merengue voice is a reedy, nasal style that occasionally manages to be haunting amid the up-tempos. Guerra is the principal exponent today. But the more richly sonorous Latin tradition is evident as well, most notably in the work of Ventura, the Dominican answer to Elvis. Choruses tend to come in threes, engaging in extended call-and-response sections with the lead, which is swapped among them when there is no superstar. Meanwhile, they engage in virtuosic floor shows, dancing in split-second formations like the Temptations on speed and maintaining an impossibly fast hand jive. Bandleaders engage in the proceedings to varying degrees. Ventura's hip-swivelling histrionics are on a par with the legendary James Brown, while trumpet great Wilfrido Vargas maintains a dignified distance from his chorus's erotic foreplay.

Double and triple entendres involving sexuality and politics are standard procedure in the **lyrics**, while direct polemics are eschewed in favour of irony. "Dominicans have a wry sense of humour," says Guerra. "Irony works better than heavy messages and it's more fun!" In his writing, a first-rate poetry emerges using surrealistic images culled from *campesino* life. More often, though, merengue is the language of escapism and its lyrics seek to banish the exhausting outside world.

The immaculate conception

There are many stories regarding the **origins of merengue**, most of them patently apocryphal. One tale dates its inception to the Dominican Revolution against Haiti in the early nineteenth century. A soldier named Tomas Torres abandoned his post during a critical battle that the Dominicans later won and the first merengue song was composed by the victors to mock poor Tomas's glaringly unpatriotic survival instinct.

The main purpose of this fabrication is to shield Dominican society from the unsavoury fact that it was probably transported from Haiti and owes a debt to the traditions of Africa as well as Europe – an acknowledgement most Dominicans couldn't bear to make. Nevertheless, a musical form called **mereng** with an alarmingly similar rhythmic structure developed in Haiti (then St-Domingue) during the eighteenth century among the landed mulatto classes. Until the colony's last years, Europeans and Africans were allowed to intermarry, permitting some of African heritage to attain a level of power and wealth, even while others were subjected to the worst plantation slavery system of them all. The Europeans brought with them an abiding love of contra dance – the primary ballroom genre throughout the colonial Caribbean. Mereng was a "danza" form infused with African rhythm and is, incidentally, still current in Haiti, in a slower and more lilting form.

Meanwhile, the European settlers of Santo Domingo were from an early date subject to chastisement by their priesthood for excessive fervour while dancing. Merengue first infiltrated the country through the pueblos, via Haitian invaders and former French gentry fleeing the machete after the revolution across the border, from whence it made its way to elite urban ballrooms. There it encountered entrenched resistance from prominent literary figures, largely on the basis of its "African-ness". Victims of the latest dance craze were likened to virgins who had soiled their good names. From that point, any bumpkin musician who happened to innocently offer a merengue during a high-society dance set could expect to have a revolver pointed at him.

Utterly taboo in the ballrooms, merengue was left to the auspices of rural Dominican folk. Partly because it was easy to dance, partly because the lyrics were irreverent and lewd, it completely took over amid the vast agricultural stretches of the Cibao valley in particular. The Cibao's central city Santiago became the focal point for *merengue típico cibaeño*, still considered the definitive form.

One final touch was needed to achieve the classic form and it came, oddly enough, via Germany. The country was an important business partner for the Dominican Republic during the latter half of the century, buying a great deal of the tobacco grown in the Cibao plantations. Many German exporters made a side business out of selling accordions, which quickly made inroads into the merengue ensemble, replacing the older string instruments. This generated huge concern for the survival of traditional merengue, partly because the first accordions in the country played only in one major key, rendering them inflexible and banishing all minor-key merengues to the dustbin of memory for a time.

Latin exodus

Merengue was finally completely adopted as the national Dominican music by all segments of society during the **isolationist regime of Trujillo** in the mid-twentieth century. Trujillo used it to emphasize his peasant roots and gain popularity with the masses and a number of major stars emerged from the era, including ballroom king **Luís Kalaff** and saxophonist **Tavito Vásquez**, often called the Dominican Charlie Parker. A top-notch big-band group would follow Trujillo around on campaign stops and state radio stations blasted favourite tunes between edicts. The entrenched antipathy of the urban elite began to melt as **El Jefe** started to frequent their salons, a pistol in his pocket and a song in his heart, causing a stately ballroom merengue to re-emerge.

After Trujillo was assassinated, merengue was removed from the closet and there was no stopping it. The end of Trujillo's isolationist policies sparked a wave of migration to the major cities of North America, where Dominicans joined Puerto Ricans, Cubans and others in the vast urban barrios that served as cultural cauldrons from which modern Latin music fomented. Back home, Johnny Ventura was busy marketing his music to compete with the North American imports. Ventura was the first of the *merengueros* to fashion for himself a **pop icon status** similar to the ones being generated up north, using large-scale advertising, trademark floor shows and a sound more closely aligned with that of the American record industry. The end result for merengue was a sharp, stuttering momentum that the old style only hinted at.

The migration continued on an even greater scale in the 1980s due to a major recession. The increased Dominican presence in New York and Miami meant a much higher profile for the music. The resultant explosion onto the world music scene is still being felt, even as the encroachment of outside influences on this previously insular style has forever transformed it.

Wilfrido Vargas was the top star of this golden era, pushing the music into uncharted harmonic and rhythmic territory. Vargas has always been an interesting mix of culture and commerce and his band had started out playing bossa novas and rock'n'roll because he thought it was the best way to make a buck. For a time he even featured disco covers, though it apparently caused him a certain degree of embarrassment. When it became financially viable for him to focus solely on merengue, he was much more open to outside elements than artists of the past, incorporating forms such as salsa, compa, zouk, reggae and recently even house music and rap into his own native idiom. His experiments initially met a certain amount of resistance from the purists, but his expansion of the vocabulary is now considered orthodoxy. Other big stars have followed suit, notably singing-great **Cuco Valoy**, whose passion is Cuban music and calypso given a political slant.

Bachata blitzkrieg

The explosion of outside influences on traditional Dominican music gave rise to the towering figure of the last two decades, **Juan Luís Guerra** and his band, **4:40**. Weaned on a mixture of traditional merengue and Western pop influences such as the Beatles and Manhattan Transfer, Guerra has contributed a vast amount to the music, injecting South African choruses and Zairian guitar work, slowing it down to a more lyrical level, infusing it with rich vocal harmonies and writing some of the most beautiful song lyrics ever conceived. "I studied literature in Santo Domingo," he says, "and the lyrics reflect my enthusiasm for poets like Neruda and Vallejo." Many of the songs, such as *I Hope it Rains Coffee in the Fields*, betray an affinity with magical realism: "[That] comes from an anonymous poem I found when I went to the city of Santiago de los Caballeros. It's probably the work of a *campesino* – a peasant – and it was such a beautiful metaphor, I had to develop it."

This sentiment conveys the spirit and conflict behind Guerra's phenomenally popular sound. For even as he incorporates an ever-widening menagerie of world music influences ("You look in Juan Luís' bag," says one collaborator, "and you see West African tapes, South African tapes, Indian music – he's listening to a whole different thing"), it is his urgent life's work to produce a populist music to which the people back home can relate. The high poetry of his lyrics focuses on Dominican images and issues, such as *The Cost of Living*, addressing long-term economic stagnation, and *Guavaberry*, an indigenous fruit that causes the skin to itch upon contact, and the outside musical colours he inserts function strictly in the service of Dominican music.

Guerra really blew the lid off the Latin music charts when he turned to a disreputable Dominican fusion of Cuban bolero and *ranchero* called **bachata**. Long popular with the Dominican underclasses, bachata began as a twangy rural guitar form performed by *campesinos* during outdoor parties and was transported to the bars and brothels of the desperately poor outer barrios around Santo Domingo during the mass urban migrations of the 1970s and 1980s. In part because of its social context, bachata – like its predecessor, merengue – was at first looked down on with extreme distaste by Dominican society and it was impossible to even purchase a bachata record in a mainstream music store. This allowed a handful of enterprising bottom-feeders like record producer Radhames Aracena and his **Radio Guarachita** a near-monopoly on the production and sales of bachata stars like **Leonardo Paniagua**, **Melida Rodríguez** and legendary guitarist and singer **Luís Segura** – whose records were hawked informally from outdoor stalls alongside fried snacks and split coconuts. The signature hit of this era was Segura's *Pena*, a typically doleful look at the pain of unrequited love that sold somewhere around 200,000 copies in 1983 – even though bachata was still banned from the record stores.

Guerra's upper-middle-class background is not that of the usual *bachatero*, but he was smart enough to see through the negative stereotypes associated locally with the music and turn out an entire album of bachatas on his legendary *Bachata Rosa*, giving them a slick, commercial production along with his trademark lyrics and vocals. The album went platinum across Latin America and was at the tops of the Latin charts in North America and Europe, instantly making him the biggest name in Dominican music and completely transforming the perception of bachata back in the home country. Many of the original *bachateros* resent Guerra's sudden co-opting of their musical form, but his success has resulted in new-found respect and fame for them as well. Segura and Paniagua – both now in their 60s – today sell more albums than they did in their youth and are in demand for concerts worldwide, while a new generation of bachata stars has arisen – pre-eminent of whom are **Luís Vargas** and **Raulín Rodriguez** – who haven't had to face the old social barriers.

Merengue mañana

Bachata's place in the Dominican musical landscape has been permanently enshrined; listen to Dominican radio today and you'll hear at least one bachata tune for every two merengues. Most bands today stick to one or the other, but a growing movement of young musicians like **Antony Santos** and **Teodoro Reyes** has fused the two into a new

---

JUAN LUÍS GUERRA – OJALÁ QUE LLUEVA CAFÉ

Ojalá que llueva café	I hope it rains coffee in the fields
Ojalá que llueva café en el campo	that there falls a shower
que caiga un aguacero de yuca y té	of yuca and tea
del cielo una jarina de queso blanco	from the sky a tub of white cheese
y al sur, un montaña	and to the south, a mountain
de berro y miel	of butter and honey
oh, oh, oh, oh	oh, oh, oh, oh
Ojalá que llueva café	I hope it rains coffee in the fields

form – **bachatarengue** – which speeds up bachata's twangy guitar arpeggios and places them within merengue's up-tempo thump. The end result is a bit of a surprise – though the African roots of the two separate forms are not always obvious at first glance, bachatarengue sounds very much like Congolese soukous, an unintentional connecting of the fragmented strands of African music that survived in the Caribbean for five hundred years, bringing it back full-circle to its origin.

Another movement that has started to catch on – particularly in the Dominican barrios of New York and Boston – is **Dominican Roots**, a more conscious attempt to pay tribute to the African aspects of Dominican culture by a set of young musicians who grew up with the traditional *Vodú* music of the *campos* and outer barrios of Santo Domingo, then immigrated to the cities of the United States. Once in the States, many of these kids were shocked to find themselves considered "black" by their new society – which in turn sparked a renewed interest in the long-buried African influence on their home country. The grandfather of Dominican Roots music is **Luís Díaz**, whose 1970s ensemble Convite was part rock band and part ethnomusicological enterprise; they scoured the countryside learning about and recording the music that was played in villages across the island, then translated this folk music into a new rock-based idiom. But while Díaz's music attracted a sizeable cult following for twenty years, it wasn't until the mid-1990s that a slew of **emerging musicians** like Willian Alemán, Edis Sánchez, Tony Vicioso and the recently deceased Boni Raposo began setting up their

RENOWNED DOMINICAN MUSIC ARTISTS

Xiomara Fortuna
This woman is a true national treasure, though she's garnered more recognition in Europe and North America than in her home country. Both a singer and composer, she fuses traditional Dominican folk music with jazz and other styles.

Fulanito
By far the best of the merenhouse bands and with a huge following across Latin America. Although, like most merenhouse bands, their music fuses merengue with reggaeton and rap, they were one of the first groups to actually use house as well.

Juan Luís Guerra
Juan Luís Guerra and his band 4:40 have cut a swath through the field of Latin American popular music with their brand of magical-realist merengue fused with discreetly erotic lyrics and mildly critical socio-political themes.

Los Hermanos Rosario
The Rosario brothers have led one of the most popular merengue bands on the island and abroad for over fifteen years.

Luís Segura
The great star of pre-Guerra bachata, known as "The Father of Bachata" with a soulful, reedy voice that's truly timeless.

Francisco Ulloa
The greatest of the merengue accordionists. On some of his songs he also incorporates the marimbula, a descendant of the African thumb piano, a wooden box with strips of metal attached that when plucked give off a deep, reverberating thrum.

Cuco Valoy
Although Cuco Valoy – "El Brujo" as he is known – is from the Dominican Republic, he is as likely to perform salsa or Cuban-style son as merengue and bachata. He's equally virtuosic in all four styles.

Wilfrido Vargas
The legendary merengue innovator and dignified elder statesman who brought the influence of a dozen different world musical forms into the family.

Johnny Ventura
The Dominican Elvis did a lot to update the music and was the first *merenguero* to fashion for himself an image as a pop icon.

own roots-based ensembles. The music that they've created varies wildly – from Raposo's straight-ahead *Vodú* drum-and-chorus lines to Sánchez's psychedelicizing of Dominican *gagá* music and Vicioso's massive ensembles combining *rara*, *palos* drums and electronics – but in all of their groups you can hear the traditional rumba, calypso and merengue beats of the Caribbean, grooving just as hard as in mainstream Latin music but with a defiantly populist slant. Taking this trend a step further is singer **Xiomara Fortuna**, who is the first Dominican musician to ride this movement to the top of the world music charts in the West. Like other Dominican Roots artists, Fortuna co-opts the lesser-known beats of the countryside like *pri-pri*, *mangulina* and *salves*, but combines them with a more forward-looking production akin to contemporary West African pop.

DISCOGRAPHY

Abusadura – **Wilfrido Vargas** (Karen, US).
One of Vargas's most striking and popular recordings, with influences across world music and merengue versions of a couple of classic bachatas.

El Disco de Oro – **Luís Segura** (Kubaney).
Two-CD tribute that contains all of his classic hits, which span over twenty years of recording. The seminal song *Pena Por Ti* is deemed so important by the compilation's producers that it's included twice – once on each disc.

Los Grandes Exitos – **Juan Luís Guerra** (Karen, US).
First issued in 1996, this greatest-hits album remains the best introduction to Guerra's extensive oeuvre.

Guataco – **Johnny Ventura** (Kubaney, US).
A classic Ventura album with many of his hits. Great singing with an old-time saxophone sound (sort of an accordion impression with arpeggios and mile-wide, furious vibrato), even as the influence of disco begins to creep in.

Kumbajei – **Xiomara Fortuna** (Circular Moves)
Heavily influenced by contemporary West African pop, this album is filled with iconoclastic renderings of various traditional Dominican rhythms – which in her hands are utterly transformed into a new pop style.

La Llave de Mi Corazon – **Juan Luís Guerra** (EMI Televisa, US).
A return to his roots earned mega-star Guerra two well-earned Latin Grammys in 2007. A series of great pop-*chata* love songs, some acoustic guitar solo pieces and plenty of slick, hard-driving merengue as well.

¡Merengue! – **Francisco Ulloa** (Globe Style, UK).
Never has the accordion sounded like this. His most famous recording, featuring frantic arpeggios from accordion and saxophone, free-sounding triple-time bass and a driving throb from the tambora.

Salsa con Coco – **Cuco Valoy** (Discolor, US).
This collection of some of Valoy's greatest hits is well worth getting, not least because it contains perhaps his most famous song, *Juliana*, and the typically loopy *La Muerte de Don Marcos*.

Y Es Fácil! – **Los Hermanos Rosario** (Karen, US).
Los Hermanos Rosario best represent the exuberant excesses of merengue since the 1980s and this is the album for which they won a Latin Grammy, a high-octane, cardiac-arresting thrill ride through hit after hit.

Bachata Roja: Acoustic Bachata from the Cabaret Era (IASO, US).
Classic acoustic bachata recordings that display the virtuosity of guitar work and lyric genius of local legends like Blas Duran, Leonardo Paniagua and Augusto Santos.

Grandes Soneros: 100% Dominicanos (Camaleón, US).
Rare recordings of the Dominican Republic's great stars in the field of Cuban son – an absolute must for any Latin music lover's collection. Includes cuts from little-known but top-notch *soneros* who frequent the dark, dicey son clubs of Santo Domingo, like Santiago Cerón, Cuco Valoy, Manolé and Los Hijos del Rey.

Other emerging artists have instead been focusing on North American hip-hop, although most of the **merenhouse rap** at the top of the charts these days has yet to approach the best of either genre and is starting to get drowned out by the hipper **reggaeton** coming out of Puerto Rico and Panama. The fusing of merengue with house music is predictably decried in more traditional circles, but the history of merengue is an account of similar reinventions and consequent destructions; merengue has always adapted and survived. The genre's regular beat structure is well suited to house music fusions and many of the dance remixes work extremely well. The result is a slew of Latin rap ensembles with one ear on the *périco ripao* grooves of their parents and the other on the multilayered industrial urban noise of young African America. Those who grew up with the music can take comfort that the old forms lie embedded in the new like geological strata. The most prominent merenhouse band, **Fulanito**, for example, pays homage to the history of their music by large-scale sampling of the accordion and other traditional instruments, whispering in the background like a ghost memory.

Baseball

The Dominican Republic is responsible for a disproportionate number of today's top baseball players: just for starters, Robinson Cano, David Ortiz and Adrian Beltré are all household names in the United States; among the very best at their positions, they command salaries in excess of ten million dollars a year. It's the result of a century-long Dominican passion for the game that makes North American baseball fanaticism pale in comparison.

Dominican boys are exposed to baseball from almost the moment they're born and playing fields can be found in even the smallest villages. Dominican professional games command huge crowds and the successes and failures of Dominicans in the major leagues are televised across the country and assiduously reported in the newspapers. The veneration heaped on these home-grown players can't be overstated; when Sammy Sosa returned from his MVP season with the Chicago Cubs in 1998, he was greeted by a line of cheering locals for the full 40km from Santo Domingo's airport to his home town of San Pedro de Macorís.

Plantations to professionalism

In the late nineteenth century, the **United States** began to export its national pastime to countries around the world, especially those where it had some sort of military presence. The game was thus spread to Cuba, Central America, Mexico, Venezuela and Japan, though it would take slightly longer for the sport to take root in the Dominican Republic. Here its history is inextricably linked to the rise of sugar plantations in the 1860s, when wealthy **Cuban plantation owners** fled a revolution in their own country that freed their slaves and destroyed much of their property. Many resettled in Santo Domingo, where they founded several youth clubs devoted to baseball that weaned local kids away from football (soccer); others headed to the DR's southeast, buying land from the government, forcibly evicting any peasants who happened to live there and establishing sugar mills around tiny fishing hamlets La Romana and San Pedro de Macorís. In the 1880s the Cuban owners began providing minimal baseball equipment to their workers as a cheap diversion to keep up morale.

By the early twentieth century, the game had been adopted to such an extent that several **semi-professional ball clubs** were formed in Santo Domingo, Santiago, San Pedro and La Romana, both to play each other and face teams from Puerto Rico and Cuba in various tournaments. The **American occupation** that lasted from 1916 to 1924 resulted in further inroads, as military administrators saw baseball as a convenient way to insinuate US culture into the country. They provided money to form amateur Dominican clubs and purchase equipment, and organized their troops into teams that regularly played Dominican squads. The Dominicans, though, saw these games as a matter of pride; whenever they defeated a military club, impromptu parties carried on well into the night.

Towards the end of the occupation, **professional baseball** in the country took on the shape and structure that remains today, with two teams in Santo Domingo – Licey and Escogido – and one each in San Pedro, La Romana and even Santiago, which at the time was an arduous four-day mule-back trek for any visiting team. When **Rafael Trujillo** came to power in 1930, though, his son Ramfis – a rabid baseball fan – forced Licey's ownership to sell out to him and in turn signed some of the best talent in the country to contracts far too lucrative for local box-office revenues to support. For the Trujillos this was no problem; they had ownership of all major industries in the country and were rich enough to write off Ramfis' pricey hobby as a public relations expense. But the other teams followed suit in order to keep up – despite the fact that their owners depended far more on baseball earnings for their profits – and a tremendous bidding war ensued for both the best Dominicans as well as the cream of the crop from other Caribbean islands and the American Negro Leagues, whose black players were unable to break into the major leagues in the States until Jackie Robinson did so, in 1948.

The legendary 1937 season

In 1936, **San Pedro de Macorís** (a city the Trujillos hated for its opposition to their rule) beat Licey in the national championship behind Dominican sluggers **Tetelo Vargas** and **Mateo de la Rosa**, the first great batsmen the island produced. In response to his defeat, Ramfis joined Licey and Escogido together into a Ciudad Trujillo super-team that he hoped would restore the family honour. To counter this, San Pedro's scouts flew off to Pittsburgh to sign the top Negro League stars from the **Pittsburgh Crawfords**, which were run by local mobster Gus Greenlee. Despite being arrested on arrival – on orders from Greenlee – the scouts did, once out of custody, manage to sign the team's three best ballplayers (all three now in the baseball hall of fame): pitcher **Satchel Paige**, slugger **Josh Gibson** and lightning-fast centre fielder **Cool Papa Bell**.

These signings should have made San Pedro de Macorís invincible, but more bad fortune was to befall the scouts. Upon the representatives' return to San Pedro, Trujillo's men threw them in jail and government troops informed the three players that they would be suiting up instead for Ciudad Trujillo. Paige, Gibson and Bell were joined on that team by several other top Negro Leaguers and infielder **Perucho Cepeda**, father of hall-of-famer Orlando Cepeda and considered the best Latin player of his day. A third team, Santiago, got into the act, signing Dominican hero **Horacio Martínez** along with Venezuelan shortstop **Luís Aparicio** and Cubans **Luís Tiant** (father of the Boston Red Sox pitching star of the same name) and hall-of-famer **Martín Dihigo**, a versatile pitcher/outfielder who had played in Mexico, Venezuela, Cuba and the US, where he had the Negro League's highest batting average and lowest ERA (the mark by which pitchers are rated) in the same year.

The hard-fought battles between these three teams are still legendary in the Dominican Republic, though for Paige, Gibson and Bell the bizarre antics of the Trujillo family were probably more memorable. After Ciudad dropped the season opener to San Pedro, Paige reported that the team was surrounded by a phalanx of soldiers who fired their automatic weapons into the air while shouting, "The Benefactor doesn't like to lose!" If a fight broke out during a game, the National Police swarmed the field and clobbered the opposing team; meanwhile, the Americans were routinely jailed the night before a game to ensure they got a good night's rest.

After a gruelling regular season, the **Ciudad Trujillo Dragones** knocked off Santiago and faced defending champion San Pedro in a best-of-seven **championship series**. Taken from their prison cells to Quisqueya Stadium under armed escort, the Dragones were edgy enough that they dropped the first three games. For his part, Paige was firmly convinced that if they didn't come from behind to win the series they'd be going back to the States in pinewood boxes; he spent the entire series popping antacid tablets as he glanced warily from the dugout at the troops who surrounded the field. Fortunately, his theory was never tested: the Dragones took the next four games to win the national championship. A week-long city festival ensued, but the vast amounts of money used to finance the 1937 season bankrupted the other owners and **ended professional Dominican baseball** for ten years, shifting local sentiment to the **amateur national** team the country put together – using a unit of the Dominican army as Trujillo's personal farm club.

The English

Though professional Dominican baseball went into a tailspin, the sport was attracting a new generation of players and fans in the rural sugar *bateyes*. The most prominent such group was the Cocolos, also known as "**The English**", impoverished immigrants from the British Caribbean who came to the DR at the turn of the century as seasonal cane cutters and settled around San Pedro de Macorís. There was little to alleviate the misery of their squalid living conditions other than benefits from the Improvement Organizations founded in the 1910s by **Marcus Garvey**'s UNIA, which collected money for workers' medical expenses, held social events and created a sports league. This sports league, however, was for **cricket**, the pastime that the Cocolos had brought over from the British Antilles, but during the hype of the 1937 baseball season many were weaned from their native sport and won over to this new Dominican obsession.

At first the English ballplayers were largely ignored in the rest of the DR and excluded from the amateur national teams. **The first wave** of Dominican players to catch the eye of the newly integrated major leagues in the early 1950s came from the talent pool that had worked its way through the army and Trujillo's amateur team, including the Alou brothers, hall-of-famers Ozzie Virgil and Juan Marichal – all of whom were signed by the San Francisco Giants – and Dodger great Manny Mota. But when a team from **Batey Consuelo** north of San Pedro whipped the military team several years in a row in the 1950s, players from the *bateyes* began to gain far more prominence, being recruited for the national team and falling under the watchful eyes of American scouts. The first Cocolo to break through to the big leagues was slugger **Rico Carty** in the 1960s; shortly thereafter the majors would be swamped with the sons of San Pedro, including Pedro Guerrero, George Bell, Juan Samuel, Tony Fernández, Alfredo Griffin, Manny Lee, Julio Franco, Joaquín Andujar, José Offerman, Mariano Duncan, and Sammy Sosa, among others.

The modern game

Today, an astounding ten percent of the players in the US major and minor leagues comes from the Dominican Republic, more, in fact, than the rest of Latin America put together. Of those professional players, an equally astounding number hail from around the city of **San Pedro**, known in baseball circles as "the city of shortstops". This pipeline of talent has been honed into a **well-oiled business**, which has not been slowed down by the **steroid controversy** in the United States that has engulfed a number of top Dominican players including Alex Rodríguez; the downside of all the success – as much wealth and fame as it may bring both to individual players and to the country as a whole – is that Dominican baseball is no longer operating nearly as independently as it once did.

The old **Dominican professional league** alignment still largely exists: two Santo Domingo teams and one each from Santiago, La Romana and San Pedro de Macorís were joined by a team from San Francisco de Macorís in 1996. The six teams face off against each other in a regular **winter season** that features a blend of Dominican stars from the majors, up-and-coming young local talent and American minor leaguers looking to sharpen their game, often coached by retired stars like Santiago's Tony Peña. The champion of the winter season goes on to face off teams from Venezuela, Puerto Rico and Cuba in the Latin American championship.

Professional teams in the Dominican Republic, however, all enter into formal agreements with **North American clubs** and act as little more than a developmental team for the parent club. Meanwhile, fewer and fewer of the **best Dominican players** are willing to endanger multimillion-dollar careers by playing back home and they're strongly discouraged from doing so by their major league club, for fear of injuries. The entire country is scoured by **scouts** from professional teams in the United States, Canada and even Japan; most kids who display some talent are signed and whisked off to a major league camp by the time they're 16 or 17. As a result, many of the top young Dominicans never play professional ball locally.

But while other North American companies that move into the DR and take control of an economic sector are resented here, baseball's major leagues are positively lionized for it. Today every North American club has a complex in the DR where they recruit and train young Dominicans for up to three years before moving the best of the bunch on to their minor league system. Major league scouts have been known to commit a variety of **abuses** in the quest for cheap Dominican talent, including signing underage players, hiding prospects from their families so that they won't be stolen by another team and failing to pay out promised signing bonuses. Some of their jobs are being taken over by unofficial **buscandos**, who track down talented youngsters, sign them to an agreement and then auction them off to the highest bidder for a percentage of the signing bonus. The competitive fever pitch in search of the next Pedro Martínez or Sammy Sosa has climbed so high that the traditional attraction for major league clubs – inexpensive talent that can be bought for less than a third of what it would take to sign a comparable kid in the United States – is very much in danger. Ten years ago, **emerging stars** would have felt lucky to sign a US$3000, three-year development contract with a North American organization, but today they're being signed to minor league contracts in excess of $1 million per year. Meanwhile, less-coveted players as young as 13 and as old as 23 regularly purchase **fake birth certificates** to claim that they're 16 or 17 years old, the optimum legal age at which to begin training.

Books

Dominican literature is not very well known worldwide, mainly because so little of it is available in translation, but in the last decade or so there has been a surge in influence by a new generation of Dominican authors, most residing in the United States and writing in English, rather than Spanish. Led by Julia Alvarez and Junot Díaz, they have enjoyed both the critical and commercial success outside of DR that eluded many of their predecessors.

HISTORY

Bartolomé de las Casas *The Devastation of the Indies* (Johns Hopkins). A translation of the document that Las Casas, a priest who fought tirelessly for the rights of the Tainos, read to Spain's Ferdinand and Isabella in an effort to end colonial injustice against Native Americans.

Robert D. Crassweller *Trujillo: The Life and Times of a Caribbean Dictator* (Macmillan). Long out of print but remains the most thorough and accurate account of Trujillo's life and regime. An engaging read and impeccably researched.

Samuel Hazard *Santo Domingo Past & Present with a Glance at Hayti* (Dominican Ministry of Culture). A lively, if sometimes unsavoury in its racist commentary, mid-nineteenth-century account of travelling the entire country, written from the perspective of an American bureaucrat trying to push forward US annexation.

★ **Kris E. Lane** *Pillaging the Empire* (Sharpe). A terrific history of piracy in the Caribbean between 1500 and 1750, including snappy accounts of the buccaneers who hunted wild animals off Hispaniola's north coast and the pirates who made a lair of the Samaná Bay – among the memorable cast of characters are Jack Banister, Cofresí, Calico Jack Rackham, Sir Francis Drake, Henry Morgan, and female pirates Ann Bonny and Mary Read.

Abraham F. Lowenthal *The Dominican Intervention* (Johns Hopkins). A blow-by-blow analysis of the chaotic events that led to American intervention in 1965. The author uses this military action to prove that foreign policies are as controlled by bad analogies (in this case "Another Cuba") and insufficient intelligence as they are by rational strategies.

W.J. Nelson *Almost a Territory* (St Martin's). A lucid history of the various nineteenth-century attempts by the United States to annex either the Dominican Republic or the Samaná Peninsula. The colourful cast of characters, including Dominican *caudillos* Buenaventura Báez and Pedro Santana and US president Ulysses S. Grant, keep the book lively.

Thomas O. Ott *The Haitian Revolution* (Tennessee). The best account currently published in English of the slave revolt that created the world's first black republic on the western end of Hispaniola, including Toussaint L'Ouverture's occupation of Santo Domingo.

★ **Frank Moya Pons** *The Dominican Republic: A National History* (Hispaniola). Written and translated by the Dominican Republic's foremost historian, this is the definitive history of the country. A blessing since it first came out in 1995, as before then a good history of the country didn't exist in English.

Eric Paul Roorda *Dictator Next Door: The Good Neighbor Policy and the Trujillo Regime, 1930–1945* (Duke). An essential history of American presidents Herbert Hoover and FDR's failed "Good Neighbor Policy" in Latin America, detailing how Trujillo managed to maintain support in Washington by siding against first the Fascists and later the Communists, despite the blatant horrors of his regime.

★ **Irving Rouse** *The Tainos* (Yale). The definitive work of scholarship on the Tainos, tracing their migration from the Amazon river basin to the Antilles and their eventual extermination at the hands of the Spaniards. This book is a must if you're planning to see some of the Taino sites spread across the DR.

Richard Lee Turits *Foundations of Despotism* (Stanford University). Explores the entire history of the Dominican Republic with an emphasis on how the Trujillo dictatorship happened, concluding that Trujillo's real power came from his patrician empowerment of the peasant classes, who were a strong base of support throughout the course of his regime. Required reading for anyone who really wants to understand what made the Trujillo era tick.

Edwin Williamson *The Penguin History of Latin America* (Penguin). This excellent history contains by far the best and most judicious account in print of Columbus's voyages and Santo Domingo's early days.

FICTION AND POETRY

Julia Alvarez *In the Name of Salomé; Homecoming: New and Collected Poems; How the García Girls Lost Their Accents; In the Time of the Butterflies; Yo!* (Plume, Penguin). A leading American writer who grew up in the Dominican Republic, Alvarez's lucid prose, by turns comic and sublime, rewards any time spent with it. *García Girls* and *Yo!* centre on middle-class Dominican immigrants in New York, while *Butterflies* recounts the tale of the Mirabal sisters, who stood up to Trujillo's repression and were assassinated for it. *Salomé* is a singular work that blends a story of immigration similar to *García Girls* with the tale of a short-lived nineteenth-century revolution inspired by Dominican poet Salomé Ureña.

Edwidge Danticat *The Farming of Bones* (Abacus/Soho). Best-selling historical novel by a young Haitian-American, set along the Haitian border during the terror of Operación Perejil (see p.270). The writing is lush and moving, and the events come vividly to life.

★**Junot Díaz** *Drown; This Is How You Lose Her; The Brief Wondrous Life of Oscar Wao* (Faber & Faber). The latter novel an account of a geeky, comic-book-loving Dominican-American kid that traverses high art prose and Spanglish street lingo, sometimes in a near-stream-of-consciousness style, won Díaz the Pulitzer Prize. The other two titles, both highly original, excellent sets of shorts stories, focus on Dominican life in New Jersey; the more recent *This Is How You Lose Her* is an inventive collection of connected narratives about different kinds of love.

Manuel Jesús de Galván & Robert Graves *The Cross and the Sword* (AMS). Robert Graves' classic English translation of *Enriquillo*, the nineteenth-century novel that transformed Dominican identity.

★**Marío Vargas Llosa** *The Feast of the Goat* (Picador). This truly outstanding novel by a Nobel Prize-winning fiction writers engages in a multilevel narrative that manages to capture the whole Dickensian panorama of destruction that took place during the Trujillo era while outlining the last days of Trujillo and the bloody outcome of his assassination. A true page-turner in the best sense.

Viriato Sención *They Forged the Signature of God* (Curbstone). Artful novel tinged with magical realism, taking a swipe at fictionalized versions of dictators Trujillo and Balaguer as it follows the lives of three young seminarians losing their innocence.

SOCIETY, POLITICS AND CULTURE

Michiel Baud *Peasants and Tobacco in the Dominican Republic, 1870–1930* (Tennessee). A detailed and surprisingly engaging account of peasant society in the Cibao valley during the great Dominican tobacco boom, with a lot of information on the intricacies of the market.

Denise Brennan *What's Love Got to Do with It?* (Duke University). A fascinating examination of the Sosúa sex-tourism business, from the perspective of sex workers, customers and facilitators.

Marcos Breton & José Luís Villegas *Away Games* (University of New Mexico). Follows the life of Oakland As' shortstop Miguel Tejada from his initial signing to a US$2000 contract through his life in the Dominican and minor leagues and up to his entry into the majors and emerging stardom. Not just fan propaganda, though; it clearly outlines the trials and troubles of the thousands of Dominican prospects who never make it that far.

Eric Thomas Chester *Rag-Tags, Scum, Riff-Raff and Commies* (New York University Press). This is an enlightening outline of the American military intervention in the Dominican Republic in 1965–66. Shows how this invasion broke Roosevelt's "Good Neighbor Policy" and initiated an era of constant American military intervention throughout Latin America.

Lauren Derby, Raymundo González and Eric Paul Roorda (eds) *The Dominican Republic Reader* (Duke). The best available collection of writing in English for anyone wanting a broad and varied introduction to Dominican history, politics and culture. Very much a book for dipping into, which works well for the appealingly diverse sections on religion, popular culture and the Dominican diaspora but means the history sections, necessarily lacking a consistent narrative, work better for those with some prior knowledge of the country's past.

★**Barbara Fischkin** *Muddy Cup* (Scribner). This remarkably well written and moving book tracks a Dominican family for four generations as they make the transition from a tiny Dominican mountain village to the barrios of New York.

Steven Gregory *The Devil Behind the Mirror* (University of California). A fascinating and kaleidoscopic view of the impact of globalization on Boca Chica and the surrounding towns, in terms of industrialization, sex tourism, Dominican–Haitian relations and a range of other fascinating angles.

José Itzigsohn *Developing Poverty* (Pennsylvania State). An analysis of the effects of industrial "free" zones and the informal economies of the Dominican Republic and Costa Rica on overall economic health and job growth. Presents a well-balanced look at the pros and cons and though the material is a bit dry, it will give you a good inside look at the inner workings of Dominican work life.

Allan M. Klein *Sugarball: The American Game, the Dominican Dream* (Yale). A fun, book-length essay on baseball in the Dominican Republic, analyzing the country's obsession with it and how it plays into the relations between the DR and the United States.

Peggy Levitt *The Transnational Villagers* (University of California). Based on detailed fieldwork by the author, this is an account of a family of Dominicans from the Dominican *campo* of Miraflores who split their time between their home town and the Jamaica Plain neighbourhood of Boston. Challenges the idea that transnationality and cultural assimilation are in conflict and provides an interesting examination of the Dominican family's experiences in the United States with regards to gender and race.

Samuel Martínez *Peripheral Migrants: Haitians and Dominican Republic Sugar Plantations* (University of Tennessee). A scholarly and sobering examination of the mass migration of Haitian labourers to Dominican sugar *bateyes*, with plenty of fascinating description of their dangerous journeys across the border and their living conditions once they arrive.

Valentina Peguero *The Militarization of Culture in the Dominican Republic, from the Captains General to General Trujillo* (University of Nebraska). Traces the interaction of the military and civilian Dominican population over the course of the island's entire post-Columbus history,

explaining how the military ethos has come to pervade every aspect of Dominican society.

Rob Ruck *The Tropic of Baseball* (Carroll & Graf). A history of baseball in the DR, including eyewitness accounts of sandlot games, profiles of major Dominican stars and a definitive history of the *Cocolos* of San Pedro de Macorís.

Helen Safa *The Myth of the Male Breadwinner: Women and Industrialization in the Caribbean* (Westview). An interesting analysis of the changing role of women in the DR, Puerto Rico and Cuba, showing how low-wage industrialization, like that in the assembly lines of Dominican industrial free zones, has altered Dominican society.

Michele Wucker *Why the Cocks Fight: Dominicans, Haitians and the Struggle for Hispaniola* (Hill & Wang). This extremely well-written, thoroughly researched account of the conflict between the Dominican Republic and Haiti is a must-read for those who want to understand the island.

MUSIC, ART AND ARCHITECTURE

Paul Austerlitz *Merengue: Dominican Music and Dominican Identity* (Temple). Engagingly written ode to merengue, including the first complete history of the music and an analysis of what it reflects about Dominican society. Indispensable for understanding Dominican music and culture.

Fatima Bercht & Estrellita Brodsky *Tainos: Pre-Columbian Art and Culture from the Caribbean* (Monacelli). A beautifully presented coffee-table book with photographs of the most impressive Taino relics extant.

★ **Deborah Pacini Hernández** *Bachata: A Social History of Dominican Popular Music* (Temple). Highly recommended journey into the heart of Dominican bachata, including an

account of its origins in various pre-existing Caribbean forms, its transmission to the cities via waves of urban migration, and the somewhat informal industry that built up around it before it gained social acceptance with the Dominican middle classes.

Veerle Poupeye *Caribbean Art* (Thames and Hudson). The best source book for information on the visual art of the Caribbean, including a generous section dedicated to contemporary Dominican painting.

Henry Shukman *Travels with my Trombone: A Caribbean Journey* (Crown). A lively account of a freelance musician's wanderings across the Spanish Caribbean, including the Dominican Republic, in various Latin bands.

RELIGION

Jan Lundius *The Great Power of God in San Juan Valley* (Lund). A wonderful, sorely needed study of rural Dominican messiah Liborio and his lasting influence on the religion of peasants in the San Juan valley. Difficult to get hold of as it's published in Sweden, but worth the effort.

David Martin *Tongues of Fire* (Westview). An analysis of the explosion of Pentecostalism in the Dominican

Republic and across Latin America over the past few decades.

Dagoberto Tejeda Ortiz *Cultura Popular e Identidad Nacional* (Instituto Dominicano de Folklore). A wonderful, two-volume survey of various aspects of Dominican folk religion, with a refreshingly frank explanation of the African as well as Spanish roots of many local festivals and beliefs.

NATURE

Ken DuPree *Whales of Samaná* (Samaná). A very informative pamphlet on the humpback whales of the Bahía de Samaná and Silver Banks Sanctuary, widely available in the city of Samaná.

Jurgen Hoppe *Flowering Trees of the Dominican Republic; National Parks of the Dominican Republic* (APEB; Fundación Barceló). Available only in Santo Domingo, these are

excellent paperback guides to the flora and fauna of the DR, with beautiful colour photographs.

Eugene Kaplan *A Field Guide to the Coral Reefs of the Caribbean and Florida* (Houghton Mifflin). An excellent and attractive guide to the region's reefs and reef life.

G.W. Lennox & S.A. Seddon *Flowers of the Caribbean; Trees of the Caribbean; Fruits and Vegetables of the*

Caribbean (Macmillan). Handy pocket-sized books, with glossy, sharp, colour photos and a good general introduction to the region's flora.

George & Roberta Poinar *The Amber Forest: Reconstruction of a Vanished World* (Princeton). A wonderful book that analyzes hundreds of animals and plants trapped in Dominican amber in order to reconstruct the tropical jungle that existed here in the time of the dinosaurs.

Herbert Raffaele *Birds of the West Indies* (Princeton). The authoritative guide to birding in the Dominican Republic and throughout the region, by far the most comprehensive, accurate and up-to-date resource on the subject.

FOOD

Clara Gonzalez *Aunt Clara's Dominican Cookbook* (Lunch Club Press). A handy and comprehensive guide to preparing a vast array of Dominican dishes, from simple staples like rice and beans and *morir soñando* through complicated day-long recipes for *sancocho* and *pescado con coco*.

Spanish

Though most people who work in the tourism industry speak English – sometimes along with German, French or Italian – you'll find that nearly everyone you meet outside the resort areas speaks only Spanish. The few places where English is spoken as a first language are parts of the Samaná Peninsula, where a community of nineteenth-century African-American migrants still exists, and in the sugar-cane *bateyes* around San Pedro de Macorís, where many of the older folk came to the Dominican Republic from English-speaking islands like St Thomas and Tortola as migrant sugar-cane cutters.

If you want to get to know Dominicans, then it makes sense to acquire some Spanish before you arrive. Dominicans are endlessly patient with those struggling to speak their language, and will not only tolerate but appreciate the attempt.

Pronunciation

The rules of **pronunciation** are pretty straightforward and strictly observed. Unless there's an accent, all words ending in l, r and z are stressed on the last syllable, all others on the second last. In the Dominican Republic the final "s" of a word sometimes gets dropped; thus you'll often hear "buena" for "buenas" or "do" for "dos". All vowel sounds are pure and short.

A somewhere between the A sound in "back" and that in "father".

E as in "get".

I as in "police".

O as in "hot".

U as in "rule".

C is soft before E and I, hard otherwise: cerca is pronounced "serka".

G works the same way: a guttural H sound (like the ch in "loch") before E or I, a hard G elsewhere: gigante becomes "higante".

H is always silent.

J is the same sound as guttural G: jamón is pronounced "hamón".

LL is pronounced as a Y at the beginning of a word, a soft J elsewhere: llama is pronounced "yama", but ballena (whale) becomes "bajzhena" instead of "bayena".

N is as in English, unless it has a tilde accent over it, when it becomes NY: mañana sounds like "manyana".

QU is pronounced like the English K.

R is rolled, RR doubly so.

V sounds more like B, vino becoming "beano".

Z is the same as the soft C: cerveza is thus "serbesa".

USEFUL WORDS AND PHRASES

BASICS

yes, no	sí, no	**with, without**	con, sin
please, thank you	por favor, gracias	**good, bad**	bueno/a, malo/a
where, when	dónde, cuándo	**big, small**	grande, pequeño/a
here, there	aquí, allí	**more, less**	más, menos
what, how much	qué, cuánto	**today, tomorrow**	hoy, mañana
now, later	ahora, más tarde	**yesterday**	ayer
open, closed	abierto/a, cerrado/a	**this, that**	esto, eso

GREETINGS AND RESPONSES

Do you speak English?	¿Habla inglés?
Good afternoon/ night	Buenas tardes/ noches
Good morning	Buenos días
Hello, goodbye	Hola, adiós
How are you?	¿Como está?
I am English	Soy inglés(a)
…American…	americano/a
…Australian…	australiano/a
…Canadian…	canadiense/a
…Irish…	irlandés(a)
…Scottish…	escosés(a)
…Welsh…	galés(a)
I don't speak Spanish	No hablo español
I don't understand	No entiendo
My name is…	Me llamo…
Not at all/you're welcome	De nada
See you later	Hasta luego
Sorry	Lo siento or Perdón
What did you say?	¿Como?
What is your name?	¿Como se llama usted?

HOTELS

Can one…?	¿Se puede…?
Do you know…?	¿Sabe…?
Do you have…?	¿Tiene…?
…the time	…la hora
…a room	…una habitación
…with two beds	…con dos camas
Don't you have anything cheaper?	¿No tiene algo más barato?
Give me… (one like that)	Deme… (uno así)
How much is it?	¿Cuánto es?
I'd like	Quisiera
I don't know	No sé
I want	Quiero
It's fine(?)	(¿)Está bien(?)
It's for one person	Es para una persona
…two persons	…dos personas
…for one night (one week)	…para una noche (una semana)
It's too expensive	Es demasiado caro
Is there a hotel nearby?	¿Hay un hotel por aquí?

TRANSPORT

How do I get to…?	¿Por dónde voy para llegar…?
…the bus station	…a la estación de autobuses?

…the nearest bank	…al banco más cercano?
…the toilet	…al baño?
Left, right	Izquierda, derecha
Straight on	Derecho
There is (is there?)	(¿) Hay (?)
Where is…?	¿Dónde está…?
Where does the bus to… leave from?	¿De dónde sale el autobus para…?
I'd like a (return) ticket to…	Quisiera un tiquete / un boleto (de ida y vuelta)
What time does it leave (arrive)?	¿A qué hora sale (llega)?

ROAD SIGNS

Ceda el paso	Give way
Pare	Stop
Una vía	One way
Doble vía	Two-way traffic
Retorno	U-turn
No estacione	No parking
No entre	No entry
Reduzca velocidad	Reduce speed
Desvio	Detour

NUMBERS AND DAYS

1	uno/una
2	dos
3	tres
4	cuatro
5	cinco
6	seis
7	siete
8	ocho
9	nueve
10	diez
11	once
12	doce
13	trece
14	catorce
15	quince
16	dieciséis
20	veinte
21	veintiuno
30	treinta
40	cuarenta
50	cincuenta
60	sesenta
70	setenta
80	ochenta
90	noventa
100	cien(to)
101	ciento uno
200	doscientos

201	doscientos uno
500	quinientos
1000	mil
2000	dos mil
2001	dos mil uno
first	primero/a
second	segundo/a
third	tercero/a

Monday	lunes
Tuesday	martes
Wednesday	miércoles
Thursday	jueves
Friday	viernes
Saturday	sábado
Sunday	domingo

FOOD AND DRINK

BASICS

¿Hay?…	Do you have? (Is there…?)
Un menú, por favor	A menu, please
La cuenta, por favor	The bill, please
Quiero…	I would like…
Soy vegetariano/a	I'm a vegetarian
Sin carne	Without meat
Dos cervezas	Two beers
¡Salud!	Cheers!
pan	bread
arroz	rice
mantequilla	butter
queso	typical white Dominican cheese
sal	salt
pimienta	pepper
cilantro	coriander
azúcar	sugar
huevos	eggs

COOKING STYLES

barbacoa	barbecued
al carbón	grilled
cómida criolla	Dominican cuisine
criolla	tomato-based creole sauce
frito	fried
guisado/a	stewed
al horno	roasted

DOMINICAN DISHES

bandera dominicana	rice and beans, sometimes with chicken
lambí	conch meat
longaniza	spicy sausage made from pork tripe, ground pork, garlic and oregano
mangú	mashed plantains with onions and oil
mofongo	pork rinds, plantains and garlic
mondongo	tripe stew

moro	black beans and rice
sancocho	stew with several kinds of meat, tubers and an array of spices

SOUPS AND SALADS

crema de habichuelas rojas	creamed red-bean soup
crema de maíz	cream of corn soup
ensalada aguacate	sliced avocados with oil and vinegar
ensalada típica	shredded cabbage and carrots with oil and vinegar
ensalada campesina	watercress, tomatoes, oregano and radishes
ensalada verde	green salad
sopa de guandules	pigeon-pea soup
sopa de morros	black bean and rice soup
sopa pescado	fish soup
sopa verdura	vegetable soup

MEAT

bistec	beefsteak
bistec encebollado	beefsteak with onions
carne ripiada	shredded beef
cerdo	pork
chicarrones	fried bits of pork or chicken
chivo	goat
chuletas de puerco	pork chops
empanadas	ground-beef-filled pastries
jamón	ham
parrillada	Argentine-style meat platter
pechuga	chicken breast
pollo al carbon	grilled chicken in a cream sauce
pollo frito	fried chicken

puerco	pork	maíz	corn
quipes	cracked-wheat fritters with ground beef	papa	potato
		papas fritas	French fries
res	beef	plátano	plantain
		tomate	tomato
SEAFOOD		tostones	double-fried plantains
atún	tuna		
calamar	squid		
camarones	shrimp	**DESSERTS**	
cangrejo	crab	arroz con leche	rice pudding
carite	kingfish	dulce con coco	coconut sweet
chillo	red snapper	dulce de leche	milk sweet
langosta	clawless lobster	flan	flan/custard
mariscos	seafood	flan de leche	milk custard
mero	sea bass	flan de maíz	corn custard
pulpo	octopus	helado	ice cream
		pudin de pan	bread pudding

FRUITS AND VEGETABLES			
aguacate	avocado	**DRINKS**	
fresas	strawberries	agua	water
fritos	fried plantain	agua purificada	purified water
guineo	banana	batida	fruit shake with pulp
lechoza	papaya	café con leche	coffee with hot milk
limón	lemon	café solo	black coffee
mango	mango	cerveza	beer
naranja, china	orange	Cuba libre	rum and Coke
piña	pineapple	jugo	juice
tamarindo	tamarind	jugo de naranja, jugo de china	orange juice
batata	sweet potato		
cassava	yuca	leche	milk
cebolla	onion	refresco	juice with sugar
habichuelas	red beans	ron	rum

Glossary

Below are some useful Spanish **terms** and some more specifically **Dominican words and phrases**. Many of them have been used throughout the guide and can commonly be heard in daily parlance in the Dominican Republic. A number of **Taino** words have also made their way into the contemporary Dominican vocabulary, though the meaning has drifted a bit over the centuries; some of the more prominent follow.

SPANISH TERMS FREQUENTLY USED IN THIS GUIDE

bachata twangy ballad music, with a steadily emphasized offbeat

bahía bay

balneario swimming hole

barrio neighbourhood

calle street

carretera main road

casa de cambio small currency-exchange shop

caudillo nineteenth-century strongman who ruled the country by force of arms

ciudad city

cordillera mountain range

iglesia church

merengue the fast-paced national dance music, less rhythmically intricate than salsa, with a repetitive thump right on the beat

parque central the square, central park in every Dominican town that generally serves as the centre of socializing and commerce

peso the unit of Dominican currency

pueblo small town

río river

sierra mountain range

son Cuban form of guitar music which is especially popular in Santo Domingo, and which many Dominicans claim was created here

Taino Native Americans who inhabited the Dominican Republic and much of the Caribbean at the time of Columbus's arrival

DOMINICAN TERMS

agua de melao shallow or without substance.

areito long narrative songs used by the Tainos to depict and celebrate battles and other important events, used by Juan Luís Guerra as the title of a famous album

Belie Belcán patron spirit of the Dominican Republic, both a benevolent protector and a military strongman

bien-bienes the wandering souls of dead *cimarrones*, who haunt the Haitian border at night, stealing food from peasants' gardens

bomba petrol station

botánica shop where folk religion items can be purchased

bracero Haitian cane cutter

buscador a "finder", or someone who offers himself as a freelance guide for tourists

cabaña turística sets of hotel rooms with attached garages and hourly rates, used mainly by local couples as sex stops

caliente dangerous (the more common meaning is hot)

campesino rural Dominican peasantry

campo settlement too small to be considered a pueblo

casa de huespedes also called *pensión*, a private home with rooms to let to travellers

cédula ID card

chin a little bit

ciguapa the souls of dead Taino women who escaped the rapacious Spanish settlers by hiding out in the Cordillera Central

cimarrones escaped slaves

cobrador conductor (common on guaguas and buses)

concho catch-all term for any makeshift vehicle used as public transport

club gallístico circular, two-tiered wooden venues for cockfights

Cocolo disparaging term referring to the English-speaking, black, seasonal sugar labourers who cut Dominican cane around the turn of the twentieth century

cofradía Dominican religious brotherhoods that involve the worship of patron African deities syncretized to Catholic saints. Most are called Hermanidad del Congo and worship Kalunda/the Holy Spirit.

colmado grocery shack, especially prevalent in the countryside

comedor small, family-run restaurant serving local food

Cuba libre servicio popular way to drink in discos and bars: two Cokes, a bottle of rum and a bucket of ice

detelengue tight clothes

Dominican York a Dominican who has emigrated to the United States, though increasingly pejorative, referring to flashy Dominican drug dealers from New York

encomienda an attempted reform of the Taino slave system by the Spanish Crown, according to which Tainos were to be paid a fair wage for their forced labour and educated in Catholicism

Evangélico a convert to the burgeoning Pentecostal movement in the Dominican Republic

fiesta patronal festival for the patron saint of a town or city

la frontera the Haitian border

gomero tyre repair shop

gourde Haitian unit of currency

guagua privately owned vans and minibuses that are the primary form of transportation in the DR

guloya style of music played by the Cocolo mummers in San Pedro de Macorís, involving fife-and-drum bands and dancing

hato a large, rural Spanish estate used for raising cattle

jevito teenager or twentysomething who always wears the latest fashion

jonrón a baseball home run

larimar semiprecious, turquoise stone unique to the Dominican Republic, mined in the Sierra Bahoruco west of Barahona

mafioso rip-off artist or thug

malecón boardwalk avenue along the ocean

mambo female priest of Haitian Voodoo

mayimbe the leader of a group, or the greatest at some skill

merengue périco ripao old-style acoustic merengue using an instrumentation of accordion, tambora, *güira* and African thumb piano

momise the Dominican mispronunciation of "mummers", dancers who parade around San Pedro de Macorís at Christmas and during the *fiesta patronal*, performing from door to door in exchange for money and rum

motoconcho small-engined motorbikes used as taxis

pájaro a popular euphemism, meaning "bird", used to refer to gay men

pensión a private home with rooms to let to travellers

plaza (comercial) shopping mall; commercial centre

público weather-beaten automobiles used as public transport in the cities and between towns along the north coast

sanky panky practice of some underpaid Dominican resort employees acting as "escorts" to tourists in exchange for money and gifts

Santera standard term used to refer to Dominican syncretism, without any of the pejorative associations of *Vodú*

tambora a lap drum that is a standard instrument in merengue bands, held and slapped by a hand at one end while it's drummed with a stick at the other

tigre thief; hooligan

yola leaky fishing boats used by Dominicans to emigrate illegally to Puerto Rico

TAINOISMS

batey the public plaza at the centre of every Taino community, today it refers to the meagre rows of shacks where Haitian cane cutters live and work.

bohío once the circular thatch homes of Taino commoners, it now means a thatch-and-mud hut of a rural Dominican farmer

cacique Taino word signifying both a political leader and the tribe which he commanded; sometimes used today to denote a corrupt town boss

caney large rectangular great-house of the Taino nobles

canoa small wooden canoes used to travel rivers

cassava the bread made from yuca root which served as the major staple in the Taino diet, and is still quite popular locally

cemi stone Taino idol with flared nostrils and inward-spiralling eyes that was believed to hold benevolent spirits

conuco originally, an environmentally sound method of Taino agriculture (in which multiple crops were grown within mulched large mounds), the word later came to denote the slash-and-burn farming settlement in the wilderness

dujo intricately carved wooden throne for a *cacique*, usually made of lignum vitae

Haiti the island of Hispaniola

hamaca hammock, which was invented by the Tainos

hupía the spirits of the recently dead, thought to return at night

Huracán the great Taino god of evil, who had to be constantly appeased in order to avoid the destruction of the community. His most visible manifestations were the hurricanes that still plague the Caribbean

macuteo a bride

maguey traditional Taino drum

mao a cotton neck garment worn by *caciques*

nagua the extremely small, hip-covering cloth worn by married Taino women

nigua an extremely small insect that buries its eggs inside your flesh, causing nasty lesions

papaya the English word for this fruit comes from the Taino language

uiku Taino liquor, made from corn masticated by teenage girls and then allowed to ferment

Small print and index

A ROUGH GUIDE TO ROUGH GUIDES

Published in 1982, the first Rough Guide – to Greece – was a student scheme that became a publishing phenomenon. Mark Ellingham, a recent graduate in English from Bristol University, had been travelling in Greece the previous summer and couldn't find the right guidebook. With a small group of friends he wrote his own guide, combining a highly contemporary, journalistic style with a thoroughly practical approach to travellers' needs.

The immediate success of the book spawned a series that rapidly covered dozens of destinations. And, in addition to impecunious backpackers, Rough Guides soon acquired a much broader readership that relished the guides' wit and inquisitiveness as much as their enthusiastic, critical approach and value-for-money ethos.

These days, Rough Guides include recommendations from budget to luxury and cover more than 120 destinations around the globe, as well as producing an ever-growing range of ebooks.

Visit **roughguides.com** to find all our latest books, read articles, get inspired and share travel tips with the Rough Guides community.

Rough Guide credits

Editor: Neil McQuillian
Layout: Ankur Guha
Cartography: Deshpal Dabas
Picture editor: Marta Bescos
Proofreader: Susanne Hillen
Senior editor: Natasha Foges
Managing editor: Alice Park
Assistant editor: Prema Dutta

Production: Emma Sparks
Cover design: Ankur Guha, Raffaella Morini, Nicole Newman
Editorial assistant: Rebecca Hallett
Senior pre-press designer: Dan May
Programme manager: Helen Blount
Publisher: Joanna Kirby
Publishing director: Georgina Dee

Publishing information

This sixth edition published November 2014 by
Rough Guides Ltd,
80 Strand, London WC2R 0RL
11, Community Centre, Panchsheel Park,
New Delhi 110017, India
Distributed by Penguin Random House
Penguin Books Ltd,
80 Strand, London WC2R 0RL
Penguin Group (USA)
345 Hudson Street, NY 10014, USA
Penguin Group (Australia)
250 Camberwell Road, Camberwell,
Victoria 3124, Australia
Penguin Group (NZ)
67 Apollo Drive, Mairangi Bay, Auckland 1310,
New Zealand
Penguin Group (South Africa)
Block D, Rosebank Office Park, 181 Jan Smuts Avenue,
Parktown North, Gauteng, South Africa 2193
Rough Guides is represented in Canada by Tourmaline
Editions Inc. 662 King Street West, Suite 304, Toronto,
Ontario M5V 1M7
Printed in Singapore by Toppan Security Printing Pte. Ltd.

© Rough Guides, 2014
Maps © Rough Guides
No part of this book may be reproduced in any form
without permission from the publisher except for the
quotation of brief passages in reviews.
312pp includes index
A catalogue record for this book is available from the
British Library
ISBN: 978-1-40935-312-6
The publishers and authors have done their best to
ensure the accuracy and currency of all the information
in **The Rough Guide to Dominican Republic**, however,
they can accept no responsibility for any loss, injury, or
inconvenience sustained by any traveller as a result of
information or advice contained in the guide.
1 3 5 7 9 8 6 4 2

MIX
Paper from
responsible sources
FSC
www.fsc.org
FSC™ C018179

Help us update

We've gone to a lot of effort to ensure that the sixth
edition of **The Rough Guide to Dominican Republic** is
accurate and up-to-date. However, things change – places
get "discovered", opening hours are notoriously fickle,
restaurants and rooms raise prices or lower standards. If
you feel we've got it wrong or left something out, we'd like
to know, and if you can remember the address, the price,
the hours, the phone number, so much the better.

Please send your comments with the subject line
"**Rough Guide Dominican Republic Update**" to ✉ mail
@uk.roughguides.com. We'll credit all contributions and
send a copy of the next edition (or any other Rough Guide
if you prefer) for the very best emails.

Find more travel information, connect with fellow
travellers and plan your trip on ⓦ roughguides.com.

ABOUT THE AUTHORS

Matt Norman lives in London where he works as an editor at The National Archives. He has been writing and researching travel guides for over fifteen years and specializes in the Spanish-speaking Caribbean.

Charles Young has been travelling since university and, as well as working on a dozen Rough Guides titles, has taught English in Catalunya, run a coffee shop in Hong Kong, was a publican in South Korea and worked in the spice trade in India. He should be older than he is.

Acknowledgements

Matt Norman would like to thank Diane Bartlett in Las Galeras for going out of the way to be helpful; Gill Thomas in particular, but also Danny Thomas and the rest of the family in Bávaro for a friendly welcome and lots of useful advice; Martina in Bayahibe; Anna in Juan Dolio; Jonathan Baldrey and Freddy in Santo Domingo for insights, conversation and getting me out of a jam; Bernard in Santo Domingo; John Wood for his understanding and flexibility; and Suzanne and Bob for a great night – hope all is well in Cincinnati; at Rough Guides, thanks to Natasha Foges for being supportive and a pleasure to work with, and to Neil McQuillian for being such a great editor and for making work on this guide so enjoyable and collaborative.

Readers' updates

Thanks to all the readers who have taken the time to write in with comments and suggestions (and apologies if we've inadvertently omitted or misspelt anyone's name):

Adrien Daneau; Konrad Kracher; Anne Youldon.

Photo credits

All photos © Rough Guides except the following:
(Key: t-top; c-centre; b-bottom; l-left; r-right)

p.1 Jeremy Horner/Corbis
p.2 Jane Sweeney/JAI/Corbis
p.5 Tatiana Taylor/Alamy Images
p.8 Caro/Alamy Images
p.9 Jane Sweeney/AWL Images
p.10 epa european pressphoto agency b.v./Alamy Images
p.11 Ingolf Pompe 7/Alamy Images
p.13 Wilmar Topshots/Alamy Images (t); Casa Sanchez Boutique Hotel (c); Soles Chill Out Bar (b)
p.14 Jane Sweeney/Corbis
p.15 age fotostock/Alamy Images (t); Sylvain Grandadam/SuperStock (c); Luciano Ippolito/Dreamstime.com (b)
p.16 Franck Guiziou/Hemis/Corbis (t); Gallo Images/Getty Images (b)
p.17 Photoshot/Xinhua (t); UIG/Getty Images (c); Vova Pomortzeff/Alamy Images (b)
p.18 Catherine Karnow/Corbis (t)
p.19 Nick Hanna/Alamy Images (t); M. Timothy O'Keefe/Alamy Images (cl); Travel Pictures/Alamy Images (cr); John Mitchell/Alamy Images (b)

p.20 Prisma Bildagentur AG/Alamy Images (tl); Stefan Ember/123RF.com (tr)
p.22 Prisma Bildagentur AG/Alamy Images
pp.44–45 Christian Kober/JAI/Corbis
p.47 Alvaro Leiva/SuperStock
pp.84–85 Robert John/Alamy Images
p.87 Richard Soberka/Hemis/Corbis
pp.120–121 Picture Alliance/Photoshot
p.123 Ainara Garcia/Alamy Images
pp.152–153 Carib Images/Alamy Images
pp.202–203 Matthew Wakem/Axiom Photographic Agency
p.205 Vova Pomortzeff/Alamy Images
pp.234–235 Franck Guiziou/Hemis/Corbis

Front cover: Las Galeras, Samaná Peninsula © Alvaro Leiva/Superstock
Back cover: beach at Las Terrenas © Jane Sweeney/AWL Images (t); Museo de Las Casas Reales, Santo Domingo © Jane Sweeney/AWL Images (bl); Cohiba cigars © Walter Bibikow/AWL Images (br)

Index

Maps are marked in grey

Map symbols

The symbols below are used on maps throughout the book

⊠ Post office	✡ Synagogue	✈ Major airport	Church (town maps)
ⓘ Information centre	🏛 Monument	✗ Municipal airport	Building
✚ Hospital	Fortress	★ Public transport stop	Stadium
⊙ Statue	🏛 Stately home	P Parking	Park
General point of interest	Cave	Waterfall	Beach
@ Internet access	▲ Mountain peak	Lighthouse	Cemetery
∴ Ruins	Fuel station	Church (regional maps)	Swamps/marshes

Listings key

- ■ Accommodation
- ● Eating
- ■ Drinking/nightlife/music venue
- ● Shopping

SO NOW WE'VE TOLD YOU
HOW TO MAKE THE MOST
OF YOUR TIME, WE WANT
YOU TO STAY SAFE AND
COVERED WITH OUR
FAVOURITE TRAVEL INSURER

WorldNomads.com
keep travelling safely

GET AN ONLINE QUOTE
roughguides.com/travel-insurance